# BUSN¹²

## Introduction to Business

**Marce Kelly**
Santa Monica College

**Chuck Williams**
Butler University

 CENGAGE

Australia • Brazil • Canada • Mexico • Singapore • United Kingdom • United States

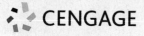

**BUSN**, 12e
**Marce Kelly and Chuck Williams**

SVP, Higher Education Product Management: Erin Joyner

VP, Product Management, Learning Experiences: Thais Alencar

Product Director: Joe Sabatino

Product Manager: Heather Thompson

Product Assistant: Hannah May

Learning Designer: Megan Guiliani

Senior Content Manager: Allie Janneck

Digital Delivery Quality Partner: Amanda Ryan

Director, Product Marketing: Danae April

Portfolio Marketing Manager: Anthony Winslow

Product Development Researcher: Cara Suriyamongkol

IP Analyst: Diane Garrity

IP Project Manager: Kumaresan Chandrakumar - Integra

Production Service: MPS Limited

Designer: Sara Greenwood

Cover Image Source: Weedezign/iStock/ Getty Images Plus/Getty Images

For product information and technology assistance, contact us at
**Cengage Customer & Sales Support, 1-800-354-9706
or support.cengage.com.**

For permission to use material from this text or product, submit all requests online at **www.copyright.com.**

Library of Congress Control Number: 2021920194

ISBN: 978-0-357-12294-5

**Cengage**
200 Pier 4 Boulevard
Boston, MA 02210
USA

Cengage is a leading provider of customized learning solutions with employees residing in nearly 40 different countries and sales in more than 125 countries around the world. Find your local representative at **www.cengage.com.**

To learn more about Cengage platforms and services, register or access your online learning solution, or purchase materials for your course, visit **www.cengage.com.**

Printed in the United States of America
Print Number: 02        Print Year: 2022

Weedezign/iStock/Getty Images Plus/Getty Images

# Contents

**Part 1**
**The Business Environment**

G-Stock Studio/Shutterstock.com

# Part 2
## Creating a Business

Monkey Business Images/Shutterstock.com

# Part 3
## Financing a Business

Fizkes/Shutterstock.com

# Part 4
## Marketing a Business

G Stock Studio/Shutterstock.com

# Part 5
## Managing a Business

Monkey Business Images/Shutterstock.com

With love and appreciation
to my amazing children
who make all things possible!

—Marce Kelly


To Jenny,
the book is done, let's play!

—Chuck Williams

The idea for this book—a whole new way of learning—began with students like you across the country. We paid attention to students who wanted to learn about business without slogging through endless pages of dry text. We listened to students who wanted to sit through class without craving a triple espresso. We responded to students who wanted to use their favorite gadgets to prepare for tests.

So, we are confident that BUSN will meet your needs. The short, lively text covers all the key concepts without the fluff. The examples are relevant and engaging, and the visual style makes the book fun to read. But the text is only part of the package. You can access a rich variety of study tools via computer or iPad—the choice is yours.

Marce Kelly

Chuck Williams

We did one other thing we hope you'll like. We paid a lot of attention to students' concerns about the high price of college textbooks. We made it our mission to ensure that our package not only meets your needs but does so without busting your budget!

This innovative, student-focused package was developed by the authors—Marce Kelly and Chuck Williams—and the experienced Cengage Learning publishers. The Cengage team contributed a deep understanding of students and professors across the nation, and the authors brought years of teaching and business experience.

Marce Kelly, who earned her MBA from UCLA's Anderson School of Management, spent the first 14 years of her career in marketing by building brands for Neutrogena and The Walt Disney Corporation. But her true love is teaching, so in 2000 she accepted a full-time teaching position at Santa Monica College. Professor Kelly has received seven Outstanding Instructor awards from the International Education Center and has been named four times to *Who's Who Among American Teachers*.

Chuck Williams' interests include employee recruitment and turnover, performance appraisal, and employee training and goal setting. Most recently, he was the Dean of Butler University's College of Business. He has taught in executive development programs at Oklahoma State University, the University of Oklahoma, Texas Christian University, and the University of the Pacific. Dr. Williams was honored by TCU's M.J. Neeley School of Business with the undergraduate Outstanding Faculty Teaching Award, was a recipient of TCU's Dean's Teaching Award, and was TCU's nominee for the U.S. Professor of the Year competition sponsored by the Carnegie Foundation for the Advancement of Teaching. He has written three other textbooks: *Management, Effective Management: A Multimedia Approach*, and *MGMT*.

We would appreciate any comments or suggestions you want to offer about this package. You can reach Chuck Williams at chuck.1.williams@gmail.com, and Marce Kelly at marcella.kelly@gmail.com. We wish you a fun, positive, productive term, and look forward to your feedback!

# 1 Business Now:
## Change Is the Only Constant

**Learning Objectives**

After studying this chapter, you will be able to:

**1-1** Discuss the role of business in the economy

**1-2** Explain the evolution of modern business

**1-3** Discuss the role of nonprofit organizations in the economy

**1-4** Outline the core factors of production and how they affect the economy

**1-5** Describe today's business environment and each key dimension

**1-6** Explain how current business trends might affect your career choices

---

**1-1** Business Now: Moving at Breakneck Speed

Day by day, the business world simply spins faster. Industries rise—and sometimes fall—in the course of a few short months. Technologies forge instant connections across the globe. Powerful new trends surface and submerge, sometimes within less than a year. In this fast-paced, fluid environment, change is the only constant. According to Charles Darwin, it is not the strongest of the species that survive, nor the most intelligent, but the one most responsive to change. And so it is with business.

Successful firms lean forward and embrace the change. They seek the opportunities and avoid the pitfalls. They carefully evaluate risks. They completely understand their market, and they adhere to ethical practices. Their core goal: to generate long-term profits by delivering unsurpassed **value** to their customers.

The business environment faced an onslaught of changes in the first two decades of the twenty-first century, including the Great Recession in 2008, the explosive growth of social media, the appearance of the #MeToo movement, the growing prominence of Generation Z in the workplace, the breakneck growth of artificial intelligence, historic tax reform, and the growing dominance of China's goliath online retailer Alibaba.

But the pivot point came with the year that none of us will ever forget: 2020. In late 2019, a new, highly contagious,

**value** The relationship between the price of a good or a service and the benefits that it offers its customers.

and deadly respiratory virus, later dubbed COVID-19, was discovered in Wuhan, China. As the virus spread around the world in the first months of 2020, the World Health Organization declared a worldwide pandemic. Countries shut down, schools closed, and the death toll mounted. By early March 2020, COVID-19 had hit the United States hard. State after state declared a "state of emergency," initiating mandatory stay-at-home orders in an effort to slow the spread and minimize the death toll. Unsurprisingly, one result was that the longest-ever U.S. economic expansion came to a screeching halt, followed by the steepest quarterly drop in economic output on record. Unemployment skyrocketed, along with food and housing insecurity. By the end of 2020, hope was in sight, as the pharmaceutical industry, working hand-in-glove with the federal government, had developed and tested two different COVID-19 vaccines; daunting logistical challenges remained, however, in terms of how to roll out the vaccines to the population at large, many of whom did not trust it.

In late May, 2020, George Floyd, an unarmed Black man, was brutally killed by police in Minneapolis, Minnesota. Video footage of the killing went viral, triggering massive protests against racism and police violence in virtually every city in the county. The protests continued

> "When the ideas are coming, I don't stop until the ideas stop because that train doesn't come along all the time."
>
> —Dr. Dre, Rapper, Record Producer, Entrepreneur

throughout the summer, fueled by the high-profile unjust shootings of more Black people.

In response to the heightened national awareness of systemic racism, a number of U.S. businesses began to examine their policies and products in an effort to root out racism. Examples:

- **Starbucks:** In 2020, Starbucks hired its first chief inclusion and diversity officer, Nzinga "Zing" Shaw, and committed $1 million in Neighborhood Grants to promote racial equity and create more inclusive and just communities.[1]

- **Quaker Oats:** After 130 years, Quaker Oats decided to retire the Aunt Jemima brand and logo, recognizing that "Aunt Jemima's origins are based on a racial stereotype," and that, "we also must take a hard look at our portfolio of brands and ensure they reflect our values and meet our consumers' expectations."[2]

- **Washington Redskins:** The owner of this DC NFL team, Dan Snyder, finally agreed to change its name, a racial slur against Native Americans. The deciding factor seemed to be pressure from two of the team's key sponsors, FedEx and Nike. Options under consideration at the time of writing were Redtails, Red Hogs, Warriors, and Red Wolves.[3]

## 1-1a Business Basics: Some Key Definitions

While you can certainly recognize a business when you see one, more formal definitions may help as you read through this book. A **business** is any organization or activity that provides goods and services in an effort to earn a profit. **Profit** is the financial reward that comes from starting and running a business. More specifically, profit is the money that a business earns in sales (or revenue), minus expenses such as the cost of goods and the cost of salaries. But clearly, not every business earns a profit all the time. When a business brings in less money than it needs to cover expenses, it incurs a **loss**. If you launch a music label, for instance, you'll need to pay your artists, lease a studio, and purchase equipment, among other expenses. If your label generates hits, you'll earn more than enough to cover all your expenses and make yourself rich. But a series of duds could leave you holding the bag. Just the possibility of earning a profit provides a powerful incentive for people of all backgrounds to launch their own enterprises.[4] People who do risk their time, money, and other resources to start and manage a business are called **entrepreneurs**.

Interestingly, as entrepreneurs create wealth for themselves, they produce a ripple effect that enriches everyone around them. For instance, if your new website becomes the next Facebook, who will benefit? Clearly, *you* will. And you'll probably spend at least some of that money enriching your local clubs, clothing stores, and car dealerships. But others will benefit, too, including your members, advertisers on your site and the staff who support them, contractors who build your facilities, and the government that collects your taxes. The impact of one successful entrepreneur can extend to the far reaches of the economy. In fact, fast-growing new firms generate about 10% of all new jobs in any given year.[5] Multiply the impact by thousands of entrepreneurs—each working in their own self-interest—and you can see how the profit motive benefits virtually everyone.

---

**business** Any organization or activity that provides goods and services in an effort to earn a profit.

**profit** The money that a business earns in sales (or revenue), minus expenses, such as the cost of goods and the cost of salaries. Revenue − Expenses = Profit (or Loss).

**loss** When a business incurs expenses that are greater than its revenue.

**entrepreneurs** People who risk their time, money, and other resources to start and manage a business.

---

## ⚠ Oops! What Were They Thinking?

### Not Every Dumb Move Is an Utter Disaster...

In the wake of disastrous mismanagement and outrageous mistakes across our economy, it might be hard to remember that some goofs are actually kind of funny. Some examples to help remind you:

- **Kim Kardashian "kimono":** Woman's shapewear is underwear that is designed to hold a part of the body in a particular form. In 2019, Kim Kardashian tried to copywrite the name "kimono" for her line of shapewear, even though it had nothing to do with the traditional Japanese garment that dates back to nearly 800 B.C.

- **Instagram *swipe bait*:** A clever sneaker manufacturer from China, called Kaiwei Ni, published a Black Friday ad on Instagram Stories in 2017 with a stray hair right in the middle of the screen. The designer of the ad made it look like it was a stray hair on the phone screen of the person viewing it, to get users to swipe up their screen in the attempt to clear the stray hair. Sneaky. Instagram removed this ad immediately for violating its policies and disabled the account from advertising.

- **Socially distant arches:** McDonald's Brazil responded to COVID-19 pandemic by separating its iconic golden arches to remind customers to engage in social distancing. They featured the new logo in television advertising and across social media. Consumers were NOT impressed, and they expressed their disdain for the "precious arches" loudly via Twitter, condemning the move for being tone deaf and exploitative.[6]

From a bigger-picture perspective, business drives up the **standard of living** for people worldwide, contributing to a higher **quality of life**. Businesses not only provide the products and services that people enjoy but also provide the jobs that people need. Beyond the obvious, business contributes to society through innovation—think cars, TVs, and tablet computers. Business also helps raise the standard of living through taxes, which the government spends on projects that range from streetlights to environmental cleanup. Socially responsible firms contribute even more by actively advocating for the well-being of the society that feeds their success.

## 1-2 The History of Business: Putting It All in Context

You may be surprised to learn that—unlike today—business hasn't always been focused on what the customer wants. In fact, business in the United States has changed rather dramatically over the past 200–300 years. Most business historians divide the history of American business into five distinct eras, which overlap during the periods of transition:

- **The Industrial Revolution:** Technological advances fueled a period of rapid industrialization in America from the mid-1700s to the mid-1800s. As mass production took hold, huge factories replaced skilled artisan workshops. The factories hired large

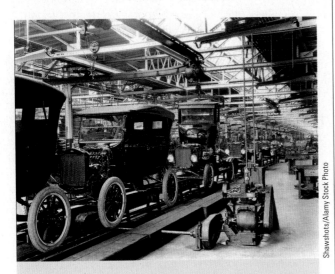

Shawshots/Alamy Stock Photo

Henry Ford's assembly line began operation on December 1, 1913. Initially developed for the Model T, this new production system allowed manufacturers of all kinds to output products like never before.

numbers of semiskilled workers who specialized in a limited number of tasks. The result was unprecedented production efficiency but also a loss of individual ownership and personal pride in the production process.

- **The Entrepreneurship Era:** Building on the foundation of the Industrial Revolution, large-scale entrepreneurs emerged in the second half of the 1800s, building business empires. These industrial titans—such as Andrew Carnegie, Cornelius Vanderbilt, JP Morgan, and Nelson Rockefeller—created enormous wealth, raising the overall standard of living across the country. But many also dominated their markets, forcing out competitors, manipulating prices, exploiting workers, and decimating the environment. Toward the end of the 1800s, the government stepped into the business realm, passing laws to regulate business and protect consumers and workers, creating more balance in the economy.

- **The Production Era:** In the early part of the 1900s, major businesses focused on further refining the production process and creating greater efficiencies. Jobs became even more specialized, increasing productivity and lowering costs and prices. In 1913, Henry Ford introduced the assembly line, which quickly became standard across major manufacturing industries. With managers focused on efficiency, the customer was an afterthought. But when customers tightened their belts during the Great Depression and World War II, businesses took notice. The "hard sell" emerged: aggressive persuasion designed to separate consumers from their cash.

- **The Marketing Era:** After World War II, the balance of power shifted away from producers and toward consumers, flooding the market with enticing choices. To differentiate themselves from their competitors, businesses began to develop brands, or distinctive identities, to help consumers understand the differences among various products. The *marketing concept* emerged: a consumer focus that permeates successful companies in every department, at every level. This approach continues to influence business decisions today as global competition heats up to unprecedented levels.

- **The Relationship Era:** Building on the marketing concept, today, leading-edge firms look beyond each immediate transaction

**standard of living** The quality and quantity of goods and services available to a population.

**quality of life** The overall sense of well-being experienced by either an individual or a group.

with a customer and aim to build long-term relationships. Satisfied customers can become advocates for a business, spreading the word with more speed and credibility than even the best promotional campaign. According to technology entrepreneur, Lisa Masiello, "Happy customers are your biggest advocates and can become your most successful sales team." And cultivating current customers is more profitable than constantly seeking new ones. One key tool is technology. Using digital resources, businesses collect enormous amounts of data, allowing them to better serve customers.

##  1-3 Nonprofits and the Economy: The Business of Doing Good

Nonprofit organizations play a critical role in the economy, often working hand in hand with businesses to improve the quality of life in our society. Focusing on areas such as health, human services, education, art, religion, and culture, **nonprofits** are business-*like* establishments, but their primary goals do not include profits. Chuck Bean, former executive director of the Nonprofit Roundtable, explains: "By definition, nonprofits are not in the business of

**nonprofits** Business-like establishments that employ people and produce goods and services with the fundamental goal of contributing to the community rather than generating financial gain.

**factors of production** Four fundamental elements—natural resources, capital, human resources, and entrepreneurship—that businesses need to achieve their objectives.

financial gain. We're in the business of doing good. However, nonprofits are still businesses in every other sense—they employ people, they take in revenue, they produce goods and services and contribute in significant ways to our region's economic stability and growth." Nationwide, nonprofits employ about one in ten workers, accounting for more paid workers than the entire construction industry and more than the finance, insurance, and real-estate sectors combined. And nonprofit museums, schools, theaters, and orchestras have become economic magnets for many communities, drawing additional investment.[7]

## 1-4 Factors of Production: The Basic Building Blocks

Both businesses and nonprofits rely on **factors of production**—four fundamental resources—to achieve their objectives. Some combination of these factors is crucial for an economic system to work and create wealth. As you read through the factors, keep in mind that they don't come free of charge. Human resources, for instance, require wages, while entrepreneurs need a profit incentive.

- **Natural Resources:** This factor includes all inputs that offer value in their natural state, such as land, fresh water, wind, and mineral deposits. Most natural resources must be extracted, purified, or harnessed; people cannot actually create them. (Note that agricultural products, which people do create through planting and tending, are not a natural resource.)

# From Basement Dwellers...to Elite Esports Athletes

Not long ago, the best an intense video game player could hope for was a comfy berth in the basement, a superfast internet connection, a respite from nagging, and a fresh bag of Doritos. But video gamers today often have bigger goals—the esports industry has ignited the imagination of millions, and filled their wallets, too. Esports tournaments pack iconic stadiums such as The Staples Center in Los Angeles and Madison Square Garden in New York. Top players can earn as much as $3.5 million annually, while streamers can make more than $1 million a month. The industry overall is expected to rake in more than $1.5 billion in advertising, media rights, and sponsorships by 2021.

Clearly, most gamers won't make it to the big leagues. But according to long-time gamer, Zandr Rose, even recreational players will hone a skillset that applies directly to both school and the workplace:

- **Strategic thinking:** Many games require players to think several moves ahead, which requires planning skills.

- **Performing under pressure:** Most games require players to consider and respond to multiple variables under a short deadline.

- **Teamwork:** No matter how skilled an individual player may be, many games will not allow him or her to succeed without effective team cooperation.

So, let the video games begin![8]

Many businesses work with nonprofits to boost their impact in the community.

The value of all-natural resources tends to rise with high demand, low supply, or both.

- **Capital:** This factor includes machines, tools, buildings, information, and technology—the synthetic resources that a business needs to produce goods or services. Computers and telecommunications capability have become pivotal elements of capital across a surprising range of industries, from financial services to professional sports. You may be surprised to learn that in this context, capital does not include money, but, clearly, businesses use money to acquire, maintain, and upgrade their capital.

- **Human Resources:** This factor encompasses the physical, intellectual, and creative contributions of everyone who works within an economy. As technology replaces a growing number of manual labor jobs, education and motivation have become increasingly important to human resource development. Given the importance of knowledge to workforce effectiveness, some business experts, such as management guru Peter Drucker, break out knowledge as its own category, separate from human resources.

- **Entrepreneurship:** Entrepreneurs are people who take the risk of launching and operating their own businesses, largely in response to the profit incentive. They tend to see opportunities where others don't, and they use their own resources to capitalize on that potential. Entrepreneurial enterprises can kick-start an economy, creating a tidal wave of opportunity by harnessing the other factors of

production. But entrepreneurs don't thrive in an environment that doesn't support them. The key ingredient is economic freedom: freedom of choice (whom to hire, for instance, or what to produce), freedom from excess regulation, and freedom from too much taxation. Protection from corruption and unfair competition is another entrepreneurial "must."

Clearly, all of these factors must be in place for an economy to thrive. But which factor is most important? One way to answer that question is to examine current economies around the world. Russia and China are both rich in natural resources and human resources, and both countries have a solid level of capital (growing in China, and deteriorating in Russia). Yet, neither country is wealthy; both rank relatively low in terms of gross national income per person. The missing ingredient seems to be entrepreneurship, limited in Russia largely through corruption and in China through government interference and taxes. Contrast those examples with, say, Hong Kong. The population is small, and the natural resources are severely limited, yet Hong Kong has consistently ranked among the richest regions in Asia. The reason: operating for many years under the British legal and economic system, the government actively encouraged entrepreneurship, which fueled the creation of wealth. Recognizing the potential of entrepreneurship, China has recently done more to relax regulations and support free enterprise. The result has been tremendous growth, which may yet bring China into the ranks of the wealthier nations.[9]

## 1-5 The Business Environment: The Context for Success

No business operates in a vacuum. Outside factors play a vital role in determining whether each individual business succeeds or fails. Likewise, the broader **business environment** can make the critical difference in whether an overall economy thrives or disintegrates. The five key dimensions of the business environment are the economic environment, the competitive environment, the technological environment, the social environment, and the global environment, as shown in Exhibit 1.1.

> **business environment** The setting in which business operates. The five key components are economic environment, competitive environment, technological environment, social environment, and global environment.

## Exhibit 1.1
## The Business Environment

Economic Environment

Social Environment

**BUSINESS**

Competitive Environment

Global Environment

Technological Environment

Each dimension of the business environment affects both individual businesses and the economy in general.

### 1-5a The Economic Environment

In September 2008, the U.S. economy plunged into the worst fiscal crisis since the Great Depression. Huge, venerable financial institutions faced collapse, spurring unprecedented bailouts by the federal government and the Federal Reserve. By the end of the year, the stock market had lost more than a third of its value, and 11.1 million Americans were out of work. Housing prices fell precipitously, and foreclosure rates reached record levels. As fear swept through the banking industry, many businesses and individuals could not borrow money to meet their needs. Economic turmoil in the United States spread quickly around the world, fueling a global economic crisis.

The U.S. economy continued to stagger through 2010 and 2011, with unemployment remaining stubbornly high, although signs of recovery began to emerge in late 2012, and certainly in 2013. The Federal Reserve—the U.S. central banking system—took unprecedented, proactive steps to encourage an economic turnaround. And former President Barack Obama spearheaded passage of a massive economic stimulus package, designed not only to create jobs but also to build

infrastructure—with a focus on renewable energy—to position the U.S. economy for stability and growth in the decades to come. (The price, of course, was more national debt, which will ultimately counterbalance some of the benefits.) Ultimately, the United States experienced the longest economic expansion ever recorded—ended by the COVID-19 pandemic in early 2020, which crippled the growing economy. The critical question is: how and when will the economy recover, and what scars will remain?[10]

The government also takes active steps on an ongoing basis to reduce the risks of starting and running a business. The result: free enterprise and fair competition flourish. Despite the economic crisis, research suggests that most budding entrepreneurs still plan to launch their firms in the next three years. One government policy that supports business is the relatively low federal tax rate, both for individuals and businesses. A number of states—from Alabama to Nevada—make their local economies even more appealing by providing special tax deals to attract new firms. The federal government also runs entire agencies that support business, such as the Small Business Administration. Other branches of the government, such as the Federal Trade Commission, actively promote fair competitive practices, which help give every enterprise a chance to succeed.

Another key element of the U.S. economic environment is legislation that supports enforceable contracts. For instance, if you contract a baker to supply your health food company with 10,000 pounds of raw kale chips at $1.00 per pound, that firm must comply or face legal consequences. The firm can't wait until a day before delivery and jack up the price to $10.00 per pound because you would almost certainly respond with a successful lawsuit. Many U.S. businesspeople take enforceable contracts for granted, but in a number of developing countries—which offer some of today's largest business

> "A banker is a fellow who lends you his umbrella when the sun is shining, but wants it back the minute it begins to rain."
>
> —Mark Twain,
> American Author

opportunities—contracts are often not enforceable (at least not in day-to-day practice).

Corruption also affects the economic environment. A low level of corruption and bribery dramatically reduces the risks of running a business by ensuring that everyone plays by the same set of rules—rules that are clearly visible to every player. Fortunately, U.S. laws keep domestic corruption mostly—but not completely—at bay. Other ethical lapses, such as shady accounting, can also increase the cost of doing business for everyone involved. But in the wake of corporate ethical meltdowns such as Enron, the federal government has passed tough-minded new regulations to increase corporate accountability. If the new legislation effectively curbs illegal and unethical practices, every business will have a fair chance at success.

Upcoming chapters on economics and ethics will address these economic challenges and their significance in more depth. But bottom line, we have reason for cautious (some would say very cautious) optimism. The American economy has a proven track record of flexibility and resilience, which will surely help us navigate this crisis and uncover new opportunities.

## 1-5b The Competitive Environment

As global competition intensifies yet further, leading-edge companies have focused on customer satisfaction like never before. The goal: to develop long-term, mutually beneficial relationships with customers. Getting current customers to buy more of your product is a lot less expensive than convincing potential customers to try your product for the first time. And if you transform your current customers into loyal advocates—vocal promoters of your product or service—they'll get those new customers for you more effectively than any advertising or discount program. Companies such as Amazon, Coca-Cola, and Northwestern Mutual life insurance lead their industries in customer satisfaction, which translates into higher profits even when the competition is tough.[11]

Customer satisfaction comes in large part from delivering unsurpassed value. The best measure of value is the size of the gap between product benefits and price. A product has value when its benefits to the customer are equal to or greater than the price that the customer pays. Keep in mind that the cheapest product doesn't necessarily represent the best value. If a 99-cent toy from Big Lots breaks in a day, customers may be willing to pay several dollars more for a similar toy from somewhere else. But if that 99-cent toy lasts all year, customers will be delighted by the value and will likely encourage their friends and family to shop at Big Lots. The key to value is quality, and

### Exhibit 1.2 Global Brand Champions

| Most Valuable | Biggest Gainers | Percentage Growth |
|---|---|---|
| Apple | Amazon | +60% |
| Amazon | Microsoft | +53% |
| Microsoft | Spotify | +52% |
| Google | Adobe | +41% |
| Samsung | Netflix | +41% |
| Coca-Cola | PayPal | +38% |
| Toyota | Salesforce | +34% |
| Mercedes-Benz | Nintendo | +31% |
| McDonald's | Mastercard | +17% |
| Disney | Visa | +15% |

Source: Interbrand Best Global Brands 2020, https://interbrand.com/best-global-brands/, accessed January 6, 2021.

virtually all successful firms offer top-quality products relative to their direct competitors.

A recent ranking study by consulting firm Interbrand highlights brands that use imagination and innovation to deliver value to their customers. Exhibit 1.2 shows the winners and the up-and-comers in the race to capture the hearts, minds, and dollars of consumers around the world.

**Leading Edge versus Bleeding Edge** Speed-to-market—the rate at which a firm transforms concepts into actual products—can be another key source of competitive advantage. And the pace of change just keeps getting faster. In this tumultuous setting, companies that stay ahead of the pack often enjoy a distinct advantage. But keep in mind that there's a difference between leading edge and bleeding edge. Bleeding-edge firms launch products that fail because they're too far ahead of the market. During the late 1990s, for example, in the heart of the dot.com boom, Webvan, a grocery delivery service, launched to huge fanfare. But the firm went bankrupt just a few years later in 2001, partly because customers weren't yet ready to dump traditional grocery stores in favor of cyber-shopping. (Online grocery shopping finally came into its own during the COVID-19 pandemic, with research indicating that 68% of American consumers ordered groceries online between April and August 2020.)[12] Leading-edge firms, on the other hand, offer products just as the market becomes ready to embrace them.[13]

**speed-to-market** The rate at which a new product moves from conception to commercialization.

McLittle Stock/Shutterstock.com

Apple provides an excellent example of leading edge. You may be surprised to learn that Apple—which controls about 70%[14] of the digital music player market—did not offer the first MP3 player. Instead, it surveyed the existing market to help develop a new product, the iPod, which was far superior in terms of design and ease-of-use. But Apple didn't stop with one successful MP3 player. Racing to stay ahead, they soon introduced the colorful, more affordable iPod mini. And before sales reached their peak, they launched the iPod Nano, which essentially pulled the rug from under the blockbuster iPod mini just a few short months before the holiday selling season. Why? If they hadn't done it, someone else may well have done it instead. And Apple is almost maniacally focused on maintaining its competitive lead.[15]

### 1-5c The Workforce Advantage

Employees can contribute another key dimension to a firm's competitive edge. Human resources firm Glassdoor published summaries of six recent studies that show clearly that investing in worker satisfaction yields tangible, bottom-line results. For each 1-star increase in a company's overall rating by employees on Glassdoor, researchers found a 7.9% average jump in the market value of a company—a powerful financial impact.[16]

While the critical difference in performance

> **business technology** Any tools—especially computers, telecommunications, and other digital products—that businesses can use to become more efficient and effective.

most likely stemmed from employee satisfaction, other factors—such as excellent product and superb top management—likely *also* played a role in both employee satisfaction and strong stock performance.[17]

Finding and holding the best talent will likely become a crucial competitive issue in the next decade as the baby boom generation begins to retire. The 500 largest U.S. companies anticipate losing about half of their senior managers over the next five to six years. Since January 1, 2011, approximately 10,000 baby boomers began to turn 65 (the traditional retirement age) every day, and the Pew Research Center anticipates that this trend will continue for 19 years. Replacing the skills and experience these workers bring to their jobs may be tough: baby boomers include about 77 million people, while the generation that follows includes only 46 million. Firms that cultivate human resources now will find themselves better able to compete as the market for top talent tightens.[18] However, job market contraction may not be an issue, because a growing number of baby boomers opt to either postpone retirement or continue working part-time during retirement, in the face of inadequate financial resources.

### 1-5d The Technological Environment

The broad definition of **business technology** includes any tools that businesses can use to become more efficient and effective. But more specifically, in today's world, business technology usually refers to computers, telecommunications, and other digital tools. Over the past few decades, the impact of digital technology on business has been utterly transformative. New industries have emerged, while others have disappeared. And some fields—such as travel, banking, and music—have changed dramatically. Even in categories with relatively unchanged products, companies have leveraged technology to streamline production and create new efficiencies. Examples include new processes such as computerized billing, digital animation, and robotic manufacturing. For fast-moving firms, the technological environment represents a rich source of competitive advantage, but it clearly can be a major threat for companies that are slow to adopt or to integrate new approaches.

# Spacing Out

Although rich retirees in your parents' generation may have opted to cruise the seven seas for a relaxing vacation, you or your children may opt instead to cruise through zero gravity. The space tourism industry—individuals traveling in space for recreation—stands ready to grow explosively. Experts estimate that the potential market value is $30 billion dollars by 2030.

There are two basic categories of space tourism: orbital and suborbital. Suborbital travel gives passengers just a few minutes in zero gravity, while orbital travel allows travelers to spend a week or even more in space. Although this industry has not quite blasted off, the competition is already fierce. And the key players will probably sound familiar:

- **Virgin Galactic:** Richard Branson, flamboyant entrepreneur, and creator of the Virgin Group, founded Virgin Galactic with the goal of initiating suborbital Space tourism. He expects to have private paying passengers by next year. The price of a zero-gravity trip will probably be in the neighborhood of $200,000 to $250,000 each.

- **Blue Origin:** Jeff Bezos, founder of Amazon, launched Blue Origin, which he funded privately, with the goal of introducing suborbital space tourism. He has not yet announced pricing, but he anticipates the prices will be comparable to the competition.

- **Space X:** Elon Musk, founder of Tesla, launched Space X with the goal of orbital space tourism. He aims to take passengers to space for about a week, for a price of roughly $50 million per person.

Clearly, the pricing for space travel is out of reach for most people. But the target market at least for the first few years is high-net-worth individuals who have demonstrated very strong demand for this luxury experience. Over time, all three entrepreneurs expect the price will drop, bringing outer space into reach for most of us. It doesn't hurt to hope! As Norman Vincent Peale once said, "Shoot for the moon. Even if you miss, you'll land among the stars."[19]

---

The creation of the **internet** has transformed not only business but also people's lives. Anyone, anywhere, anytime can use the web to send and receive images and data (as long as access is available). One result is the rise of **e-commerce** or online sales, which allow businesses to tap into a worldwide community of potential customers. In the wake of the global economic crisis, e-commerce slowed from the breakneck 20%+ growth rates of the previous five years, but unsurprisingly, the COVID-19 pandemic reignited explosive growth rates. Business-to-business selling comprises the vast majority of total e-commerce sales (and an even larger share of the profits). A growing number of businesses have also connected their digital networks with suppliers and distributors to create a more seamless flow of goods and services.[20]

Alternative selling strategies thrive on the internet, giving rise to a more individualized buying experience. If you've browsed seller reviews on eBay or received shopping recommendations from Amazon, you'll have a sense of how personal web marketing can feel. Online technology also allows leading-edge firms to offer customized products at prices that are comparable to standardized products. On the Burton website, for instance, customers can "custom build" professional quality "Custom X" snowboards while sitting at home in their pajamas. Nike offers a similar service for NikeID shoes, clothing, and gear.

As technology continues to evolve at breakneck speed, the scope of change—both in everyday life and business operations—is almost unimaginable. In this environment, companies that welcome change and manage it well will clearly be the winners.

## 1-5e The Social Environment

The social environment embodies the values, attitudes, customs, and beliefs shared by groups of people. It also covers **demographics**, or the measurable characteristics of a population. Demographic factors include population size and density and specific traits such as age, gender, race, education, and income. Clearly, given all these influences, the social environment changes dramatically from country to country. And a nation as diverse as the United States features a number of different social environments. Rather than cover the full spectrum, this section focuses on the broad social trends that have the strongest impact on American business. Understanding the various dimensions of the social environment is crucial since successful businesses must offer goods and services that respond to it.

**internet** The service that allows computer users to easily access and share information in the form of text, graphics, video, apps, and animation.

**e-commerce** Business transactions conducted online, typically via the internet.

**demographics** The measurable characteristics of a population. Demographic factors include population size and density, as well as specific traits such as age, gender, and race.

**Diversity** While the American population has always included an array of different cultures, the United States has become more ethnically diverse in recent years. Whites continue to represent the largest chunk of the population at 60%, but according to the director of the U.S. Census Bureau, "The next half century marks a turning point in continuing trends—the U.S. will become a plurality nation, where the non-Hispanic White population remains the largest single group, but no group is in the majority." This will probably happen in about 2045. The year that different populations hit "marginalized majority" status will differ dramatically by age—the number of non-White children currently surpasses the number of White children. For those age 18-29–members of the younger labor force and voting age populations—the number of non-White people will likely surpass the number of White people by 2027.[21]

The Hispanic and Asian populations will probably continue to grow faster than any other ethnic groups. By 2060, nearly one in three U.S. residents will be Hispanic, up from about one in six today. This will happen even though the overwhelming wave of immigration from Mexico to the United States has stalled and even begun to reverse in the past few years.[22] Exhibit 1.3 demonstrates the shifting population breakdown.

So, what does this mean for business? Growing ethnic populations offer robust profit potential for firms that pursue them. For instance, a number of major brands such as Coca-Cola, General Mills, Ford, Nestlé, Purina, and Walmart have invested heavily in the Hispanic market. Japanese automakers have begun targeting the Hispanic market,

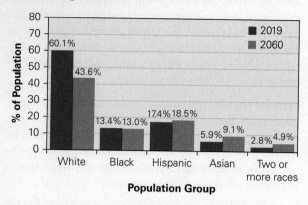

## Exhibit 1.3
## U.S. Population Estimates

Source: U.S. Census QuickFacts, Population Estimates, July 1, 2019, https://www.census.gov/quickfacts/fact/table/US#, accessed January 7, 2021.

recognizing the potential of them. Because of these efforts, Hispanic customers are reportedly 15% more likely than any other group to buy a Japanese-made car. Toyota, in particular, has been the top-selling brand among Latinos for more than ten years thanks to its highly targeted marketing. Targeting an ethnic market can also yield remarkable results for products that cross over into mainstream culture. Black rapper and songwriter, Pharrell Williams, for instance, created a streetwear empire with his Billionaire Boys Club brand.[23]

## Do You Do It?

More than 1,000 times a minute, someone in America bites into a Jack in the Box taco—one of more than a million Jack in the Box tacos sold every day. With such numbers, you might think that Jack unearthed the secret to the perfect-tasting taco . . . but you'd be wrong. Jack's taco has been variously described by its fans as:

- "a wet envelope of cat food"
- "vile and amazing"
- "disgusting and delectable"
- "repulsive and yet irresistible"

So why does the Jack in the Box taco do so well? Food writer Sophie Egan offers three possible reasons. First, it's cheap. At two for $.99 it's a real deal. Second, it's fried. As much as we like the idea of fruits and vegetables—fried stuff tastes good! Finally, it's a metaphorical flip of the bird to the "food police," who many believe are attempting to exert too much control over our rights to eat whatever we please.[24]

Eric Broder Van Dyke/Shutterstock.com

Growing diversity also affects the workforce. A diverse staff—one that reflects an increasingly diverse marketplace—can yield a powerful competitive advantage in terms of both innovation and ability to reach a broad customer base. Leading edge companies are responding—propelled in part by the social justice movement in 2020 and by recognition of their own shortcomings—by reworking their employment and hiring policies with an eye toward greater diversity and inclusion. Facebook, for example, pledged to have 50% of its workforce come from underrepresented communities by 2024. As part of this goal, Facebook says it wants to double the number of Black and Hispanic employees in the United States. Currently, Black and Hispanic women each account for less than 1% of Facebook executives. The social media goliath will clearly benefit from the influx of diverse talent into its homogenous ranks.[25]

In some cases, the call for greater diversity and inclusion has come directly from employees who are fed up with racism. Workers at Adidas, for example, presented senior management with a list of demands, including:

- 31% representation of Black and Latinx employees across all levels of the company by the end of 2021

- Overall commitment of $50 million of global sales to funding Black communities

- Partner with vetted external nonprofits to raise $100 million annually to end systematic racism and injustice for Black people

The workers implied that if the Adidas' response was insufficient, they would continue their scathing public exposing of the company's racist internal environment. Employee Aaron Ture explained his frustration in a letter to senior management: "We are an organization that exploits minorities, [B]lack, queer and so many others for commercial profit, without aiming to empower them at the workspace and in their own communities."

Adidas responded to the worker demands with a promised $20 million investment into Black American communities over the next four years and outlined investments in university scholarships for Black employees and a commitment to filling 30% of all new positions in the United States with Black and Latinx people. Ultimately, Adidas and other corporations may not respond fully to worker calls for diversity and inclusion, but many are endeavoring to head in a more positive direction.[26]

> In Asia, the average person's living standards are currently set to rise by 10,000% in one lifetime!
>
> —Newsweek

It's important to remember that true diversity also includes differences in gender, age, religion, and nationality, among other areas. Leading-edge firms have also taken proactive steps to train their entire workforce to manage diversity for top performance.[27]

Effectively managing diversity should only become easier as time goes by. Multiple studies demonstrate that young American adults are the most tolerant age group, and they are moving in a more tolerant direction than earlier generations regarding racial differences, immigrants, and homosexuality. As this generation gathers influence and experience in the workforce, they are likely to leverage diversity in their organizations to hone their edge in a fiercely competitive marketplace.[28]

**Aging Population** As life spans increase and birthrates decrease, the American population is rapidly aging. The U.S. Census Bureau projects that the nation's population age 65 and older will more than double between 2005 and 2060. By 2060, older Americans will represent just over one in five residents, up from one in seven today. Also, the number of working-age Americans will shrink from 63% to 57% of the population, dramatically increasing the number of people who are depending on each working American. And the United States isn't alone in this trend. The population is aging across the developed world, from Western Europe to Japan. China faces the same issue, magnified by its huge population. Demographers estimate that in the next 20 years the number of people in China over the age of 60 will double, leading to a nation where the retired will outnumber the entire population of Western Europe. There are currently six workers to every retiree, but China's one-child policy—in place from the early 1980s until roughly 2014—suggests that the number of people providing for the old will rapidly collapse.[29]

The rapidly aging population brings opportunities and threats for business. Companies in fields that cater to the elderly—such as healthcare, pharmaceuticals, travel, recreation, and financial management—will clearly boom. But creative companies in other fields will capitalize on the trend as well by reimagining their current products to serve older clients. Possibilities include books and movies—maybe even video games—with mature characters; low-impact fitness programs such as water aerobics; and cell phones and PDAs with more readable screens. Again, the potential payoff of age diversity is clear: companies with older employees are more likely to find innovative ways to reach the aging consumer market.

But the larger numbers of retired people also pose significant threats to overall business success. With a smaller labor pool, companies will need to compete even harder for top talent, driving up recruitment and payroll costs. As state and federal governments stretch to serve the aging population, taxes may increase, putting an additional burden on business. And as mid-career workers spend more on elder care, they may find themselves with less to spend on other goods and services, shrinking the size of the consumer market.

**Rising Worker Expectations** Workers of all ages continue to seek flexibility from their employers. Moreover, following massive corporate layoffs in the early 2000s, employees are much less apt to be loyal to their firms. According to the Bureau of Labor Statistics, the median number of years workers had been with their current employer was only 4.1 as of 2020.[30] As young people today enter the workforce, they bring higher expectations for their employers in terms of salary, job responsibility, and flexibility—and less willingness to pay dues by working extra-long hours or doing a high volume of "grunt work." Smart firms are responding to the change in worker expectations by forging a new partnership with their employees. The goal is a greater level of mutual respect through open communication, information sharing, and training. And the not-so-hidden agenda, of course, is stronger long-term performance.[31]

**Ethics and Social Responsibility** With high-profile ethical meltdowns dominating the headlines in the past few years, workers, consumers, and government alike have begun to hold businesses—and the people who run them—to a higher standard. Federal legislation demands transparent financial management and more accountability from senior executives. And recognizing their key role in business success, a growing number of consumers and workers have begun to insist that companies play a proactive role in making their communities—and often the world community—better places. Sustainability—doing business today without harming the ability of future generations to

meet their needs—has become a core issue in the marketplace, driving business policies, investment decisions, and consumer purchases on an unprecedented scale. Going beyond simply recycling, a number of innovative brands are engaged in upcycling—making use of their waste to enter entirely new markets. Swedish hosiery brand, Swedish Stockings, transforms used tights into commercial grease tanks and furniture.[32]

## 1-5f The Global Environment

The U.S. economy operates within the context of the global environment, interacting continually with other economies. In fact, over the past two decades, technology and free trade have blurred the lines between individual economies around the world. Technology has forged unprecedented links among countries, making it cost effective—even efficient—to establish computer help centers in Mumbai to serve customers in Boston, or to hire programmers in Buenos Aires to make websites for companies in Stockholm. Not surprisingly, jobs have migrated to the lowest bidder with the highest quality—regardless of where that bidder is based.

Often, the lowest bidder is based in China or India. Both economies are growing at breakneck speed, largely because they attract enormous foreign investment. Over the past couple of decades, China has been a magnet for manufacturing jobs because of the high population and low wages—about $5.50 per hour (including government-mandated benefits) versus about $27.00 in the United States—although the gap is rapidly closing due to double-digit annual wage inflation in China.[33] And India has been especially adept at attracting high-tech jobs, in part because of their world-class, English-speaking university graduates who are willing to work for less than their counterparts around the globe.[34]

The migration of jobs relates closely to the global movement toward **free trade**. In 1995, a renegotiation of the **General Agreement on Tariffs and Trade (GATT)**—signed by 125 countries—took bold steps to lower tariffs (taxes on imports) and to reduce trade restrictions worldwide. The result: goods move more freely than ever across international boundaries. Individual groups of countries have gone even further, creating blocs of nations with virtually unrestricted trade. Mexico, Canada, and the United States have laid the groundwork for a free-trade mega-market through the United States–Mexico–Canada–Agreement (USMCA), the successor to the North

**free trade** An international economic and political movement designed to help goods and services flow more freely across international boundaries.

**General Agreement on Tariffs and Trade (GATT)** An international trade agreement that has taken bold steps to lower tariffs and promote free trade worldwide.

American Free Trade Agreement (NAFTA), and 27 European countries have created a powerful free-trading bloc through the European Union (EU), which has been weakened by a severe, ongoing financial crisis. The free-trade movement has lowered prices and increased quality across virtually every product category as competition becomes truly global. We'll discuss these issues and their implications in more depth in Chapter 3.

**A Multi-Pronged Threat** In the past decade alone, war, terrorism, disease, and natural disasters have taken a horrific toll on human lives across the globe. The economic toll has been devastating as well, affecting businesses around the world. The 9/11 terrorist attacks in New York and Washington, D.C., decimated the travel industry and led to multibillion-dollar government outlays for Homeland Security. In 2002, a terrorist bombing at an Indonesian nightclub killed nearly 200 people, destroying tourism on the holiday island of Bali. Similarly, the 2015 terror attacks in Paris dealt a devastating blow to tourism throughout Europe, which was already struggling to handle an overwhelming refugee crisis. The 2003 deadly epidemic of the SARS flu dealt a powerful blow to the economies of Hong Kong, Beijing, and Toronto. And the Ebola outbreak of 2014 had a catastrophic impact on several impoverished African economies that could least afford the hit. Less than two years later, the Indian Ocean tsunami wiped out the fishing industry on long swaths of the Indian and Sri Lankan coastlines and crippled the booming Thai tourism industry. That same year, in 2005, Hurricane Katrina destroyed homes and businesses alike and brought the Gulf Coast oil industry to a virtual standstill. In 2012, Hurricane Sandy wreaked $50 billion of economic damage on the eastern seaboard states. And in 2013, Typhoon Haiyan decimated the Philippines. The wars in Afghanistan and Iraq—while a boon to the defense industry—have dampened the economic potential of both areas. With nationalism on the rise, and growing religious and ethnic tensions around the world, the global economy may continue to suffer collateral damage.[35]

## 1-6 Business and You: Making It Personal

Whatever your career choice—from video game developer to real-estate agent, to web designer—business will affect your life. Both the broader economy and your own business skills will influence the level of your personal financial success. In light of these factors, making the right career choice can be a bit scary. But the good news is that experts advise graduating students to "Do what you love." This is a hardheaded strategy, not softhearted puffery. Following your passion makes dollars and sense in today's environment, which values less-routine abilities such as creativity, communication, and caring. These abilities tend to be more rewarding for most people than routine, programmable skills that computers can easily emulate. Following your passion doesn't guarantee a fat paycheck, but it does boost your chances of both financial and personal success.[36]

Milles Studio/Shutterstock.com

## The Big Picture

Business today is complex, global, and faster moving than ever before. Looking forward, it's hard to imagine how the global economy—especially the United States—will recover from the blow of the COVID-19 pandemic. Technology will continue to change the business landscape. And a new focus on ethics and social responsibility—especially diversity and inclusion—will likely transform the role of business in society. This book will focus on the impact of change in every facet of business, from management to marketing, to money, with an emphasis on how the elements of business relate to each other and how business as a whole relates to you.

## Careers in Business

### Manager of New Media

Work with marketing team to determine what motivates and inspires consumers. Lead development and execution of digital marketing campaigns across a variety of platforms to build a deep, meaningful, and genuine relationship with consumers. Develop and manage interactive viral campaigns, integrate interactive media into the overall business strategy. According to Glassdoor, the median base salary for social media marketing managers in 2020 was $65,834, although there was significant variation based on company, location, industry, experience, and benefits. Most new media positions require experience in the field and a four-year degree in either business or communication. Many also prefer a master's degree in business (an MBA).

# 2 | Economics:
## The Framework for Business

## Learning Objectives

After studying this chapter, you will be able to:

**2-1** Define economics and discuss the global economic crisis

**2-2** Analyze the roots of the Great Recession and identify its impact on the economy

**2-3** Discuss the impact of fiscal and monetary policy on the economy

**2-4** Evaluate the free market system and supply and demand

**2-5** Evaluate planned market systems

**2-6** Describe the trend toward mixed market systems

**2-7** Discuss key terms and tools to evaluate economic performance

## 2-1 Economics: Navigating a Crisis

Understanding economics—and the role of the government, businesses, and individuals—requires understanding some basic definitions: The **economy** is essentially a financial and social system. It represents the flow of resources through society, from production to distribution, to consumption. **Economics** is the study of the choices that people, companies, and governments make in allocating those resources. The field of economics falls into two core categories: macroeconomics and microeconomics. **Macroeconomics** is the study of a country's overall economic dynamics, such as the employment rate, the gross domestic product, and taxation policies. While macroeconomic issues may seem abstract, they directly affect your day-to-day life, influencing key variables such as what jobs will

**economy** A financial and social system of how resources flow through society, from production to distribution, to consumption.

**economics** The study of the choices that people, companies, and governments make in allocating society's resources.

**macroeconomics** The study of a country's overall economic dynamics, such as the employment rate, the gross domestic product, and taxation policies.

be available for you, how much cash you'll actually take home after taxes, or how much you can buy with that cash in any given month. **Microeconomics** focuses on smaller economic units such as individual consumers, families, and individual businesses. Both macroeconomics and microeconomics play an integral role in the global economy.

The U.S. economy experienced the longest expansion in recorded history from 2009 until early 2020. The unprecedented growth jolted to a halt when COVID-19 cases reached a dangerous level, prompting government-mandated lockdowns. In March 2020, the U.S. economy experienced the biggest ever downturn in response to

> "Every time you spend money, you're casting a vote for the kind of world you want."
>
> —Anna Lappe,
> Sustainable Food Advocate

the government-mandated economic lockdowns. Millions of workers were thrust into unemployment, thousands of businesses closed their doors permanently, and most chilling of all, more than 400,000 Americans had lost their lives to the virus as of January, 2021.

The Federal response to the crisis was mixed, at best. Federal relief spending kept hunger and homelessness at bay, at least temporarily, and also fueled a short-term economic rebound three months into the pandemic. But a year after the pandemic hit, the need for strategic economic recovery planning had become painfully clear. The obvious first step was COVID-19 vaccinations to allow the economy to reopen. By the end of 2020,

**microeconomics** The study of smaller economic units such as individual consumers, families, and individual businesses.

the pharmaceutical industry had developed, tested, and gained emergency FDA approval for two different COVID-19 vaccinations. Distributing those vaccinations was among the highest priorities of the incoming Biden administration in early 2021. The logistics were daunting—especially since much of the population did not trust that the vaccines would be either effective or harmless.

## 2-2 Economics and the Great Recession

A deep understanding of today's economy requires a look back at the Great Recession and its historical roots. Through the last half of the 1990s, America enjoyed unprecedented growth. Unemployment was low, productivity was high, inflation was low, and the real standard of living for the average American rose significantly. The American economy grew by more than $2.4 trillion, a jump of nearly 33% in just five years. But the scene changed for the worse when the dot-com bubble burst in 2000, followed by the 9/11 terrorist attacks in 2001. As the stock market dropped and unemployment rose, economic experts feared that the country was hovering on the brink of a full-blown recession.[1]

> "The financial crisis is a stark reminder that transparency and disclosure are essential in today's marketplace."
>
> —U.S. Senator Jack Reed

### 2-2a Managing the Crisis

In an effort to avert a recession by increasing the money supply and encouraging investment, the Federal Reserve—the nation's central bank—decreased interest rates from 6.5% in mid-2000 to 1.25% by the end of 2002. As a result, the economy was awash with money, but opportunities to invest yielded paltry returns. This is when *subprime mortgage loans* came into play. Most experts define subprime mortgages as loans to borrowers with low credit scores, high debt-to-income ratios, or other signs of a reduced ability to repay the money they borrow.

These subprime mortgage loans were attractive to borrowers and lenders alike. For the borrowers, getting a loan suddenly became a cinch, and for the first time ever, hundreds of thousands of people could afford homes. The lenders were all too willing to give them mortgage loans, sometimes with little or no documentation (such as proof of income), and sometimes with little or no money down.

As demand for homes skyrocketed, prices continued to rise year after year. Borrowers took on adjustable-rate loans assuming that when their loans adjusted up—usually sharply up—they could simply refinance their now-more-valuable homes for a new low starter rate and maybe even pull out some cash.

## A Trillion Dollars? Say What?

Between stimulating the economy and managing the federal debt, "a trillion dollars" is a figure you may have heard a lot lately. But getting your mind around what that actually means may be a little tricky, since it's just so much money. To understand the true magnitude of a trillion dollars, consider this:

- If you had started spending a million dollars a day—every day, without fail—at the start of the Roman Empire, you still wouldn't have spent a trillion dollars by 2020; in fact, you'd have more than $250 billion left over.

- One trillion dollars, laid end-to-end, would stretch farther than the distance from the earth to the sun. You could also wrap your chain of bills more than 12,000 times around the earth's equator.

- If you were to fly a jet at the speed of sound, spooling out a roll of dollar bills behind you, it would take you more than 14 years to release a trillion dollars. But your plane probably couldn't carry the roll, since it would weigh more than one million tons.

Turning the economy around may take even more than a trillion dollars, but make no mistake when you hear those numbers thrown around on the news—a trillion dollars is an awful lot of money![2]

Subprime loans were attractive to lenders because they provided a higher return than many other investments, and—given the growth in housing prices—they seemed relatively low risk. Banks and investment houses invented a range of stunningly complex financial instruments to slice up and resell the mortgages as specialized securities. Hedge funds swapped the new securities, convinced that they were virtually risk-free. With a lack of regulation—or any other government oversight—financial institutions did *not* maintain sufficient reserves in case those mortgage-backed funds lost value.

And they did indeed lose value. In 2006, housing prices peaked, and in the months that followed, prices began falling precipitously (refer to Exhibit 2.1), dropping nearly 35% from the market peak in 2006 through the market trough in 2009. Increasing numbers of subprime borrowers found themselves "upside down"—they owed their lenders more than the value of their homes. Once this happened, they couldn't refinance to lower their payments. Foreclosure rates climbed at an increasing pace. RealtyTrac, a leading online marketplace for foreclosure properties, reported that foreclosure rates were 33% higher in 2010 than they were in all of 2009. In 2011, the foreclosure rate dropped to the lowest level since 2007, when the recession began. And by January 2014, the inventory of foreclosed homes had experienced 16 consecutive months of year-to-year double-digit declines, signaling that the fragile economic recovery had finally taken hold.[3]

As mortgage values dropped, financial institutions began to feel the pressure—especially firms such as Bear Stearns that specialized in trading mortgage-backed securities, and firms such as Washington Mutual that focused on selling subprime mortgages. When financial institutions actually began to face collapse, a wave of fear washed over the entire banking industry. Banks became unwilling to lend money to each other or to clients, which meant that funds were not available for businesses to finance either day-to-day operations or longer-term growth. Company after company—from General Motors to Yahoo!, to American Express, to countless small employers— began to announce layoffs. The December 2008 unemployment rate hit 7.2%. About 2.6 million Americans lost their jobs in 2008, making 2008 the worst year for jobs since 1945. And the unemployment rate continued to rise, hitting 9.3% in 2009 and 9.6% in 2010, leading to total Great Recession job losses of nearly 8 million, many of which will never come back as the economy continues to change and old skills become obsolete.[4] The national average unemployment rate began to drop in late 2011 until it reached a near historic low of 3.5% in February 2020.

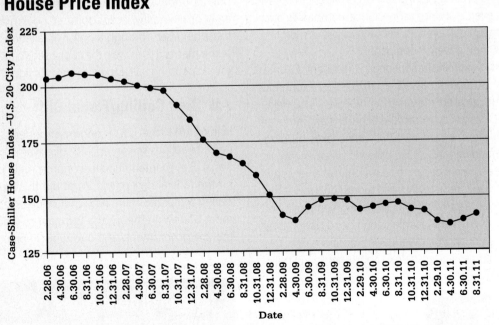

## Exhibit 2.1
## House Price Index

Source: Housing's Rise and Fall in 20 Cities, December 27, 2011, The *New York Times* website, http://www.nytimes.com/interactive/2011/05/31/business/economy/case-shiller-index.html#city/IND20, accessed January 25, 2012.

## 2-2b Moving in a Better Direction

Although the benefits were not immediately obvious in the face of a downward trend, the federal government and the Federal Reserve—known as "the Fed"—intervened in the economy at an unprecedented level to prevent total financial disaster. In March 2008, the Fed staved off bankruptcy at Bear Stearns. In early September 2008, the U.S. Department of the Treasury seized Fannie Mae and Freddie Mac, which owned about half of the U.S. mortgage market. A week later, the Fed bailed out tottering global insurance giant AIG with an $85 billion loan. But the bleeding continued.

The negative spiral spurred Congress to pass a controversial $700 billion economic bailout plan in early October 2008, called TARP (the Troubled Assets Relief Program). By the end of the year, the Treasury had spent the first half of that money investing in banks, although early results were imperceptible for the economy. Just as the Treasury began to release funds to the banks, GM and Chrysler, two of the Big Three U.S. automakers, announced they also desperately needed a bailout. Both firms suggested that bankruptcy was imminent without government assistance. (Ford, the other member of the Big Three, also admitted to financial problems but claimed that it was not in the dire straits faced by its domestic competitors.) Facing the loss of more than 2.5 million jobs related to the auto industry, the Treasury agreed to spend a portion of what remained of the $700 billion in a partial auto industry bailout.[5] Although much of the public railed against the expensive government bailout program, by 2010 it appeared likely that TARP could end up costing taxpayers far less than anticipated, or even nothing, as insurance companies and banks began to break even, or in many cases earn profits, and pay back their government loans.[6]

As the new administration began, President Obama proposed, and Congress passed, an $825 billion economic stimulus package called the American Recovery and Reinvestment Act, designed to turn the economy around over the next two years. The plan included cutting taxes, building infrastructure, and investing $150 billion in green energy. In late 2011, the economy began to turn around at a very slow pace. Employment grew slowly for 49 months in a row—the best run since at least World War II. Although employment numbers improved, many people traded good-paying jobs for part-time work and/or lower-paying positions. This has constrained incomes and restrained consumer spending in the years since.[7]

All of these moves by the federal government and the Federal Reserve are part of fiscal and monetary policy.

> **fiscal policy** Government efforts to influence the economy through taxation and spending.

## 2-3 Managing the Economy Through Fiscal and Monetary Policy

While the free market drives performance in the American economy, the federal government and the Federal Reserve can help *shape* performance. During the recent crisis, both the government and the Fed have taken proactive—some say heavy-handed—roles to mitigate this economic contraction. The overarching goal is controlled, sustained growth, and both fiscal and monetary policy can help achieve this objective.

### 2-3a Fiscal Policy

**Fiscal policy** refers to government efforts to influence the economy through taxation and spending decisions that are designed to encourage growth, boost employment, and curb inflation. Clearly, fiscal strategies are closely tied to political philosophy. But regardless of politics, most economists agree that lower taxes can boost the economy by leaving more money in people's pockets for them to spend or invest. Most also agree that government spending can boost the economy in the short term by providing jobs, such as mail carrier, bridge repairer, or park ranger; and in the long term by investing in critical public assets, such as a national renewable energy grid. Done well, both taxation and spending can offer economic benefits. The tricky part is finding the right balance between the two approaches. As American economist Henry Hazlitt pointed out, it's important to keep in mind that "[e]ither immediately or ultimately, every dollar of government spending must be raised through a dollar of taxation; once we look at the matter in this way, the supposed miracles of government spending will appear in another light."

### 2-3b Debt Ceiling/Fiscal Cliff

In mid-2011, the U.S. economy shuddered again as the news headlines screamed with dire warnings about a national or even international economic meltdown when we hit the federal *debt ceiling*. What did this mean? The debt ceiling is the maximum amount Congress lets the government borrow. In theory, this is meant to limit the amount that the government can borrow, but in practice, voting on

> ## "Government does not solve problems; it subsidizes them."
>
> —U.S. President Ronald Reagan

## Exhibit 2.2
## Federal Government Revenue and Expenses

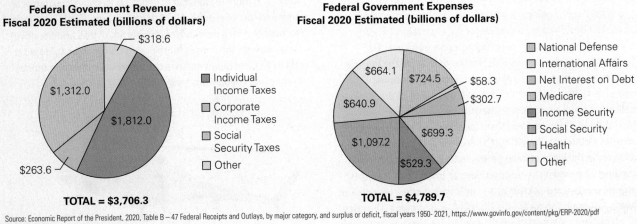

**Federal Government Revenue**
Fiscal 2020 Estimated (billions of dollars)

$318.6
$1,312.0
$1,812.0
$263.6

- ☐ Individual Income Taxes
- ☐ Corporate Income Taxes
- ☐ Social Security Taxes
- ☐ Other

**TOTAL = $3,706.3**

**Federal Government Expenses**
Fiscal 2020 Estimated (billions of dollars)

$664.1
$724.5
$58.3
$640.9
$302.7
$699.3
$1,097.2
$529.3

- ☐ National Defense
- ☐ International Affairs
- ☐ Net Interest on Debt
- ☐ Medicare
- ☐ Income Security
- ☐ Social Security
- ☐ Health
- ☐ Other

**TOTAL = $4,789.7**

Source: Economic Report of the President, 2020, Table B – 47 Federal Receipts and Outlays, by major category, and surplus or deficit, fiscal years 1950- 2021, https://www.govinfo.gov/content/pkg/ERP-2020/pdf /ERP-2020-table47.pdf, accessed January 10, 2021.

the debt ceiling happens separately from voting on taxes and spending, so the debt ceiling ends up being mostly about whether the federal government can pay for debts that it has already incurred. Typically, debt ceiling hikes are fairly routine; in fact, Congress has raised the debt ceiling 74 times since 1962, and ten times since 2001, all with little or no notice. But as federal debt began to nudge the ceiling in 2011, it garnered unprecedented political and journalistic attention because various political groups saw the issue as an opportunity to further their political agenda. Those who wanted to raise the debt ceiling portrayed others as irresponsible buffoons who were willing to shut down the government simply to make a point without any real long-term change in spending. Those who did not want to raise the debt ceiling argued that the others are spendthrift bureaucrats who must learn to live within their means like the Americans who elected them.

After weeks of high-profile wrangling, Congress finally agreed to raise the debt ceiling, which temporarily averted a shutdown crisis, but the deal they reached to do so created the fiscal cliff. The *fiscal cliff* was a package of draconian across-the-board spending cuts and sharp tax hikes scheduled to hit at the same time that could dramatically decrease the U.S. budget deficit. Going over the *fiscal cliff* could potentially cripple the U.S. economy, and possibly even cause the United States to default on some of its debt, which could send world markets into a tailspin. But once again, Congress could not reach a reasonable long-term agreement, so they simply passed last-minute legislation that pushed the

really tough tax and spending decisions farther down the road. The federal government actually did shut down for 16 days in October 2013 after much congressional squabbling failed to produce a budget agreement. The government reopened with passage of another temporary agreement that again delayed the tough fiscal choices. If the country continues to fracture along political lines, it may become increasingly difficult to reach a federal budget agreement, leading to more regular government shutdowns, such as the two very brief shutdowns at the start of 2018. In the middle of December 2020, Congress averted a government shutdown by passing yet another temporary funding bill.[8]

Every year, the government must create a budget, or a financial plan, that outlines expected revenue from taxes and fees, and expected spending. If revenue is higher than spending, the government incurs a **budget surplus** (rare in recent years, but usually quite welcome!). If spending is higher than revenue, the government incurs a **budget deficit** and must borrow money to cover the shortfall. The sum of all the money borrowed over the years and not yet repaid is the total **federal debt**. Exhibit 2.2 shows an estimate of key sources of revenue and key expenses

**budget surplus** Overage that occurs when revenue is higher than expenses over a given period of time.

**budget deficit** Shortfall that occurs when expenses are higher than revenue over a given period of time.

**federal debt** The sum of all the money that the federal government has borrowed over the years and not yet repaid.

# What Does It Really Mean to Call an Uber?

If you're like most people, the first thing that comes to mind when you think about "calling an Uber" is hailing a car for a local trip or maybe arranging a food delivery to satisfy a craving via UberEATS. But if you are a member of the entertainment elite, calling an Uber may well mean hailing a helicopter via Uber Copter to get to the Cannes Film Festival or to avoid the bumper-to-bumper traffic between Manhattan and the Hamptons on a steamy New York weekend. Airbus expanded its private helicopter service into all-new markets by joining forces with Uber in 2016. The partnership was launched as demand from some of Airbus's traditional customers—oil and gas companies—dropped in the wake of falling commodity prices. But Uber has expanded beyond just helicopter rides. In India, Uber's services include on-demand rickshaws, and in Turkey, it offers on-demand boats. Although the cost of the Uber Copter is sky high (the price of a flight from Manhattan's Wall Street to JFK airport was roughly

$220 in 2019, depending on demand), the price of hailing a rickshaw is more reasonable in India and Pakistan, starting at a minimum fare of roughly $0.74. Motorcycle hailing is even more reasonable with a base fare of roughly $0.37 U.S., and the driver shows up with the helmet for the rider. It's fun to imagine what calling an Uber might mean in the future—on-demand drones? On-demand robots? Time will tell.[9]

Shutterstock.com

for the federal government in 2018. Note that spending significantly outstrips receipts, creating a one-year budget deficit of more than a trillion dollars. Clearly, any additional spending without corresponding tax increases could dramatically increase the shortfall. Also note that these numbers changed dramatically with the onset of the pandemic in 2020, although that data was not available at the time of writing.

By the end of 2020, the total U.S. federal debt stood at $26.95 trillion and growing, a staggering $82,000 for every U.S. citizen.[10]

The debt has only grown bigger every year since 1957, and the pace of growth will likely increase further in the wake of the COVID-19 pandemic. This matters to each taxpayer because as the government repays the debt—not to mention paying the skyrocketing interest to finance this debt—less and less money will be available for other uses; services may be eliminated (e.g., student loans, veterans' benefits, housing subsidies), or taxes will soar, or perhaps even both.

Analysts agree that the federal tax reform that Congress passed in late 2017 will add an estimated $1.5 trillion to the deficit over ten years due to a decrease in corporate taxes from 35% to 21% and a decrease in individual income taxes.[11]

**monetary policy** Federal Reserve decisions that shape the economy by influencing interest rates and the supply of money.

**commercial banks** Privately owned financial institutions that accept demand deposits and make loans and provide other services for the public.

## 2-3c Monetary Policy

**Monetary policy** refers to actions that shape the economy by influencing interest rates and the supply of money. The Federal Reserve—essentially the central bank of the United States—manages U.S. monetary policy. For the first time in its history, the Fed has also taken an activist role in bailing out and propping up shaky financial firms during the economic crisis. Other Fed functions include banking services for member banks and the federal government.

The Fed is headed by a seven-member Board of Governors. The president appoints each member of the Board to serve a single 14-year term—though a member can also complete a former member's unexpired term and still be appointed to a full term of their own. These terms are staggered, with one expiring every two years, so that no single president can appoint all of the members. This structure helps ensure that the Fed can act independently of political pressure.

In addition to setting monetary policy, the Board of Governors oversees the operation of the 12 Federal Reserve Banks that carry out Fed policies and perform banking services for **commercial banks** in their districts. Interestingly, the federal government does not own these Federal Reserve Banks. Instead, they're owned by the member commercial banks in their individual districts.

The president appoints one of the seven members of the Board of Governors to serve as its chair—a position so powerful that many consider him or her the second most powerful person on earth. For nearly 19 years, the chair was Alan Greenspan. When Greenspan retired in early 2006, President Bush appointed economist Ben Bernanke to the chair role. Bernanke led the Fed's proactive efforts to turn the ailing economy around. In early 2014, the Senate confirmed economist Janet Yellen as new chair of the Fed. Yellen was the first female chair, and she focused primarily on fighting unemployment by encouraging economic expansion. In late 2017, President Trump appointed Jerome Powell to succeed Janet Yellen as new chair of the Fed. Although analysts anticipated that Powell would continue Yellen's policies, he was quite different from recent Fed Chairs because he has a business background, rather than an academic background.

The core purpose of the Fed is to influence the size of the **money supply**—or the total amount of money within the overall economy. Clearly, you know what money is. But the formal definition of **money** is anything generally accepted as a medium of exchange, a measure of value, or a means of payment. The two most commonly used definitions of the money supply are M1 and M2:

- **M1:** All currency—paper bills and metal coins—plus checking accounts and traveler's checks.

- **M2:** All of M1 plus most savings accounts, money market accounts, and certificates of deposit (low-risk savings vehicles with a fixed term, typically less than one year).

By the end of 2020, the M1 money supply totaled more than $6.5 trillion, and the M2 version of the money supply totaled about $19.1 trillion. In practice, the term "money supply" most often refers to M2. (Note that credit cards are not part of the money supply, although they do have an unmistakable impact on the flow of money through the economy.)[12]

When the economy contracts, the Fed typically increases the money supply. If more money is available, interest rates usually drop, encouraging businesses to expand and consumers to spend. But when prices begin to rise, the Fed attempts to reduce the money supply. Ideally, if less money is available, interest rates will rise. This will reduce spending, which should bring inflation under control. Specifically, the Fed uses three key tools to expand and contract the money supply: open market operations, discount rate changes, and reserve requirement changes.

**Open Market Operations** This is the Fed's most frequently used tool. **Open market operations** involve buying and selling government securities, which include treasury bonds, notes, and bills. These securities are the IOUs the government issues to finance its deficit spending.

How do open market operations work? When the economy is weak, the Fed *buys* government securities on the open market. When the Fed pays the sellers of these securities, money previously held by the Fed is put into circulation. This directly stimulates spending. In addition, any of the additional funds supplied by the Fed that are deposited in banks will allow banks to make more loans, making credit more readily available. This encourages even more spending and further stimulates the economy.

When inflation is a concern, the Fed *sells* securities. Buyers of the securities write checks to the Fed to pay for securities they bought, and the Fed withdraws these funds from banks. With fewer funds, banks must cut back on the loans they make, credit becomes tighter, and the money supply shrinks. This reduces spending and cools off the inflationary pressures in the economy.

Open market operations are set by the aptly named Federal Open Market Committee, which consists of the seven members of the Board of Governors and 5 of the 12 presidents of the Federal Reserve district banks. Each year, the Federal Open Market Committee holds eight regularly scheduled meetings to make decisions about open market operations, although they do hold additional meetings when the need arises. Both businesses and markets closely watch Open Market Committee rate setting and outlook statements in order to guide decision making.

**Discount Rate Changes**
Just as you can borrow money from your bank, your bank can borrow funds from the Fed. And just as you must pay interest on your loan, your bank must pay interest on loans from the Fed. The **discount rate** is the interest rate the Fed charges on its loans to commercial banks. When the Fed reduces the discount rate, banks can obtain funds at a lower cost and use these funds to make more loans to their

**money supply** The total amount of money within the overall economy.

**money** Anything generally accepted as a medium of exchange, a measure of value, or a means of payment.

**M1 money supply** Includes all currency plus checking accounts and traveler's checks.

**M2 money supply** Includes all of M1 money supply plus most savings accounts, money market accounts, and certificates of deposit.

**open market operations** The Federal Reserve function of buying and selling government securities, which include treasury bonds, notes, and bills.

**discount rate** The rate of interest that the Federal Reserve charges when it loans funds to banks.

# Looking to Multiply Your Money? Look No Further Than Your Local Bank!

Everyone knows that banks help people save money, but most people don't realize that banks actually create money. While the process is complex, a simplified example illustrates the point. Say you deposit $5,000 in the bank. How much money do you have? Obviously, $5,000. Now imagine that your neighbor Anne goes to the bank for a loan. In line with Federal Reserve requirements, the bank must hold onto about 10% of its funds, so it loans Anne $4,500. She uses the money to buy a used car from your neighbor Jake, who deposits the $4,500 in the bank. How much money does Jake have? Clearly, $4,500. How much money do you have? Still, $5,000. Thanks to the banking system, our "money supply" has increased from $5,000 to $9,500. Multiply this phenomenon times millions of banking transactions, and you can see why cold, hard cash accounts for only about 10% of the total U.S. M2 money supply. But what happens if everyone goes to the bank at once to withdraw their money? The banking system would clearly collapse. And in fact, in 1930 and 1931, a run on the banks caused wave after wave of devastating bank failures. Panicked customers lost all their savings, ushering in the worst years of the Great Depression. To restore public confidence in the banking system, in 1933 Congress established the

**Federal Deposit Insurance Corporation (FDIC).** The FDIC insures deposits in banks and thrift institutions for up to $100,000 per customer, per bank. In the wake of the banking crisis, the FDIC temporarily increased its coverage to $250,000 per depositor at the end of 2008. Since the FDIC began operations on January 1, 1934, no depositor has lost a single cent of insured funds as a result of a bank failure.

Syda Productions/Shutterstock.com

own customers. With the cost of acquiring funds from the Fed lower, interest rates on bank loans also tend to fall. The result: businesses and individuals are more likely to borrow money and spend it, which stimulates the economy. Clearly, the Fed is most likely to reduce the discount rate during recessions. In fact, during the early months of the Great Recession, the Fed cut the rate to less than 1%. The Fed kept the rate well below 1% throughout the recovery, eventually nudging it up at the end of 2015 and again at the end of 2016. As the recovery continued, the Fed continued raising rates slowly—*very* slowly.

But in response to the COVID-19-pandemic-driven economic crash in March 2020, the Fed decreased the discount rate back down to .25%.[13]

**Reserve Requirement Changes** The Fed requires that all of its member banks hold funds, called "reserves," equal to a stated percentage of the deposits held by their customers. This percentage is called the **reserve requirement** (or required reserve ratio). The reserve requirement helps protect depositors who may want to withdraw their money without notice. Currently, the reserve requirement stands at about 10%, depending on the size and type of a bank's deposits. If the Fed increases the reserve requirement, banks must hold more funds, meaning they will have fewer funds available to make loans. This makes credit tighter and causes interest rates to rise. If the Fed decreases the reserve requirement, some of the funds that banks were required to hold become available for loans. This increases the availability of credit and causes interest rates to drop. Since changes in the reserve requirement can have a dramatic impact on both the economy and the financial health of individual banks, the Fed uses this tool quite infrequently.

**Other Fed Functions** In addition to monetary policy, the Fed has several other core functions, including regulating financial institutions and providing banking services both for the government and for banks. In its role as a regulator, the Fed sets and enforces rules of conduct for banks and oversees mergers and acquisitions to ensure fairness and compliance with government policy. In its role as a banker for banks, the Fed coordinates the

**Federal Deposit Insurance Corporation (FDIC)** A federal agency that insures deposits in banks and thrift institutions for up to $250,000 per customer, per bank.

**reserve requirement** A rule set by the Fed, which specifies the minimum amount of reserves (or funds) a bank must hold, expressed as a percentage of the bank's deposits.

check-clearing process for checks on behalf of any banks that are willing to pay its fees. And as the government's bank, the Fed maintains the federal government's checking account and keeps the U.S. currency supply in good condition.

## 2-4 Capitalism: The Free Market System

It's a simple fact—more clear now than ever before—no one can get everything they want all of the time. We live in a world of finite resources, which means that societies must determine how to distribute resources among their members. An **economic system** is a structure for allocating limited resources. Over time and around the globe, nations have instituted different economic systems. But a careful analysis suggests that no system is perfect, which may explain why there isn't one standard approach. The next sections of this chapter examine each basic type of economic system and explore the trend toward mixed economies.

The economic system of the United States is called **capitalism**, also known as a "private enterprise system" or a "free market system." Brought to prominence by Adam Smith in the 1700s, capitalism is based on private ownership, economic freedom, and fair competition. One core capitalist principle is the paramount importance of individuals, innovation, and hard work. In a capitalist economy, individuals, businesses, or nonprofit organizations

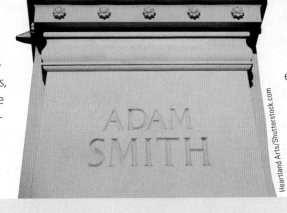

Adam Smith (1723–1790) has often been called the "father of modern economics."

privately own the vast majority of enterprises (with only a small fraction owned by the government). These private-sector businesses are free to make their own choices regarding everything from what they will produce to how much they will charge, to whom they will hire and fire. Correspondingly, individuals are free to choose what they will buy, how much they are willing to pay, and where they will work.

To thrive in a free enterprise system, companies must offer value to their customers—otherwise, their customers will choose to go elsewhere. Businesses must also offer value to their employees and suppliers in order to attract top-quality talent and supplies. As companies compete to attract the best resources and offer the best values, quality goes up, prices remain reasonable, and choices proliferate, raising the standard of living in the economy as a whole.

### 2-4a The Fundamental Rights of Capitalism

For capitalism to succeed, the system must ensure some fundamental rights—or freedoms—to all of the people who live within the economy.

■ *The right to own a business and keep after-tax profits:* Remember that capitalism doesn't guarantee that anyone will actually *earn* profits. Nor does it promise that there won't be taxes. But if you do earn profits, you get to keep your after-tax income and spend it however you see fit (within the limits of the law, of course). This right acts as a powerful motivator for business owners in a capitalist economy; the lower the tax rate, the higher the motivation. The U.S. government strives to maintain low tax rates to preserve the after-tax profit incentive that plays such a pivotal role in the free enterprise system.

**economic system** A structure for allocating limited resources.

**capitalism** An economic system—also known as the private enterprise or free market system—based on private ownership, economic freedom, and fair competition.

- *The right to private property:* This means that individuals and private businesses can buy, sell, and use property—which includes land, machines, and buildings—in any way that makes sense to them. This right also includes the right to will property to family members. The only exceptions to private property rights are minimal government restrictions designed to protect the greater good. You can't, for instance, use your home or business to produce cocaine, abuse children, or spew toxic smoke into the air.

- *The right to free choice:* Capitalism relies on economic freedom. People and businesses must be free to buy (or not buy) according to their wishes. They must be free to choose where to work (or not work) and where to live (or not live). Freedom of choice directly feeds competition, creating a compelling incentive for business owners to offer the best goods and services at the lowest prices. U.S. government trade policies boost freedom of choice by encouraging a wide array of both domestic and foreign producers to compete freely for our dollars.

- *The right to fair competition:* A capitalist system depends on fair competition among businesses to drive higher quality, lower prices, and more choices. Capitalism can't achieve its potential if unfair practices—such as deceptive advertising, predatory pricing, and broken contracts—mar the free competitive environment. The government's role is to create a level playing field by establishing regulations and monitoring the competition to ensure compliance.

## 2-4b Four Degrees of Competition

Although competition is essential for the free market system to function, not all competition works the same. Different industries experience different degrees of competition, ranging from pure competition to monopolies.

- **Pure competition** is a market structure with many competitors selling virtually identical products. Since customers can't (or won't) distinguish one product from another, no single producer has any control over the price. And new producers can easily enter and leave purely competitive markets. In today's U.S. economy, examples of pure competition have virtually disappeared. Agriculture probably comes closest—corn is basically corn, for example—but with the dramatic growth of huge corporate farms and the success of major agricultural cooperatives such as Sunkist, Sun-Maid, and Land O'Lakes, the number of competitors in agriculture has dwindled, and new farmers have trouble entering the market. Not only that, segments of the agriculture market—such as organic farms and hormone-free dairies—have emerged with hit products that command much higher prices than the competition.

- **Monopolistic competition** is a market structure with many competitors selling differentiated products. (Caution! Monopolistic competition is quite different from a *monopoly*, which we will cover shortly.) Producers have some control over the price of their wares, depending on the value that they offer their customers. And new producers can fairly easily enter categories marked by monopolistic competition. In fact, in monopolistic competition, a successful product usually attracts new suppliers quite quickly. Examples of monopolistic competition include the clothing industry and the restaurant business.

Think about the clothing business, for a moment, in local terms. How many firms do you know that sell T-shirts? You could probably think of at least 50 without too much trouble. And the quality and price are all over the board: designer T-shirts can sell for well over $100, but plenty of options go for less than $10. How hard would it be

Which of the four degrees of competition does the soft drink market represent?

Roman Tiraspolsky/Shutterstock.com

to start your own T-shirt business? Probably not hard at all. In fact, chances are strong that you know at least one person who sells T-shirts on the side. In terms of product and price variation, number of firms, and ease of entry, the T-shirt business clearly demonstrates the characteristics of monopolistic competition.

- **Oligopoly** is a market structure with only a handful of competitors selling products that can be similar or different. The retail gasoline business and the car manufacturing industry, for instance, are both oligopolies, even though gas stations offer very similar products, and car companies offer quite different models and features. Other examples of oligopoly include the soft drink industry, the computer business, and network television. Breaking into a market characterized by oligopoly can be tough because it typically requires a huge upfront investment.

You could start making T-shirts in your kitchen, for instance, but you'd need a pretty expensive facility to start manufacturing cars. Oligopolies typically avoid intense price competition, since they have nothing to gain—every competitor simply makes less money. When price wars do flare up, the results can be devastating for entire industries.

**Monopoly** is a market structure with just a single producer completely dominating the industry, leaving no room for any significant competitors. Monopolies usually aren't good for anyone but the company that has control, since without competition there isn't any incentive to hold down prices or increase quality and choices.

The EU slapped Google with a $1.7 billion fine for preventing rivals from competing fairly in the online ad market.

Because monopolies can harm the economy, most are illegal according to federal legislation such as the Sherman Antitrust Act of 1890 and the Clayton Antitrust Act of 1914. In the mid-1990s, Microsoft ran afoul of antimonopoly laws due to its position and policies in the software business. Even though Microsoft is not an actual monopoly, it was convicted of "monopolistic practices" that undermined fair competition. In 2020, the Justice Department accused Google of illegally protecting its monopoly over search and search advertising markets, which may ultimately reshape how consumers use the internet.[14]

However, in a few instances, the government not only allows monopolies but actually encourages them. This usually occurs when it would be too inefficient for each competitor to build its own infrastructure to serve the public. A **natural monopoly** arises. Public utilities offer a clear example. Would it really make sense for even a handful of competitors to pipe neighborhoods separately for water? Clearly, that's not practical. Just imagine the chaos! Instead, the government has granted exclusive rights—or monopolies—to individual companies for limited geographic areas and then regulated them (with mixed results) to ensure that they don't abuse the privilege. In addition to natural monopolies, the government grants patents and copyrights, which create artificial monopoly situations (at least temporarily) to encourage innovation.

### 2-4c Supply and Demand: Fundamental Principles of a Free Market System

In a free market system, the continual interplay between buyers and sellers determines the selection of products and prices available in the economy. If a business makes something that few people

**pure competition** A market structure with many competitors selling virtually identical products. Barriers to entry are quite low.

**monopolistic competition** A market structure with many competitors selling differentiated products. Barriers to entry are low.

**oligopoly** A market structure with only a handful of competitors selling products that can be similar or different. Barriers to entry are typically high.

**monopoly** A market structure with one producer completely dominating the industry, leaving no room for any significant competitors. Barriers to entry tend to be virtually insurmountable.

**natural monopoly** A market structure with one company as the supplier of a product because the nature of that product makes a single supplier more efficient than multiple, competing ones. Most natural monopolies are government sanctioned and regulated.

## Exhibit 2.3
## The Supply Curve and Demand Curve

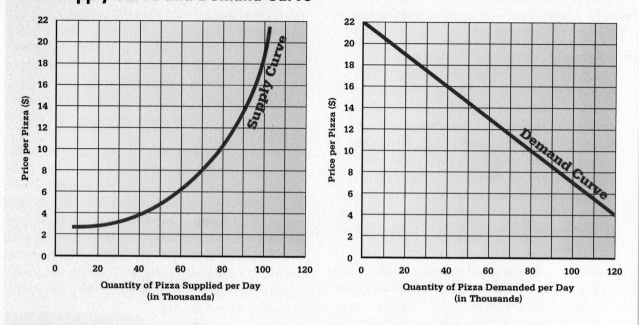

actually want, sales will be low, and the firm will typically yank the product from the market. Similarly, if the price of a product is too high, low sales will dictate a price cut. But if a new good or service becomes a hit, you can bet that similar offerings from other firms will pop up almost immediately (unless barriers—such as government-granted patents—prevent new entrants). The concepts of supply and demand explain how the dynamic interaction between buyers and sellers directly affects the range of products and prices in the free market.

**Supply Supply** refers to the quantity of products that producers are willing to offer for sale at different market prices. Since businesses seek to make as much profit as possible, they are likely to produce more of a product that commands a higher market price and less of a product that commands a lower price. Think about

it in terms of pizza. Assume it costs a local restaurant about $5 to make a pizza. If the market price for pizza hits, say, $20, you can bet that restaurant will start cranking out pizza. But if the price drops to $6, the restaurant has much less incentive to focus on pizza and will probably invest its limited resources in cooking other, pricier dishes.

The relationship between price and quantity from a supplier standpoint can be shown on a graph called the **supply curve**. The supply curve maps quantity on the *x*-axis (or horizontal axis) and price on the *y*-axis (or vertical axis). In most categories, as the price rises, the quantity produced rises correspondingly, yielding a graph that curves up as it moves to the right. Exhibit 2.3 shows a possible supply curve for pizza.

**Demand Demand** refers to the quantity of products that consumers are willing to buy at different market prices. Since consumers generally seek to get the products they need (or want) at the lowest possible prices, they tend to buy more products with lower prices and fewer products with higher prices. Pizza and tacos, for instance, are both popular meals. But if pizza costs a lot less than tacos, most people will get pizza more often than tacos. Likewise, if the price of pizza were out

**supply** The quantity of products that producers are willing to offer for sale at different market prices.

**supply curve** The graphed relationship between price and quantity from a supplier standpoint.

**demand** The quantity of products that consumers are willing to buy at different market prices.

## Exhibit 2.4
## Equilibrium

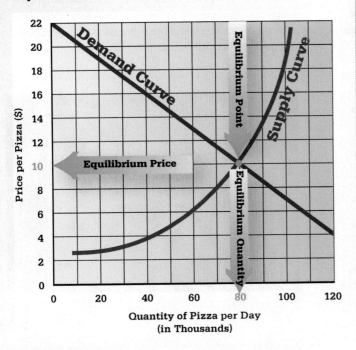

of hand, people would probably order tacos (or some other option) more often, reserving their pizza-eating for special occasions.

The relationship between price and quantity from a demand standpoint can be shown on a graph called the **demand curve**. Like the supply curve, the demand curve maps quantity on the *x*-axis and price on the *y*-axis. But different from the supply curve, the demand curve for most goods and services slopes downward as it moves to the right, since the quantity demanded tends to drop as prices rise. Exhibit 2.3 shows how a demand curve for pizza could look.

**Equilibrium Price** It's important to remember that supply and demand don't operate in a vacuum. The constant interaction between the two forces helps determine the market price in any given category. In theory, market prices adjust toward the point where the supply curve and the demand curve intersect (refer to Exhibit 2.4). The price associated with this point of intersection—the point where the quantity demanded equals the quantity supplied—is called the **equilibrium price**, and the quantity associated with this point is called the "equilibrium quantity."

## 2-5 Planned Economies: Socialism and Communism

In capitalist economies, private ownership is paramount. Individuals own businesses, and their personal fortunes depend on their success in the free market. But in planned economies, the government plays a more heavy-handed role in controlling the economy. The two key categories of planned economies are socialism and communism.

### 2-5a Socialism

**Socialism** is an economic system based on the principle that the government should own and operate key enterprises that directly affect public welfare, such as utilities, telecommunications, and healthcare. Although the official government goal is to run these enterprises in the best interest of the overall public, inefficiencies and corruption often interfere with effectiveness. Socialist economies also tend to have higher taxes, which are designed to distribute wealth more evenly through society. Tax revenues typically fund services that citizens in free enterprise systems would have to pay for themselves in countries with lower tax rates. Examples range from free childcare to free university education, to free public healthcare systems. Critics of the recent government intervention in the U.S. economy believe that the new moves have pushed us too far in a socialist direction.

Most Western European countries—from Sweden to Germany, to the United Kingdom—developed powerful socialist economies in the decades after World War II. But more recently, growth in these countries has languished. Although many factors have contributed to the slowdown, the impact of high taxes on the profit incentive and lavish social programs on the work incentive has clearly played a role. Potential entrepreneurs may migrate to countries that let them keep more of their profits, and workers with abundant benefits may find

**demand curve** The graphed relationship between price and quantity from a customer demand standpoint.

**equilibrium price** The price associated with the point at which the quantity demanded of a product equals the quantity supplied.

**socialism** An economic system based on the principle that the government should own and operate key enterprises that directly affect public welfare.

# Competitive Carbon

Achieving sustainability begins with measuring sustainability. We all know that the more we consume, the worse it is for the planet. But wouldn't it be nice if we could make better choices based on a good understanding of the environmental impact of each of the goods and services that we buy? A growing number of brands are differentiating themselves by labeling the "carbon footprint" or" carbon cost" of each item they sell. This includes Swedish pop-up shop, the "klimatbutik," where items are priced according to their carbon footprint—each customer has a weekly budget of 18.6 kg. In September 2020, Just Salad was the first U.S. restaurant chain to put carbon labels on its entire menu. Similarly, Allbirds footwear brand prints the carbon emissions on the sole of its popular sneakers. According to Allbirds' sustainability lead Hana Kajimura, they believe that printing carbon omissions on their products is an important step in helping their customers develop an understanding of carbon footprints in the same way that they already have for calories or other nutrition facts on food. As an overall consumer focus on sustainability continues to develop, companies that better educate consumers about the true cost of their products will gain a substantial competitive edge.[15]

themselves losing motivation. Over the last decade, many of these economies have imposed stiff austerity measures to control government spending, eliminating some public benefits many took for granted.

## 2-5b Communism

**Communism** is an economic and political system that calls for public ownership of virtually all enterprises, under the direction of a strong central government. The communist concept was the brainchild of political philosopher Karl Marx, who outlined its core principles in his 1848 *Communist Manifesto*. The communism that Marx envisioned was supposed to dramatically improve the lot of the worker at the expense of the super-rich.

But countries that adopted communism in the 1900s—most notably the former Soviet Union, China, Cuba, North Korea, and Vietnam—did not thrive. Most imposed authoritarian governments that suspended individual rights and choices. People were unable to make even basic choices such as where to work or what to buy. Without the free market to establish what to produce, crippling shortages and surpluses developed. Corruption infected every level of government. Under enormous pressure from their own people and the rest of the world, communism began to collapse across the Soviet Union and its satellite nations. At the end of the 1980s, it was replaced with democracy and the free market. Over the past two decades, China has also introduced significant free market reforms across much of the country, fueling a torrid growth rate that has only recently begun to slow. And in the 1990s, Vietnam launched free market reforms, stimulating rapid, sustained growth. The remaining communist economic systems—North Korea and Cuba—continue to falter, their people facing drastic shortages and even starvation.

## 2-6 Mixed Economies: The Story of the Future

In today's world, pure economies—market or planned—are practically nonexistent, since each would fall far short of meeting the needs of its citizens. A pure market economy would make insufficient provision for the old, the young, the sick, and the environment. A pure planned economy would not create enough value to support its people over the long term. Instead, most of today's nations have

**communism** An economic and political system that calls for public ownership of virtually all enterprises, under the direction of a strong central government.

# Big Brother Is Watching . . . or Is He?

One of the underlying principles of communism and socialism is that most people are willing to sacrifice self-interest for the good of the overall society. That may be true, but a new study suggests that may *only* be true if other people are watching. Researchers at the psychology department of a major university recently ran an experiment whereby they changed the price list at an honor system–based coffee bar in the faculty and staff break room. The prices themselves remained unchanged, but each week the photocopied picture above the prices varied between flowers and the eyes of real faces. The faces changed, but the eyes on the faces always looked directly at the observer. During the weeks with faces on the list, staff members paid nearly three times as much for their drinks as during the weeks with flowers. These results suggest that self-interest may be more natural and comfortable than fairness for most people. We're happy to be generous, but only when we think someone is watching—even if that someone is just a cutout picture of a face with observant eyes. Our deep-seated interest in our own well-being over everyone else's may be one reason why socialism and communism haven't created as much wealth over the long term as free enterprise has.[16]

Rangizzz/Shutterstock.com

**mixed economies**, falling somewhere along a spectrum that ranges from pure planned at one extreme to pure market at the other.

Even the United States—one of the most market-oriented economies in the world—does not have a *pure* market economy. The various departments of the government own a number of major enterprises, including the postal service, schools, parks, libraries, entire systems of universities, and the military. In fact, the federal government is the nation's largest employer, providing jobs for more than 4 million Americans. And—although the government does not directly *operate* firms in the financial sector—the federal government has become part owner in a number of financial institutions as part of the recent bailouts. The government also intervenes extensively in the free market by creating regulations that stimulate competition and protect both consumers and workers. Regulations are likely to become stronger in the wake of the economic crisis.[17]

Over the past 30 years, most economies of the world have begun moving toward the market end of the spectrum. Government-owned businesses have converted to private ownership via a process called **privatization**. Socialist governments have reduced red tape, cracked down on corruption, and created new laws to protect economic rights. Extravagant human services—from free healthcare to education subsidies—have shrunk. And far-reaching tax reform has created new incentives for both domestic and foreign investment in once-stagnant planned economies.[18]

Unfortunately, the price of economic restructuring has been a fair amount of social turmoil in many nations undergoing market reforms. Countries from France to China have experienced sometimes violent demonstrations in response to social and employment program cutbacks. Change is challenging, especially when it redefines economic winners and losers. But countries that have taken strides toward the market end of the spectrum—from small players such as the Czech Republic, to large players such as China—have seen the payoff in rejuvenated growth rates that have raised the standard of living for millions of people.

ПРОЛЕТАРИИ ВСЕХ СТРАН, СОЕДИНЯЙТЕСЬ!

Ekaterina Bykova/Shutterstock.com

Karl Marx (1818–1883) was a Prussian-born theorist who helped develop the political ideology of communism.

**mixed economies** Economies that embody elements of both planned and market-based economic systems.

**privatization** The process of converting government-owned businesses to private ownership.

# Has the American Dream Become a Nightmare?

In the late 1800s and early 1900s, millions of peasants from around the world set sail for the United States in search of the American Dream. Sometime between then and now, however, the American Dream lost its shine. According to a recent poll, only 25% of those surveyed agreed that "capitalism works for the ordinary American." Capitalism is charged with being fixated on shareholder returns, myopically short term, inherently monopolistic, antidemocratic, amoral, rootless, and bad for the planet. But according to experts writing for *Fortune* magazine, these indictments confuse the concept of capitalism with its implementation. They also point out that "capitalism is simply a tool—one that channels savings into investment and rewards risk-takers.

Blaming capitalism for its misapplication is like blaming sex for overpopulation, teenage pregnancies, and sexually transmitted diseases. We can address these problems without all becoming celibate."

Maybe the lack of enthusiasm for capitalism should not be surprising, given the swell of support for Democratic Socialist Bernie Sanders during the 2016 and 2020 presidential elections. But as the text highlights, every economic system has advantages and disadvantages. Perhaps Winston Churchill had it right when he said, "Capitalism is the worst economic system, except for all the others."[19]

## 2-7 Evaluating Economic Performance: What's Working?

Clearly, economic systems are complex—very complex. So you probably won't be surprised to learn that no single measure captures all the dimensions of economic performance. To get the full picture, you need to understand a range of terms and measures, including gross domestic product, employment level, the business cycle, inflation rate, and productivity.

### 2-7a Gross Domestic Product

Real **gross domestic product (GDP)** measures the total value of all final goods and services produced within a nation's physical boundaries over a given period of time, adjusted for inflation. (Nominal GDP does not include an inflation adjustment.) All domestic production is included in the GDP, even when the producer is foreign owned. The U.S. GDP, for instance, includes the value of Hyundai Sonatas built in Alabama, even though Hyundai is a Korean firm. Likewise, the Indonesian GDP includes the value of Gap clothing manufactured in Indonesian factories, even though Gap is an American firm.

GDP is a vital measure of economic health. Businesspeople, economists, and political leaders use GDP to measure the economic performance of individual nations and to compare the growth among nations. Interestingly, GDP levels tend to be somewhat understated since they don't include any activities such as volunteer work, bartering, and homemakers—which can represent a significant portion of some countries' production. The GDP also ignores legal goods that are not reported to avoid taxation, plus output produced within households.[20] Check out Chapter 3 for a survey of the world's key economies according to total GDP and GDP growth rate.

### 2-7b Employment Level

The overall level of employment is another key element of economic health. When people have jobs, they have money, which allows them to spend and invest, fueling economic growth. Most nations track employment levels largely through the **unemployment rate**, which includes everyone age 16 and older who doesn't have a job and is actively seeking one. The U.S. unemployment rate climbed precipitously through the Great Recession, rising from 5.8% in 2008 to 9.3% in 2009, then dropping to 8.1% in 2012 as the economy began its glacially slow turnaround. Unemployment didn't move below 8% until September of 2012, and then it dropped slowly throughout 2013 to end the year at an annual average of 7.4% as the recovery began to take hold. Unemployment continued dropping, hitting 4.7% in December 2016. The unemployment rate dropped throughout 2017, ending the year at 4.1%, remaining at 4.1% through mid-2018, ultimately falling to 3.5% in February, 2020, before shooting up to 14.8% by April 2020 in response to COVID-19-pandemic-related lockdowns.[21] But unfortunately, about

**gross domestic product (GDP)** The total value of all final goods and services produced within a nation's physical boundaries over a given period of time.

**unemployment rate** The percentage of people in the labor force over age 16 who do not have jobs and are actively seeking employment.

## Exhibit 2.5
## The Business Cycle

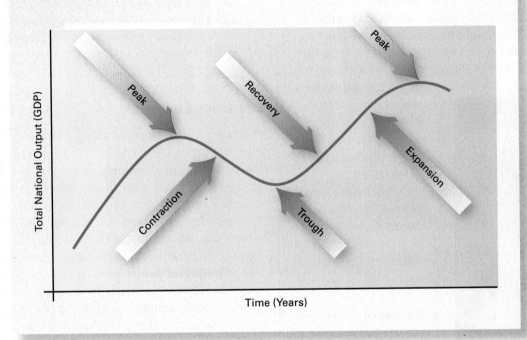

half of the 8 million jobs lost during the recession were middle-income jobs, and about half of the new jobs created since have been in low-wage sectors of the economy, leading to stagnant household incomes.[22]

Interestingly, some unemployment is actually good—it reflects your freedom to change jobs. If you have an awful boss, for instance, you may just quit. If you quit, are you unemployed? Of course, you are. Are you glad? You probably are, and in normal times, the chances are good that you'll find another position that's a better fit for you. This type of job loss is called *frictional unemployment*, and it tends to be ultimately positive. *Structural unemployment*, on the other hand, is usually longer term. This category encompasses people who don't have jobs because the economy no longer needs their skills. In the United States, growing numbers of workers in the past decade have found themselves victims of structural unemployment as manufacturing jobs have moved overseas. Often their only option is expensive retraining. Two other categories of unemployment are *cyclical*, which involves layoffs during recessions, and *seasonal*, which involves job loss related to the time of year. In some areas of the country, construction and agricultural workers are seasonally unemployed, but the best example may be the department-store Santa who has a job only during the holiday season!

> Raising a child born in 2015 from birth to age 17 costs about $233,610 (not including college!)— almost $14,000 every year.
>
> —U.S. Department of Agriculture

### 2-7c  The Business Cycle

The **business cycle** is the periodic contraction and expansion that occur over time in virtually every economy. But the word "cycle" may be a little misleading, since it implies that the economy contracts and expands in a predictable pattern. In reality, the phases of the cycle are different each time they happen, and—despite the efforts of countless experts—no one can accurately predict when changes will occur or how long they will last. Those who make the best guesses stand to make fortunes, but bad bets can be financially devastating. The two key phases of the business cycle are contraction and expansion, shown in Exhibit 2.5.

**business cycle** The periodic contraction and expansion that occur over time in virtually every economy.

- **Contraction** is a period of economic downturn, marked by rising unemployment. Businesses cut back on production, and consumers shift their buying patterns to more basic products and fewer luxuries. The economic "feel-good factor" simply disappears. Economists declare an official **recession** when GDP decreases for two consecutive quarters. A **depression** is an especially deep and long-lasting recession. Fortunately, economies seldom spiral into severe depressions, thanks in large part to proactive intervention from the government.

  The last depression in the United States was the Great Depression of the 1930s. Whether a downturn is mild or severe, the very bottom of the contraction is called the "trough," as shown in Exhibit 2.5.

- **Recovery** is a period of rising economic growth and increasing employment following a contraction. Businesses begin to expand. Consumers start to regain confidence, and spending begins to rise. The recovery is essentially the transition period between contraction and expansion.

- **Expansion** is a period of robust economic growth and high employment. Businesses expand to capitalize on emerging opportunities. Consumers are optimistic and confident, which fuels purchasing, which fuels production, which fuels further hiring. As Exhibit 2.5 demonstrates, the

height of economic growth is called the peak of the expansion. The U.S. economy had the longest growth spurt on record during the ten-year period from 1991 to 2001. After a relatively mild slowdown in 2001–2002, the U.S. economy again expanded for several years before it plunged into a full-blown recession in 2008, leading to another expansion, until the COVID-19 pandemic in 2020.[23]

## 2-7d Price Levels

The rate of price changes across the economy is another basic measure of economic well-being. **Inflation** means that prices, on average, are rising. Similar to unemployment, a low level of inflation is not so bad. It reflects a healthy economy—people have money, and they are willing to spend it. But when the Federal Reserve—the nation's central bank—manages the economy poorly, inflation can spiral out of control, which can lead to **hyperinflation**, when average prices increase more than 50% per month. In Hungary, for example, inflation in its unstable, post–World War II economy climbed so quickly that prices doubled every 15 hours in 1946. More recently, prices in the war-torn former Yugoslavia doubled every 16 hours between October 1993 and January 1994.

When the rate of price increases slows down, the economy is experiencing **disinflation**, which was the situation in the United States in the mid-1990s and more recently in the second half of 2008. But when prices actually decrease, the economy is experiencing **deflation**, typically a sign of economic trouble that goes hand-in-hand with very high unemployment. People don't have money and simply won't spend unless prices drop. During the Great Depression in the 1930s, the U.S. economy experienced deflation, with prices dropping 9% in 1931 and nearly 10% in 1932. Despite some economic turmoil, inflation in the United States was relatively low from 2000 to 2007, hovering at around 3%. But inflation picked up in the first half of 2008, only to fall during the first months of the Great Recession. Inflation has remained low throughout the last decade, hovering in the neighborhood of 2%–despite very low interest rates, set by the Federal Reserve. In 2020, inflation fell to 1.2%.[24]

The government uses two major price indexes to evaluate inflation: the **consumer price index (CPI)** and the **producer price index (PPI)**. The CPI measures the change in weighted-average price over time in

Productivity is calculated by dividing the output by the input. Everything else being equal, the more circuit boards (output) assembled per hour of work (input), the higher the productivity.

a consumer "market basket" of goods and services that the average person buys each month. The U.S. Bureau of Labor Statistics creates the basket—which includes hundreds of items such as housing, transportation, haircuts, wine, and pet care—using data from more than 30,000 consumers. Although the market basket is meant to represent the average consumer, keep in mind that the "average" includes a lot of variation, so the CPI may not reflect your personal experience. For example, as a college student, you may be painfully sensitive to increases in tuition and the price of textbooks—a fact the authors of this particular textbook fully realize! But tuition and textbook prices aren't a big part of the "average" consumer's budget, so increases in these prices have a relatively small impact on the CPI.

The PPI measures the change over time in the prices that businesses pay each other for goods and services on a weighted average. Changes in the PPI can sometimes predict changes in the CPI because producers tend to pass on price increases (and sometimes also price decreases) to consumers within a month or two of the changes.

## 2-7e Productivity

**Productivity** refers to the relationship between the goods and services that an economy produces and the resources needed to produce them. The amount of output—goods and services—divided by the amount of input (e.g., hours worked) equals productivity. The goal, of course, is to produce more goods and services, using fewer hours and other inputs. A high level of productivity typically correlates with healthy GDP growth, while low productivity tends to correlate with a more stagnant economy.

Over the past couple of decades, the United States has experienced strong productivity growth, due largely to infusions of technology that help workers produce more output, more quickly. But keep in mind that productivity doesn't measure quality. That's why it's so important to examine multiple measures of economic health rather than relying on simply one or two dimensions.

> **productivity** The basic relationship between the production of goods and services (output) and the resources needed to produce them (input) calculated via the following equation: output/input = productivity.

## The Big Picture

From a business standpoint, one key goal of economics is to guide your decision making by offering a deeper understanding of the broad forces that affect both your business and your personal life. Knowing even basic economic principles can help you make better business decisions in virtually every area—from production, to marketing, to accounting, to name just a few—regardless of your specific function or level within an organization.

But you won't find an economics department within many (if any) businesses—rather, you'll find people across the organization applying economic theories and trends to their work, even in the face of continual economic flux. As you read through the other chapters in this book, take a moment to consider both the macroeconomic and microeconomic forces that affect each area you study. You're likely to find a surprising number of examples.

## Careers in Business

### Business Economist

Collect, analyze, and distribute data to explain economic phenomena and forecast economic trends, particularly with regard to supply and demand. Create and present clear, concise reports on economic trends to senior management on a monthly basis. Manage and motivate a small team of financial analysts and statisticians.

# 3 | The World Marketplace:
## Business without Borders

### Learning Objectives

After studying this chapter, you will be able to:

**3-1** Discuss dramatic changes in U.S. trade policy over the last decade

**3-2** Describe business opportunities in the world economy

**3-3** Explain the key reasons for international trade

**3-4** Describe the tools for measuring international trade

**3-5** Analyze strategies for reaching global markets

**3-6** Discuss barriers to international trade and strategies to surmount them

**3-7** Describe the free-trade movement, and discuss key benefits and criticisms

Rawpixel.com/Shutterstock.com

## 3-1 A Dramatic Change

For the second half of the 20th century and through the start of the 21st century, official U.S. trade policy moved the country, and indeed the world, toward increased free-trade and globalization. The result was a dramatic increase in the average standard of living (the amount of stuff each person can buy)—although many would argue that the price was a significant decrease in the average quality-of-life (sense of well-being). At the beginning of his administration, President Donald Trump linked American trade policy directly to national security. American trade policy—a cornerstone of his foreign policy—became a zero-sum game; if America had a trade deficit with any nation, that nation was violating the rules in his view. And in his opinion, the biggest violator was China.

Early in his administration, President Trump slapped huge tariffs (import taxes) on aluminum and steel. While these tariffs were ostensibly aimed at China, the United States imports most of its steel and aluminum from its allies such as Europe, Canada, and Mexico, and very little from China. The unfortunate result was higher prices for American

consumers. President Trump imposed further tariffs on about $360 billion in Chinese goods—well over half of what Beijing ships to the United States every year. Retaliatory tariffs from China and the EU were aimed at quint-essentially American products such as Kentucky whiskey, Mack trucks, Florida boats, and American farm products. But the upshot of the Trump trade deal was a great deal of uproar with little result. In early 2020, Trump had negotiated and signed the "first phase" of the trade agreement with China that requires the Chinese to purchase $40 billion worth of U.S. agricultural products over two years. Unfortunately, as of September 2020, China's agricultural purchases were barely half of what they'd need to be to reach the agreed target for 2020. Meanwhile, heavy tariffs remained in place on both sides. The second phase of the agreement seems unlikely to happen as China sails out of the COVID-19 pandemic with a robust economy, the United States struggles to recover, and the U.S. trade deficit with China remains higher than ever.

Looking forward, the United States continues to face major "structural issues" in its relationship with China, as pointed out by President Trump, who accused China of showing strong favoritism to state-owned industries, of intellectual property theft, and of forcing U.S. companies to "transfer

> "The world is more malleable than you think and it's waiting for you to hammer it into shape."
>
> —Bono, Musician and Humanitarian

technology" to the Chinese government when they were operating in China. President Trump was unable to resolve these issues before the end of his administration, so they were left in the hands of the incoming Biden administration at the beginning of 2021—the results could determine the global economic structure for generations to come.[1]

## 3-2 The Global Marketplace: A Huge Business Opportunity

Individual economies around the world have become more interdependent than ever before. The result is a tightly woven global economy marked by intense

## Exhibit 3.1 Selected Population and GDP Figures

| Nation | Population* | Per Capita GDP (PPP basis)** | GDP Growth Rate*** |
|---|---|---|---|
| China | 1,394,015,977 | $8,014 | +6.1% |
| India | 1,351,209,574 | $2,100 | +4.5% |
| European Union | 453,007,803 | $40,900 | +2.3% |
| United States | 332,639,102 | $55,761 | +2.2% |
| Indonesia | 267,026,366 | $4,455 | +5.0% |
| Pakistan | 233,500,636 | $1,404 | +5.4% |

Source: CIA World Factbook, https://www.cia.gov/the-world-factbook/countries/, accessed January 16, 2021.
*CIA World FactBook Population July 2021 Estimates
**CIA World FactBook 2019 GDP Estimates
***CIA World FactBook 2020 GDP Growth Estimates

competition and huge, shifting opportunities. Overall, during the last decade, global economic growth has been slow but relatively steady. The long-term potential for U.S. business is enormous.[2] Refer to Exhibit 3.1 for a sampling of some specific higher- and lower-growth countries.

A quick look at population trends validates the global business opportunity, especially in developing nations. In mid-2020, the world's population stands at about 7.8 billion people. With more than 332 million people, the United States accounts for less than 4.5% of the world's total population. More than 7.4 billion people live beyond our borders, representing more than 95% of potential customers for U.S. firms. But most of these nations remain behind the United States in terms of development and prosperity, posing considerable challenges for foreign firms. (In other words, most of their populations may not have the resources to buy even basic goods and services and their infrastructure and technology may not be developed enough to support contemporary business.) Exhibit 3.1, a comparison of population, gross domestic product (GDP) growth rate, and per capita GDP for the world's six largest nations, highlights some of the discrepancies. Note that even though U.S. and EU consumers clearly have money, China and India represent a much bigger opportunity in terms of both sheer size and economic growth.

### 3-2a So Where Exactly Will the Opportunity Be?

**Projections for the future:** Looking forward, economists see reasons for optimism in world markets. The International Monetary Fund (IMF) projects solid growth of 5.4% in 2021, led by emerging and developing countries, and followed by opening economies in the United States and Europe. Investment bank Morgan Stanley projects even stronger growth—also led by emerging markets—saying,

"We maintain that consumers have driven the recovery, and investment growth—a reflection of the private corporate sector's risk tolerance and a key feature of any self-sustaining recovery—is bouncing back as well."

Growth projections for China—the world's largest developing economy—in 2021 range from +8.2% to +9.0%, with all economists urging caution regarding growth forecasts as they depend on the rollout of COVID-19 vaccinations, *and* effective, progrowth government policies. Growth projections across the rest of Asia are somewhat uneven, but all positive: the forecast for India ranges from +8.0% to +9.8%, and the forecast for Southeast Asia (which includes Indonesia, Malaysia, and the Philippines) is +5.2%.

Africa, home to 1.3 billion people, is another important part of the emerging-market picture. However, recent analysis suggests that the conventional narrative of Africa's rising middle class may be somewhat flawed. Collecting statistics in Africa is notoriously difficult. One challenge is simply how to define the middle class. One economist distinguishes the middle class from the poor by the ability to earn a steady income. And poverty itself is an enormous problem, growing rampantly. Nigeria, for example, recently overtook India as the country with the largest number of people living in extreme poverty, with an estimated 87 million Nigerians, or around half of the country's population, thought to be living on less than $1.90 per day. Nevertheless, the IMF projects respectable 3.5% growth for sub-Saharan Africa in 2021.[3]

### 3-2b The Cell Phone Connection

The growing number of people with cell phones offers an interesting indicator of economic growth. Several recent studies have found that if a country increases cell phone penetration by 10 percentage points, GDP will likely increase by anywhere from +0.5% to +1.2%. That may

# Kicking Over a Really Big Anthill

The Chinese government recently pulled the plug on what would've been a record-setting IPO ($34 billion) of the Ant Group. The government apparently perceived that founder Jack Ma was thumbing his nose at regulators. The Ant Group was founded in 2004 as Alipay, the financial services arm of Alibaba—conceived to build trust between buyers and sellers doing business on the e-commerce giant. Alipay, which continued to grow and innovate over the years, was rebranded as Ant Financial Services in 2014. As of 2020, its mobile payment app, Alipay, had over 1 billion users, making it the world's most popular app outside social media networks. Ant is continuously cross-selling and upselling higher-value financial products to users of its payments network and expects engagement with its customers to grow tenfold in the coming five years. Its platform takes just three minutes to process a loan and 1 second to disburse the loan, with zero human intervention.

Just as Ant's massive stock debut was coming together in late 2020, Jack Ma gave a speech at a Shanghai finance conference, criticizing the risk-averse Chinese banking system and its tight financial regulatory structure. Shortly later, government regulators shut down the IPO. One social media commentator correctly observed that Ma's remarks comprised "the most expensive speech ever."

So why is such a huge company named for such a tiny insect? According to former CEO Eric Jing, the company named itself after the small insect because it "serves the little guys," just like they do.[4]

This trend is particularly marked across Africa, where cell phone penetration rates continue to grow explosively. Most of the penetration growth involves feature phones, but smartphone penetration is growing as well, providing access to the Internet for the first time ever to huge swaths of the population. David Knapp, general director of Motorola Vietnam, points out that many developing nations "can leapfrog technology." And Vietnamese micro-entrepreneur Nguyen Huu Truc says, "It's no longer something that only the rich can afford. Now, it's a basic means

seem small, but it equates to somewhere between $49 and $118 billion for an economy the size of China. In other words, when the percentage of the population with cell phones goes up, the entire economy benefits.

Not surprisingly, cell phone penetration in India and China is skyrocketing. China currently boasts the world's largest base of cell phone users—more than 1 billion—and the growth will likely continue. India's subscriber base just crossed the 1 billion mark; it has grown explosively over the past five years and seems likely to follow suit in the next decade. Most of those phones are "feature phones," which are cell phones that typically don't support apps, have limited storage, and limited Internet connectivity. Clearly, smartphones and smartphone penetration are more directly applicable to business opportunity. Mobile smartphone usage skyrocketed between 2016 and 2020, and by 2021 experts predict that nearly half the people on the planet will own a smartphone. Smartphone penetration around the world varies dramatically. In 2020, penetration in China hit nearly 60%, and in India, only 25%. Meanwhile, smartphone penetration in Brazil was less than 50%, and up near 80% for most developed countries. In the United States, Europe, and Japan, cell phones followed landlines, but large swaths of developing nations aren't bothering to build conventional phone service. Rather, they're moving directly to cell phone networks.

As penetration increases, smartphones weave into every aspect of Indian culture.

of communication." As more people get the chance to get connected, better communication will likely feed economic growth. According to Muhammad Yunus, founder of Grameen Bank in Bangladesh, "A mobile phone is almost like having a card to get you out of poverty in a couple of years." The upshot is that millions of people worldwide will have a higher standard of living.[5]

## 3-3 Key Reasons for International Trade

Companies engage in global trade for a range of reasons beyond the obvious opportunity to tap into huge and growing new markets. The benefits include better access to factors of production, reduced risk, and an inflow of new ideas.

- *Access to factors of production:* International trade offers a valuable opportunity for individual firms to capitalize on factors of production that simply aren't present in the right amount for the right price in each individual country. India, China, and the Philippines, for example, attract multibillion-dollar investments because of their large cohort of technically skilled university graduates who work for about one-fifth the pay of comparable American workers. Russia and the Organization of the Petroleum Exporting Countries (OPEC) nations offer a rich supply of oil, and Canada, like other forested nations, boasts an abundant supply of timber. The United States offers plentiful capital, which is less available in other parts of the world. International trade helps even out some of the resource imbalances among nations.

- *Reduced risk:* Global trade reduces dependence on one economy, lowering the economic risk for multinational firms. When the Japanese economy entered a deep, sustained slump in the 1990s, for instance, Sony and Toyota thrived through their focus on other, healthier markets around the world. But a word of caution is key: as national economies continue to integrate, an economic meltdown in one part of the world can have far-reaching impact. Major foreign banks, for example, were badly burned by the U.S. subprime market mess, due to heavy investments in U.S. mortgage markets.

> Although Africans represent more than 70% of the world's poorest people, the continent is also home to 30% of the world's mineral reserves, 8% of its natural gas, 12% of its oil reserves, 40% of its gold, and up to 90% of its chromium and platinum.
>
> —United Nations and The Brookings Institute

- *Inflow of innovation:* International trade can also offer companies an invaluable source of new ideas. Japan, for instance, is far ahead of the curve regarding cell phone service. Japanese cell phone "extras," including games, ringtones, videos, and stylish new accessories, set the standard for cell service around the world. In Europe, meanwhile, consumers are showing a growing interest in traditional and regional foods, which allow them to picture where their ingredients come from. Companies with a presence in foreign markets experience budding trends like these firsthand, giving them a jump in other markets around the world.[6]

### 3-3a Competitive Advantage

Beyond individual companies, industries tend to succeed on a worldwide basis in countries that enjoy a competitive advantage. But to understand competitive advantage, you need to first understand how **opportunity cost** relates to international trade. When a country produces more of one good, it must produce less of another good (assuming that resources are finite). The value of the second-best choice—the value of the production that a country gives up in order to produce the first product—represents the opportunity cost of producing the first product.

A country has an **absolute advantage** when it can produce more of a good than other nations, using the same amount of resources. China, for example, has an absolute advantage in terms of clothing production, relative to the United States. But having an absolute advantage isn't always enough. Unless they face major trade barriers, the industries in any country tend to produce products for which they have a **comparative advantage**— meaning that they tend to turn out those goods that have

**opportunity cost** The opportunity of giving up the second-best choice when making a decision.

**absolute advantage** The benefit a country has in a given industry when it can produce more of a product than other nations using the same amount of resources.

**comparative advantage** The benefit a country has in a given industry if it can make products at a lower opportunity cost than other countries.

the lowest opportunity cost compared to other countries. The United States, for instance, boasts a comparative advantage versus most countries in movie and television program production; Germany has a comparative advantage in the production of high-performance cars; and South Korea enjoys a comparative advantage in electronics.

But keep in mind that comparative advantage seldom remains static. As technology changes and the workforce evolves (through factors such as education and experience), nations may gain or lose comparative advantage in various industries. China and India, for example, are both seeking to build a comparative advantage versus other nations in technology production by investing in their infrastructure and their institutions of higher education.

Pla2na/Shutterstock.com

 ## 3-4 Global Trade: Taking Measure

Global trade dropped dramatically in the wake of COVID-19 pandemic-related lockdowns and travel restrictions in 2020. Correspondingly, global GDP dropped as the financial impact was felt worldwide. In 2021, experts anticipate that both global GDP and global trade will rebound, but the recovery depends of course on the decreasing number of COVID-19 cases, the vaccine rollout, and on the easing of trade tensions.[7]

Measuring the impact of international trade on individual nations requires a clear understanding of balance of trade, balance of payments, and exchange rates.[8]

### 3-4a Balance of Trade

The **balance of trade** is a basic measure of the difference between a nation's exports and imports. If the total value of exports is higher than the total value of imports, the country has a **trade surplus**. If the total value of imports is higher than the total value of exports, the country has a **trade deficit**. Balance of trade includes the value of both goods and services, and it incorporates trade with all foreign nations. Although a trade deficit signals the wealth of an economy that can afford to buy huge amounts of foreign products, a large deficit can be destabilizing. It indicates, after all, that as goods and services flow into a nation, money flows out—a challenge with regard to long-term economic health. The United States has had an overall trade deficit since 1976, and as the American appetite for foreign goods has grown, the trade deficit has ballooned.

### 3-4b Balance of Payments

**Balance of payments** is a measure of the total flow of money into or out of a country. Clearly, the balance of trade plays a central role in determining the balance of payments. But the balance of payments also includes other financial flows such as foreign borrowing and lending, foreign aid payments and receipts, and foreign investments. A **balance of payments surplus** means that more money flows in than out, while a **balance of payments deficit** means that more money flows out than in. Keep in mind that the balance of payments typically corresponds to the balance of trade because trade is, in general, the largest component.

### 3-4c Exchange Rates

**Exchange rates** measure the value of one nation's currency relative to the currency of other nations. While the exchange rate does not directly measure global commerce, it certainly has a powerful influence on how global trade affects individual nations and their trading partners. The exchange rate of

**balance of trade** A basic measure of the difference in value between a nation's exports and imports, including both goods and services.

**trade surplus** Overage that occurs when the total value of a nation's exports is higher than the total value of its imports.

**trade deficit** Shortfall that occurs when the total value of a nation's imports is higher than the total value of its exports.

**balance of payments** A measure of the total flow of money into or out of a country.

**balance of payments surplus** Overage that occurs when more money flows into a nation than out of that nation.

**balance of payments deficit** Shortfall that occurs when more money flows out of a nation than into that nation.

**exchange rate** A measurement of the value of one nation's currency relative to the currency of other nations.

a given currency must be expressed in terms of another currency. The table below shows some examples of how the exchange rate can influence the economy, using the dollar and the euro. In recent years, for example, a number of currencies underwent value swings versus the U.S. dollar (e.g., the EU euro, the Japanese yen, the Indian rupee, the Canadian dollar, and the British pound). One result was multibillion-dollar earnings hits against U.S. corporations with a strong international presence, including Johnson & Johnson and Philip Morris International. Many firms opt to present their earnings reports stripped of the effects of currency translations, but in today's global economy, that clearly offers a misleading picture of performance.[9]

| Strong Dollar versus Euro: Who Benefits? (Example: $1.00 = 1.20 euros) | Weak Dollar versus Euro: Who Benefits? (Example: $1.00 = 0.60 euros) |
|---|---|
| *U.S. travelers to Europe:* Their dollars can buy more European goods and services. | *European travelers to the United States:* Their dollars buy more American goods and services. |
| *American firms with European operations:* Operating costs—from buying products to paying workers—are lower. | *European firms with American operations:* Operating costs—from buying products to paying workers—are lower. |
| *European exporters:* Their products are less expensive in the United States, so Europe exports more, and we import more. | *American exporters:* Their products are less expensive in Europe, so we export more, and Europe imports more. |

### 3-4d Countertrade

A complete evaluation of global trade must also consider exchanges that don't actually involve money. A surprisingly large chunk of international commerce—possibly as much as 25%—involves the barter of products for products rather than for currency. Companies typically engage in **countertrade** to meet the needs of customers who don't have access to hard currency or credit, usually in developing countries. Individual countertrade agreements range from simple barter to a complex web of exchanges that end up meeting the needs of multiple parties. Done poorly, countertrading can be a confusing nightmare for everyone involved. But done well, countertrading is a powerful tool for gaining customers and products that would not otherwise be available.[10] Not surprisingly, barter opportunities tend to increase during economic downturns.

**countertrade** International trade that involves the barter of products for products rather than for currency.

## Seizing the Opportunity: Strategies for Reaching Global Markets

There is no one "right way" to seize the opportunity in global markets. In fact, the opportunity may not even make sense for every firm. While international trade can offer new profit streams and lower costs, it also introduces a higher level of risk and complexity to running a business. Being ready to take on the challenge can mean the difference between success and failure.

Firms ready to tap the opportunity have a number of options for how to move forward. One way is to seek foreign suppliers through outsourcing and importing. Another possibility is to seek foreign customers through exporting, licensing, franchising, and direct investment. These market development options fall in a spectrum from low cost–low control to high cost–high control, as shown in Exhibit 3.2. In other words, companies that choose to export products to a foreign country spend less to enter that market than companies that choose to build their own factories. But companies that build their own factories have a lot more control than exporters over how their business unfolds. Keep in mind that profit opportunity and risk—which vary along with cost and control—also play a critical role in how firms approach international markets.

Smaller firms tend to begin with exporting and move along the spectrum as the business develops. But larger firms may jump straight to the strategies that give them more control over their operations. Large firms are also likely to use a number of different approaches in different countries, depending on the goals of the firm and the structure of the foreign market. Regardless of the specific strategy, most large companies—such as General Electric, Nike, and Disney—both outsource

## Exhibit 3.2
### Market Development Options

LOWER Risk · Exporting · Licensing · Franchising · Direct Investment · HIGHER Risk

LESS Control · MORE Control

with foreign suppliers and sell their products to foreign markets.

### 3-5a Foreign Outsourcing and Importing

**Foreign outsourcing** means contracting with foreign suppliers to produce products, usually at a fraction of the cost of domestic production. H&M, for instance, relies on a network for manufacturers around the globe, mostly in less developed parts of the world, including Kenya, Cambodia, Indonesia, Myanmar, Sri Lanka, and Bangladesh. Apple depends on firms in China and Taiwan to produce the iPhone. And countless small companies contract with foreign manufacturers as well. The key benefit, of course, is dramatically lower wages, which drive down the cost of production.

But while foreign outsourcing lowers costs, it also involves significant risk. Quality control typically requires very detailed specifications to ensure that a company gets what it actually needs. Another key risk of foreign outsourcing involves social responsibility. A firm that contracts with foreign producers has an obligation to ensure that those factories adhere to ethical standards. Deciding what those standards should be is often quite tricky, given different cultures, expectations, and laws in different countries. And policing the factories on an ongoing basis can be even harder than determining the standards. But companies that don't get it right face the threat of significant consumer backlash in the United States and Europe. This has been a particular issue with products produced in China. In the recent past, for instance, product defects forced U.S. firms to recall a host of Chinese-produced toys, including Thomas the Tank Engine trains that were coated with toxic lead paint, ghoulish fake eyeballs that were filled with kerosene, and Polly Pocket dolls that posed a swallowing hazard. In 2019, the European Environmental Bureau sounded the alarm that the EU was facing a "flood" of dangerously contaminated Chinese toys, most of them infused with illegal levels of toxic chemicals.[11]

Many Americans have become personally familiar with the quality/cost trade-off as a growing number of companies have outsourced customer service to foreign call centers. Research suggests that the approximate cost of offering a live, American- or Canadian-based customer service agent averages about $0.75–$0.90 per minute, while outsourcing those calls to live agents in another country drops the average cost down to about $0.35–$0.45 per minute. But customers end up paying the difference in terms of satisfaction, reporting high levels of misunderstanding, frustration, and inefficiency.[12]

A number of firms—such as JetBlue and Amazon.com—have enjoyed the best of both worlds by outsourcing customer service calls to U.S. agents who work from their own homes.[13]

**Importing** means buying products from overseas that have already been produced, rather than contracting with overseas manufacturers to produce special orders. Imported products, of course, don't carry the brand name of the importer, but they also don't carry as much risk. Pier 1 Imports, a large, now exclusively online retail chain, has built a powerful brand around the importing concept, curating a range of merchandise that gives the customer the sense of a global shopping trip without the cost or hassle of actually leaving the country.

### 3-5b Exporting

**Exporting** is the most basic level of international market development. It simply means producing products domestically and selling them abroad. Exporting represents an especially strong opportunity for small and mid-sized companies. Planetary Design, for instance, in Missoula, Montana, sells a stellar line of stainless-steel coffee, tea, and other kitchen products around the world. Exports to countries such as Canada, Ecuador, Iceland, and Korea account for more than 15% of its total sales and support 10% of its workforce.[14]

### 3-5c Foreign Licensing and Foreign Franchising

Foreign licensing and foreign franchising, the next level of commitment to international markets, are quite similar. **Foreign licensing** involves a

Dmitry Melnikov/Shutterstock.com

# Help Unwanted

Worldwide, there are approximately 1.3 billion young people between the ages of 15 and 24. Significantly, young people are three times as likely as adults (25 years and older) to be unemployed. Around 497 million young people, or roughly 41% of the global youth population, are in the labor force. Of these, 429 million are employed, while nearly 68 million are looking for, and are available for, work (these people are defined as unemployed).

Also, more than half of young people—around 776 million—are outside the labor force, meaning that they are not in employment and are not looking and available for a job. Many of these young people are gaining an education. But 20% of young people worldwide are neither gaining experience in the labor market, nor receiving an income from work, nor enhancing their education and skills. Clearly, their full potential is not being realized, although many may be contributing to the economy through unpaid work, which is particularly true of young women.

Even among young people who are employed, their situation can be dire. Of the 429 million young workers worldwide, around 55 million, or 13%, are suffering extreme poverty (living on an income below $1.90 per day), while 71 million of them, or 17%, live in moderate poverty (an income below $3.20 per day). Labor challenges, such as these, in the early stages of a young person's

career can lead to a number of scarring effects, including lower employment and earnings prospects decades later.

The transition of these young people into the labor market has long-term impacts on both their lives *and* on the socioeconomic development of their countries. It is thus essential to understand their pathways into the world of work and how they are engaging—or not, as the case may be—in employment.

An integrated policy framework to support young people in securing decent jobs in this context is critical for future socioeconomic progress. Failure to act would mean growing numbers of discouraged young people in many countries, ultimately undermining socioeconomic development.[15]

domestic firm granting a foreign firm the rights to produce and market its product or to use its trademark/patent rights in a defined geographical area. The company that offers the rights, or the *licensor*, receives a fee from the company that buys the rights, or the *licensee*. This approach allows firms to expand into foreign markets with little or no investment, and it also helps circumvent government restrictions on importing in closed markets. But maintaining control of licensees can be a significant challenge. Licensors also run the risk that unethical licensees may become their competitors, using information that they gained from the licensing agreement. Foreign licensing is especially common in the food and beverage industry. The most high-profile examples include Coke and Pepsi, which grant licenses to foreign bottlers all over the world.

**Foreign franchising** is a specialized type of licensing. A firm that

**foreign franchising** A specialized type of foreign licensing in which a firm expands by offering businesses in other countries the right to produce and market its products according to specific operating requirements.

Foreign franchisers offer franchisees the rights to produce and market their products. According to Entrprepreneur .com, the top global franchises in 2020 were McDonald's, KFC, Pizza Hut, 7-Eleven, and Dunkin' Donuts.

expands through foreign franchising, called a *franchisor*, offers other businesses, or *franchisees*, the right to produce and market its products if the franchisee agrees to specific operating requirements—a complete package of how to do business. Franchisors also often offer their franchisees management guidance, marketing support, and even financing. In return, franchisees pay both a start-up fee and an ongoing percentage of sales to the franchisor. One key difference between franchising and licensing is that franchisees assume the identity of the franchisor. A McDonald's franchise in Paris, for instance, is clearly a McDonald's, not, say, a Pierre's Baguette outlet that also carries McDonald's products.

### 3-5d Foreign Direct Investment

**Direct investment** in foreign production and marketing facilities represents the deepest level of global involvement. The cost is high, but companies with direct investments have more control over how their business operates in a given country. The high-dollar commitment also represents significant risk if the business doesn't go well. Most direct investment takes the form of either acquiring foreign firms or developing new facilities from the ground up. Another increasingly popular approach is strategic alliances or partnerships that allow multiple firms to share risks and resources for mutual benefit.

Foreign acquisitions enable companies to gain a foothold quickly in new markets. In 2009, for example, Italian carmaker Fiat took over struggling U.S. auto giant Chrysler, with plans to more fully exploit the American market in the wake of the Great Recession. A number of other global giants, such as Microsoft, General Electric, and Nestlé, tend to follow a foreign acquisition strategy.[16]

Developing new facilities from scratch—or "offshoring"—is the most costly form of direct investment. It also involves significant risk. But the benefits include complete control over how the facility develops and the potential for high profits, which makes the approach attractive for corporations that can afford it. Intel,

for instance, built a $2.5 billion specialized computer chip manufacturing plant in northeastern China. And foreign car companies, from German Daimler-Benz to Korean Hyundai, to Japanese Toyota, have built factories in the southern United States.[17]

**Joint ventures** involve two or more companies joining forces—sharing resources, risks, and profits, but not merging companies—to pursue specific opportunities. A formal, long-term agreement is usually called a **partnership**, while a less formal, less encompassing agreement is usually called a **strategic alliance**. Joint ventures are a popular, though controversial, means of entering foreign markets. Often a foreign company connects with a local firm to ease its way into the market. In fact, some countries, such as India and Malaysia, require that foreign investors have local partners. But research from Harvard finance professor Mihir Desai finds that joint ventures between multinational firms and domestic partners can be more costly and less rewarding than they initially appear. He and his team suggest that they make sense only in countries that require local political and cultural knowledge as a core element of doing business.[18]

## 3-6 Barriers to International Trade

Every business faces challenges, but international firms face more hurdles than domestic firms. Understanding and surmounting those hurdles is the key to success in global markets. Most barriers to trade fall into the following categories: sociocultural differences, economic differences, and legal/political differences. As you think about these barriers, keep in mind that each country has a different mix of barriers. Often countries with the highest barriers have the least competition, which can be a real opportunity for the first international firms to break through.

**direct investment** (or foreign direct investment) When firms either acquire foreign firms or develop new facilities from the ground up in foreign countries.

**joint ventures** When two or more companies join forces—sharing resources, risks, and profits, but not actually merging companies—to pursue specific opportunities.

**partnership** A voluntary agreement under which two or more people act as co-owners of a business for profit.

**strategic alliance** An agreement between two or more firms to jointly pursue a specific opportunity without actually merging their businesses. Strategic alliances typically involve less formal, less encompassing agreements than partnerships.

> "Whether you think you can, or you think you can't—you're right."
>
> —Henry Ford, Founder of Ford Motor Company

### 3-6a Sociocultural Differences

**Sociocultural differences** include differences among countries in language, attitudes, and values. Some specific, and perhaps surprising, elements that affect business include nonverbal communication, forms of address, attitudes toward punctuality, religious celebrations and customs, business practices, and expectations regarding meals and gifts. Understanding and responding to sociocultural factors are vital for firms that operate in multiple countries. But since the differences often operate at a subtle level, they can undermine relationships before anyone is aware that it's happening. The best way to jump over sociocultural barriers is to conduct thorough consumer research, cultivate firsthand knowledge, and practice extreme sensitivity. The payoff can be a sharp competitive edge. Hyundai, for instance, enjoyed a whopping 28% share of the passenger SUV market in India in 2020.[19] It beats the competition with custom features that reflect Indian culture, such as elevated rooflines to provide more headroom for turban-wearing motorists.[20]

### 3-6b Economic Differences

Before entering a foreign market, it's critical to understand and evaluate the local economic conditions. Key factors to consider include population, per capita income, economic growth rate, currency exchange rate, and stage of economic development. But keep in mind that low scores for any of these measures don't necessarily equal a lack of opportunity. In fact, some of today's biggest opportunities are in countries with low per capita income. For example, the Indian division of global giant Unilever gets 50% of its sales from rural India by selling products to individual consumers in tiny quantities, such as two-cent sachets of shampoo. The rural Indian market has been growing so dramatically that in 2010, the chair of Hindustan Unilever declared, "What we have done in the last 25 years we want to do it in the next two years," scaling up the reach of its consumer products from about 250,000 rural retail outlets to about 750,000. In a recent TED Talk, the chair of Hindustan Unilever passionately argued that including value, purpose, and sustainability in top-level decision-making is not just savvy—it's the only way to run a twenty-first-century business responsibly. And Hewlett-Packard has recently joined forces with Unilever to give microdistributors in rural India the ability to check prices and place orders online from "what are now distinctively offline villages and regions." After the initial financial hit from the COVID-19 pandemic, Hindustan Unilever experienced a stronger bounce back in its rural business than in its urban business. Also capitalizing on the rapid growth and increased demand, Samsung has introduced Guru, a mobile phone that can be charged with solar power, to rural India. Other mobile companies are scrambling to keep up.[21]

Effectively serving less developed markets requires innovation and efficiency. Emerging consumers often need different product features, and they almost always need lower costs. C. K. Prahalad, an influential business scholar, believed that forward-thinking companies can make a profit in developing countries if they make advanced technology affordable. Many markets are simply so large that high-volume sales can make up for low profit margins.

Overall, the profit potential is clear and growing. And as consumers in developing countries continue to gain income—although at a much slower pace in the wake of the economic crisis—companies that established their brands early will have a critical edge over firms that enter the market after them.

**Infrastructure** should be another key economic consideration when entering a foreign market. Infrastructure refers to a country's physical facilities that support economic activity. It includes basic systems in each of the following areas:

- Transportation (e.g., roads, airports, railroads, and ports)

- Communication (e.g., TV, radio, Internet, and cell phone coverage)

- Energy (e.g., utilities and power plants)

- Finance (e.g., banking, checking, and credit)

The level of infrastructure can vary dramatically among countries. In Africa, for instance, only 29% of the population has Internet access, compared to 83% in Europe.[22] In Vietnam and Thailand, many consumers buy products directly from vendors in small boats, compared to firmly grounded stores in Europe. Although credit card purchases are still relatively low in much of the world, particularly in Asia, recent growth has been explosive and will probably continue for the next few years.[23]

### 3-6c Political and Legal Differences

Political regimes obviously differ around the world, and their policies have a dramatic impact on business.

**sociocultural differences** Differences among cultures in language, attitudes, and values.

**infrastructure** A country's physical facilities that support economic activity.

# Familiar Favorites with a Brand New Twist

Travel around the world and you're likely to see American fast-food franchisees in virtually every city. Although you'll surely recognize the names of these fast-food behemoths, you may not be as familiar with the food that they serve, since many of the dishes have been completely changed in response to local culture.

**Burger King:**

- Japan: A limited-time offer of a Whopper with 15 strips of bacon added. Soon after, pigs were listed in the Endangered Species Registry in Japan (just kidding). You could also order a black-colored "Ninja Burger," with charcoal infused in the beef and cheese to achieve the startling color.

- Austria: X-tra Long Burger (sub sandwich–length burger with three beef patties topped with either chili cheese or BBQ sauce AND onion rings).

- Egypt: Cheesy Whopper (a Whopper with a patty of deep-fried, breaded cheese on the beef).

- United Kingdom: Sprout Surprise Whopper. In case your Whopper tastes too good, this version adds a disk made of breaded Brussels sprouts and swiss cheese (surprise!).

**Pizza Hut:**

- Japan: Crust stuffed with shrimp nuggets and injected with mayonnaise.

- South Korea: Crust filled with sweet potato mousse.

- China: Lemon-flavored salmon pastry roll and scallop croquettes with crushed seaweed.

- Middle East: Crown Crust (a pizza/cheeseburger hybrid studded with "cheeseburger gems," which are cheeseburger sliders attached to the outside of a meaty pizza that's topped with lettuce and tomato and drizzled with "special sauce," served with a side of Pepto Bismol).

- Singapore: Double Decker Pizza: The second layer is comprised of turkey and ham rolls topped with mango mayonnaise (for the truly calorie deprived).

**KFC:**

- China: Spicy tofu chicken rice, rice porridge breakfast (congee).

- India: Chana Snacker (a chickpea burger topped with Thousand Island sauce).

- Philippines: Double Down Dog (a hot dog wrapped in a fried chicken bun).

**McDonald's:**

- India: Paneer Salsa Wrap (cottage cheese with Mexican-Cajun coating).

- Australia: Bacon and Egg Roll ("rashers of quality bacon and fried egg").

- Brazil: Cheese Quiche.

- Kuwait: Veggie Surprise Burger (no detailed description ... yikes!).[24]

- Austria: McItaly Adagio burger topped with "eggplant mousse" and chopped almonds.

- Italy: Nutella Burger (a sweet bun filled with a chocolate and hazelnut spread). This one sounds yummy!

Morumotto/Shutterstock.com

The specific laws and regulations that governments create around business are often less obvious, yet they can still represent a significant barrier to international trade. To compete effectively—and to reduce risk—managers must carefully evaluate these factors and make plans to respond to them both now and as they change.

**Laws and Regulations** International businesses must comply with international legal standards, the laws of their own countries, and the laws of their host countries. This can be a real challenge since many developing countries change business regulations with little notice and less publicity. The justice system can pose another key challenge, particularly with regard to legal enforcement of ownership and contract rights. Since 2003, the World Bank has published a "Doing Business" report that ranks the ease of doing business for small and medium-sized companies in 190 different countries. The 2020 "Doing Business" report showed that New Zealand leads in the ease of doing business, followed by Singapore, Hong Kong SAR, Denmark, Korea, and the United States. Countries that scored well in "Doing Business" tended to benefit from higher levels of entrepreneurial activity and lower levels of corruption. Overall, the Eastern Europe and Central Asia regions continued to show a faster rate of improvement than any other regions according to "Doing Business" indicators. The "Doing Business" project examines the ease of doing business from ten different angles, including the ease of dealing with construction permits, paying taxes, and enforcing contracts.[25] The key benefit of an effective legal system is that it reduces risk for both domestic and foreign businesses.

Bribery, the payment of money for favorable treatment, and corruption, the solicitation of money for favorable treatment, are also major issues throughout the world. While bribery and corruption are technically illegal in virtually every major country, they are often accepted as a standard way of doing business. Regardless, U.S. corporations and American citizens are subject to prosecution by U.S. authorities for offering bribes in any nation. Refer to Chapter 4 for more details.

**Political Climate** The political climate of any country deeply influences whether that nation is attractive to foreign business. Stability is crucial. A country subject to strife from civil war, riots, or other violence creates huge additional risk for foreign business. Yet, figuring out how to operate in an unstable environment, such as Russia, Bolivia, or the Middle East, can give early movers a real advantage. Grant Winterton, Coca-Cola's regional manager for Russia, commented to *Time* magazine that "the politics do concern us." But having snagged 50% of the $1.9 billion carbonated-soft-drink market, he concludes that "the opportunity far outweighs the risk." Poor enforcement of intellectual property rights across international borders is another tough issue for business. The Business Software Alliance's piracy-tracking study found that worldwide piracy rates hover at about 42%, with piracy rates in emerging markets towering over those in mature markets—68% versus 24%. The total value of software theft hit a record $63.4 billion. The highest-piracy countries are Georgia, Zimbabwe, Moldova, and Libya, all 90% or higher. Somewhat ironically, business decision makers admit to pirating software more frequently than other computer users do.[26]

**International Trade Restrictions** National governments also have the power to erect barriers to international business through a variety of international trade restrictions. The arguments for and against trade restrictions—also called **protectionism**—are summarized below. As you

## Troubled Waters

Planet Earth does not produce more fresh water—it simply recycles what it has—which isn't nearly enough in light of the planet's exploding human population; in fact, according to the World Health Organization, more than 2.4 million people die every year from lack of access to clean water, which is not surprising, given that 1 in 10 people lack access to clean water. Amazingly, the problem only stands to worsen. By 2050, one in five developing countries will face water shortages, many of them severe. By 2030, China, the world's most populous country, may no longer be self-sufficient in terms of wheat and corn production. Clearly, the growing water shortage is a human crisis, but it also will be a business crisis. Obviously, food and beverage companies depend on water. But when it comes right down to it, every industry from pharmaceuticals to semiconductors, to mining, to clothing manufacturing depends on water at some point in its supply or usage chain. Investment in clean water can pay off—big time. According to Water.org, every $1 invested in water and sanitation provides a $4 economic return. *Fortune* magazine suggests that agricultural firms can begin preparing now by investing in the development of GMO crops, precision agriculture, and high-tech irrigation. According to brand consultancy *Interbrand*, other businesses would also be wise to prepare by designing and executing an enterprise-wide strategy for water stewardship—not just for their own operations but for their entire value chains.[27]

Santiparp Wattanaporn/Shutterstock.com

## Exhibit 3.3 Reasons to Create and Eliminate Trade Restrictions

| Reasons to Create Trade Restrictions | Reasons to Eliminate Trade Restrictions |
|---|---|
| Protect domestic industry (e.g., the U.S. steel industry) | Reduce prices and increase choices for consumers by encouraging competition from around the world |
| Protect domestic jobs in key industries (but perhaps at the cost of domestic jobs in other industries) | Increase domestic jobs in industries with a comparative advantage versus other countries |
| Protect national security interests | Increase jobs—both at home and abroad—from foreign companies |
| Retaliate against countries who have engaged in unfair trade practices | Build exporting opportunities through better relationships with other countries |
| Pressure other countries to change their policies and practices | Use resources more efficiently on a worldwide basis |

read, note that most economists find the reasons to eliminate trade restrictions much more compelling than the reasons to create them (refer to Exhibit 3.3).

Just as trade restrictions have a range of motivations, they can take a number of different forms. The most common trade restrictions are tariffs, quotas, voluntary export restraints, and embargoes.

- **Tariffs** are taxes levied against imports. Governments tend to use protective tariffs either to shelter fledgling industries that couldn't compete without help, or to shelter industries that are crucial to the domestic economy. During the four years of the Trump presidency, the United States, China, the EU, Canada, and Mexico levied tariffs and counter-tariffs on each other as discussed at the beginning of this chapter. The main result seemed to be higher prices for consumers.

- **Quotas** are limitations on the amount of specific products that may be imported from certain countries during a given time period. Russia, for instance, has specific quotas for U.S. meat imports.

- **Voluntary export restraints (VERs)** are limitations on the amount of specific products that one nation will export to another nation. Although the government of the exporting country typically imposes VERs, they usually do so out of fear that the importing country would impose even more onerous restrictions. As a result, VERs often aren't as "voluntary" as the name suggests. The United States, for instance, insisted on VERs with Japanese auto exports in the early 1980s (which many economists believe ultimately precipitated the decline of the U.S. auto industry).

- An **embargo** is a total ban on the international trade of a certain item, or a total halt in trade with a particular nation. The intention of most embargoes is to pressure the targeted country to change political

> **Around the world, one in three children lives in poverty, compared to one in six adults.**
> —UN 2020 Poverty Index

policies or to protect national security. The U.S. embargo against trade with Cuba offers a high-profile example.

Quotas, VERs, and embargoes are relatively rare compared to tariffs, and tariffs are falling to new lows. But as tariffs decrease, some nations are seeking to control imports through nontariff barriers such as:

- Requiring red-tape-intensive import licenses for certain categories

- Establishing nonstandard packaging requirements for certain products

- Offering less-favorable exchange rates to certain importers

- Establishing standards on how certain products are produced or grown

- Promoting a "buy national" consumer attitude among local people

**protectionism** National policies designed to restrict international trade, usually with the goal of protecting domestic businesses.

**tariffs** Taxes levied against imports.

**quotas** Limitations on the amount of specific products that may be imported from certain countries during a given time period.

**voluntary export restraints (VERs)** Limitations on the amount of specific products that one nation will export to another nation.

**embargo** A complete ban on international trade of a certain item, or a total halt in trade with a particular nation.

In October 2016, President Barack Obama lifted limits on cigars and rum imported from Cuba, easing the embargo imposed on the small Caribbean nation in 1962. Here, a woman prepares cigars for shipment at La Bodeguita del Medio in Havana, Cuba.

Nontariff barriers tend to be fairly effective because complaints about them can be hard to prove and easy to counter.[28]

## 3-7 Free Trade: The Movement Gains Momentum

Perhaps the most dramatic change in the world economy has been the global move toward **free trade**—the unrestricted movement of goods and services across international borders. Even though *complete* free trade is not a reality, the emergence of regional trading blocks, common markets, and international trade agreements has moved the world economy much closer to that goal.

**free trade** The unrestricted movement of goods and services across international borders.

**General Agreement on Tariffs and Trade (GATT)** An international trade treaty designed to encourage worldwide trade among its members.

**World Trade Organization (WTO)** A permanent global institution to promote international trade and to settle international trade disputes.

**World Bank** An international cooperative of 189 member countries, working together to reduce poverty in the developing world.

### 3-7a GATT and the World Trade Organization

The **General Agreement on Tariffs and Trade (GATT)** is an international trade accord designed to encourage worldwide trade among its members. Established in 1948 by 23 nations, GATT has undergone a number of revisions. The most significant changes stemmed from the 1986–1994 Uruguay Round of negotiations, which took bold steps to slash average tariffs by about 30% and to reduce other trade barriers among the 125 nations that signed.

The Uruguay Round also created the **World Trade Organization (WTO)**, a permanent global institution to promote international trade and to settle international trade disputes. The WTO monitors provisions of the GATT agreements, promotes further reduction of trade barriers, and mediates disputes among members. The decisions of the WTO are binding, which means that all parties involved in disputes must comply to maintain good standing in the organization. During his presidency, Donald Trump attacked the WTO as being irrelevant, unfair, and outdated. Experts anticipate, however, that President Joe Biden will increase cooperation with the WTO.

Ministers of the WTO meet every two years to address current world trade issues. As the world economy has shifted toward services rather than goods, the emphasis of WTO meetings has followed suit. Controlling rampant piracy of intellectual property is a key concern for developed countries. For less-developed countries, one central issue is U.S. and European agricultural subsidies, which may unfairly distort agricultural prices worldwide.

In fact, both the broader agenda and the individual decisions of the WTO have become increasingly controversial over the past ten years. Advocates for less-developed nations are deeply concerned that free trade clears the path for major multinational corporations to push local businesses into economic failure. A local food stand, for instance, probably won't have the resources to compete with a global giant such as McDonald's. If the food stand closes, the community has gained inexpensive hamburgers, but the entrepreneurs have lost their livelihood, and the community has lost the local flavor that contributes to its unique culture. Other opponents of the WTO worry that the acceleration of global trade encourages developing countries to fight laws that protect the environment and workers' rights, for fear of losing their low-cost advantage on the world market. The concerns have sparked significant protests during the past few meetings of the WTO ministers, and the outcry may well grow louder as developing nations gain economic clout.

### 3-7b The World Bank

Established in the aftermath of World War II, the **World Bank** is an international cooperative of 189 member countries, working together to reduce poverty in the developing world. The World Bank influences the global

christianthiel.net/Shutterstock.com

economy by providing financial and technical advice to the governments of developing countries for projects in a range of areas, including infrastructure, communications, health, and education. The financial assistance usually comes in the form of low-interest loans. But to secure a loan, the borrowing nation must often agree to conditions that can involve rather arduous economic reform.

### 3-7c The International Monetary Fund

Like the World Bank, the **International Monetary Fund (IMF)** is an international organization accountable to the governments of its 190 member nations. The basic mission of the IMF is to promote international economic cooperation and stable growth. Funding comes from the member nations, with the United States contributing more than twice as much as any other country. To achieve these goals, the IMF:

- Supports stable exchange rates

- Facilitates a smooth system of international payments

- Encourages member nations to adopt sound economic policies

- Promotes international trade

- Lends money to member nations to address economic problems

Although all of its functions are important, the IMF is best known as a lender of last resort to nations in financial trouble. This policy has come under fire in the past few years. Critics accuse the IMF of encouraging poor countries to borrow more money than they can ever hope to repay, which actually cripples their economies over the long term, creating even deeper poverty.

In 2020, to help address the impact of the COVID-19 pandemic, the IMF offered immediate debt relief for 25 of their poorest member countries. The Managing Director of the IMF pointed out that the debt relief would help the recipients "channel more of their scarce financial resources toward vital medical and other relief efforts."[29]

### 3-7d Trading Blocs and Common Markets

Another major development in the past decade is the emergence of regional **trading blocs**, or groups of countries that have reduced or even eliminated all tariffs, allowing the free flow of goods among the member nations. A **common market** goes even further than a trading bloc by attempting to harmonize all trading rules. The United States, Mexico, and Canada have formed the largest trading bloc in the world, and the 27 countries of the European Union have formed the largest common market.

**USMCA** The **United States–Mexico–Canada Agreement (USMCA)** is the treaty that governs trading among the United States, Mexico, and Canada. The agreement was negotiated by former President Trump to replace NAFTA with the goal of securing more favorable terms for the United States. The USMCA took effect in 2020, and most experts anticipate that the impact will be minor since the changes to the treaty are incremental at best.

**International Monetary Fund (IMF)** An international organization of 190 member nations that promotes international economic cooperation and stable growth.

**trading bloc** A group of countries that have reduced or even eliminated tariffs, allowing for the free flow of goods among the member nations.

**common market** A group of countries that have eliminated tariffs and harmonized trading rules to facilitate the free flow of goods among the member nations.

**United States–Mexico–Canada Agreement (USMCA)** The treaty among the United States, Mexico, and Canada that eliminated trade barriers and investment restrictions over a 15-year period starting in 1994.

## Exhibit 3.4
## European Union 2020

But critics of North American free trade point out that the U.S. trade deficit with both Mexico and Canada has skyrocketed. While exports to both nations have increased, imports have grown far faster; both countries are among the top ten contributors to the total U.S. trade deficit, threatening the long-term health of the American economy. Other criticisms include increased pollution and worker abuse. Companies that move their factories to Mexico to capitalize on lower costs also take advantage of looser environmental and worker-protection laws, creating major ethical concerns. But the full impact—for better or for worse—is tough to evaluate because so many other variables affect all three economies.[30]

**European Union** Composed of 27 nations and more than half a billion people, and boasting a combined GDP of nearly $15.6 trillion, the **European Union (EU)** is the world's largest common market. Exhibit 3.4 shows a map of the 2020 EU countries plus six countries that have applied to join.[31]

The overarching goal of the EU is to bolster Europe's trade position and to increase its international political and economic power. To help make this happen,

**European Union (EU)** The world's largest common market, composed of 27 European nations.

# Hurting in Hong Kong

Great Britain ceded control of its former colony, Hong Kong, back to China in 1997 with the understanding that there would be "one country two systems." However, in June 2020, China imposed the Hong Kong National Security Law, which rolled back democracy and basic civil rights in the freewheeling, market-based, economic hub. The move triggered massive protests from terrified civilians in the streets of Hong Kong. But the business community lined up for the most part behind China. Commercial renters bolstered the Hong Kong property market soon after protests began; both Alibaba, the e-commerce giant and ByteDance, the parent company of the video app TikTok, signed leases for expensive new office space. Also, in recent years China has issued new rules making it easier for its homegrown companies to list on the Hong Kong stock exchange, so Hong Kong has attracted more Chinese businesses that support the national security legislation. Meanwhile, on the streets of Hong Kong, the protests and arrests continue.[32]

Protesters in Hong Kong push back against China's National Security Law.

the EU has removed all trade restrictions among member nations and unified internal trade rules, allowing goods and people to move freely among EU countries. The EU has also created standardized policies for import and export between EU countries and the rest of the world, giving the member nations more clout as a bloc than each would have had on its own. Perhaps the EU's most economically significant move was the introduction of a single currency, the euro, in 2002. Of the 15 EU members at the time, 12 adopted the euro (exceptions were the United Kingdom, Sweden, and Denmark). The EU also affects the global economy with its leading-edge approach to environmental protection, quality production, and human rights.

In mid-2016, the United Kingdom, which includes England, Scotland, Wales, and Northern Ireland, held a referendum on whether to exit the European Union. After an intense and divisive campaign, the UK public voted to leave the EU in a very close vote. Dubbed *Brexit* (a combination of the words "British" and "exit"), the decision to leave was quite unexpected.[33] Many political and economic analysts have voiced deep concerns about the impact that Brexit will have on the United Kingdom as well as the rest of the world—especially in light of London's position as an international banking center. The initial vote is likely to be final, but the implementation of Brexit will not be immediate. There will be an initial two-year negotiation with the EU about the terms of withdrawal. This negotiation was relatively unfavorable toward Britain, in part so that the EU could discourage other countries from withdrawing. The EU has leverage with regard to items such as terms of trade.

So why did Britain want out? The two major issues at play were immigration and self-determination. Many British citizens, especially older and more rural populations in England, were concerned that the country's unemployment and social services would be swamped under the weight of new immigrant arrivals as mandated by the EU. Many Brits were also concerned that the country's identity and direction would increasingly be determined by the EU and become fused into a continental identity. The ultimate impact of the British exit will be unclear for months, and likely years, to come. The next several years in particular will be critical to the shape, size, and structure of the European economy. The UK voted to leave the European Union and actually departed on January 31, 2020.[34]

## The Big Picture

The past decade has been marked by extraordinary changes in the world economy. The boundaries between individual countries have fallen lower than ever before, creating a new level of economic connectedness. The growing integration has created huge opportunities for visionary companies of every size. But integration also means risk. The dangers became all too clear in 2020 when the COVID-19 pandemic reverberated around the globe, shutting down virtually every economy in its wake.

To succeed abroad—especially in tough economic times—individual firms must make the right choices about how to structure their operations, surmount barriers to trade, meet diverse customer needs, manage a global workforce, and handle complex logistics. Human rights and environmental protection continue to be especially critical for international businesses. Both are vital components of social responsibility and will only gain importance as advocates raise awareness around the world. In the face of economic, political, and social flux, effective global business leaders must master both strategy and implementation at a deeper level than ever before.

## Careers in International Business

### International Sports Marketing Manager

Implement marketing plans outside the United States with a focus on Europe, Australia, and New Zealand. Work with global brand marketing team to develop and execute events that incorporate athletes. Participate in the scouting process to identify and pursue up-and-coming athletes in relevant sports. Provide support for the endorsement contract negotiation process.

# 4 | Business Ethics and Social Responsibility:
## Doing Well by Doing Good

## Learning Objectives

After studying this chapter, you will be able to:

**4-1** Explain ethics and universal ethical standards

**4-2** Describe business ethics and ethical dilemmas

**4-3** Discuss how ethics relates to both the individual and the organization

**4-4** Examine the impact of social responsibility on stakeholder groups

**4-5** Explain the role of social responsibility in the global arena

**4-6** Describe how companies evaluate their efforts to be socially responsible

## 4-1 Ethics and Social Responsibility: A Close Relationship

Ethics and social responsibility—often discussed in the same breath—are closely related, but they are definitely not the same. Ethics refers to sets of beliefs about right and wrong, good and bad; business ethics involve the application of these issues in the workplace. Clearly, ethics relate to individuals and their day-to-day decision making. Just as clearly, the decisions of each individual can affect the entire organization.

Social responsibility is the obligation of a business to contribute to society. The most socially responsible firms feature proactive policies that focus on meeting the needs of all their stakeholders—not just investors but also employees, customers, the broader community, and the environment. The stance of a company regarding social responsibility sets the tone for the organization and clearly influences the decisions of individual employees.

Although this chapter discusses ethics and social responsibility separately, keep in mind that the two areas have a dynamic, interactive relationship that plays a vital role in building both profitable businesses and a vibrant community.

### 4-1a Defining Ethics: Murkier Than You'd Think

In the most general sense, **ethics** refer to sets of beliefs about right and wrong, good and bad. While your individual ethics stem from who you are as a human being, your family, your social group, and your culture also play a significant role in shaping

**ethics** A set of beliefs about right and wrong, good and bad.

# BUSINESS ETHICS

your ethics. And therein lies the challenge: in the United States, people come from such diverse backgrounds that establishing broad agreement on specific ethical standards can be daunting. The global arena only amplifies the challenge.

A given country's legal system provides a solid starting point for examining ethical standards. The function of laws in the United States (and elsewhere) is to establish and enforce ethical norms that apply to everyone within our society. Laws provide basic standards of behavior. But truly ethical behavior goes beyond the basics. In other words, your actions can be completely legal, yet still unethical. But since the legal system is far from perfect, in rare instances your actions can be illegal, yet still ethical. Exhibit 4.1 shows some examples of how business conduct can fall within legal and ethical dimensions. Clearly, legal and ethical actions should be your goal. Legality should be the floor—not the ceiling—for how to behave in business and elsewhere.

Do all actions have ethical implications? Clearly not. Some decisions fall within the realm of free choice with no direct link to right and wrong, good and bad. Examples might include what color T-shirt you choose to wear, what levels your game development company includes

> "When the culture of an organization mandates that it is more important to protect the reputation of a system and those in power than it is to protect the basic human dignity of individuals or communities, you can be certain that shame is systemic, money drives ethics, and accountability is dead."
>
> —Brené Brown, American Professor, Lecturer, Author, and Podcast Host

in its new video game, or what sunglasses you decide to purchase.

## 4-1b Universal Ethical Standards: A Reasonable Goal or Wishful Thinking?

Too many people view ethics as relative. In other words, their ethical standards shift depending on the

## Exhibit 4.1 | Legal-Ethical Matrix

| Legal and Unethical | Legal and Ethical |
|---|---|
| Promoting high-calorie/low-nutrient foods with inadequate information about the risks | Producing high-quality products |
| Producing products that you know will break before their time | Rewarding integrity<br>Leading by example |
| Paying nonliving wages to workers in developing countries | Treating employees fairly<br>Contributing to the community<br>Respecting the environment |

| Illegal and Unethical | Illegal and Ethical |
|---|---|
| Embezzling money | Providing rock-bottom prices *only* to distributors in underserved areas |
| Engaging in sexual harassment | Collaborating with other medical clinics to guarantee low prices in low-income counties (collusion) |
| Practicing collusion with competitors | |
| Encouraging fraudulent accounting | |

situation and how it relates to them. Here are a few examples:

- "It's not okay to steal paper from the office supply store…*but* it's perfectly fine to 'borrow' supplies from the storage closet at work to use at home. Why? The company owes me a bigger salary."

- "It's wrong to lie…*but* it's okay to call in sick when I have personal business to take care of. Why? I don't want to burn through my limited vacation days."

- "Everyone should have a level playing field. . .*but* it's fine to give my brother the first shot at my company's contract. Why? I know he really needs the work."

This kind of two-faced thinking is dangerous because it can help people rationalize bigger and bigger ethical deviations. But the problem can be fixed by identifying **universal ethical standards** that apply to everyone across a broad spectrum of situations. Some people argue that we could never find universal standards for a country as diverse as the United States. But the nonprofit, nonpartisan Character Counts organization has worked with a diverse group of educators, community leaders, and ethicists to identify six core

**universal ethical standards** Ethical norms that apply to all people across a broad spectrum of situations.

values, listed in Exhibit 4.2, that transcend political, religious, class, and ethnic divisions.

## Exhibit 4.2 | Universal Ethical Standards

| | |
|---|---|
| Trustworthiness | Be honest.<br>Don't deceive, cheat, or steal.<br>Do what you say you'll do. |
| Respect | Treat others how you'd like to be treated.<br>Be considerate.<br>Be tolerant of differences. |
| Responsibility | Persevere.<br>Be self-controlled and self-disciplined.<br>Be accountable for your choices. |
| Fairness | Provide equal opportunity.<br>Be open-minded; listen to others.<br>Don't take advantage of others. |
| Caring | Be kind.<br>Be compassionate.<br>Express gratitude. |
| Citizenship | Contribute to the community.<br>Protect the environment.<br>Cooperate whenever feasible; volunteer. |

Source: ©2021 Character Counts, https://charactercounts.org/character-counts-overview/six-pillars/. Reprinted from the Josephson Institute's Report Card on the Ethics of American Youth Summary with permission.

## 4-2 Business Ethics: Not an Oxymoron

Quite simply, **business ethics** is the application of right and wrong, good and bad in a business setting. But this isn't as straightforward as it may initially seem. The most challenging business decisions seem to arise when values are in conflict...when whatever you do will have negative consequences, forcing you to choose among bad options. These are true **ethical dilemmas**. (Keep in mind that ethical *dilemmas* differ from ethical *lapses*, which involve clear misconduct.) Here are three examples of ethical dilemmas:

- Imagine that you did a great job on a recent project at your company. Your boss has been very vocal about acknowledging your work and the increased revenue that resulted from it. Privately, she said that you clearly earned a bonus of at least 10%, but due to company politics, she was unable to secure the bonus for you. She also implied that if you were to submit inflated expense reports for the next few months, she would look the other way, and you could pocket the extra cash as well-deserved compensation for your contributions.

- Uber: Are Uber drivers employees of the Uber Corporation, or are they their own bosses (independent contractors)? It depends on who you ask. According to the Uber Corporation, its drivers are definitely independent contractors. In fact, the company requires all new drivers to sign a form acknowledging as much. This means that drivers do not get access to benefits or other protections such as workers' compensation, paid sick time, and accident and unemployment insurance, or pensions, which leaves them financially vulnerable as they continue to contribute to the enormous value of the world's largest ride-sharing company. Is this fair? It would seem not. The company, in fact, argues that their drivers are essentially mini-entrepreneurs, who have complete flexibility in terms of their schedules, and who can (and often do) toggle back and forth between working for them and their competitors. The National Labor Relations Board issued a memo in 2019, siding with Uber by designating its drivers as independent contractors on the federal level—but there was still a patchwork of designations on a state-by-state level. In 2020, this issue became a ballot initiative in

California. Uber claimed that if they were forced to classify drivers as employees rather than independent contractors, they would also be forced to hire fewer drivers and to set driver schedules, eliminating the flexibility that makes driving such an attractive gig, leading to longer wait times and higher prices for consumers. Uber, Lyft, and DoorDash spent more than $200 million promoting their side of this ballot measure. So, for the time being, gig drivers will continue to be independent contractors in the highest population state in the union.[1]

- Facebook: Most people, when they join a private Facebook group expect their information to stay private, right? This is especially true for those who join the group to discuss a private or intimate health condition in order to find information and support from peers with a similar condition. Private groups include those who are trying to kick an addiction, those who share a genetic condition, and those who've been diagnosed with stigmatized diseases. Imagine the surprise of breast cancer research advocate, Andrea Downing, and cybersecurity analyst, Fred Trotter, when they discovered a security loophole that they believed would allow developers, marketers, and others to download the membership lists of Facebook groups for thousands of diseases and conditions, from Alcoholics Anonymous to survivors of sexual assault. Facebook changed their privacy settings in 2018 to close the loophole. Furthermore, in response to a vulnerability report that Downing and Trotter filed with Facebook in 2019, they claimed that "people who are concerned about their membership in groups being seen by others are able to simply not use the Groups product, or can limit their usage to secret groups. Some people may have legitimate reasons to want to create groups which have different feature-sets than the functionality we provide today...If people are confused about the privacy of their membership in a group that is an unfortunate situation and we are committed to finding ways to reduce such occurrences."[2]

> **business ethics** The application of right and wrong, good and bad, in a business setting.
>
> **ethical dilemma** A decision that involves a conflict of values; every potential course of action has some significant negative consequences.

# Who Should Die? And Who Should Decide?

Imagine that your driverless robotic car blows a tire while careening down a lovely mountain road. Your car still has some degree of control, but it is quickly becoming clear that this is not going to end well. On one side of you is oncoming traffic (several cars and a family of bicyclists), and on the other is a very, very steep cliff. Should the car slam into the oncoming traffic to save your life, or send you careening over the cliff to save others? This is not just an abstract question—it's an authentic ethical dilemma that businesses will increasingly need to face as more and more consumer machinery takes on a superhuman ability to react to danger.

A major hurdle in programming a robot to make ethical decisions is anticipating the virtually endless number of scenarios that the robot might face. One possible solution is to randomize the robot's response, but that approach completely evades human responsibility and negates the potential positive power

of human judgment. Courts, insurance companies, and governments around the world will certainly weigh in on how robots are and should be programmed. Clearly, contemporary "moral math" is nothing if not complex.

Martial Red/Shutterstock.com

---

 ## 4-3 Ethics: Multiple Touchpoints

Although all people must make their own ethical choices, the organization can have a significant influence on the quality of those decisions.

### 4-3a Ethics and the Individual: The Power of One

Ethical choices begin with ethical individuals. Your personal needs, your family, your culture, and your religion all influence your value system. Your personality traits—self-esteem, self-confidence, independence, and sense of humor—play a significant role as well. A recent study suggested that personal empathy—"identification with and understanding of another's situation, feelings, and motives"—is another strong predictor of ethical leadership. In fact, business leaders who scored highest on empathy also exhibited the highest levels of ethical leadership. These factors all come into play as you face ethical dilemmas. The challenge can be overwhelming, which has led a range of experts to develop frameworks for reaching ethical decisions. While the specifics vary, the key principles of most decision guides are very similar:

- Do you fully understand each dimension of the problem?

- Who would benefit? Who would suffer?

- Are the alternative solutions legal? Are they fair?

- Does your decision make you comfortable at a "gut feel" level?

- Could you defend your decision on the nightly TV news?

- Have you considered and reconsidered your responses to each question?[3]

The approach seems simple, but in practice it really isn't. Workers—and managers, too—often face enormous pressure to do what's right for the company or right for their career, rather than simply what's right. And keep in mind that it's completely possible for two people to follow the framework and arrive at completely different decisions, each feeling confident that they have made the right choice.

### 4-3b Ethics and the Organization: It Takes a Village

Although all people are clearly responsible for their own actions, the organization can influence those actions to a startling degree. Not surprisingly, that influence starts at the top, and actions matter far more than words. The president of the Ethics Resource Center states, "CEOs in particular must communicate their personal commitment to high ethical standards and consistently drive the message down to employees through their actions." Any other approach—even just the *appearance* of shaky ethics—can be deeply damaging to a company's ethical climate. Here are a couple of examples:

- **High Flyers:** When the CEOs of General Motors, Fiat Chrysler, and Ford Motor Company—two of them hovering on the edge of bankruptcy—went to Washington to request a $25 billion bailout package in the wake of the Great Recession, they flew in three separate corporate jets at an estimated cost of $20,000 per round-trip flight. All three were operating in line with official corporate travel policies, but it just didn't look right. One lawmaker pointedly asked, "Couldn't you all have downgraded to first class or jet-pooled or something to get here? It would have at least sent a message that you do get it." Not surprisingly, the execs left empty-handed.[4]

- **Boardroom Bullies:** More recently, boardroom bullies have been ejected from their powerful positions. In 2018, the CEO of "athleisure" giant Lululemon, Laurent Potdevin, stepped down due to behavior that apparently fell short of the company standards. Lululemon said that it "expects all employees to exemplify the highest levels of integrity and respect for one another" and Potdevin apparently did not. In a statement to the press, the Lululemon Board asserted that culture is at the core of the organization, and that

> **"Real integrity is doing the right thing, knowing that nobody's going to know whether you did it or not."**
>
> —Oprah Winfrey

Potdevin did not protect the organization's culture. Also, in 2018, Barnes & Noble fired its chief executive for "sexual harassment, bullying behavior, and other violations of company policies."[5]

Are these decisions wrong? Unethical?[6] How do you feel about the business decisions described in Exhibit 4.3?

## 4-3c Creating and Maintaining an Ethical Organization

Research from the Ethics Resource Center (ERC) suggests that organizational culture has more influence than any other variable on the ethical conduct of individual employees. According to the ERC, key elements of a strong culture include displays of ethics-related actions at all levels of an organization and accountability for actions. The impact of these elements can be dramatic.

According to Ethics & Compliance Initiative research conducted in 2019, more than 20% of workers worldwide felt pressure of one sort or another to break the rules at work. So, the question becomes: what causes the pressure? And what can reduce the pressure? Unsurprisingly, the research showed that employee pressure to bend the rules was higher among those who perceived their leaders as having weak commitment to organizational values and ethical leadership (49%) compared with those who perceived their leaders as having strong commitment

---

### Exhibit 4.3 Ethics at Work: How Would You Judge the Actions of These Business Leaders?[7]

Pierre Omidyar: Founder of eBay, he has contributed $100 million to the Tufts University Micro Finance Fund. His goal is to give economic power to impoverished people around the world through small business loans. Ultimately, he hopes to create entrepreneurial self-sufficiency as eBay has done for so many avid users.

Elizabeth Holmes: Founder of Silicon Valley biotech firm Theranos, she claimed to develop the revolutionary new blood testing technology. But due to her firm's deceptive practices, she was charged with defrauding her investors out of more than $700 million. Holmes relinquished control of Theranos in 2018. Her trial is scheduled for 2021.

Jeff Bezos: Founder of Amazon, he drew a great deal of negative press in 2020 for failing to provide adequate protection for Amazon warehouse workers during the COVID-19 pandemic. He also created a $2 billion Housing Equity Fund to create or preserve 20,000 affordable homes in all three of Amazon's headquarters regions.

Elon Musk: Founder of Tesla, Musk reopened the Fremont, CA plant in mid-March, 2020, despite a countrywide health order for all but essential businesses to remain closed due to the COVID-19 pandemic. Employees were forced to choose between their health and their income.

Bill Gates: Co-founder of Microsoft, he made some ethically shaky moves, but he and his wife also established the Bill and Melinda Gates Foundation, by far the largest U.S. charity. Working for the foundation, Gates applies his famous problem-solving skills to global health, global development, and American education.

Jessica Alba: As a follow-up to her successful acting career, Alba launched The Honest Company to promote health products that were "honestly free" of dangerous chemicals. However, Alba faced a number of lawsuits from disgruntled consumers who claimed that her products contained unnatural ingredients and that her firm engages in deceptive marketing. The Honest Company managed and learned from their lawsuits, experiencing growth during the COVID-19 pandemic by focusing on *not* overselling their products and growing in the digital space where their customers are concentrated.

(13%). Also, unsurprisingly, employee pressure to bend the rules increased with weak supervisor leadership (48%) compared with strong direct supervisor leadership (18%). Perhaps the biggest surprise in the research was that employees who self-identified as being part of top management experienced pressure to bend the rules almost two times higher than that of employees who self-identified as individual contributors (30% vs. 17%). Note: The Ethics & Compliance Initiative researchers also observed that the rate of misconduct increases noticeably in organizations undergoing significant change. They speculate, therefore, that the dramatic changes wrought by the COVID-19 pandemic may have caused a high level of misconduct.[8]

Clearly, there are myriad ways to be ethical, and unethical—some of them more expensive than others. According to the Association of Certified Fraud Examiners, organizations lose roughly 5% of their revenue each year to fraud. Owners and executives commit only 20% of total occupational frauds, but they cause the largest losses by far on a dollar basis.[9]

Robert Lane, former CEO of Deere, a historically high-performing corporation, believes in the importance of senior management commitment to ethics, but he points out that the "tone at the top" must be reinforced by the actual behavior observed by suppliers, dealers, customers, and employees. At Deere, this is summed up in the highly visible, frequently referenced shorthand known as "the how." Lane declares that to establish an ethical culture, ethical words must be "backed up with documented practices, processes, and procedures, all understood around the globe."[10]

ERC research further supports the need for senior manager commitment by showing that when employees perceive more management commitment, they tend to be more fully engaged. More-engaged employees are much less likely to behave badly, and much more likely to report others who do, which dramatically lowers the risk for the company.[11]

A strong organizational culture works in tandem with formal ethics programs to create and maintain ethical work environments. A written **code of ethics** is the cornerstone of any formal ethics program. The purpose of a written code is to give employees the information they need to

3D Generator/Shutterstock.com

**Strong Ethics Is Good Business**

World's Most Ethical Companies honorees have historically out-performed others financially, demonstrating the connection between good ethical practices and performance that's valued in the marketplace.

Every year, the Ethisphere Institute publishes a list of the world's most ethical companies. Ethisphere's 2020 list featured 131 honorees from 21 countries and 50 industries and included 14 first-time honorees and seven companies that have been named to the list every year since its inception. The list included familiar names such as Best Buy, Dell, Hilton, Salesforce, L'Oréal, and Sony. For the complete list, visit worldsmostethicalcompanies.ethisphere.com/honorees.

make ethical decisions across a range of situations. Clearly, an ethics code becomes even more important for multi-national companies, since it lays out unifying values and priorities for divisions that are rooted in different cultures. But a written code is worthless if it doesn't reflect living principles. An effective code of ethics flows directly from ethical corporate values and leads directly to ongoing communication, training, and action.

Specific codes of ethics vary greatly among organizations. Perhaps the best-known code is the Johnson & Johnson Credo, which has guided the company profitably—with a soaring reputation—through a number of crises that would have sunk lesser organizations. One of the striking elements of the credo is the firm focus on fairness. It carefully refrains from overpromising financial rewards, committing instead to a "fair return" for stockholders.

To bring a code of ethics to life, experts advocate a forceful, integrated approach to ethics that virtually always includes the following steps:

1. Get executive buy-in and commitment to follow through. Top managers need to

## Exhibit 4.4
## The Spectrum of Social Responsibility

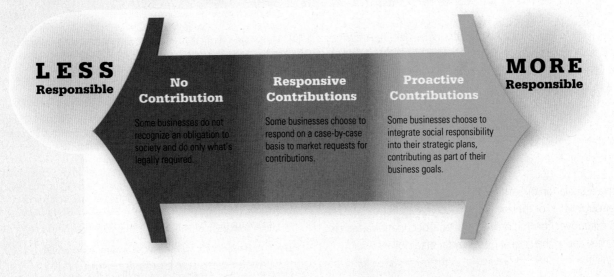

**LESS** Responsible

**No Contribution**
Some businesses do not recognize an obligation to society and do only what's legally required.

**Responsive Contributions**
Some businesses choose to respond on a case-by-case basis to market requests for contributions.

**Proactive Contributions**
Some businesses choose to integrate social responsibility into their strategic plans, contributing as part of their business goals.

**MORE** Responsible

---

communicate—even overcommunicate—about the importance of ethics. But talking works only when it's backed up by action: senior management must give priority to keeping promises and leading by example.

2. Establish expectations for ethical behavior at all levels of the organization, from the CEO to the nighttime cleaning crew. Be sure that outside parties such as suppliers, distributors, and customers understand the standards.

3. Integrate ethics into mandatory staff training. From new-employee orientation to ongoing training, ethics must play a role. Additionally, more specialized training helps employees who face more temptation (e.g., purchasing agents, overseas sales reps).

4. Ensure that your ethics code is both global and local in scope. Employees in every country should understand both the general principles and the specific applications. Be sure to translate it into as many languages as necessary.

5. Build and maintain a clear, trusted reporting structure for ethical concerns and violations. The structure should allow employees to seek anonymous guidance for ethical concerns and to report ethics violations anonymously.

6. Establish protection for **whistle-blowers**, people who report illegal or unethical behavior. Be sure that no retaliation occurs, in compliance with both ethics and the Sarbanes–Oxley legislation. Some have even suggested that whistle-blowers should receive a portion of the penalties levied against firms that violate the law.

7. Enforce the code of ethics. When people violate ethical norms, companies must respond immediately and—whenever appropriate—publicly to retain employee trust. Without enforcement, the code of ethics becomes meaningless.

## 4-4 Defining Social Responsibility: Making the World a Better Place

**Social responsibility** is the obligation of a business to contribute to society. Similar to ethics, the broad definition is clear, but specific implementation can be complex. Obviously, the number-one goal of any business is long-term profits; without profits, other contributions are impossible. But once a firm achieves a reasonable return, the balancing act begins: How can a company balance the need to contribute against the need to boost profits, especially when the two conflict? The answer depends on the business's values, mission, resources, and management philosophy, which lead in turn to its position on social responsibility. Business approaches fall across the spectrum, from no contribution to proactive contribution, as shown in Exhibit 4.4.

> **whistle-blowers** Employees who report their employer's illegal or unethical behavior to either the authorities or the media.
>
> **social responsibility** The obligation of a business to contribute to society.

## Exhibit 4.5 | Social Responsibility at Work

**How Would You Judge the Actions of These Firms?**[12]

Kraft: To celebrate National Noodle Day (who knew that existed?) in 2020, Kraft Heinz released a provocative digital campaign that featured a blurred picture of a bowl of mac and cheese with the headline encouraging consumers to "Send Noods." The first 7,000 consumers using the hashtag #SendNoods were eligible to have Kraft send a box of Mac & Cheese to friends and family. According to a Kraft spokesperson, the campaign was intended to be funny. But according to thousands of outraged mothers on social media—not so much.

Pharmaceutical companies: In late 2019, Federal prosecutors publicized an investigation into the role that six pharmaceutical companies may have played in the opioid crisis. One company shipped 3.7 million hydrocodone pills between 2008 and 2011 to a pharmacy in a West Virginia town of about 400 people. Purdue Pharma reached a multibillion-dollar settlement with thousands of cities, counties, and tribes, as well as 23 states for its role in the opioid crisis. Under the deal, the company filed for bankruptcy and restructured with its OxyContin proceeds going to victims of the opioid addiction epidemic.

Patagonia: The activist outdoor clothing maker transforms trash—in the form of used soda bottles and unusable manufacturing waste—into new polyester fibers for clothing. Their extensive field testing shows it performs just as well, if not better, than gear made from virgin polyester. Furthermore, using recycled fabrics limits their dependence on petroleum as a source of raw materials and prolongs landfill life, while also reducing toxic emissions from incinerations.

Subway: There might be something fishy about Subway tuna sandwiches, according to a lawsuit filed against the sandwich giant in early 2021, which alleged that its tuna sandwiches and wraps contain absolutely none of the popular fish but are made instead from a "mixture of various concoctions that do not constitute tuna yet have been blended together by defendants to imitate the appearance of tuna." The publicity from this accusation has been devastating for Subway, which had only recently recovered from a wave of bad publicity about the revelation in 2014 that it used a chemical also found in yoga mats (since discontinued) to make its bread.

USC: The of University of Southern California, a private university, offered free COVID-19 testing during the global pandemic for local students, faculty, and university personnel, giving them a welcome sense of caring and coverage at a time that was fraught for many in their large local university community.

High tech: Technology firms from social media giants, to email hosts, to grocery store scanners constantly vacuum up our data, slice it, dice, sell it, and serve it back to us in the form of customized marketing opportunities for us and other like us—sometimes without our permission, and almost always without paying us for the use of our personal data.

## 4-4a The Stakeholder Approach: Responsibility to Whom?

**Stakeholders** are any groups that have a stake—or a personal interest—in the performance and actions of an organization. Different stakeholders have different needs, expectations, and levels of interest. The federal government, for instance, is a key stakeholder in pharmaceutical companies but a very minor stakeholder in local art studios. The community at large is a key stakeholder for a coffee shop chain but a minor stakeholder for a web design firm. Enlightened organizations identify key stakeholders for their business and consider stakeholder priorities in their decision making. The goal is to balance their needs and priorities as effectively as possible, with an eye toward building their business over the long term. Core stakeholder groups for most businesses are employees, customers, investors, and the broader community.

**Responsibility to Employees: Creating Jobs That Work** Jobs alone aren't enough. The starting point for socially responsible employers is to meet legal standards, and the requirements are significant. How would you judge the social responsibility of the firms listed in Exhibit 4.5? Employers must comply with laws that include equal opportunity, workplace safety, minimum-wage and overtime requirements, protection from sexual harassment, and family and medical unpaid leaves. We will discuss these legal requirements (and others) in Chapter 15 on Human Resource Management.

But socially responsible employers go far beyond the law. They create a workplace environment that respects the dignity and value of each employee. They ensure that hard work, commitment, and talent pay off. They move beyond minimal safety requirements to establish proactive protections, such as ergonomically correct chairs and computer screens that reduce eyestrain. And the best employers respond to the ongoing employee search for a balance between work and personal life. With an increasing number of workers facing challenges such as raising kids and caring for elderly parents, responsible companies are stepping in with programs such as on-site day care, company-sponsored day camp, and referral services for elder care.

**Responsibility to Customers: Value, Honesty, and Communication** One core responsibility of business is to deliver consumer value by providing quality products at fair prices. Honesty and communication are critical components of this equation.

**stakeholders** Any groups that have a stake—or a personal interest—in the performance and actions of an organization.

**Consumerism**—a widely accepted social movement—suggests that consumer rights should be the starting point. In the early 1960s, President Kennedy defined these rights, which most businesses respect in response to both consumer expectations and legal requirements:

- The Right to Be Safe: Businesses are legally responsible for injuries and damages caused by their products—even if they have no reason to suspect that their products might cause harm. This makes it easy for consumers to file suits. In some cases, the drive to avert lawsuits has led to absurdities such as the warning on some coffee cups: "Caution! Hot coffee is hot!" (No kidding…)

- The Right to Be Informed: The law requires firms in a range of industries—from mutual funds, to groceries, to pharmaceuticals—to provide the public with extensive information. The Food and Drug Administration, for instance, mandates that most grocery foods feature a very specific "Nutrition Facts" label. Beyond legal requirements, many firms use the Web to provide a wealth of extra information about their products. KFC, for example, offers an interactive Nutrition Calculator that works with all of its menu items (and it's fun to use, too).

- The Right to Choose: Freedom of choice is a fundamental element of the capitalist U.S. economy. Our economic system works largely because consumers freely choose to purchase the products that best meet their needs. As businesses compete, consumer value increases. Socially responsible firms support consumer choice by following the laws that prevent anticompetitive behavior such as predatory pricing, collusion, and monopolies.

- The Right to Be Heard: Socially responsible companies make it easy for consumers to express legitimate complaints. They also develop highly trained customer service people to respond to complaints. In fact, smart businesses view customer complaints as an opportunity to create better products and stronger relationships. Statistics suggest that 1 in 50 dissatisfied customers takes the time to complain. The other 49 quietly switch brands. By soliciting feedback, you're not only being responsible but also building your business.[13]

Delivering quality products is another key component of social responsibility to consumers. **Planned obsolescence**—deliberately designing products to fail in order to shorten the time between consumer repurchases—represents a clear violation of social responsibility. In the long term, the market itself weeds out offenders. After all, who would repurchase a product that meets a premature end? But in the short term, planned obsolescence thins consumer wallets and abuses consumer trust.

Here are several examples of corporations that violated their social responsibility to consumers:

- Wells Fargo: In mid-2016, the Consumer Financial Protection Bureau, the Office of the Comptroller of the Currency (OCC), and the city and county of Los Angeles fined Wells Fargo Bank a total of nearly $185 million. This fine, along with other financial actions against Wells Fargo executives totaling roughly $200 million, represented a combination of penalties to punish the bank for a scandal that included creating fake accounts in customers' names, resulting in millions of dollars in fines, and damaging the credit scores of some customers. Management was pressuring salespeople to open the fake accounts to meet outlandish monthly sales goals. In response to the misconduct, Wells Fargo has paid $110 million to settle a class-action lawsuit. The new Wells Fargo CEO has apologized extensively. The bank has created an Office of Ethics, Oversight, and Integrity to handle complaints from employees and to monitor sales practices. It has also eliminated sales goals.[14]

- Equifax: At a time when public concern over privacy was especially high, Equifax—one of the three biggest credit

**consumerism** A social movement that focuses on four key consumer rights: (1) the right to be safe, (2) the right to be informed, (3) the right to choose, and (4) the right to be heard.

**planned obsolescence** The strategy of deliberately designing products to fail in order to shorten the time between purchases.

reporting agencies in the United States—stoked the flames of mistrust by allowing a breach of its databases to occur over a period of six months in 2017, exposing the personal data of more than 147 million Americans, which could lead to identity theft and fraud. Equifax apparently knew it was vulnerable to a hack, but did nothing to fix the exposure until after the data was stolen. As part of a global settlement for its security failure, Equifax agreed to pay at least $575 million, and potentially up to $700 million. Much of that money will be used to help people affected by the data breach.[15]

■ Mylan: Pharmaceutical behemoth Mylan, producer of the EpiPen, found itself at the center of a pricing controversy, which landed its CEO, Heather Bresch, at a congressional hearing in 2017 to testify about outrageous increases in the price of prescription drugs. The EpiPen is a self-injection device that temporarily reverses the effects of severe allergies by allowing people who are affected to inject themselves with a small dose of epinephrine. The device is a lifesaver that people with severe allergies—and their caregivers—have learned to keep at hand in case of emergencies. But unfortunately, the list price of the EpiPen soared from about $103.50 in 2009 to more than $608.61 in 2016. According to Bresch, the price rose because the company made an investment to the market, and because so many other entities in the pharmaceutical supply chain take a "piece of pie." She declared that the pricing controversy was a "window into a broken system." But she stopped well short of reducing the price.[16]

**Responsibility to Investors: Fair Stewardship and Full Disclosure** The primary responsibility of business to investors is clearly to make money—to create an ongoing stream of profits. But companies achieve and maintain long-term earnings in the context of responsibility to *all* stakeholders, which may mean trading short-term profits for long-term success. Responsibility to investors starts by meeting legal requirements, and in the wake of recent corporate scandals, the bar is higher than ever. The 2002 **Sarbanes–Oxley Act** limits conflict-of-interest issues by restricting the consulting services that

**Sarbanes–Oxley Act**
Federal legislation passed in 2002 that sets higher ethical standards for public corporations and accounting firms. Key provisions limit conflict-of-interest issues and require financial officers and CEOs to certify the validity of their financial statements.

# Profits and So Much More

If the corporation you're dealing with does not have profits as a first priority, it may well be a B-Corp, or benefit corporation. B-Corps are a new corporate structure that value profits, but not more than other priorities such as employees, suppliers, the community, and the environment. Benefit corporations do not receive special tax treatment, but B-Corp status, like the food producer's organic certification, can offer a real advantage, especially for firms competing in crowded markets. Tim Frick, a B-Corp executive at MightyBytes, says that being a benefit corporation is "being part of a larger global movement of making sure that business is being used as a force for good and not for evil." It can also keep companies focused on what makes them different, especially since firms must undergo comprehensive annual audits to keep their status. Current B-Corps fall across a range of industries and include businesses of all different sizes. One example is Cotopaxi, an outdoor gear company. The company donates 2% of its yearly revenue to ending poverty by funding local organizations working on sustainable solutions. Cotopaxi not only makes high-quality products, but also puts out a Repurposed Collection of limited-edition gear made out of scraps. The company encourages employees to participate in a skills-based volunteering initiative that leverages their time and talent to respond to community needs, such as a card-writing initiative that provides a paid "first job" for refugees in Salt Lake City. The program provides youth with professional development, work experience, a competitive wage, and the opportunity to practice their English language skills. Higher purpose seems to be woven into Cotopaxi's DNA.[17]

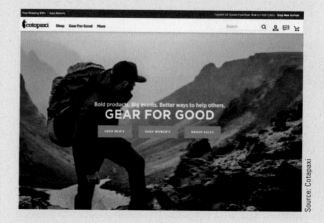

Source: Cotapaxi

accounting firms can provide for the companies they audit. Sarbanes–Oxley also requires that financial officers and CEOs personally certify the validity of their financial statements. (Refer to Chapter 8 for more detail on the Sarbanes–Oxley Act.)

But beyond legal requirements, companies have a number of additional responsibilities to investors. Spending money wisely would be near the top of the list. For instance, are executive retreats to the South Pacific on the company tab legal? They probably are. Do they represent a responsible use of corporate dollars? Now that seems unlikely. Honesty is another key responsibility that relates directly to financial predictions. No one can anticipate exactly how a company will perform, and an overly optimistic or pessimistic assessment is perfectly legal. But is it socially responsible? It probably isn't, especially if it departs too far from the objective facts—which is, of course, a subjective call.

**Responsibility to the Community: Business and the Greater Good Beyond** increasing everyone's standard of living, businesses can contribute to society in two main ways: philanthropy and responsibility. **Corporate philanthropy** includes all business donations to nonprofit groups, including both money and products. The Giving USA Foundation reported that total corporate donations increased +11.4% in 2019, a banner year for giving across all sources (perhaps due to the robust economy).[18] Corporate philanthropy also includes donations of employee time; in other words, some companies pay their employees to spend time volunteering at nonprofits. Patagonia, for example, allows workers after one year of service to apply for two-month internships with environmental not-for-profits, during which time they're still paid by Patagonia.[19]

## "We're in Business to Save Our Home Planet."

—Mission Statement, Patagonia Website

Some companies contribute to nonprofits through **cause-related marketing**. This involves a partnership between a business and a nonprofit, designed to spike sales for the company and raise money for the nonprofit. Unlike outright gifts, these dollars are not tax deductible for the company, but they can certainly build the company's brands.

**Corporate responsibility** relates closely to philanthropy but focuses on the actions of the business itself rather than donations of money and time. More than 100 major corporations have signed onto the Fair Chance Business Pledge reducing barriers in employment for those with a criminal record and creating a pathway for a second chance—signatories include American Airlines, The Coca-Cola Company, Facebook, Georgia Pacific, Google, The Hershey Company, PepsiCo, Prudential, Starbucks, Uber, Under Armour/Plank Industries, Unilever, and Xerox. Taking a different approach to corporate responsibility, A to Z Wineworks in Oregon aims "not only to be the best in the world, but to be the best for the world." That commitment includes management is 50% women, one third of staff members are from underrepresented populations, and all workers are paid above the minimum wage. Chocolatier Madécasse noticed that Africa grows 70% of the world's cocoa yet produces less than 1% of the world's chocolate. The company decided to change this statistic by making its chocolate entirely in Africa. Madécasse now empowers Madagascar's cocoa farmers with skills training and higher wages to make its chocolate right on the island. So far, the company has created meaningful income for more than 200 people in Madagascar across a wide variety of specialties, including chocolate making, packaging, shipping, and of course the farming of the cocoa, spices, and fruits. And Madécasse's chocolate tastes delicious, too![20]

**Responsibility to the Environment** Protecting the environment is perhaps the most crucial element of responsibility to the community. Business is a huge consumer of the world's limited resources, from oil to timber, to fresh water, to minerals. In some cases, the production process decimates the environment and spews pollution into the air, land, and water, sometimes causing

Rangizzz/Shutterstock.com

Protecting the environment has become the most crucial element of responsibility to businesses across the globe.

**corporate philanthropy**
All business donations to nonprofit groups, including money, products, and employee time.

**cause-related marketing**
Marketing partnerships between businesses and nonprofit organizations, designed to spike sales for the company and raise money for the nonprofit.

**corporate responsibility**
Business contributions to the community through the actions of the business itself rather than donations of money and time.

irreversible damage. And the products created by business can cause pollution as well, such as the smog generated by cars and the sometimes-toxic waste caused by junked electronic parts.

The government sets minimum standards for environmental protection at the federal, state, and local levels. But a growing number of companies are going further, developing innovative strategies to build their businesses while protecting the environment. Many have embraced the idea of **sustainable development**: doing business to meet the needs of this generation without harming the ability of future generations to meet their needs. This means weaving environmentalism throughout the business decision-making process. Since sustainable development can mean significant long-term cost savings, the economic crisis may even push forward environmentally friendly programs.

The results of sustainability programs have been impressive across a range of industries. McDonald's, for instance, produces mountains of garbage each year, as do virtually all major fast-food chains. But the Golden Arches stands above the others in its attempts to reduce the problem. Following are some encouraging statistics:

- In 2018, McDonald's Japan initiated a toy recycling program with the Japanese Ministry of the Environment to collect plastic Happy Meal toys and convert them into restaurant serving trays. As part of this program, McDonald's Japan collected around 1.27 million used plastic toys (3.4 million in 2019) that were turned into over 165,000 trays.
- In 2020, McDonald's Netherlands launched a customer campaign "You Bin It You Win It," awarding prizes to customers who disposed of their waste correctly.

## Sorry! So, So Sorry!

Why is it so compelling to watch the rich and powerful squirm? It's hard to explain, but when CEOs of big companies apologize for their mistakes, people love to watch, and their apologies often go viral. Sometimes the apologies are sincere and heartfelt, and everyone moves on; and sometimes they become targets of ridicule. Here are a few noteworthy examples of high-profile corporate apology fails. Reading through them will at the very least give you some ideas of how NOT to apologize for a business blunder.

- In 2013, Chip Wilson, former CEO and co-founder of Lululemon, stated to the press that "some women's bodies just don't actually work" for Lululemon's yoga pants. He apologized via a YouTube video in which he declared, "I'm really sad. I'm sad for the repercussions of my actions." He didn't even bother to address his offended customers.

- After BPs Deepwater Horizon oil rig exploded in 2010, causing the worst marine oil spill *in history*, and killing 11 workers, former BP CEO Tony Hayward's many apologies included the following: "I want my life back," and "The Gulf of Mexico is a very big ocean. The amount and volume of oil and dispersant we are putting into it is tiny in relation to the total water volume."[21]

- In 2017, United Airlines overbooked one of its flights from Chicago to Louisville. After requesting that volunteers give up their seats in favor of airline personnel, they called the police, who violently yanked a man out of his seat and dragged him off the plane when he wouldn't "voluntarily" give up his seat for an airline employee. United chief executive, at the time, Oscar Munoz's apology included the following: "This is an upsetting event to all of us here at United, I apologize for having to re-accommodate these customers." The Twitter response was swift and scathing, including a suggestion that somebody ought to "re-accommodate" Oscar Munoz.[22]

**sustainable development**
Doing business to meet the needs of the current generation, without harming the ability of future generations to meet their needs.

**carbon footprint** Refers to the amount of harmful greenhouse gases that a firm emits throughout its operations, both directly and indirectly.

- In the UK, McDonald's, its suppliers, and its waste service providers all use biodiesel-fueled trucks. Over 16,700 metric tons of $CO_2$ emissions were saved in 2019 from using biodiesel when compared to ultralow-sulfur diesel. And that's not all—the plant that converts the waste to oil also runs on energy generated from kitchen food waste, such as coffee grounds and eggshells.

Reducing the *amount* of trash is better than recycling, but recycling trash clearly beats dumping it in a landfill. McDonald's participates in this arena as well, through their extensive recycling programs, but more importantly as an innovator in the field of reusable packaging and a big buyer of recycled products.[23]

Taking an even broader perspective, some firms have started to measure their carbon footprint, with an eye toward reducing it. **Carbon footprint** refers

# Diversity Making a Difference

A recent study published in *Harvard Business Review* suggests that gender could make a real difference to profitability. A global study of nearly 22,000 firms found that in 2014, almost 60% of these firms had no female board members. Just over half had no female senior executives, and fewer than 5% had a female CEO—although there was considerable variation among countries and industries. A second, similar study showed that among the world's largest 500 companies, only 10.9% of senior executives are women, and 21% of the companies have only one woman in senior leadership. Both studies showed that these numbers matter to the bottom line. Going from having no women in corporate leadership to a 30% share of women is associated with a 1% increase in net margin, which translates to a 15% increase in profitability for a typical firm—wow! This performance improvement seems to come from two key factors: (1) increased skill diversity within top management and (2) less gender discrimination throughout the management ranks, which helps the company recruit, promote, and retain talent. The key question is *how* to best achieve the goal of more talented women in executive leadership.

**Beyond gender diversity:** By 2021, forward-leaning corporations were actively pursuing diversity of age, thought, race, and experience on their boards. But experts agreed that they will only realize the benefits of diversity if the most senior leadership actively cultivates an environment for the development and sharing of diverse perspectives.[24]

Andrey Popov/Shutterstock.com

---

to the amount of harmful greenhouse gases that a firm emits throughout its operations, both directly and indirectly. The ultimate goal is to become carbon neutral—either to emit zero harmful gases or to counteract the impact of emissions by removing a comparable amount from the atmosphere through projects such as planting trees. In early 2021, General Motors shifted its commitment toward green energy into overdrive. The automobile behemoth announced a goal of making the vast majority of the vehicles it produces electric by 2035, and the entire company carbon neutral, including operations, five years after that. GM also unveiled a new corporate logo that features lowercase letters intended to highlight the company's electric car future by evoking the look of an electrical outlet and using a shade of blue intended to suggest the "clean skies of a zero-emissions future."[25]

According to the Conference Board, business leaders have begun to see their carbon footprint—both measurement and reduction—as a burgeoning opportunity.[26] Many large corporations track three different types of emissions. The first, called Scope 1, refers to direct emissions produced by corporate operations. The second, called Scope 2, refers to emissions that result from purchased electricity, heat, and steam. Scope 3 emissions, which are more complex to track, are emissions that occur outside a company's boundary, but over which it has some control. This category includes areas such as employee commutes, supplier emissions, and product-use emissions. When Stonyfield Farms, maker of organic yogurt and other dairy products, examined their Scope 3 emissions, they came to the rather startling (and somewhat gross!) conclusion that most of their emissions did not come from manufacturing or transporting their products, but from the methane gas produced by the cows back at their suppliers' farms! Interest in Scope 3 emissions is still somewhat new but seems sure to grow as environmental accounting methods become more sophisticated.[27]

A growing number of companies use **green marketing** to promote their businesses. This means marketing environmental products and practices to gain a competitive edge. Toyota, for example, has advertised its Prius as offering "More Green for Less Green." In the past, green marketing has represented a tough challenge: while most people supported the idea of green products, the vast majority wouldn't sacrifice

> **green marketing**
> Developing and promoting environmentally sound products and practices to gain a competitive edge.

price, performance, or convenience to actually buy those products. But National Geographic has reported a positive change. "Younger generations are buying differently and are willingly throwing support behind sustainable-marketed products. These products have a 39% higher price premium over conventional products. They have shown seven-times faster growth, too. That's huge because technology around reuse drives better quality, lower costs, and drives premium price points for greater profit."[28]

## 4-5 Ethics and Social Responsibility in the Global Arena: A House of Mirrors?

Globalization has made ethics and social responsibility even more complicated for workers at every level. Bribery and corruption are among the most challenging issues faced by companies and individuals that are involved in international business. Transparency International, a leading anticorruption organization, published its yearly index of "perceived corruption" across 180 countries in 2020. No country scored a completely clean 100 out of 100, and the United States scored a troubling 67, which was quite a bit higher than India at 40 and China at 42, but lower than most of the European countries that dominated the top of the list. Not surprisingly, the world's poorest countries fall largely in the bottom half of the index, with African and Central Asian countries clustered at the very bottom, suggesting that rampant corruption is part of their business culture.[29]

Corruption wouldn't be possible if companies didn't offer bribes. U.S. corporations are forbidden to offer bribes since 1977 under the Foreign Corrupt Practices Act, but still show a disturbing inclination to flout the law. Running afoul of this legislation can lead to multimillion-dollar losses—yet violators have included Ralph Lauren, Oracle, Eli Lilly, Pfizer, and Tyco.[30]

Some questions to consider:

- When does a gift become a bribe? The law is unclear, and perceptions differ from country to country.

- How can corporations monitor corruption and enforce corporate policies in their foreign branches?

- What are other ways to gain a competitive edge in countries where bribes are both accepted and expected?

> **Every five weeks, 9,500 brand new electric buses take to the roads in China.**
>
> —Bloomberg News

Other challenging issues revolve around business responsibility to workers abroad. At minimum, businesses should pay a living wage for reasonable hours in a safe working environment. But exactly what this means is less clear-cut. Does a living wage mean enough to support an individual or a family? Does "support" mean enough to subsist day to day or enough to live in modest comfort? Should American businesses ban child labor in countries where families depend on their children's wages to survive? Companies must address these questions individually, bringing together their own values with the laws of both the United States and their host countries.

The most socially responsible companies establish codes of conduct for their vendors, setting clear policies for human rights, wages, safety, and environmental impact. In 1991, Levi Strauss became the first global company to establish a comprehensive code of conduct for its contractors. Over the years, creative thinking has helped it maintain its high standards, even in the face of cultural clashes. An example from Bangladesh, outlined in the *Harvard Business Review*, illustrates its preference for win–win solutions. In the early 1990s, Levi Strauss "discovered that two of its suppliers in Bangladesh were employing children under the age of 14—a practice that violated the company's principles but was tolerated in Bangladesh. Forcing the suppliers to fire the children would not have ensured that the children received an education, and it would have caused serious hardship for the families depending on the children's wages. In a creative arrangement, the suppliers agreed to pay the children's regular wages while they attended school and to offer each child a job at age 14. Levi Strauss, in turn, agreed to pay the children's tuition and provide books and uniforms." This creative solution allowed the suppliers to maintain their valuable contracts from Levi Strauss, while Levi Strauss upheld its values and improved the quality of life for its most vulnerable workers.[31]

Clearly, codes of conduct work best with monitoring, enforcement, and a commitment to finding solutions that work for all parties involved. Upscale athleisure

# Choosing between a Loaf of Bread and a Packet of Shampoo

The World Bank estimates that roughly 150 million people around the world will live in extreme poverty (less than $1.90 per day) by the end of 2021. But the late C.K. Prahalad, a well-respected consultant and economist, claimed that if the "aspirational poor" had a chance to consume, they could add about $13 trillion in annual sales to the global economy. Unilever, a global marketing company headquartered in Europe, has aggressively pursued this market with consumer products. Its customers might not have electricity, running water, or even enough for dinner, but many of its customers do have packets of Sunsilk shampoo and Omo detergent. Unilever's success stems from local knowledge gained over decades of operating in developing markets—Unilever has been in Indonesia since 1933 and India since 1888. Electronics companies have experienced marketing success as well. In Dharavi, for instance—one of the largest urban areas characterized by substandard housing and squalor in India—more than 85% of households own a television.

Critics suggest that the corporate push to reach impoverished consumers will enrich multinationals at the expense of their customers, representing exploitation of the world's poorest people. Ashvin Dayal, former East Asia director for the antipoverty group Oxfam UK, expressed concern to *Time* magazine that corporate marketing might unseat locally produced products or encourage overspending by those who truly can't afford it. Citing heavily marketed candy and soda, he points out that "companies have the power to create needs rather than respond to needs."

But Prahalad countered that many people at the bottom of the economic pyramid accept that some of the basics—running water, for instance—are not likely to ever come their way. Instead, they opt to improve their quality of life through affordable "luxuries," such as single-use sachets of fragrant shampoo. He argued, "It's absolutely possible to do very well while doing good." Furthermore, he suggested that corporate marketing may kick-start the poorest economies, triggering entrepreneurial activity and economic growth. Since globalization continues apace, let's hope that he's right.[32]

What do you think? Is targeting the poor with consumer goods exploitation or simply smart marketing?

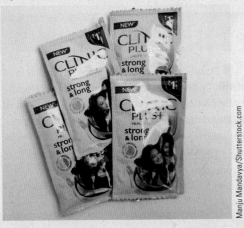

Manju Mandavya/Shutterstock.com

---

clothing brand Patagonia offers an encouraging example. Patagonia publishes a rigorous Supplier Code of Conduct for its supply chain. The Code of Conduct focuses on worker well-being and sustainability in the countries from which they source their products. It includes a zero-tolerance policy for any worker treatment violations, and it mandates both unannounced and announced visits to assess working conditions. Patagonia helps their suppliers move from basic to leadership sustainability practices. Patagonia also insists that workers are paid enough to meet the needs of themselves and their families, with some discretionary income—an unusually generous stance for producers who outsource overseas.[33]

Patagonia and Levi Strauss seem to be "doing their part," but the world clearly needs universal standards and universal enforcement to ensure that the benefits of globalization don't come at the expense of the world's most vulnerable people.[34]

## 4-6 Monitoring Ethics and Social Responsibility: Who Is Minding the Store?

Actually, many firms are monitoring themselves. The process is called a **social audit**, which is a systematic evaluation of how well a firm is meeting its ethics and social responsibility objectives. Establishing goals is the starting point for a social audit, but the next step is to determine how to measure the achievement of those goals, and measurement can be a bit tricky. As You Sow, an organization dedicated to promoting corporate social responsibility, recommends that companies measure their success by evaluating a "double bottom line," one

> **social audit** A systematic evaluation of how well a firm is meeting its ethics and social responsibility goals.

Investors count on companies to spend money wisely and fully disclose all key facts.

that accounts for traditional financial indicators, such as earnings, and one that accounts for social-responsibility indicators, such as community involvement.

Other groups are watching as well, which helps keep businesses on a positive track. Activist customers, investors, unions, environmentalists, and community groups all play a role. In addition, the threat of government legislation keeps some industries motivated to self-regulate. One example is the entertainment industry, which uses a self-imposed rating system for both movies and TV, largely to fend off regulation. Many people argue that the emergence of fruit and salads at fast-food restaurants represents an effort to avoid regulation as well.

## The Big Picture

Clearly, the primary goal of any business is to earn long-term profits for its investors. But profits alone are not enough. As active participants in society, firms must also promote ethical actions and social responsibility throughout their organizations and their corresponding customer and supplier networks. Although every area matters, a few warrant special mention:

- In tough economic times, effective business leaders focus more than ever on integrity, transparency, and a humane approach to managing the workforce—especially during cutbacks.

- Building or maintaining a presence in foreign markets requires particularly careful attention to human rights and local issues.

- Sustainable development and other environmentally sound practices are not only fiscally prudent and customer-friendly but also crucial for the health of our planet.

## Careers in Business Ethics and Social Responsibility

### Ethics Officer

Work with senior management to provide leadership, advice, and guidance in all matters pertaining to ethics, including training, enforcement, financial disclosure, and gift rules. Ensure that the company's code of ethics remains in strict compliance with all relevant laws. Model the highest standards of honesty and personal ethics at all times to foster an ethical climate in the organization. Arrange and facilitate employee ethics training. Work with HR to examine ethics complaints and to ensure that all investigations of employee misconduct are handled fairly and promptly. Assist in the resolution of ethical dilemmas wherever needed throughout the organization.

# 5 | Business Communication: Creating and Delivering Messages That Matter

## Learning Objectives

After studying this chapter, you will be able to:

**5-1** Explain the importance of excellent business communication

**5-2** Describe the key elements of nonverbal communication

**5-3** Identify effective communication channels

**5-4** Choose the right words for effective communication

**5-5** Write more effective business memos, letters, and emails

**5-6** Deliver successful verbal presentations

Girts Ragelis/Shutterstock.com

---

## 5-1 Excellent Communication Skills: Your Invisible Advantage

Much of your success in business will depend on your ability to influence the people around you. Can you land the right job? Close the deal that makes the difference? Convince the boss to adopt your idea? Motivate people to buy your products? Excellent communicators are not only influential but also well liked, efficient, and effective. Great communication skills can dramatically boost your chance for success, while poor communication skills can bury even the most talented people.

So what exactly are "excellent communication skills"? Many students believe that great business communication equates to a knack for speaking or a flair for writing. But if that's where you stop, you're likely to hit a brick wall again and again as you attempt to achieve your goals. Effective **communication** happens only when you transmit meaning—*relevant* meaning—to your audience.

Communication must be dynamic, fluid, and two-way, which includes listening. Seeking and understanding feedback from your audience—and responding appropriately—form the core of successful business communication. And it isn't as easy as you may think. American novelist Russell Hoban neatly summarized the issue: "When you come right down to it, how many people speak the same language even when they speak the same language?"

> **communication** The transmission of information between a sender and a recipient.

### 5-1a Communication Barriers: "That's Not What I Meant!"

Why is effective communication so challenging? The key issue is **noise**, which is any interference that causes the message you send to be different from the message your audience understands. Some experts define noise in terms of **communication barriers**, which arise in a number of different forms. As you read the definitions, keep in mind that with a bit of extra effort, most are surmountable, and we'll discuss strategies and tips as we move through the chapter.

- **Physical Barriers:** These can range from a document that looks like a wall of type to a room that's freezing cold, to chairs in your office that force your visitors to sit at a lower level than you.

- **Language Barriers:** Clearly, if you don't speak the language, you'll have trouble communicating. But even among people who do share the same language, slang, jargon, and regional accents can interfere with meaning.

- **Body Language Barriers:** Even if your words are inviting, the wrong body language can alienate and

"If a leader can't get a message across clearly, and motivate others to act on it, then having a message doesn't even matter."

—Gilbert Amelio, Former CEO, Jazz Semiconductor Corp.

distract your audience so completely that they simply won't absorb the content of your message.

- **Perceptual Barriers:** How your audience perceives you and your agenda can create a significant obstacle to effective communication. If possible, explore their perceptions—both positive and negative—in advance!

**noise** Any interference that causes the message you send to be different from the message your audience understands.

**communication barriers** Obstacles to effective communication, typically defined in terms of physical, language, body language, cultural, perceptual, and organizational barriers.

# Where in the World?

According to former Secretary General of the United Nations Dag Hammarskjold, the *unspoken* dialogue between two people can never be put right by anything they say. To avoid making devastating gaffes when engaging in international business, consider researching other cultures where you hope to do business. And don't just read books and articles—seek out and interact with people who are part of the target culture. Some examples of intercultural communication differences that you may encounter:

■ **Time:** Arriving late is shockingly rude from a Swedish perspective, while tardiness is almost expected in many Central American countries. Don't be caught by surprise!

■ **Greetings:** In Saudi Arabia, male acquaintants kiss on the cheek, and some even walk through the streets holding hands. In Germany and China, on the other hand, most businesspeople actively avoid unnecessary touching.

■ **Gestures:** When Japanese colleagues nod their heads and say, "hai," it doesn't necessarily mean that they agree with you, but rather that they hear you—big difference! When people in some parts of the Middle East give you the thumbs-up, it doesn't mean "good job." Quite the opposite—it's equivalent to flipping the bird in the United States.

■ **Directness:** U.S. culture deeply values directness, which can lead people from other countries to view Americans as abrupt and crass. When doing business in countries such as Lebanon and India, an indirect approach can be much more effective.

■ **Hospitality:** In many eastern countries such as China, the culture values hospitality—and getting to know business partners better before anything is agreed upon—especially by eating and drinking together—is very important, and it can take a long time before plans are made. For an American partner, this approach can seem frustrating and counterproductive.

■ **Business practices:** From giving gifts to exchanging business cards, business practices vary widely from culture to culture. As in each of the other cultural arenas, advanced preparation definitely pays off![1]

Metamorworks/Shutterstock.com

---

■ **Organizational Barriers:** Some companies have built-in barriers to effective communication, such as an unspoken rule that the people at the top of the organization don't talk to the people at the bottom. These barriers are important to understand but hard to change.

■ **Cultural Barriers:** These can include everything from how you greet colleagues and establish eye contact to how you handle disagreement, eat business meals, and make small talk at meetings. As globalization gains speed, **intercultural communication** will become increasingly pivotal to long-term business success. Identifying and understanding communication barriers is a vital first step toward dismantling them in order to communicate more effectively with any audience.

**intercultural communication**
Communication among people with differing cultural backgrounds.

**nonverbal communication**
Communication that does not use words. Common forms of nonverbal communication include gestures, posture, facial expressions, tone of voice, and eye contact.

## 5-2 Nonverbal Communication: Beyond the Words

Most of us focus on what we want to say, but *how* we say it is just as important. There is plenty of research on the importance of nonverbal communication—and it all points in the same general direction: in face-to-face communication, your body language and tone of voice communicate roughly as much as the content of your message.[2]

The goal of **nonverbal communication** should be to reinforce the meaning of your message. Random facial expressions and disconnected body language—arbitrary arm thrusts, for example—are at best distracting, and at worst clownish. But strong, deliberate nonverbal communication can dramatically magnify the impact of your messages. Here are a few examples of how this can work (but keep in mind that these examples do not necessarily translate from culture to culture):

■ **Eye Contact:** Within American culture, sustained eye contact (different from a constant cold stare) indicates integrity, trust, and respectful attention,

# If You See It in the News, It's Got to Be True . . . Psych!!!

Satirical news shows have long had a prominent seat in the spectrum of American entertainment. However, fake news rose to new prominence toward the end of the 2016 presidential election cycle as each side accused the other of planting fake news stories to sway the election. Fake news catapulted to a whole new level of prominence when former President Trump began labeling legitimate news organizations—such as *The New York Times* and CNN—as "fake news."

Outside of politics, more and more businesses depend on world events, filtered through the news, to guide their decision making. Millions of dollars hang in the balance, so the credibility of the news is crucial. But since mock news programs and websites enjoy more popularity than ever, business decision makers must make sure that they are in on the joke instead of the butt of the joke, which can't be as easy as it sounds, given the number of times legitimate news outlets and high-profile individuals have mistaken satirical or joke news for legitimate news. Some examples:

- Based on a fake story in *The Onion*, China's People's Daily Online exuberantly reported that North Korea's leader, Kim Jong-un, was the "Sexiest Man Alive" even though some believe that he possesses traits that aren't conventionally attractive.

- On April Fool's Day 2016, Yahoo's news service published an article reporting that Trader Joe's would close its more than 450 grocery stores in 2017. Furious Trader Joe's fans took to Twitter in a firestorm of fury and outrage—even though the end of the article clarified that it was just a joke.

- In 2019, a video surfaced on the internet (and quickly went viral) allegedly showing a Tesla "self-driving vehicle" slam into a robot prototype at CES, a consumer electronics show attended by tech reporters from across the globe. The vehicle "killed" the robot. BUT the video was apparently a total fake—the "dead" robot was in fact part of an elaborate publicity stunt conjured up by the Russian firm that developed it. Unless it was, as some cybersecurity experts speculated, a deliberate attack on the American stock market by "foreign actors" trying to undermine consumer acceptance and trust in self-driving cars and drive down stock prices in companies that develop them.[3]

The lesson here is that if something seems too silly to be true, it may not be, and it certainly merits further investigation. Otherwise, it may be the jokers who get the last laugh![4]

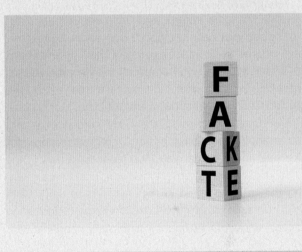

Monster Ztudio/Shutterstock.com

whether you're communicating with a subordinate, a superior, or a peer.

- **Tone of Voice:** Variation is the key to effectiveness, since paying attention to a monotone voice takes more concentration than most people are willing to muster. Also, even when you're angry or frustrated, try to keep your voice in a lower pitch to encourage listeners to stay with your message.

- **Facial Expressions:** People vary widely in terms of how much emotion they show on their faces, but virtually everyone communicates, whether or not they know it, through a wide range of expressions that include shy smiles, focused frowns, clenched jaws, squinted eyes, and furrowed brows.

- **Gestures and Posture:** How you handle your body speaks for you. For example, leaning forward can

indicate interest, shrugging can suggest a lack of authority, and fidgeting can imply either impatience or nervousness. To increase the power of your message, both your gestures and your posture should be confident, open, and coherent.

When disgraced cyclist Lance Armstrong confessed to doping in a 2013 interview with Oprah Winfrey, body language expert Tonya Reiman noticed that despite the confidence of his words, he betrayed anxiety nonverbally by not meeting Ms. Winfrey's eyes, biting his lip, and repeatedly touching his face. She also pointed out that he "'fig-leafed,' or nervously covered his groin with his hands, several different times…That's a sign of somebody who's under pressure."[5] Reiman has also pointed out that when people swallow hard after making strong assertions, they are clearly lying. As silly as it sounds, one of the easiest, most effective ways to improve your body language is to

## Exhibit 5.1 Tips for Better Listening

| Listening Dos | Listening Don'ts |
|---|---|
| Use your extra mental capacity to summarize (to yourself!) what the speaker is saying. Ask yourself: Why does this matter? What's the key point? | Don't even glance at your emails or text messages. You won't fool anyone with those surreptitious peeks. |
| Take a few notes. It will not only help you concentrate but will also communicate to the speaker that their thoughts really matter. | Don't begin speaking the moment the person stops talking. Take a brief pause to indicate that you're absorbing the message. |
| Listen with both your ears and your eyes. Notice any inconsistency between the speaker's words and body language. | Don't get overly comfortable. If your body is too relaxed, your mind may wander more easily. |
| Use nonverbal communication—nods, smiles, leaning forward—to indicate interest in the speaker. | Don't pick up your phone—or even look at your phone—when you're listening. And whenever it's practical, set your cell phone to vibrate when others are speaking. |
| Use verbal feedback and questions to indicate understanding and empathy: "So you're saying that…," or "Why do you think that?" | Don't interrupt or finish other people's sentences. There are few better ways to cut off future communication. |

practice nonverbal communication in front of the mirror. Check out your gestures, notice your facial expressions, and focus on eye contact. If you have the time and ability, it's also helpful (though humbling!) to videotape yourself delivering both a formal and informal message and ask a trusted friend to dissect the results with you.

Accurately discerning the body language of others is another powerful business communication tool. But keep in mind that you must evaluate others in the context of common sense. When your boss keeps yawning, they may be bored, *or* they may just be tired. When your colleague crosses their arms, they may be indicating defensiveness, *or* they might just normally stand that way.

### 5-2a Active Listening: The Great Divider

How we listen (or don't listen) also sends a high-impact, nonverbal message. In fact, an old Chinese proverb asserts that to listen well is as powerful a means of influence as to speak well. Those who do both are unstoppable.

Strong listening skills—**active listening**—play an obvious role in business success. The higher you go in an organization, the more you find that people are listening. Hourly employees may spend 30% of their time listening, while managers often spend 60%, and executives might spend 75% or more. Interestingly, top salespeople also tend to spend about 75% of their communication time listening.[6]

**active listening** Attentive listening that occurs when the listener focuses their complete attention on the speaker.

**communication channels** The various ways in which a message can be sent, ranging from one-on-one in-person meetings to internet message boards.

According to the International Listening Association website, 85% of our learning is derived from listening, yet listeners are distracted, forgetful, and preoccupied 75% of the time. If listening is so crucial, why do most of us have such a hard time engaging completely? One reason may be that people *listen* at about 125 to 250 words per minute, but *think* at about 1,000 to 3,000 words per minute—that's a significant gap. Common ways to fill the void include daydreaming, thinking about the past (e.g., last night), and planning for the future (e.g., later in the day).[7]

When you listen, try to use the extra thinking time to make yourself pay closer attention to the speaker. You'll find that people tend to tell more to those who listen better, so if you polish your listening skills, you're also likely to buff up the quality of what you know and when you know it. Exhibit 5.1 highlights some listening dos and don'ts (specific to American culture).[8]

### 5-3 Choose the Right Channel: A Rich Array of Options

Figuring out the right way to send a message can be a daunting challenge, especially in light of the growing number of choices. The various options are called **communication channels**. Understanding the impact of each channel will help you make the best decision regarding which to use.

Communication channels differ from one another in terms of how much information—or richness—they communicate to the recipient. Exhibit 5.2 provides a brief overview of key channels. Other channels might include

Exhibit 5.2 | Communication Channels

| Communication Channel | Channel Richness | When Should You Use This Channel? |
|---|---|---|
| **Texting** | Very low: Because so many of us text with as few words as possible, your audience will pick up only the basics. | When your content is uncontroversial<br><br>When you want a quick response regarding relatively simple issues<br><br>When you know that your audience won't be annoyed by it (if you don't know—ask!) |
| **Memos/Reports** | Very low: Your audience won't gain any information from your tone or your body language. | When your content is uncontroversial<br><br>When you must reach a number of people with the same message<br><br>When you must communicate lengthy or detailed information |
| **Email** | Very low: Here, too, your audience learns nothing beyond your words themselves. | When your content is uncontroversial<br><br>When you must reach a number of people with the same message |
| **Voice Mail** | Low: Your audience has the benefit of hearing your tone but not seeing your body language. | When your content is uncontroversial<br><br>When you don't need a record of your message (but don't forget that the recipient can easily save or forward your voice mail) |
| **Telephone Conversation** | Moderate: Your audience benefits from hearing your tone and how it changes through the call. | When you need to either deliver your message or get a response quickly<br><br>When your content is more personal or controversial<br><br>When you need or want a spontaneous, dynamic dialogue with the recipient |
| **Videoconferencing** | High: Especially with state-of-the-art equipment, the channel conveys much of the richness of actually being there. | When you need to reach multiple people with complex or high-priority content<br><br>When you need or want a spontaneous, dynamic dialogue with an audience that you cannot reach in person |
| **In-Person Presentation** | High: Your audience directly experiences every element of your communication, from verbal content to tone, to body language. | When you need to reach a large audience with an important message<br><br>When you need or want to experience the immediate response of your audience |
| **Face-to-Face Meeting** | Very high: Your audience experiences your full message even more directly. | When your message is personal, emotional, complex, or high priority (but if the recipient might be volatile, consider using a less immediate channel)<br><br>When you need or want instant feedback from your audience |

intranet postings, WebEx, Facebook, and instant messaging. Where would these additional channels fall on the spectrum? Why?

## 5-3a The Dramatic Rise of Videoconferencing

In March 2020, millions of workers made the pivot to remote work in response to government-mandated economic shutdowns associated with the COVID-19 pandemic. As a result, videoconferencing—especially via the Zoom platform—suddenly catapulted to the mainstream as a primary channel of business communication. The adjustment to the new channel was rough for many. But eventually, a set of best practices emerged. Here is a summary:

- Try to keep your video camera on to help build trust and more personal connections with your colleagues.

- Mute your audio when you are not speaking to minimize background noise for other participants.

- Try to find a simple, and distraction-free, background for your camera—if this isn't possible, consider using a virtual background.

- If possible, position yourself with light in front of you so that your face is visible. If there is a window—or some other light—directly behind you, you risk looking like a dark, expressionless silhouette on the video call.

- Try to keep your eyes on the camera during the call so that you will give the appearance of making eye contact with your colleagues. If you look at their faces on screen—or if you check yourself out on screen—you will simply appear distracted.

- Do your best not to multitask—it appears every bit as rude on camera as it would in person.

- Maintain your clothing and personal grooming as you would if you were in the office (at least from the waist up!). Your appearance should not be a distraction from the content of the call.

- Filters and frames can be funny, but leave that cute cat, pig, crown, or potato for calls with family and friends. It's just not professional for business video calls.

Leveraging video conferencing effectively as a communication channel will become increasingly important as a growing number of businesses move their employees to remote work at least a day or two per week on a permanent basis.[9]

## 5-3b Consider the Audience: It's Not about You!

Clearly, the needs and expectations of your audience play a crucial role in your choice of communication channel. Even if the recipient's preferences seem absurd—for example, we probably all know someone who refuses to check email or voice mail—remember that your first priority is to communicate your message. If you send it through a channel that the audience doesn't expect, understand, or like, you've risked your chance for successful communication.

Analysis and consideration of your audience should also be a top priority after you choose your communication channel. Meeting the needs of your audience will give you a crucial edge in developing a message that works.

## 5-4 Pick The Right Words: Is That Car Pre-Loved or Just Plain Used?!

Mark Twain once said, "The difference between the right word and almost the right word is the difference between lightning and the lightning bug." Perhaps that's a little extreme, but it may not be too far from the truth. In the business world, where your messages are competing with so many others for the all-too-limited attention of the recipient, the right words can encourage your audience to stay with you long enough to absorb your message.

**bias** A preconception about members of a particular group. Common forms of bias include gender bias; age bias; and race, ethnicity, or nationality bias.

## 5-4a Analyze Your Audience

To find the right words, begin with the needs of your audience. Consider:

- **Expectations:** What kind of language do most people use in the organization? Is it formal or informal? Is it direct or roundabout? Should you differ from the norm? Why or why not?

- **Education:** The education level of the audience should drive the level of vocabulary and the complexity of the message.

- **Profession:** Some professions (e.g., website development) are rife with jargon and acronyms. How should this influence your message?

## 5-4b Be Concise

Comedian Jerry Seinfeld once said, "I will spend an hour editing an eight-word sentence into five." While Jerry might be going a bit too far, it pays to be clear and concise in business communication. But don't be concise at the expense of completeness; include all information that your audience may need. (It'll save you time down the road.)

## 5-4c Avoid Slang

Unless you're absolutely certain that your audience will understand and appreciate it, do not use slang in either written or verbal communication. The risk of unintentionally alienating yourself from your audience is simply too high.

## 5-4d Avoid Bias

Intentionally or unintentionally, words can communicate biases that can interfere with your message, alienate your audience, and call your own character into question. As a result, you will be less effective in achieving the immediate goals of your communication (and possibly any future communication as well). Three kinds of **bias** are common.

**Gender Bias** Gender bias consists of words that suggest stereotypical attitudes toward a specific gender.

"Improvement in a firm's communication effectiveness is associated with a nearly 16% increase in its market value."

—Watson Wyatt, Consulting Firm

## Oops! #Flushthatjobdownthetoilet

Common sense dictates that your work friends should not be your Facebook friends, especially if your private life is not suitable for your work realm (and in most cases—even if it isn't as racy as you might prefer—it simply isn't appropriate), but you might be surprised to learn that Twitter grew from 30 million to 330 million users between 2010 and 2019, and more than 80% of its users live outside the United States. And unlike Facebook posts, tweets are in the public arena, which means that workers must know, understand, and carefully follow their companies' social media policies or risk fairly certain consequences. Job seekers should be particularly careful about what they post on social media.[10]

Seventy percent of employers use social networking sites to research job candidates, according to a recent CareerBuilders.com national survey, and 57% of them said they've found content that caused them to not hire the candidate. Here are some of the key reasons:

- Job candidates posted provocative or inappropriate photographs or information (40%).

- Job candidates posted information about themselves drinking or using drugs (36%).

- Job candidates bad-mouthed their previous company or fellow employee (25%).

- Job candidates had poor communication skills (27%).

- Job candidates had discriminatory comments related to race, gender, religion, and so on (31%).

What do you think? Is it reasonable for employers to use social media to screen applicants? Why or why not? Does it represent a violation of privacy?

Even after landing the perfect job, workers should use social media cautiously if they want to *keep* that job. In 2019, for example, Hussien Mehaidli, who was a general manager for a construction material wholesaler in Canada, was fired after he complained on his anonymous Twitter account that the company's Christmas gift—a $6 bottle of BBQ sauce—was chintzy, counter-seasonal, and disproportionately small, relative to the Christmas gift the firm gave to its American employees. Unfortunately—and somewhat foolishly—Mehaidli tagged his employer on the disgruntled tweet. And since another photo on the same account featured his computer and his workplace in the background, he was identified and fired for a "violation of standards of conduct." According to a lawyer familiar with the case, issues like Mehaidli's, where employees are disciplined for complaining publicly on social media, are becoming more and more common.[11]

Sattalat Phukkum/Shutterstock.com

Avoiding bias becomes tricky when you simply don't know the gender of your audience, which often happens when you apply for a job in writing. The best solution, of course, is to find out the recipient's name, but if you can't do that, do not address your message to "Dear Sir" or "Dear Madam"; rather, use the title of the position (e.g., "Dear Hiring Manager").

Another common challenge is to establish agreement in your sentences without creating gender bias. Consider the following example:

*The manager who loses his temper must apologize.*

Technically, this sentence is correct, but it implies that all managers are men. A simple solution would be to convert to plural:

*Managers who lose their temper must apologize.*

Effective business communication requires an analysis of the audience.

Bleakstar/Shutterstock.com

**Age Bias** Age bias refers to words that suggest stereo-typical attitudes toward people of specific ages. In American culture, older people tend to experience negative age bias much more often than younger people. This happens despite specific federal legislation outlawing employment discrimination against people more than 40 years old. The reason may be that American culture associates youth with highly valued qualities such as creativity, speed, independence, and individualism. This bias will become increasingly detrimental as the workforce ages. Here is an example of age bias:

*We need someone young and dynamic in this position!*

You could easily eliminate the negative bias by simply deleting the word "young" or by replacing it with the word "energetic." One clear benefit of eliminating bias in this case would be a broader applicant pool that might include an older person who is more dynamic than any of the younger applicants.

**Race, Ethnicity, and Nationality Bias** Words can also suggest stereotypical attitudes toward specific races, ethnicities, and nationalities. Leaving aside prejudice—which is clearly wrong—bias sometimes stems from unarticulated assumptions about a person's attitudes, opinions, and experiences. Your best plan for avoiding bias is to forgo any references to race, ethnicity, or nationality unless they are directly relevant and clearly necessary. And of course, never simply assume that one person embodies the attitudes, opinions, and experiences of a larger group. If you communicate with each person as an individual, you will not only avoid bias but also develop deeper, more effective channels of communication.

### 5-4e Use the Active Voice Whenever Possible

Active voice facilitates direct, powerful, concise communication. You have used the **active voice** when the subject of your sentence *is* doing the action described by the verb. You have used the **passive voice** when the subject of your sentence *is not* doing the action described by the verb.

Here's an example of a sentence that uses the active voice:

*Our team did not hit our sales goal.*

Our team, the subject of the sentence, did the action described by the verb

> **active voice** Sentence construction in which the subject performs the action expressed by the verb (e.g., The accountant did the taxes.). The active voice works better for the vast majority of business communication.
>
> **passive voice** Sentence construction in which the subject does not do the action expressed by the verb; rather, the subject is acted upon (e.g., The taxes were done by our accountant.). The passive voice tends to be less effective for business communication.

(missing the sales goal). The same sentence in the passive voice would read as follows:

*The sales goal was not reached.*

In this version, the subject of the sentence is the sales goal, which clearly did not do the action. As you can see from these examples, another benefit of active voice is accountability, which can create deeper trust between you and your audience.

## 5-5 Write High-Impact Messages: Breaking Through the Clutter

For many businesspeople, checking email—or even regular mail—is like approaching a fire hose for a sip of water. Goal number one is to crank down the pressure to get what you need without being knocked over by all the rest. To attain this goal, many people simply press the delete button.

Your challenge as a writer is to make your message a must-read, and the starting point should be the needs of your audience. Consider how the audience will respond to your message—think about how they will feel, not what they will do—and use that information to guide your writing. But keep in mind that it's hard to know for sure how the recipient will respond. For instance, each of the responses in Exhibit 5.3 could be reasonable for different people.

How do you know how your audience will respond? In most cases, you must simply guess based on as much

**Exhibit 5.3** | **Messages and Responses**

| Message | Anticipated Recipient Response |
|---|---|
| *Please note the new computer password procedures.* | Positive: *Great! We've really needed this.*<br>Neutral: *Okay, no big deal.*<br>Negative: *Not another change. …* |
| *The company plans to reassign your project team at the end of the year.* | Positive: *I can hardly wait to work with new people!*<br>Neutral: *It's all part of the job …*<br>Negative: *Not another change!* |

evidence as you can find. The value of making a thoughtful guess is that the chances of achieving your goal will soar if you happen to be correct.

The anticipated audience response should directly affect how you structure your writing.

- If the recipient will feel positive or neutral about your message, the memo or email should begin with your bottom line. What is your request or recommendation or conclusion? Why should the audience care? After you've clarified those points, follow up with your rationale and explanations (keeping in mind that less is usually more for time-starved businesspeople).

- If the recipient will feel negative about your message, start the memo or email with a couple of lines that present the rationale before you give the bottom line. Follow up with alternatives if there are any and be sure to end on a positive note (rather than an apology). This structure is less straightforward, but it's a more effective way to communicate your message.

Refer to Exhibit 5.4 for sample emails based on different anticipated responses to messages in an internet game development firm.

### 5-5a Strike the Right Tone

Good business writing sounds natural—it flows like spoken language and reads like a conversation on paper. To strike the right tone for any given message, remember that you can choose from a wide variety of conversational styles, from formal to chatty. Imagine yourself speaking to the recipient of your message, and you'll find that the right tone emerges naturally. A few guidelines will also help:

- Use common words in most situations (e.g., *use* vs. *utilize*).

- Use the active voice (e.g., *We made a mistake* vs. *A mistake was made*).

- Use personal pronouns (*I, you*) whenever appropriate.

- Use contractions (*I'll, don't, here's*) as often as you would when speaking.

### 5-5b Don't Make Grammar Goofs

Grammatical errors distract your reader from your writing and undermine your credibility. Most businesspeople are aware of the more common grammatical errors, so they tend to jump off the page before the content of the message. But if you're uncertain about a particular point, look at how professionally edited publications handle similar issues. Finally, don't be afraid to do a commonsense check on any grammatical question.

Edward P. Bailey, noted professor and business communication author, points out that many writers make grammar mistakes based on phantom knowledge— "mythical" grammar rules that aren't even in grammar handbooks. His research firmly reassures us that:

- It is okay to end a sentence with a preposition when doing so sounds natural and does not involve excess

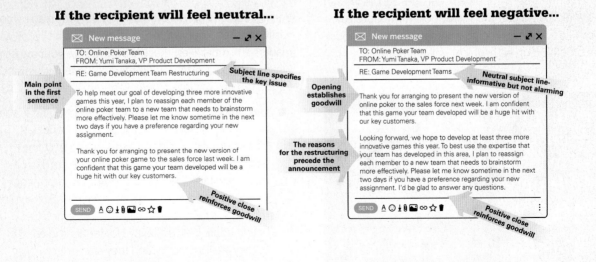

## Exhibit 5.4
## Sample Emails: Same Message, Different Approach

**If the recipient will feel neutral...**

Main point in the first sentence

New message — ⤢ ×
TO: Online Poker Team
FROM: Yumi Tanaka, VP Product Development
RE: Game Development Team Restructuring

Subject line specifies the key issue

To help meet our goal of developing three more innovative games this year, I plan to reassign each member of the online poker team to a new team that needs to brainstorm more effectively. Please let me know sometime in the next two days if you have a preference regarding your new assignment.

Thank you for arranging to present the new version of your online poker game to the sales force last week. I am confident that this game your team developed will be a huge hit with our key customers.

SEND

Positive close reinforces goodwill

**If the recipient will feel negative...**

Opening establishes goodwill

New message — ⤢ ×
TO: Online Poker Team
FROM: Yumi Tanaka, VP Product Development
RE: Game Development Teams

Neutral subject line- informative but not alarming

Thank you for arranging to present the new version of online poker to the sales force next week. I am confident that this game your team developed will be a huge hit with our key customers.

The reasons for the restructuring precede the announcement

Looking forward, we hope to develop at least three more innovative games this year. To best use the expertise that your team has developed in this area, I plan to reassign each member to a new team that needs to brainstorm more effectively. Please let me know sometime in the next two days if you have a preference regarding your new assignment. I'd be glad to answer any questions.

SEND

Positive close reinforces goodwill

## What's the Trick to Getting More People to Respond to Your Emails?

Do you often find yourself left hanging after sending an email? One helpful trick may be changing your sign-off. According to a recent study on email written to request help or advice, fewer than half received a response (47.5%). However, the response rate increased a whopping 36% on average when email had a "thankful closing" such as "thanks in advance," "thanks," or "thank you." Overall, email with a thankful closing garnered a 62% response rate. Other popular sign-offs were total duds in comparison:

- Cheers: 54% response rate

- Regards: 54% response rate

- Best: 51% response rate

So always keep in mind: if you want your email to result in action, a little thanks goes a long way.[12]

words (e.g., *Where is this book from?* is much better than *From where is this book?*).

- It is okay to begin sentences with "And" or "But" (e.g., *Most teens enjoy video games with a moderate level of violence. But a small, vocal minority strongly advocates a more clean-cut approach.*).

- It is okay to split infinitives (e.g., *Try to effectively film the next scene* is a perfectly acceptable sentence, even though "effectively" is inserted between "to" and "film.").

If you follow these principles, your writing not only will sound more natural but also will flow more easily. Winston Churchill, a renowned writer and speaker, was on-board with this commonsense approach decades ago, as we can see from his joking comment that poked fun at tortured writing: "From now on, ending a sentence with a preposition is something up with which I will not put."[13]

> "Your grammar is a reflection of your image. Good or bad, you have made an impression. And like all impressions, you are in total control."
>
> — Jeffrey Gitomer,
> American Author and Professional Speaker

### 5-5c Use Block Paragraphs

There are three elements to block paragraphs: (1) use single spacing, (2) double space between paragraphs, and (3) do not indent the first sentence of your paragraphs. This approach has become standard for business writing over the past decade, as writers have begun to include an increasing number of additional elements such as headings and illustrations. The block paragraphs create a more organized look for your page, guiding the reader's eye through the key elements of your structure.

### 5-5d Use Headings and Bulleted Lists Wherever Appropriate

Both headings and bulleted lists guide your reader more easily through your writing. And the easier it is for your readers, the more likely that they will absorb your message, which is, of course, your ultimate goal. Refer to Exhibit 5.5 for the ten tips to write an excellent email.

- **Headings:** A heading is not a title; rather, it is a label for one of several parts. If you have only one part, skip the heading, and use a title or a subject line. Consider using informative headings (e.g., "Recruitment has stalled," rather than simply "Recruitment") or question headings (e.g., "Have we met our recruitment goals for this campaign?"). And remember, headings are just as effective for letters and emails as they are for memos, and they are perfectly okay in one-page documents.

# Mind Your Digital Manners! Not as Easy as You Might Think...

Technology today makes almost everything easier. We can use navigation programs to find even the most obscure address and never struggle with an uncooperative paper map. We can use cheap or free video chat programs to see the faces of friends and family around the world. We can use health apps to monitor our own heart rate and sleeping patterns.

But technology doesn't make it easier to mind our manners as we communicate with each other—or with our devices—in the rapidly changing digital world. In fact, Kevin Sintumuang, columnist for *The Wall Street Journal*, noted, "More devices will have us talking (or yelling) into the air—crying out, as if to the Almighty, 'Please play the workout mix!'" Sintumuang points out that it's rude to text at a nice restaurant and to take selfies at disaster sites. He also comments that while some people are absolutely fluent in emojis, others swear that the cute cartoon symbols are destroying "real" human language. British researchers and other digital etiquette experts tried to help by developing a list of golden etiquette rules for the digital age. A sampling:

- Don't overshare on social media.
- Don't look for hook-ups on LinkedIn or any other professional platform.
- Don't even *glance* at your phone or smartwatch when you're having a face-to-face conversation—it's rude, and you're not fooling anyone.

- Use your email client's vacation responder so people won't be left hanging when you're out of town.
- Never text, email, or use social media while drunk, angry, or emotional.
- Never end a business relationship by text or social media.
- Don't look through your business partner's phone.

So, what are the right answers? Well, until technology stops—which we hope won't be anytime soon—and the proper etiquette sorts itself out, all of us should probably let common sense and old-fashioned consideration be our guides.[14]

Robert Kneschke/Shutterstock.com

---

- **Bulleted Lists:** A bulleted list is an invaluable tool that you can use to engage your reader's attention whenever you have more than one of anything in your writing (e.g., next steps, similar sections, questions). By formatting your lists with bullets, you are directing your reader's eye through your writing.

> "The single biggest problem in communication is the illusion that it has taken place."
>
> —George Bernard Shaw

## 5-6 Deliver Successful Verbal Presentations: Hook 'Em and Reel 'Em In!

What do people fear most? The *Book of Lists* asserts that public speaking ranks number one for the majority of people, high above the fear of death at number four. So, when people say they would rather die than give a speech, they may really mean it! This section is designed to mitigate any fear you might have about public speaking by giving you guidance on how to create and deliver a high-impact verbal presentation.

As with most communication, the needs of the audience are the best place to begin. How does your audience feel about you and your topic? Are they interested? Hostile? Positive? What were they doing before your presentation? Dragging themselves out of bed after a late night at a sales meeting? Eating lunch? Use this information to guide how you develop your presentation. For instance, an eager, engaged audience might not need as much background as a more lethargic, less-interested audience.

### 5-6a Opening

The opening of your presentation gives you a chance to grab the attention of the audience. If your opening hooks them, you've boosted the likelihood that you will hold their attention throughout the presentation. But developing that hook can be a challenge. The following are some suggestions for effective hooks:

- **An Interesting or Startling Statistic:** In a presentation from a nonprofit foodbank seeking to partner with a grocery chain, you could open by sharing that "the U.S. has the largest number of homeless women and children of any industrialized nation, and 57% of homeless kids spend at least one day a month completely without food. How could we improve these devastating numbers?"

- **Audience Involvement:** Pulling the audience into your opening can be very effective. For instance, in a presentation for a clothing company: "Imagine yourself with me at 11 P.M. on a Friday night, standing in line for admission to the hottest club in New York. As we inch forward, we suddenly realize that three other women in line are wearing the exact same dress as you...."

- **A Compelling Story or Anecdote:** This approach works best when it's completely genuine, using specific details that are directly relevant to the audience. For instance, in a presentation about employee benefits, you might want to share the story of a colleague who beat cancer using the company's innovative healthcare program.

- **A Relevant Simile or Metaphor:** Patricia Fripp, an award-winning keynote speaker, shares a simile that worked well to open a presentation for a colleague: "Being a scientist is like doing a jigsaw puzzle in a snowstorm at night...you don't have all the pieces ... and you don't have the picture to work from."

- **Engaging Questions:** In a presentation about customer service, you could open by asking: "How many of you have spent far too long waiting on hold for customer service that was finally delivered by a surly agent who clearly knew nothing about your question?"

### 5-6b Body

The most common presentation mistake is to include too many key ideas in the body of your presentation. Audiences simply cannot absorb more than two to four main points, and three are ideal. Specific examples and vivid comparisons will illustrate your points and bring them to life, while trusted sources, specific data, and expert quotations will increase your credibility and persuasiveness.

### Exhibit 5.5 Ten Tips for Excellent Email

Consider both your primary and secondary readers. In other words, never forget that your reader may forward your email without considering the potential impact on you.

Keep it short! Many readers won't scroll down past whatever shows on their screen, so be sure to get your bottom line close to the top of your message.

Don't forget to proofread. This is especially important if you're asking someone to do something for you. And remember that your spell-checker won't catch every mistake.

Use standard writing. Smiley faces, abbreviations, and five exclamation points are all fine if you're emailing your buddies, but in more formal messages they can make you look silly (or like you just don't care).

Avoid attachments if possible. They take time and space to open, and they don't always translate well to smartphones and tablets. Instead, cut and paste relevant sections of the attachment into your email.

Don't assume privacy. Think of your emails as postcards that anyone (especially computer system administrators and managers) can read along the way. In that light, try not to use email to communicate negative, critical, or highly personal messages.

Respond promptly to emails. If you don't have time to respond to the email itself, consider sending a message such as "Sorry, but I'm swamped right now—will get back to you early next week."

Assume the best. Because emails are often brief, they can cause unintentional offense. If you receive an off-key message, don't be afraid to inquire: "I'm not sure what you mean ... could you please explain?"

Create a compelling subject line. Make your reader want to open your message. Briefly communicate the topic of your message and why your reader should care.

Think before you write and think again before you send! Too many people send messages in an emotional moment that they later regret. Take time to think and think again.

Giving great presentations may be easier than you think.

Monkey Business Images/Shutterstock.com

Regardless of the length of your presentation, be sure to use clear transitions as you move from point to point.

Just before launching into the body of your presentation, you should tell the audience your key points, ideally with visual reinforcement. Then as you move to each new point, you can refer to the blueprint that you established upfront. A clear, explicit structure will help the audience track with you as you move through your material.

## 5-6c Close

Ideally, the close of your presentation will summarize your key points. Then circle back to your introduction, so that the beginning and the end serve as "bookends" for the body of your presentation. For instance, if you began by asking questions, end by answering them. If you began with an anecdote, end by referring to the same story. As an alternative (or maybe an addition), consider sharing a quotation or a bit of humor relevant to your content.

Also, keep in mind that you should verbally signal to your audience that you are about to conclude. After you do so—by saying, "In summary," for instance—be sure that you actually do conclude. Nothing alienates an audience more quickly than launching into another point after you've told them you're finished! Your body language will support your conclusion if you turn off your projector and move toward the audience to answer questions. And even if you aren't so eager to field questions, try to paste a receptive look on your face—it'll increase your credibility and set a positive tone for the Q&A session.

## 5-6d Questions

At the start of your presentation, decide whether you want to handle questions throughout your talk or save them for the end. Tell your audience your preference upfront; most of the time they will respect it. But if you do receive unwanted questions in the middle of your presentation, don't ignore them. Simply remind the questioner that you'll leave plenty of time for questions at the end.

Not surprisingly, the best tip for handling questions is to be prepared. Since it's tough to anticipate questions for your own presentation, you may want to enlist the help of a trusted colleague to brainstorm the possibilities. And don't just come up with the questions—prepare the answers, too!

## 5-6e Visual Aids

Studies suggest that three days after a presentation, people retain 10% of what they heard from an oral presentation, 35% from a visual presentation, and 65% from a combined visual and oral presentation. The numbers are compelling: visual aids matter. Depending on your audience, effective, high-impact visual aids could range from props to charts to mounted boards. But in business communication, PowerPoint slides are the most common option. If you use PowerPoint, consider these suggestions:

- **Showing Works Better Than Simply Telling:** Use pictures and other graphics whenever possible.

- **Less Is More:** Keep this helpful guideline in mind: no more than seven words per line, no more than seven lines per slide.

- **Don't Just Read Your Slides Aloud:** Instead, paraphrase, add examples, and offer analysis and interpretation.

- **Go Easy on the Special Effects:** Too many sounds and too much animation can be painfully distracting.

- **Don't Let Your Slides Upstage You:** Look at your audience, not at the slides. And dim the screen when you're not specifically using it.[15]

## 5-6f Google Presentations

Although Microsoft PowerPoint remains the software option of choice for business presentations, Google Presentations software is swiftly gaining ground. Google Slides is one of a growing number of applications based in "the cloud." Another popular option is Prezi, which includes pan and zoom features that give presentations an engaging cinematic feel. Cloud-based presentation software means that when you buy a new computer, you don't need to spend hundreds of dollars buying PowerPoint. You simply log into your Google account, for instance; use the Google Presentations software; and save your finished product on

Google's servers. Since your work is stored on the internet, you can access it from any device with a web connection—you don't need to email it to yourself, or store it on a temperamental local drive, or worry about saving your changes as you move from work to home, to school.

But cloud-based software is far from perfect. If you temporarily lose your internet connection—while on a plane or a bus, for instance—you cannot access your work. Security might be a worry, since web-based data may be vulnerable to hackers. If Google disables your account for any reason, your work is lost. The price, though, for both Google Presentations and Prezi is pretty attractive: free! And that includes new versions and updates.

From a long-term perspective, another key benefit of Google Presentations—and all other cloud computing applications—is environmental. *Newsweek* writer Brian Braiker points out that "conducting affairs in the cloud is not only convenient, it's also greener: less capital and fewer printouts means less waste." All of which suggests that the forecast for Google Presentations is far from cloudy.[16]

## 5-6g Handling Nerves

Believe it or not, most experts agree that nervousness can be useful before a presentation. A little adrenaline can help you perform better, think faster, and focus more completely. But we all know that out-of-control nerves can interfere with effectiveness. Here are some ideas to mitigate speech anxiety:

- Send yourself positive messages; visualize success. Examples: "I will be dynamic and engaging." "They will completely support my new product idea."

- Take ten slow, deep breaths—use the yoga approach of breathing in through your nose and out through your mouth.

- Take a sip of water to loosen your throat muscles and mitigate a shaking voice. (Water also gives you a way to fill pauses.)

- Pick a friendly face or two in the audience, and imagine yourself speaking only to those people (but don't pin them down with a cold stare!).

- Remind yourself that the audience wants you to succeed. Focus on their needs rather than your own nerves.

If possible, have a handful of one-on-one conversations with audience members before your presentation. This will almost certainly reinforce that they want you to succeed, which will likely take the edge off your nerves.

## 5-6h Handling Hostility

We've all seen hostile questioners who seem determined to undermine presenters. It can be awful to watch, but it's surprisingly easy to handle. Here are a few tips:

- Stay calm and professional. Rightly or wrongly, the hostile questioner has won the day if you get defensive or nervous.

- Don't be afraid to pause before you answer to gather your thoughts and allow the hostility to diffuse. (A sip of water can provide good cover for a thought-gathering moment.)

- Once you've answered the question, don't reestablish eye contact with the questioner. Doing so would suggest that you are seeking approval for your response, which only invites further hostile follow-up.

- If the questioner insists on follow-up, you may need to agree to disagree. If so, be decisive: "Sounds like we have two different points of view on this complex issue."

- Use body language to reinforce that you are done interacting with the questioner. Take a couple of steps away and ask another part of the group whether they have any questions.

## 5-6i Incorporating Humor

Everyone likes to be funny but incorporating humor in a business presentation can be risky. Only do it if you're very, very sure that it's funny. Even so, double-check that your jokes are appropriate and relevant. You should never, ever laugh at the expense of any member of your audience. Even laughing at yourself is chancy, since you risk diminishing your credibility. (But a joke at your own expense is always effective if you make a mistake; there's no better way to recover the goodwill of your audience.)

Pathdoc/Shutterstock.com

## 5-6j A Spot on the Back Wall?

Many people have heard the old myth that no one will know the difference if you calm your nerves by looking at a spot on the back wall rather than at the audience. Don't do it! While *you* may be more comfortable, your audience will be mystified . . . more often than not, they'll keep turning around to find out what's so interesting back there!

## 5-6k Delivery

Some people are naturals, but for the rest of us, **dynamic delivery** is a learned skill. It begins and ends with preparation, but keep in mind that practice doesn't always make perfect—in fact, practice more often just makes permanent. So be sure that you practice with an eye toward improvement. If possible, you should set up a practice situation that's close to the real thing. If you'll be standing to present, stand while you practice, since standing makes many people feel more vulnerable. Consider practicing in front of a mirror to work on eye contact and gestures. Also, try recording your voice to work on a lively tone.

| Exhibit 5.6 | Ten Tips for Dynamic Delivery |
| --- | --- |

1. PRACTICE!
2. Know your material, but never memorize it word for word.
3. Look directly at members of your audience at least 50% of the time.
4. Vary your voice, your facial expressions, and your body language.
5. Use selective notes (but keep them inconspicuous).
6. Stick to your allotted time.
7. Slow down and listen to yourself.
8. Don't apologize (unless you really did something wrong!).
9. Remember to use natural gestures.
10. PRACTICE!

Finally, practice in front of a trusted friend or two who can give you valuable feedback. Refer to Exhibit 5.6 for Ten Tips for Dynamic Delivery.

**dynamic delivery** Vibrant, compelling presentation delivery style that grabs and holds the attention of the audience.

## The Big Picture

Effective communication saves time and money—boosting performance and morale—across every area of business. But one vital principle holds true regardless of the more specific nature of your communication: the best way to achieve your goals is to focus on your audience, not on yourself. If you understand the goals, expectations, and needs of your audience, you can tailor your communication to boost your chances (sometimes dramatically) of accomplishing your objectives.

As globalization and technological change continue to accelerate, new communication challenges will likely develop across the spectrum of business. To ensure that your communication continues to be effective, keep an open mind. Pay attention to differences among cultures, to language usage in professional publications, and to new communication technology. And don't be afraid to consult an up-to-date communication website or handbook every so often. When other resources aren't available, rely on courtesy, consideration, and common sense—valuable tools to guide your communication in any situation.

## Careers in Business Communication

### Public Relations Manager

Plan and implement strategies to build and maintain a positive image for the organization. Build strong relationships and open channels of communication with relevant members of the press. Write and distribute compelling press releases about the organization via both traditional and digital media. Respond to requests for information from the media. Work with senior management to develop crisis management plans when necessary. Work with marketing to create events and stunts that build the company's public image. Perform an effective liaison role with an outside public relations agency when there is one.

# 6 | Business Formation:
## Choosing the Form That Fits

### Learning Objectives

After studying this chapter, you will be able to:

**6-1** Describe the characteristics of the four basic forms of business ownership

**6-2** Discuss the advantages and disadvantages of a sole proprietorship

**6-3** Evaluate the pros and cons of the partnership as a form of business ownership

**6-4** Explain why corporations have become the dominant form of business ownership

**6-5** Explain why limited liability companies are becoming an increasingly popular form of business ownership

**6-6** Evaluate the advantages and disadvantages of franchising

## 6-1 Business Ownership Options: The Big Four

One of the most important decisions an entrepreneur makes when starting a new business is which form of business ownership to use. This choice affects nearly every aspect of starting and running a company, including the initial cost of setting up the business, the way profits are distributed, the types of taxes the business pays, and the kinds of regulations it must follow. The form of business ownership chosen also determines the degree to which each owner is personally liable for the firm's debts and the sources of funds available to the firm to finance future expansion.

Finally, choosing the right business form helps entrepreneurs battle the steep odds against survival. Twenty percent of new businesses fail within one year, while one-third fail within two. Fifty-one percent fail within five years, and two-thirds close their doors after ten. Even 37% of large, established, and highly successful Fortune 500 and S&P 500 firms can be expected to fail every five years.[1] While these numbers make clear just how difficult it is to make a business succeed, the global COVID-19 pandemic crushed the aspirations of millions of business owners:

- Ten months into the pandemic, 17% of restaurants were permanently closed or had closed for an

extended time.[2] According to the National Restaurant Association, "On average, permanently closed restaurants had been in business for 16 years."[3]

■ Fifteen percent of small businesses with a Facebook presence were "forced out of business."[4]

■ An International Monetary Fund study found that the pandemic increased the business failure rate by 9% across 17 countries.[5]

■ The Federation of Small Businesses estimated that 250,000 companies in the United Kingdom would go out of business as a result of multiple COVID-19 pandemic-related lockdowns.[6]

The COVID-19 pandemic, however, also produced record numbers of new businesses. New company registrations surged by 82% in the United States, 20% in France, 14% in Japan, and 30% in the United Kingdom.[7] Steven Hamilton, an economist at George Washington University, explained that, "As horrible as [the pandemic] is, and as badly as it has affected so many people, it has pushed people to come up with new ideas and products and services."[8] The question, as with the formation of any new business, is how many businesses started

"The limited liability corporation is the greatest single discovery of modern times."

—Nicholas Murray Butler, President of Columbia University, 1902–1945

during the COVID-19 pandemic will succeed—and for how long?

The vast majority of businesses are owned and organized under these four forms:

1. A **sole proprietorship** is a business that is owned, and usually managed, by a single individual. As far as the law is concerned, a sole proprietorship is simply an extension of the owner. Company earnings are treated just like the owner's income. Likewise, any debts the company incurs are considered the owner's personal debts.

> **sole proprietorship** A form of business ownership with a single owner who usually actively manages the company.

This means that a business owner's personal financial assets, such as cash, bank accounts, their home or investments, can be seized to pay unpaid company debts. This is known as **unlimited liability**.

2. A **partnership** is a voluntary agreement under which two or more people act as co-owners of a business for profit. As we'll see later in the chapter, there are several types of partnerships. In its most basic form, known as a **general partnership**, each partner has the right to participate in the company's management and share in its profits. Each partner, however, also has unlimited liability for company debts.

3. A **corporation** is a business entity created by filing a form (known in most states as the **articles of incorporation**) with the appropriate state agency, paying the state's incorporation fees, and meeting other requirements. (The specifics vary among states.) Unlike a sole proprietorship or a partnership, a corporation is considered to be a legal entity that is separate and distinct from its owners. In many ways, a corporation is like an artificial person. It can legally engage in virtually any business activity a natural person can pursue. For example, a corporation can enter into binding contracts, borrow money, own property, pay taxes, and initiate legal actions (such as lawsuits) in its own name. It can even be a partner in a partnership or an owner of another corporation. Because of a corporation's status as a separate legal entity, the owners of a corporation have **limited liability**—meaning they aren't personally responsible for the debts and obligations of their company.

4. A **limited liability company (LLC)** is a hybrid form of business ownership that is similar in some respects to a corporation while having other characteristics that are similar to a partnership. Like a corporation, an LLC is considered a legal entity separate from its owners. Also like a corporation—and as its name implies—an LLC offers its owners limited liability for the debts of their business. But it offers more flexibility than a corporation in terms of tax treatment; in fact, one of the most interesting characteristics of an LLC is that its owners can elect to have their business taxed either as a corporation *or* a partnership.[9] A third option allows individuals to form a single-person LLC that is taxed as part of the owner's personal tax return.[10] But, as discussed in Section 6-5b (on the Advantages of LLCs), there is a key tax difference between single-person LLCs and sole proprietorships.

Sole proprietorships, partnerships, and corporations have been around in some form since the beginning of our nation's history, but limited liability companies are a relatively new form of ownership in the United States. In 1977, Wyoming passed the first state statute allowing LLCs, and Florida became the second state to do so in 1982. But it wasn't until a ruling by the IRS in 1988 clarifying the tax treatment of LLCs that most other states followed suit. Today every state has enacted LLC legislation, and the LLC has become a very popular ownership option. In many states, filings to form LLCs now outnumber filings to form corporations.[11]

Exhibits 6.1 and 6.2 provide some interesting insights about the relative importance of each form of ownership. As shown in Exhibit 6.1, the sole proprietorship is by far the most common type of business organization in the United States. In 2018, 27.12 million individuals reported operating nonfarm sole proprietorships. This represented 72% of the total number of business enterprises. As a group, these sole proprietorships reported $1.59 trillion in revenue and $349 billion in net income (profit). But while these figures are impressive in the aggregate, most individual sole proprietorships are quite small. According to the Internal Revenue Service (IRS), about 70% of all sole proprietorships reported annual revenue of less than $25,000, while less than 1% reported receipts in excess of $1 million.[12] So, while sole proprietorships make up 72% of all businesses, they only account for 4.34% of total revenues and 10.27% of total profits. Still, 59% of sole proprietorships break even or are profitable.[13]

As Exhibit 6.2 shows, when it comes to economic impact, the corporate form of ownership rules. Though corporations comprised only 16.9% of all business entities, in 2018 they reported nearly 80% of all business revenues

**unlimited liability** When businesses formed as sole proprietorships or business partnerships cannot pay their bills, all or part of the business owner's personal financial assets, such as cash, bank accounts, investments, or homes, can be seized to pay the business debts.

**partnership** A voluntary agreement under which two or more people act as co-owners of a business for profit.

**general partnership** A partnership in which all partners can take an active role in managing the business and have unlimited liability for any claims against the firm.

**corporation** A form of business ownership in which the business is considered a legal entity that is separate and distinct from its owners.

**articles of incorporation** The document filed with a state government to establish the existence of a new corporation.

**limited liability** When owners are not personally liable for claims against their firm. Owners with limited liability may lose their investment in the company, but their other personal assets are protected.

**limited liability company (LLC)** A form of business ownership that offers both limited liability to its owners and flexible tax treatment.

## Exhibit 6.1
## Total Number of Businesses by Form of Ownership

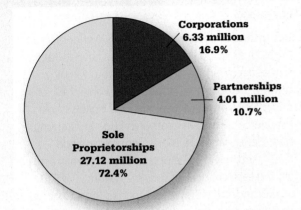

Corporations
6.33 million
16.9%

Partnerships
4.01 million
10.7%

Sole
Proprietorships
27.12 million
72.4%

Source: "Table 1. Nonfarm Sole Proprietorships: Business Receipts, Selected Deductions, Payroll, and Net Income, by Industrial Sectors, Tax Year 2018," Internal Revenue Service, September 2020, https://www.irs.gov/pub/irs-soi/18sp01br.xls, accessed January 11, 2021; "Table 1. All Partnerships: Total Assets, Trade or Business Income and Deductions, Portfolio Income, Rental Income, and Total Net Income (Loss), by Industrial Sector, Tax Year 2018," Internal Revenue Service, April 2020, https://www.irs.gov/pub/irs-soi/18pa01.xlsx, accessed January 11, 2021; "Table 1. Selected Income Statement, Balance Sheet and Tax Items and Coefficients of Variation, by Minor Industry, Tax Year 2017," Internal Revenue Service, September 2020, https://www.irs.gov/pub/irs-soi/17co01ccr.xlsx, accessed January 11, 2021.

and 67% of all business profits. Corporations such as Walmart and Amazon (retail), Exxon Mobile (energy) Apple (technology), CVS Health (pharmacies), Berkshire Hathaway (investing), United Health Group (health insurance), McKesson (medical supplies), AT&T (data & wireless communication), and AmerisourceBergen (pharmaceutical distributor) have annual sales revenues measured in the hundreds of billions of dollars.[14] But not all corporations are multibillion-dollar enterprises. In fact, 24.1% of all corporations reported total revenues of less than $25,000.[15]

> "Corporation: an ingenious device for obtaining profit without individual responsibility."
>
> —Ambrose Bierce, 19th-century compiler of the Devil's Dictionary

## Exhibit 6.2
## Total Revenue and Net Income by Form of Ownership

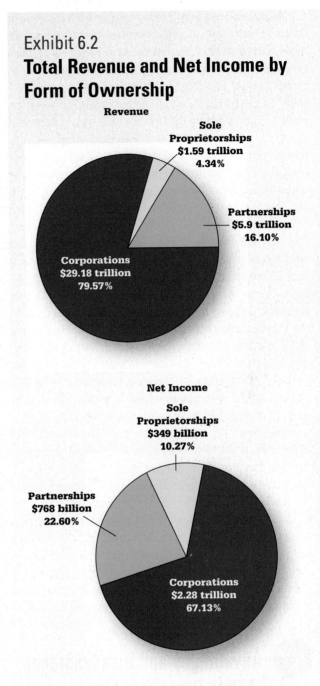

**Revenue**

Sole
Proprietorships
$1.59 trillion
4.34%

Partnerships
$5.9 trillion
16.10%

Corporations
$29.18 trillion
79.57%

**Net Income**

Sole
Proprietorships
$349 billion
10.27%

Partnerships
$768 billion
22.60%

Corporations
$2.28 trillion
67.13%

Source: "Table 1. Nonfarm Sole Proprietorships: Business Receipts, Selected Deductions, Payroll, and Net Income, by Industrial Sectors, Tax Year 2018," Internal Revenue Service, September 2020, https://www.irs.gov/pub/irs-soi/18sp01br.xls, accessed January 11, 2021; "Table 1. All Partnerships: Total Assets, Trade or Business Income and Deductions, Portfolio Income, Rental Income, and Total Net Income (Loss), by Industrial Sector, Tax Year 2018," Internal Revenue Service, April 2020, https://www.irs.gov/pub/irs-soi/18pa01.xlsx, accessed January 11, 2021; "Table 1. Selected Income Statement, Balance Sheet and Tax Items and Coefficients of Variation, by Minor Industry, Tax Year 2017," Internal Revenue Service, September 2020, https://www.irs.gov/pub/irs-soi/17co01ccr.xlsx, accessed January 11, 2021.

As you can see from Exhibit 6.1, partnerships are less common than sole proprietorships or corporations. Still, more than 4 million businesses were classified as partnerships in the United States. And partnerships tend to be both larger and more profitable than sole proprietorships. As Exhibit 6.2 shows, in the aggregate, partnerships earned 2.2 times more total net income than sole proprietorships, despite the fact that sole proprietorships outnumbered partnerships by a ratio of almost seven to one![16] Altogether, partnerships earned 16.1% of business revenues and 22.6% of business profits.

You've probably noticed that Exhibits 6.1 and 6.2 don't include specific information about limited liability companies. That's because these exhibits are based on information taken from annual tax returns submitted to the IRS. The IRS doesn't track LLC information separately. Instead, it classifies each LLC based on the tax treatment the company selects. LLCs that choose to be taxed as partnerships are classified as partnerships, while those choosing to be taxed as corporations are classified as corporations. Single-person LLCs are taxed as sole proprietorships where the business taxes are handled and paid as part of the owner's personal tax returns.[17] (The vast majority of LLCs elect to be taxed as partnerships, so most LLC earnings are reported in the partnership category.)

We'll see that each form of ownership has distinct advantages and disadvantages. As a company grows and matures, the form of ownership it needs may change. Fortunately, the form of ownership for a business isn't set in stone. For example, it is possible—and in fact quite common—for business owners to convert from a sole proprietorship to a corporation, or from a corporation to an LLC. Conversions from one business form to another became much more common after significant changes to federal business tax laws in 2018.[18] Refer to the "Converting Your Business Form to Lower Business Taxes" boxed feature for an explanation.

## 6-2 Advantages and Disadvantages of Sole Proprietorships

Our look at Exhibits 6.1 and 6.2 raises two questions about sole proprietorships. First, why is this form of ownership so popular? Second, why do sole proprietorships usually remain relatively small? A look at the advantages and disadvantages of sole proprietorships helps answer these questions.

### 6-2a Advantages

Sole proprietorships offer very attractive advantages to people starting a business:

- **Ease of Formation:** Compared to the other forms of ownership, the paperwork and costs involved in forming a sole proprietorship are minimal. No special forms must be filed, and no special fees must be paid. Entrepreneurs who are eager to get a business up and running quickly can find this a compelling advantage.

- **Retention of Control:** As the only owner of a sole proprietorship, you're in control. You have the ability to manage your business the way you want. If you want to "be your own boss," a sole proprietorship might look very attractive. Nicholas Hollows, sole proprietor of Hollows Leather in Eugene, Oregon, says, "Being hands on is the whole reason I do this."[19] And, having one person in charge may actually increase chances of success. A study of 3,526 crowdfunded Kickstarter companies (on Kickstarter.com entrepreneurs invite the public to fund specific startup products or services) found that while sole proprietors initially raised less money, they outlasted and out earned startups with more people. Study co-author Jason Greenberg said, "The more cooks you put into the kitchen, the more likely there is to be disagreement about what ingredients you should use and so forth."[20]

- **Pride of Ownership:** One of the main reasons many people prefer a sole proprietorship is the feeling of pride and the personal satisfaction they gain from owning and running their own business.

- **Retention of Profits:** If your business is successful, all the profits go to you—minus your personal taxes, of course.

- **Possible Tax Advantage:** No taxes are levied directly on the earnings of sole proprietorships as a business. Instead, the earnings are taxed only as income of the proprietor. As we'll see when we discuss corporations, this avoids the undesirable possibility of double taxation of earnings.

### 6-2b Disadvantages

Entrepreneurs thinking about forming sole proprietorships should also be aware of some serious drawbacks:

- **Limited Financial Resources:** Raising money to finance growth can be tough for sole proprietors. With only one owner responsible for a sole proprietorship's debts, banks and other financial institutions are often reluctant to lend it money. Likewise, suppliers may be unwilling to provide supplies on credit. This leaves sole proprietors dependent on their own wealth plus the money that their firms generate. And most small businesses, especially sole proprietorships, don't generate a lot of cash. For example, the typical small business with monthly expenses of $10,000 doesn't have enough cash on hand to cover two weeks of spending.[21]

- **Unlimited Liability:** Because the law views a sole proprietorship as an extension of its owner, the debts of the firm become the owner's personal debts. The owner of Erie County Farms, a grocery store in Erie, Pennsylvania, never incorporated his business, so the store operated as a sole proprietorship. Accordingly, when Erie County Farms went bankrupt, the bankruptcy court seized the owner's home and personal assets to pay $650,000 in unpaid bills.[22] Likewise, if someone sues your business and wins, the court can seize your personal possessions—even those that have nothing to do with your business—and sell them to pay the damages. This unlimited personal liability means that operating as a sole proprietorship is a risky endeavor.

- **Limited Ability to Attract and Maintain Talented Employees:** Most sole proprietors are unable to pay the high salaries and substantial perks that highly qualified, experienced employees get when they work for big, well-established companies.

- **Heavy Workload and Responsibilities:** Being your own boss can be very rewarding, but it can also mean very long hours and lots of stress. Sole proprietors—as the ultimate authority in their business—often must perform tasks or make decisions in areas where they lack expertise.

- **Lack of Permanence:** Because sole proprietorships are just extensions of their owners, they lack permanence. If the owner dies, retires, or withdraws from the business for some other reason, the company legally ceases to exist. Even if the company continues to operate under new ownership, in the eyes of the law, it becomes a different firm.

## 6-3 Partnerships: Can Two Heads (and Bankrolls) Be Better Than One?

There are several types of partnerships, each with its own specific characteristics. We'll focus our discussion mainly on the most basic type, known as a general partnership. However, we'll also take a quick look at limited partnerships and limited liability partnerships (LLPs).

Sharing responsibilities and complementary skills are one of the advantages of general business partnerships.

### 6-3a Formation of General Partnerships

There is no limit on the number of partners who can participate in a general partnership, but most partnerships consist of only a few partners—often just two. The partnership is formed when the partners enter into a voluntary partnership agreement. It is legally possible to start a partnership on the basis of a verbal agreement, but doing so is often a recipe for disaster. It's much safer to get everything in writing and to seek expert legal assistance when drawing up the agreement. A typical partnership agreement spells out details, such as the initial financial contributions each partner will make, the specific duties and responsibilities each will assume, how they will share profits (and losses), how they will settle disagreements, and how they will deal with the death or withdrawal of one of the partners. Well-written agreements can prevent common misunderstandings, and even potential lawsuits.

### 6-3b Advantages of General Partnerships

Partnerships offer some key advantages relative to both sole proprietorships and corporations:

- **Ability to Pool Financial Resources:** With more owners investing in the company, a partnership is likely to have a stronger financial base than a sole proprietorship.

- **Ability to Share Responsibilities and Capitalize on Complementary Skills:** Partners can share the burden of running the business, which can ease the workload. Tasks and jobs can also be divided based on complementary skills, using each partner's talents to best advantage.

- **Ease of Formation:** In theory, forming a partnership is easy. As we've already noted, it's possible (but not advisable) to establish a partnership based on a simple verbal agreement. But we shouldn't overemphasize this advantage. Working out all of the details of a partnership agreement can sometimes be a complex and time-consuming process.

- **Possible Tax Advantages:** Similar to a sole proprietorship, the earnings of a partnership "pass through" the business—untouched by the IRS—and are taxed only as the partners' personal income. Again, this avoids the potential for double taxation endemic to corporations.

> "It is rare to find a business partner who is selfless. If you are lucky it happens once in a lifetime."
>
> —Michael Eisner, former Disney CEO

### 6-3c Disadvantages of General Partnerships

General partnerships also have some serious disadvantages. Well-written partnership agreements, however, can mitigate some of these major drawbacks:

- **Unlimited Liability:** As a general partner, you're not only liable for your own mistakes but also for those of your partners. In fact, all general partners have unlimited liability for the debts and obligations of their business. So, if the assets they've invested in the business aren't sufficient to meet these claims, the personal assets of the partners are at risk. When someone sues a general partnership, the lawsuit can target *any* individual partner or group of partners. In fact, lawsuits often go after the partners with the deepest pockets, even if they did not personally participate in the act that caused the legal action. In other words, if you have more personal wealth than the other partners, you could lose more than they do even if they were the ones at fault!

- **Potential for Disagreements:** If general partners can't agree on how to run the business, the conflict can complicate and delay decision making. A well-drafted partnership agreement usually specifies how disputes will be resolved, but disagreements among partners can create friction and hard feelings that

harm morale and undermine the cooperation needed to keep the business on track. An unfortunate example comes from a lawsuit between business partners who also happened to be sisters. The lawsuit, filed by a sister against her half-sister, alleged "an absolutely shocking record of fraud, tax fraud, deceit, breach of fiduciary duties, gross negligence and incompetence, oppressive and unfair dealings toward the other… partners," and that the half-sister had "dementia or another mental disorder."[23] Friction and hard feelings, indeed.

- **Lack of Continuity:** If a current partner withdraws from the partnership, the relationships among the participants will clearly change, potentially ending the partnership. This creates uncertainty about how long a partnership will remain in business.

- **Difficulty in Withdrawing from a Partnership:** A partner who withdraws from a partnership remains personally liable for any debts or obligations the firm had *at the time of withdrawal*—even if those obligations were incurred by the actions of other partners.

### 6-3d Limited Partnerships

The risks associated with unlimited liability make general partnerships unattractive to many individuals who would otherwise be interested in joining a business partnership. Fortunately, two other types of partnerships allow some partners to limit their personal liability to some extent, although each comes with particular requirements.

The first of these, known as a **limited partnership**, is a partnership arrangement that includes at least one general partner *and* at least one limited partner. Both types of partners contribute financially to the company and share in its profits. But in other respects they play different roles:

- General partners have the right to participate fully in managing their partnership, but they also assume unlimited personal liability for any of its debts—just like the partners in a general partnership.

- Limited partners *cannot* actively participate in its management, but they have the protection of limited liability. This means that, as long as they do not actively participate in managing the company, their personal wealth is not at risk.

**limited partnership** A partnership that includes at least one general partner who actively manages the company and accepts unlimited liability and one limited partner who gives up the right to actively manage the company in exchange for limited liability.

# Converting Your Business Form to Lower Business Taxes

Conversions from one business form to another became much more common after changes to federal business tax laws in 2018. Why? First, the tax rate for corporations fell from 35% to 21%. Second, many pass-through businesses (PTBs), where the earnings pass through to the owner's personal tax returns, became eligible for a Qualified Business Income deduction that cut their tax base by 20%. For example, if your PTB earned $100, you would only be taxed on $80 on your personal tax return. With these changes, which is right for your business?

*Convert to a C Corporation When:*

- The 21% tax rate for C corporations is lower than the personal income tax rates (shown below) used for PTBs:

    - 22% at $40,525 or $81,050 for married couples filing jointly (MCFJ).

    - 24% at $86,375 or $172,750 for MCFJ.

    - 32% at $164,925 or $329,850 for MCFJ.

    - 35% at $209,425 or $418,850 for MCFJ.

    - 37% at $523,600 or $628,300 for MCFJ.

- You retain earnings by reinvesting profits in the business.

    - Because retained earnings are *not* taxed, they avoid double taxation on corporate dividends, which are profits paid to owners.

- Changing to a C corporation will benefit the firm for some time.

    - Firms converting to C corporations cannot switch to another business form for five years.

*Convert to a PTB when:*

- Your PTB is eligible for the Qualified Business Income deduction:

- Many PTBs are eligible, but most service businesses, such as legal and accounting firms, are *not.*

- Taxable income on your personal tax return is under $164,900 for single filers and $329,800 for joint filers.

- Using the QBI deduction lowers your tax rate (taxes for PTBs are paid on the owner's personal tax returns) below the combined tax rate for C corporations.

    - Double taxation is 21% for business profits followed by another 15% to 20% tax on corporate dividends.

    - For example, a $100 profit for a C corporation becomes $79 after taxes. If that $79 is paid to shareholders, it becomes $63 after taxes (assuming a 20% tax rate on dividends). The effective double taxation rate is 37%.

These are the key issues, but it can be much more complicated. So, don't convert your business form without consulting your attorney and tax accountant. But don't hesitate to change if it benefits your business.[24]

Sean Locke Photography/Shutterstock.com

## 6-3e Limited Liability Partnerships

The **limited liability partnership (LLP)** is another partnership arrangement that is attractive to partners who want to limit their personal risk. It is similar to a limited partnership in some ways, but it has the advantage of allowing *all* partners to take an active role in management while also offering *all* partners some form of limited liability. In other words, there's no need to distinguish between limited and general partners in an LLP.

The amount of liability protection offered by LLPs varies among states. In some states, LLPs offer "full-shield" protection, meaning that partners have limited liability for all claims against their company, except those resulting from *their own* negligence or malpractice. In other states, partners in LLPs have a lesser "partial-shield" protection. In these states, each partner has limited liability for the negligence or malpractice of other partners but still has unlimited liability for any other debts. Another drawback is that some states only allow specific types of professional businesses to form LLPs. For example, California law allows only accountants, lawyers, and architects to form LLPs.

Thanks to full- and partial-shield protections, LLPs are often preferred over general partnerships because according to

> **limited liability partnership (LLP)** A form of partnership in which all partners have the right to participate in management and have limited liability for company debts.

attorneys Randy Evans, Shari Klevens, and Suzanne Badawi, "The one thing that many partners fear most is being held personally liable for something they did not do and knew nothing about."[25]

## 6-4 Corporations: The Advantages and Disadvantages of Being an Artificial Person

There are several types of corporations. The most common is called a **C corporation**; when people use the term "corporation" without specifying which type, they are generally referring to a C corporation. Because it's the most common, we'll devote most of our discussion to C corporations. However, we'll also describe three other types of corporations: S corporations, statutory close (or closed) corporations, and nonprofit corporations.

### 6-4a Forming a C Corporation

As mentioned earlier, the formation of a corporation requires filing articles of incorporation and paying filing fees. It also requires the adoption of **corporate bylaws**, which are detailed rules that govern the way the corporation is organized and managed. Many states also require that new corporations name a board of directors, issue stock certificates to initial shareholders, and appoint a registered agent to receive legal and tax documents on behalf of the new corporation.[26] Because of these requirements, forming a corporation tends to be more expensive and complex than forming a sole proprietorship or partnership.

The requirements, however, vary among the states. Some states are known for their simple forms, inexpensive fees, low corporate tax rates, and "corporation-friendly" laws and court systems. In those states, forming a corporation is not much harder or more expensive than setting up a sole proprietorship and sometimes can be simpler than forming a partnership. Not surprisingly, many large companies choose to incorporate in states with such favorable

environments—even if they intend to do the majority of their business in other states. Delaware, in particular, has been very successful at attracting corporations. You may not think of Delaware as the home of corporate power, but more than half of all publicly traded corporations—and 66% of the firms listed in the *Fortune 500*—are incorporated in Delaware.[27] When the Carlyle Group, a global investment firm with $230 billion in assets and 30 offices on six continents, converted from a publicly traded partnership to a C corporation, the Washington D.C.-based firm formed its new C corporation in Delaware.[28]

### 6-4b Ownership of C Corporations

Ownership of C corporations is represented by shares of stock, so owners are called "**stockholders**" (or "shareholders"). Common stock represents the basic ownership interest in a corporation, but some firms also issue preferred stock. One key difference between the two types of stock involves voting rights; common stockholders normally have the right to vote in stockholders' meetings, while preferred stockholders do not. As shown in Exhibit 6.3, many large corporations issue billions of shares of stock and have hundreds of thousands—or even millions—of stockholders.

Stock in large corporations is usually publicly traded, meaning that anyone with the money and inclination to do so can buy shares—and that anyone who owns shares is free to sell them. But many smaller corporations are owned by just a handful of stockholders who don't actively trade their stock. It's even possible for individuals to incorporate their business and be the sole shareholder in their corporation.[29]

Stockholders don't have to be individuals. **Institutional investors**, such as mutual funds, insurance companies, pension funds, and endowment funds, pool money from a large number of individuals and use these funds to buy stocks and other securities. As Exhibit 6.3 illustrates, institutional investors own the majority of stock in many large corporations, ranging from 96% in Visa, the credit card company, to 30% in Walmart. The reason that Visa has so few stockholders, just 338 as of January 2021, is that institutional investors bought and held most of its stock when first issued in 2008.[30]

### 6-4c The Role of the Board of Directors

It's not practical for all of the stockholders of a large corporation to actively participate in the management of their company. Besides, most stockholders don't have the

**C corporation** The most common type of corporation, which is a legal business entity that offers limited liability to all of its owners, who are called stockholders.

**corporate bylaws** The basic rules governing how a corporation is organized and how it conducts its business.

**stockholder** An owner of a corporation.

**institutional investor** An organization that pools contributions from investors, clients, or depositors and uses these funds to buy stocks and other securities.

## Exhibit 6.3 Stock Ownership in Major U.S. Corporations

| Corporation | Shares of Common Stock Outstanding | Total Number of Stockholders | Percentage of Shares Owned by Institutional Investors |
|---|---|---|---|
| Visa | 1,700,000,000 | 338 | 96% |
| JPMorganChase | 3,050,000,000 | 195,467 | 72% |
| Microsoft | 7,560,000,000 | 91,674 | 72% |
| Johnson & Johnson | 2,630,000,000 | 135,953 | 70% |
| Google | 329,870,000 | 2,455 | 68% |
| Procter & Gamble | 2,480,000,000 | 4,000,000 | 66% |
| Apple | 16,800,000,000 | 22,797 | 60% |
| Amazon | 500,890,000 | 3,169 | 59% |
| Walmart | 2,830,000,000 | 217,840 | 30% |

Sources: Shares outstanding and percentage of institutional ownership are from the Key Statistics for each corporation reported in Yahoo! Finance (https://finance.yahoo.com/); Information about the number of shareholders is found in Item 5 (Market for the Company's Common Equity) of each firm's 2015/2016 10-K annual report filed with the SEC accessed through the Edgar database (https://www.sec.gov/edgar.shtml) accessed January 13, 2021.

time, management skills, or desire to effectively manage such a complex business enterprise. Thus, in accordance with corporate bylaws, the stockholders elect a **board of directors** and rely on this board to oversee the operation of their company and protect their interests.

The board of directors establishes the corporation's mission and sets its broad objectives. But board members seldom take an active role in the day-to-day management of their company. Instead, again in accordance with corporate bylaws, the board appoints a chief executive officer (CEO) and other corporate officers (i.e., top executives) to manage the company on a daily basis. The board also sets the level of compensation for these officers and monitors their performance to ensure that they act in a manner consistent with stockholder interests. When General Electric (GE) missed five out of its six strategic performance goals in a year of disastrous financial performance, GE's board of directors cut top executive pay by *not* paying sizable cash bonuses to 3,800 managers for the first time in the company's 125-year history.[31] Boards also provide advice to top executives on broad policy issues, approve their major proposals, and ensure that the company adheres to major regulatory requirements.

### 6-4d Advantages of C Corporations

Corporations have become the dominant form of business ownership for several reasons:

- **Limited Liability:** As already explained, stockholders are not personally liable for the debts of their company. If a corporation goes bankrupt, the stockholders might find that their stock is worthless, but their other personal assets are protected.

- **Permanence:** Unless the articles of incorporation specify a limited duration, corporations can continue operating as long as they remain financially viable and the majority of stockholders want the business to continue. Unlike a sole proprietorship or partnership, a general corporation is unaffected by the death or withdrawal of an owner.

- **Ease of Transfer of Ownership:** It's easy for stockholders of publicly traded C corporations to withdraw from ownership—they simply sell their shares of stock.

- **Ability to Raise Large Amounts of Financial Capital:** Corporations can raise large amounts of financial capital by issuing shares of stock or by selling formal IOUs called corporate bonds. The ability to raise money by issuing these securities gives corporations a major financial advantage over most other forms of ownership. For example, Zoom raised $1.75 billion by selling 5.15 million shares of stock for $340 each. It will use that money for strategic acquisitions and international growth.[32] You'll learn more about raising capital in financial markets in Chapter 10.

- **Ability to Make Use of Specialized Management:** Large corporations often find it easier to hire highly qualified professional managers than proprietorships and partnerships. Major corporations can typically offer attractive salaries and benefits, and their

> **board of directors** The individuals who are elected by stockholders of a corporation to represent their interests.

# Improve Your Board of Directors: Buddy Them Up and Send Them Into the Wild

From hiring the right leaders to challenging top management's assumptions, boards are critical to company success. But few are run well, and board members rarely have the deep understanding they need to provide good advice. Here are two steps top companies are taking to improve board effectiveness.

## Buddy System

According to Carol Bartz, a longtime Cisco director (who also was a CEO), the biggest benefit of the buddy system, "is having an effective board member faster." Bartz helped coach new director Amy Chang, meeting with her three times before Chang's first board meeting. According to Chang, who had been a board member at another company, "She really took the time to walk me through things," including other board members' business concerns and Cisco's complex global business.

## Attending Senior Management Meetings

At Netflix, board members regularly observe one of three senior management meetings: a monthly meeting of the top seven leaders, a quarterly meeting of the top 90 leaders, or a quarterly business review with the top 500 employees. Watching managers operate "in the wild" says CEO Reed Hastings, "is an efficient way for the board to understand the company better." According to one Netflix board member, "You see a different level of dynamic of the executive team... and you see the dynamic with the CEO. You see how the topics that have been discussed, resolved, and reported on in a board meeting actually got processed."

So, to improve your board's effectiveness, buddy them up and send them into the wild.[33]

Larcsky789/Shutterstock.com

Michael Vi/Shutterstock.com

permanence and potential for growth offer managers opportunities for career advancement.

## 6-4e Disadvantages of C Corporations

In addition to their significant benefits, C corporations have a number of drawbacks:

- **Expense and Complexity of Formation and Operation:** As we've already seen, establishing a corporation can be more complex and expensive than forming a sole proprietorship or partnership. Corporations are also subject to more formal operating requirements. For example, they are required to hold regular board meetings and keep accurate minutes.

- **Complications When Operating in More Than One State:** When a business that's incorporated in one state does business in other states, it's called a "*domestic* corporation" in the state where it's incorporated, and a "*foreign* corporation" in the other states. A corporation must register (or "qualify") as a foreign corporation in order to do business in any state other than the one in which it is incorporated. This typically requires additional paperwork, fees, and taxes. But registration as a foreign corporation is only necessary if the company is involved in substantial business activities within the state. Businesses that only engage in minor business activities are typically exempt from the registration requirement. For example, a firm operating a production facility or maintaining a district office in a state other than its corporate home would need to register as a foreign corporation, but a firm that simply held a bank account or solicited sales to customers in that state through the mail would not be required to do so.

## Exhibit 6.4
## How Double Taxation Reduces Earnings for Stockholders

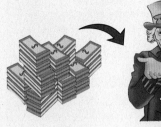

| Pre-Tax Corporate Earnings | Corporate Taxes | After Tax Corporate Earnings | Stockholders | Personal Income Taxes | Stockholders' After-Tax Income |

- **Double Taxation of Earnings and Additional Taxes:** The IRS considers a C corporation to be a separate legal entity and taxes its earnings accordingly. Then, as shown in Exhibit 6.4, any dividends (earnings the corporation distributes to stockholders) are taxed *again* as the personal income of the stockholders (though typically at the lower capital gains rate of 15% to 20%). This double taxation can take a big bite out of earnings that are distributed to shareholders. But note that corporations often reinvest some or all of their profits back into the business. Shareholders don't pay income taxes on these *retained earnings*. Many states also impose separate income taxes on corporations. Most states also impose an annual franchise tax on both domestic and foreign corporations that operate within their borders.

- **More Paperwork, More Regulation, and Less Secrecy:** Corporations are more closely regulated and are required to file more government paperwork than other forms of business. Large, publicly traded corporations are required to send annual statements to all shareholders and to file detailed 10-Q (quarterly), 10-K (annual), and 8-K (current reports, which if needed, are filed between quarterly and annual reports) with the Securities and Exchange Commission (SEC). The 10-K annual report filed with the SEC is often hundreds of pages long and includes a wealth of information about the company's operations and financial condition. For example, Apple's 10-K breaks out key financial information by product (iPhone, Mac, iPad, wearables, home and accessories, and services) as well as geographically (Americas, Europe, China, Japan, and the rest of Asia Pacific).[34] Because companies with publicly traded shares are public, anyone can look at these reports at https://www.sec.gov/edgar.shtml.

- **Possible Conflicts of Interest:** The corporate officers appointed by the board are supposed to further the interests of stockholders. But some top executives pursue policies that further their *own* interests (such as prestige, power, job security, high pay, and attractive perks) at the expense of the stockholders. The board of directors has an obligation to protect the interests of stockholders, but in recent years the boards of several major corporations have come under criticism for continuing to approve high compensation packages for top executives, even when their companies performed poorly.

"General Electric, one of the largest corporations in America, filed a whopping 57,000-page federal tax return ...[which] would have been 19 feet high if printed out and stacked."

—Weekly Standard

## Exhibit 6.5 — Characteristics of S, Statutory Close, and Nonprofit Corporations

| Type | Key Advantages | Limitations |
|---|---|---|
| S Corporation | ■ The IRS does not tax earnings of S corporations separately. Earnings pass through the company and are taxed only as income to stockholders, thus avoiding the problem of double taxation associated with C corporations.<br>■ Stockholders have limited liability. | ■ It can have no more than 100 stockholders.<br>■ With only rare exceptions, each stockholder must be a U.S. citizen or permanent resident of the United States (no ownership by foreigners or other corporations). |
| Statutory Close (or Closed) Corporation | ■ Operate under simpler arrangements than conventional corporations. For example, they don't have to elect a board of directors or hold an annual stockholders' meeting.<br>■ All owners can actively participate in management while still having limited liability. | ■ The number of stockholders is limited. (The number varies among states but is usually no more than 50.)<br>■ Stockholders normally can't sell their shares to the public without first offering the shares to existing owners.<br>■ Not all states allow formation of this type of corporation. |
| Nonprofit (or Not-for-Profit) Corporation | ■ Earnings are exempt from federal and state income taxes.<br>■ Members and directors have limited liability.<br>■ Individuals who contribute money or property to the nonprofit can take a tax deduction, making it easier for these organizations to raise funds from donations. | ■ It has members (who may pay dues) but cannot have stockholders.<br>■ It cannot distribute dividends to members.<br>■ It cannot contribute funds to a political campaign.<br>■ It must keep accurate records and file paperwork to document tax-exempt status. |

Sources: "S Corporations," Internal Revenue Service, November 9, 2020, https://www.irs.gov/businesses/small-businesses-self-employed/s-corporations, accessed January 14, 2021; "Close Corporation Tax," *UpCounsel*, https://www.upcounsel.com/close-corporation-tax, accessed January 14, 2021; "Federal Tax Obligations of Non-Profit Corporations," Internal Revenue Service, September 19, 2020, https://www.irs.gov/charities-non-profits/federal-tax-obligations-of-non-profit-corporations, accessed January 14, 2021.

## 6-4f Other Types of Corporations: Same but Different

Now that we've described C corporations, let's take a quick look at three other types of corporations: **S corporations**, **statutory close corporations**, and **nonprofit corporations**. Like C corporations, each is created by filing the appropriate paperwork with a government agency. Also, like general corporations, these corporations are considered legal entities that stand apart from their owners and can enter into contracts, own property, and take legal action in their own names. But in other key respects they are quite different from C corporations—and from each other. Exhibit 6.5 summarizes the basic features of these corporations.

**S corporation** A form of corporation that avoids double taxation by having its income taxed as if it were a partnership.

**statutory close (or closed) corporation** A corporation with a limited number of owners that operates under simpler, less formal rules than a C corporation.

**nonprofit corporation** A corporation that does not seek to earn a profit and differs in several fundamental respects from C corporations.

**acquisition** A corporate restructuring in which one firm buys another.

## 6-4g Corporate Restructuring

Large corporations constantly look for ways to grow and achieve competitive advantages. Some corporations work to achieve these goals, at least in part, through mergers, acquisitions, and divestitures. We'll close our discussion of corporations by taking a quick look at these forms of corporate restructuring.

**Mergers and Acquisitions** In the news and casual conversation, the terms "merger" and "acquisition" are often used interchangeably. However, there's a difference between the two. An **acquisition** occurs when one firm buys another firm. For example, Microsoft paid $7.5 billion to acquire Bethesda Softworks, maker of popular videogame series such as *Elder Scrolls, Doom, Wolfenstein, Dishonored, Fallout, Prey,* and *The Evil Within.* Since 2019, Microsoft has used an acquisition strategy to expand its Xbox Game Studios network from 15 to 23 videogame studios.[35] The firm making the purchase (Microsoft) is called the "acquiring firm," and the firm being purchased (Bethesda) is called the "target firm." After the acquisition, the target firm ceases to exist as an independent entity while the purchasing firm continues in operation, and its stock is still traded. But not all acquisitions, like Microsoft and Bethesda, are on friendly terms. When the acquiring firm buys the target firm despite the opposition of the

## Exhibit 6.6 Types of Mergers and Acquisitions

| Type of Merger/Acquisition | Definition | Common Objective | Example |
|---|---|---|---|
| **Horizontal** | A combination of firms in the same industry. | Increase size and market power within the industry. Improve efficiency by eliminating duplication of facilities and personnel. | U.S.-based Pioneer Natural Resources, an oil and natural gas driller, acquired Parsley Energy Inc., an independent oil and natural gas company, for $4.5 billion. |
| **Vertical** | A combination of firms that are at different stages in the production of a good or service, creating a "buyer-seller" relationship. | Provide tighter integration of production and increased control over the supply of crucial inputs. | Apple, maker of iPhones, iPads, and Mac computers, acquired Vilynx, which uses artificial intelligence to automatically analyze and tag video content so it can be made searchable, for $50 million. |
| **Conglomerate** | A combination of firms in unrelated industries. | Reduce risk by making the firm less vulnerable to adverse conditions in any single market. | Chinese-based Midea, a maker of consumer appliances and heating, ventilation, and air-conditioning systems, acquired Kuka AG, a German-based robotics and automation systems company, for $5 billion. |

Sources: W. Anderson, "Parsley Energy Officially Bought by Pioneer Natural Resources For $4.5B, *Austin Business Journal*, January 13, 2021, https://www.bizjournals.com/austin/news/2021/01/13/pioneer-resources -closes-buyout-parsley-energy.html, accessed January 14, 2021; M. Gurman, "Apple Buys Vilynx Self-Learning AI Video Startup to Improve Apps," *Bloomberg*, October 27, 2020, https://www.bloomberg.com/news/articles /2020-10-27/apple-buys-self-learning-ai-video-startup-to-improve-apps?sref=xXo7CWym, accessed January 14, 2021; P. Basu, "Midea Completes Acquisition of German Robot Maker Kuka," S&P Global Market Intelligence, January 8, 2017, https://www.spglobal.com/marketintelligence/en/news-insights/blog/amazon-ecommerce-sales-soar-amid-covid19, accessed January 14, 2021.

target's board and top management, the result is called a "hostile takeover."

In a **merger**, instead of one firm buying the other, the two companies agree to a combination of equals, joining together to form a new company out of the two previously independent firms. For example, Knight Transportation and Swift Transportation merged to form the largest trucking and transportation company in the United States.[36] The two companies maintained their distinct brands, but merged all management, financial, and operational systems to become Knight–Swift Transportation Holdings Inc. Together, Knight–Swift has 26,000 drivers and 65 truck terminals in North America.[37]

Exhibit 6.6 describes the three most common types of corporate combinations.

**Divestitures: When Less Is More** Sometimes corporations restructure by subtraction rather than by addition. A **divestiture** occurs when a firm transfers total or partial ownership of some of its operations to investors or to another company. Firms often use divestitures to rid themselves of a part of their company that no longer fits well with their strategic plans. This allows them to streamline their operations and focus on their core businesses. For example, Constellation Brands, which adopted a strategy of selling premium brand beer, wine, and spirits, divested its Paul Masson Grande Amber Brandy (a bottle of which typically sells for $15 or less) for $265 million, and also sold a collection of wine and spirits brands (typically selling for $11 a bottle or less) for $810 million.[38] In many (but not all) cases, divestitures involve the sale of assets to outsiders, which raises financial capital for the firm. Constellation Brands will use the $1.075 billion from divestitures to pay off company debt.

One common type of divestiture, called a "spin-off," occurs when a company issues stock in one of its own divisions or operating units and sets it up as a separate company—complete with its own board of directors and corporate officers. It then distributes the stock in the new company to its existing stockholders. After the spin-off, the stockholders

**horizontal merger** A combination of two firms that are in the same industry.

**vertical merger** A combination of firms at different stages in the production of a good or service.

**conglomerate merger** A combination of two firms that are in unrelated industries.

**merger** A corporate restructuring that occurs when two formerly independent business entities combine to form a new organization.

**divestiture** The transfer of total or partial ownership of some of a firm's operations to investors or to another company.

Constellation Brands divested its Paul Masson Grande Amber Brandy brand ($15 a bottle) for $265 million after adopting a strategy of selling premium beer, wine and spirits.

therapy company (treating disease by repairing or replacing genes) is spinning off its cancer-drug division into a new company, Oncology Newco, with its own publicly traded stock.[39] While a spin-off allows a corporation to eliminate a division that no longer fits in its plans, it doesn't actually generate any additional funds for the firm.

A "carve-out" is like a spin-off, in that the firm converts a particular unit or division into a separate company and issues stock in the newly created corporation. However, instead of distributing the new stock to its current stockholders, it sells the stock to outside investors, thus raising additional financial capital. In many cases, the firm sells only a minority of the total shares, so that it maintains majority ownership. Sharp Corporation, a manufacturer of electronic and computer components, as well as consumer electronics products, will carve out its LCD panel business into a separate company. The LCD panel unit earns revenues of $7 billion a year. The money Sharp raises by issuing new stock will be used to invest in the next generation of panel technologies.[40]

end up owning two separate companies rather than one. They can then buy, sell, or hold either (or both) stocks as they see fit. For example, Blue-Bird Bio, a gene

# Cheese Off! Divestiture Helps Kraft Heinz Focus on Fewer Brands

Companies use divestiture to sell some of their operations. When a part of a company no longer fits strategically, divesting allows the firm to streamline operations and refocus on its core business.

When Miguel Patricio became CEO, one of his goals for Kraft Heinz was to slice the number of new product introductions in half. As Patricio said, "My role is to simplify this business. Fewer big bets." When Kraft and Heinz merged, they became the fifth largest food company in the world, but one with so many brands that its products were found in 56 sections of the grocery store. Patricio said, "If you try to innovate in 56 different categories, you can't execute on all of them. We need to be more selective."

And that's where divestiture comes in. In millions of households, Kraft brands, like Velveeta or Kraft Macaroni and Cheese, are synonymous with cheese. So, it came as a surprise that Kraft Heinz sold a variety of cheese businesses to Lactalis, a French-based global dairy company that sells President brand cheeses in the United States.

For $3.2 billion, Lactalis bought Kraft Heinz's shredded and block cheese businesses, Athenos Greek cheeses, Breakstone's cottage cheese and sour cream, Cracker Barrel cheeses, Knudsen cottage cheese and sour cream, and Polly-O Italian cheeses. This came two years after Kraft Heinz divested its Canadian natural cheese business to Parmalat, an Italian-based Lactalis company, for $1 billion.

With fewer brands and $3.2 billion to put toward debt reduction and product improvement, Kraft Heinz hopes to regain focus by reorganizing into six "consumer-driven product platforms." CEO Patricio said, "First, we had to stabilize the business. Now, we are building a strategy for the future."[41]

# 6-5 The Limited Liability Company: The New Kid on the Block

As the newest form of business ownership, state laws concerning the legal status and formation of LLCs are still evolving. Several states have recently revised their statutes to make forming LLCs simpler and to make transfer of ownership easier. Other states have kept more restrictive requirements intact. This diversity of state requirements, and the continuing evolution of LLC statutes, makes it difficult to provide meaningful generalizations about this form of ownership.[42]

## 6-5a Forming and Managing an LLC

In many respects, forming an LLC is similar to forming a corporation. As with corporations, LLCs are created by filing a document (which goes by a variety of names, such as *certificate of organization* or *articles of organization*) and paying filing fees in the state where the business is organized. Organizers of most LLCs also draft an operating agreement, which is similar to the bylaws of a corporation. Some states also require LLCs to publish a notice of intent to operate as an LLC.

Because LLCs are neither corporations nor partnerships, their owners are called *members* rather than stockholders or partners. Members of LLCs often manage their own company under an arrangement similar to the relationship among general partners in a partnership. However, some LLCs hire professional managers who have responsibilities much like those of the CEO and other top officers of corporations.

## 6-5b Advantages of LLCs

Why are LLCs so popular? This form of ownership offers significant advantages:

- **Limited Liability:** Similar to a corporation, all owners of an LLC have limited liability.

- **Tax Pass-Through:** As mentioned at the beginning of this chapter, for tax purposes the owners of LLCs may elect to have their companies treated as either a corporation or a partnership—or even as a sole proprietorship if owned by a single person. The default tax classification for LLCs with more than one owner—and the one most LLCs choose—is the partnership option. Under this arrangement, there is no separate tax on the earnings of the company. Instead, earnings "pass through" the company and are taxed only as

income of the owners. This eliminates the double taxation of profits that is endemic to general corporations.

However, there are some cases where it makes sense for LLCs to elect to be taxed as a corporation. For example, the owner of a single-person LLC can avoid paying self-employment taxes (meaning Social Security and Medicare taxes) by electing to have the LLC treated as a corporation (typically an S Corporation) rather than as a sole proprietorship. Why do this? Because Social Security and Medicare taxes are only paid on the salary that the single-person LLC pays themselves, rather than as a percentage of *all* earnings as is done with a sole proprietor. While profits are still taxed as part of the owner's personal tax return, a single-person LLC that is treated as a corporation does *not* pay self-employment taxes on profits.[43] The IRS does require that single-person LLCs pay themselves a demonstrably reasonable salary. In other words, you can't pay yourself a salary of $1 a year to avoid paying Social Security and Medicare taxes.

- **Simplicity and Flexibility in Management and Operation:** Unlike corporations, LLCs aren't required to hold regular board meetings. Also, LLCs are subject to less paperwork and fewer reporting requirements than corporations.

- **Flexible Ownership:** Unlike S corporations, LLCs can have any number of owners. Also, unlike S corporations, the owners of LLCs can include foreign investors and other corporations. However, some states do make it difficult to transfer ownership to outsiders.

## 6-5c Limitations and Disadvantages of LLCs

Despite their increasing popularity, LLCs have some limitations and drawbacks:

- **Complexity of Formation:** Because of the need to file articles of organization and pay filing fees, LLCs can take more time and effort to form than sole proprietorships. But in most states, choosing an LLC name, completing the paperwork, and paying the LLC processing fee can be done easily at a Secretary of State website (e.g., https://www.sos.texas.gov/corp/sosda/index.shtml),. While costs vary, the average fee to establish an LLC is $132.[44] And, in most cases, it takes no more than 30 minutes to form and register an LLC—if that.

Is forming an LLC more difficult than creating a partnership? As mentioned earlier, the formation of a partnership requires a "meeting of the minds" of the partners, which isn't always easy to achieve. So, in some cases, the formation of a partnership can prove to be every bit as challenging as the formation of an LLC, if not more. The bigger issue is choosing the correct business form, LLC or partnership.

- **Annual Franchise Tax:** Even though they may be exempt from corporate income taxes (LLC earnings are taxed as part of the owners' personal taxes), many states require LLCs to pay an annual franchise tax (which is not a tax on franchise businesses, as discussed in Section 6-6). For example, the average LLC annual franchise tax is $91 but can reach as high as $800 in California.[45]

- **Foreign Status in Other States:** Like corporations, LLCs must register or qualify to operate as "foreign" companies when they do business in states other than the state in which they were organized. This results in additional paperwork, fees, and taxes.

- **Limits on Types of Firms that Can Form LLCs:** Most states do not permit banks, insurance companies, and nonprofit organizations to operate as LLCs.

- **Differences in State Laws:** As we've already mentioned, LLC laws and their specific requirements vary considerably among the states. In 2006, the National Conference of Commissioners on Uniform State Laws created a Revised Uniform Limited Liability Company Act that could be used as a model by all states. To date, 21 states have adopted this law.[46] Until there is more uniformity in state laws, operating LLCs in more than one state is likely to remain a complex endeavor.[47]

# Maximizing Earnings Potential: Start Fresh or Franchise?

While millions dream of running their own businesses, cost and inexperience are the biggest reasons one-third of small businesses fail within two years. Inexperienced entrepreneurs often struggle to get customers to buy from them rather than from existing businesses. And a great deal of start-up capital is often needed to pay for offices, facilities, transportation, insurance, and salaries (but probably not for themselves until the business establishes itself financially). It's not easy!

Aspiring entrepreneurs don't need to build new businesses from scratch, however. With franchising, a franchisor licenses the franchisee to use its name, trademark, products, and business methods. In short, franchising allows a businessperson to launch a new business with the support of a successful brand and backed by a proven business model. Moreover, starting a franchise can cost less than starting a fresh new business.

While franchises are less likely to fail than new independent businesses, how do they compare in terms of earning potential? Well, it depends on the industry, the success of the franchisor, the level of competition, and, frankly, the terms of the franchise contract. According to one estimate, the median annual franchise income is $70,000, which is nearly identical to the $70,300 average income for small business owners.

But what if as a franchisee you want to do much better than average? The best strategy is to own multiple franchises. As mentioned in Section 6-6a, Dawn Lafreeda, who now owns 90 Denny's restaurants, bought her first at age 23. Jeff Rahn also bought multiple franchises, but with different franchisors in plumbing, heating and air conditioning, and electrical services.

Franchising is not for everyone, but for millions franchising remains a great business opportunity, and a fantastic way to provide for themselves and their families.[48]

one photo/Shutterstock.com

## 6-6 Franchising: Proven Methods for a Price

A **franchise** is a licensing arrangement under which one party (the **franchisor**) allows another party (the **franchisee**) to use its name, trademark, patents, copyrights, business methods, and other property in exchange for monetary payments and other considerations. Franchising has become a very popular way to operate a business and an important source of employment and income. According to the International Franchise Association, in the U.S. economy:

- 732,000 U.S. businesses are franchises.

- Franchising provides 8% of private sector jobs, meaning 7.6 million employees work directly for franchisees.

- Another 13.2 million jobs are provided by companies that support franchise businesses.

- Overall, franchising accounts for 5.3% of private GDP.[49]

And according to a Census Bureau study, franchise establishments dominate several major markets such as fast food, auto dealerships, convenience stores, and private mail distribution centers.[50]

The two most popular types of franchise arrangements are **distributorships** and **business format franchises**. In a distributorship, the franchisor makes a product and grants distributors a license to sell it. The most common example of this type of franchise is the arrangement between automakers and the dealerships that sell their cars. Another example of a distributorship franchise is Advanced Beverages & Bar Supplies, which sells supplies (soft drinks, fruit juices, and drink mixes), dispensing equipment (soda fountain and alcohol "guns"), and maintenance and repair services for bars, taverns, and restaurants.[51]

In a business format franchise, the franchisor grants the franchisee the right to both make *and* sell its good or service. Under this arrangement, the franchisor usually provides a wide range of services to the franchisee, such as help with site selection, training, and help in obtaining financing, but also requires the franchisee to follow very specific guidelines while operating the business. Chick-fil-A, Domino's Pizza, and Baskin-Robbins ice cream are all business format franchises.

### 6-6a Franchising in Today's Economy

Franchising is now a well-established method of operating a business—but that doesn't mean it's static. Let's look at some ways the world of franchising is changing.

Tim Gray/Shutterstock.com

While franchises are usually associated with restaurants, any kind of business can be operated as a franchise. Some non-restaurant franchises in the United States include convenience store 7-Eleven, hotel chain Marriott International, Chem-Dry Carpet Cleaning, Century 21 real estate, and Kumon child education franchises.[52]

One of the biggest trends in franchising for the past several years has been an expansion into foreign markets. Franchisors in a variety of industries have found that opportunities for franchise growth are greater in foreign countries because competition is less intense, and markets are less saturated than in the United States. In 2020, McDonald's had 23,196 franchise outlets in foreign countries (10,021 more than it had in the United States), Subway had 17,471, and 7–11 had 59,193.[53] Of course, operating in foreign countries can pose special challenges. Differences in culture, language, laws, demographics, and economic development mean that franchisors, like other types of business owners, must adjust their business methods—and

**franchise** A licensing arrangement under which a franchisor allows franchisees to use its name, trademark, products, business methods, and other property in exchange for monetary payments and other considerations.

**franchisor** The business entity in a franchise relationship that allows others to operate its business using resources it supplies in exchange for money and other considerations.

**franchisee** The party in a franchise relationship that pays for the right to use resources supplied by the franchisor.

**distributorship** A type of franchising arrangement in which the franchisor makes a product and licenses the franchisee to sell it.

**business format franchise** A broad franchise agreement in which the franchisee pays for the right to use the name, trademark, and business and production methods of the franchisor.

the specific products they offer—to meet the needs of foreign consumers.

Another notable trend has been the growth in the number of women franchisees. Reliable statistics on women in franchising are difficult to find, but according to *Franchise Business Review*, 26% of U.S. franchises are solely owned by women, with another 9% of franchises co-owned by women. That 24% increase, compared to ten years ago, is accelerating as in the last two years 41% of new franchises have been started by women.[54] Dawn Lafreeda, who started as a waitress, owns 90 Denny's restaurant franchises. Lafreeda, Denny's largest franchisee, took a big risk by maxing out her credit cards at age 23 when she bought her first Denny's franchise.[55]

Minority participation in franchises has grown consistently over the last 20 years. African Americans, Hispanics, Asian Americans, and Native Americans make up 32% of the population and now own 30% of franchises, up from 20% in 2016. Nonfranchised businesses, by comparison, are just 18% minority-owned.[56]

In addition to franchisor's strong efforts to actively recruit minority franchisees, which can include reduced fees or subsidized payment plans, two major initiatives were started to boost minority franchising.[57] The first, known as the National Minority Franchising Initiative (NMFI), was founded in 2000. For roughly a decade, the NMFI's website actively maintained a directory of more than 500 franchisors who actively promoted minority franchise ownership. The second initiative, DiversityFran (franchisefoundation.org/programs/diversityfran), was established in early 2006 by the IFA.[58] This initiative, which is now a part of the IFA's Diversity Institute, has the cooperation of a variety of organizations interested in promoting racial and ethnic business ownership, including the National Urban League, the Association of Small Business Development Centers, the U.S. Pan Asian American Chamber of Commerce, and the Minority Business Development Agency. Franchisors participating in the program receive information and marketing materials designed to help them reach potential minority franchisees more effectively.

## 6-6b Advantages of Franchising

Both the franchisee and the franchisor must believe they'll benefit from the franchise arrangement; otherwise, they wouldn't participate. The advantages of franchising for the franchisor are fairly obvious. It allows the franchisor to expand the business and bring in additional revenue (in the form of franchising fees and royalties) without investing its own capital. Also, franchisees—business owners who are motivated to earn a profit—may have a greater incentive than salaried managers to do whatever it takes to maximize the success of their outlets. From the franchisee's perspective, franchising offers several advantages:

■ **Less Risk:** Franchises offer access to a proven business system and product. The systems and methods offered by franchisors have an established track record. Dawn Lafreeda, who owns 90 Denny's restaurant franchises, agrees, saying, "Do you want to spend two years of your life creating something, or do you want to say, 'I really like that concept, I wonder if I could open one?' It's a much shorter path to ownership than starting from ground zero."[59] People who are interested in buying a franchise can do research to see how stores in the franchise have performed and can talk to existing franchisees before investing.

■ **Training and Support:** The franchisor normally provides the franchisee with extensive training and support. For example, Subway offers two weeks of training at its headquarters and additional training via online training courses and a minimum of 70 hours of hands-on learning with Subway corporate team members as new stores open.[60] The franchisor also sends out newsletters, provides Internet support, maintains a toll-free number for phone support, and provides on-site evaluations.[61]

■ **Brand Recognition:** Operating a franchise gives the franchisee instant brand-name recognition, which can be a big help in attracting customers.

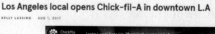

**Los Angeles local opens Chick-fil-A in downtown L.A**

KELLY LASSING   AUG 1, 2017

INSIDE CHICK-FIL-A
Welcome to the first Chick-fil-A in DTLA!

Source: Chick-fil-A

Ashley Lamothe is one of the youngest franchise owners in Chick-fil-A history starting up her franchise in Los Angeles at the age of 26.

## Exhibit 6.7  Franchisee Costs for Selected Franchises

| Franchise | Type of Business | Initial Franchisee Fee | Initial Investment | Cash Requirement | Ongoing Royalty* |
|---|---|---|---|---|---|
| Budget Blinds | Window coverings & film | $19,950 | $125,340 to $254,370 | $75,340 | $300–$2,000 per month |
| Dunkin' (Donuts) | Donuts, coffee, and other baked goods | $40,000 to $90,000 | $199,700 to $1,688,200 | $125,000 to $250,000 | 5.9% |
| Great Clips | Hair styling | $20,000 | $132,250 to $253,100 | $75,000 to $250,000 | 6% |
| Jersey Mike's Subs | Fast food | $18,500 | $169,001 to $804,045 | $100,000 | 6.5% |
| Kumon | Tutoring | $1,000 | $74,428 to $156,590 | $70,000 | $34–$38 per student per month |
| Pizza Hut | Pizza | $25,000 | $367,000 to $2,063,500 | $350,000 | 6% |
| Planet Fitness | 24/7 fitness club | $20,000 | $968,100 to $4,113,000 | $1,500,000 | 7% |
| The UPS Store | Mailing and business services | $29,950 | $137,849 to $566,585 | $60,000 to $100,000 | 5% |

*Royalty is expressed as a percentage of gross revenues unless otherwise specified.

Source: Individual franchise opportunity pages for each listed franchise on the Entrepreneur.com website, https://www.entrepreneur.com/franchiseopportunities/index.html, accessed January 16, 2021.

■ **Easier Access to Funding:** Bankers and other lenders may be more willing to lend money if the business is part of an established franchise than if it is a new, unproven business.

### 6-6c  Disadvantages of Franchising

Franchising also has some drawbacks. From the franchisor's perspective, operating a business with perhaps thousands of semi-independent owner–operators can be complex and challenging. With such a large number of owners, it can be difficult to keep all of the franchisees satisfied, and disappointed franchisees sometimes go public with their complaints, damaging the reputation of the franchisor. In fact, it isn't unusual for disgruntled franchisees to sue their franchisors.

Franchisees are also likely to find some disadvantages:

■ **Costs:** The typical franchise agreement requires franchisees to pay an initial franchise fee when they enter into the franchise agreement and an ongoing royalty (usually a percentage of monthly sales revenues) to the franchisor. In addition, the franchisor may assess other fees to support national advertising campaigns or for other purposes. These costs vary considerably, but for high-profile franchises, they can be substantial. Exhibit 6.7 compares the initial franchise fees, initial investment, cash requirements, and ongoing royalties for several well-established franchises. Initial investment reflects the fact that the cost of starting a franchise generally requires the franchisee to invest in property, equipment, and inventory in addition to paying the franchise fee. Cash requirements reflect that additional funds are usually needed to start and grow business at a new franchise location. In other words, the actual total investment that franchisees make is often substantially higher than "initial" fees and investments.

■ **Lack of Control:** The franchise agreement usually requires the franchisee to follow the franchisor's procedures to the letter. People who want the freedom and flexibility to be their own boss can find these restrictions frustrating.

■ **Negative Halo Effect:** The irresponsible or incompetent behavior of a few franchisees can create a negative perception that adversely affects not only the franchise as a whole but also the success of other franchisees.

■ **Growth Challenges:** While growth and expansion are definitely possible in franchising (many franchisees own multiple outlets), strings are attached. Franchise agreements usually limit the franchisee's territory and require franchisor approval before expanding into other areas.

> "In business for yourself, not by yourself."
>
> —Ray Kroc, founder, McDonald's Restaurants

# What Happens When Franchisees Disagree With Franchisors?

One of the biggest challenges in franchising is keeping franchisees satisfied. Disappointed franchisees sometimes go public with their complaints or sue the franchisor. Here are three instances in which franchisees and franchisors disagreed.

**7-Eleven Plays Hardball.** Mitoshi Matsumoto owns a 7-Eleven franchise in Japan where 7-Eleven convenience stores must be open 24 hours a day, 365 days a year. Matsumoto, whose wife died two years ago, worked daily 14-hour shifts, even after his son came home from college to help. Japan's shrinking, aging population makes it difficult to hire staff. For his health and sanity, he reduced his store hours to 6 a.m. to 1 a.m., even after 7-Eleven informed him that doing so would result in a $155,000 breach of contract penalty. So, when Matsumoto then decided to close for New Year's Day, one of Japan's national holidays, 7-Eleven played hardball, terminating his franchise "because of customer complaints." 7-Eleven's logistics system immediately stopped daily deliveries, leaving Matsumoto with a mostly empty store. Matsumoto sued, asking Japanese courts to reverse 7-Eleven's decision. A decision has not yet been handed down.

**Domino's Pizza Franchises Band Together in the United Kingdom.** Under most franchise contracts, franchisees are billed for cost increases for supplies, updating and modernizing stores, or new technology, like touchscreen ordering systems. Franchisees push back when franchisors pile on too many cost increases too quickly. Eleven of Domino's Pizza's largest UK franchisees declared "war" when Domino's aggressively raised their prices, forming the Domino's Franchise Association UK & Ireland (DFA UK&I) to consolidate negotiations with the franchisor. DFA UK&I members also objected to corporate's aggressive store opening plans, which hurt sales at existing stores. Domino's CEO admitted to "a period of intense commercial discussions with franchisees," but was "very optimistic of finding a solution."

**Cadillac Gives Dealers a Choice on Electric Vehicles.** GM is transitioning to a future based on electric vehicles (EVs), so it gave its 880 Cadillac dealers a choice: spend $200,000 for charging stations and EV tools, or accept a franchise buyout worth $300,000 to $1 million+. One hundred fifty dealers took the payout to end their Cadillac franchises. Most sold few Cadillacs, but held multiple GM franchises, selling Chevy, Buick, and GMC vehicles, too. With EVs holding just 2% of the market, many dealers were skeptical about their future. South Carolina dealer Claude Burns made the investment, however. As Burns said, "It looks to me like this electric-vehicle market might be fixing to take off. So, I decided I'm going to hang with Cadillac."[62]

Mitoshi Matsumoto stands in front of his 7-Eleven Store in Higashiosaka in Osaka Prefecture, western Japan.

*Kyodo News/Getty Images*

- **Restrictions on Sale:** Franchise agreements normally prevent franchisees from selling their franchises to other investors without prior approval from the franchisor.

**franchise agreement** The contractual arrangement between a franchisor and franchisee that spells out the duties and responsibilities of both parties.

- **Poor Execution:** Not all franchisors live up to their promises. Sometimes the training and support are of poor quality, and sometimes the company does a poor job of screening franchisees, leading to the negative halo effect we mentioned previously.

These considerations suggest that before buying a franchise, potential owners should carefully research the franchise opportunity.

## 6-6d Entering into a Franchise Agreement

To obtain a franchise, the franchisee must sign a **franchise agreement**. This agreement is a legally binding contract that specifies the relationship between the franchisor and the franchisee in great detail. There's no standard form for the contract, but some of the key items normally covered include the following:

- **Terms and Conditions:** The franchisee's rights to use the franchisor's trademarks, patents, and signage, and any restrictions on those rights. It also covers how long the agreement will last and under what terms (and at what cost) it can be renewed.

- **Fees and Other Payments:** The fees the franchisee must pay for the right to use the franchisor's products and methods, and when these payments are due.

- **Training and Support:** The types of training and support the franchisor will provide to the franchisee.

- **Specific Operational Requirements:** The methods and standards established by the franchisor that the franchisee is required to follow.

- **Conflict Resolution:** How the franchisor and franchisee will handle disputes.

- **Assigned Territory:** The geographic area in which the franchisee will operate and whether the franchisee has exclusive rights in that area.

It's vital for anyone thinking about entering into a franchise agreement to know all the facts before signing on the dotted line. Fortunately, the Federal Trade Commission (FTC) requires franchisors to provide potential franchisees with a document known as a **Franchise Disclosure Document (FDD)**. This long, complex document (covering 23 separate major topics and sometimes running well over 100 pages) can be an invaluable source of information about virtually every aspect of the franchise arrangement. For example, the FDD must provide contact information for at least 100 current franchisees. (If the franchisor has fewer than 100 current franchisees, it must list all of them.) This gives a potential franchisee the ability to contact other franchisees and ask them about their experiences with the franchisor. As an added bonus, the FTC requires the FDD to be written in "plain English" rather than in the complex legal jargon that often characterizes such documents. This rule means you actually have a chance to understand what you're reading![63]

Under FTC rules, the franchisor must give the franchisee at least 14 calendar days to review the FDD before the franchise agreement can be signed. A careful study of the FDD can go a long way toward ensuring that the franchisee makes an informed decision. Even though the FDD is written in "plain English," it's a good idea to have a lawyer who is knowledgeable about franchise law review it. You'll have to pay for any legal advice, but entering into a bad franchise agreement can be a lot more expensive (and stressful) than a lawyer's fees.

> **Franchise Disclosure Document (FDD)** A detailed description of all aspects of a franchise that the franchisor must provide to the franchisee at least 14 calendar days before the franchise agreement is signed.

## The Big Picture

This chapter discusses the four major forms of business ownership. Each form of ownership has both advantages and limitations, so no single form of ownership is the best in all situations.

Sole proprietorships are appealing to entrepreneurs who want to start a business quickly, with few formalities or fees, and who want to be their own boss. But sole proprietorships aren't well suited for raising financing from external sources, so growth opportunities are limited. And sole proprietors have unlimited liability for their company's debts and obligations.

General partnerships allow two or more owners to pool financial resources and take advantage of complementary skills. But each owner must assume the risk of unlimited liability, and disagreements among partners can complicate and delay important decisions.

Corporations are more complex and expensive to create than other forms of business. Another potentially serious drawback is the double taxation of earnings. But corporations have the greatest potential for raising financial capital and provide owners with the protection of limited liability.

The limited liability company (LLC) is a relatively new form of business ownership that offers many of the advantages of corporations without as many regulations. One major advantage of LLCs compared to corporations is that its earnings can be taxed as if the company is a partnership, thus avoiding double taxation. But the laws governing limited liability companies vary considerably among states, making it a challenge to operate an LLC in multiple states.

## Careers in Franchising

### Franchise Store Manager

Responsible for running day-to-day retail store operations. Required to open and close the store; manage schedules and productivity; provide world-class customer service; monitor cost control, payroll, and expenses; provide weekly and monthly reports to the franchise owner; recruit, train, and coach employees; and develop and implement store marketing program. Ultimately accountable for profit/loss, continuous improvement, service delivery levels, personnel management, and business development. The ideal candidate has a college degree, a dynamic personality, two years of retail store operations experience, strong management skills, excellent computer knowledge, and is a good listener who can motivate a team and run good meetings.

# 7 | Small Business and Entrepreneurship:
## Economic Rocket Fuel

### Learning Objectives

After studying this chapter, you will be able to:

**7-1** Explain the key reasons to launch a small business

**7-2** Describe the typical entrepreneurial mindset and characteristics

**7-3** Discuss funding options for small business

**7-4** Analyze the opportunities and threats that small businesses face

**7-5** Discuss ways to become a new business owner and tools to facilitate success

**7-6** Explain the size, scope, and economic contributions of small business

**7-1** Launching a New Venture: What's in It for Me?

In the two years prior to the COVID-19 global pandemic, the US economy reported record levels of entrepreneurial activity, which was unsurprising, given the booming economy overall during that time period. Also, unsurprisingly, in the first month of the pandemic, the rate of new business start-ups plummeted in the face of the public health crisis and the economic lockdowns. But after a couple of months, entrepreneurial activity rebounded. By mid-August 2020, there were actually 56% more new business applications than in mid-August 2019, and the strong year-over-year growth continued into early 2021, especially for "high propensity businesses" (likely to have employees). The recovery of entrepreneurship felt staggering to many in the midst of a crisis, but in reality, it represented the resilience and optimism that tend to be characteristic of entrepreneurs.[1]

Looking ahead, many expect the entrepreneurial surge to continue, fueled by the energy and innovation of Generation Z—those born after 1996. Many of these young people were drawn to entrepreneurship at a very young age. According to a recent Gallup poll, 40% of students surveyed from grades five to 12 stated they wanted to run their own business. Then, 24% said they had already started. Many Generation Z entrepreneurs have succeeded via leveraging collaboration, disruption, and mentorship with powerful results.[2]

Starting a new business can be tough—very tough. Yet, for the right person, the advantages of business ownership far outweigh the risk and hard work. Although people start their own ventures for a variety of reasons, most are seeking some combination of greater financial success, independence, flexibility, and challenge. Others are simply seeking survival.

## 7-1a Greater Financial Success

Although you can make a pretty good living working for someone else, your chances of getting really rich may be higher if you start your own business. The *Forbes* magazine annual list of the 400 richest Americans is dominated by **entrepreneurs**, such as Bill Gates and Paul Allen

"If you know too much before the start, then you will get overwhelmed. Come up with an original idea, and don't copy because there will be no passion. You need that otherworldly passion. Just start."

—Jeni Britton Bauer, Founder of Jeni's Splendid Ice Creams

(founders of Microsoft), Oprah Winfrey (founder of Harpo Productions), Phil Knight (founder of Nike), Michael Dell (founder of Dell Inc.), and Sergey Brin and Larry Page (founders of Google). And many people feel that their chances of even moderate financial success are higher if they're working for themselves rather than someone else. The opportunity to make more money is a

**entrepreneurs** People who risk their time, money, and other resources to start and manage a business.

primary motivator for many entrepreneurs, although other factors clearly play a role as well.[3]

## 7-1b Independence

Being your own boss is a huge benefit of starting your own business. You answer to no one other than yourself and any investors whom you invite to participate in your business. Bottom line: You are the only one who is ultimately responsible for your success or failure. This setup is especially compelling for people who have trouble being subordinates because of their personalities (and we probably all know someone who fits that description!). But while independence is nice, it's important to keep in mind that every business depends on meeting the needs of its customers, who can be even more demanding than the toughest boss.

## 7-1c Flexibility

The ability to set your own hours and control your own schedule is a hugely appealing benefit for many business owners, especially parents seeking more time with their kids or retirees looking for extra income. Given current technological tools—from Slack to Zoom—it's easy for

> "You can make money without doing evil."
>
> —Sergey Brin, Co-founder, Google

small business owners to manage their firms on the go or after hours. Of course, there's often a correlation between hours worked and dollars earned. (It's rare to work less and earn more.) But when more money isn't the primary goal, the need for flexibility can be enough to motivate many entrepreneurs to launch their own enterprise.

## 7-1d Challenge

Running your own business provides a level of challenge unmatched by many other endeavors. Most business

> "Help young people. Help small guys. Because small guys will be big. Young people will have the seeds you bury in their minds, and when they grow up, they will change the world."
>
> —Jack Ma, Founder, Alibaba

# Eccentric Entrepreneurs

Do quirky people become entrepreneurs, or does successful entrepreneurship breed quirkiness? Hard to know which comes first, but it's not hard to find quirky entrepreneurs. Some highlights:

- Mark Zuckerberg, founder of Facebook, personally butchered all the animals he ate in 2011.

- Sandy Lerner, co-founder of both Cisco Systems and Urban Decay, enjoys jousting so much that she breeds her own horses, owns Elizabethan costumes, and has allegedly read Jane Austin's *Persuasion* more than 60 times.

- Automobile tycoon Henry Ford ate weeds from his garden, and even ate sandwiches filled with weeds.

- Dustin Moscovitz, Zuckerberg's college roommate at Harvard and Facebook's third employee, still rides his bicycle to work despite being the world's youngest billionaire at age 29.

- Marc Andreessen, founder of Netscape, blogs in his underwear.

- David Karp, CEO of Tumblr, prides himself on ignoring email.

- Paul Graham, founder of Y Combinator, wrote an essay titled "Why Nerds Are Unpopular."

- Co-founder of Apple, Steve Jobs, would eat only one type of food, such as carrots or apples, for weeks at a time. He

reportedly ate so many carrots at one time that his skin turned bright orange. Jobs also believed that his restrictive, vegan diet meant that his body was free from body odor and allowed him to bathe only once per week.

- John Harvey Kellogg (pictured), founder of the cereal empire, began his career as a medical doctor, and was once the chief physician at the Western Health Reform Institute of Battle Creek, where he argued that people should have yogurt enemas on a daily basis. Perhaps we should all be thankful that his corn flakes went mainstream, rather than his other ideas about health.

So, if you're a quirky individual, you may want to consider nurturing your quirks, not hiding them. Who knows? Even if you're not the world's next billionaire, your quirks may give you a common interest with them, which could ultimately land you a great job![4]

AP Images

owners—especially new business owners—never find themselves bored! Starting a business also offers endless opportunities for learning that can provide more profound satisfaction for many people than grinding out the hours as an employee.

### 7-1e Survival

Although most entrepreneurs launch their business in response to an opportunity with hopes of improving their lives, some entrepreneurs—called "necessity entrepreneurs"—launch their business because they believe it is their *only* economic option. Necessity entrepreneurs range from middle-aged workers laid off from corporate jobs, to ex-convicts, to those who experience discrimination in the standard workplace. For each of these types of people, small business ownership can be the right choice in the face of few other alternatives.

## 7-2 The Entrepreneur: A Distinctive Profile

Successful entrepreneurs tend to stand out from the crowd in terms of both their mindset and their personal characteristics. As you read this section, consider whether you fit the entrepreneurial profile.

### 7-2a The Entrepreneurial Mindset: A Matter of Attitude

Almost every entrepreneur starts as a small business-person—either launching a firm or buying a firm—but not every small businessperson starts as an entrepreneur. The difference is a matter of attitude. From day one, a true entrepreneur—such as Sam Walton of Walmart, Robyn "Rihanna" Fenty of Fenty Beauty, or Jeff Bezos of Amazon—aims to change the world through blockbuster goods or services. That isn't the case for all small business owners. Most people who launch new firms expect to better themselves, but they don't expect huge, transformative growth. In fact, nearly 70% of small business owners say they don't want to grow any larger.[5]

However, classic entrepreneurs who deliver on the promise of their best ideas can dramatically change the economic and social landscape worldwide. Examples of business owners who thought and delivered big include Henry Ford, founder of the Ford Motor Company and originator of assembly line production; Walt Disney, founder of The Walt Disney Company and creator of Mickey Mouse; Mary Kay Ash, founder of a cosmetics powerhouse; Martha Stewart, lifestyle innovator for the masses; Joanna Gaines, co-creator of the *Fixer-Upper* and the Magnolia cable network; and Mark Zuckerberg, founder of Facebook.

## Exhibit 7.1
## Entrepreneurial Characteristics

Vision

Self-Reliance

Energy

Confidence

Tolerance of Uncertainty

Tolerance of Failure

Take A Pix Media/Shutterstock.com

## 7-2b Entrepreneurial Characteristics

While experts sometimes disagree about the specific characteristics of successful entrepreneurs, virtually all include vision, self-reliance, energy, confidence, tolerance of uncertainty, and tolerance of failure (refer to Exhibit 7.1). Most successful entrepreneurs have all of these qualities and more, but they come in a huge variety of combinations that highlight the complexity of personality: there is no one successful entrepreneurial profile.

**Vision** Most entrepreneurs are wildly excited about their own new ideas, which many seem to draw from a bottomless well. Entrepreneurs find new solutions to old problems, and they develop new products that we didn't even know we needed until we had them. And entrepreneurs stay excited about their ideas, even when friends and relatives threaten to call the loony bin. For instance, Fred Smith, founder of the FedEx empire, traces the concept for his business to a term paper he wrote at Yale, which supposedly received a C from a skeptical professor. But that didn't stop him from creating a business logistics system that transformed the industry, and along with UPS, enabled e-commerce to flourish.

**Self-Reliance** As an entrepreneur, the buck stops with you. New business owners typically need to do everything themselves, from getting permits to motivating employees, to keeping the books—all in addition to producing the product or service that made them start the business in the first place. Self-reliance seems to come with an **internal locus of control**, or a deep-seated sense that the individual is personally responsible for what happens in their life. When things go well, people with an internal locus of control feel that their efforts have been validated, and when things go poorly, those same people feel that they need to do better next time. This sense of responsibility encourages positive action. In contrast, people with an **external locus of control** rely less on their own efforts, feeling buffeted by forces such as random luck and the actions of others, which they believe will ultimately control their fate.

**Energy** Entrepreneurs simply can't succeed without an enormous amount of energy. Six or seven 12-hour workdays are not atypical in the start-up phase of running a business. In fact, 61% of small business owners report working six or more days per week, compared to only 22% of workers in the general population. And for small business owners, even a day off isn't *really* off. Only 27% of small business owners define a day off as not working at all, while 57% of small business owners say they always or most of the time work on holidays. But Discover Financial Services also learned that many small business owners seem to find the grind worthwhile: 47% of small business owners said that if they won $10 million in the lottery, they would still work in their current job. Only 9% would stop working, and 8% would combine work, volunteering, and other areas of interest.[6]

**Confidence** Successful entrepreneurs typically have confidence in their own ability to achieve, and their confidence encourages them to act boldly. But too much confidence has a downside. Entrepreneurs must take care not to confuse likelihood with reality. In fact, many could benefit from the old adage "Hope for the best and plan for the worst." A study for the Small Business Administration Office of Advocacy confirmed that entrepreneurs are typically overconfident regarding their own abilities. As a result, they're sometimes willing to plunge into a new business, but they don't always have the skills to succeed.[7]

**Tolerance of Uncertainty** More often than others, entrepreneurs see the world in shades of gray rather than simply black and white. They tend to embrace uncertainty in the business environment, turning it to their advantage rather than shying away. Uncertainty also relates to risk, and successful entrepreneurs tend to more willingly accept risk—financial risk, for instance, such as mortgaging their home for the business, and professional risk, such as staking their reputation on the success of an unproven product.

**Tolerance of Failure** Even when they fail, entrepreneurs seldom label themselves losers. They tend to view failure as a chance to learn rather than as a sign that they just can't do it (whatever "it" may be for them at any given moment). Interestingly, Isaac Fleischmann, director of the U.S. Patent Office for 36 years, pointed out: "During times of economic decline when unemployment increases, so does the

> "A lot of times, people don't know what they want until you show it to them."
>
> —Steve Jobs, Co-founder, Apple

> "To learn to succeed, you must first learn to fail."
>
> —Michael Jordan, Athlete and Entrepreneur

**internal locus of control** A deep-seated sense that the individual is personally responsible for what happens in their life.

**external locus of control** A deep-seated sense that forces other than the individual are responsible for what happens in their life.

number of patents. Dark days often force us to become more ingenious, to monitor and modify the ways we reached failure and reshape them into a new pattern of success." Failure can actually be an effective springboard for achievement.[8]

A surprising number of twentieth-century entrepreneurial stars experienced significant failure in their careers yet bounced back to create wildly successful ventures. Early in his career, for instance, Walt Disney was fired from an ad agency (in hindsight, a rather foolish ad agency) for a "singular lack of drawing ability." Ray Kroc, the man who made McDonald's into a fast-food empire, couldn't make a go of real estate, so he sold milkshake machines for much of his life. He was 52 years old, and in failing health, when he discovered the McDonald brothers' hamburger stand and transformed it into a fast-food empire. Steve Jobs, founder of Apple computer, found himself unceremoniously dumped by his board of directors less than ten years after introducing the world's first personal computer. After another decade, he returned in triumph, restoring Apple's polish with blockbuster new products such as the iPod and the iPhone. And J. K. Rowling, creator of the $15 billion Harry Potter empire, had her initial book rejected by 12 shortsighted publishers. So, the next time you fail, keep your eyes open for opportunity—your failure may be the first step of the next big thing.[9]

## 7-3 Finding the Money: Funding Options for Small Businesses

For many entrepreneurs, finding the money to fund their business is the top challenge of their start-up year. The vast majority of new firms are funded with the personal resources of their founder. In fact, about 95% of entrepreneurs raise start-up funds from personal accounts, family, and friends. Other key funding sources include bank loans, angel investors, and venture capital firms.[10]

### 7-3a Personal Resources

While the idea of using just your own money to open a business sounds great, and more than three-quarters of small business owners spend their own savings as a source

# Big Lies about Entrepreneurship

There's no shortage of advice about entrepreneurship in the business world. However, that doesn't mean that it's all *good* advice. *Inc.* magazine asked a handful of entrepreneurs and experts to share the biggest whoppers they ever heard about entrepreneurship. Here are some highlights:

- **All you need is a good idea.** "An excellent idea is an important first step, but your business will not take off as a success unless you have a smart strategy and put passionate effort behind it." —*Sherry Harnett, a marketing and leadership consultant, professor, and a judge for Get Started Pensacola 2016*

- **Being an entrepreneur is glamorous.** "Being an entrepreneur is harder than a 9–5 job. You must eat, sleep, and dream it. This ain't for the weary or weak." —*Duncan Kabinu, co-founder of Gainesville Dev Academy, a software training center; and a judge for Get Started Gainesville 2016*

- **Do what you love, and the money will follow.** "No words have ever created more failed entrepreneurs than the notion that just because you love doing something, it will be a successful business and you will make tons of money. In fact, oftentimes, a person's love for doing something becomes a problem because instead of running their business, they just focus on delivering the service they enjoy so much, as the business around them crumbles." —*Topher Morrison, executive director of Key Person*

of Influence, a growth accelerator that has worked with more than 2,000 entrepreneurs

- **Entrepreneurship is a young person's game.** Not always. "Success is much more likely to find a mid-career professional who has identified a market opportunity through their own professional and life experience and has the financial capital and network required to take the risk, assemble the team, and network to advance a new venture." —*Garret Westlake, executive director of the da Vinci Center, a unique collegiate model that advances innovation and entrepreneurship through cross-disciplinary collaboration at Virginia Commonwealth University*

So, as always, don't believe everything you hear. A little extra research may serve you well before you turn your dream into reality.[11]

Billion Photos/Shutterstock.com

of start-up funding,[12] the financial requirements of most new firms typically force entrepreneurs to also tap personal resources such as family, friends, and credit cards. According to the Small Business Administration, more than 64% of total start-up financing comes from personal resources.[13] If you do borrow from family or friends, virtually every small business expert recommends that you keep the relationship as professional as possible. If the business fails, a professional agreement can preserve personal ties. And if the business succeeds, you'll need top-quality documentation of financing from family and friends to get larger-scale backing from outside sources.[14]

Personal credit cards can be an especially handy—though highly risky—financing resource. In fact, a recent survey found that roughly 20% of all start-ups are funded with plastic, and 37% of start-ups founded by those aged 21 to 36 are funded with plastic. (It's no wonder, given that those solicitations just keep on coming.) Credit cards do provide fast, flexible money, and many offer easy approval and the ability to earn points and cash back. But watch out—if you don't pay back your card company fast, you'll find yourself socked with financing fees that can take years to pay off.[15]

### 7-3b Loans

Getting commercial loans for a new venture can be tough. Banks and other lenders are understandably hesitant to fund a business that doesn't have a track record. And when they do, they require a lot of paperwork and often a fairly long waiting period. Given these hurdles, only 16.5% of new business owners launch with commercial loans.[16] And virtually no conventional lending source—private or government—will lend 100% of the start-up dollars for a new business. Most require that the entrepreneur provide a minimum of 25% to 30% of total start-up costs from personal resources.[17]

Another source for loans may be the U.S. Small Business Administration (SBA). The SBA doesn't give free money to start-up businesses—neither grants nor interest-free loans—but it does partially guarantee loans from local commercial lenders. This reduces risk for the lenders, who are, in turn, more likely to lend money to a new business owner. The SBA also has a microloan program that lends small amounts of money—$13,000 on average—to start-up businesses through community nonprofit organizations.[18]

Peer-to-peer lending offers yet another potential funding source for new business start-ups. Websites such as Prosper.com and LendingClub.com bring together borrowers and investors so that both can benefit financially. Many entrepreneurs have found this is an easier way to get money, at more favorable terms, than through more-established sources.

### 7-3c Crowdfunding

Crowdfunding is the process of funding ventures by raising money from a large number of investors via the internet. Crowdfunding began to appear in the mid-2000s, and quickly gained traction, becoming a $14 billion funding source by 2019. Experts anticipate that global crowdfunding could grow to nearly $29 billion by 2025.[19] Many crowdfunding sites are used to fund nonprofits. The largest crowdfunding sites in terms of traffic are gofundme.com, kickstarter.com, and indiegogo.com. Two examples of big

## Online Dating Is Better than Ever... Thanks to Bumble Founder Whitney Wolfe Herd

Bumble went public in early 2021, making 31-year-old Whitney Wolfe Herd the newest member of a rarefied club of self-made female billionaires. Wolfe Herd, who began her career at Tinder, initially intended Bumble to be a "female-only social network for women to send each other compliments," but the app evolved into a popular dating service where women make the first move. Bumble aggressively works to eliminate sexual aggression, harassment, ghosting, and other issues endemic to the online dating world. Bumble has become the second-most-popular dating app in the United States with the help of inspiring ads such as: "Be the CEO your parents always wanted you to marry." Big picture, Wolfe Herd hopes to "empower women to make the first move in every area of their lives."[20]

The Washington Post/Getty Images

crowdfunding successes are (1) the Pebble smart watch, which raised $1 million in just 28 hours and eventually went on to raise more than $10 million, and (2) SkyBell, the smart video doorbell, which sends live video of a homeowner's front door to their smartphone, raised $600,000 in a 30-day campaign on Indiegogo. Since then, the doorbell has become one of the most popular smart home products on the market, and the business ranks as one of the most successful crowdfunded companies of all time.[21]

> "If people are doubting how far you can go, go so far you can't hear them anymore."
>
> —Michelle Ruiz, Entrepreneur

Center for Venture Research anticipates that angels will respond to the economic fallout from the COVID-19 global pandemic by consolidating their resources in support for their current portfolios rather than seeking an abundance of newer, higher risk early-stage start-ups. They point out that "any potential decline of the foundational, and critical seed and start-up financing provided by angel investors could lead to significant, and lasting, repercussions throughout the risk capital ecosystem."[22, 23]

### 7-3d Angel Investors

**Angel investors** aren't as saintly—or as flighty—as they sound. They are wealthy individuals who invest in promising start-up companies for one basic reason: to make money for themselves. According to Jeffrey Sohl, director of the Center for Venture Research, angels look for companies that seem likely to grow at 30% to 40% per year and will then either be bought or go public. He estimates that 10% to 15% of private companies fit that description, but points out that finding those firms isn't easy. It doesn't help, he says, that "80% of entrepreneurs think they're in that 10% to 15%." The

### 7-3e Venture Capital

**Venture capital firms** fund high-potential, new companies in exchange for a share of ownership, which can sometimes be as high as 60%. These deals tend to be quite visible, but keep in mind that only a tiny fraction of new businesses receive any venture capital money.

**angel investors** Individuals who invest in start-up companies with high growth potential in exchange for a share of ownership.

**venture capital firms** Companies that invest in start-up businesses with high growth potential in exchange for a share of ownership.

## Diversity Making a Difference

Diversity in the workplace is a hot topic. And it should be: the data is clear—businesses with diverse workforces outperform their peers on virtually every business metric. Yet according to research done by Silicon Valley Bank, only 26% of start-ups are making deliberate efforts to improve diversity among their leadership teams. This lack represents a significant unmined asset in at least three ways:

- *Broader vision*: Typical entrepreneurs attract and hire people who are similar to them—maybe mostly people they already know, or who are even part of their family. Clearly, this can lead to a shortage of perspectives that are different from those of the founder—and the more different perspectives, the smarter the decision-making. According to product development specialist, Maxim Savelyev, "Listening to underrepresented voices highlights concerns and issues that others tend to ignore, and that creates opportunity. For start-ups, this could mean gaining the inside track on a new market that others have missed."

- *International opportunity*: Start-ups with geographic and cultural diversity can open windows to international markets that start-up may not have considered without that talent onboard, creating a powerful competitive advantage.

- *Greater innovation*: By surrounding the leadership team with people from a wide variety of backgrounds, start-ups can unleash the best in everyone, which ultimately leads to innovation and out-of-the-box thinking.

Diversity is not a fad. It's a potential competitive edge that too many start-ups fail to hone. By actively pursuing diversity, start-ups will benefit from fresh ideas and perspectives that can help them both achieve their goals. With more diverse leadership teams, start-ups may also gain access to capital sources that value diversity. [24]

Vitalii Vodolazskyi/Shutterstock.com

The advice and guidance that come with the dollars can also be quite significant. David Barger, former chief executive officer of JetBlue Airways, remembers that he and JetBlue's founder, David Neeleman, originally planned to call the airline Taxi and to fly bright yellow planes. But an influential venture capitalist changed their minds. He called them into his office and said, "If you call this airline Taxi, we're not going to invest." The name changed, and the venture capitalist stayed.[25]

## 7-4 Opportunities and Threats for Small Business: A Two-Sided Coin

Most small businesses enjoy a number of advantages as they compete for customers. But they also must defuse a range of daunting potential threats to succeed over the long term.

### 7-4a Small Business Opportunities

Small businesses enjoy a real competitive edge across a range of different areas. Because of their size, many small firms can exploit narrow but profitable **market niches**, offer personal customer service, and maintain lower overhead costs. And due to advances in technology, small firms can compete more effectively than ever in both global and domestic markets.

**Market Niches** Many small firms are uniquely positioned to exploit market niches. These sparsely occupied spaces in the market tend to have fewer competitors because they simply aren't big enough— or high-profile enough—for large firms. They nonetheless offer more than enough potential for small, specialized companies. For example, Kazoo & Company, a relatively small toy store, competes effectively with Walmart, Target, and Kmart by stocking different—and complementary—products, deliberately zigging when the big players zag.[26]

**Personal Customer Service** With a smaller customer base, small firms can develop much more personal relationships with individual customers. Shel Weinstein, for instance, former owner of a Los Angeles corner pharmacy, knew his customers so well that they would call him at home in the middle of the night for help with medical emergencies. The personal touch can be especially beneficial in some foreign markets, where clients prize the chance to deal directly with top management.

**market niche** A small segment of a market with fewer competitors than the market as a whole. Market niches tend to be quite attractive to small firms.

Founded in 2015 by entrepreneur Sky White, Wendigo Tea Co. offers imperial-grade loose-leaf teas named after mythic beasts like Bigfoot and Nessy (the Loch Ness Monster). Wendigo uses branding and marketing strategies modeled after the craft beer industry to reach the market niche of young, hip tea drinkers.

**Lower Overhead Costs** With entrepreneurs wearing so many hats, from CEO to customer service rep, many small firms have lower overhead costs. They can hire fewer managers and fewer specialized employees. Perhaps more importantly, smaller firms—due to a lack of resources—tend to work around costs with tactics such as establishing headquarters in the owner's garage or offering employees flexible schedules instead of costly healthcare benefits. Apple, for instance, was famously launched in Steve Job's parents' garage.

**Technology** The internet has played a powerful role in opening new opportunities for small businesses. Using a wealth of online tools, from eBay to eMachineshop, companies-of-one can create, sell, publish, and even manufacture goods and services more easily than ever before. The internet has also created international opportunities, transforming small businesses into global marketers. The London-based Anything Left-Handed retail store, for instance, evolved into an award-winning global wholesaler of left-handed items within a year of launching its website. Founder Keith Milsom comments that "our website has allowed us to communicate with potential customers and market our business worldwide at very little cost, making international development possible."[27]

### 7-4b Small Business Threats

While small businesses do enjoy some advantages, they also face intimidating obstacles, from a high risk of failure to too much regulation.

**High Risk of Failure** Starting a new business involves risk—a lot of risk—but the odds improve significantly if you make it past the first five years. Check out the ten-year survival rate in Exhibit 7.2. Notice that it declines much more slowly in Years 7–10. Not surprisingly, new research also shows that the five-year survival rate depends fairly heavily on the industry, ranging from 51.3% at the high end for manufacturing to 36.4% at the low end for construction, as illustrated in Exhibit 7.3. So clearly, it pays to choose your industry carefully when you launch a new business.

Even though these numbers may look daunting, it's important to remember that owners shut down their businesses for many reasons other than the failure of the firm itself. The possibilities include poor health, divorce, better opportunities elsewhere, and interestingly, an unwillingness to make the enormous time commitment of running a business. Small business expert David Birch jokingly calls this last reason—which is remarkably common—the "I had no idea!" syndrome. It highlights the importance of anticipating what you're in for *before* you open your doors.[28]

**Lack of Knowledge and Experience** People typically launch businesses because they either have expertise in a particular area—such as designing websites or cooking Vietnamese food—or because they have a breakthrough idea—such as a new way to develop computer chips or run an airline. But in-depth knowledge in a specific area doesn't necessarily mean expertise in running

| Exhibit 7.3 | New Business Four-Year Survival Rates by Industry |
|---|---|
| Finance, Insurance, and Real Estate | 58% |
| Education and Health | 56% |
| Agriculture | 56% |
| Services | 55% |
| Wholesale | 54% |
| Mining | 51% |
| Manufacturing | 49% |
| Construction | 47% |

Source: Here Are the Startup Failure Rates by Industry, by Kristin Pryor, January 12, 2016, Tech.co website, http://tech.co/startup-failure-rates-industry-2016-01, accessed May 18, 2016.

a business. Successful business owners must know everything from finance to human resources, to marketing.

**Too Little Money** The media are filled with stories of business owners who made it on a shoestring, but lack of start-up money is a major issue for most new firms. Ongoing profits don't usually begin for a while, which means that entrepreneurs must plan on some lean months—or even years—as the business develops momentum. That means a real need to manage money wisely and to resist the temptation to invest in fixed assets, such as fancy offices and advanced electronics, before sufficient regular income warrants it. It also requires the nerve to stay the course despite initial losses.[29]

**Bigger Regulatory Burden** Complying with federal regulations can be challenging for any business, but it can be downright overwhelming for small firms. But relief may be on the way: Congress continues to examine ways to reduce the growing regulatory burden on small businesses—an urgent need in the face of the struggling economy.[30]

**Higher Health Insurance Costs** Administrative costs for small health plans are much higher than for large businesses, making it even tougher for small firms to offer coverage to their employees. Given skyrocketing healthcare costs in general, the best employees are likely to demand a great insurance plan, putting small business at a real disadvantage in terms of building a competitive workforce. But this may all change as Republicans and Democrats struggle to enact their own versions of healthcare reform. Currently, under the Affordable Care Act, all but the very smallest businesses are required to offer "affordable" health insurance to their full-time employees. Navigating the complexities of constantly changing legislation has been a significant challenge for many small business owners. However, they may

| Exhibit 7.2 | New Business Survival Rates | |
|---|---|---|
| **Year in Business** | **Survival Rate** | **Change vs. Prior Year (percentage points)** |
| Year 1 | 100.0% | — |
| Year 2 | 78% | −22 |
| Year 3 | 66% | −12 |
| Year 4 | 56% | −10 |
| Year 5 | 50% | −6 |
| Year 6 | 45% | −5 |
| Year 7 | 42% | −3 |
| Year 8 | 40% | −2 |
| Year 9 | 37% | −3 |
| Year 10 | 35% | −2 |

Source: Entrepreneurship and the U.S. Economy, Bureau of Labor Statistics website, http://www.bls.gov/bdm/entrepreneurship/bdm_chart3.htm, accessed May 18, 2016.

find the whole ordeal worth it if they come out the other side being able to offer their workers top-quality health insurance at competitive rates.[31]

**7-5 Launch Options: Reviewing the Pros and Cons**

When you imagine starting a new business, the first thought that comes to mind would probably be the process of developing your own big idea from an abstract concept to a thriving enterprise. But that's not the only option. In fact, it may make more sense to purchase an established business, or even buy a franchise such as a Pizza Hut or Subway restaurant. Each choice, of course, involves pros and cons. The trick is finding the best fit for you: the combination that offers you the least harmful downsides and the most meaningful upsides. Broadly speaking, it's less risky to buy an established business or franchise, but it can be more satisfying to start from scratch. Exhibit 7.4 offers a more detailed overview of the pros and cons.

**Small Business Administration (SBA)** An agency of the federal government designed to maintain and strengthen the nation's economy by aiding, counseling, assisting, and protecting the interests of small businesses.

**7-5a Making It Happen: Tools for Business Success**

Whatever way you choose to become a small business owner, several strategies can help you succeed over the long term: gain experience in your field, learn from others, educate yourself, access **Small Business Administration (SBA)** resources, and develop a business plan.

**Gain Experience** Getting roughly three years of experience working for someone else in the field that interests you is a good rule of thumb. That way, you can learn what does and doesn't fly in your industry with relatively low personal risk (and you'd be making any mistakes on someone else's dime). You can also start developing a

**Exhibit 7.4  Pros and Cons of Starting a Business from Scratch versus Buying an Established Business**

**Starting Your Business from Scratch**

| Key Pros | Key Cons |
|---|---|
| It's all *you*: your concept, your decisions, your structure, and so on. | It's all *you*. That's a lot of pressure. |
| You don't have to deal with the prior owner's bad decisions. | It takes time, money, and sheer sweat equity to build a customer base. |
| | Without a track record, it's harder to get credit from both lenders and suppliers. |
| | From securing permits to hiring employees, the logistics of starting a business can be challenging. |

**Buying an Established Business**

| Key Pros | Key Cons |
|---|---|
| The concept, organizational structure, and operating practices are already in place. | Working with someone else's idea can be a lot less fun for some entrepreneurs. |
| Relationships with customers, suppliers, and other stakeholders are established. | You may inherit old mistakes that can range from poor employee relations to pending lawsuits. |
| Getting financing and credit is less challenging. | |

**Buying a Franchise**

| Key Pros | Key Cons |
|---|---|
| In most cases, you're buying your own piece of a well-known brand and proven way of doing business. | You have less opportunity for creativity since most agreements tie you to franchise requirements. |
| Typically, management expertise and consulting come with the franchise package. | If something goes wrong with the national brand (e.g., *E. coli* at a burger joint), your business will suffer, too. |
| Franchisors occasionally offer not just advice but also the financing that can make the purchase possible. | The initial purchase price can be steep, and that doesn't include the ongoing percent-of-sales royalty fee. |
| These advantages add up to a very low 5% first-year failure rate. | |

Source: Five Reasons Why Franchises Flop, by Steve Strauss, February 28, 2005, USA Today Money website, http://www.usatoday.com/money/smallbusiness/columnist/strauss/2005-02-28-franchise_x.htm.

vibrant, relevant network before you need to ask for favors. But if you stay much longer than three years, you may get too comfortable to take the plunge and launch your own venture.

**Learn from Others** You should actively seek opportunities to learn from people who've succeeded in your field. If you don't know anyone personally, use your network to get introductions. And don't forget industry associations, local events, and other opportunities to build relationships. Also, remember that people who failed in your field may be able to give you valuable insights (why make the same mistakes they did?). As a bonus, they may be more willing to share their ideas and their gaffes if they're no longer struggling to develop a business of their own.

**Educate Yourself** The opportunities for entrepreneurial learning have exploded in the past decade. Many colleges and universities now offer full-blown entrepreneurship programs that help students both develop their plans and secure their initial funding. But education shouldn't stop there. Seek out relevant press articles, workshops, websites, and blogs so that your ongoing education will continue to boost your career.

**Access SBA Resources** The SBA offers a number of resources beyond money (which we'll discuss in the next section). The SBA website, www.sba.gov, provides a wealth of information from industry-specific statistics, to general trends, to updates on small business regulations.

> More than 30% of the richest people in the world do not have a college degree, but 57% of those who start a business in high-income countries do have a college degree.
>
> —Global Entrepreneurship Monitor and Forbes

The SBA also works hand in hand with individual states to fund local **Small Business Development Centers (SBDCs)**. SBDCs provide a range of free services for small businesses, from developing your concept to consulting on your business plan, to helping with your loan applications. And the SBA supports **SCORE**, the **Service Corps of Retired Executives**, at www .score.org. They provide free, comprehensive counseling for small businesses from qualified volunteers.

**Develop a Business Plan** Can a business succeed without a plan? Of course. Many do just fine by simply seizing opportunity as it arises, and changing direction as needed. Some achieve significant growth without a plan. But a **business plan** does provide an invaluable way to keep you and your team focused on success. And it's absolutely crucial for obtaining outside funding, which is why many entrepreneurs write a business plan after they've used personal funding sources (such as savings, credit cards, and money from family and friends) to get themselves up and running. Even then, the plan may be continually in flux if the industry is rapidly changing.

An effective business plan, which is usually 25 to 50 pages long, takes about six months to write. While the specifics may change by industry, the basic elements of any business plan answer these core questions:

- What service or product does your business provide, and what needs does it fill?

- Who are the potential customers for your product or service, and why will they purchase it from you?

- How will you reach your potential customers?

- Where will you get the financial resources to start your business?

- When can you expect to achieve profitability?

A business plan can help entrepreneurs stay focused.

Rawpixel.com/Shutterstock.com

**Small Business Development Centers (SBDCs)** Local offices—affiliated with the Small Business Administration—that provide comprehensive management assistance to current and prospective small business owners.

**SCORE (Service Corps of Retired Executives)** An organization—affiliated with the Small Business Administration—that provides free, comprehensive business counseling for small business owners from qualified volunteers.

**business plan** A formal document that describes a business concept, outlines core business objectives, and details strategies and timelines for achieving those objectives.

The final document should include all of the following information:

- Executive summary (two to three pages)

- Description of business (include both risks and opportunities)

- Marketing

- Competition (don't underestimate the challenge)

- Operating procedures

- Personnel

- Complete financial data and plan, including sources of start-up money (be realistic!)

- Appendix (be sure to include all your research on your industry)[33]

Check out the SBA business-planning site for more information on how to write your own business plan and for samples of actual business plans (https://www.sba.gov/business-guide). Other excellent resources (among many) on the internet include the sample business plan resource center (www.bplans.com) and the business plan pages of AllBusiness.com (www.allbusiness.com).

## 7-6 Small Business and the Economy: An Outsized Impact

The most successful entrepreneurs create goods and services that change the way people live. Many build blockbuster corporations that power the stock market and dominate pop culture through ubiquitous promotion. But small businesses—despite their lower profile—also play a vital role in the U.S. economy. Here are a few statistics from the U.S. Small Business Administration:

- Small businesses comprise 99.9% of all businesses in the United States

- Small businesses account for 47.1% of all private sector employees.

- Yet the opening of new businesses has accounted for over 65% of net new jobs in the U.S. economy over the past two decades.

The statistics, of course, depend on the definition of small business. For research purposes, the SBA defines small business as companies with up to 500 employees, including the self-employed. But the SBA also points out that the meaning of small business differs across industries. To officially count as "small," the number of employees can range from fewer than 100 to 1,500, and the average revenue can range from $0.75 million to $28.5 million, depending on the type of business. But regardless of the specific definition, the fact is clear: small business is a big player in the U.S. economy.[34]

Beyond the sheer value of the goods and services they generate, small businesses make a powerful contribution to the U.S. economy in terms of creating new jobs, fueling innovation, and vitalizing inner cities.

- Creating New Jobs: Small businesses with employees start up at a rate of about 600,000 per year. Five years after they launch, about half of those businesses—and many of the jobs they create—remain viable. But while small businesses are quick to add new jobs, they're often the first to contract

Chaay_Tee/Shutterstock.com

when times are tough; instability comes with the territory.[35]

- Fueling Innovation: Small businesses are much more likely to develop revolutionary new ideas. Small patenting firms produce about 16 times more patents per employee than their large-firm counterparts, and those patents are twice as likely to be found among the top 1% of highest-impact patents. Small firms tend to be effective innovators for a number of reasons. Perhaps most importantly, their very reason for being often ties to a brand-new idea. In the early years, they need innovation to simply survive. And they often display a refreshing lack of bureaucracy that allows new thinking to take hold.[36]

- Vitalizing Inner Cities: Research shows that small businesses are the backbone of urban economies, finding opportunity in niches that may not be worthwhile for larger firms. Small business comprises more than 99% of inner-city business establishments. In addition to creating new jobs, these small businesses generate 80% of total employment in American inner cities, providing a springboard for economic development.[37]

### 7-6a  Entrepreneurship around the World

Research suggests that entrepreneurship has an economic impact in countries around the world. Societies need entrepreneurs to ensure that new ideas actualize and to ensure that people are able to self-employ when their economy does not provide for their basic needs. For more than 20 years, the Global Entrepreneurship Monitor (GEM) has measured the annual rate of new business start-ups across a range of countries across the globe. The 21st annual GEM study included 50 economies. According to GEM, the most effective way to evaluate entrepreneurship levels is by phase. A country's total early-phase entrepreneurship rate includes the percentage of adults who have been running their own business from three months to 3.5 years. The current entrepreneurship rate varies dramatically from country to country, ranging from a low of less than 4% in Italy and Pakistan, while more than one in three adults are starting and running their own business in Chile and Ecuador. The differences among countries seem to depend largely on several key factors: What is the national per capita income? What will the entrepreneur need to give up (i.e., the opportunity costs)? How much competition is there? How high is the risk of failure? How strongly do the national culture and political environment support business start-ups?[38]

**Per Capita Income**  In lower-income countries, such as China and Chile, a high percentage of entrepreneurs start their own businesses because they simply have no other options. This contributes heavily to the startlingly high overall level of entrepreneurship. The rate of such "necessity entrepreneurship" declines in higher-income countries, such as the United States and Japan, where entrepreneurs are more likely to strike out on their own in response to an opportunity that they spot in the marketplace.

**Opportunity Costs**  Entrepreneurship rates are significantly lower in countries that provide a high level of employment protection (it's hard to get fired) and strong unemployment insurance (financial support if you do get fired). With these benefits in place, the sense of urgency regarding entrepreneurship tends to fall, in part because fear of failure is much lower. The European Union provides a number of clear examples.

**Cultural/Political Environment**  Extensive, complex regulations can hinder entrepreneurship by raising daunting barriers. And a lack of cultural support only compounds the problem. These factors certainly contribute to the relatively low entrepreneurship rates in much of the European Union and Japan. Entrepreneurs in more supportive nations such as the United States and New Zealand get a boost from limited regulation and strong governmental support. A thriving "cowboy culture" helps, too—standout individuals who break free of old ways attract attention and admiration in many of the countries with higher entrepreneurship rates.[39]

Successful entrepreneurs need more than simply a great idea. Bringing that idea to market—and earning a profit in the process—requires deep knowledge of every area of business. Finding money, attracting customers, and absorbing risk are only some of the challenges. But for the right person, the payoff can be huge in terms of everything from financial success to scheduling flexibility. The key is finding something you love to do that offers value to others. While that doesn't guarantee success, building on a passion suggests that you'll at least enjoy the journey. Looking forward from the global economic crisis, entrepreneurship seems likely to become a way of life, either part-time or full-time, for a growing swath of the population. The ideal result would be a higher standard of living—and a higher quality of life—for business owners and their customers worldwide.

## Careers in Entrepreneurship

### Clothing Company Founder

Design unique items that appeal to young people via innovative styles, attention-grabbing slogans, and distinctive fabrics. Build relationships with business funders. Oversee suppliers to ensure timely order delivery and ethical manufacturing practices. Build solid base of retail accounts. Develop a creative social media marketing campaign to boost sales. Meet profitability goals every quarter.

# 8 Accounting:
## Decision Making by the Numbers

## Learning Objectives
After studying this chapter, you will be able to:

**8-1** Describe the role of accounting in business and how accounting information is used by various stakeholders

**8-2** Identify the purposes and goals of generally accepted accounting principles

**8-3** Describe the key elements of the major financial statements

**8-4** Describe several methods stakeholders can use to obtain useful insights from a company's financial statements

**8-5** Explain how the budget process can help managers plan, motivate, and evaluate their organization's performance

**8-6** Discuss the role of managerial accounting and the various cost concepts identified by managerial accountants

## 8-1 Accounting: Who Needs It—and Who Does It?

**Accounting,** the "language of business," is a system for recognizing, organizing, analyzing, and reporting information about the financial transactions that affect an organization. The goal of this system is to provide relevant, timely information that helps its users make better economic decisions. Let's examine the business stakeholders who use accounting information and the dire consequences that occur when that information can't be trusted.

### 8-1a Accounting: Who Uses It?

**accounting** A system for recognizing, organizing, analyzing, and reporting information about the financial transactions that affect an organization.

Key users of accounting information include:

■ Managers: Marketing managers, for instance, need information about sales in various regions and for various product lines. Financial managers need up-to-date facts about debt, cash, inventory, and capital. Patisserie Holdings, the parent company of the UK café chain Patisserie Valerie, once valued at $750 million, was stunned to find that instead of $38 million in cash in Patisserie Valerie's bank accounts, there was $15 million in bank overdrafts. Forensic accountants subsequently uncovered

"thousands of false entries into the company's ledgers."[1]

- Stockholders: As owners of the company, most stockholders have a keen interest in its financial performance, especially as indicated by the firm's financial statements. Has management generated a strong-enough return on their investment? How profitable is the business? Should I invest more money in this company or not? Patisserie Valerie's accounting fraud not only wiped out initial investors, it also destroyed the investments of shareholders who (in exchange for new shares of stock) gave the firm an *additional* $20 million to save the company *after* the accounting fraud became public. Laith Khalaf, a senior analyst at Hargreaves Lansdown, the UK's largest savings and investment firm, said "It's one thing to see a company's shares wiped out by poor trading conditions, or even bad management decisions, it's quite another to see your investment disappear as a result of fraudulent activity."[2]

> "The pen is mightier than the sword, but no match for the accountant."
>
> —Jonathan Glancey, British Journalist

- Employees: Strong financial performance would help employees make their case for nice pay raises and hefty bonuses. But if earnings drop—especially multiple times—layoffs might be in the offing, so many employees might decide to polish their résumés! If you were one of the 3,000 employees at Patisserie Valerie's 200 UK restaurants, wouldn't you have wanted to know the company's real financial situation?[3] Especially since laid off employees were *not* paid for their last month of work.[4]

- Creditors: The late, great comedian Bob Hope once defined a bank as a place that would only lend you money if you could prove you didn't really need it. That's a bit of an exaggeration, but it is true that before granting a loan, responsible bankers and other lenders want to assess a firm's creditworthiness by looking at its financial statements. After the accounting fraud was identified, Patisserie Valerie's bankers refused to renew its bank loans, forcing the company into "administration," which is similar to "Chapter 11 bankruptcy/reorganization" in the United States. This meant bringing in a new accounting firm to examine its books, settling with creditors, reorganizing finances, and closing 70 restaurants.[5]

- Suppliers: Like bankers, companies that provide supplies want to know that the company can pay for the orders it places. Matt Scaife, of Causeway Capital, a turnaround fund that eventually bought Patisserie Valerie out of administration for just $17 million, explained that "They had a really, really long list of small suppliers that they had stretched terms on and that they weren't paying because they didn't have the money to do it. There was a whole team whose job it was to stretch creditors and as a result the pricing [from suppliers] wasn't great because they'd stretched the payment terms."[6]

- Government agencies: Accurate accounting information is critical for meeting the reporting requirements of the Internal Revenue Service (IRS), the Securities and Exchange Commission (SEC), and other federal and state agencies. The UK's Serious Fraud Office "is conducting a criminal investigation into the business and accounting practices of individuals associated with Patisserie Holdings PLC. Several arrests have been made in relation to this investigation, including one re-arrest."[7] Likewise, the firm's accountants, Grant Thornton, are being sued for $250 million for being "negligent in the preparation and conduct of… financial statements."[8] Grant Thornton strongly contested the lawsuit, responding that, "We will rigorously defend the claim. Patisserie Valerie is a case that involves sustained and collusive fraud, including widespread deception of the [Grant Thornton] auditors. The claim ignores the board's and management's own failings."[9]

A number of other groups—including the news media, competitors, and unions—also have a real interest in a firm's accounting information—whether the firm wants them to have it or not!

If you want to manage, invest in, or work for a business, the ability to understand accounting information is extremely valuable. And, you don't have to be an accountant to speak the "language of business."

### 8-1b Accounting: Who Does It?

Accountants work in a variety of positions to provide all of this information. Let's take a quick look at some of the roles accountants play:

- *Public accountants* provide services such as tax preparation, external auditing (a process we'll describe later in this chapter), and management consulting to clients on a fee basis.

- *Management accountants* work within a company and provide analysis, prepare reports and financial statements, and assist managers in their own organization. *Internal auditors* also work within their organizations to detect internal problems such as waste, mismanagement, embezzlement, and employee theft.

- *Government accountants* perform a variety of accounting functions for local, state, or federal government agencies. Some ensure that the government's own tax revenues and expenditures are recorded and reported in accordance with regulations and requirements. Others work for the IRS to audit tax returns, or for other government agencies such as the SEC, which makes sure investors get accurate and timely information about firms' financial performance, and the Federal Deposit Insurance Corporation (FDIC), which ensures that banks and other financial institutions comply with the rules and regulations governing their behavior.

Many jobs performed by accountants require expertise in complex subject areas. For this reason, accountants who want to move up in their profession often seek certification in a particular field. But achieving such recognition isn't easy. For example, in order to be recognized as a *certified public accountant*, a candidate must complete the equivalent of 150 semester hours (five years) of college education with a heavy emphasis in accounting and other business-related courses; must pass a rigorous two-day, four-part exam (very few candidates pass all four parts on their first try); and must complete at least one year of direct work experience in the field of accounting.[10] Individuals seeking to become *certified management accountants* (who can explain the "why" behind accounting numbers) or *certified fraud examiners* (who help companies detect and deter fraud) must satisfy similar requirements.[11]

## 8-2 Financial Accounting: Intended for Those on the Outside Looking in

**Financial accounting** is the branch of accounting that addresses the needs of external stakeholders, including stockholders, creditors, and government regulators. These stakeholders are seldom interested in poring over detailed accounting information about the individual departments or divisions within a company. Instead, they're interested in the financial performance of the firm as a whole. They often want to know how a firm's financial condition has changed over a period of several years.

For example, Exhibit 8.1 shows how, over a three-year period, Netflix's revenue jumped from $15.4 billion to $24.6 billion, while its paid memberships grew from 139 million to nearly 204 million accounts. And while average revenue per member (i.e., per customer account) increased steadily in the United States and Canada, it barely increased in its Europe, Middle East, and Africa markets and declined in its Latin America and Asia-Pacific markets.[12] We return to the importance of examining financial information over several years later in the chapter in Section 8-4c, "Looking for Trends in Comparative Statements."

Investors are also interested in comparing a company's financial results to other firms in the same industry. We examine this in detail in Chapter 9, Section 9-2a, "Using Ratio Analysis to Identify Current Strengths and Weaknesses."

The major output of financial accounting is a set of financial statements, balance sheets (Section 8-3a), income statements (Section 8-3b), and cash flows (Section 8-3c), designed to provide fundamental information about a company's past and future financial performance. But first, let's learn about the rules that guide the use of financial statements and the independent professional group that governs those rules.

### 8-2a Role of the Financial Standards Accounting Board

Imagine how confused and frustrated investors, creditors, and regulators would become if every firm could make its own financial accounting rules as it went along and change them whenever it wanted! To reduce confusion and provide external stakeholders with consistent and accurate financial statements, the

**financial accounting** The branch of accounting that prepares financial statements for use by owners, creditors, suppliers, and other external stakeholders.

### Exhibit 8.1 — Netflix Streaming Revenue and Membership by Region Over Three Years

| Netflix Streaming Revenue and Membership Information by Region (in thousands, except for average revenue per membership) | 2018 | 2019 | 2020 |
|---|---|---|---|
| **United States and Canada (UCAN)** | | | |
| Revenues | $8,281,532.00 | $10,051,208.00 | $11,455,396.00 |
| Paid memberships at end of period | 64.8 million | 67.7 million | 73.9 million |
| Average revenue per membership | $11.16 | $12.57 | $13.32 |
| **Europe, Middle East, and Africa (EMEA)** | | | |
| Revenues | $3,963,707.00 | $5,543,067.00 | $7,772,252.00 |
| Paid memberships at end of period | 37.8 million | 51.8 million | 66.7 million |
| Average revenue per membership | $10.45 | $10.33 | $10.72 |
| **Latin America (LATAM)** | | | |
| Revenues | $2,237,697.00 | $2,795,434.00 | $3,156,727.00 |
| Paid memberships at end of period | 26.1 million | 31.4 million | 37.5 million |
| Average revenue per membership | $8.19 | $8.21 | $7.45 |
| **Asia-Pacific (APAC)** | | | |
| Revenues | $945,816.00 | $1,469,521.00 | $2,372,300.00 |
| Paid memberships at end of period | 10.6 million | 16.2 million | 25.5 million |
| Average revenue per membership | $9.33 | $9.24 | $9.12 |
| Total Revenues | $15,428,752.00 | $19,859,230.00 | $24,756,675.00 |
| Total Paid Memberships | 139.3 million | 167.1 million | 203.7 million |

Adapted from "Q4 2020 Financial Statements: Streaming Revenue and Membership Information by Region," Netflix, January 19, 2021, https://s22.q4cdn.com/959853165/files/doc_financials/2020/q4/Q4'20 -Website-Financials.xlsx, accessed January 22, 2021.

# Accounting Fraud: China's Luckin Coffee Makes Its Own Bad Luck

After opening 2,000 stores in 2018, Luckin Coffee opened 2,500 more in 2019, overtaking Starbucks' 3,600 stores to become China's largest coffee chain. By undercutting Starbucks on price, developing an app for ordering and cashless payment, and promising mobile delivery within 30 minutes, Luckin's ultimate goal was 10,000 stores by 2021.

Thanks to private investors and an IPO to sell stock to the public, Luckin had already raised and burned through $1.8 billion. But in April 2020, Luckin's auditors found "management personnel engaged in fabricated transactions which led to the inflation of the company's income, costs, and expenses." A subsequent internal investigation made public revealed $310 million of fake transactions, half of company sales. Luckin's stock plunged 75%. A second round of public funding worth $2.5 billion dried up. The Nasdaq stock exchange delisted Luckin's stock. Luckin's board of directors fired the CEO and COO, while suspending six others.

So, how do you fake $310 million of coffee sales?

- Hire a Chief Financial Officer, but only make him responsible for cultivating western investors.

- "Sell" tens of millions of dollars of coffee vouchers to fake companies owned by the controlling shareholder and the chair of Luckin's board of directors.

- "Sell" to fake business accounts registered to legitimate cellphone numbers ostensibly associated with companies across China.

According to the *Wall Street Journal*, one such company "bought 960,000 yuan ($134,000) worth of Luckin vouchers in a single order… more than a hundred similar purchases [were made on that fake account] from May to November of 2019."

- Create a fictitious employee to approve $140 million of payments to fake companies for supplies and services that were never received.

- Route fake payments to the CEO for internal approval to avoid rousing the CFO's suspicions.

Luckin survived because it was quick to reveal and take action against accounting fraud. Today, after paying a $180 million SEC fine, and shrinking from 4,500 to 3,900 stores, 60% of its stores are profitable and it has resumed taking franchise applications.[13]

Shutterstock.com

---

accounting profession has adopted a set of **generally accepted accounting principles (GAAP)** that guide the practice of financial accounting. In the United States, the Securities and Exchange Commission (SEC) has the ultimate legal authority to set and enforce accounting standards. In practice, however, the SEC has delegated the responsibility for developing these rules to an independent, private-sector, nonprofit organization known as the **Financial Accounting Standards Board (FASB)**.[14] This board consists of seven members appointed by the Financial Accounting Foundation. Each member serves a five-year term and can be reappointed to serve one additional term. In order to preserve independence and impartiality, the full-time

**generally accepted accounting principles (GAAP)** A set of accounting standards that is used in the preparation of financial statements.

**Financial Accounting Standards Board (FASB)** The private board that establishes the generally accepted accounting principles used in the practice of financial accounting.

> "If my father had hugged me even once, I'd be an accountant right now."
>
> —Ray Romano, Comedian

members are required to sever all ties with any firms or institutions they served prior to joining the board.[15]

Through GAAP, the FASB aims to ensure that financial statements are:

- Relevant: They must contain information that helps the user understand the firm's financial performance and condition.

- Reliable: Companies must provide information that is objective, accurate, and verifiable.

- Consistent: Firms must provide financial statements based on the same core assumptions and procedures

A variety of business stakeholders, managers, stockholders, employees, creditors, suppliers, and government agencies use accounting information.

over time; if a firm introduces any significant changes in how it prepares its financial statements, GAAP requires it to clearly identify and describe these changes so that anyone using those results understands what the non-GAAP numbers mean and how they were calculated.

- Comparable: Companies must present accounting statements in a reasonably standardized way, allowing users to track the firm's financial performance over a period of years and compare its results with those for other firms.

How well do companies adhere to GAAP practices? In 2019, only 3% of S&P 500 companies reported strict GAAP-based results, down significantly from 25% in 2006 and 41% in 1996. The remaining 97% of companies reported what's called "adjusted" or non-GAAP accounting in addition to their GAAP-based results.[16]

So, why does this matter? According to Harvard and MIT researchers, using non-GAAP methods inflates earnings estimates by 15% compared to GAAP calculated earnings![17] Former SEC Chief Accountant Lynn Turner described non-GAAP earnings as including, "everything but the bad stuff."[18]

The problem with non-GAAP accounting is that the numbers may not be relevant, reliable, consistent, or comparable. Andrew Clarke, former CFO of logistics company C.H. Robinson Worldwide, explains, "What one company says is adjusted might be different to what another company says is adjusted. . . . It lends itself to inconsistency. We believe in providing [stockholders] with a [GAAP-based] clean number as to how we perform so that they can make an informed decision."[19]

## 8-2b Ethics in Accounting

Even clear and well-established accounting principles won't result in accurate and reliable information if managers and accountants don't use them. Caterpillar, $580 million; Waste Management, $1.5 billion; Olympus, $1.7 billion; HealthSouth, $2.7 billion; Autonomy, a software company purchased by Hewlett-Packard, $8.8 billion; WorldCom, $11 billion, and the two biggest, Lehman Brothers, $50 billion, and Madoff Investment Securities, $65 billion, are all unfortunate examples of exorbitant accounting fraud where debts were hidden or earnings were wildly overstated. Once their accounting improprieties became known, most of these firms suffered severe financial difficulties.[20]

These scandals have repeatedly served as a wake-up call to the accounting profession that their ethical training and standards needed major improvement. In the wake of the scandals, many state accounting boards passed new ethics-related requirements.

## 8-3 Financial Statements: Read All about Us

One of the major responsibilities of financial accounting is the preparation of three basic financial statements: the balance sheet, income statement, and statement of cash flows. Taken together, these financial statements provide external stakeholders with a broad picture of an organization's financial condition and its recent financial performance. Large corporations with publicly traded stock must provide an annual report containing all three statements to all stockholders. As we learned in Chapter 6, they also file quarterly (10-Q) and annual (10-K) reports with the SEC that contain these three financial statements. Let's take a look at the information that balance sheets, income statements, and statements of cash flows provide.

### 8-3a The Balance Sheet: What We Own and How We Got It

The **balance sheet** summarizes a firm's financial position at a specific point in time. Though the balance sheets of different firms vary in specifics, all of them are organized to reflect the most

> **balance sheet** A financial statement that reports the financial position of a firm by identifying and reporting the value of the firm's assets, liabilities, and owners' equity.

## Exhibit 8.2
## The Balance Sheet for McDonald's Corporation

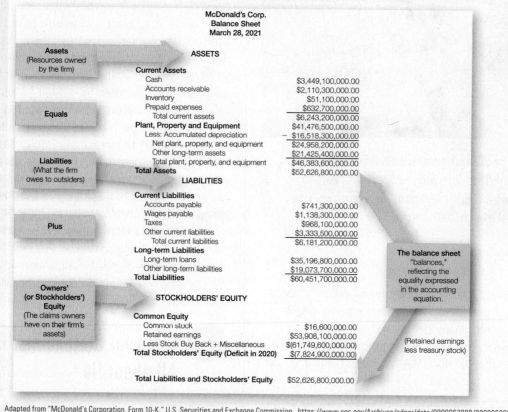

McDonald's Corp.
Balance Sheet
March 28, 2021

**Assets** (Resources owned by the firm)

**ASSETS**

| Current Assets | |
| --- | --- |
| Cash | $3,449,100,000.00 |
| Accounts receivable | $2,110,300,000.00 |
| Inventory | $51,100,000.00 |
| Prepaid expenses | $632,700,000.00 |
| Total current assets | $6,243,200,000.00 |
| Plant, Property and Equipment | $41,476,500,000.00 |
| Less: Accumulated depreciation | − $16,518,300,000.00 |
| Net plant, property, and equipment | $24,958,200,000.00 |
| Other long-term assets | $21,425,400,000.00 |
| Total plant, property, and equipment | $46,383,600,000.00 |
| **Total Assets** | $52,626,800,000.00 |

**Equals**

**Liabilities** (What the firm owes to outsiders)

**LIABILITIES**

| Current Liabilities | |
| --- | --- |
| Accounts payable | $741,300,000.00 |
| Wages payable | $1,138,300,000.00 |
| Taxes | $968,100,000.00 |
| Other current liabilities | $3,333,500,000.00 |
| Total current liabilities | $6,181,200,000.00 |
| Long-term Liabilities | |
| Long-term loans | $35,196,800,000.00 |
| Other long-term liabilities | $19,073,700,000.00 |
| **Total Liabilities** | $60,451,700,000.00 |

**Plus**

The balance sheet "balances," reflecting the equality expressed in the accounting equation.

**Owners'** (or Stockholders') **Equity** (The claims owners have on their firm's assets)

**STOCKHOLDERS' EQUITY**

| Common Equity | |
| --- | --- |
| Common stock | $16,600,000.00 |
| Retained earnings | $53,908,100,000.00 |
| Less Stock Buy Back + Miscellaneous | $(61,749,600,000.00) |
| **Total Stockholders' Equity (Deficit in 2020)** | $(7,824,900,000.00) |

(Retained earnings less treasury stock)

| **Total Liabilities and Stockholders' Equity** | $52,626,800,000.00 |
| --- | --- |

famous equation in all of accounting—so famous that it is usually referred to simply as the **accounting equation**:

Assets = Liabilities + Owners' Equity

Exhibit 8.2 shows a simplified balance sheet for McDonald's Corporation, which we'll use to illustrate the information provided by financial statements. Notice that the three major sectors of this statement reflect the key terms in the accounting equation. Once we've defined each of these terms, we'll explain the logic behind the accounting equation and how the balance sheet illustrates this logic.

- **Assets** are things of value that the firm owns. Balance sheets usually classify assets into at least two major categories. The first category, called *current assets,* consists of cash, $3.449 billion, and other assets that the firm expects to use up or convert

into cash within a year. For example, in McDonald's balance sheet, the value for *accounts receivable,* $2.110 billion, refers to money owed to McDonald's by franchise restaurants who bought its goods on credit. (These receivables are converted into cash when the franchise restaurants pay their bills.) *Inventory*, also a current asset, represents the $51.1 million of burgers, fries, and other foods and ingredients used in McDonald's restaurants. If this strikes you as not very much, you're right. It isn't, because McDonald's never has more than three to four days of inventory on hand in its restaurants. McDonald's has $632.7 million of *prepaid expenses,* such as insurance, or prepaid advertising, that have been paid before they are due.

The other major category of assets on McDonald's balance sheets is *Property, plant, and equipment*. It lists the value, in this case $41.476 billion, of the company's land, buildings, machinery, equipment, and other long-term assets. With the

**accounting equation**
Assets = Liabilities + Owners' Equity

**assets** Resources owned by a firm.

exception of land, these assets have a limited useful life, so accountants subtract *accumulated depreciation,* $16.518 billion, from the original value of these assets (resulting in $24.958 billion in net property, plant, and equipment), to reflect the fact that these assets are being used up over time. McDonald's also has $21.425 billion in other long-term assets.

Though not shown here, some companies list another category of assets, called *intangible assets.* These are assets that have no physical existence—you can't see or touch them—but they still have value. Examples include patents, copyrights, trademarks, and even the goodwill a company develops with its stakeholders. McDonald's trademarks, such as Ronald McDonald and the golden arches, clearly have tremendous value to the company. For more on the growing importance of intangible assets, refer to the boxed feature "Can Intangible Assets Tell Us What Digital Companies Are Worth?"

- **Liabilities** indicate what the firm owes to nonowners—in other words, the claims nonowners have against the firm's assets. Balance sheets usually organize liabilities into two broad categories: current liabilities and long-term liabilities. *Current liabilities,* totaling $6.181 billion for McDonald's, are debts that come due within a year of the date on the balance sheet. McDonald's has, for example, $741.37 million in accounts payable, that is, how much it owes suppliers on credit. Wages payable, $1.138 billion for McDonald's, what the firm owes to workers for work they have already performed, is another current liability, as are taxes, which amount to $968.1 million for McDonald's. *Long-term liabilities* are debts that don't come due until more than a year after the date on the balance sheet. McDonald's has $35.196 billion in long-term loans and $19.073 billion in other long-term liabilities.

- **Owners' (or Stockholders') equity** refers to the claims the owners have against their firm's assets. The specific accounts listed in the owners' equity section of a balance sheet depend on the form of business ownership. As Exhibit 8.2 shows, common stock is a key owners' equity account for corporations. For corporations like McDonald's, the owners' equity section is usually titled *stockholders' equity.* Also notice that retained earnings, which are the accumulated earnings reinvested in the company (rather than paid to owners), are another major components of the owners' equity section. McDonald's has $16.6 million in common stock and $53.908 billion in retained earnings, which are put back into growing and improving the company. McDonald's incurred a $7.824 billion deficit in total stockholders' equity by virtue of cumulative stock buy backs over the years now valued at more than $67 billion. Buying stock back from shareholders

is another way, besides stock dividends (refer to Chapter 9), of returning earnings to shareholders. The cumulative value of these large stock buy backs, which have been a strategic goal for the company, reduced retained earnings by $7.824 billion, and flipped retained earnings from positive to negative.

The logic behind the accounting equation is based on the fact that firms must finance the purchase of their assets, and owners and nonowners are the only two sources of funding. The accounting equation tells us that the value of a firm's assets must equal the amount of financing provided by owners (as measured by owners' equity) plus the amount provided by creditors (as indicated by the firm's liabilities) to purchase those assets. Because a balance sheet is based on this logic, it must *always* be in balance. In other words, the dollar value of the assets *must* equal the dollar value of the liabilities plus owners' equity. This is true for *all* firms, from the smallest sole proprietorship to the largest multinational corporation. Notice in Exhibit 8.2 that the $52.626 billion in total assets listed on McDonald's balance sheet matches the $52.626 billion in liabilities plus owners' equity.

### 8-3b The Income Statement: So, How Did We Do?

The **income statement** summarizes the financial results of a firm's operations over a given period of time. The figure that attracts the most attention on the income statement is net income, which measures the company's profit or loss. In fact, another name for the income statement is the *profit and loss statement* (or, informally, the *P&L*). Just as with the balance sheet, we can use a simple equation to illustrate the logic behind the organization of the income statement:

$$\text{Revenue} - \text{Expenses} = \text{Net Income}$$

In this equation:

- **Revenue** represents the increase in the amount of cash and other assets (such as accounts receivable) the firm earns in a given time period as the result of its business activities. For example, Exhibit 8.3 shows that McDonald's has $19.207 billion in revenues, with $8.139 billion

**liabilities** Claims that outsiders have against a firm's assets.

**owners' equity** The claims a firm's owners have against their company's assets (often called "stockholders' equity" on balance sheets of corporations).

**income statement** The financial statement that reports the revenues, expenses, and net income that resulted from a firm's operations over an accounting period.

**revenue** Increases in a firm's assets that result from the sale of goods, provision of services, or other activities intended to earn income.

## Exhibit 8.3
## Income Statement for McDonald's

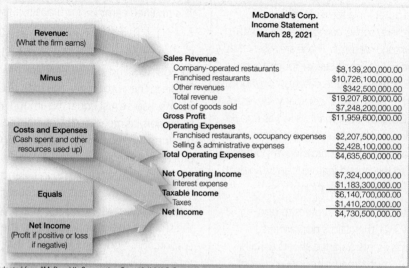

| | McDonald's Corp.<br>Income Statement<br>March 28, 2021 |
|---|---|
| **Revenue:**<br>(What the firm earns) | |
| **Sales Revenue** | |
| Company-operated restaurants | $8,139,200,000.00 |
| Franchised restaurants | $10,726,100,000.00 |
| **Minus** | |
| Other revenues | $342,500,000.00 |
| Total revenue | $19,207,800,000.00 |
| Cost of goods sold | $7,248,200,000.00 |
| **Gross Profit** | $11,959,600,000.00 |
| **Operating Expenses** | |
| **Costs and Expenses**<br>(Cash spent and other<br>resources used up) | |
| Franchised restaurants, occupancy expenses | $2,207,500,000.00 |
| Selling & administrative expenses | $2,428,100,000.00 |
| **Total Operating Expenses** | $4,635,600,000.00 |
| **Net Operating Income** | $7,324,000,000.00 |
| **Equals** | |
| Interest expense | $1,183,300,000.00 |
| **Taxable Income** | $6,140,700,000.00 |
| Taxes | $1,410,200,000.00 |
| **Net Income** | $4,730,500,000.00 |
| **Net Income**<br>(Profit if positive or loss<br>if negative) | |

Adapted from "McDonald's Corporation, Form 10-K," U.S. Securities and Exchange Commission, https://www.sec.gov/Archives/edgar/data/0000063908/000006390821000013/mcd-20201231.htm, accessed March 29, 2021. Because the accounting information found in the annual report is much more detailed than presented here, some of the accounting numbers shown here will differ from similar numbers shown in McDonald's income statement in its 10-K.

coming from company-owned restaurants and $10.726 billion coming from franchised restaurants and $342.5 million coming from other revenues. A firm normally earns revenue by selling goods or by charging fees for services (or both). Accountants use **accrual-basis accounting** when recognizing revenues. Under the accrual approach, revenues are recorded when they are earned, and payment is reasonably assured. It's important to realize that this is not always when the firm receives cash from its sales. For example, if a firm sells goods on credit, it reports revenue before it receives cash. (The revenue would show up initially as an increase in accounts receivable rather than as an increase in cash.)

■ **Expenses** indicate the cash a firm spends, or other assets it uses up, to carry out the business activities necessary to generate its revenue. Under accrual-basis accounting, expenses aren't necessarily recorded when cash is paid. Instead, expenses are matched to the revenue they help generate. The specific titles given to the costs and

expenses listed on an income statement vary among firms—as do the details provided. But the general approach remains the same: costs are deducted from revenue in several stages to show how net income is determined. The first step in this process is to deduct *costs of goods sold*, $7.248 billion for McDonald's, which are costs directly related to buying, manufacturing, or providing the goods and services the company sells. (Manufacturing companies often use the term *cost of goods manufactured* for these costs.) The difference between the firm's revenue and its cost of goods sold is its *gross profit*, which was $11.959 billion for McDonald's. The next step is to deduct *operating expenses*, totaling $4.635 billion for McDonald's, from gross profit. Operating expenses are costs the firm incurs in the regular operation of its business. Most income statements divide operating expenses into *selling expenses* (such as salaries and commissions to salespeople and advertising expenses) and *general* (or *administrative*) *expenses* (such as rent, insurance, utilities, and office supplies), which combined total $2.428 billion for McDonald's. McDonald's, however, typically owns the land and the building of franchised restaurants. So, it has another large, but specialized operating expense of $2.207 billion to pay for

**accrual-basis accounting** The method of accounting that recognizes revenue when it is earned and matches expenses to the revenues they helped produce.

**expenses** Resources that are used up as the result of business operations.

# Can Intangible Assets Tell Us What Digital Companies Are Worth?

In corporate accounting, assets are things of value that a firm owns. Tangible assets like plant, property, and equipment, have a physical form—you can touch them and see them. With well-established corporate markets for office space, distribution warehouses, or specialized factory machines, and companies and consultants who earn their livings doing nothing but helping firms buy or sell assets, tangible assets are relatively easy to put a price on.

Intangible assets have no physical existence—you can't see or touch them. Examples include patents, copyrights, trademarks, and software. Intangible assets have value, but that value is typically much more difficult to determine, especially for digital companies like Facebook (FB).

Indeed, how do we determine the value of FB's acquired technologies, one of FB's largest set of intangible assets? For example, FB acquired RedKix, now "Workplace from Facebook," for $100 million. Workplace, which competes with Slack, Microsoft Teams, and Google Chat, is an online platform for discussion channels and chat rooms for projects, teams, departments, and entire companies. Is Workplace worth more or less the $100 million FB paid for it three years ago?

One accepted method of estimating value is paying a multiple for a firm's annual earnings (e.g., 5 times earnings or 10 times earnings). The basic idea is that a firm in a low-growth industry will see its future earnings grow slowly over time, so you might pay a standard 5 times earnings. But for a firm in a high-growth industry you might pay 10 or 15 times earnings or more, because the future earnings from owning that firm will be much larger. You pay more today via a higher multiple to get more future earnings. Workplace had 5 million daily users in 2020. If they all paid the corporate rate of $96 a year, then Workplace's total revenue was $480 million. If we assume a profit margin similar to FB, 45%, then Workplace's net annual earnings were $216 million. Multiply that by 24, which is a common earnings multiple for software companies, and the estimated value is $5.1 billion.

But is that really what Workplace is worth, given that FB acquired 25 companies in the last five years, but reports a total value of *just* $1.15 billion for *all* of its acquired technologies? Does FB think that Workplace is worth less now than what it paid for it?

Is Workplace really worth $5.1 billion, given that Microsoft Office subscribers pay *nothing* for Microsoft Teams since it is available at no extra cost along with Word, Excel, PowerPoint, and other Microsoft Office apps? Indeed, Microsoft Teams usage grew 50% to 115 million daily users in 2020, 23 times the number of daily Workplace users.

Or is Workplace worth much more than $5.1 billion because it looks, acts, and feels exactly like FB, but for work?

The hard reality is there's no easy answer to this question. Which is a problem for accountants because intangible assets, like those at Facebook and Workplace, account for over 90% of the value of today's S&P 500 companies, compared to just 17% in 1975.[21]

---

franchised restaurants' occupancy expenses. The difference between gross profit and operating expenses is *net operating income,* which is $7.324 billion for McDonald's. Finally, interest expenses and taxes are deducted from net operating income to determine the firm's net income. After paying $1.183 billion in interest expenses and $1.410 billion in taxes, McDonald's net income is $4.730 billion.

> "It sounds extraordinary, but it's a fact that balance sheets can make fascinating reading."
>
> —Baroness Mary Archer, Cambridge University Lecturer and Chairwoman of the National Energy Foundation

- **Net income** is the profit or loss the firm earns in the time period covered by the income statement. If net income is positive, the firm has earned a profit. If it's negative, the firm has suffered a loss. Net income is called the "bottom line" of the income statement because it is such an important measure of the firm's operating success.

### 8-3c The Statement of Cash Flows: Show Me the Money

The last major financial statement is the **statement of cash flows**. Cash is the lifeblood of any business organization. A firm must have enough cash to pay what it owes to workers, creditors, suppliers, and

**net income** The difference between the revenue a firm earns and the expenses it incurs in a given time period.

**statement of cash flows** The financial statement that identifies a firm's sources and uses of cash in a given accounting period.

taxing authorities—hopefully, with enough left to pay a dividend to its owners! So, it's not surprising that a firm's stakeholders are very interested in how and why a company's cash balance changed over the past year. Cash flow statements commonly begin with net income. Why? Because it represents an increase (or decrease in the case of a loss) to the cash available to the company. Indeed, since McDonald's net income was $4.730 billion in 2020 we see that amount at the beginning of cash flow statement in Exhibit 8.4. The statement of cash flows identifies the amount of cash that flowed into and out of the firm from three types of activities:

1. Cash flows from *operating activities* show the amount of cash that flowed into the company from the sale of goods or services, as well as cash from dividends and interest received from ownership of the financial securities of other firms. It also shows the amount of cash used to cover expenses resulting from operations and

> ## "Happiness is a positive cash flow."
>
> —Fred Adler

any cash payments to purchase securities held for short-term trading purposes. Remember that under the accrual method, not all revenues and expenses on the income statement represent cash flows, so operating cash flows may differ substantially from the revenues and expenses shown on the income statement. Exhibit 8.4 shows that McDonald's operating cash flow comes from three sources:

a. $1.746 billion in adjustments to cash from operations (which consists of highly detailed accounting issues beyond the scope of this introductory chapter),

b. less $68.6 million for purchasing inventory used in restaurants,

c. less $143.5 million spent on cash or short-term expenses (such as accounts payable).

All of which comes to $1.534 billion in net cash from operations.

## Exhibit 8.4
## McDonald's Statement of Cash Flows

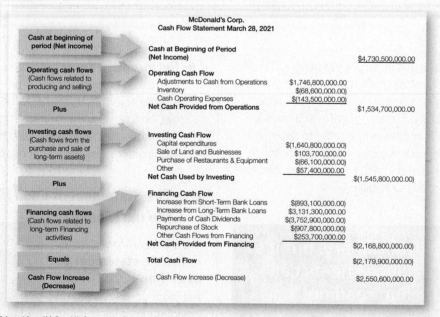

| McDonald's Corp. Cash Flow Statement March 28, 2021 | | |
|---|---|---|
| **Cash at Beginning of Period (Net Income)** | | $4,730,500,000.00 |
| **Operating Cash Flow** | | |
| Adjustments to Cash from Operations | $1,746,800,000.00 | |
| Inventory | $(68,600,000.00) | |
| Cash Operating Expenses | $(143,500,000.00) | |
| **Net Cash Provided from Operations** | | $1,534,700,000.00 |
| **Investing Cash Flow** | | |
| Capital expenditures | $(1,640,800,000.00) | |
| Sale of Land and Businesses | $103,700,000.00 | |
| Purchase of Restaurants & Equipment | $(66,100,000.00) | |
| Other | $57,400,000.00 | |
| **Net Cash Used by Investing** | | $(1,545,800,000.00) |
| **Financing Cash Flow** | | |
| Increase from Short-Term Bank Loans | $(893,100,000.00) | |
| Increase from Long-Term Bank Loans | $3,131,300,000.00 | |
| Payments of Cash Dividends | $(3,752,900,000.00) | |
| Repurchase of Stock | $(907,800,000.00) | |
| Other Cash Flows from Financing | $253,700,000.00 | |
| **Net Cash Provided from Financing** | | $(2,168,800,000.00) |
| **Total Cash Flow** | | $(2,179,900,000.00) |
| Cash Flow Increase (Decrease) | | $2,550,600,000.00 |

Labels at left of diagram:
- Cash at beginning of period (Net income)
- Operating cash flows (Cash flows related to producing and selling)
- Plus
- Investing cash flows (Cash flows from the purchase and sale of long-term assets)
- Plus
- Financing cash flows (Cash flows related to long-term Financing activities)
- Equals
- Cash Flow Increase (Decrease)

Adapted from "McDonald's Corporation, Form 10-K," U.S. Securities and Exchange Commission, https://www.sec.gov/Archives/edgar/data/000 0063908/000006390821000013/mcd-20201231.htm, accessed March 29, 2021. Because the accounting information found in the annual report is much more detailed than presented here, some of the accounting numbers shown here will differ from similar numbers shown in McDonald's cash flow statements in its 10-K.

2. Cash flows from *investing activities* show the amount of cash received from the sale of fixed assets (such as land and buildings) and financial assets bought as long-term investments to grow or improve the business. It also shows any cash used to buy fixed assets or make long-term financial investments. McDonald's:

   a. put $1.640 billion toward capital expenditures (primarily for building and opening new restaurants or remodeling existing restaurants),

   b. brought in $103.7 million from the sale of land and businesses,

   c. used $66.1 million for new restaurants or to upgrade equipment in existing restaurants (which is an abnormally small amount, primarily due to the COVID-19 pandemic),

   d. brought in an additional $57.4 million in cash on "other" investing activities.

   In total, McDonald's invested $1.545.8 billion in cash flows toward growing and improving its business.

3. Cash flows from *financing activities* show the cash the firm received from issuing additional shares of its own stock or from taking out short-term and long-term loans:

   a. McDonald's aggressively paid off short-term loans, thus reducing cash by $893.1 million.

   b. But thanks to long-term loans (mostly bonds), cash flows increased by $3.131 billion.

   c. Payments of dividends to shareholders reduced cash by $3.752 billion.

   d. McDonald's also decreased cash flow by spending $907.8 million to repurchase shares of McDonald's stock.

   e. Other cash flows from financing activities increased cash flows by $253.7 million.

   In all, cash flows from financing activities were negative for McDonald's at $2.168. billion more in cash outflows than inflows.

   Exhibit 8.4 shows that McDonald's cash flows increased in 2020 by 2,550 billion, primarily because of cash from long-term loans which increased cash flow by $3.131 billion.

### 8-3d  Other Statements: What Happened to the Owners' Stake?

In addition to the three major statements we've just described, firms usually prepare either a statement of retained earnings or a stockholders' equity statement. Let's take a quick look at each.

The *statement of retained earnings* is a simple statement that shows how retained earnings have changed from one accounting period to the next. The change in retained earnings is found by subtracting dividends paid to shareholders from net income.

Firms that have more complex changes in the owners' equity section sometimes report these changes in notes to the financial statements in the annual report. But they often disclose these changes by providing a *stockholders' equity statement*. Like the statement of retained earnings, this statement shows how net income and dividends affect retained earnings. But it also shows other changes in stockholders' equity, such as those that arise from the issuance of additional shares of stock.

## 8-4  Interpreting Financial Statements: Digging beneath the Surface

The financial statements we've just described contain a lot of important information. But they don't necessarily tell the whole story. In fact, the numbers they report can be misleading if they aren't put into proper context. Thus, in addition to looking at the statements, it's also important to check out the independent auditor's report and read the management discussion and footnotes that accompany them. It's also a good idea to compare the figures reported in current statements with those from earlier statements to see how key account values have changed.

External auditors carefully examine a company's financial records before rendering their opinion.

Rocketclips,Inc/Shutterstock.com

# Should Your Business Quit Using Cash? Is External Auditing Broken? Can It Be Fixed?

Publicly traded corporations are required to hire independent CPA firms to perform *external audits* verifying that financial statements are accurate and prepared in accordance with generally accepted accounting principles (GAAP). But as we saw with the UK's Patisserie Valerie, auditors aren't always right, and financial statements are sometimes wildly inaccurate.

Another notable audit failure occurred in Germany in 2020 with Wirecard, a digital payment services company, that fabricated $2 billion in cash that it did *not* have in its accounts. Ernst & Young (EY), Wirecard's auditors, claimed, "There are clear indications that this was an elaborate and sophisticated fraud, involving multiple parties around the world in different institutions, with a deliberate aim of deception." However, it appears one of EY's employees warned the firm four years earlier that Wirecard's top managers may have committed fraud and tried to bribe an auditor.

Attorney Marc Liebscher, whose Berlin law firm represents Wirecard investors, said, "We feel Ernst & Young's auditing work was a disaster. Our clients are convinced, Ernst & Young should stand trial." According to the *Financial Times*, "EY failed for more than three years to request crucial account information from a Singapore bank where Wirecard claimed it had up to $1.1 billion in cash a routine audit procedure that could have uncovered the vast fraud at the German payments group... Instead, EY relied on documents and screenshots provided by a third-party trustee and Wirecard itself." A senior auditor at another firm commented that getting bank statements directly from Wirecard's bank, which EY did not do, is "equivalent to day-one training at audit school."

Because they are paid by the firms whose accounts they certify, professor of business and public policy, Karthik Ramanna, explains that "The big issue is [that audit firms are] too deferential to clients' senior management."

- Should auditors be held financially liable for accounting fraud committed by others? Perhaps, but might that incentivize auditors to not report fraud?

- Should stock exchanges pay for audits? Because, after all, financial statements are audited to ensure investors have accurate numbers and information.

- Or should accounting firms divest their auditing practices into separate businesses, as the UK's Financial Reporting Council is requiring by 2024?

However it's done improvements must be made. Auditing is too important to investors' decisions, the integrity of financial markets, and government finances.[22]

## 8-4a The Independent Auditor's Report: Getting a Stamp of Approval

U.S. securities laws require publicly traded corporations in the United States to have an independent CPA firm (an accounting firm that specializes in providing public accounting services) perform an annual *external audit* of their financial statements. And many companies that aren't publicly traded also obtain external audits even though they aren't legally required to do so.

The purpose of an audit is to verify that a company's financial statements were properly prepared in accordance with generally accepted accounting principles and fairly present the financial condition of the firm. So external auditors don't just check the figures, they also examine the accounting *methods* used to *obtain* those figures. For example, auditors interview the company's accounting and bookkeeping staff to verify that they understand and properly implement procedures that are consistent with GAAP. They also examine a sample of specific source documents (such as sales receipts or invoices) and verify that the transactions they represent were properly posted to the correct accounts. Auditors also look for signs of fraud or falsified records. They often conduct an actual physical count of goods or supplies in inventory to determine the accuracy of the figures reported in the company's inventory records and contact the company's banker to verify its account balances. The audit process is rigorous, but it's important to realize that in large, public companies, it would be impossible for auditors to check the accuracy of every transaction. And, as we learned with Patisserie Valerie's accounting fraud at the beginning of the chapter, auditors can be fooled by fraudulent transactions and accounts.

The results of the audit are presented in an *independent auditor's report*, which is included in the annual report the firm sends to its stockholders. If the auditor doesn't find any problems with the way a firm's financial statements were prepared and presented, the report will offer an *unqualified* (or *"clean"*) *opinion*—which is by far the most common outcome. If the auditor identifies some minor concerns but believes that on balance the firm's statements remain a fair and accurate representation of the company's financial position, the report will offer a *qualified opinion*. But when auditors discover more serious and widespread problems with a firm's statements, they offer an *adverse opinion*. An adverse opinion indicates that the auditor believes the financial statements are seriously flawed and that they may be misleading and unreliable. (An adverse opinion must include an explanation of the specific reasons for the opinion.) Adverse opinions are very rare, so when an auditor renders one, it should set off alarm bells, warning stakeholders to view the information in the firm's financial statements with real skepticism. For example, KPMG, a global "big four" accounting firm, issued an adverse opinion for British Telecom (BT), the UK's largest telecommunication company. KPMG's auditor concluded that BT, "did not maintain effective internal control over financial reporting…," which means that BT was doing a poor job of ensuring the accuracy of the numbers used to calculate its financial results.[23]

For CPA firms to perform audits with integrity, they must be independent of the firms they audit. During the 1990s, many of the major CPA firms entered into very lucrative consulting contracts with some of the businesses they were auditing. It became increasingly difficult for these CPA firms to risk losing these high-paying contracts by raising issues about accounting practices when they audited the books of their clients. In other words, the auditors ceased to be truly independent and objective. The lack of rigorous oversight by external auditors contributed to some of the accounting scandals we mentioned earlier in this chapter.

In the aftermath, Congress passed the Sarbanes-Oxley Act of 2002 (commonly referred to as "SOX" or "Sarbox"). This law banned business relationships that might create conflicts of interest between CPA firms and the companies they audit. It also established a private-sector nonprofit corporation known as the Public Company Accounting Oversight Board (PCAOB). The PCAOB defines its mission as overseeing "the audits of public companies and SEC-registered brokers and dealers in order to protect investors and further the public interest in the preparation of informative, accurate, and independent audit reports."[24]

Despite Sarbanes-Oxley and the U.S. Securities and Exchange Commission's strict enforcement of GAAP accounting rules, 169 class-action lawsuits were filed against companies in 2019 for improper accounting statements, which are alleged to have cost investors $54 billion in losses.[25]

To encourage accountants and auditors to report illegal or unethical accounting practices, the International Ethics Standards Boards for Accountants (IESBA) developed a new code of ethics for professional accountants that went into effect in July 2017. It was updated in 2018 and can be downloaded at https://www.ethicsboard.org/international-code-ethics-professional-accountants.[26] Stavros Thomadakis, former chair of the IESBA, says, "The standards clarify that professional accountants must be active and not turn a blind eye to noncompliance. It's trying to bring about early, early detection, if you will, but also early action by management or authorities."[27]

## 8-4b Checking Out the Notes to Financial Statements: What's in the Fine Print?

Some types of information can't be adequately conveyed by numbers alone. Annual reports include notes (often *many* pages of notes) that disclose additional information about the firm's operations, accounting practices, and special circumstances that clarify and supplement the numbers reported on the financial statements. These notes can be *very* revealing.

As mentioned earlier, GAAP often allows firms to choose among several options when it comes to certain accounting procedures—and the choices the firm makes can affect the value of assets, liabilities, and owners' equity on the balance sheet and the revenues, costs, and net income on the income statement. The notes to financial statements explain the specific accounting methods used to recognize revenue, value inventory, and depreciate fixed assets. They might also provide details about the way the firm funds its pension plan or health insurance for its employees. They must also disclose *changes* in accounting methods that could affect the comparability of the current financial statements to those of previous years. Even more interesting, the notes might disclose important facts about the status of a lawsuit against the firm or other risks the firm faces. For example, Microsoft's 2020 annual report acknowledges that, because of its 2013 acquisition of mobile phone maker Nokia, it is a defendant in 40 lawsuits alleging that mobile phone

# Three Ways the COVID-19 Pandemic Affected Accounting

Like every aspect of business, the practice of accounting was affected by the COVID-19 pandemic, especially inventory counts, canceled orders, and write-downs.

**Inventory Counts.** Because of the huge amounts of money involved, counting raw materials, work-in-process, and finished products inventory is central to "closing the financial books" each year. But that becomes difficult when working from home. So, accountants turned to live worksite video feeds showing inventories, location-data confirmations from mobile phones, and calculating the difference between sales and purchase receipts obtained directly from vendors and customers.

**Canceled Orders.** In the apparel business, "Big companies don't pay upfront," explains Florian Schneider who works in merchandise sourcing. Until delivery, a bank letter of credit guarantees payment from retail stores to clothing suppliers. But when the COVID-19 hit, struggling retailers, desperate to conserve cash, laid off workers and canceled clothing orders. They also stopped honoring letters of credit. Roughly two weeks before widespread virus lockdowns fell into place, European retailer Primark issued a letter of credit to order $386,000 of jeans from Denim Expert Ltd., a Bangladeshi factory owned by Mostafiz Uddin. When the order was ready to ship, Primark refused to pay. Uddin, who must pay his employees and suppliers, said, "I am losing hope."

**Write-downs and Write-offs.** A *write-down* happens when an asset loses parts of its value, meaning it's worth less than previously indicated on the company balance sheet. As accounting consultant Steve Hills said, "You have assets at least for a period of time generating zero—or close to zero—revenue," so they become less valuable. A *write-off* is when an asset loses all of its value. When a bank loan goes bad because the borrower can't make payments, the bank writes the loan off because it's not getting the money back. M&T bank wrote off $530 million in loans that empty hotels, lacking customers because of the coronavirus, were no longer able to pay.[28]

Fabio Balbi/Shutterstock.com

---

"radio emissions" cause brain tumors.[29] Stakeholders who ignore these notes are likely to miss out on important information.

Another important source of information is the section of the annual report usually titled "Management's Discussion and Analysis." As its name implies, this is where the top management team provides its take on the financial condition of the company. SEC guidelines require top management to disclose any trends, events, or risks likely to have a significant impact on the firm's financial condition in this section of the report. For 2020, the most significant item for McDonald's was how it dealt with the COVID-19 pandemic. In "Management's Discussion and Analysis," McDonald's explained how it partnered with the Mayo Clinic to identify 50 best practices to control the spread of the virus in its restaurants.

## 8-4c Looking for Trends in Comparative Statements

The SEC requires publicly traded corporations to provide *comparative financial statements*. This simply means that the balance sheet, income statement, and statement of cash flows must list two or more years of figures side by side, making it possible to see how account values have changed over a period of time. Many firms that aren't publicly traded also present comparative statements, even though they are not required to do so by GAAP.

Comparative balance sheets allow users to trace what has happened to key assets and liabilities over the past two or three years, and whether its owners' equity had increased. Comparative income statements show whether the firm's net income increased or decreased and what has happened to revenues and expenses over recent years. For example, comparative income statements in Microsoft's

> In 2004 a horse named "Read The Footnotes" ran in the Kentucky Derby.
>
> **Securities and Exchange Commission**

2020 10-k showed revenues rising from $110.4 billion in 2018 to $125.8 billion in 2019 to $143 billion in 2020, with nearly all of the increase coming from service revenues in Microsoft's cloud computing business.[30] Using comparative statements to identify changes in key account values over time is called **horizontal analysis**.

## 8-5 Budgeting: Planning for Accountability

Management accountants also play an important role in the development of budgets. **Budgeting** is a management tool that explicitly shows how a firm will acquire and allocate the resources it needs to achieve its goals over a specific time period. The budgetary process facilitates planning by requiring managers to translate goals into measurable quantities and identify the specific resources needed to achieve these goals. But budgeting offers other advantages as well. If done well, budgeting:

- Helps managers clearly specify how they intend to achieve the goals they set during the planning process. This should lead to a better understanding of how the organization's limited resources will be allocated.

- Encourages communication and coordination among managers and employees in various departments within the organization. For example, the budget process can give middle and first-line managers and employees an opportunity to provide top managers with important insights about the

Budgeting encourages communication and coordination among managers and employees.

challenges facing their specialized areas—and the resources they need to meet those challenges. But, as we will explain in the next section, the extent to which this advantage is realized depends on the specific approach used in the budgeting process.

- Serves as a motivational tool. Good budgets clearly identify goals *and* demonstrate a plan of action for acquiring the resources needed to achieve them. Employees tend to be more highly motivated when they understand the goals their managers expect them to accomplish and when they view these goals as ambitious but achievable.

- Helps managers evaluate progress and performance. Managers can compare actual performance to budgeted figures to determine whether various departments and functional areas are making adequate progress toward achieving their organization's goals. If actual performance falls short of budgetary goals, managers can look for reasons and, if necessary, take corrective action.

### 8-5a Preparing the Budget: Top-Down or Bottom-Up?

There are two broad approaches to budget preparation. In some organizations, top management prepares the budget with little or no input from middle and supervisory managers—a process known as *top-down budgeting*. Supporters of this approach point out that top management knows the long-term strategic needs of the company and is in a better position to see the big picture when making budget decisions.

The other approach to budgeting is called *bottom-up (or participatory) budgeting*. Organizations that use a participatory process allow middle and supervisory managers to participate actively in the creation of the budget. Proponents of this approach maintain that it has two major advantages. First, middle and supervisory managers are likely to know more about the issues and challenges facing their departments—and the resources it will take to address them—than top management. Second, middle and first-line managers are likely to be more highly motivated to achieve budgetary goals when they have a say in how those goals are developed. On the negative side, the bottom-up approach is more time

**horizontal analysis** Analysis of financial statements that compares account values reported on these statements over two or more years to identify changes and trends.

**budgeting** A management tool that explicitly shows how a firm will acquire and use the resources needed to achieve its goals over a specific time period.

consuming and resource intensive to carry out than the top-down approach. Also, some middle managers may be tempted to overstate their needs or set low budget goals in order to make their jobs easier—an outcome known as *budgetary slack*.[31] Despite these drawbacks, the participatory approach currently is more common than the top-down process.

## 8-5b Developing the Key Budget Components: One Step at a Time

The budgeting process actually requires the preparation of several different types of budgets. But all of these individual budgets can be classified into two broad categories: operating budgets and financial budgets.

**Operating budgets** are budgets that identify projected sales and production goals and the various costs the firm will incur to meet these goals. These budgets are developed in a specific order, with the information from earlier budgets used in the preparation of later budgets.

The preparation of operating budgets begins with the development of a *sales budget* that provides quarterly estimates of the number of units of each product the firm expects to sell, the selling price, and the total dollar value of expected sales. For example, *Jeopardy*, the popular syndicated TV game show, bases its sales budget on syndication licensing fees paid by local TV stations and TV commercials. With an average of 10 to 11 million viewers per show, *Jeopardy* charges "low six figure [weekly] license fees" in the United States' two largest TV markets, L.A. and New York City, but less in smaller markets.[32] Likewise, while the revenue from running TV commercials during *Jeopardy* episodes varies by market (it's less in Fargo than in Miami), both TV commercial revenues and licensing revenues are predetermined by contract, making it relatively easy for *Jeopardy* to forecast its sales budget each year.[33]

The sales budget *must* be created first because many of the production and cost figures that go into other operating budgets depend on the level of sales. Once the sales budget is complete, the budgeted sales level can be used to develop the production budget, the administrative expenses, and the selling expenses budgets. And once the production budget is completed, the information it contains is used to prepare budgets for direct labor costs, direct materials costs, and manufacturing overhead. At *Jeopardy*, the key costs are the host's salary, production costs, and the prize budget. The late Alex Trebek, who hosted *Jeopardy* for 36 years, reportedly earned $10 million a year. Production costs are estimated at $5 million a year for 220 shows.[34] While *Jeopardy's* prize budget is estimated at $4.4 million a year or $20,000 a show, that budget was smashed by contestant James Holzhauer, a professional gambler, whose daily winnings averaged $74,673 during his 33-show win streak.[35] Bob Boden, who was head of programming at the Game Show Network said, "James' performance, I'm sure, is causing grief for an accountant somewhere."[36]

The final stage in the preparation of operating budgets is the creation of a *budgeted income statement*. This budget looks much like the income statement we described earlier, but instead of describing the actual results of the firm's past operations, it combines the revenue projections from the sales budget and the cost projections from the other operating budgets, to present a forecast of *expected* net income. After subtracting the operating budget from the sales budget, *Jeopardy's* producers typically come up with a budgeted income statement of $60 million to $70 million a year.[37]

**Financial budgets** focus on the firm's financial goals and identify the resources needed to achieve these goals. The two main financial budget documents are the *cash budget* and the *capital expenditure budget*. The cash budget identifies short-term fluctuations in cash flows, helping managers identify times when the firm might face cash flow problems—or when it might have a temporary surplus of cash that it could invest. The capital expenditure budget identifies the firm's planned investments in major fixed assets and long-term projects. The information from these two financial budgets and the budgeted income statement are combined to construct the *budgeted balance sheet*. This is the last financial budget; it shows how the firm's operations, investing, and financing activities are expected to affect all of the asset, liability, and owners' equity accounts.

The firm's **master budget** organizes the operating and financial budgets into a unified whole, representing the firm's overall plan of action for a specified time period. In other words, the master budget shows how all of the pieces fit together to form a complete picture. Exhibit 8.5 shows all of the budget documents that are included in a typical master budget. The arrows indicate the order in which the budgets are developed, starting with the sales budget and ending with the budgeted balance sheet.

**operating budgets** Budgets that communicate an organization's sales and production goals and the resources needed to achieve these goals.

**financial budgets** Budgets that focus on the firm's financial goals and identify the resources needed to achieve these goals.

**master budget** A presentation of an organization's operational and financial budgets that represents the firm's overall plan of action for a specified time period.

## Exhibit 8.5
## Development of the Master Budget

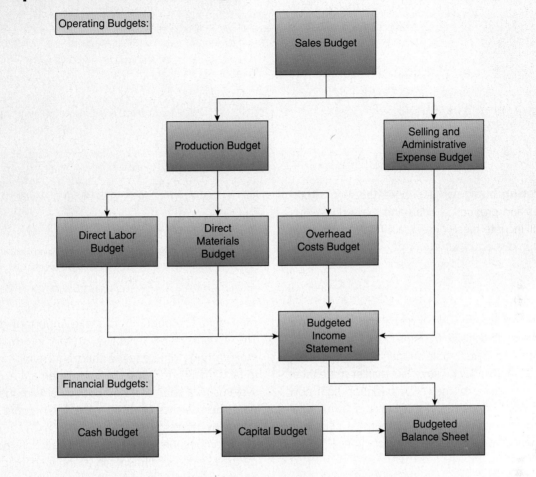

## 8-5c Being Flexible: Clearing Up Problems with Static Budgets

The budget process, as we've described it so far, results in a *static* budget, meaning that it is based on a single assumed level of sales. Static budgets are excellent tools for planning, but they have weaknesses when they are used to measure progress, evaluate performance, and identify problem areas that need correcting.

The problem with a static budget is that real-world sales can (and often do) vary considerably from their forecasted value—often for reasons that aren't under the control of the firm's management. Within days of the start of widespread shelter-in-place restrictions, 150 publicly traded companies warned that previous sales and earning predictions would be affected by the COVID-19 pandemic. Anheuser–Busch InBev predicted a global sales drop of $285 million for the first quarter of the year. The world's largest liquor company, Diageo, estimated a drop of $260 million just from China and Asia alone. Finally, Delta Airlines withdrew previous sales and earnings estimates, "until we have more clarity on the duration and severity of the current situation."[38] As mentioned earlier, many cost figures in budgets are based on the level of sales specified in the sales budget. When actual sales differ significantly from the sales volume assumed in a static budget, the budget figures based on those sales estimates will be wrong, and in extreme cases like the coronavirus, useless.

One common way managerial accountants avoid this problem is to develop a *flexible budget* for control purposes. A flexible budget is one that isn't based on a single assumed level of sales. Instead, it is developed over a *range* of possible sales levels, and is designed to show the appropriate budgeted level of costs for each different level of sales. This flexibility enables managers to make more meaningful comparisons between actual costs and

## Exhibit 8.6 Comparison of Financial and Managerial Accounting

| | Financial Accounting | Managerial Accounting |
|---|---|---|
| **Purpose** | Primarily intended to provide information to external stakeholders, such as stockholders, creditors, and government regulators. Information provided by financial accounting is available to the general public. | Primarily intended to provide information to internal stakeholders, such as the managers of specific divisions or departments. This information is proprietary—meaning that it isn't available to the general public. |
| **Type of Information Presented** | Focuses almost exclusively on financial information. | Provides both financial and nonfinancial information. |
| **Nature of Reports** | Prepares a standard set of financial statements. | Prepares customized reports to deal with specific problems or issues. |
| **Timing of Reports** | Presents financial statements on a predetermined schedule (usually quarterly and annually). | Creates reports upon request by management rather than according to a predetermined schedule. |
| **Adherence to Accounting Standards?** | Governed by a set of generally accepted accounting principles (GAAP). | Uses procedures developed internally that are not required to follow GAAP. |
| **Time Period Focus** | Summarizes past performance and its impact on the firm's present condition. | Provides reports dealing with past performance but also involves making projections about the future when dealing with planning issues. |

budgeted costs. But the sudden global halt to consumer and global spending arising from the COVID-19 pandemic is well beyond standard flexible budgets. At the beginning of the pandemic, Quincy Krosby, chief market strategist at Prudential Financial, explained, "The backdrop right now is different. We don't know… under the coronavirus what happens to the economy, what happens to consumer spending, what happens to [capital expenditures]."[39]

## 8-6 Inside Intelligence: The Role of Managerial Accounting

Now that we've looked at financial accounting, let's turn our attention to the other major branch of accounting, **managerial (or management) accounting**. As its name implies, this branch of accounting is designed to meet the needs of a company's managers, though in recent years many firms have empowered other employees and given them access to some of this information as well. Exhibit 8.6 identifies several ways that managerial accounting differs from financial accounting.

Managers throughout an organization rely on information created by

managerial accountants to make important decisions. The accuracy and reliability of this information can make a huge difference in the performance of a firm. In fact, many firms view their management accounting systems as a source of competitive advantage and regard the specifics of these systems as highly valuable company secrets.[40]

It's impossible to describe all the functions performed by managerial accountants in a single chapter. So, we'll be selective and focus on only two of them—but the two we'll discuss often play a crucial role in managerial decision making: measuring and assigning costs, and developing budgets.

### 8-6a Cost Concepts: A Cost for All Reasons

Without good information on costs, managers would be operating in the dark as they try to set prices, determine the most desirable mix of products, and locate areas where efficiency is lagging. A firm's management accounting system helps managers throughout an organization measure costs and assign them to products, activities, and even whole divisions.

Accountants define **cost** as the value of what is given up in exchange for something else. Depending on the type of problem they are analyzing, managerial accountants actually measure and evaluate several different types of costs. We'll begin our discussion by describing some of the cost concepts commonly used by managerial accountants.

The bricks, the mortar, the gloves, and the wages paid for the labor are all out-of-pocket costs.

At the most basic level, accountants distinguish between out-of-pocket costs and opportunity costs. **Out-of-pocket costs** (also called *explicit costs*) are usually easy to measure because they involve actual expenditures of money or other resources. The wages a company pays to its workers, the payments it makes to suppliers for raw materials, and the rent it pays for office space are examples.

But accountants realize that not all costs involve a monetary payment; sometimes what is given up is the *opportunity* to use an asset in some alternative way. Such opportunity costs are often referred to as **implicit costs**. For example, suppose a couple of lawyers form a partnership and set up their office in a building one of the partners already owns. They feel good about their decision because they don't have to make any out-of-pocket payments for rent. But a good managerial accountant would point out to the partners that they still incur an implicit cost, because by using the building themselves they forgo the opportunity to earn income by renting the office space to someone else.

Managerial accountants also distinguish between fixed costs and variable costs. As the name implies, **fixed costs** don't change when the firm changes its level of production. However, it's important to understand that fixed costs are really only fixed for a "relevant range" of output. For example, if a company sees a dramatic rise in sales, it might have to move into bigger facilities, thus incurring higher rent.

Examples of fixed costs include interest on a bank loan, property insurance premiums, rent on office space, and other payments that are set by a contract or by legal requirements. With most office buildings empty for well over a year, and many companies realizing that they didn't need as much office space, cash-strapped businesses looked at unused office space as an opportunity to reduce fixed costs. Ruth Colp-Haber, CEO of Wharton Property Advisors, said, "When it comes to making decisions about office leases, the words are postpone, adjourn and delay."[41] Michael Colacino, president of SquareFoot, a commercial real estate broker, agreed, saying. "What's the point of signing a lease with a 15 percent decrease in rent if you think it's going to go lower?"[42]

**Variable costs** are costs that rise (vary) when the firm produces more of its goods and services. As a company ramps up its production, it is likely to need more labor and materials and to use more electrical power. Thus, payments for many types of labor, supplies, and utilities are variable costs. With e-commerce sales increasing by nearly 20% in 2020, online retailers saw product returns surge by 70%![43] With such a dramatic increase in this variable cost ($10 to $20 just to process a return, plus 5% to 20% of the item's cost for return shipping), retailers have figured out that for some products it's just cheaper to tell the customer, "keep it." When Lorie Anderson tried to return makeup to Target and batteries to Walmart, they gave her refunds and told her to keep the items. Anderson agreed, saying, "They were inexpensive, and it wouldn't make much financial sense to return them by mail."[44]

### 8-6b Assigning Costs to Products: As (Not So) Simple as ABC?

Finally, accountants often want to assign costs to specific *cost objects*, such as one of the goods or services their firm produces. When they assign costs to specific cost objects, accountants distinguish between *direct costs* and *indirect costs*. **Direct costs** can be directly traced to the production of the product. For example, the wage payments made to workers directly involved in producing a good or service would be a direct cost for that product. On the other hand, the costs a firm incurs for plant maintenance, quality control, or depreciation on office equipment are usually classified as **indirect costs** since they tend to be the result of the firm's general operation rather than the production of any specific product.

Direct costs for labor and materials are usually easy to measure and assign, since they have an easily

**out-of-pocket cost** A cost that involves the payment of money or other resources.

**implicit cost** The opportunity cost that arises when a firm uses owner-supplied resources.

**fixed costs** Costs that remain the same when the level of production changes within some relevant range.

**variable costs** Costs that vary directly with the level of production.

**direct cost** Costs that are incurred directly as the result of some specific cost object.

**indirect costs** Costs that are the result of a firm's general operations and are not directly tied to any specific cost object.

identifiable link to the object. Unfortunately, indirect costs aren't tied in such a simple and direct way to the production of a specific product. In the past, managerial accountants usually relied on simple rules to assign indirect costs to different products—and in some cases they still do. One such approach is to allocate indirect costs in proportion to the number of direct labor hours involved in the production of each product. Under this method, products that require the most labor to produce are assigned the most indirect costs. But while this approach is simple, it can provide very misleading information. There is simply no logical reason for many types of indirect costs to be related to the amount of direct labor used to produce a product.

In recent years, managerial accountants have developed more sophisticated ways to allocate costs.

**activity-based costing (ABC)** A technique to assign product costs based on links between activities that drive costs and the production of specific products.

One relatively new method is called **activity-based costing (ABC)**.

This approach is more complex and difficult to implement than the direct labor method. Basically, it involves a two-stage process. The first stage is to identify specific activities that create indirect costs, and then determine the factors that "drive" the costs of these activities. The second stage is to tie these cost drivers to the production of specific goods (or other cost objects). Once the relationships between cost drivers and specific products are identified, they can be used to determine how much of each indirect cost is assigned to each product.

Clearly, ABC is much more complex to implement than a system that assigns costs based on a simple "one size fits all" rule, such as the direct labor method. However, it's likely to provide more meaningful results because it is based on a systematic examination of how indirect costs are related to individual goods.

## The Big Picture

Accounting provides vital information to both the internal and external stakeholders of a firm. The balance sheet, income statement, and statement of cash flows that are the main output of financial accounting help external stakeholders, such as owners and creditors, evaluate the financial performance of a firm. And managerial accounting helps managers throughout an organization make better decisions by providing them with relevant and timely information about the costs and benefits of the choices they have to make. Clearly, a basic knowledge of accounting concepts will help you succeed in just about any career path you choose.

## Careers in Accounting

### Staff Accountant

Responsible for daily cash reconciliation, preparation of monthly financial reports, including balance sheets and profit and loss statements, preparing spreadsheets and financial forecasts and analyses for the accounting manager and/or controller, and ensuring compliance with GAAP and Sarbanes-Oxley requirements. The ideal candidate has a bachelor's or master's degree in accounting, technical accounting knowledge, strong oral and written communication skills, a problem-solving attitude, the ability to prioritize tasks and work under deadlines, pays close attention to detail, and is eligible to sit for the CPA exam or is CPA certified.

# 9 | Finance:
## Acquiring and Using Funds to Maximize Value

### Learning Objectives

After studying this chapter, you will be able to:

**9-1** Identify the goal of financial management and the issues financial managers confront as they seek to achieve this goal

**9-2** Describe the tools financial managers use to evaluate their company's current financial condition and develop financial plans

**9-3** Evaluate the major sources of funds available to meet a firm's short-term and long-term financial needs

**9-4** Identify the key issues involved in determining a firm's capital structure

**9-5** Describe how financial managers acquire and manage current assets

**9-6** Explain how financial managers evaluate capital budgeting proposals to identify the best long-term investment options for their company

tckes/Shutterstock.com

### 9-1 What Motivates Financial Decisions?

**Financial capital** refers to the funds a firm uses to acquire its assets and finance its operations. Firms use some of their capital to meet short-term obligations, such as paying bills from suppliers, meeting payroll, repaying bank loans, and paying taxes to the government. Early in the COVID-19 pandemic some independently owned restaurants, knowing their survival was at stake, issued "dining bonds" in which customers paid $75 for a $100 coupon to be redeemed toward a meal at a later date. With virus lockdowns falling into place, restaurants scrambled to find funds to meet (what they hoped would be) short-term obligations for rent, employee wages, and suppliers' bills.[1] They were right to worry. In January 2021, 10 months into the pandemic, Hudson Riehle, senior vice president at the National Restaurant Association declared that, "2020 was certainly the worst year for the restaurant industry in its history."[2]

**financial capital** The funds a firm uses to acquire its assets and finance its operations.

Other funds are used to finance major long-term investments, such as building a new manufacturing plant and filling it with newly bought machines and equipment, or launching a new product line. Unlike independent restaurants, Domino's Pizza, a huge pizza franchiser with 17,200 stores in 90 countries, viewed the pandemic as an opportunity to invest in long-term growth. As the largest pizza delivery company in the world, Domino's was perfectly situated to thrive in virus lockdowns. Chief financial officer (CFO) Jeffrey Lawrence said, "This is not a time to pinch pennies. This is a time to do the right thing for your team members, for your customers."[3] So Domino's made plans to hire 10,000 new employees and invest millions of dollars more into a contactless "Carside Delivery" service where customers who order via Domino's website or mobile app notify the store that they've arrived, what their vehicle looks like, and whether their pizza order should be put in the passenger's side seat, the back seat, or a trunk, all without risking contact with others. CFO Lawrence explained that, "We don't think… [these investments are] just going to help us for a couple months. We think a lot of these could help us for years."[4]

Finally, firms need funds to pay a financial return to the owners in exchange for their investment in the

> "Money is like a sixth sense— and you can't make use of the other five without it."
>
> —William Somerset Maugham, English Playwright, Novelist, and Short Story Writer

company. Billionaire entrepreneur Elon Musk's four companies—The Boring Company, SolarCity, SpaceX, and Tesla Motors—are worth $1 trillion. It's estimated that Musk has invested half a billion dollars of his personal funds to purchase shares in The Boring Company, Tesla, and SolarCity (figures are not available for SpaceX, which is privately funded).[5] Musk said, "If I ask investors to put money in, then I feel morally I should put money in as well. I should not ask people to eat from the fruit bowl if I have not myself been willing to eat from the fruit bowl."[6] In addition to direct contributions from owners like Elon Musk, companies can also acquire financial capital through reinvestment of earnings, loans from banks, credit provided by suppliers, and (for corporations) newly issued stocks or bonds. This isn't a complete list by

## Exhibit 9.1

## Risk-Return Trade-Off: Average, High, and Low Financial Returns, 1928–2020

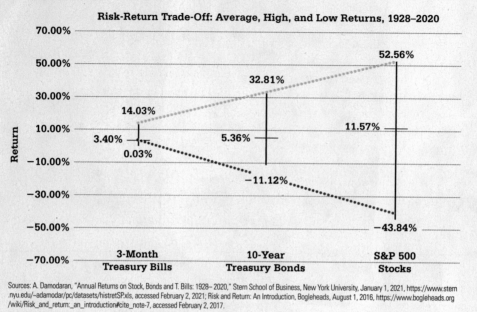

Risk-Return Trade-Off: Average, High, and Low Returns, 1928–2020

Sources: A. Damodaran, "Annual Returns on Stock, Bonds and T. Bills: 1928– 2020," Stern School of Business, New York University, January 1, 2021, https://www.stern.nyu.edu/~adamodar/pc/datasets/histretSP.xls, accessed February 2, 2021; Risk and Return: An Introduction, Bogleheads, August 1, 2016, https://www.bogleheads.org/wiki/Risk_and_return:_an_introduction#cite_note-7, accessed February 2, 2017.

any means—in fact, we'll discuss additional sources later in the chapter—but you get the idea: firms often have several ways to raise money.

In a nutshell, **finance** is the functional area of business that is responsible for finding the best sources of funds *and* the best ways to use them. But which sources and uses are "best" depends on the goals targeted by financial managers. Historically, the most widely accepted goal of financial management has been to *maximize the value of the firm to its owners*. For corporations with publicly traded stock, this translates into finding the sources and uses of financial capital that will maximize the market price of the company's common stock. After all, the stockholders are the ones with their money at risk.

Financial managers emphasize the goal of maximizing the market price of stock because they have a legal and ethical obligation (called a *fiduciary duty*) to make decisions consistent with the financial interests of their firm's owners. The legal foundation of this fiduciary duty was established in a famous 1919 court case, *Dodge v. Ford Motor Co.*, in which the court ruled that "a business corporation is organized and carried on primarily for the profit of the stockholders."[7] Recent legal rulings and scholarship reaffirm this fiduciary duty.[8]

Another reason for emphasizing shareholder wealth is more pragmatic. Firms that fail to create shareholder wealth are unlikely to be viewed as attractive investments. So, to continue attracting the financial capital needed to achieve its other goals, a firm must provide value to its stockholders.

But finding the mix of sources and uses of funds that maximize shareholder value isn't a simple process. Let's look at two major issues, shareholder value and social responsibility, and the risk-return trade-off, that financial managers confront as they search for the best sources of funds and the best ways to use them.

### 9-1a Shareholder Value and Social Responsibility: Does Good Behavior Pay Off?

The emphasis that financial managers place on maximizing shareholder value may seem to conflict with the modern view that a socially responsible firm has an

**finance** The functional area of business that is concerned with finding the best sources and uses of financial capital.

obligation to respect the needs of *all* stakeholders—not just its owners, but also its employees, customers, creditors, suppliers, and even society as a whole. The good news is that being socially responsible *can* be (and often is) a good strategy for also achieving the goal of shareholder wealth maximization—especially if managers take a *long-term* perspective.

When a company respects the needs of customers by providing high-quality goods and services at competitive prices, and when it listens and responds fairly to their concerns, those customers are more likely to keep coming back—and to recommend the company to friends and relatives. Similarly, when a firm provides its employees with a good work environment, those employees are likely to have better morale and greater loyalty, resulting in higher productivity and lower employee turnover. And when a company supports its local community through corporate philanthropy or cause-related marketing, the resulting goodwill may boost sales and create a more favorable business climate. All of these outcomes suggest that a commitment to meeting social responsibilities can contribute to a more profitable company and an increase in shareholder value.[9]

But things aren't always that simple. Being socially responsible requires a long-term commitment to the needs of many different stakeholders. Incentives for top executives (in the form of raises, bonuses, and other perks), however, are often tied to their firm's *short-term* performance. In such cases, some managers focus on policies that make their firm's stock price rise in the short run, but which are unsustainable over the long haul. And when managers fix their attention on raising the market price of the company's stock in the next year (or next quarter), concerns about social responsibility sometimes get lost in the shuffle.

It is also worth noting that responding to the needs of all stakeholders isn't always a simple and straightforward task. For example, public utilities across the world are closing coal-fired electricity plants or converting them to natural gas, solar, and wind power.[10]

- While good for the environment, these changes often put workers out of high-paying union jobs, hurting local economies.

- On the other hand, local farmers benefit financially by signing long-term leases with solar panel companies that pay substantially better than raising crops.

- But converting productive farmland to solar production reduces crop production, potentially leading to higher food prices (unless crop yields keep rising).

- Likewise, utilities are not doing this just to be socially responsible, but because switching significantly lowers their long-term costs, which probably raises profits and benefits shareholders.[11]

- Finally, a large percentage of the polysilicon production used in solar panels reportedly violates human rights because of reliance on forced labor.[12]

As this example makes clear, finding the right balance among the competing interests of diverse stakeholder groups can be difficult. But when conflicts occur between the long-term interests of owners and other stakeholders, the fiduciary duty required of financial managers generally leads them to make decisions that are most consistent with the interests of ownership.

## 9-1b Risk and Return: A Fundamental Trade-Off in Financial Management

One of the most important lessons in financial management is that there is a trade-off between risk and return. In financial management, **risk** refers to the degree of uncertainty about the actual outcome of a decision. The **risk-return trade-off** suggests that sources and uses of funds that offer the potential for high rates of return tend to be riskier than sources and uses of funds that offer lower returns.

Financial managers want to earn an attractive rate of return for shareholders. But they also must realize that the higher the expected return they seek, the more they expose their company to risk. Exhibit 9.1 illustrates the risk-return trade-offs of three kinds of investments from 1928 to 2020. As discussed in section 9-5a, treasury bills, or "T-bills," are backed by the U.S. government and are basically risk-free. They are often considered a "cash equivalent." Because of their short-term nature and nearly zero risk, the average return on T-bills is just 3.43%. Given their extremely low risk, T-bills have the smallest range of returns, from a low of 0.03% to a high of 14.30%. Ten-year treasury bonds generally produce higher returns because of the increased risk of holding the bond for such a long time. Therefore, not only is the average return from 10-year treasury bonds higher at 5.36%, the range of returns (the risk) is greater, with a low return of −11.12% and a high of 32.81%. (Section 10-3c explains why bond yields or returns vary from year to

> **risk** The degree of uncertainty regarding the outcome of a decision.
>
> **risk-return trade-off** The observation that financial opportunities that offer high rates of return are generally riskier than opportunities that offer lower rates of return.

We can analyze McDonald's strengths and weaknesses by comparing the company's financial ratios to industry averages.

year.) Investing in stocks—that is, investments in company ownership—produces the highest average return at 11.57%. That higher return comes with much more risk. Indeed, annual stock returns ranged from a low of −43.84% to a high of 52.56%. The risk-return relationship is expressed in this exhibit via the green dotted line (representing highest returns) and red dotted line (representing lowest returns). The vertical distance between the green- and red-dotted lines represents the risk, or range of returns. This distance increases as the average return rises from left to right via T-bills, treasury bonds, and stocks.[13]

Why does this matter? Because financial managers must consider risk-return trade-offs in two fundamental ways. First, as they allocate the firm's financial resources, sometimes they should choose less risk and smaller returns (see section 9-5 on "Acquiring and Managing Current Assets") and other times they should choose riskier investments with hopefully higher returns (see section 9-6 "Capital Budgeting: In It for the Long Haul"). Finally, in trying to earn an attractive rate of return for shareholders, risk-return trade-offs help financial managers understand how potential investors view their company and what the company needs to do to attract their investment dollars.

**financial ratio analysis** Computing ratios that compare values of key accounts listed on a firm's financial statements.

**liquid asset** An asset that can quickly be converted into cash with little risk of loss.

**liquidity ratios** Financial ratios that measure the ability of a firm to obtain the cash it needs to pay its short-term debt obligations as they come due.

## 9-2 Identifying Financial Needs: Evaluation and Planning

Before financial managers can determine the best financial strategies for their firms, they must identify existing financial strengths and weaknesses. Then they must devise financial plans that provide a roadmap for improving financial performance and acquiring the resources needed to achieve short-term and long-term objectives.

### 9-2a Using Ratio Analysis to Identify Current Strengths and Weaknesses

One way financial managers evaluate a firm's current strengths and weaknesses is by computing ratios that compare values of key accounts listed on their firm's financial statements—mainly its balance sheet and income statement. This technique is called **financial ratio analysis**. Over the years, financial managers have developed an impressive array of specific ratios. The most important fall into four basic categories: liquidity, asset management, leverage, and profitability. Because financial needs differ across industries, for example, the automobile industry is capital intensive (it takes billions of dollars to design new cars and build or refurbish factories), whereas the software industry is not (the marginal cost of producing another copy of a software program or app is close to zero); standard practice is to compare a firm's financial ratios to industry averages. We'll do just that as we work through the financial ratios below by continuing our financial analysis of McDonald's, which we began in Chapter 8 on accounting, where you learned the basics of income statements, balance sheets, and cash flows.[14]

1. **Liquidity ratios:** In finance, a **liquid asset** is one that can be quickly converted into cash with little risk of loss. **Liquidity ratios** measure the ability of an organization to convert assets into the cash it needs to pay off liabilities that come due in the next year.

   One of the simplest and most commonly used liquidity ratios is the *current ratio*, which is computed by dividing a firm's current assets by its current liabilities. Current assets include cash and other assets expected to be converted into cash in the next year, while current liabilities are the debts that must be repaid in the next year. The larger the current ratio, the easier it is for a firm to pay its short-term debts. A current ratio below 1.0 signifies that a company does not have enough current assets to pay short-term liabilities. In March 2020, McDonald's current ratio was 1.01 compared to the industry average of 1.46. So, while McDonald's has 1% more current assets than liabilities the industry has a stronger financial liquidity ratio with 46% more current assets than liabilities. When we discuss how firms manage cash and other liquid assets, you'll learn that it is also possible to have too much liquidity.

2. **Asset management ratios: Asset management ratios** (also sometimes called *activity ratios*) measure how effectively an organization uses its assets to generate net income. For example, the *inventory turnover ratio*—computed by dividing the firm's cost of goods sold by average inventory levels—measures how many times a firm's inventory is sold and replaced each year.

For example, if a company keeps an average of 100 finished widgets in inventory each month, and it sold 1,000 widgets this year, then it turned its inventory ten times. A high turnover ratio is good because it indicates that a firm can continue its daily operations with a small amount of inventory on hand. It's expensive to have unsold inventory sitting on shelves, that is, low inventory turns. Companies with high inventory turns, which replenish inventory levels more frequently, have less cash tied up in inventory, which means those funds can be used elsewhere. However, inventory turnover ratios can be *too* high. When that happens, the company isn't keeping enough goods in stock, causing stockouts, which frustrates customers and results in lost sales if they take their business elsewhere.

In March 2020, McDonald's inventory turnover ratio of 187 was much stronger than the industry average of 63. In other words, McDonald's carries 1.95 days' worth of inventory on average, compared to the average fast-food restaurant, which carries 5.79 days of inventory.

For firms that sell a lot of goods on credit, the *average collection period* is another important asset management ratio. This ratio is computed by dividing accounts receivable by average daily

iStockPhoto/Mgkaya

credit sales. A value of 45 for this ratio means that customers take 45 days (on average) to pay for their credit purchases. In general, the smaller the ratio, the better, since a lower value indicates that the firm's customers are paying for their purchases more quickly. But we'll see in our discussion of working capital management that low collection periods can also have drawbacks. In March 2020, McDonald's average collection period was 37 days, compared to the fast-food industry average of 8 days. Typically, average collection periods under 30 days are considered to be very strong.

3. **Leverage ratios: Financial leverage** is the use of debt to meet a firm's financing needs; a *highly leveraged* firm is one that relies heavily on debt. While the use of leverage can benefit a firm when times are good, a high degree of leverage is very risky. As we mentioned earlier, the extensive use of debt financing by big banks and major Wall Street firms played a major role in the financial meltdown that began during the latter part of the past decade.

**Leverage ratios** measure the extent to which a firm uses financial leverage. One common measure of leverage is the *interest coverage*, which is computed by dividing a firm's annual earnings before interest and taxes by its annual interest expenses on loans and bonds. Because interest payments cannot be skipped without dire consequences, the interest coverage ratio is closely watched by banks and financial markets. The larger the interest coverage ratio, the less leveraged the firm is. Interest coverage ratios below 2.0 signal potential problems in covering future interest payments. In March 2020, McDonald's interest coverage ratio was 11.17, compared to the industry

**asset management ratios** Financial ratios that measure how effectively a firm is using its assets to generate revenues or cash.

**financial leverage** The use of debt in a firm's capital structure.

**leverage ratios** Ratios that measure the extent to which a firm relies on debt financing in its capital structure.

## Exhibit 9.2 | Key Financial Ratios

| Ratio Name | Type | What It Measures | How It Is Computed |
|---|---|---|---|
| **Current** | Liquidity: measures ability to pay short-term liabilities as they come due. | Compares current assets (assets that will provide cash in the next year) to current liabilities (debts that will come due in the next year). | $\dfrac{Current\ Assets}{Current\ Liabilities}$ |
| **Inventory Turnover** | Asset management: measures how effectively a firm is using its assets to generate revenue. | How quickly a firm sells its inventory to generate revenue. | $\dfrac{Cost\ of\ Goods\ Sold}{Average\ Inventory}$ |
| **Average Collection Period** | Asset management: measures how effectively a firm is using its assets to generate revenue. | How long it takes for a firm to collect from customers who buy on credit. | $\dfrac{Accounts\ Receivable}{\left(\dfrac{Annual\ Credit\ Sales}{365}\right)}$ |
| **Interest Coverage** | Leverage: measures the extent to which a firm relies on debt to meet its financing needs. | The ratio of a firm's annual earnings (before interest and taxes) to its annual interest expenses. Higher is better. This is another way of measuring the degree of financial leverage, or debt, the firm is using. | $\dfrac{Earnings\ before\ Interest\ and\ Taxes}{Annual\ Interest\ Expenses}$ |
| **Net Profit Margin** | Profitability: compares the amount of profit to some measure of resources invested or earnings gained. | Indicates the percentage that a firm earns on each dollar of revenue, after paying all operating expenses, interest, and taxes. | $\dfrac{Net\ Income}{Total\ Revenue}$ |

interest coverage ratio of 5.8. This indicates that McDonald's was half as leveraged as the rest of the fast food industry in term of relying on loans.

4. **Profitability ratios:** Firms are in business to earn a profit, and **profitability ratios** provide measures of how successful they are at achieving this goal. There are many different profitability ratios, but we'll just look at *net profit margin*, which is calculated by dividing net income by total revenue. The larger the percentage of net profit margin, the more profit a firm earns on each dollar of revenue. For example, a 5% net profit margin means that if a firm earns one hundred dollars, it will be left with a net profit of $5 after paying for costs of goods sold, operating expense, interest expense, and taxes. In March 2020, McDonald's net profit margin was a very strong 25.92%, compared to an industry average of 11.86%, so McDonald's is more than two times as profitable as the fast-food industry on average.

Exhibit 9.2 defines each of the ratios we've just described and shows how it is computed. As you look at the exhibit, keep in mind that it represents only a sample of the financial ratios used by financial managers.

### 9-2b Planning Tools: Creating a Road Map to the Future

Ratio analysis helps managers identify their firm's current financial strengths and weaknesses. The next step is to develop plans that build on the firm's strengths and correct its weaknesses. Financial planning is an important part of the firm's overall planning process. Assuming that the overall planning process has established appropriate goals and objectives for the firm, financial planning must answer the following questions:

- What specific assets must the firm obtain to achieve its goals?

- How much additional financing will the firm need to acquire these assets?

- How much financing will the firm be able to generate internally (through additional earnings), and how much must it obtain from external sources?

- When will the firm need to acquire external financing?

- What is the best way to raise these funds?

**profitability ratios** Ratios that measure the rate of return a firm is earning on various measures of investment.

The planning process involves input from a variety of areas. In addition to seeking input from managers in various functional areas of their business, financial managers usually work closely with the firm's accountants during the planning process.

## 9-2c Basic Planning Tools: Budgeted Financial Statements and the Cash Budget

The budgeting process provides financial managers with much of the information they need for financial planning. The **budgeted income statement** and **budgeted balance sheet** (also refer to section 8-5b in the accounting chapter) are two key financial planning tools. Also called *pro forma financial statements*, they provide a framework for analyzing the impact of the firm's plans on the financing needs of the company.

- The budgeted income statement uses information from the sales budget and various cost budgets (as well as other assumptions) to develop a forecast of net income for the planning period. This can help the firm evaluate how much internal financing (funds generated by earnings) will be available.

- The budgeted balance sheet forecasts the types and amounts of assets a firm will need to implement its future plans. It also helps financial managers determine the amount of additional financing (liabilities and owners' equity) the firm must arrange to acquire those assets.

The **cash budget** is another important financial planning tool. Cash budgets normally cover a one-year period and show projected cash inflows and outflows for each month. Financial managers use cash budgets to get a better understanding of the *timing* of cash flows within the planning period. This is important because most firms experience uneven inflows and outflows of cash over the course of a year, which can lead to cash shortages and sometimes large cash surpluses. For example, the video game industry experiences sizable increases in cash flows when new blockbuster games (such as *Call of Duty, Marvel's Spider-Man,* or *Animal Crossing*) are released; and in November and December, during which holiday sales often exceed combined sales from the rest of the year. But video game industry cash surpluses become enormous when Sony and Microsoft introduce new versions of their PlayStation and Xbox gaming consoles (typically every 7 years).[15] When the Sony PlayStation 5 and the Xbox Series X/S next generation consoles were introduced in November 2020, videogame hardware sales, which

were already up a record 34% (yes, we know what many of *you* were doing during the pandemic), jumped 58% in November and 38% in December.[16] Why the drop in December? Widespread shortages of both consoles. Sony CFO Hiroki Totoki said, "We are doing our best on production so that we can ship as many units as possible at the earliest timing."[17]

Projecting cash flows helps financial managers determine when the firm is likely to need additional funds to meet short-term cash shortages, and when surpluses of cash will be available to pay off loans or to invest in other assets. With stores closed and revenues sharply down at the beginning of the COVID-19 pandemic, apparel retailer Gap faced a huge cash shortage. So, it stopped a planned cash dividend payment to shareholders, skipped three months of store rent payments to Simon Property Group (the largest U.S. shopping mall owner), issued bonds (to borrow funds from investors), and drew cash out of its bank's line of credit.[18]

Even firms with growing sales can experience cash flow problems, especially if many of their customers buy on credit. To meet increasing sales levels, a growing firm must hire more labor and buy more supplies. These workers and suppliers may expect to be paid long before the company's customers pay their bills, leading to a temporary cash crunch.

Exhibit 9.3 illustrates this type of situation by presenting a partial cash budget for a hypothetical firm called Oze-Moore. The cash budget shows that, despite its increasing sales, Oze-Moore will have cash shortages in March and April. Knowing this in advance gives financial managers time to find the best sources of short-term financing to cover these shortages. The cash budget also shows that Oze-Moore will experience a big cash surplus in May as the customers start paying for the purchases they made in March and April. Knowing this ahead of time helps managers forecast when they will be able to repay the loans they took out to cover their previous cash shortages. It also gives them time to evaluate short-term interest-earning investments they could make to temporarily "park" their surplus cash.

**budgeted income statement** A projection showing how a firm's budgeted sales and costs will affect expected net income. (Also called a pro forma income statement.)

**budgeted balance sheet** A projected financial statement that forecasts the types and amounts of assets a firm will need to implement its future plans and how the firm will finance those assets. (Also called a pro forma balance sheet.)

**cash budget** A detailed forecast of future cash flows that helps financial managers identify when their firm is likely to experience temporary shortages or surpluses of cash.

## Exhibit 9.3
## Cash Budget for Oze-Moore

**Cash Budget for Oze-Moore**

|  | February | March | April | May |
|---|---|---|---|---|
| **Sales** | $75,000 | $110,000 | $125,000 | $90,000 |
| Cash balance at beginning of month | | $10,000 | $10,000 | $10,000 |
| **Receipts of Cash** | | | | |
| Cash sales | | $16,500 | $18,750 | $13,500 |
| Collection of accounts receivable from last month's sales | | $63,750 | $93,500 | $106,250 |
| **Total Cash Available** | | $90,250 | $122,250 | $129,750 |
| | | | | |
| **Disbursements of Cash** | | | | |
| Payment of accounts payable | | $60,500 | $68,750 | $49,500 |
| Wages and salaries | | $27,500 | $31,250 | $22,500 |
| Fixed costs (rent, interest on debt, etc.) | | $8,000 | $8,000 | $8,000 |
| Purchase of new computers | | | $6,500 | |
| **Total Cash Payments** | | $96,000 | $114,500 | $80,000 |
| | | | | |
| **Excess or Deficit of Cash for Month** | | -$5,750 | $7,750 | $49,750 |
| Loans needed to maintain cash balance of $10,000 | | $15,750 | $2,250 | $0 |
| Amount of cash available to repay short-term loans | | $0 | $0 | $39,750 |
| Cash balance at end of month | | $10,000 | $10,000 | $31,750 |
| Cumulative loans | | $15,750 | $18,000 | $0 |

*Sales increase in both March and April. But since most of Oze-Moore's customers buy on credit, its receipt of cash lags behind these sales increases.*

*While receipts of cash lag behind sales, Oze-Moore's payments of wages and accounts payable are due in the same month as sales.*

*Despite big increases in sales in March and April, Oze-Moore suffers a shortfall of cash because of the difference in* timing *between cash receipts and cash payments.*

*Financial managers want to have at least $10,000 in the cash balance at the beginning of each month. When cash falls below this amount, they take out a short-term loan.*

*In May, Oze-Moore has a surplus in cash. This gives it enough cash to pay off the loans from earlier months.*

# 9-3 Finding Funds: What Are the Options?

Once financial managers have identified the amount of financial capital needed to carry out their firm's plans, the next step is to determine which sources of funds to tap. The most appropriate sources of funds for a business depend on several factors. One of the most important considerations is the firm's stage of development. Start-up firms face different challenges and have different needs than more established firms. Another factor is the reason the funds are needed. Funds used to meet short-term needs, such as meeting payroll, paying suppliers, or paying taxes, typically come from different sources than funds used to finance major investments in plants, property, and equipment.

The financing options available to new firms are generally much more limited than those available to more mature firms with an established track record. In fact, for start-up firms the main source of funds is likely to be the personal wealth of the owner (or owners), supplemented by loans from relatives and friends. Given how risky new business ventures are, banks and other established lenders often hesitate to make loans to new, unproven companies. (In some cases, the Small Business Administration overcomes this reluctance by guaranteeing loans for start-ups and other small businesses that satisfy its criteria.) As the firms grow and become more established, they typically are able to obtain financing from other sources.

Some start-ups with the potential for generating rapid growth may be able to attract funds from wealthy individuals, called *angel investors*, or from venture capital firms. Both angel investors and venture capitalists typically invest in risky opportunities that offer the possibility of high rates of return. Both also typically provide funds in exchange for a share of ownership. Long before home-rental company Airbnb raised $100 billion in its 2020 initial public offering (IPO), it received significant funds from Sequoia Capital, a leading venture capital firm.[19] Sequoia paid $585,000 for 58 million stock shares in 2009 when Airbnb had only 2,500 rentals listed on its website. Sequoia invested a total of $280 million that became worth $12 billion with Airbnb's IPO.[20]

## 9-3a Sources of Short-Term Financing: Meeting Needs for Cash

Firms that have survived the start-up phase of the business life cycle often have several sources of short-term financing. Let's take a look at some of the most common options.

# How the COVID-19 Pandemic Affected Corporate Finance

Like every aspect of business, the practice of finance was affected by COVID-19 .

**Withdrawing guidance.** Public companies in which people hold stock provide financial guidance to let investors know whether their financial performance is likely to meet, exceed, or fall short of expectations. Two-hundred ninety-five of the 1,500 companies in the S&P Composite 1500 index withdrew guidance about forecasted profits, unable to predict how severely the pandemic would affect their businesses.

**Credit drawdowns.** Two-hundred sixty of those companies drew down credit from existing bank credit lines, adding $221 billion in cash to their balance sheets. Analysts at investment firm Morgan Stanley described the intense demand for cash as "a full-blown liquidity scramble."

**Top management pay cuts.** One-hundred forty-five of those 1,500 companies cut the base salaries of their top executives.

**Layoffs and furloughs.** Just one month into the pandemic, only 100 of 1,500 those companies had temporarily furloughed employees (expecting to call them back to work when the economy improved) or had permanently laid off employees from their jobs.

**Stop paying rent to landlords.** Large retailers like Dick's Sporting Goods, Petco Animal Supplies, Victoria's Secret, Staples, and Ross Dress for Less stores told their landlords that they would temporarily stop paying monthly rent for their stores. Mall landlords were only collecting 10% to 25% of rent owed them from nonessential business, and just 50% to 60% of rent owed from essential businesses like grocery stores and pharmacies.

**Issuing new stock.** Through June 2020, companies whose stocks were listed on U.S. stock exchanges had raised $148 billion by issuing new stock.

These are just some of the ways that financial managers preserved cash, used or expanded bank credit, or raised new funds in capital markets.[21]

---

**Trade Credit** One of the most important sources of short-term financing for many firms is **trade credit**, which arises when suppliers ship materials, parts, or goods to a firm without requiring payment at the time of delivery. By allowing the firms to "buy now, pay later," they help the firm conserve its existing cash, thus avoiding the need to acquire funds from other sources.

In most cases, the terms of trade credit are presented on the invoice the supplier includes with the shipment. For example, the invoice might list the terms as 2/10 net 30. The "net 30" indicates that the supplier allows the buyer 30 days before payment is due. But the "2/10" tells the buyer that the supplier is offering a 2% discount off the invoice price if the buyer pays within 10 days.

At first glance, the 2% discount in our example may not seem like a big deal. But failing to take the discount can be very costly. Consider the terms we mentioned above: 2/10, net 30. If the firm fails to pay within 10 days, it loses the discount and must pay the full amount 20 days later. Paying 2% more for the use of funds for only 20 days is equivalent to an *annual* finance charge of over 37%![22]

Suppliers will grant trade credit only after they've evaluated the creditworthiness of the firm. But once they've granted this credit to a company, they generally continue offering it as long as the firm satisfies the terms of the credit arrangements. Trade credit is sometimes called **spontaneous financing** because it is granted when the company places its orders without requiring any additional paperwork or special arrangements. The level of trade credit automatically adjusts as business conditions change and the company places larger or smaller orders with its suppliers.

Although firms of all sizes use this type of financing, trade credit is a particularly important source of financing for small businesses. The Federal Reserve Board's *Survey of Small Business Finances* indicates that about 60% of small firms rely on trade credit as a major source of short-term financial capital.[23]

**Factoring** The money that customers owe a firm when they buy on credit shows up in accounts receivable on the company's balance sheet. A **factor** buys the accounts receivables of other firms. The factor makes

> **trade credit** Spontaneous financing granted by sellers when they deliver goods and services to customers without requiring immediate payment.
>
> **spontaneous financing** Financing that arises during the natural course of business without the need for special arrangements.
>
> **factor** A company that provides short-term financing to firms by purchasing their accounts receivables at a discount.

a profit by purchasing the receivables at a discount and collecting the full amount from the firm's customers.

Although firms that use factors don't receive the full amount their customers owe, factoring offers some definite advantages. Instead of having to wait for customers to pay, the firm gets its money almost immediately. Also, since the factor is responsible for collection efforts, the firm using the factor may be able to save money by eliminating its own collection department. Finally, the factor typically assumes the risk for bad debts on any receivables it buys. However, factors typically perform a careful evaluation of the quality of accounts receivable before they buy them and may refuse to buy receivables that are high risk. Taiwan-based Foxconn Technology Group, which manufactures iPhones for Apple, has used factoring to provide $157 million in loans to its parts suppliers. Managing director Jack Lee explained why this is a good business risk for Foxconn, saying, "We know the suppliers' business status better than anyone because we are their customer."[24] According to the Commercial Finance Association, factoring has typically provided more than $247 billion in short-term funds on an annual basis to American businesses in recent years.[25]

**Short-Term Bank Loans** Banks are another common source of short-term business financing. Short-term bank loans are usually due in 30 to 90 days, though they can be up to a year in length. When a firm negotiates a loan with a bank, it signs a *promissory note*, which specifies the length of the loan, the rate of interest the firm must pay, and other terms and conditions of the loan. Banks sometimes require firms to pledge collateral, such as inventories or accounts receivable, to back the loan. That way, if the borrower fails to make the required payments, the bank has a claim on specific assets that can be used to pay off the amount due.

Rather than going through the hassle of negotiating a separate loan each time they need more funds; many firms work out arrangements with their bankers to obtain preapproval so that they can draw on funds as needed. One way they do this is by establishing a **line of credit**. Under this arrangement, a bank agrees to provide the firm with funds up to some specified limit, as long as the borrower's credit situation doesn't deteriorate, and the bank has sufficient funds—conditions that aren't always met, as the recent financial meltdown clearly illustrated.

A **revolving credit agreement** is similar to a line of credit, except that the bank makes a formal, legally binding commitment to provide the agreed-upon funds. In essence, a revolving credit agreement is a *guaranteed* line of credit. In exchange for the binding commitment to provide the funds, the bank requires the borrowing firm to pay a commitment fee based on the *unused* amount of funds. Thus, under the terms of a revolving credit agreement, the firm will pay interest on any funds it borrows, and a commitment fee on any funds it does not borrow. The commitment fee is lower than the interest on the borrowed funds, but it can amount to a fairly hefty charge if the firm has a large unused balance. In March 2020, Hilton, the global hotel company, was using 89% of its $1.75 billion revolving credit agreement. However, it tapped the remaining $195 million that was available, "to increase its cash position and preserve financial flexibility in light of current uncertainty in the global markets resulting from the COVID-19 outbreak."[26] In total, U.S. companies borrowed $310 billion against their revolving credit agreements through the first half of 2020.[27]

**Commercial Paper** Well-established corporations have some additional sources of short-term financial capital. For instance, many large corporations with strong credit ratings issue **commercial paper**, which consists of short-term promissory notes (IOUs). Historically,

Banks are a common source of short-term business financing. When a firm negotiates a loan with a bank, it signs a promissory note, which specifies the length of the loan, the rate of interest the firm must pay, and other terms and conditions of the loan.

**line of credit** A financial arrangement between a firm and a bank in which the bank preapproves credit up to a specified limit, provided that the firm maintains an acceptable credit rating.

**revolving credit agreement** A guaranteed line of credit in which a bank makes a binding commitment to provide a business with funds up to a specified credit limit at any time during the term of the agreement.

**commercial paper** Short-term (and usually unsecured) promissory notes issued by large corporations.

commercial paper issued by corporations has been unsecured, which means it isn't backed by a pledge of collateral. Because it is normally unsecured, commercial paper is only offered by firms with excellent credit ratings; firms with less than stellar financial reputations that try to issue unsecured commercial paper are unlikely to find buyers. In recent years, a new class of commercial paper has emerged, called *asset-backed commercial paper,* which, as its name implies, is backed by some form of collateral.

Commercial paper can be issued for up to 270 days, but most firms typically issue it for much shorter periods—typically 30 days, but sometimes for as little as two days. One key reason commercial paper is popular with companies is that it typically carries a lower interest rate than commercial banks charge on short-term loans. By far the biggest issuers of commercial paper are financial institutions, but other large corporations also use this form of financing.

Why use commercial paper? According to the Consumerist, "The commercial paper market works like a credit card for big companies. Some days they have money, and some days they do not. So, if they need money Tuesday, but will have money Friday, they'll go to the commercial paper market and borrow some money. Then on Friday they will pay back the money, plus interest."[28] According to the U.S. Federal Reserve, the average rate for 30-day commercial paper was just 0.08% in February 2021.[29] That means a firm would pay a phenomenally low $800 in interest to use $1 million over 30 days. Commercial paper is sold at a discount, so the interest cost is deducted up front. In this instance, the firm would get $999,200 for 30 days, after which it would need to pay back $1,000,000 ($999,200 + $800 = $1,000,000).[30] Energy company Exxon Mobile ($25.3 billion), pharmaceutical company Pfizer ($12.3 billion), and entertainment firm the Walt Disney Company ($10.6 billion) were the largest users of commercial paper in 2020, during which a total of just over $1 trillion of commercial paper was issued.[31]

## 9-3b Sources of Long-Term Funds: Providing a Strong Financial Base

The sources of financial capital we've looked at so far have been appropriate for dealing with cash needs that arise from short-term fluctuations in cash flows. But financial managers typically seek more permanent funding to finance major investments and provide a secure financial base for their company. Let's take a look at some of the more common sources of long-term funds.

**Direct Investments from Owners** One key source of long-term funds for a firm is the money the owners themselves invest in their company. For corporations, this occurs when it sells *newly issued* stock—and it's important to realize that the *only* time the corporation receives financial capital from the sale of its stock is when it is initially issued. When Tesla issues *new* shares of stock, all the funds go to Tesla. In 2020, Tesla issued new stock three times, selling $2 billion of shares in February, $5 billion in September, and another $5 billion in December, raising $12 billion to expand and build new manufacturing facilities for Tesla cars and batteries in China, Germany, and the United States.[32] But once you own Tesla's stock, if you decide to sell your shares to another investor, Elon Musk and Tesla get nothing.

Another way firms can meet long-term financial needs is by reinvesting their earnings. The profits that a firm reinvests are called **retained earnings**. This source isn't a pool of cash; it simply reflects the share of the firm's earnings used to finance the purchase of assets, pay off liabilities, and reinvest in the business. At the end of 2020, Tesla reported an "accumulated deficit" of $6.1 billion for 2020 retained earnings. What that means is over its nearly two decades in business, Tesla had cumulative losses of $6.1 billion that would have totaled $6.8 billion except for Tesla's first-ever profit of $720 million in 2020.[33] This explains why Tesla, without a reliable source of profits to reinvest in the business as retained earnings, raised $12 billion by issuing stock three times in 2020.

It's important to understand that retained earnings and cash aren't the same thing. If you want to know how much cash a firm has, check the figure in the cash account at the top of its balance sheet. You'll typically find that the cash account is different from the amount listed for retained earnings! For example, Microsoft had 34.6 billion in retained earnings compared to $13.6 billion in cash and cash equivalents.[34]

Retained earnings are a major source of long-term capital for many corporations, but the extent to which they are used depends on the state of the economy. When the economy is booming and profits are high, retained earnings tend to soar. But when the economy slides into a recession, most corporations find they have few earnings to reinvest.

The decision to retain earnings involves a trade-off because firms have another way to use their earnings: they can pay out some or all of their profits to their owners by declaring a dividend. You might think that stockholders would be unhappy with a firm that retained most of its earnings, since that would mean they would receive a smaller dividend. But many stockholders actually prefer their companies to reinvest earnings—at least if

> **retained earnings** The part of a firm's net income it reinvests.

management invests them wisely—because doing so can help finance their firm's growth. And a growing, more profitable firm usually translates into an increase in the market price of the firm's stock.

Billionaire Warren Buffett's company, Berkshire Hathaway, has never paid dividends, choosing to reinvest all of its substantial profits. This strategy paid off handsomely for stockholders. Between June 8, 1990 and February 4, 2021, Berkshire's stock soared from $7,325 to $354,527 per share.[35] Despite the fact that it paid them no dividend, you can bet that most of Berkshire's shareholders were pleased with the capital gains that resulted from this strategy!

**Long-Term Debt** In addition to contributions from owners, firms can also raise long-term funds by borrowing from banks and other lenders or by issuing bonds.

**Term Loans** There are many different types of long-term loans, but the most typical arrangement—sometimes simply called a *term loan*—calls for a regular schedule of fixed payments sufficient to ensure that the principal (the amount initially borrowed) and interest are repaid by the end of the loan's term.

Lenders often impose requirements on long-term loans to ensure repayment. Most lenders require that the loans be backed by a pledge of some type of collateral. Banks and other lenders also often include *covenants* in their loan agreements. A **covenant** is a requirement a lender imposes on the borrower as a condition of the loan. One common covenant requires the borrower to carry a specified amount of liability insurance. Another requires the borrower to agree not to borrow any *additional* funds until the current loan is paid off. Covenants sometimes even restrict the size of bonuses or pay raises the firm can grant to employees. The purpose of covenants is to protect creditors by preventing the borrower from pursuing policies that might undermine its ability to repay the loan. While covenants are great for lenders, borrowers often view them as highly restrictive.[36]

**Corporate Bonds** Rather than borrow from banks or other lenders, corporations sometimes issue their own formal IOUs, called *corporate bonds*, which they sell to investors. Bonds often have due dates (maturities) of ten or more years after issuance. For example, wireless carrier T-Mobile sold $19 billion in 30-year bonds to help pay for its acquisition of former competitor, Sprint.[37] Like corporate stock, bonds are marketable, meaning that bondholders can sell them to other investors before they mature. But it is important to realize that unlike shares of stock, which represent ownership in a corporation, bonds are certificates of debt.

## 9-4 Leverage and Capital Structure: How Much Debt Is Too Much Debt?

Most firms use a combination of **equity** and **debt financing** to acquire needed assets and to finance their operations. Owners provide equity financing, while creditors (lenders) provide debt financing. Thus, when a company issues and sells new stock or uses retained earnings to meet its financial needs, it is using equity financing. But when it takes out a bank loan, or issues and sells corporate bonds, it is relying on debt financing.

Both equity and debt financing have advantages and drawbacks. The extent to which a firm relies on various forms of debt and equity to satisfy its financing needs is called that firm's **capital structure**. To simplify our discussion, we'll focus mainly on the capital structure of corporations, but many of the basic principles apply to other forms of ownership.

### 9-4a Pros and Cons of Debt Financing

When a firm borrows funds, it enters into a contractual agreement with the lenders. This arrangement creates a *legally binding* requirement to repay the money borrowed (called the principal) *plus interest*. These payments take precedence over any payments to owners. Lenders often require the firm to pledge collateral, such as real estate, financial securities, or equipment, to back the loan. If the firm is unable to make the required payments, the lenders can use this collateral to recover what they are owed. Norwegian Cruise Lines put up a 268-acre Caribbean island, a second island off Belize, and several of its cruise ships as collateral for $700 million in junk bonds (high-risk,

**covenant** A restriction lenders impose on borrowers as a condition of providing long-term debt financing.

**equity financing** Funds provided by the owners of a company.

**debt financing** Funds provided by lenders (creditors).

**capital structure** The mix of equity and debt financing a firm uses to meet its permanent financing needs.

> "When you combine ignorance and leverage, you get some pretty interesting results."
>
> —Warren Buffett

# Could Netflix Run Out of Cash?

Have you binged *Bridgerton*, the costume drama? Are all of you "cool cats and kittens" hoping for another season of the *Tiger King* true crime documentary? Did you brush the dust off your chess set because of *The Queen's Gambit*? What do these three very different shows have in common? They're Netflix Originals. What's the finance angle? Netflix needs billions of dollars of external funding each year to produce them. Here's how the sources of those funds have changed in Netflix's 25 years in business.

In the beginning, Netflix paid huge licensing fees for the rights to air movies and TV shows, like *Friends* and *The Office*, produced by other movie studios and TV networks. Initially, Netflix paid for those licensing fees with monthly subscription revenue, funds from startup investors, and bank loans. Growth was slow. Long-term debt was small. Profits were small to nonexistent, so there were few funds (retained earnings) to reinvest in the business. In 2002, an initial public stock offer raised $82.5 million to put toward licensing fees for more shows. In 2003, Netflix reached 1 million subscribers.

With the launch of Netflix Originals in 2009, Netflix needed substantially more money to attract producers, directors, writers, and actors to create Netflix exclusive shows. From 2009 to 2015, Netflix's long-term debt rose in direct proportion to its program budget, from $500 million to $8 billion per year. By 2017, long-term debt had nearly doubled to $15.4 billion. From 2018 to the end of 2020, long-term debt jumped from $20.7 billion to $26.4 billion and finally to $28.2 billion! By contrast, its net income from 2018 to 2020 ($1.2 billion, $1.8 billion, and $2.7 billion) paled in comparison to debt levels.

Many doubted the company's business model. Mike Vorhaus, president of Vorhaus Advisors, a media and digital video consultancy, said, "Nobody is ever the dominant player forever.

I think they're going to need some luck in not drowning in debt..." Co-CEO Reed Hastings admitted, "That's a lot of capital up front..." Hastings said Netflix would "be free-cash-flow negative for many years." In other words, it would continue borrowing to fund and grow Netflix Originals.

But in January 2021, Netflix announced "we believe we no longer have a need to raise external financing for our day-to-day operations." What explains this amazing change?

- Netflix added 37 million subscribers(!) in 2020 to bypass 200+ million total subscribers.

- Revenue grew by $25 billion! Almost as much as the company's total long-term debt ($28.2 billion).

- Operating profits grew by 76% compared to 2019.

- Netflix raised prices $2 per month in 2019 and again in 2021.

Media analyst Rich Greenfield, co-founder of research firm LightShed Partners, says the conventional wisdom on Netflix has changed from "when they are going to run out of money?" to "how are they going to spend all this cash?"[38]

sitthiphong/Shutterstock.com

high-interest bonds) to help it survive the COVID-19 disruption of the passenger cruise industry. Tim Conduit of London-based Allen & Overy, an international law firm specializing in global business, said, "I get that some fixed-income investor is not going to want to be the owner of a Caribbean island. But they are going to want to be in a better position as a creditor. 'Some collateral is better than no collateral' is probably what investors are thinking."[39]

Debt financing used to be less expensive because every dollar of interest payments made on debt was tax-deductible. Companies could raise needed funds and

lower taxes. But because of U.S. corporate tax law changes in 2018, firms may now only deduct interest expenses up to 30% of earnings before interest, taxes, depreciation, and amortization (EBITDA). In addition, with the top corporate tax rate lowered to 21% from 39%, interest payment tax deductions are roughly half as valuable as before. Together, these changes make debt financing significantly more expensive.

Another advantage of debt was that firms acquired more funds without asking existing stockholders for more money or issuing new stock to new investors. So, assuming proper investment of the borrowed funds, debt financing improved shareholders' return on equity by not diluting existing shares of stock. But, because of much higher costs stemming from changes in U.S. tax laws, debt financing is less likely to increase shareholders' return on equity. We'll further illustrate these issues in section 9-4c's discussion of using debt financing to leverage or magnify financial gains and losses.

One obvious disadvantage of debt is the requirement to make fixed payments. This can create real problems when the firm finds itself in an unexpectedly tight financial situation. In bad times, required interest payments can eat up most (or all) of the earnings, leaving little or no return to the firm's owners. And if the firm is unable to meet these payments, its creditors can force it into bankruptcy. Exactly one month after skipping a $12 million interest payment to bondholders, retailer JCPenney filed for Chapter 11 bankruptcy to reorganize its finances, close stores, and seek a buyer who could improve the more than 100-year-old company's financial situation.[40] After discussions with its major bondholders, 70% agreed to restructure, meaning they were willing to take less than what they were owed. But because Penney's was unable to pay back 100% of its bonds, its largest lenders forgave 20% of Penney's debt in exchange for ownership of 150 Penney stores.[41] In November 2020, Penney's exited bankruptcy, purchased by the Simon Property Group (the largest mall owner in the United States) and Brookfield Asset Management.[42]

As we mentioned earlier, another disadvantage of debt financing is that creditors often impose covenants on the borrower. These covenants can hamper the firm's flexibility and might result in unintended problems. For example, a covenant that restricts bonuses and pay raises to employees might undermine the morale of key workers and tempt them to seek employment elsewhere. Similarly, restrictions on dividends or on the ability of the firm to borrow additional funds may make it difficult for the firm to raise more money.

## 9-4b Pros and Cons of Equity Financing

For corporations, equity financing comes from two major sources: retained earnings and money directly invested by stockholders who, as we saw with Tesla, purchase newly issued stock. Equity financing is more flexible and less risky than debt financing. Unlike debt, equity imposes no required payments. A firm can skip dividend payments to stockholders without having to worry that it will be pushed into bankruptcy. And a firm doesn't have to agree to burdensome covenants to acquire equity funds.

On the other hand, equity financing doesn't yield the same tax benefits as debt financing. In addition, existing owners might not want a firm to issue more stock, since doing so might dilute their share of ownership. Finally, a company that relies mainly on equity financing forgoes the opportunity to use financial leverage. But as we've already noted, leverage can be a two-edged sword. We'll illustrate the risks and rewards of leverage in our next section.

## 9-4c Financial Leverage: Using Debt to Magnify Gains (and Losses)

The discussion of financial ratios explained that firms using a lot of debt in their capital structure are highly leveraged. The main advantage of financial leverage is that it magnifies the return on the stockholders' investments. We'll illustrate how that works with two hypothetical companies, Eck-Witty and Oze-Moore, shown in Exhibit 9.4. The main disadvantage is that the cost of leverage or debt financing is now significantly higher because of changes to the 2018 U.S. corporate tax laws. We'll illustrate the real-world consequences of those higher costs for First Data Corporation later in this section.

Exhibit 9.4 shows the revenues, expenses, and earnings that two firms—Eck-Witty Corporation and Oze-Moore

## Exhibit 9.4
## How Financial Leverage Affects the Return on Equity

**Eck-Witty** (Capital structure is all only equity)

| Equity (Funds supplied by owners) | | $1,000,000 |
|---|---|---|
| Debt (Funds obtained by borrowing) | | $0 |

| | Strong Sales | Weak Sales |
|---|---|---|
| EBITDA | $160,000 | $80,000 |
| Deductible Debt Interest (Limited to 30% of EBITDA) | 0.00 | 0.00 |
| Taxable income | 160,000 | 80,000 |
| Taxes | 32,000 | 16,000 |
| After-tax earnings | 128,000 | 64,000 |
| ROE | 12.8% | 6.8% |

**Oze-Moore** (Capital structure is 20% equity and 80% debt)

| Equity (Funds supplied by owners) | | $200,000 |
|---|---|---|
| Debt (Funds obtained by borrowing) | | $800,000 |

| | Strong Sales | Weak Sales |
|---|---|---|
| EBIT | $160,000 | $80,000 |
| Interest | 48,000 | 24,000 |
| Taxable income | 112,000 | 56,000 |
| Taxes | 22,400 | 11,200 |
| After-tax earnings | 137,600 | 68,800 |
| ROE | 68.8% | 34.4% |

# Cash, the "Business Vaccine" for the COVID-19 Pandemic

It's said that "cash is king." But when the COVID-19 pandemic hit, cash was not only king, it was also the difference between business survival and bankruptcy.

For some companies, this meant selling long-held investments. Fox Corporation, the news, sports, and entertainment firm, an early investor in Roku the streaming device company, sold its 5% share for $350 million. Anticipating the stresses that the pandemic placed on its banks, PNC Financial Services sold its $13 billion stake in BlackRock, a global investment firm, a position PNC had held for 25 years.

Others, like Carnival Corporation, raised cash by selling assets, in this case, six cruise ships. Hilton Worldwide Holdings, the global hotel company, presold $1 billion of customer loyalty points to credit card and travel services company American Express.

Finally, home builder Lennar Corporation postponed buying land (on which to build houses) for three months. Vice President

and CFO Diane Bessette said, "The endgame of all that was an intense focus on managing cash and preserving the strength of our balance sheet."[43]

Nagy Bagoly Arpad/Shutterstock.com

---

International—would experience for two different levels of sales, one representing a strong year and the other a weak year. To make the impact of leverage easy to see, we'll assume that Eck-Witty and Oze-Moore are *identical* in all respects *except* their capital structure. In particular, our example assumes that the two companies have the same amount of assets and experienced exactly the same earnings before interest, taxes, depreciation, and amortization (abbreviated as EBITDA). Thus, any differences in the net income of these firms results from differences in their use of debt and equity financing. We'll use return on equity (ROE) to measure the financial return each firm offers its stockholders. ROE is calculated by dividing after-tax earnings by equity (funds supplied by owners).

Note that both firms have a total of $1 million in assets, but they've financed the purchase of their assets in very different ways. Eck-Witty used only common stock and retained earnings in its capital structure, so it has $1 million in equity financing and no debt. Oze-Moore's capital structure consists of $200,000 in owners' equity and $800,000 in debt, so it is highly leveraged. The interest rate on its debt is 10%, so Oze-Moore has to make required interest payments of $80,000 per year to its lenders. While the highest

> "Debt is one person's liability, but another person's asset."
>
> —Nobel Prize–Winning Economist Paul Krugman

U.S. corporate tax rate is 21% as of 2018, we will use a 20% tax rate in Exhibit 9.4 to simplify the calculations.

As Exhibit 9.4 shows, debt financing significantly increases Oze-Moore's ROE compared to Eck-Witty's equity financing when sales are strong or weak. Why? Because Oze-Moore's interest payments are partially tax-deductible, its tax bill will be lower and its after-tax income will be higher. Furthermore, those higher profits are based on a smaller amount of equity, $200,000 for Oze-Moore versus $1,000,000 for Eck-Witty, so Oze-Moore's ROE is naturally higher. Let's dig further into the specifics to see how this works.

When sales are strong, Oze-Moore's use of leverage results in a 68.8% ROE compared to Eck-Witty's 12.8%. Oze-Moore's interest payments are fixed. It pays its creditors $80,000 in interest—no more, no less—whether sales are strong or weak. With the interest deduction capped at 30% of EBITDA (earnings before interest, taxes, depreciation, and amortization), Oze-Moore can deduct $48,000 of its $80,000 of interest payments from earnings (30% of $160,000 in earnings is $48,000). This makes Oze-Moore's taxable income $112,000. By contrast, with no debt and no interest to deduct, Eck-Witty's taxable income is $160,000.

In turn, Oze-Moore only pays $22,400 in taxes compared to $32,000 for Eck-Witty. That means that Oze-Moore's after-tax earnings are higher than Eck-Witty's, thanks to debt financing. Likewise, Oze-Moore's ROE of 68.8% ($137,600 in after-tax earnings divided by $200,000 in equity) is much higher than Eck-Witty's ROE of 12.8% ($128,000 in after-tax earnings divided by $1,000,000 in equity). So, compared to equity financing, debt financing leverages or magnifies financial gains.

This also happens when sales are weak. But, because of weaker sales, Oze-Moore can only deduct $24,000 of its $80,000 of interest payments from earnings (30% of $80,000 in earnings is $24,000). This makes Oze-Moore's taxable income $56,000. By contrast, with no debt and no interest to deduct, Eck-Witty's taxable income is $80,000. In turn, Oze-Moore only pays $11,200 in taxes compared to $16,000 for Eck-Witty. That again means that Oze-Moore's after-tax earnings are higher than Eck-Witty's, thanks to debt financing. Likewise, Oze-Moore's ROE of 34.4% ($68,800 in after-tax earnings divided by $200,000 in equity) is much higher than Eck-Witty's ROE of 6.4% ($64,000 in after-tax earnings divided by $1,000,000 in equity). So, even when sales are weak, debt financing magnifies financial gains.

But what Exhibit 9.4's comparison of debt versus equity financing doesn't show is that debt financing has become significantly more expensive for highly leveraged firms under the 2018 tax laws. For example, First Data Corporation had $18.5 billion in debt, for which it paid $964 million in annual interest. Under prior tax law, it could deduct 100% of that interest, thus lowering its tax bill and increasing its after-tax income. But with annual earnings of $2.7 billion, First Data can now only deduct $810 million of debt interest (30% of its $2.7 billion in annual earnings). As a result, First Data Corporation's taxes were now $154 million higher. Which is another way of saying that debt financing now cost First Data Corporation $154 million more a year under the new tax law. This shows how the cost of leveraging financial gains via debt financing is significantly more expensive than it used to be.

History offers another real-world lesson about debt financing. Debt leverage not only magnifies financial gains, but it also magnifies financial losses! During the economic boom between 2003 and 2007, many companies used debt leverage to magnify their ROEs. When the economy slowed, the required interest and principal payments on their debt became a heavy burden. Many of those highly leveraged firms ended up in bankruptcy. The moral of the story: if the financial returns of leverage seem too good to be true,

over the long run they probably are. Sound financial management requires keeping a level head and balancing the risk and return of financial decisions.[44]

In the wake of the financial crisis, the federal government enacted the 2010 **Dodd-Frank Act**, which required large financial firms to hold more equity and less debt. The 2018 changes to U.S. corporate tax laws will also encourage less debt financing and more equity financing. Limiting deductions on debt-based interest payments to no more than 30% of EBITDA makes debt financing significantly more expensive than before and will likely reduce corporate profits. Likewise, reducing the corporate tax rate from 39% to 21% will significantly boost companies' retained earnings, leading to much greater use of this form of equity financing.[45]

## 9-5 Acquiring and Managing Current Assets

Let's turn our attention to how a firm determines the amount and type of current assets to hold. As we'll see, holding current assets involves trade-off; either too much or too little of these assets can spell trouble.

### 9-5a Managing Cash: Is It Possible to Have Too Much Money?

A company must have cash to pay its workers, suppliers, creditors, and taxes. Many firms also need cash to pay dividends. And most firms also want to hold enough cash to meet unexpected contingencies. But cash has one serious shortcoming compared to other assets: it earns little or no return. If a firm holds much more cash than needed to meet its required payments, stockholders are likely to ask why the excess cash isn't being invested in more profitable assets. And if the firm can't find a profitable way to invest the money, the stockholders are likely to ask management why it doesn't use the excess cash to pay them a higher dividend—most shareholders can think of plenty of ways

**Dodd-Frank Act** A law enacted in the aftermath of the financial crisis of 2008–2009 that strengthened government oversight of financial markets and placed limitations on risky financial strategies such as heavy reliance on leverage.

"The Dodd-Frank Act was 2,319 pages in length. Apparently there was a lot about our financial system in 2010 that Congress wanted to change!"

—David Skeel, in The New Financial Deal

*they'd* like to use the cash! Indeed, firms were sitting on $4 trillion in cash in 2020, up from $2.7 trillion in 2010 and $1.6 trillion in 2000.[46]

In the narrowest sense, a firm's cash refers to its holdings of currency (paper money and coins issued by the government) plus demand deposits (the balance in its checking account). However, when most firms report their cash holdings on their balance sheet, they take a broader view, including **cash equivalents** along with their actual cash. Cash equivalents are very safe and highly liquid assets that can be converted into cash quickly and easily. Commercial paper, U.S. Treasury Bills (T-bills), and money market mutual funds are among the most popular cash equivalents. The advantage of these cash equivalents is that they offer a better financial return (in the form of interest) than currency or demand deposits.

As we explained in our discussion of short-term sources of funds, major corporations with strong credit ratings often *sell* commercial paper to raise needed short-term funds. On the other side of such transactions are firms that *buy* commercial paper as part of their portfolio of cash equivalents because—at least under normal economic conditions—it is a safe and liquid way to earn some short-term interest. But during economic downturns the appeal of commercial paper as a cash equivalent plummets due to increased risk.

**U.S. Treasury Bills, or "T-bills,"** are short-term IOUs issued by the U.S. government. Most T-bills mature (come due) in 4, 13, or 26 weeks. There is a very active secondary market for T-bills, meaning that their owners can sell them to other investors before they mature. Thus, T-bills are highly liquid. And, unlike commercial paper, T-bills are backed by the U.S. government, so they are essentially risk-free. The safety and liquidity of T-bills make them very attractive cash equivalents even in times of economic distress. As discussed earlier in the chapter, the average return on T-bills from 1928 to 2020 was just 3.43%. Over the past decade T-bills have had an average return of 0.51%.

**Money market mutual funds** raise money by selling shares to large numbers of investors. They then pool these funds to purchase a portfolio of short-term, liquid securities. (In fact, money market mutual funds often include large holdings of commercial paper and T-bills.) Money market mutual funds are an affordable way for small investors to get into the market for securities, which would otherwise be beyond their means. This affordability also makes these funds a particularly attractive cash equivalent for smaller firms. One example is Vanguard's Cash Reserves Federal Money Market Fund, "which invests at least 99.5% of its total assets in cash, U.S. government securities, and/or repurchase agreements that are collateralized solely by U.S. government securities or cash (collectively,

A U.S. Treasury bill's Treasury yield is its return on investment expressed as a percentage. In February 2021, the Treasury yield on a 10-year T-bill was 1.19%.

government securities)."[47] Considered to be one of Vanguard's most conservative funds, it has had an average annual return of 0.63% over the past decade.[48]

## 9-5b Managing Accounts Receivable: Pay Me Now or Pay Me Later

Accounts receivable represents what customers who buy on credit owe the firm. Allowing customers to buy on credit can significantly increase sales. However, as our discussion of the cash budget showed, credit sales can create cash flow problems because they delay the receipt of cash the firm needs to meet its financial obligations. Customers who pay late or don't pay at all only exacerbate the problem. So it's important for firms to have a well-thought-out policy that balances the advantages of offering credit with the costs. The key elements of this policy should include:

- Setting credit terms: For how long should the firm extend credit? What type of cash discount should the firm offer to encourage early payments?

- Establishing credit standards: How should the firm decide which customers qualify for

**cash equivalents** Safe and highly liquid assets that many firms list with their cash holdings on their balance sheet.

**U.S. Treasury bills (T-bills)** Short-term marketable IOUs issued by the U.S. federal government.

**money market mutual funds** A mutual fund that pools funds from many investors and uses these funds to purchase very safe, highly liquid securities.

# When Is Paying Dividends to Shareholders a "Moral Imperative?"

Financial managers have a fiduciary duty to act in the best interest of company ownership by increasing the value of the firm's stock price. In publicly owned firms, this is accomplished in three ways:

- Earn higher profits.

- Buy back existing shares of publicly held stock. With fewer shares outstanding, earnings per share (EPS), a key metric in valuing stock performance, will rise.

- Pay cash dividends, that is, a portion of annual profits, directly to shareholders.

To conserve cash, many companies stopped paying dividends during the first six months of the COVID-19 pandemic. Globally, 2020 dividend payments dropped by 11.4% in the third quarter, which was an improvement over the second quarter's steeper 18.3% decline.

But once firms start paying dividends, there's a strong expectation they won't stop. Simply put, investors see dividends as a long-term promise to share profits with shareholders. So, was it wrong for companies to stop dividend payments because of the pandemic?

Keith Skeoch, former CEO of Standard Life Aberdeen, an asset and wealth management firm, says, "If there is a moral issue, it is that there is a substantial part of our society that is dependent on retirement income, and dividends, particularly at the time when interest rates are incredibly low, are an important part of that support for retirement income."

Federated Hermes fund manager Daniel Peris agrees, saying, "Even pension funds at the end of the day are people. Dividends are a way to sustain the population at a time of great stress... We're saying, as smaller shareholders, whatever profits are left after the necessary investments and debt should be distributed."

So, yes, there is a moral imperative to paying dividends. But even Skeoch says that "moral imperative" applies to companies with the "economic wherewithal" to pay them. Businesses laying off staff, closing stores, and not paying suppliers shouldn't pay dividends.[49]

---

credit? What type of credit information should it require? How strict should its standards be?

- Deciding on an appropriate collection policy: How aggressive should the firm be at collecting past-due accounts? At what point does it make sense to take (or at least threaten to take) legal action against late-paying customers, or to turn over the accounts to collection agencies? When does it make sense to work out compromises?

In each area, financial managers face trade-offs. For example, a firm that extends credit for only 30 days will receive its payments sooner than a firm that allows customers 90 days. But setting short credit periods may also result in lost sales. Similarly, setting high credit standards reduces the likelihood a firm will have problems with customers who pay late (or not at all). However, strict standards may prevent many good customers from getting credit, resulting in lower sales. Finally, an aggressive collection policy may help the firm collect payments that it would otherwise lose. But an aggressive policy is costly, and it might alienate customers who make honest mistakes, causing them to take future business to competitors.

Some businesses have found that being flexible can help them get at least some of what they are owed. Global apparel company Levi Strauss & Co. switched to extended payment plans for many of its 50,000 retailers, many of whom were forced to close during the COVID-19 pandemic. CFO Harmit Singh said, "I am calling the big retailers, saying, 'You are owing me money; when are you paying me?' My feedback to all of them is I need [just] a little bit of money every week."[50]

## 9-5c Managing Inventories: Taking Stock of the Situation

Inventories are stocks of finished goods, work-in-process, parts, and materials that firms hold as a part of doing business. Clearly, businesses must hold inventories to operate. For example, you'd probably be disappointed if you visited a Best Buy store and were confronted with empty shelves rather than with a wide array of electronic gadgets to compare and try out. Similarly, a manufacturing firm wouldn't be able to assemble its products without an inventory of parts and materials.

But for many firms, the costs of storing, handling, and insuring inventory items are significant expenses. In recent years, many manufacturing firms, especially automotive manufacturers, have become very aggressive about keeping inventories as low as possible in an attempt to reduce

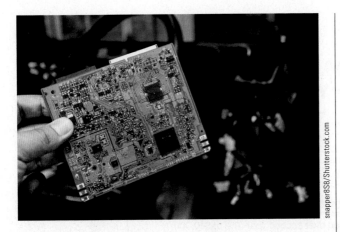
snapper8S8//Shutterstock.com

costs and improve efficiency. Such "lean" inventory policies can be very effective, but they leave the firm vulnerable to supply disruptions. In January 2021, Toyota, Fiat Chrysler, and Ford Motor Company all shut down factories because of computer chip shortages. Dan Hearsch, a managing director at consulting firm AlixPartners, said, "Consumer electronics exploded. Everybody and their brother wanted to buy an Xbox and PlayStation and laptops, while automotive shut down. Then automotive [sales] came back faster than expected, and that's where you get into this problem."[51] Michael Hogan, senior vice president at computer chip maker GlobalFoundries, said, "We are doing everything humanly possible to prioritize our output for automotive."[52] The problem, said Gary Silberg, who heads the global automotive practice at the Big Four accounting firm KPMG, is that automotive firms "are not [at] the front of the line for chips anymore."[53]

## 9-6 Capital Budgeting: In It for the Long Haul

We'll conclude the chapter with a look at how firms evaluate proposals to invest in long-term assets or undertake major new projects. **Capital budgeting** refers to the procedure a firm uses to plan for investments in assets or projects that it expects will yield benefits for more than a year. Fast-growing Spotify, the world's largest music and podcast streaming service, made $213 million in capital investments in 2019 and 2020 to build offices in Stockholm, New York, Boston, London, São Paolo, Los Angeles, Berlin, Singapore, and Miami.[54]

The capital budgeting process evaluates proposals such as:

- Replacing old machinery and equipment with new models to reduce cost and improve the efficiency of current operations

- Buying additional plant, machinery, and equipment to expand production capacity in *existing* markets

- Investing in plant, property, and equipment needed to expand into *new* markets

- Installing new, or modifying existing, plant and equipment to achieve goals not directly related to expanding production, such as reducing pollution or improving worker safety

The number of capital budgeting proposals a firm considers each year can be quite large. But it's unlikely that all proposals will be worth pursuing. How do financial managers decide whether or not to accept a proposal?

### 9-6a Evaluating Capital Budgeting Proposals

Financial managers measure the benefits and costs of long-term investment proposals in terms of the cash flows they generate. These cash flows are likely to be negative at the start of a project because money must be spent to get a long-term investment project up and running before it begins generating positive cash flows. But a project must eventually generate enough positive cash flows to more than offset these negative initial cash outflows if it is to benefit the company.

### 9-6b Accounting for the Time Value of Money

One of the most challenging aspects of the evaluation of a long-term project's cash flows is that they are spread out over a number of years. When financial managers compare cash flows that occur at different times, they must take the **time value of money** into account. The time value of money reflects the fact that, from a financial manager's perspective, a dollar received today is worth *more* than a dollar received in the future because the sooner you receive a sum of money, the sooner you can put that money to work to earn even *more* money.

Suppose, for example, that you were given the choice of receiving $1,000 either today or the same amount one year from today. If you think like a financial manager, this choice is a no-brainer! Let's be conservative and say that if you receive the money today you can deposit it in an

**capital budgeting** The process a firm uses to evaluate long-term investment proposals.

**time value of money** The principle that a dollar received today is worth more than a dollar received in the future.

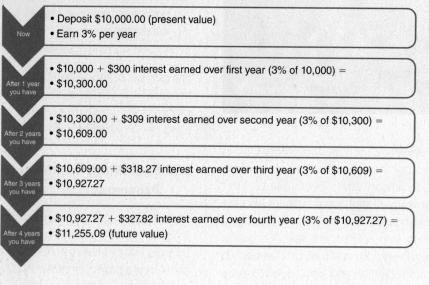

## Exhibit 9.5

### How a Present Value of $10,000 Grows to a Future Value of $11,255.09 in Four Years

**Now**
- Deposit $10,000.00 (present value)
- Earn 3% per year

**After 1 year you have**
- $10,000 + $300 interest earned over first year (3% of 10,000) =
- $10,300.00

**After 2 years you have**
- $10,300.00 + $309 interest earned over second year (3% of $10,300) =
- $10,609.00

**After 3 years you have**
- $10,609.00 + $318.27 interest earned over third year (3% of $10,609) =
- $10,927.27

**After 4 years you have**
- $10,927.27 + $327.82 interest earned over fourth year (3% of $10,927.27) =
- $11,255.09 (future value)

insured one-year **certificate of deposit (CD)** at your local bank that pays 3% interest. (A CD is similar to a savings account, except that it requires the funds to remain on deposit for a fixed term; in our example, the term is one year. You would incur a penalty if you withdrew your funds early.) Investing in your 3% CD means that a year from today you would have $1,030 (the $1,000 you deposited plus $30 in interest). But if you wait until next year to receive the $1,000, you'll lose the opportunity to earn that $30 in interest. Clearly, receiving the cash today is the better option.

Because money has a time value, a cash flow's value depends not only on the *amount* of cash received but also on *when* it is received. Financial managers compare cash flows occurring at different times by converting them to their present values. The **present value** of a cash flow received in a future time period is the amount of money that, if invested *today* at an assumed rate of interest (called the *discount rate*), would grow to become that future amount of money. Exhibit 9.5 shows

that $10,000 invested today at 3% grows to a future value of $11,255.09 in four years. Thus, $10,000 is the present value of $11,255.09 received in four years.

### 9-6c The Risk-Return Trade-Off Revisited

Unfortunately, financial managers don't have crystal balls, so they don't know the *actual* cash flows a proposed project will generate. Instead, they base their analysis on the cash flows the proposal is *expected* to generate. Once a company actually invests in a project, it may find that the *actual* cash flows are quite different from these estimated flows. This uncertainty means that capital budgeting decisions must consider risk.

In general, projects with the potential for high returns are also the projects with a high degree of uncertainty and risk. This is another example of the risk-return trade-off we introduced at the beginning of this chapter. Clearly, financial managers must take this trade-off into account when they compare different capital budgeting proposals; they must determine whether riskier proposals generate a high enough expected return to justify their greater risk.

One common way financial managers try to do this is to use a higher discount rate when they compute the present values of cash flows for risky projects than when they compute present values for less risky

**certificate of deposit (CD)** An interest-earning deposit that requires the funds to remain deposited for a fixed term. Withdrawal of the funds before the term expires results in a financial penalty.

**present value** The amount of money that, if invested today at a given rate of interest (called the discount rate), would grow to become some future amount in a specified number of time periods.

projects. This reflects the idea that a higher return is required to compensate for the greater risk.

### 9-6d Net Present Value: A Decision Rule for Capital Budgeting

The most common method financial managers use to evaluate capital budgeting proposals is to compute their **net present value (NPV)**. The NPV of an investment proposal is found by adding the present values of *all* of its estimated future cash flows and subtracting the initial cost of the investment from the sum. A positive NPV means that the present value of the expected cash flows from the project is greater than the cost of the project. In other words, the benefits from the project exceed its cost even after accounting for the time value of money. Financial managers approve projects with positive NPVs. A negative

| Exhibit 9.6 | Decision Rule for Capital Budgeting |
| --- | --- |
| **Result of NPV Calculation** | **Decision** |
| NPV ≥ 0 | Accept proposal ✔ |
| NPV < 0 | Reject proposal ✘ |

NPV means that the present value of the expected future cash flows from the project is less than the cost of the investment. This would indicate that the cost of the project outweighs its cash flow benefits. Financial managers would reject proposals with negative NPVs. (Refer to Exhibit 9.6.)

> **net present value (NPV)** The sum of the present values of expected future cash flows from an investment, minus the cost of that investment.

## The Big Picture

In this chapter, we described the tasks financial managers perform as they attempt to find the "best" sources and uses of financial resources—meaning those that will maximize the value of the firm to its owners. We saw that in their attempts to achieve this goal, financial managers face two challenges. The first is to balance the needs of owners against those of the other stakeholders; the second is to balance the potential rewards of their decisions against the risks.

Recent history illustrates how important sound financial management is to the success of a firm—and how devastating poor financial decisions can be. Indeed, the recent decline and fall of some of the biggest and best-known U.S. corporations can be traced in large measure to poor financial

decisions—especially decisions that failed to adequately take risk into account, resulting in the use of too much leverage.

These lessons from the recent past will probably result in a different approach to financial management over the next several years. While memories of the Great Recession are still relatively fresh, firms may be more conservative in their view of what constitutes the best sources and uses of funds. In particular, they are likely to shy away from excessive debt and put more emphasis on equity financing. They also are less likely to use their funds to invest in highly risky or speculative assets. These more conservative tendencies are likely to be reinforced by the major regulatory reforms, designed to curb aggressive (and risky) behavior, introduced by the Dodd-Frank Act.

## Careers in Finance

### Financial Analyst

Responsible for financial planning; preparing complex financial analyses and recommendations; establishing and maintaining internal financial controls; creating and analyzing monthly, quarterly, and annual reports; and ensuring financial information has been recorded accurately; working closely with business unit leaders to align company and financial goals;

and performing Sarbanes-Oxley assessments and testing. The ideal candidate has a bachelor's or master's degree in finance, expert spreadsheet and analytical skills, strong oral and written communication skills, strong understanding of financial analysis and reporting, and effective time and project management skills including the ability to simultaneously manage multiple projects and priorities as well as to work under pressure to meet deadlines.

# 10 | Financial Markets:
## Allocating Financial Resources

### Learning Objectives

After studying this chapter, you will be able to:

**10-1** Explain the role of financial markets in the U.S. economy and the key players in these markets

**10-2** Identify the key laws that govern the way financial markets operate and the impact of each law

**10-3** Compare the major types of securities that are traded in securities markets

**10-4** Explain how securities are issued in the primary market and traded on secondary markets

**10-5** Compare several strategies that investors use to invest in securities

**10-6** Interpret the information provided in the stock quotes available on financial websites

Katjen/Shutterstock.com

## 10-1 The Role of Financial Markets and Their Key Players

**Financial markets** perform a vital function: they transfer funds from savers (individuals and organizations willing to defer using some of their income to earn a financial return and build their wealth) to borrowers (individuals and organizations that need additional funds to achieve their financial goals). For example, Zoom, the videoconference company, raised $348 million from investors who purchased Zoom stock in its initial public offering in 2020. Investors came back for more in 2021, buying an additional $2 billion of shares when Zoom issued another round of new stock.[1] Zoom also borrowed $350 million from investors in 2021 by selling bonds, due in 2029, which pay bondholders an annual interest of 3.875%.[2] Without financial markets, companies like Zoom would find it difficult to obtain the funds needed to meet payrolls, invest in new facilities, develop new products, and compete

**financial markets** Markets that transfer funds from savers to borrowers.

effectively in global markets. For more on Zoom's IPO, read the boxed feature, "Before Buying Zoom's IPO Stock, Read the S-1 Registration First!"

But it's not just businesses that benefit. You do, too, through your involvement in both sides of financial markets. You participate as a borrower when using your credit card to finance daily purchases or when taking out a loan for college tuition. You also participate as a saver and investor, growing your financial portfolio to fund your children's education, accumulate a down payment for a home mortgage, or pay for retirement. For example, since stocks historically average a 10% annual return (6.5% from stock price appreciation and 3.5% from stock dividends paid to shareholders), a $3,000 investment in stocks in 1920 would have grown to $41 million by 2020.[3] Of course, very few of us have 100 years to invest our money. Most people, however, have 50 years if they begin investing in their early 20s and then start paying for retirement in their early 70s.

> "The stock market is a device for transferring money from the impatient to the patient."
>
> —Warren Buffett

An initial investment of $3,000 in the stock market—without any additional funds—would grow to $352,000 at the end of 50 years. But if you contributed $3,000 *annually*, your financial portfolio would grow to $3.8 million in 50 years![4] In other words, you can secure your financial future by buying ownership in companies and lending your money to corporate bond issuers. We'll learn more in section 10-5, "Personal Investing," and in *BUSN's* "Personal Finance Appendix."

In the United States and other well-developed market economies, the vast majority of financing occurs indirectly, with *financial intermediaries, such as banks and brokers,* coming between the ultimate savers and borrowers. We'll see that they perform a variety of functions, but what they all have in common is that they help channel funds from savers to borrowers.

# Before Buying Zoom's IPO Stock, Read the S-1 Registration First!

Are you Zoomed out? Who isn't? But all that "Zoom fatigue" has been great for Zoom Video Communications, Inc., the company behind the Zoom app powering online classes, work-from-home meetings and "we-can't-hear-you-so-click-the-unmute-button" family get togethers.

Zoom filed an S-1 Registration Statement with the U.S. Security and Exchange Commission in April 2019 for its initial public offering (IPO) of stock in April 2020. Zoom hoped to raise somewhere between $305 million and $348 million by offering "10,877,446 shares of our Class A common stock" at a price "between $28.00 and $32.00 per share."

How could ordinary investors decide whether to buy Zoom's IPO stock? By reading Zoom's S-1.

**Why Zoom is a good investment. . .**

- Revenue grew from $60.8 million in 2017 to $151.5 million in 2018 to $330.5 million in 2019. Zoom broke even in 2017,

had a small loss of $3.8 million in 2019, and earned a profit of $7.6 million in 2020.

- Zoom uses a video-first architecture, which means that unlike pre-existing conference call and chat apps, it was built from the ground up for cloud-based video and audio.

- Zoom is easy to use, requires little technical support, and is compatible with all digital platforms such as Microsoft Office and Google Docs.

**Why Zoom is a risky investment. . .**

- Zoom's business depends on its ability to attract new customers, convert them to annual subscribers, and to get them to renew annual Zoom subscriptions despite many competing products.

- Zoom's video services are price sensitive. Zoom's competitors "offer, lower-priced or free products or services that compete with our platform or may bundle and offer a broader range of products and services." For example, Microsoft offers Teams, a Zoom alternative, at no additional cost to Microsoft Office subscribers.

- Unlike Microsoft and Google, which control and run the data centers that run Microsoft Teams and Google Chat, Zoom does not control the 13 co-located data centers in Australia, Brazil, Canada, China, Germany, India, Japan, the Netherlands, and the United States that it uses to run Zoom video conferences.

- Was Zoom's IPO a good investment? Zoom's stock rose 72% on the day of its IPO. Zoom's second issuance of stock in 2021 which raised $2 billion, was priced at $340 a share, more than 10 times the IPO stock price. Are Zoom's IPO investors happy? So far, they're elated![5]

*Ymphotos/Shutterstock.com*

## 10-1a Depository Institutions

**Depository institutions** are financial intermediaries that obtain funds by accepting checking and savings deposits from individuals, businesses, and other institutions, and then lending those funds to borrowers.

- Commercial banks are the most common depository institutions. When you make a deposit into a checking or savings account at your bank, you are providing

funds that the bank can use for making loans to businesses, governments, or other individuals.

Halfway through 2020, more than half (54%) of total bank assets were in the form of loans, including over $5.7 trillion in real estate and mortgage loans, more than $2.1 trillion in consumer loans.[6]

- **Credit unions** are cooperatives, meaning that they are not-for-profit organizations that are owned by their depositors. As not-for-profit organizations, they strive to pay higher interest rates on member deposits and charge lower interest rates on loans.

Credit unions are open to individuals who belong to a specific "field of membership." For example, membership in some credit unions is limited to the employees who work for a specific employer and their family members; other credit unions base membership on church or union affiliation or are open to people living in a certain geographic area.[7]

Credit unions are a much smaller player in financial markets than commercial banks, but in 2020 they held more than $595 billion in mortgage financing and $478 billion in consumer credit on their books.[8]

■ **Savings and loan associations** (also called "S&Ls" or "thrifts") traditionally accepted only savings account deposits and used them to make mortgage loans. During the early 1980s, regulations on S&Ls were relaxed, allowing them to accept checking account deposits and make a broader range of loans. Still, the major focus of the savings and loan industry remains mortgage loans.

■ At the end of 2013 (the last year the Federal Reserve collected these data), S&Ls held $452 billion in mortgages—a big drop from 2006 when the figure peaked at $1.25 trillion.[9] In large part, this reflected a collapse of the housing market beginning in 2008. But S&Ls began declining in importance well before the Great Recession.[10]

## 10-1b Nondepository Financial Institutions

In addition to banks and other depository institutions, a number of other financial intermediaries play important roles in financial markets.

■ **Institutional investors** don't accept deposits but amass huge pools of financial capital from other sources and use these funds to acquire a portfolio of many different assets:

■ Mutual funds obtain money by selling shares to investors.

■ Insurance companies obtain money by collecting premiums from policyholders.

■ Retirement funds obtain money by collecting funds employers and their employees contribute for the employees' retirement.

These institutions invest heavily in corporate stock; institutional investors hold the majority of shares in most major U.S. corporations. They are also major holders of corporate bonds and government securities. Exhibit 10.1 lists the world's largest institutional investors, with New York-based BlackRock and Pennsylvania-based Vanguard Group topping the list with $6.8 trillion and $6.2 trillion in holdings, respectively.

■ **Securities brokers** act as agents for investors who want to buy or sell financial securities, such as corporate

### Exhibit 10.1 World's Largest Institutional Investors

| Institutional Investors | Headquarters Location | Financial Holdings (in U.S. dollars) |
|---|---|---|
| BlackRock | New York, New York, USA | $6.84 trillion |
| Vanguard Group | Valley Forge, Pennsylvania, USA | $6.2 trillion |
| UBS Group | Co-headquartered in Zurich and Basel, Switzerland | $3.26 trillion |
| Fidelity Investments | Boston, Massachusetts, USA | $3.2 trillion |
| State Street Global Advisors | Boston, Massachusetts, USA | $3.12 trillion |
| Allianz | Munich, Germany | $2.36 trillion* |
| J.P. Morgan Asset Management | New York, New York, USA | $1.9 trillion |
| Bank of New York Mellon | New York, New York, USA | $1.9 trillion |
| Capital Group | Los Angeles, California, USA | $1.8 trillion |
| PIMCO | Newport Beach, California, USA | $1.76 trillion |

Source: T. Lemke, "The 10 Largest Investment Management Companies Worldwide," *The Balance*, April 9, 2020, https://www.thebalance.com/which-firms-have-the-most-assets-under-management-4173923, accessed February 9, 2021.

*Not including PIMCO, which was acquired by Allianz in 2000.

stocks or bonds. In addition to handling the trades, many brokers provide their clients with additional services, such as financial planning and market research. Brokers are compensated by charging fees and commissions for the services they provide. Charles Schwab ($6.69 trillion in client assets) and Fidelity Investments ($8.8 trillion in client assets) are two of the largest U.S. securities brokers.[11]

■ **Securities dealers** participate directly in securities markets, buying and selling stocks and bonds for their own account, but not for others like

**savings and loan association** A depository institution that has traditionally obtained most of its funds by accepting savings deposits, which have been used primarily to make mortgage loans.

**securities broker** A financial intermediary who acts as an agent for investors who want to buy and sell financial securities. Brokers earn commissions and fees for the services they provide.

**securities dealer** A financial intermediary who participates directly in securities markets, buying and selling stocks and other securities for its own account.

securities brokers. They earn a profit by selling securities for higher prices than they paid to purchase them. (The difference between the prices at which they buy and sell a security is called the *spread*.)

- **Investment banks** are financial intermediaries that help firms issue new securities to raise financial capital. Goldman Sachs, founded in 1869, is one of the world's most prestigious investment banks. In 2020, its investment banking division earned $9.42 billion in revenue.[12] Sometimes investment banks actually buy the newly issued securities themselves; in other cases, they simply help arrange for their sale. Many of today's investment banks aren't actually independent companies. Instead, they are typically divisions of huge bank holding companies that also own commercial banks. JPMorgan Chase, for example, is both a commercial bank for businesses and individuals (Chase Bank), and, an investment bank (JP Morgan), the latter of which earned $3.3 billion from investment banking services in 2020.[13]

## 10-2 Regulating Financial Markets to Protect Investors and Improve Stability

Financial markets work well only when savers and borrowers have confidence in the soundness of key financial institutions and in the fairness of the market outcomes. When depositors lose confidence in their banks, or when investors discover that financial markets are rigged by practices such as insider trading or unethical and deceptive accounting, the financial system breaks down.

The financial crisis of 2008 is a recent example of the disruptions that result when financial markets malfunction. Indeed, the lessons learned in 2008, such as the Federal bank cutting interests rates to make it easier to borrow money, may have helped minimize the effects on financial markets during the early days of the COVID-19 pandemic in 2020.[14] From the early twentieth century to the present day, the U.S. economy has experienced several other major financial crises. The economy experienced massive bank failures in 1907 and in the early 1930s. It also weathered a savings and loan crisis in the late 1980s that brought the failure of over 1,000 S&Ls and required a federal bailout that cost over $120 billion.[15] And a variety of scandals involving ethical lapses (and in many cases outright fraud) roiled financial markets at the turn of the century.

### 10-2a Financial Regulation: Early Efforts

During most of the twentieth century, the federal government responded to financial upheavals by introducing new laws and regulations. This trend first emerged in the wake of the banking panic of 1907, which created pressure for Congress to find a way to stabilize the nation's banking system. The result was the **Federal Reserve Act of 1913**. As its name implies, this act created the Federal Reserve System (the Fed) to serve as the central bank in the United States. The law gave the Fed the primary responsibility for overseeing our nation's banking system.

Unfortunately, the creation of the Fed didn't solve all of the nation's banking problems. Another wave of bank failures occurred in the early 1930s as the economy sank into the Great Depression. Congress responded by passing the **Banking Act of 1933**, also known as the *Glass-Steagall Act*. This law established the Federal Deposit Insurance Corporation, which insured depositors against financial losses when a bank failed. The insurance initially covered only $2,500 of deposits—but $2,500 bought a lot more in the 1930s than it does today! Over the years, coverage has been increased several times. Today, the Federal Deposit Insurance Corporation (FDIC) insures up to $250,000 of your deposits per bank.[16] To get full FDIC coverage for $500,000, for example, put $250,000 in one bank and $250,000 in another. Accounts for trusts, retirement accounts, and businesses are also FDIC insured. Refer to "How Are My Deposit Accounts Insured by the FDIC?" at fdic.gov/deposit/covered/categories.html for specific coverage guidelines.

Another major provision of the Glass-Steagall Act banned commercial banks from dealing in securities markets, selling insurance, or otherwise competing with non-depository institutions such as insurance companies and investment banks. The rationale for these restrictions was that involvement in such activities exposed banks and their depositors to higher levels of risk.

Congress responded to the stock market crash that occurred in 1929 with two laws that are still the foundation of U.S. securities markets regulation. The first of these was the **Securities Act of 1933**, which dealt mainly

**investment bank** A financial intermediary that specializes in helping firms raise financial capital by issuing securities in primary markets.

**Federal Reserve Act of 1913** The law that established the Federal Reserve System as the central bank of the United States.

**Banking Act of 1933** The law that established the Federal Deposit Insurance Corporation (FDIC) to insure bank deposits. It also prohibited commercial banks from selling insurance or acting as investment banks.

**Securities Act of 1933** The first major federal law regulating the securities industry. It requires firms issuing new stock in a public offering to file a registration statement with the SEC.

# GameStop: What Goes Up Must Come Down

A decade ago, GameStop sold video game discs for computers and game consoles, such as the PlayStation or Xbox, which could only be purchased and picked up at its 6,000 stores. It sold each game twice, as a new game and again as a traded-in used game. Today, Sony, Microsoft, Nintendo, and others sell video games directly to gamers who download games to their PCs or consoles, all without GameStop. GameStop made $230 million in 2018, but lost $795 million in 2019, and $464 million in 2020. Since 2018 it has closed nearly 900 of its 6,000 stores.

So, it wasn't a surprise that institutional investors were shorting GameStop's stock, betting it would fall. Shorting is when investors "borrow" a stock via a margin loan from their broker. If that stock was $100 when "borrowed," but drops to $50, the investor sells the stock to make $50 a share. But if the stock rises to $150, the investor loses $50 a share. Shorting is risky. By using loans to buy much more stock than normal, investors can make huge profits, or huge losses.

On January 4, 2020, GameStop stock sold for $17.25. But things were about to change. By January 25, it had risen to $76.79 thanks to the millions of members of Reddit's subreddit WallStreetBets who encouraged each other to buy GameStop, feeling it was undervalued. The stock peaked at $483 two days later. By February 2, it was $90. By mid-February it was $50. The "shorts," who expected GameStop's problem to get worse, lost billions of dollars as the price surged. But so did ordinary investors who, swept up in the frenzy, bought in late hoping for the stock price to rise even higher. Michael, a corporate accountant, reallocated the investments in his $69,000 retirement fund to GameStop as it fell to $230 per share. The next day he got out, having turned $69,000 into a $42,000 loss in 24 hours.

GameStop's stock bubble is nothing new. In 1636 and 1637, the market for rare tulip bulbs in Amsterdam surged. Foreign and amateur investors, who normally did not buy tulip bulbs, began speculative buying, hoping to ride the surging prices to short-term profits. At peak, with prices up 28-fold in just two weeks, one tulip bulb could be traded for a house. Soon after, as with GameStop, prices crashed back to normal levels.

The lesson is that stock market investors are sometimes irrational. GameStop's basic business hadn't changed. The digitization of video games hadn't suddenly swung in GameStop's favor. But for a multitude of reasons, thousands of investors convinced themselves otherwise, temporarily propping up a stock price well beyond the value of its shrinking business. Chasing quick returns rarely works. Michael, the 27 year-old accountant who lost his entire retirement fund, said, "In a moment of intense hype, in a moment of weakness for me, I messed it all up in a matter of a day… I should've known better."[17]

Hanson L/Shutterstock.com

with the process of issuing new securities. It prohibited misrepresentation or other forms of fraud in the sale of newly issued stocks and bonds. It also required firms issuing new stock in a public offering to file a registration statement with the SEC. The next year, Congress passed the **Securities Exchange Act of 1934**, which regulated the trading of previously issued securities. This law created the **Securities and Exchange Commission** (SEC) and gave it broad powers to oversee the securities industry. The law required that all publicly traded firms with at least 500 shareholders and $10 million in assets file quarterly and annual financial reports with the SEC, and that brokers and dealers register with the SEC.

The Securities Exchange Act also gave the SEC the power to prosecute individuals and companies that engaged in fraudulent securities market activities. For example, the SEC has the authority to go after individuals who engage in illegal *insider trading*, which is the practice of using inside information (important information about a

**Securities and Exchange Act of 1934** A federal law dealing with securities regulation that established the Securities and Exchange Commission to regulate and oversee the securities industry.

**Securities and Exchange Commission** The federal agency with primary responsibility for regulating the securities industry.

IgorGolovniov/Shutterstock.com

company that isn't available to the general investing public) to profit unfairly from trading in a company's securities. The United Kingdom's Financial Conduct Authority, which is the UK's equivalent to the SEC, ordered a convicted stock trader, Walid Choucair, to pay back $4.5 million in stock earnings resulting from inside information received from Fabiana Abdel-Malek, a senior compliance officer at investment bank UBS AG. Abdel-Malek used burner phones to let Choucair know about five planned corporate mergers that UBS was facilitating *before* they were publicly announced. Choucair immediately purchased shares of those companies which rose in value after the mergers were announced.[18]

### 10-2b Deregulation During the 1980s and 1990s: Temporarily Reversing Course

The passage of these laws ushered in a period of more stable financial markets. But critics argued that the laws—especially the Glass-Steagall Act—represented an onerous government intrusion into the financial sector that stifled competition and impeded financial innovation. During the 1980s and 1990s Congress responded to these criticisms by easing restrictions on banks and other depository institutions. For instance, the **Financial Services Modernization Act of 1999**, also known as the *Gramm-Bliley-Leach Act*, reversed the Glass-Steagall Act's prohibition of banks selling insurance or acting as investment banks.

The financial sector initially seemed to prosper under its less regulated environment. It responded to its increased freedom with a variety of new services. Also, new technologies such as

ATMs and online banking made financial transactions easier and more convenient.

### 10-2c Recent Developments: Reregulation in the Aftermath of Financial Turmoil

But the wave of deregulation didn't last. A series of accounting scandals at the beginning of the twenty-first century, followed by a near collapse of the financial system in 2008, created pressure for new laws.

Congress reacted to the accounting scandals in the first years of the new century by passing the Sarbanes-Oxley Act in 2002. This law included provisions to ensure that external auditors offered fair, unbiased opinions when they examined a company's financial statements. It also increased the SEC's authority to regulate financial markets and investigate charges of fraud and unethical behavior.[19]

In the wake of the financial crisis of 2008–2009 Congress passed the Dodd-Frank Act of 2010. This far-reaching law expanded the Fed's regulatory authority over nondepository financial institutions, such as hedge funds and mortgage brokers that had previously operated with little regulatory oversight or accountability. It also created the Financial Stability Oversight Council to identify emerging risks in the financial sector so that action could be taken to rein in risky practices *before* they led to a crisis. The council was given the authority to recommend new rules to the Federal Reserve that would limit risky practices of the nation's largest, most complex financial institutions.[20]

### 10-3 Investing in Financial Securities: What Are the Options?

Financial securities markets are critical to corporations that rely on them to obtain much of their long-term financial capital. They also provide one of the most important venues that individuals can use to build their long-term wealth and earn significant financial returns.

### 10-3a Common Stock: Back to Basics

**Common stock** is the basic form of ownership in a corporation. Exhibit 10.2 shows a stock certificate for The Columbus Southern Railway Company. As owners of corporations, common stockholders have certain basic rights:

- **Voting Rights:** Owners of common stock have the right to vote on important issues at the annual stockholders' meeting. Under the most common arrangement, stockholders can cast one vote for each share of stock they own. One of the key issues that stockholders

## Exhibit 10.2

## Stock Certificates Represent Shares of Ownership in a Corporation

**Common stock is the basic form of ownership in a corporation.**

Robert Brown Stock/Shutterstock.com

vote on is the selection of members to the corporation's board of directors, but they also may vote on other major issues, such as the approval of a merger with another firm or a change in the corporation's by-laws. Ninety-nine percent of shareholders approved the merger between the Italian-American automaker Fiat Chrysler, which produces the Chrysler, Dodge, Ram, Jeep, Fiat, Alfa Romeo, Maserati, and Lancia auto brands, and the French PSA Groupe, which makes Peugeot, Citroën, DS, Opel, and Vauxhall cars.[21] The merger created the world's fourth largest automaker.

- **Right to Dividends:** Dividends are a distribution of earnings to the corporation's stockholders. All common stockholders have the right to receive a dividend *if* their corporation's board of directors declares one. In January 2021, the boards of chemical company Linde, railroad company Norfolk Southern, and consumer products company Kimberly-Clark approved payment of quarterly dividends to shareholders of $1.06, $0.99, and $1.14 per share, respectively.[22] The "catch" is that the board has no legal obligation to declare a dividend. Companies sometimes skip dividends to reinvest most or all of their earnings to finance growth. Vodafone, a European wireless carrier, cut its dividend by 40% to help pay the enormous cost of building out its new 5G network.[23]

- **Capital Gains:** Stockholders receive another type of return on their investment, called a **capital gain**, *if* the price of the stock rises above the amount they paid for it. Because of huge demand for at-home workouts during the COVID-19 pandemic, shareholders of Peloton Interactive, maker of the Peloton bike whose workouts are led by virtual spin class instructors, saw the price of their stock rise from $30.60 in January 2020 to $148.75 on February 10, 2021.[24] Capital gains can create very attractive financial returns for stockholders. Of course, there is no guarantee the stock's price will rise. If it falls, stockholders incur a capital loss rather than a capital gain.

- **Preemptive Right:** If a corporation issues new stock, existing stockholders sometimes have a preemptive right to purchase new shares in proportion to their existing holdings before the stock is offered to the other investors. For example, if you own 5% of the existing shares of stock, then the preemptive right gives you the right to purchase 5% of the new shares. This could be important for large stockholders who want to maintain their share of ownership. However, the conditions under which existing stockholders have preemptive rights vary among the states. In several states, a preemptive right is only available if it is specifically identified in the corporation's charter.

- **Right to a Residual Claim on Assets:** The final stockholder right is a residual claim on assets. If the corporation goes out of business and liquidates its assets, stockholders have a right to share in the proceeds in proportion to their ownership. But note that this is a *residual* claim—it comes *after all other claims* have been satisfied. In other words, the firm must pay any back taxes, legal expenses, wages owed to workers, and debts owed to creditors before the owners get anything. By the time all of these other claims have been paid, nothing may be left for the owners.

### 10-3b Preferred Stock: Getting Preferential Treatment

Common stock is the basic form of corporate ownership, but some companies also issue **preferred stock**, so named because it offers its holders preferential treatment in two respects:

- **Claim on Assets:** Holders of preferred stock have a claim on

**capital gain** The return on an asset that results when its market price rises above the price the investor paid for it.

**preferred stock** A type of stock that gives its holder preference over common stockholders in terms of dividends and claims on assets.

assets that comes before common stockholders if the company goes out of business. This gives preferred stockholders a better chance than common stockholders of recovering their investment if the company goes bankrupt.

- **Payment of Dividends:** Unlike dividends on common stock, dividends on preferred stock are usually a stated amount. For example, in February 2021, Wells Fargo bank sold $3.5 billion shares of preferred stock with a dividend of 3.9%. With each share selling for $1,000, the annual dividend payment is $39.[25]

- And a corporation can't pay *any* dividend to its common stockholders unless it pays the full stated dividend on its preferred stock. Still, it is important to note that a corporation has no *legal* obligation to pay a dividend to *any* stockholders, not even those who hold preferred stock.

Preferred stock sometimes includes a *cumulative feature*. This means that if the firm skips a preferred dividend in one period, the amount it must pay the next period is equal to the dividend for that period *plus* the amount of the dividend it skipped in the previous period. Additional skipped dividends continue to accumulate, and the firm can't pay *any* dividends to common stockholders until *all* accumulated dividends are paid to preferred stockholders. In the midst of the lowest oil prices in two decades, Oklahoma-based Chesapeake Energy suspended its 2016 annual dividends to save $240 million. After significant restructuring and cost cutting, Chesapeake reinstated dividends in February 2017. But before resuming quarterly dividends, the company paid preferred stockholders the four quarterly dividends (that is, dividends in arrears) that it had missed in 2016.[26]

Preferred stock isn't necessarily "preferred" to common stock in all respects. For instance, preferred stockholders normally don't have voting rights, so they can't vote on issues that come up during stockholders' meetings. And even though preferred stockholders are more likely to receive a dividend, they aren't guaranteed a *better* dividend; the board can declare a dividend to common stockholders that offers a higher return.[27] Finally, when a company

experiences strong earnings, the market price of its common stock can—and often does—appreciate more in value than the price of its preferred shares, thus offering common shareholders a greater capital gain.

### 10-3c Bonds: Earning Your Interest

A **bond** is a formal IOU issued by a corporation or government entity. Bonds come in many different forms. Our discussion will focus on the basic characteristics of long-term bonds issued by corporations.

The date a bond comes due is called its **maturity date**, and the amount the issuer owes the bondholder at maturity is called the bond's **par value** (or face value). Long-term bonds issued by corporations usually mature 10 to 30 years after issuance, but longer maturities are possible. In 2020, aerospace manufacturer Boeing sold $6 billion of bonds with par values of $1,000 that will mature in 20 years.[28]

Bondholders can sell their bonds to other investors before they mature, but the price they receive might not correspond to the bond's par value because bond prices fluctuate with conditions in the bond market. When a bond's market price is above its par value, it is selling at a *premium*; when its price is below par value, it is selling at a *discount*.

Most bonds require their issuers to pay a stated amount of interest to bondholders each year until the bond matures. The **coupon rate** on the bond expresses the annual interest payment as a percentage of the bond's par value. Boeing's 20-year bonds maturing in 2050 have a coupon rate of 5.705% and a par value of $1,000.[29] So investors who own those bonds receive $57.05 in interest (5.705% of $1,000) each year until the bonds reach maturity—or until they sell their bonds to someone else. But since bonds can sell at a premium or a discount, the coupon rate doesn't necessarily represent the rate of return that investors earn on the amount they actually *paid* for the bond. The **current yield** expresses a bond's interest payment as a percentage of the bond's *current market price* rather than its par value. In February 2021, the market price of Boeing's 2020/2040 bonds was selling for a premium of $1,130.25, making the current yield 5.05% (found by dividing the $57.05 interest payment by $1,130.25).[30]

---

**bond** A formal debt instrument issued by a corporation or government entity.

**maturity date** The date when a bond will come due.

**par value (of a bond)** The value of a bond at its maturity; what the issuer promises to pay the bondholder when the bond matures.

**coupon rate** The interest paid on a bond, expressed as a percentage of the bond's par value.

**current yield** The amount of interest earned on a bond, expressed as a percentage of the bond's current market price.

In 2018, private-equity firm Silver Lake Group LLC paid movie theater chain AMC Entertainment Holdings $600 million to buy its convertible bonds. When the price of AMC's stock quadrupled in less than a week, fueled by buying surges from Reddit subgroup members backing the stock, Silver Lake converted the bonds to stock, which it then sold for $713 million, locking in a $113 million capital gain.

Unlike dividends on stock, a firm has a *legal obligation* to pay interest on bonds—and to pay the bondholder the par value of the bond when it matures. Thus, bondholders are more likely to receive a financial return than stockholders. But that doesn't mean that bonds are without risk. As we discussed in Chapter 9 when JCPenney's skipped a 12 million bond interest payment a month before filing for bankruptcy, corporations that get into serious financial difficulties sometimes *default* on their bonds, meaning that they are unable to make required payments.[31] When that happens, bankruptcy proceedings usually allow bondholders to recover some (but not all) of what they are owed; historically, the average amount recovered has been about 72 cents on the dollar.[32] While that is better than what stockholders can expect, it is far short of being risk free. Indeed, during the COVID-19 pandemic, bondholders recovered just 55 cents to 60 cents on the dollar on bond defaults.[33]

### 10-3d Convertible Securities: The Big Switch

Corporations sometimes issue **convertible securities**, which are bonds or shares of preferred stock that investors can exchange for a given number of shares of the issuing corporation's common stock. A *conversion ratio* indicates the number of shares of common stock exchanged for each convertible security. Berkshire Hathaway is an American multinational conglomerate holding company headquartered in Omaha, Nebraska. Berkshire Hathaway's Class A stock was $360,290 per share when this was written. And yes, that's the most expensive share of stock in the world! Berkshire's Class B stock, however, traded for $239.92 on that same day. Each share of Berkshire's Class A stock can be converted into 1,500 Class B shares. At those prices, 1,500 shares of the Class B stock are worth $359,880, or $410 less than the class A stock. Because the conversion produces a $410 loss, Class A shareholders are not likely to convert their stock.[34] The ratio is set at the time the convertible securities are issued so that it is only financially desirable to convert the securities if the price of the common stock increases.

Owning a convertible security allows investors to gain from an increase in the price of common stock, while limiting their risk if the price of the stock falls. If the price of the common stock increases, the holders of convertible securities can convert them into the now more valuable stock. But if the price of the company's common stock falls, investors can continue to hold their convertible securities and collect their interest or preferred dividends.

The firm also can benefit from issuing convertible bonds, because the popularity of this feature with investors allows it to offer a lower coupon rate on convertible bonds (or a lower dividend on preferred stock), thus reducing its fixed payments. And if investors convert to common stock, the firm no longer has to make these fixed payments at all. In 2018, private-equity firm Silver Lake Group LLC paid movie theater chain AMC Entertainment Holdings $600 million to buy its convertible bonds. When the price of AMC's stock quadrupled in less than a week in 2021, fueled by buying surges from Reddit subgroup members backing the stock, Silver Lake converted the bonds to stock, which it then sold for $713 million, locking in a $113 million capital gain.[35] Converting those bonds to stock reduced AMC's $6 billion of debt by 10%. With Silver Lake now holding stocks rather than bonds, AMC no longer has to pay Silver Lake bond interest payments, nor does it have to repay Silver Lake $600 million when the bonds mature.[36]

But there is one important group that may be unhappy with this arrangement; the corporation's existing stockholders may be displeased if the new stock issued to holders of convertible securities dilutes their share of ownership—and their share of profits!

**convertible security** A bond or share of preferred stock that gives its holder the right to exchange it for a stated number of shares of common stock.

# Robinhood: The Unintended Costs of Free Stock Trading

Robinhood (RH), the investing app that played a large role in GameStop's stock bubble, touts itself as "Investing for Everyone." RH's commission-free trades can be a good deal for disciplined investors, but when combined with RH's frequent feedback on stock performance, could encourage poor investing habits.

For example, frequent buying and selling runs counter to nearly all long-term investment advice. But with zero commissions, new investors don't worry about trading costs. Julian Emanuel, chief equity and derivatives strategist at investment firm BTIG, says, "When you can engage in an activity that used to cost you something and no longer seemingly costs you anything, the inclination is, particularly if you're making money doing it, you're likely to do it more often. It's a perfect example of the law of unintended consequences."

Likewise, while intended to provide meaningful feedback to stock market newbies, the "Vegas-y look" in the RH app may also encourage frequent trading. *Wall Street Journal* investment advice columnist Jason Zweig says, "Whenever a stock's price changes, Robinhood updates it not just by showing an uptick in green and a downtick in red [the traditional method], but also by spinning the digits up and down like a slot machine. This flux of direction and color quickly becomes hypnotic… the ever-changing numbers and colors put me into a kind of trance."

RH says that 98% of its customers use buy-and-hold strategies. But sticking to a long-term strategy could be difficult, said Zweig, because "Robinhood kept sending me alerts, lighting up my phone anytime anything I owned moved more than 5%."

RH is making it easier and cheaper for stock market rookies to start investing. But those investors need to be mindful of the unintended costs of free trades and the gamified feedback generated by the RH app.[37]

## 10-3e Mutual Funds and ETFs: Diversification Made Easy

**Financial diversification**—the practice of holding many different securities in many different sectors—is generally considered a desirable strategy because it helps reduce (but not completely eliminate) risk. If you hold many different securities in different sectors of the economy, then losses on some securities may be offset by gains on others.

Many investors who want to hold diversified portfolios find that investing in large numbers of individual stocks and bonds is prohibitively expensive. And even if they could afford to do so, investors often lack the time and expertise to select a large number of individual securities. Faced with these limitations, many investors find that **mutual funds** and exchange-traded funds are attractive options.

**Mutual Funds: Portfolios Made Easy** There are two ways mutual funds can be structured. A *closed-end fund* issues a fixed number of shares and invests the money received from selling these shares in a portfolio of assets. Shares of closed-end funds can be traded among investors much like stocks. This means that after initial funding, closed-end funds do not accept new investors. So, if you put $10,000 "into" an established closed-end fund, you're not giving the fund managers $10,000 more to invest, you're simply buying $10,000 of the closed-end fund shares from another investor in that fund. Many investors find closed-end funds confusing.[38] They have fallen in popularity compared to open-end funds and exchanged-traded funds, discussed next.

**financial diversification** A strategy of investing in a wide variety of securities in order to reduce risk.

**mutual fund** An institutional investor that raises funds by selling shares to investors and uses the accumulated funds to buy a portfolio of many different securities.

Mutual funds are one of the best ways for individual investors to diversify investment portfolios across different sectors of the economy.

Natee K Jindakum/Shutterstock.com

An *open-end mutual fund* doesn't have a fixed number of shares, nor are its shares traded like stocks. Instead, the fund issues additional shares when demand increases and redeems (buys back) old shares when investors want to cash in. So, if you put $10,000 into an open-end fund, you *are* giving the fund managers $10,000 more to invest. Instead of buying shares from another investor, as with closed-end funds, you're buying shares directly from the mutual fund. The price at which shares of an open-end mutual fund are issued and redeemed is based on the fund's **net asset value per share** (NAVPS), which is computed by dividing the total value of the fund's cash, securities, and other assets (less any liabilities) by the number of fund shares outstanding. Though the NAVPS is the basis for the price of a fund's shares, investors often also pay commissions and purchase fees.

Several features make mutual funds a popular choice for investors:

- **Diversification at Relatively Low Cost:** By pooling the funds of thousands of investors, mutual funds have the financial resources to invest in a broader portfolio of securities than individual investors could afford. This high level of diversification can help reduce risk. For instance, Vanguard's Total Stock Market Index Fund, which is an open-end fund, allows investors to diversify because it holds more than 3,500 U.S. stocks representing "the investment return of the overall stock market."[39]

- **Professional Management:** Most mutual funds are managed by a professional fund manager who selects the assets in the fund's portfolio. This can be appealing to investors who lack the time and expertise to make complex investment decisions.

- **Variety:** Whatever your investment goals and philosophy, you can probably find a fund that's a good match. There are many different types of funds; some invest only in certain types of securities (such as municipal bonds or stocks of large corporations), others invest in specific sectors of the economy (such as energy, technology, or healthcare), and yet others seek more balanced and broad-based portfolios. Some funds simply invest in a portfolio of stocks that matches those in a specific stock index, such as the Standard & Poor's 500 or the Wilshire 5000. These *index funds* have become very popular in recent years.

- **Liquidity:** It's easy to withdraw funds from a mutual fund. For a closed-end fund, you simply sell your shares. For an open-end fund, you redeem your shares from the fund itself. However, regardless of when you initiate your withdrawal, redemptions of an open-end fund are not carried out until its NAVPS is determined after the *next* trading session is completed.

Mutual funds do have some drawbacks. Perhaps the most serious is that the professional management touted by many funds doesn't come cheap. Investors in mutual funds pay a variety of fees that typically range from 1% to 3% of the amount invested. The fees charged by mutual funds can make a serious dent in the overall return received by the fund's investors. And funds assess these fees even when they perform poorly. One reason for the popularity of index funds is that they don't require professional management, so their fees are lower. For example, the average fee for index funds and exchanged-traded funds (discussed next) is 0.48%.[40]

Another drawback of actively managed funds is that when their professional managers engage in a lot of trading, significant tax consequences are associated with those financial gains. It is also important to realize that some of the specialized mutual funds that invest in only one sector of the economy or only one type of security may not provide enough diversification to reduce risk significantly.

### 10-3f Exchange Traded Funds: Real Basket Cases (and We Mean That in a Good Way)

An **exchange traded fund (ETF)** is similar to a mutual fund in some respects but differs in how it is created and how its shares are initially distributed. ETFs allow investors to buy ownership in what is called a market basket of many different securities. In fact, the market basket for most ETFs reflects the composition of a broad-based stock index, much like an index mutual fund. But in recent years more specialized ETFs that focus on narrower market baskets of assets have appeared on the market. First Trust, for example, sells a Cybersecurity ETF (CIBR) investing in companies "engaged in the cybersecurity segment of the tech and

**net asset value per share** The value of a mutual fund's securities and cash holdings minus any liabilities, divided by the number of shares of the fund outstanding.

**exchange traded fund (ETF)** Shares traded on securities markets that represent the legal right of ownership over part of a basket of individual stock certificates or other securities.

industrial sectors," as well as a Clean Edge Smart Grid Infrastructure ETF (GRID) that, "targets companies engaged in the 'smart grid' movement which seeks to upgrade America's electricity grid with 21st century technologies."[41] Like closed-end mutual funds—but unlike the more common open-end funds—ETFs are traded just like stocks. Thus, you can buy and sell ETFs any time of the day.

Compared to most actively managed mutual funds, ETFs usually have lower costs and fees. However, since ETFs are bought and sold like stocks, you do have to pay brokerage commissions every time you buy or sell shares.

## 10-4 Issuing and Trading Securities: The Primary and Secondary Markets

There are two distinct types of securities markets: the primary securities market and the secondary securities market. The **primary securities market** is where corporations raise additional financial capital by selling *newly issued* securities. The **secondary securities market** is where *previously issued* securities are traded.

### 10-4a The Primary Securities Market: Where Securities Are Issued

There are two methods of issuing securities in the primary market:

- In a **public offering**, securities are sold (in concept, at least) to anyone in the investing public who is willing and financially able to buy them.

- In a **private placement**, securities are sold to one or more private

investors (who may be individuals or institutions) under terms negotiated between the issuing firm and the private investors.

**Public Offerings** Many corporations are initially owned by a small number of people who don't sell the stock to outsiders. But growing corporations often need to obtain more financial capital than such a small group can provide. Such firms may *go public* by issuing additional stock and offering it to investors outside their group. The first time a corporation sells its stock in a public offering, the sale is called an **initial public offering (IPO)**.

Going public is a complicated and high-stakes process; obtaining sufficient funds in an IPO is often critical to the firm's success. So, almost all firms that go public enlist the help and advice of an investment bank that specializes in helping firms issue new securities. The investment bank assists the firm at every step of the IPO, from the planning and market assessment phase until the actual securities are distributed to investors after the offering is conducted.

One of the key responsibilities of the investment bank is to arrange for the actual sale of the securities. The investment bank uses either a *best efforts* or a *firm commitment* approach. Under the best efforts approach, the bank provides advice about pricing and marketing the securities and assists in finding potential buyers. But it doesn't guarantee that the firm will sell all of its securities at a high enough price to meet its financial goals. The investment bank earns a commission on all of the shares sold under a best efforts approach.

Under a *firm commitment* arrangement, the investment bank **underwrites** the issue. This means that the investment bank itself purchases *all* of the shares at a specified price negotiated with the company, thus guaranteeing that the firm issuing the stock receives a specific amount of new funds. The investment bank that underwrites the offer seeks to earn a profit by reselling the stock to investors at a higher price. For large public offerings, a group of investment banks, called an *underwriting syndicate*, may temporarily work together to underwrite the securities. Exhibit 10.3 shows the 23 companies making up the underwriting syndicate for the 2020 IPO for data storage company Snowflake. Snowflake's underwriting syndicate of 23 companies purchased 28,000,000 shares at $120 each, guaranteeing Snowflake $3.36 billion from its IPO. However, Snowflake's shares closed at $254 per share on the first day of trading, more than double the estimated IPO price of $120 and well beyond what Snowflake and its underwriters expected.[42]

Before going public, a firm must file a **registration statement** with the Securities and Exchange

## Exhibit 10.3 Snowflake's Initial Public Offering Underwriting Syndicate

| Underwriters | Number of Shares |
|---|---|
| Goldman Sachs & Co. LLC | 9,156,000 |
| Morgan Stanley & Co. LLC | 5,756,800 |
| J.P. Morgan Securities LLC | 2,097,200 |
| Allen & Company LLC | 2,094,400 |
| Citigroup Global Markets Inc. | 2,094,400 |
| Credit Suisse Securities (USA) LLC | 1,047,200 |
| Barclays Capital Inc. | 798,000 |
| Deutsche Bank Securities Inc. | 798,000 |
| Mizuho Securities USA LLC | 798,000 |
| Trust Securities, Inc. | 798,000 |
| BTIG, LLC | 260,400 |
| Canaccord Genuity LLC | 260,400 |
| Capital One Securities, Inc. | 260,400 |
| Cowen and Company, LLC | 260,400 |
| D.A. Davidson & Co. | 260,400 |
| JMP Securities LLC | 260,400 |
| Oppenheimer & Co. Inc. | 260,400 |
| Piper Sandler & Co. | 260,400 |
| Stifel, Nicolaus & Company, Incorporated | 260,400 |
| Academy Securities, Inc. | 54,600 |
| Loop Capital Markets LLC | 54,600 |
| Samuel A. Ramirez & Company, Inc. | 54,600 |
| Siebert Williams Shank & Co., LLC | 54,600 |
| Total | 28,000,000 |

Source: "Snowflake, Inc. Rule 424(b)(4) Registration," US Securities and Exchange Commission, February 11, 2021, https://www.sec.gov/Archives/edgar/data/1640147/000162828020013667/snowflake424b4.htm, accessed February 12, 2021.

Commission (SEC). Exhibit 10.4 shows the registration statement that Snowflake filed regarding its IPO in 2020. This long, complex document must include the firm's key financial statements plus additional information about the company's management, its properties, its competition, and the intended uses for the funds it plans to obtain from the offering. The corporation cannot legally offer its new securities for sale until the SEC has examined this statement and declared it effective.

## Exhibit 10.4
### Snowflake, Inc. Registration Statement for Initial Public Offering

As filed with the Securities and Exchange Commission on September 14, 2020.

**UNITED STATES**
**SECURITIES AND EXCHANGE COMMISSION**
WASHINGTON, D.C. 20549

**Amendment No. 2**
to
**FORM S-1**
**REGISTRATION STATEMENT**
UNDER
THE SECURITIES ACT OF 1933

**Snowflake Inc.**
(Exact name of Registrant as specified in its charter)

7372
(Primary Standard Industrial Classification Code Number)

450 Concar Drive
San Mateo, CA 94402
(844) 766-9355
(Address, including zip code, and telephone number, including area code, of Registrant's principal executive offices)

Frank Slootman
Chief Executive Officer
Snowflake Inc.
450 Concar Drive
San Mateo, CA 94402
(844) 766-9355
(Name, address, including zip code, and telephone number, including area code, of agent for service)

Copies to:
Derk Lupinek
General Counsel
Snowflake Inc.
450 Concar Drive
San Mateo, CA 94402
(844) 766-9355

Source: "Snowflake Inc. Form S-1 Registration Statement," US Securities and Exchange Commission, September 14, 2020, https://sec.report/Document/0001628280-20-013518/snowflakes-1a2.htm, accessed February 12, 2021.

> "Investors must keep in mind that there's a difference between a good company and a good stock. After all, you can buy a good car but pay too much for it."
> —Richard Thaler, American Economist

**Private Placements** In a private placement, the issuing firm negotiates the terms of the offer directly with a small number of **accredited investors**. These are individuals, businesses, or other organizations that meet specific financial requirements set by the SEC. Private placements are usually quicker, simpler, and less expensive than

> **accredited investor** An organization or individual investor who meets certain criteria established by the SEC and so qualifies to invest in unregistered securities.

public offerings. The investment bank often helps the firm identify and contact accredited investors and assists the firm as it negotiates the terms of the private placement.

The main reason private placements are simpler and less expensive than public offerings is that privately placed securities are exempt from the requirement to register with the SEC. The ability to obtain financing without having to prepare complex registration documents can be a real attraction. But because the pool of potential investors is limited to accredited investors, private placements normally don't have the potential to raise as much money as public offerings. Another drawback is that securities that haven't been registered with the SEC can't be sold to anyone except other accredited investors.

## 10-4b Secondary Securities Markets: Let's Make a Deal

The firms that issue stocks and bonds don't receive any additional funds when their securities are traded in the secondary markets. But few investors would want to buy securities issued in the primary markets without the liquidity and possibility of earning capital gains provided by the opportunity to sell these securities in the secondary markets.

**Stock (Securities) Exchanges** The stocks of most large publicly traded corporations are listed and traded on a **stock (or securities) exchange**. A securities exchange provides an organized venue for stockbrokers and securities dealers to trade listed stocks and other securities. Each exchange establishes its own requirements for the securities it lists. The requirements vary among the exchanges, but they're typically based on the earnings of the company, the number of shares of stock outstanding, and the number of shareholders. In addition to meeting listing requirements, exchanges require firms to pay an initial fee at the time their securities are first listed, and an annual listing fee to remain listed on the exchange.

**stock (or securities) exchange** An organized venue for trading stocks and other securities that meet its listing requirements.

**market makers** Securities dealers that make a commitment to continuously offer to buy and sell the stock of a specific corporation listed on the NASDAQ exchange or traded in the OTC market.

**over-the-counter (OTC) market** The market where securities that are not listed on exchanges are traded.

**electronic communications network (ECN)** An automated, computerized securities trading system that automatically matches buyers and sellers, executing trades quickly and allowing trading when securities exchanges are closed.

The New York Stock Exchange, owned by Intercontinental Exchange (which runs 10 exchanges across North America, Europe, and Asia), trades stock in 2,300 companies worth $26 trillion dollars, making it the world's largest stock exchange.[43] NASDAQ, the second-largest stock exchange, is part of NASDAQ OMX, which runs exchanges in the United States and seven in Europe. Today, NASDAQ trades stock in 3,000 companies worth a combined $19.3 trillion.[44] The stocks of many of today's high-profile technology companies, such as Amazon, Apple, Google, Microsoft, and Tesla, are traded on the NASDAQ market.

The key players in the NASDAQ market are known as **market makers**. These are securities dealers that make a commitment to continuously offer to buy and sell (make a market in) specific NASDAQ-listed stocks. Each NASDAQ stock has several market makers who compete against each other by posting two prices for each stock: the *bid price* indicates how much the market maker will pay per share to buy a stated quantity of the stock, while the *ask price* indicates the price per share at which it will sell the same stock. The ask price is higher than the bid price; the difference is called the *bid/ask spread* (or just the *spread*) and is the source of the market maker's profit.

**The Over-the-Counter Market** Many corporations with publicly traded stock don't meet the requirements to have their shares listed on an organized exchange; others choose not to list on exchanges because they don't want to pay the listing fees. The **over-the-counter market (OTC)** is where the stocks of 12,000 such companies are traded.[45] OTC stocks are traded through a system of market makers much like stocks are traded on the NASDAQ exchange. However, the market for most OTC stocks is much less active than for stocks listed on the major exchanges. Because of this, most stocks listed on the OTC have only a few market makers. The lack of competition often leads to much higher spreads between bid and ask prices for stocks traded in the OTC than normally exist for stocks traded on the NASDAQ exchange.

**Electronic Communications Networks** The newest development in stock market technology involves the rise of **electronic communications networks (ECNs)**. The SEC classifies ECNs as alternative trading systems because they represent an alternative to established stock exchanges as a venue for buying and selling securities. ECNs are entirely automated and computerized trading systems that allow traders to bypass the market makers used in the NASDAQ and OTC markets. However, individuals can only take advantage of this venue by opening an account with a broker-dealer that subscribes to an ECN. Instinet and NYSE ARCA operate as ECNs.

If you place an order to buy a security on an ECN, the computer system checks to see if there is a matching order from another trader to sell the same security. If so, it immediately and automatically executes the transaction in a process that typically takes less than a second to complete. ECNs obviously speed up transactions. They also make it possible for investors to trade securities "after hours" when the U.S. exchanges are closed.

## 10-5 Personal Investing

Would investing in stocks, bonds, and other securities make sense for you? If so, how could you get started? What are the potential risks and rewards of various investment strategies?

Investing in securities requires you to think carefully about your specific situation, your personal goals, and your attitudes:

- What are your short-term and long-term goals?

- Given your budget, how much are you able to invest?

- How long can you leave your money invested?

- How concerned are you about the tax implications of your investments?

- How much tolerance do you have for risk?

Notice that the last question deals with your attitudes toward risk. Most people are not comfortable with high levels of risk. But no investment strategy completely avoids risk. And in general, the riskier the approach, the greater the *potential* rewards. To achieve your goals, you'll need to find the balance between risk and return that works for you.

### 10-5a Choosing a Broker: Gaining Access to the Markets

Members of the general public cannot directly trade stocks and other securities on the exchanges, the over-the-counter market, or the ECNs we described earlier in the chapter. Thus, most investors enlist the services of a brokerage firm to carry out their trades. Choosing the right broker is the first step in implementing your investment plans.

*Discount brokers* provide the basic services needed to buy and sell stocks, mutual funds, exchange-traded funds, and bonds and bond funds. For most investors, that's all they'll need, especially with the easy access and extensive information provided by discount brokers' websites and apps. Vanguard is the quintessential discount broker.[46]

By contrast *full-service brokers* provide a wide range of services—such as market research, personalized investment advice, and tax planning. In addition to executing standard trades, full-service brokers allow investors to buy and sell foreign securities, stock options, foreign exchange (currencies), and to buy on margin (putting say, 10% down to buy securities and then borrowing the remaining 90% from the broker). E*TRADE and TD Ameritrade (now owned by Charles Schwab) and Merrill Lynch are full-service brokers.

Discount brokers used to charge significantly lower prices than full-service brokers, but in the last decade fees and commissions have dropped dramatically at all brokers. Today, many charge nothing for online trades that customers make themselves (using broker websites and apps) or for buying and selling the broker's own investment funds (which are often very good investments). But if you need broker assistance to buy or sell an investment, expect to pay something like $25 per trade. Likewise, less expensive flat fees, such as E*TRADE's $6.95 fee for OTC trades, have replaced more expensive commission fees based on a percentage of the value of the securities bought or sold.[47]

The result is that today's investors have excellent options when choosing brokers. Full-service firms have lowered fees or eliminated commissions to stop clients from defecting to discount brokers. Discount brokers have cut their prices even more and have broadened the range of basic services they offer. Many brokerage firms, such as Charles Schwab or Fidelity, go even further, offering investors their choice of either discount or full-service accounts. So, investing is much less expensive than it used to be. But brokerage firms aren't free. All brokers, discount or full-service, charge a variety of fees, such as annual fees, maintenance fees for Individual Retirement Accounts (IRAs), minimum balance fees, and, sometimes, "inactivity fees" if you don't place enough orders!

With technology driving many of these changes, the financial planning industry now uses robo advisors to help people automatically set, track, stick to (that's the hard part), and eventually achieve their financial goals. Wealthfront and Betterment, two of the largest robo advisor services, use computer algorithms to automatically invest clients' wealth in a way that maximizes returns and minimizes taxes. Based on criteria set by the user, these services automatically deposit bank funds into retirement accounts each month; retrieve and then invest extra cash that would otherwise not earn a return; and rebalance stock portfolios by selling fast-moving stocks (capturing the gains) and investing in underweighted (and perhaps cheaper) stocks. Not only do robo advisors do all this automatically and based on individualized financial goals, they do so with lower annual fees than traditional advisors. Robo advisors typically charge 0.25% to 0.50% of assets, compared to 1% to 2% among human advisors.[48]

# Direct Listings: Your Best Chance to Buy Stock When a Company Goes Public

"Going public" is when a firm first sells stock to outside investors. Firms that go public typically use investment banks to manage this complex process, including determining the initial stock price.

But if you're a regular investor, buying a company's stock on the day it is issued can be difficult. What happens is that investment banks and IPO underwriters (refer to Exhibit 10.3) work with the company to establish an initial stock price. Underwriters buy shares at that price, guaranteeing the company its money. In turn, they sell most of those shares to large institutional investors before the stock is issued on a stock exchange. Because early investors and employees cannot sell their stock until six months later, these factors combine to reduce the amount of available stock on the day of the IPO.

The U.S. Securities and Exchange Commission, however, has approved a new method of going public proposed by the New York Stock Exchange (NYSE). *Direct listings* are different in three ways:

- First, there is no lockup period. All stock shares can be sold at the IPO.

- Second, the NYSE takes selling orders (from the company, early investors, and employees) and buying orders from members of the public. But no stock is sold until a firm market price emerges. That market-determined price becomes the price at which the stock opens on the NYSE. Recall that data storage company Snowflake's IPO stock, set at $120 by an investment bank, closed at $254 on its first day. The hope is that market-determined prices will be more accurate, thus raising more funds for firms, rather than for investment banks, IPO underwriters, and institutional investors.

- Third, there are no IPO underwriters. Which means that investment banks and institutional investors don't get a bite of the apple before ordinary investors. The IPO is truly public, open to all buyers.

Only a few direct listings have been tried so far. But online gaming firm Roblox switched from an IPO to a direct listing for its first public stock sale. Keep an eye out. There will be more. Direct listings are your best chance to buy stock when a company goes public.[49]

Orhan akkurt/Shutterstock.com

---

Once you've decided on a broker, you need to open an account. This is a fairly simple process; it requires filling out some forms (usually available online) and making an initial investment. The minimum initial investment varies, but $1,000 to $3,000 is fairly typical.

## 10-5b Buying Securities: Let's Make a Deal

Once you've set up your account, you can trade securities by using your broker's website or app to specify the security you want to trade and the quantity you want to buy or sell. You can also specify the type of order you want to place. The most common are market orders and limit orders:

- **Market orders** instruct your broker's website or app to buy or sell a security at the current market price. Placing a market order virtually guarantees that your order will be executed. The downside is that you may end up buying at a higher price than you expected to pay or selling your stock for less than you expected to receive. It just depends on whether the market price drops or rises.

- **Limit orders** place limits on the prices at which orders are executed. A *buy limit order* tells your broker's website or app to buy a stock *only* if its price is at or below a specified value. You'd use this approach if you wanted to make sure you didn't pay more for the stock than you thought it was worth. Similarly, a *sell limit order* ensures that you sell the shares only if the price is at or above a specified value. This prevents your stock from selling at a price you believe is too low.

## 10-5c Strategies for Investing in Securities

There are several strategies you can use to guide your investment decisions. We'll provide an overview of the more

**market order** An order telling a broker to buy or sell a specific security at the best currently available price.

**limit order** An order to a broker to buy a specific stock only if its price is below a certain level, or to sell a specific stock only if its price is above a certain level.

Agencja Fotograficzna Caro/Alamy Stock Photo

Stockbrokers place orders to buy and sell stocks and other securities for their clients.

common approaches, but none of these approaches is foolproof—alas, there is no known strategy that is guaranteed to earn you millions.

**Investing for Income** Some investors focus on buying bonds and preferred stocks to generate a steady, predictable flow of income. This approach is popular with retirees who want to supplement their retirement income. But the return on such low-risk securities is relatively low, and their market value seldom increases much over time. Thus, it probably isn't the best strategy for younger investors who are trying to grow their wealth.

**Market Timing** Investors who rely on *market timing* use a variety of analytical techniques to try to predict when prices of specific stocks are likely to rise and fall. Market timers try to make quick gains by buying low and selling high over a relatively short time horizon. One approach, called "buying the dip," is to aggressively buy stocks after large one-day market declines, such as the 7% drop on March 9, 2020 at the beginning of the COVID-19 pandemic, or the 11% drop on October 28, 1929 which triggered the historic stock market crash of 1929.[50] Over the last 30 years, buying the dip produces a 25% return within one year.[51] The problem, however, is determining which dips to buy. For example, after the 7% drop on March 9, 2020, markets dropped 13% on March 16, 2020, with two days of 7% and 9% gains in between. Identifying "the dip" in such turbulent market conditions is very difficult.

As these wild swings show, the problem with market timing is that it's tough to consistently identify the timing and direction of changes in stock prices. Market timing also requires investors to make frequent trades which, given the fees paid on trades and the much higher taxes incurred on short-term capital gains (stocks held for less than one year), significantly reduce overall returns. Most investors are better off using *dollar cost averaging* (DCA) in which the same amount is invested in the market every month, no matter whether stock prices are up or down. DCA reduces the average cost paid for shares and outperforms "buying the dip" 70% of the time. If investors mistime buying the dip by just two months, DCA works better 97% of the time. One analyst concluded, "Even God couldn't beat dollar-cost averaging."[52]

**Value Investing** Investors who favor *value investing* try to find stocks that are undervalued in the market. They believe that the market price will rise over time to reflect its true value, thus generating a capital gain. This approach requires intensive research to identify discrepancies between a company's true (or intrinsic) value and its current market price. The drawback is that thousands of investors are all trying to do the same thing, so the competition to locate undervalued stocks is intense. Unless you're among the first to discover a good value, the investors who beat you to it will rush to buy up the stock, increasing demand and driving up the stock's price so that it is no longer undervalued.

A simple approach to value investing is buying "Dogs of the Dow." It works like this: "After the stock market closes on the last day of the year, of the 30 stocks that make up the Dow Jones Industrial Average (DJIA), select the ten stocks which have the highest dividend yield. Then simply get in touch with your broker and invest an equal dollar amount in each of these ten high yield stocks. Then hold these ten 'Dogs of the Dow' for one year. Repeat these steps each and every year. That's it!"[53] On average, "Dogs of the Dow" slightly outpaces average market returns. Buying low helps, but perhaps more important is that DJIA companies pay strong dividends, even when financial performance drops.[54]

**Investing for Growth** Investors who focus on growth look for companies that have the potential to grow much faster than average for a sustained time, which they believe will lead to a steady (and sometimes spectacular) rise in the stock's price. Investors using this strategy often invest in stocks of relatively new companies with innovative products in a hot sector of the economy.

Investing for growth entails significant risk. Small new companies lack established track records. And rapidly expanding industries tend to attract many start-up companies, so competition can be intense. Finally, given the rapid pace of technological change, today's hot prospects may soon be dethroned by the next big thing. It's hard to predict which firms will be winners; even experts often make the wrong choice. Venture capitalists (VCs) and angel investors are primary sources of initial funding for new companies with high growth potential. But because of poor performance, just over half (56%) of those new companies get a second round of funding from VCs and angel investors. In subsequent funding rounds— round 3 (33%), round 4 (19%), round 5(10%), and round 6 (4%)—fewer and fewer companies get additional funds.[55] If venture capitalists and angel investors, who often work directly with these firms to make them more successful, find it so difficult to pick high growth winners, are you likely to do better?

**Buying and Holding** If you're a patient person with steady nerves, a buy-and-hold approach might appeal to you. This strategy involves purchasing a diversified set of securities and holding them for a long period of time. Buy-and-hold investors put their faith in the ability of the *overall market* to continue the long-run upward trend it has exhibited throughout its history. One way that many buy-and-hold investors do this is by investing in index mutual funds and ETFs. The buy-and-hold strategy seldom allows investors to "get rich quick," but it usually results in a solid financial return over the long haul and minimizes capital gains taxes and broker fees and commissions.

Obviously, the buy-and-hold strategy will work only if you can afford to leave your money invested for a long time. When the stock market takes a dive, it can sometimes take years for stocks to recover and start to show solid returns. *The Wall Street Journal* investment columnist Jason Zweig explains, "Since 1929, the S&P 500 has suffered 14 bear markets, defined by S&P Dow Jones Indices as losses of at least 20%. The shortest and shallowest was the 20% drop that lasted less than three months in late 1990. The deepest was the 86.2% collapse from September 1929 to June 1932; the longest, the 60% plunge from March 1937 to April 1942. On average, bear markets lasted 19 months and dealt a 39% loss."[56]

Some people who think they're comfortable with a buy-and-hold strategy end up getting "happy feet" after a few weeks of declining stock prices. They panic and sell off their stocks at exactly the wrong time, locking in big losses. For the buy-and-hold strategy to work, you've got to have the patience—and mental toughness—to ride out short-term downturns in the market. Recall this chapter's opening quote from Warren Buffet, perhaps the most successful investor of all time, "The stock market is a device for transferring money from the impatient to the patient."

### 10-6 Keeping Tabs on the Market

Once you've begun to invest in securities, you'll want to keep track of how your investments are doing. Using the internet, you can easily find information about both general market trends and the performance of specific securities.

#### 10-6a Stock Indices: Tracking the Trends

One of the most common ways to track general market conditions and trends is to follow what's happening to various stock indices. A **stock index** tracks the prices of a large group of stocks that meet certain defined criteria. Many investors like to compare how the stocks in their own portfolio compare to the performance of these broad indices. Two of the best-known indices are the Dow Jones Industrial Average and the S&P 500.

- The **Dow Jones Industrial Average (DJIA)**: Often called just "the Dow," this is the most widely followed stock index. The Dow is based on the adjusted average price of 30 stocks picked by the editors of *The Wall Street Journal*. All of the Dow firms are large, well-established corporations, such as Apple, Johnson & Johnson, Coca-Cola, McDonald's, Verizon, and Disney.

- The **Standard & Poor's 500**: With 500 stocks instead of just 30, the S&P 500 is a much broader index than the DJIA. Still, like the Dow, the companies included in the S&P 500 are large, well-established American corporations such as 3M, Adobe Systems, Amazon, Apple, Google, Facebook, and Pfizer.

Exhibit 10.5 identifies several other well-known indices, including some that track prices of stocks in foreign securities markets.

**stock index** A statistic that tracks how the prices of a specific set of stocks have changed.

**Dow Jones Industrial Average (DJIA)** An index that tracks stock prices of 30 large, well-known U.S. corporations.

**Standard & Poor's 500** A stock index based on prices of 500 major U.S. corporations in a variety of industries and market sectors.

## Exhibit 10.5  Major Stock Price Indices

| Index | What It Tracks |
|---|---|
| **NASDAQ Composite** | All of the domestic and foreign common stocks traded on the NASDAQ exchange. |
| **Wilshire 5000** | Stock prices of all U.S. corporations with actively traded stock. Despite the 5,000 in its name, this index actually includes well over 6,000 stocks. (The exact number changes frequently.) |
| **Russell 2000** | Stock prices of 2,000 relatively small but actively traded U.S. corporations. |
| **FTSE 100** | Stock prices of 100 of the largest and most actively traded companies listed on the London Stock Exchange. |
| **Nikkei 225** | Stock prices of 225 of the largest and most actively traded companies listed on the Tokyo Stock Exchange. |
| **SSE Composite** | Stock prices of all stocks listed on the Shanghai Stock Exchange. |

## Exhibit 10.6  Yahoo! Finance Quote for a Stock

**McDonald's Corp. Common St (NYSE: McD)**
**Real-time 213.90 ↓ 0.37 (0.17%) At close:**
**February 12, 2021, 4:00 PM EST**

| | | | |
|---|---|---|---|
| Last Trade: | 214.27 | Day's Range: | 213.00–214.70 |
| Trade Time: | 3:59 PM EST | 52wk Range: | 124.23–231.91 |
| Change: | ↓ 0.37 (0.17%) | Volume: | 2,781,322 |
| Prev Close: | 214.27 | Avg Vol (3m): | 3,194,768 |
| Open: | 214.00 | Market Cap: | 159.38B |
| Bid: | 213.89 × 800 | P/E (ttm): | 33.92 |
| Ask: | 214.05 × 800 | EPS (ttm): | 6.31 |
| 1y Target Est: | 241.93 | Div & Yield: | 5.16 (2.41%) |

Source: Yahoo! Finance stock quote, accessed February 9, 2017.

## 10-6b  Tracking the Performance of Specific Securities

Many financial websites offer detailed stock quotes that provide the current price of a company's stock and a wealth of related information. To check out a specific stock, you simply type its *stock symbol*—a short combination of letters that uniquely identifies a corporate security—into a "Get Quote" box. (Most sites have a lookup feature that finds the symbol if you type in the company's name.)

Exhibit 10.6 illustrates the information a popular financial website, Yahoo! Finance (https://finance.yahoo .com/), provides about McDonald's common stock. Some of the key figures reported for McDonald's include:

- *Last trade*: The price of McDonald's common stock for the most recent trade was $214.27.

- *Change*: The last trade of McDonald's stock was $0.37 lower than the closing price for the stock on the previous day.

- *Bid and Ask*: The highest price currently offered (bid) to buy McDonald's stock is $213.89 x 800 shares. The lowest price currently offered (asked) to sell the stock is $214.05 x 800 shares.

- *Day's range*: The highest price for the stock during the day was $214.70 and the lowest price was $213.00.

- *52-Week range*: The highest price for McDonald's stock over the previous 52 weeks was $231.91 while its lowest price was $124.23.

- *Volume*: 2,781,322 shares of the stock have been traded up to this point in the current trading session—below the average of 3,194,768 shares.

- *Market Cap*: The total market value of all shares of McDonald's common stock outstanding was 159.38 billion. This is found by multiplying the price per share times the number of shares of common stock outstanding.

- *P/E*: The price-to-earnings of 33.92 is found by dividing the stock's price per share by its earnings per share. In general, a higher P/E ratio means investors expect a greater growth in earnings over time.

- *EPS (earnings per share)*: McDonald's earned $6.31 per share of common stock outstanding. EPS is computed by dividing the net income available to common stockholders by the number of shares of common stock outstanding.

- *Div & Yield*: The sum of dividends paid by McDonald's over the past 12 months was $5.16 per share. Yield is found by dividing the dividend per share by the previous day's price per share. It tells us that at that price the dividend paid by McDonald's represented a 2.41%% return to the investor. (But since the total return to stockholders may also include a capital gain or loss, this yield doesn't tell us the whole story.)

Financial websites also provide information about other types of securities such as mutual funds, ETFs, and bonds.

## The Big Picture

Many different organizations participate in financial markets, including banks, finance companies, securities brokers and dealers, investment banks, and institutional investors such as mutual funds, insurance companies, and pension funds. Although they differ in their functions, each of these participants helps financial markets achieve their primary purpose of channeling funds from savers to borrowers.

In this chapter, we focused on one particular type of financial market, namely the market for financial securities. The financial capital that corporations raise when they issue stocks and bonds in these markets is critical to every functional area of their operations. Without these funds, the marketing department would lack the resources needed to develop new products; information technology professionals would be unable to update hardware and software; and operations managers would be unable to acquire the machinery and equipment needed to produce the goods and services the company sells to earn its profits.

On the other side of these markets, investors who buy corporate securities do so to acquire assets that they believe will help them achieve their own financial goals. But investing in securities involves risk. Over any short-run time period, there is simply no guarantee that stocks and bonds will provide investors with the returns they expect. The good news—at least if you plan to invest—is that history shows that, over the long run, the return on these securities is positive. Given enough time and patience, investing in stocks and other securities is likely to result in a substantial increase in wealth.

## Careers in Business

### Stockbroker

Responsible for meeting and getting to know clients and their financial needs, offering financial advice on investment recommendations (for a diversified mix of stocks, fixed-income investments including bonds and certificates of deposit, mutual funds and annuities, as well as a wide range of insurance options, including life insurance, long-term disability, and long-term care), and placing trades. The ideal candidate has a bachelor's or master's degree, Series 7 license, a strong sales and/or management background, strong interpersonal skills that provide the ability to develop meaningful relationships, the drive to set and achieve goals in a performance-driven atmosphere, and the ability to work autonomously from your own neighborhood office.

# 11 Marketing: Building Profitable Customer Connections

G Stock Studio/Shutterstock.com

## Learning Objectives

After studying this chapter, you will be able to:

**11-1** Discuss the objectives, the process, and the scope of marketing

**11-2** Identify the role of the customer in marketing

**11-3** Explain each element of marketing strategy

**11-4** Describe the consumer and business decision-making process

**11-5** Discuss the key elements of marketing research

**11-6** Explain the roles of social responsibility and technology in marketing

## 11-1 Marketing: Getting Value by Giving Value

What comes to mind when you hear the term **marketing**? Most people think of the radio ad they heard this morning or the billboard they saw while driving to school. But advertising is only a small part of marketing; the whole story is much bigger. The American Marketing Association defines marketing as *the activity, set of institutions, and processes for creating, communicating, delivering, and exchanging offerings that have value for customers, clients, partners, and society at large.*

**marketing** An organizational function and a set of processes for creating, communicating, and delivering value to customers and for managing customer relationships in ways that benefit the organization and its stakeholders.

**utility** The ability of goods and services to satisfy consumer "wants."

The ultimate benefit that most businesses seek from marketing is long-term profitability. But attaining this benefit is impossible without first delivering value to customers and other stakeholders. A successful marketer delivers value by filling customer needs in ways that exceed their expectations. As a result, you get sales today and sales tomorrow and sales the next day, which—across the days and months and years—can translate into long-term profitability. Alice Foote MacDougall, a successful entrepreneur in the 1920s, understood this thinking early on: "In business you get what you want by giving other people what they want." **Utility** is the ability of goods and services to satisfy these wants. And since there is a wide

range of wants, products can provide utility in a number of different ways:

- *Form utility* satisfies wants by converting inputs into a finished form. Clearly, the vast majority of products provide some kind of form utility. For example, Jamba Juice blends fresh fruits, juices, and vegetables into healthy and delicious smoothies, and UGG Australia stretches, treats, and sews sheepskins and wool into comfortable, stylish boots.

- *Time utility* satisfies wants by providing goods and services at a convenient time for customers. For example, Amazon Prime offers free two-hour delivery for qualifying orders in some areas, many dry cleaners offer one-hour service, 24 Hour Fitness is virtually always open, some fast-food restaurants offer 24-hour drive-through windows, and ATMs and online services have turned banking into an all-hours industry.

- *Place utility* satisfies wants by providing goods and services at a convenient place for customers. For example, Starbucks has been known to build coffee shops on both sides of a busy boulevard to spare drivers the need to make a U-turn, Denny's and Waffle House offer inexpensive food at the bottom of

> ## "A thrilled customer is the most potent marketing asset your organization can leverage."
>
> —John Jantsch, Author, Duct Tape Marketing

many freeway off ramps, and vending machines refuel tired students on virtually every college campus.

- *Ownership utility* satisfies wants by smoothly transferring ownership of goods and services from seller to buyer. Virtually every product provides some degree of ownership utility, but some offer more than others. Consider that many car dealerships offer financing options. These dealerships and other lenders operate around the premise of ownership utility: if borrowers make the specified number of payments, they will eventually own the product free and clear. Banks also provide ownership utility by offering mortgage loans. Few customers can afford to buy homes with cash, but a mortgage loans allows them to make payments over the course of years, with the goal of eventual full ownership.

Satisfying customer wants—in a way that exceeds expectations—is a job that never ends. Jay Levinson, a recognized expert in breakthrough marketing, comments, "Marketing is … a process. You improve it, perfect it, change it, even pause it. But you never stop it completely."

## 11-1a  The Scope of Marketing: It's Everywhere!

For many years, businesspeople have actively applied the principles of marketing to goods and services that range from cars to fast food, to liquor, to computers, to movies. But within the past decade or two, other organizations have successfully adopted marketing strategies and tactics to further their goals.

Nonprofit organizations—in both the private and public sectors—play a significant role in our economy, employing more people than the federal government and all 50 state governments combined (not to mention an army of volunteers!). These organizations use marketing, sometimes quite assertively, to achieve their objectives. The U.S. Army's marketing communications budget, for example, sometimes approaches as much as $200 million per year. Your own college probably markets itself to both prospective students and potential alumni donors. Private-sector nonprofit organizations also use marketing strategies for everything from marshaling AYSO soccer coaches for kids to boosting attendance at the local zoo, to planning cultural events.[1]

Nonprofit organizations play a pivotal role in the expansion of marketing across our economy to include people, places, events, and ideas. But for-profit enterprises have also begun to apply marketing strategies and tactics beyond simply goods and services.

Athletic, cultural, and charitable events are all activities that rely on sponsorships as part of their event marketing approach.

■ **People Marketing:** Sports, politics, and art dominate this category, but even some businesspeople merit mentioning. In 2020, for example, the U.S. government banned former Wells Fargo CEO John Stumpf from *ever* working at a bank again as part of the punishment for his role in the scandal in which millions of fake accounts were set up to meet sales quotas. In the political arena, democrat Alexandria Ocasio-Cortez made history in the U.S. midterm elections of 2018 to become the youngest woman in Congress in American history at the age of 29. Ocasio-Cortez frequently uses Instagram's live-streaming feature to engage with her supporters and answer questions. She adds a unique touch to her live streams by conducting these streams in a very casual manner; for instance, she recently held a session with her followers while assembling IKEA furniture. Ocasio-Cortez has leveraged social media to establish a highly relatable online presence for herself among her supporters.

Countless entertainers and athletes have used people marketing to their advantage as well. Consider the Kardashians, for example. While the Kardashian sisters may appear simply 'famous for being famous," a little digging uncovers some savvy people marketing. Each sister has created and maintained a niche brand with the focus ranging from family life to cosmetics to weight loss. They actively court all publicity—good and bad. They nurture a huge social media presence, consistently posting on their own and each other's properties. In fact, in 2021, Kim Kardashian West made her debut on the *Forbes* "Worlds Billionaire List."[2]

In fact, as you pursue your personal goals—whether you seek a new job, university admission, or a Friday night date—people marketing principles can help you achieve your objective. Start by figuring out what your "customer" needs, and then ensure that your "product" (you!) delivers above and beyond expectations.[3]

■ **Place Marketing:** This category involves drawing people to a particular place. Cities and states use place marketing to attract businesses. Delaware, for instance, the second-smallest state in the Union, is home to more than half of the Fortune 500 firms because it deliberately developed a range of advantages for corporations. But more visibly, cities, states, and nations use place marketing to attract tourists. Thanks to powerful place marketing, most people have probably heard that "What happens in Vegas stays in Vegas." In late 2008, Las Vegas shelved the high-rolling campaign in favor of a more "recession-proof," but less successful strategy: the "Take a Break USA" campaign. By late 2009, Vegas had reverted to the "What Happens . . ." campaign that fueled visitors since its launch in 2003, leading to a record-breaking 42.9 million visitors in 2016.[4] The campaign continued to fuel more than 40 million visitors per year until the global pandemic, when visitors dropped more than 54%. As Vegas rebuilds, experts anticipate that its marketing may revolve around big-ticket sporting events.[5]

- **Event Marketing:** This category includes marketing—or sponsoring—athletic, cultural, or charitable events. Partnerships between the public and private sectors are increasingly common. Examples include the Olympics, the Super Bowl, and the FIFA World Cup.

- **Idea Marketing:** A whole range of public and private organizations market ideas that are meant to change how people think or act. Recycle, don't drink and drive, buckle your seatbelt, conserve water, support our political party, donate blood, and don't smoke are all examples of popular causes. Often, idea marketing and event marketing are combined, as we see in the annual Avon Breast Cancer Crusade. The planners actively market the idea of annual mammograms, as they solicit contributions for breast cancer research and participation in the event itself.

## 11-1b The Evolution of Marketing: From the Product to the Customer

The current approach to marketing evolved through a number of overlapping stages, as you'll see in Exhibit 11.1. But as you read about these eras, keep in mind that some businesses have remained lodged—with varying degrees of success—in the thinking of a past era.

**Production Era** Marketing didn't always begin with the customer. In fact, in the early 1900s, the customer was practically a joke. Henry Ford summed up the prevailing mindset when he reportedly said, "You can have your Model T in any color you want as long as it's black." This attitude made sense from a historical perspective, since consumers didn't have the overwhelming number of choices that are currently available; most products were purchased as soon as they were produced and distributed to consumers. In this context, the top business priority was to produce large quantities of goods as efficiently as possible.

**Selling Era** By the 1920s, production capacity had increased dramatically. For the first time, supply in many categories exceeded demand, which caused the emergence of the hard sell. The selling focus gained momentum in the 1930s and 1940s, when the Depression and World War II made consumers even more reluctant to part with their limited money.

**Marketing Era** The landscape changed dramatically in the 1950s. Many factories that had churned out military

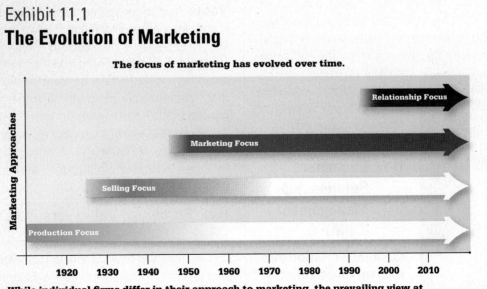

Exhibit 11.1
**The Evolution of Marketing**

The focus of marketing has evolved over time.

While individual firms differ in their approach to marketing, the prevailing view at leading-edge firms has changed over time as shown here.

supplies converted to consumer production, flooding the market with choices in virtually every product category. An era of relative peace and prosperity emerged, and—as soldiers returned from World War II—marriage and birthrates soared. To compete for the consumer's dollar, marketers attempted to provide goods and services that met customer needs better than anything else on the market. As a result, the marketing concept materialized in the 1950s. The **marketing concept** is a philosophy that makes customer satisfaction—now and in the future—the central focus of the entire organization. Companies that embrace this philosophy strive to delight customers, integrating this goal into all business activities. The marketing concept holds that delivering unmatched value to customers is the only effective way to achieve long-term profitability.

**Relationship Era** The marketing concept has gathered momentum across the economy, leading to the current era, unfolding over the past decade, which zeros in on long-term customer relationships. Acquiring a new customer can cost five times more than keeping an existing customer. Retaining your current customers—and getting them to spend additional dollars—is clearly cost-effective. Moreover, satisfied customers can develop into advocates for your business, becoming powerful generators of positive "word of mouth."

## 11-2 The Customer: Front and Center

When the internet emerged, the marketplace experienced an enormous shift in power from producers to consumers. With an abundance of information at their fingertips, consumers could compare and contrast producers with enormous ease, and rate their performance. Since smart marketers aim to deliver value, they leveraged the abundant information to develop customized products for and deeper relationships with their customers. The end game from a marketing standpoint is higher customer satisfaction, which leads to more loyal customers.

### 11-2a Customer Relationship Management (CRM)

**Customer relationship management (CRM)** is the centerpiece of successful, twenty-first-century marketing. Broadly defined, CRM is the ongoing process of acquiring, maintaining, and growing profitable customer relationships by delivering unmatched value. CRM works best when marketers combine marketing communication with one-on-one personalization. Amazon is a champion player at CRM, greeting customers by name, recommending specific products, and providing streamlined checkout. Clearly, information is an integral part of this process—you simply can't do CRM without collecting, managing, and applying the right data at the right time for the right person (and every repeat customer is the "right person"!).

**Limited Relationships** The scope of your relationships will depend not just on the data you gather but also on your industry. Colgate-Palmolive, for example, can't forge a close personal bond with every person who buys a bar of Irish Spring soap. However, the company does invite customers to call its toll-free line with questions or comments, and it maintains a vibrant website with music, an e-newsletter, special offers, and an invitation to contact the company. You can bet that the company actively gathers data and pursues a connection with customers who initiate contact.

**Full Partnerships** If you have a high-ticket product and a smaller customer base, you're much more likely to pursue a full partnership with each of your key clients. Colgate-Palmolive, for instance, has dedicated customer service teams working with key accounts such as Walmart and Costco. With a full partnership, the marketer gathers and leverages extensive information about each customer and often includes the customer in key aspects of the product development process.

**Value** You know you've delivered **value** when your customers believe that your product has a better relationship between the cost and the benefits than any competitor. By this definition, low cost does not always mean high value. In fact, a recent survey suggests that loyal customers are often willing to pay *more* for their products rather than switch to lower-cost competitors. Apple provides a clear example. We probably all know at least a handful of Apple fanatics who gladly pay far more for their iPhones or iPads than they would pay for a competing product.

### 11-2b Perceived Value versus Actual Value

The operative idea here is *perceived*. Simply creating value isn't enough; you also must help customers believe that your product is uniquely qualified to meet their needs. This becomes a particular challenge when you're a new business competing against a market leader with disproportionately strong perceived value.

**marketing concept** A business philosophy that makes customer satisfaction—now and in the future—the central focus of the entire organization.

**customer relationship management (CRM)** The ongoing process of acquiring, maintaining, and growing profitable customer relationships by delivering unmatched value.

**value** A customer perception that a product has a better relationship than its competitors between the cost and the benefits.

### 11-2c Customer Satisfaction

You know you've satisfied your customers when you deliver perceived value above and beyond their expectations. But achieving **customer satisfaction** can be tricky. Less savvy marketers frequently fall into one of two traps:

- The first trap is overpromising. Even if you deliver more value than anyone else, your customers will be disappointed if your product falls short of overly high expectations. The messages that you send regarding your product influence expectations—keep them real!

- The second trap is underpromising. If you don't set expectations high enough, too few customers will be willing to try your product. The result will be a tiny base of highly satisfied customers, which usually isn't enough to sustain a business.

Finding the right balance is tricky but clearly not impossible. According to their scores on the 2020 American Customer Satisfaction Index, Nordstrom took the top spot in Internet Retail, followed by Etsy and Costco, which tied for second place, edging out perennial winner Amazon, which suffered a somewhat surprising loss of −4.8% the first year of the COVID-19 pandemic. Hilton dominated their industry in terms of customer satisfaction, far outscoring Wyndham, Best Western, and Motel 6. Among airlines, Southwest continued to hold its enduring customer satisfaction lead, scoring 79, while bargain airline Spirit took up the rear of the pack with a score of 65.[6]

### 11-2d Customer Loyalty

**Customer loyalty** is the payoff for delivering value and generating satisfaction. Loyal customers purchase from you again and again—and they sometimes even pay more for your product. They forgive your mistakes. They provide valuable feedback. They may require less service. They refer their friends (and sometimes even strangers). Moreover, studying your loyal customers can give you a competitive edge for acquiring new ones, since people with a similar profile would likely be a great fit for your products.[7]

Prostock-studio/Shutterstock.com

Perhaps in no other industry is there more customer loyalty than when purchasing a new vehicle.

## 11-3 Marketing Strategy: Where Are You Going, and How Will You Get There?

In marketing terms, the questions become: Who is your target audience, and how will you reach them? Many successful firms answer this question by developing a formal **marketing plan**, updated on a yearly basis; other firms handle their planning on a more informal basis. But regardless of the specific approach, the first step in planning your marketing strategy should be to determine where to target your efforts. Who are those people who are most likely to buy your products? The first step is **market segmentation**—dividing your marketing into groups of people, or segments, that are similar to one another and different from everyone else. One or more of these segments will be your target market. Once you've identified your target market, your next step is to determine how you can best use marketing tools to reach them. And finally, you need to anticipate and respond to changes in the external environment. This section will define target market, explain market segmentation, introduce the marketing mix, and review the key factors in the marketing environment. Taken together, these elements will shape an effective marketing strategy, as shown in Exhibit 11.2.

The marketer creates the marketing mix but responds to the marketing environment with a single-minded focus on the target market.

### 11-3a Target Market

Your **target market** is the group of people who

**customer satisfaction** When customers perceive that a good or service delivers value above and beyond their expectations.

**customer loyalty** When customers buy a product from the same supplier again and again—sometimes paying even more for it than they would for a competitive product.

**marketing plan** A formal document that defines marketing objectives and the specific strategies for achieving those objectives.

**market segmentation** Dividing potential customers into groups of similar people, or segments.

**target market** The group of people who are most likely to buy a particular product.

## Exhibit 11.2
## Marketing Strategy

are most likely to buy your product. This is where you should concentrate your marketing efforts. But why not target your efforts toward everyone? After all, even if *most* middle-aged women wouldn't buy purple polka-dotted miniskirts, an adventurous few just might do it. Well, you can always hope for the adventurous few, but virtually every business has limited resources, and marketing toward the people who are most likely to buy your flamboyant minis—say, teenage girls—will maximize the impact of each dollar you spend. A well-chosen target market embodies the following characteristics:

- Size: There must be enough people in your target group to support a business.

- Profitability: The people must be willing and

able to spend more than the cost of producing and marketing your product.

- Accessibility: Your target must be reachable through channels that your business can afford.

- Limited competition: Look for markets with limited competition; a crowded market is much tougher to crack.

### 11-3b Consumer Markets versus Business Markets

**Consumer marketers (B2C)** direct their efforts to people who are buying products for personal consumption (e.g., granola bars, toothpaste, and clothing), whereas **business marketers (B2B)** direct their efforts to customers who are buying products to use either directly or indirectly to produce other products (e.g., lumber, insulation, and robots). But keep in mind that the distinction between the market categories is not in the products themselves; rather, it lies in how the buyer will use the product. For instance, shoes that you buy for yourself are clearly a consumer product, but shoes that a bowling alley buys for its customers are a business product. Similarly, a computer that you buy for yourself is a consumer product, but a computer that your school buys for the computer lab is a business product. Both B2C and B2B marketers need to choose the best target, but they tend to follow slightly different approaches.

### 11-3c Consumer Market Segmentation

Choosing the best target market (or markets) for your product begins with dividing your market into segments, or groups of people who have similar characteristics. But people can be similar in a number of different ways, so, not surprisingly, marketers have several options for segmenting potential consumers.

**Demographic** B2C **demographic segmentation** refers to dividing the market based on measurable characteristics about people such as age, income, ethnicity, and gender. Demographics are a vital starting point for most marketers. Chapstick, for instance, targets young women with the Shimmer version of its lip balm, and Chevy Camaro targets young men with money. Sometimes the demographic makeup of a given market is tough to discern; Black artists, for instance, create the bulk of rap music, yet White suburban males form the bulk of the rap music market.

**Geographic** B2C **geographic segmentation** refers to dividing the market based on where consumers live.

---

**consumer marketers (also known as business-to-consumer or B2C)** Marketers who direct their efforts toward people who are buying products for personal consumption.

**business marketers (also known as business-to-business or B2B)** Marketers who direct their efforts toward people who are buying products to use either directly or indirectly to produce other products.

**demographic segmentation** Dividing the market into smaller groups based on measurable characteristics about people, such as age, income, ethnicity, and gender.

**geographic segmentation** Dividing the market into smaller groups based on where consumers live. This process can incorporate countries, cities, or population density as key factors.

This process can incorporate countries, or cities, or population density as key factors. For instance, Ford Expedition does not concentrate on European markets, where tiny, winding streets and nonexistent parking are common in many cities. Cosmetic surgeons tend to market their services more heavily in urban rather than rural areas. And finding the perfect surfboard is easy in Hawaii but more challenging in South Dakota.

**Psychographic** B2C **psychographic segmentation** refers to dividing the market based on consumer attitudes, interests, values, and lifestyles. Toyota Prius, for instance, targets consumers who care about protecting the environment. A number of companies have found a highly profitable niche providing upscale wilderness experiences for people who seek all the pleasure with none of the pain (you enjoy the great outdoors, while someone else lugs your gear, pours your wine, slices your goat cheese, and inflates your extra-comfy air mattress). Both magazine racks and the internet are filled with products geared toward psychographic segments, including adventure travel websites, shoe-selling mega site Zappos.com, and business and financial powerhouse wsj.com (*The Wall Street Journal*). *Note:* Marketers typically use psychographics to complement other segmentation approaches rather than to provide the core definition.

**Behavioral** B2C **behavioral segmentation** refers to dividing the market based on how people behave toward various products. This category includes both the benefits that consumers seek from products and how consumers use the product. The Neutrogena Corporation, for example, built a multimillion-dollar hair care business by targeting consumers who wanted an occasional break from their favorite shampoo. Countless products such as

Miller Lite actively target the low-carbohydrate consumer. But perhaps the most common type of behavioral segmentation is based on usage patterns. Fast-food restaurants, for instance, actively target heavy users (who, ironically, tend to be slender): young men in their 20s and 30s. This group consumes about 17% of their total calories from fast food, compared to 12% for adults in general. Understanding the usage patterns of your customer base gives you the option of either focusing on your core users or trying to pull light users into your core market.

### 11-3d Business Market Segmentation

B2B marketers typically follow a similar process in segmenting their markets, but they use slightly different categories:

**Geographic** B2B geographic segmentation refers to dividing the market based on the concentration of customers. Many industries tend to be highly clustered in certain areas, such as technology in California and auto suppliers in the "auto corridor" that stretches south from Michigan to Tennessee. Geographic segmentation, of course, is especially common on an international basis, where variables such as language, culture, income, and regulatory differences can play crucial roles.

**Customer-Based** B2B customer-based segmentation refers to dividing the market based on the characteristics of customers. This approach includes a range of possibilities. Some B2B marketers segment based on customer size. Others segment based on customer type. Johnson & Johnson, for example, has a group of salespeople dedicated exclusively to retail accounts such as Target and Publix, while other salespeople focus solely on motivating doctors to recommend their products. Other potential B2B markets include institutions—schools and hospitals, for instance, are key segments for Heinz Ketchup—and the government.

**Product-Use–Based** B2B product-use–based segmentation refers to dividing the market based on how customers will use the product. Small and midsized companies find this strategy especially helpful in narrowing their target markets. Possibilities include the ability to support certain software packages or production systems or the desire to serve certain customer groups, such as long-distance truckers or restaurants that deliver food.

Who do you think is the target customer for the Chrysler Pacifica?

Angel DiBilio/Shutterstock.com

**psychographic segmentation** Dividing the market into smaller groups based on consumer attitudes, interests, values, and lifestyles.

**behavioral segmentation** Dividing the market based on how people behave toward various products. This category includes both the benefits that consumers seek from products and how consumers use the products.

## Exhibit 11.3
## Marketing Mix

**Product Strategy**

**Pricing Strategy**

**Promotion Strategy**

**Distribution Strategy**

### 11-3e The Marketing Mix

Once you've clearly defined your target market, your next challenge is to develop compelling strategies for product, price, distribution, and promotion. The blending of these elements becomes your **marketing mix**, as shown in Exhibit 11.3.

- **Product Strategy:** Your product involves far more than simply a tangible good or a specific service. Product strategy decisions range from brand name, to product image, to package design, to customer service, to guarantees, to new product development, and more. Designing the best product clearly begins with understanding the needs of your target market.

- **Pricing Strategy:** Pricing is a challenging area of the marketing mix. To deliver customer value, your prices

**marketing mix** The blend of marketing strategies for product, price, distribution, and promotion.

must be fair, relative to the benefits of your product. Other factors include competition, regulation, and public opinion. Your product category plays a critical role as well. A low-cost desk, for instance, might be appealing, but who would want discount-priced knee surgery?

- **Distribution Strategy:** The goal is to deliver your product to the right people, in the right quantities, at the right time, in the right place. The key decisions include shipping, warehousing, and selling outlets (e.g., the web versus network marketing versus brick-and-mortar stores). The implications of these decisions for product image and customer satisfaction can be significant.

- **Promotion Strategy:** Promotion includes all of the ways that marketers communicate about their products. The list of possibilities is long and growing, especially as the internet continues to evolve at breakneck speed. Key elements today include advertising, personal selling, sales promotion, public relations, word of mouth, and product placement. Successful promotional strategies typically evolve in response to both customer needs and competition. A number of innovative companies are even inviting their customers to participate in creating their advertising through venues such as YouTube. Refer to Exhibit 11.4 to see how easily you can analyze promotional strategies.

### 11-3f The Global Marketing Mix

As you decide to enter foreign markets, you'll need to re-evaluate your marketing mix for each new country. Should it change? If so, how should it change? Many business goods simply don't require much change in the marketing mix, since their success isn't dependent on culture. Examples include heavy machinery, cement, and farming equipment. Consumer products, however, often require completely new marketing mixes to effectively reach their consumers.

Nike's approach to marketing in China offers an interesting example of how one firm managed the complex process of building a successful business in a foreign market. When Nike first entered China in the 1990s, the company seemed to face an insurmountable challenge: not only did a pair of Nike sneakers cost twice the Chinese average monthly salary, but most Chinese just didn't play sports, according to Terry Rhoads, then

> "Don't find customers for your products, find products for your customers."
>
> —Seth Godin,
> Entrepreneur and Author

## Exhibit 11.4
## Analyzing Promotional Strategies

**Who is the target audience for each of these smartphone websites? How does each site position the product relative to the competition? Which strategy is most effective? Why?**

iPhone 12 and iPhone 12 mini
**Blast past fast.**

SAMSUNG    Galaxy 5G    Mobile    TV & Audio    Home Appliances    Smart Home    Computing    Offers    Collections    Explore    Support    Business

**Galaxy S21 5G | S21+ 5G**

From $99.99 or $2.78/mo for 36 mos® with the highest online instant trade-in values.²

Learn more    Buy now

Google Store

Google Pixel 5    Overview    Tech Specs    Compare    Trade-In & Financing    Get Started

**The ultimate 5G Google phone.**

Buy

Source: Apple Inc; Source: Samsung; Source: Google Inc.

director of Nike sports marketing. So he boldly set out to change that. Rhoads created a Nike high-school basketball league, which has since spread to 17 cities. To loosen up fans, he blasted canned cheering during games and arranged for national TV coverage of the finals. He even leveraged connections with the NBA to bring Michael Jordan for visits.

The gamble quickly paid off, as the Chinese middle class emerged—along with more individualistic values, which are a strong fit with the Nike ethos. By 2001, Nike had dubbed its marketing approach "hip hoop," which they described as an effort to "connect Nike with a creative lifestyle." Sales in 2011 exceeded $2 billion, driven largely by basketball shoes, although sales began to soften in 2012 and 2013, due to fierce competition and deep discounting. In 2014, Nike continued to lose traction in China, due in part to fierce competition from Adidas. Analysts also pointed out that among other reasons, "Nike's branding is based on encouraging strong identification with iconic sports-stars it uses to endorse its products. In a culture where parents are excessively focused on academic achievement, such a strategy has limited appeal." Nike emerged from its slump in 2015 with a powerful sales surge in China. By 2019, China accounted for more than $6 billion of Nike's $37 billion total brand sales, and almost two-fifths of Nike's earnings before interest and tax for the year. And Nike's sales in China continued to soar as China's economy recovered from the global pandemic in late 2020.[8]

### 11-3g The Marketing Environment

While marketers actively influence the elements of the marketing mix, they must anticipate and respond to the elements of the external environment, which they typically cannot control. **Environmental scanning** is a key tool; the goal is simply to continually collect information from sources that range from informal networks to industry newsletters, to the general press, to customers, to suppliers, to the competition, among others. The key elements of the external environment include the following components:

**Competitive** The dynamic competitive environment probably affects marketers on a day-to-day basis more than any other element. Understanding the competitive environment often begins with analysis of **market share**, or the percentage of the marketplace that each firm controls. To avoid ambushes—and to uncover new opportunities—you must continually monitor how both dominant and emerging competitors handle each element of their marketing mix. And don't forget indirect competitors, who meet the same consumer needs as you, but with a completely different product (e.g., Altoids vs. Scope).

**Economic** The only certainty in the economic environment is change, but the timing of expansions and

**environmental scanning** The process of continually collecting information from the external marketing environment.

**market share** The percentage of a market controlled by a given marketer.

# Color me ... hungry?!

Have you ever noticed that fast-food restaurants typically feature vivid shades of red, yellow, and orange in both their logos and their décor? Think McDonald's, KFC, Burger King, and Pizza Hut. The color choice is no coincidence.

Marketing researchers have learned that consumers in the United States associate red with energy, passion, and speed. Yellow suggests happiness and warmth, while orange suggests playfulness, affordability, and fun. A simulated cocktail party study found that partygoers in red rooms reported feeling hungrier and thirstier than others, and guests in yellow rooms ate twice as much as others. The implication? Surrounding customers with red, yellow, and orange encourages them to eat a lot quickly and leave, which aligns nicely with the goals of most fast-food chains.

Color psychology is a powerful—though often overlooked—marketing tool. Colors evoke emotions and trigger specific behaviors, which can dramatically influence how people buy your product. Here is a list of common colors and some of their associations in U.S. mainstream culture.

But there is more for marketers to consider than simply color associations. Research shows that the relationship between brands and color hinges on the perceived appropriateness of the color being used for the particular brand (in other words, the color must "fit" what is being sold). Purchasing intent is greatly affected by colors due to the impact that colors have on how a brand is perceived. This means that colors influence how consumers view the "personality" of the brand in question. For example, picture a stick of deodorant targeted at women, and then picture a stick of deodorant targeted at men. Research suggests that men prefer bold colors while women prefer softer ones. Interestingly, blue dominates as the favorite color for both men and women.

Keep in mind that while some color associations are universal, others can differ significantly among cultures. White, for instance, signifies death and mourning in Chinese culture, while purple represents death in Brazil.

**RED** – Love, passion, warmth, food, excitement, action, danger, need to stop

**BLUE** – Power, trustworthiness, calm, success, seriousness, boredom

**GREEN** – Money, nature, health, healing, decay, illness

**ORANGE** – Playfulness, affordability, youth, fun, low quality, cheap

**PURPLE** – Royalty, luxury, dignity, spirituality, nightmares, craziness

**WHITE** – Purity, innocence, simplicity, mildness

**BLACK** – Sophistication, elegance, seriousness, sexuality, mystery, evil

David P. Smith/Shutterstock.com

As a marketer, your goal should be to align your color choice with the perceptions of your target market and the features of your product. The result should be more green for your bottom line![9]

---

contractions is virtually impossible to predict. Your goal as a marketer is to identify and respond to changes as soon as possible, keeping in mind that a sharp eye sees opportunity even in economic downturns. For instance, affordable luxuries and do-it-yourself enterprises can thrive during recessions.

**Social/Cultural** The social/cultural element covers a vast array of factors, including lifestyle, customs, language, attitudes, interests, and population shifts. Trends can change rapidly, with a dramatic impact on marketing decisions. Anticipating and responding to trends can be especially important in industries such as entertainment, fashion, and technology. In late 2009, for instance, Facebook removed some key privacy controls from its News Feed. The social media giant did not anticipate the black eye it received from outraged consumers who believed that Facebook had violated their privacy. Facebook was also surprised that the privacy controls it implemented in May 2010, which required consumers to opt

# Marketing Now: Targeting Generation Z

Generation Z (Gen Z)—people born between 1996 and the early 2000s—represents a juicy target market. They account for more than a quarter of the population. Their buying power is $44 billion and expands to $600 billion when including the influence they have on their parents' spending. Members of Gen Z are more racially and ethnically diverse than any previous generation; they are also digital natives who have little or no memory of the world as it existed before smartphones. So, it isn't surprising that about 75% choose smart phones as their "device of choice," and they spend more than five hours on their phones every day, highlighting the importance of a robust mobile marketing strategy. Tech savvy Gen Z consumers have famously short attention spans, and little patience for slow-loading web-based bells and whistles—so streamline your technology and don't keep them waiting!

Gen Z consumers make purpose a priority. They actively seek and support brands that they believe are socially and environmentally responsible.

Overall, Gen Z consumers are less interested in brands than their millennial predecessors. But when a brand does grab their attention, they seek to engage at a meaningful level. Specifically, according to recent Gen Z research:

■ 42% would participate in an online game for a brand campaign

■ 38% would attend an event sponsored by a brand

■ 44% said they'd be interested in submitting ideas for product designs

■ 36% would create digital content for a brand

Gen Z consumers are also super savvy about digital privacy. If marketers do not establish their trust about how they will use

and protect sensitive personal data, Gen Z is unlikely to provide that data, which would make it difficult for marketers to offer a customized shopping experience.

Generation Z will be at the heart of smart marketing for years to come. They are complex consumers but getting to know them could pay major dividends in terms of sales and profitability for a wide range of products and services.[10]

---

out of sharing, would not be enough to appease privacy advocates.[11] From 2010 through 2020, Facebook was embroiled in a series of far-reaching privacy and data abuse scandals that led to lawsuits and closer monitoring by the U.S. Congress, the Federal Trade Commission, and the European Union.[12]

**Technological** Changes in technology can be very visible to consumers (e.g., the introduction of the iPhone). However, technology often affects marketers in ways that are less directly visible. For example, technology allows mass customization of Levi's blue jeans at a reasonable price and facilitates just-in-time inventory management for countless companies that see the results in their bottom lines.

**Political/Legal** The political/legal area includes laws, regulations, and political climate. Most U.S. laws and regulations are clear (e.g., those declaring dry counties in certain states), but others are complex and evolving (e.g., qualifications for certain tax breaks). Political climate includes changing levels of governmental support for various business categories. Clearly, the political/ legal issues affect heavily regulated sectors (e.g., telecommunications and pharmaceuticals) more than others.

## 11-3h The Global Marketing Environment

As the internet has grown, the world market has become accessible to virtually every business. This boosts the importance of understanding each element of the marketing

## Exhibit 11.5 Elements That Influence the Consumer Decision-Making Process

| Influence | Description |
|---|---|
| **Cultural** | **Culture:** The values, attitudes, and customs shared by members of a society |
| | **Subculture:** A smaller division of the broader culture |
| | **Social Class:** Societal position driven largely by income and occupation |
| **Social** | **Family:** A powerful force in consumption choices |
| | **Friends:** Another powerful force, especially for high-profile purchases |
| | **Reference Groups:** Groups that give consumers a point of comparison |
| **Personal** | **Demographics:** Measurable characteristics such as age, gender, or income |
| | **Personality:** The mix of traits that determines who you are |
| **Psychological** | **Motivation:** Pressing needs that tend to generate action |
| | **Attitudes:** Lasting evaluations of (or feelings about) objects or ideas |
| | **Perceptions:** How people select, organize, and interpret information |
| | **Learning:** Changes in behavior based on experience |

environment—competitive, economic, social/cultural, technological, and political/legal—in each of your key markets. Among the biggest global challenges are researching opportunities in other countries and delivering your product to customers in other countries.

## 11-4 Customer Behavior: Decisions, Decisions, Decisions!

If successful marketing begins with the customer, then understanding the customer is critical. Why do people buy one product, but not another? How do they use the products they buy? When do they get rid of them? Knowing the answers to these questions will clearly help you better meet customer needs.

### 11-4a Consumer Behavior

**Consumer behavior** refers specifically to how people act when they are buying products for their own personal consumption. The decisions they make often seem spontaneous (after all, how much thought do you give to buying a pack of gum?), but they often result from a complex set of influences, as shown in Exhibit 11.5.

Marketers, of course, add their own influence through the marketing mix. For instance, after smelling pretzels in the mall and tasting pretzel morsels from the sample tray, many of us would at least be tempted to cough up the cash for a hot, buttery pretzel of our own . . . regardless of any other factors! Similarly, changes in the external environment—for example, a series of hurricanes in Florida—dramatically affect consumer decisions about items such as flashlights, batteries, and plywood.

All these forces shape consumer behavior in each step of the process regarding purchase decisions. Exhibit 11.6 shows how the consumer decision process works.

Clearly, marketing can influence the purchase decision every step of the way, from helping consumers identify needs (or problems), to resolving that awful feeling of **cognitive dissonance** (or kicking oneself) after a major purchase. Some marketers attempt to avoid cognitive dissonance altogether by developing specific programs to help customers validate their purchase choices. One example might be post-purchase mailings that highlight the accolades received by an expensive product.

But does every consumer go through every step of the process all the time? That's clearly not the case! People make low-involvement decisions (such as buying that candy bar) according to habit . . . or even just on a whim. But when the stakes are high—either financially or socially—most people move through the five steps of the classic decision-making process. For example, most of us wouldn't think of buying a car, a computer, or the "right" pair of blue jeans without stepping through the decision-making process.

**consumer behavior**
Description of how people act when they are buying, using, and discarding goods and services for their own personal consumption. Consumer behavior also explores the reasons behind people's actions.

**cognitive dissonance**
Consumer discomfort with a purchase decision, typically for a higher-priced item.

## Exhibit 11.6
## Consumer Decision Process

**Need Recognition**
Your best friend suddenly notices that she is the only person she knows who still wears high-rise blue jeans to class ... problem alert!

**Information Search**
Horrified, your friend not only checks out your style but also notices what the cool girls on campus are wearing. AND she snitches your copy of *Cosmo* to leaf through the ads.

**Evaluation of Alternatives**
Your friend compares the prices and styles of the various brands of blue jeans that she identifies.

**Purchase Decision**
After a number of conversations, your friend finally decides to buy True Religion jeans for $215.

**Post-Purchase Behavior**
Three days later, she begins to kick herself for spending so much money on jeans because she can no longer afford her daily Starbucks habit.

### 11-4b Business Buyer Behavior

**Business buyer behavior** refers to how people act when they're buying products to use either directly or indirectly to produce other products (e.g., chemicals, copy paper, computer servers). Business buyers typically have purchasing training and apply rational criteria to their decision-making process. They usually buy according to purchase specifications and objective standards, with a minimum of personal judgment or whim. Often, business buyers are integrating input from a number of internal sources, based on a relatively formal process. And finally, business buyers tend to seek (and often secure) highly customized goods, services, and prices.

## 11-5 Marketing Research: So, What Do They Really Think?

If marketing begins with the customer, marketing research is the foundation of success. **Marketing research** involves gathering, interpreting, and applying information to uncover opportunities and challenges. The goal, of course, is better marketing decisions: more value for consumers and more profits for businesses that deliver. Companies use marketing research to:

- Identify external opportunities and threats (from social trends to competition).
- Monitor and predict customer behavior.
- Evaluate and improve each area of the marketing mix.

Most successful marketers rely on research to develop breakthrough products and effective marketing programs. But research will never replace the creative potential of the gifted individual. Steve Jobs, founder of Apple, famously declared, "A lot of times, people don't know what they want until you show it to them."

### 11-5a Types of Data

There are two main categories of marketing research data—**secondary data** and **primary data**—each with its own set of benefits and drawbacks, as shown in Exhibit 11.7.

Clearly, it makes sense to gather secondary data before you invest in primary research. Look at your company's internal information. What does previous research say? What does the press say? What can you find on the web? Once you've looked at the secondary research, you may find that primary research is unnecessary. But if not, your secondary research will guide your primary research and make it more focused and relevant, which ends up saving time and money.

### 11-5b Primary Research Tools

There are two basic categories of primary research: observation and survey. **Observation research** happens when the researcher *does not* directly interact with the research subject. The key advantage of watching versus asking is that what people actually *do* often differs from what they *say*—sometimes quite innocently. For instance, if an amusement park employee stands outside an attraction and records which way people turn when they exit, he may be conducting observation research to determine where to place a new lemonade stand. Watching would be better than asking

**business buyer behavior** Describes how people act when they are buying products to use either directly or indirectly to produce other products.

**marketing research** The process of gathering, interpreting, and applying information to uncover marketing opportunities and challenges, and to make better marketing decisions.

**secondary data** Existing data that marketers gather or purchase for a research project.

**primary data** New data that marketers compile for a specific research project.

**observation research** Marketing research that does not require the researcher to interact with the research subject.

**"If you can't be a good example, then you'll just have to serve as a horrible warning."**

Even the heavy hitters make marketing gaffes. Their biggest mistakes are often entertaining, but they also serve as a powerful warning to consult with the customer (or to at least think it through) before taking action—especially online, where social media goofs can dog a marketer for years. A few amusing examples:

- In 2017, the St. Louis Cardinals hawked their world series replica ring with this Tweet: "You love baseball, she loves jewelry, on May 17, it's a win-win." The Twitter-verse informed the Cardinals in no uncertain terms that many women love bling AND baseball.

- In 2014, LG sent a tweet mocking the iPhone 6 for bending issues…from an iPhone!

- The U.S. Department sent a tweet during Black History Month in 2017 honoring iconic civil rights activist W.E.B. Du Bois

and misspelled his name. The department then issued an apology, which was also misspelled.

- In 2018, Chick-fil-A responded via Twitter to a customer who asked if they were planning to open a store in North Pole, Alaska (a *real* town), by tweeting, "Although we have no immediate plans of expanding beyond North America at this time, we appreciate your feedback!"[13]

These fiascos only highlight the importance of marketing research (combined with common sense). But sometimes the best planning does not forestall a big goof. At that point, the priority should shift to dealing with the mistake openly, honestly, and quickly, which can help a company win the game, despite the gaffe.

| Exhibit 11.7 | Research Data Comparison |
| --- | --- |

| Secondary Data | Primary Data |
| --- | --- |
| Existing data that marketers gather or purchase | New data that marketers compile for the first time |
| Tends to be lower cost | Tends to be more expensive |
| May not meet your specific needs | Customized to meet your needs |
| Frequently outdated | Fresh, new data |
| Available to your competitors | Proprietary—no one else has it |
| Examples: U.S. Census, *The Wall Street Journal*, *Time* magazine, your product sales history | Examples: Your own surveys, focus groups, customer comments, mall interviews |

because many people could not honestly say which way they'd likely turn. Examples of observation research include:

- Scanner data from retail sales

- Traffic counters to determine where to place billboards

- Garbage analysis to measure recycling compliance

Observation research can be both cheap and amazingly effective. A car dealership, for instance, can survey the preset radio stations on every car that comes in for service. That information helps them choose which stations to use for advertising. But the biggest downside of observation research is that it doesn't

yield any information on consumer motivation—the reasons behind consumer decisions. The preset radio stations wouldn't matter, for example, if the bulk of drivers listen only to their iPods in the car.

**Survey research** happens when the researcher *does* interact with research subjects. The key advantage is that you can secure information about what people are thinking and feeling, beyond what you can observe.

> "Marketing without data is like driving with your eyes closed."
>
> —Dan Zarrella, Social Media Scientist, HubSpot

**survey research** Marketing research that requires the researcher to interact with the research subject.

# There Is No "Me" in Sustainability—but Maybe There Should Be!

Recent research suggests that an overwhelming majority of people around the world care about sustainability. What's more, they are finally willing to put their money where their mouth is and actually buy eco-friendly products—even if they are a little pricier than conventional products or are not quite the same quality. Even so, a surprisingly small number of eco-friendly products have broken through into the mainstream in a significant way. One example of a big success is hybrid cars. The reason may be that hybrid cars answer the age-old question of "What's in it for me?" While most eco-friendly products offer broad planetary benefits such as cleaner oceans or more trees or cleaner air, they don't offer direct personal benefits. Hybrid cars offer planetary benefits, to be sure, but they also offer the direct personal benefits of better gas mileage and a highly visible symbol that tells the rest of the world that the driver has adopted an eco-friendly technology (and is paying a little extra to do so). There is much to be said for appealing to our better intentions and higher purpose, but perhaps there is more marketing success to be had in promising customers direct personal benefits. Unilever's sustainable living hub expands on this idea:

> Recycling is mainly a guilt-avoidance activity, but could it actually be a fun teachable moment with your kids? Eating sustainably can mean better tasting food and weight loss, with less pesticides or unhealthy food additives. Natural body care products may smell nicer and are gentle on sensitive skin. Washing your hair less or in a shorter shower maintains natural shine and prevents split ends. These are tiny benefits, but when was the last sustainability campaign that promised any direct personal benefits at all?[14]

Syda Productions/Shutterstock.com

For example, a carmaker might observe that the majority of its purchasers are men. They could use this information to tailor their advertising to men, or they could do survey research and possibly learn that even though men do the actual purchasing, women often make the purchase decision . . . a very different scenario! But the key downside of survey research is that many people aren't honest or accurate about their experiences, opinions, and motivations, which can make survey research quite misleading. Examples of survey research include:

- Telephone and online questionnaires
- Door-to-door interviews
- Mall-intercept interviews
- Focus groups
- Mail-in questionnaires

## 11-5c An International Perspective

Doing marketing research across multiple countries can be an overwhelming challenge. In parts of Latin America,

for instance, many homes don't have telephone connections, so the results from telephone surveys could be very misleading. Door-to-door tends to be a better approach. But in parts of the Middle East, researchers could be arrested for knocking on a stranger's door, especially if they aren't dressed according to local standards. Because of these kinds of issues, many companies hire research firms with a strong local presence (often based in-country) to handle their international marketing research projects.

## 11-6 Social Responsibility and Technology: A Major Marketing Shift

Two key factors have had a dramatic impact on marketing in the past couple of decades: a surge in the social responsibility movement, and the dramatic emergence of the internet and digital technology. This section will cover how each factor has influenced marketing.

# Innovation: Unleashed!

In today's hyper-competitive marketplace, businesses must differentiate their products from an astonishing array of alternatives. While life-changing innovation is rare, many successful products simply provide a new twist on an existing product. Examples include Heinz's mash-up sauces (e.g., Hanch, which is a combination of hot sauce and ranch, and Wasabioli, spicy wasabi and garlic aioli), Nike's neon-colored Flyknit athletic shoes, and Yoplait's squeezable, Go-Gurt yogurt snack tubes.

To help you make those kinds of jumps, the game in this box uses rebus puzzles to stretch your creativity. Rebus puzzles present common words and phrases in novel orientation to each other. The goal is to determine the meaning. The puzzles are below, and the answers are to the right of the box.

| ARREST YOU'RE | HISTORY HISTORY HISTORY | SK8 iiiiiiiiiii iiiiiiiii | print | BAN ANA | Shut Sit |
|---|---|---|---|---|---|
| funny funny words words words words | ST4ANCE | herring | MEREPEAT | Jack | Symphon |

**Answers:** You're under arrest; too funny for words; history repeats itself; for instance; skate on thin ice; red herring; small print; repeat after me; banana split; Jack-in-the-Box; sit down and shut up; unfinished symphony.

---

> 75% of the engagement on a Facebook post happens in the first five hours.
>
> —Digital Insights

## 11-6a Marketing and Society: It's Not Just about You!

Over the past couple of decades, the social responsibility movement has accelerated in the United States, demanding that marketers actively contribute to the needs of the broader community. Leading-edge marketers have responded by setting a higher standard in key areas such as environmentalism, abolishment of sweatshops, and involvement in the local community. Starbucks, Target, and General Electric, for instance, all publish corporate responsibility reports that evaluate the social impact of how the companies run their businesses, and all highlight their programs on their corporate websites.

**Green Marketing** Companies employ **green marketing** when they actively promote the ecological benefits of their products. Toyota has been especially successful promoting the green benefits of its Prius. (Toyota did struggle during the COVID-19 pandemic,

> **green marketing** Developing and promoting environmentally sound products and practices to gain a competitive edge.

although it seemed to recover more quickly and robustly than other carmakers.)[15] Its strategy highlights fuel economy and performance, implying that consumers can "go green" without making any real sacrifices. Environmentally friendly fashion offers another emerging example of green marketing. Over the past few years, a number of designers have rolled out their versions of upscale eco-fashion. In addition to clothing made of organic cotton, recent entries include vegan stilettos with four-inch heels, bamboo dresses, biodegradable umbrellas, and solar-powered jackets. (These jackets feature solar cells, integrated into the collar, which collect solar energy and route it to charge devices.) Green marketing items are aimed at a growing number of consumers who make purchase decisions based (at least in part) on their convictions. But reaching these consumers may be an increasing challenge in tough economic times, when low prices trump all other considerations for a growing swath of the population.[16]

## 11-6b Technology and Marketing: Power to the People!

The emergence of the digital age has revolutionized every element of marketing. Perhaps the most dramatic change has been a shift in power from producers to customers. The internet gives customers 24/7 access to information and product choices from all over the world. In response, competition has intensified as marketers strive to meet an increasingly high standard of value.

But technology has also created opportunities for marketers. The internet has opened the door for **mass customization**: creating products tailored for individual consumers on a mass basis. Using sophisticated data collection and management systems, marketers can now collect detailed information about each customer, which allows them to develop one-on-one relationships and to identify high-potential new customers. Through the web, marketers can tap into (or even create) communities of users that yield valuable information about their goods and services. Technology also helps marketers lower costs, so they can deliver greater value to their customers.

The digital boom has also created an abundance of promotional opportunities, as marketers reach out to consumers via new tools, such as interactive advertising, virtual reality displays, text messaging, and video kiosks. We'll discuss these tools in more detail in Chapter 12.

**mass customization** The creation of products tailored for individual consumers on a mass basis.

## The Big Picture

Since the ultimate goal of most marketing is long-term profitability, a core marketing principle must infuse every facet of a successful organization: the need to deliver products that exceed customer expectations. The customer must come first for *every* department—including finance, accounting, engineering, manufacturing, and human resources—although the specifics of how that plays out will clearly differ for each organizational function. Competition in the future will only intensify. Customer choices will continue to multiply as globalization and technology march forward. While these forces will weed out the weaker players, firms with a deeply engrained marketing orientation and a strong customer focus will continue to flourish—delivering value to their stakeholders, and dollars to their bottom line.

## Careers in Marketing

### Brand Manager

Drive the overall performance and profitability of a brand or group of brands. Establish the brand image and position in relation to competitors. Formulate and implement creative and effective marketing strategies. Manage and motivate creative teams that support the brand's development. Understand and integrate overall corporate goals into brand strategies. Communicate brand performance to senior management. Communicate key brand information to both internal and external stakeholders.

# 12 | Product and Promotion:
## Creating and Communicating Value

*Frantic00/Shutterstock.com*

## 12-1 Product: It's Probably More Than You Thought

When most people hear the term "**product**," they immediately think of the material things that we buy, use, and consume every day: for example, a can of Pepsi, or a pair of True Religion jeans. But from a marketing standpoint, product means much more. A product can be anything that a company offers to satisfy consumer needs and wants; the possibilities include not only physical goods but also services and ideas. A charity event, cosmetic surgery, and a cooking lesson all qualify as products.

When you buy a product, you also "buy" all of the attributes associated with the product. These encompass a broad range of qualities, such as the brand name, the image, the packaging, the reputation, and the guarantee. From a consumer standpoint, these attributes (or the lack of these attributes) are part of the product purchase, even if they don't add to its value. As a marketer, it's worth your while to carefully consider each element of your product to ensure that you're maximizing value without sacrificing profitability. Apple established its reputation for creating value through product design in 1998 by introducing translucent desktop computers in a range of eyepopping colors (the iMac), at a time when other PC manufacturers completely overlooked design, churning out look-alike inventories of boring, beige boxes. Over the years, Apple has continued to polish its reputation by introducing sleek, elegantly designed products such as its iPad tablet computers and its iPhones.

> **product** Anything that an organization offers to satisfy consumer needs and wants, including both goods and services.

### 12-1a Services: A Product by Any Other Name

If a "product" includes anything that satisfies consumer needs, services clearly fit the bill. But services have some obvious differences from tangible goods. You often cannot see, hear, smell, taste, or touch a service, and you can virtually never "own" it. After math tutoring, for example, you might possess sharper algebra skills, but you don't own the tutoring experience (at least not literally). Most services embody these qualities:

- **Intangibility:** You typically cannot see, smell, taste, or touch a service before you buy it. Clearly, this creates a lot of uncertainty. Will the purchase really be worthwhile? Smart marketers mitigate the uncertainty by giving clues that suggest value. Many medical professionals, for example, hang framed versions of their degrees and certifications in their offices to bolster their credibility and increase the confidence of their patients.

- **Inseparability:** Try as you might, you simply can't separate the buyer of a service from the person who renders it. Delivery requires interaction between the buyer and the provider, and the customer directly contributes to the quality of the service. Consider a trip to the doctor. If you accurately describe your

> "Don't find customers for your products; find products for your customers."
>
> —Seth Godin,
> Entrepreneur and Author

symptoms, you're likely to get a correct diagnosis. But if you simply say, "I just don't feel normal," the outcome will likely be different.

- **Variability:** This one ties closely to inseparability. A talented massage therapist would probably help you relax, whereas a mediocre one might actually create tension. And even the talented massage therapist might give better service at the end of the day than at the beginning, or worse service on the day she is coming down with a cold. Variability also applies to the difference among providers. A massage at a top-notch spa is likely to be better than a massage at your local gym.

- **Perishability:** Marketers cannot store services for delivery at peak periods. A restaurant, for instance, only has so many seats; they can't (reasonably) tell

## Exhibit 12.1
### Goods and Services Spectrum

**Pure Goods** ⟷ **Pure Services**

Bottle of Ketchup
Package of Socks

Financial Consulting
Piano Lesson

### 12-1c Product Layers: Peeling the Onion

When customers buy products, they actually purchase more than just the good or service itself. They buy a complete product package that includes a core benefit, the actual product, and product augmentations. Understanding these layers is valuable, since the most successful products delight consumers at each one of them.

their 8 p.m. dinner customers to come back the next day at 5 p.m. Similarly, major tourist destinations, such as Las Vegas, can't store an inventory of room service deliveries or performances of Cirque du Soleil. This creates obvious cost issues; is it worthwhile to prepare for a peak crowd but lose money when it's slow? The answer depends on the economics of your business.

### 12-1b Goods versus Services: A Mixed Bag

Identifying whether a product is a good or a service can pose a considerable challenge, since many products contain elements of both. A meal at your local Italian restaurant obviously includes tangible goods: you definitely own that calzone. But someone else took your order, brought it to the table, and (perhaps most importantly) did the dishes! Service was clearly a crucial part of the package.

A goods and services spectrum can provide a valuable tool for analyzing the relationship between the two (refer to Exhibit 12.1.) At one extreme, **pure goods** don't include any services. Examples include a bottle of ketchup or a package of socks. At the other extreme, **pure services** don't include any goods. Examples include financial consulting or a piano lesson. Other products—such as a meal at Pizza Hut—fall somewhere between the poles.

**pure goods** Products that do not include any services.

**pure services** Products that do not include any goods.

Amero/Shutterstock.com

**Core Benefit** At the most fundamental level, consumers buy a core benefit that satisfies their needs. When you buy a smartphone, the core benefit is communication. When you go to a movie, the core benefit is entertainment. And when you go to the doctor, the core benefit is better health. Most products also provide secondary benefits that help distinguish them from other goods and services that meet the same customer needs. A secondary benefit of a smartphone might include entertainment, since it probably plays your music, too.

### 12-1d Actual Product

The *actual product* layer, of course, is the product itself: the physical good or the delivered service that provides the core benefit. The Samsung Galaxy Z Fold 2 is an actual good that provides the benefit of communication. A movie theater screening of *Without Remorse* is an actual service that provides the benefit of entertainment. Identifying the actual product is sometimes tough when the product is a service. For example, the core benefit of visiting a doctor might be better health, but the actual product may be someone in a white coat poking and prodding you. Keep in mind that the actual product includes all of the attributes that make it unique, such as the brand name, the features, and the packaging.

**Augmented Product** Most marketers wrap their actual products in additional goods and services, called the *augmented product*, that sharpen their competitive edge. Augmentations come in a range of different forms. Many upscale movie theaters in L.A. display props from movies that have played in that theater. Most smartphones come with warranties or insurance and offer at least some customer service. And some doctors might give you sample pills until you can get your prescription filled.

### 12-1e Product Classification: It's a Bird, It's a Plane...

Products fall into two broad categories—consumer products and business products—depending on the reason for the purchase. **Consumer products** are purchased for personal use or consumption, while **business products** are purchased to use either directly or indirectly in the production of another product. The shoes in your closet at home are a consumer product, while the shoes that you rent at the bowling alley are a business product.

**Consumer Product Categories** Marketers further divide consumer products into several different subcategories, as shown below. Understanding the characteristics of the subcategories can help marketers develop better strategies.

- *Convenience products* are the inexpensive goods and services that consumers buy frequently with limited consideration and analysis. Distribution tends to be widespread, with promotion by the producers. Examples include staples such as toothpaste and shampoo, impulse items such as magazines and candy bars, and emergency products such as headache tablets and plumbing services.

- *Shopping products* are the more expensive products that consumers buy less frequently. Typically, as consumers shop, they search for the best value and learn more about features and benefits through the shopping process. Distribution is widespread but more selective than for convenience products. Both producers and retailers tend to promote shopping products. Examples include cars, computers, and cell phone service.

- *Specialty products* are those much more expensive products that consumers seldom purchase. Most people perceive specialty products as being so important that they are unwilling to accept substitutes. Because of this, distribution tends to be highly selective. (Consumers are willing to go far out of their way for the "right" brand.) Both producers and retailers are apt to promote specialty products but to a highly targeted audience. Some specialty product examples are high-end sports cars, branded jewelry, and weight reduction surgery.

- *Unsought products* are the goods and services that hold little interest (or even negative interest) for consumers. Price and distribution vary wildly, but promotion tends to be aggressive to drum up consumer interest. Disability insurance and prepaid burial plots (especially for young people) and blood donations are some examples.

**Business Product Categories** Marketers also divide business products into subcategories. Here, too, understanding the subcategories can lead to better marketing strategies.

- *Installations* are large capital purchases designed for a long, productive life. The marketing of installations emphasizes personal selling and customization. Examples include industrial robots, new buildings, airplanes, and railroad cars.

- *Accessory equipment* includes smaller, movable capital purchases, designed for a shorter productive life than installations. Marketing focuses on personal selling but includes less customization than installations. Examples include personal computers, power tools, and furniture.

- The *maintenance, repair, and operating products* category consists of small-ticket items that businesses consume on an ongoing basis but don't become part of the final product. Marketing tactics emphasize efficiency. Examples include cleaning supplies, lightbulbs, and copy paper.

- *Raw materials* include the farm and natural products used in producing other products. Marketing emphasizes price and service rather than product differentiation. Examples include cotton, timber, and wheat.

- *Component parts and processed materials* include finished (or partially finished) products used in producing other products. Marketing emphasizes product quality as well as price and service. Examples include batteries and spark plugs for cars, aluminum ingots for soda cans, and Intel computer chips.

- *Business services* are those services that businesses purchase to facilitate operations. Marketing focuses on quality and relationships; the role of price can vary. Examples include payroll services, janitorial services, and legal services.

**consumer products** Products purchased for personal use or consumption.

**business products** Products purchased to use either directly or indirectly in the production of other products.

# A Fascination with Failure—So Bad It's Good!

A brand-new museum is opening in Sweden, with the goal of celebrating "the absurd and hilarious wrong turns that companies have taken in their product development." According to museum founder Samuel West, "Every failure is uniquely spectacular, while success is nauseatingly repetitive. True innovation requires learning from the complexities of each failure." Some highlights from the museum:

- Toothpaste company Colgate offered frozen food like beef lasagna in the 1980s.
- Coca-Cola offered Coca-Cola BlaK—a coffee-flavored cola drink—from 2004 until 2006.
- Cult motorcycle brand Harley Davidson flopped delightfully with its "Hot Road" perfume.
- The DeLorean motorcar, showcased in the *Back to the Future* movie series as a time machine, was marketed as a luxury sports car, but with a severely underpowered engine, it was apparently painfully slow, and was pulled from the market in two short years.

## 12-2 Product Differentiation and Planning: A Meaningful Difference

While some products have succeeded with little or no forethought, you'll dramatically boost your chance of a hit with careful planning. **Product differentiation** should be a key consideration. Winning products must embody a real or perceived difference versus the glut of goods and services that compete in virtually every corner of the market. But different alone isn't enough; different from, and better than, the competition are both critical in order to create the shortest path to success. A quick look at some high-profile product failures illustrates the point.

- **Vegetable Jell-O:** Few kids today would name Jell-O as their favorite dessert, and back in the 1960s, even fewer were fans of vegetable-flavored Jell-O (think celery, tomato, mixed vegetable, and Italian salad), which was soon yanked from the market.

- **Gerber Singles**—in the mid-1970s, Gerber—yes, the classic baby food company—introduced puréed adult foods, such as "Beef Burgundy," "Sweet and Sour Pork," and "Mediterranean Vegetables" in single servings sold in little glass jars, targeted toward college students and young adults. Gerber Singles were a quick, spectacular failure, in part, perhaps, because both the name and concept just screamed "loser!" to the target audience.

- **Clear Beer:** In the 1990s, several companies introduced clear beers, reflecting an ill-fated obsession with clear products, including shampoo, soap, and the short-lived, clear Crystal Pepsi.

- **Lumia 900:** Nokia introduced the Lumia 900 phone in early 2012 for just $100 with a two-year contract. The price soon dropped to $50, but even that didn't spur sales, mostly due to a dearth of apps for its Windows operating system. By 2013, Nokia, once the dominant player in cell phones, had sold its entire handset business to Microsoft.

- **Funky French Fries:** In 2002, Ore-Ida introduced Funky Fries. The flavors included cinnamon-sugar, chocolate, and "radical blue." Not surprisingly, they were off the market in less than a year.

- **Cocaine Energy Drink:** In 2006, Redux Beverages brought Cocaine Energy Drink to market, calling it a "legal alternative" to the illegal drug in form of an energy drink, and describing the beverage, which had no actual cocaine in it, as a "fruity, atomic fireball" drink. Redux was forced to pull Cocaine off the shelves in the United States in 2007 when the FDA declared that its producers were "illegally marketing their drink as an alternative to street drugs."[1]

### 12-2a Product Quality

Product quality relates directly to product value, which comes from understanding

**product differentiation**
The attributes that make a good or service different from other products that compete to meet the same or similar customer needs.

> "Give them quality. That's the best kind of advertising."
>
> —Milton Hershey, Founder, The Hershey Chocolate Company

## Exhibit 12.2 | Product Quality Indicators

| Product Category | Some Quality Indicators |
|---|---|
| Cell Phones | Design, brand, number of apps, graphics, memory, battery life, memory, and customer service |
| Kids' Toys | Safety, expert endorsements, and educational and entertainment value |
| Cars | Horsepower, design, fuel efficiency, brand, resale value, reliability, and awards |
| Water Parks | Thrill factor, design, cleanliness, variety, and setting |
| Coffee | Taste, brand, price, country of origin, and additives (or lack of) |

your customer. Peter Drucker, a noted business thinker, writer, and educator, declared:

> Quality in a product or service is not what the supplier puts in. It's what the customer gets out and is willing to pay for. A product is not quality because it is hard to make and costs a lot of money . . . this is incompetence. Customers pay only for what is of use to them and gives them value. Nothing else constitutes quality.

In other words, a high-quality product does a great job meeting customer needs. Siemens, a huge electronics conglomerate, embodies this thinking in its approach to quality: "Quality is when our customers come back and our products don't."

But the specific definition of quality—and the attributes that indicate quality—changes across product categories. Refer to Exhibit 12.2 for a few examples.

Regardless of product category, the two key aspects of quality are level and consistency. **Quality level** refers to how well a product performs its core functions. You might think that smart companies deliver the highest possible level of performance, but this is seldom profitable, or even desirable. For instance, only a tiny group of consumers would pay for a speedboat to go 200 mph, when 80 mph offers a sufficient thrill (at least for most of us!). The right level of product performance is the level that meets the needs of your consumers, and those needs include price. Decisions about quality level must also consider the competition. The goal is to outperform the other players in your category while maintaining profitability.

The second dimension of quality is **product consistency**. How consistently does your product actually deliver the promised level of quality? With a positive relationship between price and performance, consistent delivery can offer a competitive edge at almost any quality level.

Honda offers an excellent example. When most people consider the Accord, the Civic, and the CRV, all

Honda-owned models, quality quickly comes to mind. And all three dominate their markets. But clearly, the quality *levels* (and price) are different for each. The Accord serves the upper, more conservative end of the market; the Civic tends to appeal to younger, hipper, more budget-minded consumers; the CRV tends to appeal to middle-of-the-road shoppers seeking a reliable, small SUV. In short, Honda succeeds at delivering product consistency at several markedly different quality levels.

### 12-2b  Features and Benefits

**Product features** are the characteristics of the product you offer. If a product is well designed, each feature corresponds to a meaningful **customer benefit**. The marketer's challenge is to design a package of features that offers the highest level of value for an acceptable price. And the equation must also account for profitability goals.

One winning formula may be to offer at least some low-cost features that correspond to high-value benefits. Creating an "open kitchen" restaurant, for instance, has limited impact on costs but gives patrons an exciting, up-close view of the drama and hustle of professional food preparation. Exhibit 12.3 lists some other examples of product features and their corresponding customer benefits.

### 12-2c  Product Lines and the Product Mix

Some companies focus all of their efforts on one product, but most offer a number of different products to enhance their revenue and profits. A **product line** is a group of products that are closely related to each other in terms of either how they work or the customers they serve. Sony, for example, carries a wide range of digital cameras and accessories, to meet the needs of as many different customers as possible. A **product mix** is the total number of product lines and individual items sold by a single firm. Sony's product mix ranges from cameras to electronics, to phones, to music, to video game consoles, to entertainment (games, movies, music, etc.).

Decisions regarding how many items to include in each product line and in the overall product mix can have a huge impact on a

**quality level** How well a product performs its core functions.

**product consistency** How reliably a product delivers its promised level of quality.

**product features** The specific characteristics of a product.

**customer benefit** The advantage that a customer gains from specific product features.

**product line** A group of products that are closely related to each other, either in terms of how they work or the customers they serve.

**product mix** The total number of product lines and individual items sold by a single firm.

## Exhibit 12.3 Product Features and Customer Benefits

| Product | Product Feature | Customer Benefit |
|---------|-----------------|------------------|
| Subway Sandwiches | Lower fat | Looser pants |
| Costco | Rock-bottom prices on a huge range of higher end products and services | More cash for other needs |
| Whole Foods Market | Organic produce | A healthier planet |
| Stella McCartney Clutch | Highly fashionable | Feeling chic |
| Triple Latte | Caffeine, caffeine, caffeine | More time to, uh, study |

firm's profits. With too few items in each line, the company may be leaving money on the table. With too many items, the company may be spending unnecessarily to support its weakest links.

One reason that firms add new product lines is to reach completely new customers. Gap, for instance, added Old Navy to reach younger, lower-income customers, and Banana Republic to reach older, higher-income customers. Each line includes a range of different products designed to meet the needs of their specific customers. But one risk of adding new lines—especially lower-priced lines— is **cannibalization**, which happens when a new entry "eats" the sales of an existing line. This is especially dangerous when the new products are lower-priced than the current ones. You could see the problem, for instance, if a $20 blue jean purchase from Old Navy replaces a $50 blue jean purchase from Gap; the company has lost more than half its revenue on the sale. Like other companies with multiple lines, Gap carefully monitors the cannibalization issue and works to differentiate its lines as fully as possible.

### 12-2d Branding

At the most basic level, a **brand** is a product's identity that sets it apart from other players in the same category. Typically, brands represent the combination of elements such as product name, symbol, design, reputation, and image. But today's most powerful emerging brands go far beyond the sum of their attributes. They project a compelling group identity that creates brand fanatics: loyal customers who advocate for the brand better than any advertising a marketer could buy. The overall value of a brand to an organization—the extra money that consumers will spend to buy that brand—is called **brand equity**.

**cannibalization** When a producer offers a new product that takes sales away from its existing products.

**brand** A product's identity— including product name, symbol, design, reputation, and image— that sets it apart from other players in the same category.

**brand equity** The overall value of a brand to an organization.

Since 2001, Interbrand, a leading brand consultancy, has published a ranking of the 100 Best Global Brands by dollar value. The top ten brands are listed in Exhibit 12.4, but you can find the complete list at Interbrand's website.

**Brand Name** A catchy, memorable name is among the most powerful elements of your brand. While the right name will never save a bad business, it can launch a good business to new heights. But finding the right name can be tough. According to the respected Brighter Naming consulting group, the following characteristics can help:

1. Short, sweet, and easy to pronounce and spell: Examples include Sprite, H&M, GE, Nike, and Visa.

2. Unique within the industry: Think Caterpillar, Yahoo!, Starbucks, Zara, and Google.

3. Good alliteration, especially for long names: The words should roll off your tongue. Some examples are Coca-Cola, BlackBerry, Dunkin', WW (Weight Watchers), and Minute Maid.[2]

## Exhibit 12.4 Interbrand Top Ten Global Brands 2020

| Brand | Country of Ownership |
|-------|----------------------|
| Apple | United States |
| Amazon | United States |
| Microsoft | United States |
| Google | United States |
| Samsung | South Korea |
| Coca-Cola | United States |
| Toyota | Japan |
| Mercedes-Benz | Germany |
| McDonald's | United States |
| The Walt Disney Company | United States |

Source: Interbrand Best Global Brands 2020, https://www.interbrand.com/thinking/best-global-brands-2020-download/, accessed April 29, 2021.

## Exhibit 12.5 Brand Name Categories

| Category | Description | Examples |
|---|---|---|
| **Location-Based** | Refers to either the area served or the place of origin | Southwest Airlines, Bank of America, Best Western Hotels |
| **Founder's Name** | Can include first name, last name, or both | McDonald's, Dell Computer, Ford, Disney, Jenny Craig |
| **Descriptive or Functional** | Describes what the product is or how it works | eBay, U.S. News and World Report, Subway, Krispy Kreme, Reddi-wip |
| **Evocative** | Communicates an engaging image that resonates with consumers | Yahoo!, Craftsman, Virgin, Intel, Cosmopolitan, Starbucks, Apple, SpaceX, Oculus Rift, Trader Joe's, Amazon |

Brand names typically fall into four categories, as described in Exhibit 12.5.

**Line Extensions versus Brand Extensions** As companies grow, marketers look for opportunities to grow their businesses. **Line extensions** are similar products offered under the same brand name. Possibilities include new flavors, sizes, colors, ingredients, and forms. One example is Lay's potato chips, which offers more than 45 versions, including Barbecue, Baked, Flamin' Hot, Chile Limón, Dill Pickle, and Chedder Jalepeno. The marketing challenge is to ensure that line extensions steal market share from competitors rather than from the core brand. Pringles, which offers 34 varieties of the curiously addicting dehydrated potato chip, continually monitors its flavors, to ensure that each one is profitable. In 2020, Pringles discontinued Kickin' Chicken Taco. But it did offer an alternative for any disappointed customers: stacking its Rotisserie Chicken, Cheddar Cheese, and Fire Roasted Jalapeño chips to achieve the same flavor.[3]

**Brand extensions**, on the other hand, involve launching a product in a new category under an existing brand name. The Bic brand, for instance, is quite elastic, stretching nicely to include diverse products such as pens, glue, cigarette lighters, and disposable razors. The Virgin brand demonstrates similar elasticity, covering more than 350 companies that range from airlines to cell phones, to soft drinks, to cars. But the concept of brand extension becomes most clear (and most entertaining) through examining brand extension failures. Examples include, Budweiser Dry, Cosmopolitan (yes, the magazine brand!) yogurt, and Bic perfume. Apparently, there is some mysterious link between lighter fluid and perfume; Zippo offers perfume, too.[4]

**Licensing** Some companies opt to license their brands from other businesses. **Licensing** means purchasing—often for a substantial fee—the right to use another company's brand name or symbol. The benefits are instant name recognition, an established reputation, and a proven track record. On a worldwide basis, the best-known licensing arrangements are probably character names, which range from Bart Simpson to SpongeBob and appear on everything from cereal to toys, to underwear. Many movie producers also do high-profile licensing, turning out truckloads of merchandise that features movie properties such as *Batman* and *Frozen*.

Another fast-growing area is the licensing of corporate or college names. Coca-Cola, for instance, claims to have more than 300 licensees who sell over a billion dollars of licensed merchandise each year. The potential benefits for Coca-Cola are clear: more promotion, increased exposure, and enhanced image. But the risk is significant. If licensed products are of poor quality or overpriced, the consumer backlash hits the core brand rather than the producer of the licensed product.

**Cobranding Cobranding** is when established brands from different companies join forces to market the same product. This cooperative approach has a long history but is currently enjoying a new popularity. Examples include:

- Starbucks and Spotify work together to create curated playlists to benefit both partners and customers in Starbucks cafes around the world.

- Dairy Queen worked with Girl Scouts to offer the hugely popular limited-edition Thin Mint Blizzard.

Cobranding can offer huge advantages to both partners, by leveraging their strengths to enter new markets and gain more exposure.

**line extensions** Similar products offered under the same brand name.

**brand extension** A new product, in a new category, introduced under an existing brand name.

**licensing** Purchasing the right to use another company's brand name or symbol.

**cobranding** When established brands from different companies join forces to market the same product.

Archer Farms, Target's high-quality food label, is one of the most popular and successful store brands.

But cobranding can be risky. If one partner makes a major goof, the fallout can damage the reputation of the other partner as well.

**National Brands versus Store Brands** **National brands**, also called *manufacturers' brands*, are brands that the producer owns and markets. Many are well known and widely available, such as Oreo cookies, Dial soaps, and Nutella. Although most retailers carry lots of national brands, an increasing number have opted to also carry their own versions of the same products, called **store brands**, or *private label*. Deep discounters, such as Walmart and Costco, have had particular success with their private-label brands (e.g., Sam's Choice and Kirkland). *Private labels* play a growing role in grocery stores as well. In the United States, more than one out of four grocery purchases is private label, and the numbers are even higher in Europe, hitting half of all grocery sales in a number of markets. Since the global recession, private-label brand sales have grown more than twice as fast as national brand sales. The growing influence and increasing quality of low-end, private-label brands increase the pressure on national brands to continually innovate while holding down prices.[5]

At the upper end of the market—especially in the clothing business—key retailers specialize in private brands to create and protect a consistent, upscale image. Examples include Neiman Marcus, Bloomingdales, and Saks Fifth Avenue.[6]

### 12-2e Packaging

Great packaging does more than just hold the product. It can protect the product, provide information, facilitate storage, suggest product uses, promote the product brand, and attract buyer attention. Great packaging is especially important in the crowded world of grocery stores and mass merchandisers. In the average supermarket, the typical shopper passes about 300 items per minute and makes anywhere from 20% to 70% of purchases on sheer impulse. In this environment, your package must call out to your target customers and differentiate your product from all the others lined up beside it. Yet, in attracting consumer attention, a good package cannot sacrifice the basics such as protecting the product.[7]

Bottom line: great packaging stems from consumer needs, but it usually includes at least a smidge of creative brilliance. Examples include yogurt in a pouch that doesn't need a spoon, soup-to-go that can be microwaved in the can, "anti-theft" clear sandwich bags printed with mold-like green splotches (seriously!), and single-serving baby carrot packets that are easy to toss into a lunch.

### 12-3 Innovation and the Product Life Cycle: Nuts, Bolts, and a Spark of Brilliance

For a business to thrive long term, effective new product development is vital. And the process works only if it happens quickly. As technological advances hit the market at breakneck speed, current products are becoming obsolete faster than ever before. The need for speed compounds as hungry competitors crowd every niche of the market. But the rush is risky, since new product development costs can be in the millions, and the success rate is less than a third. Marketers who succeed in this challenging arena devote painstaking effort to understanding their customers, but they also nurture the creativity they need to generate new ideas. An example of how this can work: the 3M Corporation—makers of Post-it Notes and Scotch Tape—introduces about 500 new products per year by pushing its employees to "relentlessly ask, 'What if?'" Some innovative firms, such as Google, Facebook, and LinkedIn, also encourage workers to spend 20% of their work time (paid work time!) on projects of personal interest, which then belong to the firm.[8]

### 12-3a Types of Innovation

Clearly, the first personal computer represented a higher degree of newness than the first personal computer with a color screen. And the computer with a color screen represented a higher degree of newness than the first low-cost knockoff. Levels of innovation fall along a spectrum, as shown in Exhibit 12.6.

**Discontinuous Innovation** *Discontinuous innovations* are brand-new ideas that radically change how people live. Examples include the first car, the first television,

**national brands** Brands that the producer owns and markets.

**store brands** Brands that the retailer both produces and distributes (also called private-label brands).

## Exhibit 12.6
## Levels of Innovation

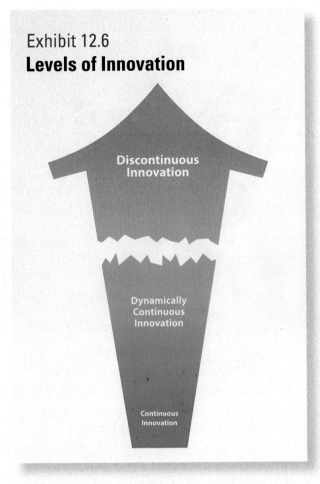

and the first computer. Affordable space tourism will also represent discontinuous innovation. These dramatic innovations require extensive customer learning, which should guide the marketing process.

**Dynamically Continuous Innovation** *Dynamically continuous innovations* are characterized by marked changes to existing products. Examples include cell phones, Blu-ray Discs, digital cameras, and driverless cars. These types of innovations require a moderate level of consumer learning in exchange for significant benefits.

**Continuous Innovation** A slight modification of an existing product is called a *continuous innovation*. Examples include new sizes, flavors, shapes, packaging, and design. The goal of continuous innovation is to distinguish a product from the competition. The goal of a knockoff is simply to copy a competitor and offer a lower price.

### 12-3b The New Product Development Process

An efficient, focused development process will boost your chances of new product success. The standard model includes six stages:

> "You can't wait for inspiration, you have to go after it with a club."
>
> —Jack London, Author

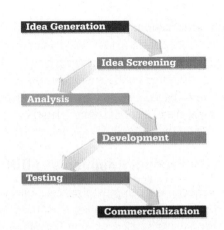

Each stage requires management to "green light" ideas before moving forward, to ensure that the company doesn't waste resources on marginal concepts.

1. **Idea Generation:** Some experts estimate that it takes 50 ideas for each new product that makes it to market, so you should definitely cast a wide net. Ideas can come from almost anywhere, including customer research, customer complaints, salespeople, engineers, suppliers, and competitors.

2. **Idea Screening:** The purpose of this stage is to weed out ideas that don't fit with the company's objectives and ideas that would clearly be too expensive to develop. The Walt Disney Company, for instance, would certainly eliminate the idea of an XXX cable channel because it just doesn't fit their mission.

3. **Analysis:** The purpose of the analysis stage is to estimate costs and forecast sales for each idea to get a sense of the potential profit and of how the product might fit within the company's resources. Each idea must meet rigorous standards to remain a contender.

4. **Development:** The development process leads to detailed descriptions of each concept with specific product features. New product teams sometimes also make prototypes, or samples, that consumers can actually test. The results help fully refine the concept.

5. **Testing:** This stage involves the formal process of soliciting feedback from consumers by testing the product concept. Do they like the features? Are the benefits meaningful? What price makes sense? Some companies also test-market their products or sell them in a limited area to evaluate the consumer response.

6. **Commercialization:** This stage entails introducing the product to the general market. Two key success factors are gaining distribution and launching promotions. But a product that tested well doesn't always mean instant success. The VW Beetle, for example, sold only 330 cars during its first year in the United States, but it later became a hit.

## 12-3c New Product Adoption and Diffusion

In order to become a commercial success, new products must spread throughout a market after they are introduced. That process is called *diffusion*. But diffusion clearly happens at different speeds, depending on the individual consumer and on the product itself.

**Product Adoption Categories** Some consumers like to try new things; others seem terrified of change. These attitudes clearly affect the rate at which individual people are willing to adopt (or begin buying and using) new products. The first adopters, about 2.5% of the total, are adventurous risk takers. The laggards, about 16% of the total, sometimes adopt products so late that earlier adopters have already moved to the next new thing. The rest of the population falls somewhere in between. Keep in mind that individuals tend to adopt new products at different rates. For instance, we probably all know someone who is an innovator in technology but a laggard in fashion, or vice versa.

**Product Diffusion Rates** Some new products diffuse into the population much more quickly than others. For example, Apple iPods and Segway Human Transporters appeared on the market around the same time; iPods became a pop culture icon, while Segways remained on the fringe. What accounts for the difference? Researchers have identified five product characteristics that affect the rate of adoption and diffusion. The more characteristics a product has, the faster it will diffuse into the population.

- **Observability:** How visible is the product to other potential consumers? Some product categories are easier to observe than others. If you adopt a new kind of car, the whole neighborhood will know, plus anyone else who sees you on the streets and highways.

- **Trialability:** How easily can potential consumers sample the new product? Trial can be a powerful way to create new consumers, which is why many markets fill their aisles with sample tables during popular shopping hours. Other examples of trial-boosting strategies include test-driving cars, sampling music, and testing new fragrances.

- **Complexity:** Can potential consumers easily understand what your product is and how it works?

Around 2005, portable media players like Apple's iPod were rocketing into the growth phase. Now, they are well into the decline stage thanks to the proliferation of always-connected smartphones.

If your product confuses people—or if they find it hard to explain to others—adoption rates will slow. For example, many people who test-ride Segway Human Transporters love the experience, but they have trouble explaining to others how it works or why it beats other transportation options.

- **Compatibility:** How consistent is your product with the existing way of doing things? Cordless phones, for example, caught on almost instantly, since they were completely consistent with people's prior experiences—only better!

- **Relative Advantage:** How much better are the benefits of your new product compared to existing products? When gas prices climb, for example, the benefits of hybrid and electric cars take on a much higher value relative to gasoline-powered cars. As a result, demand skyrockets.

## 12-3d The Product Life Cycle: Maximizing Results over Time

When marketers introduce a new product, they hope it will last forever, generating sales and profits for years to come. But they also realize that all products go through a

## Exhibit 12.7
## Product Life Cycle for a Typical Product Category

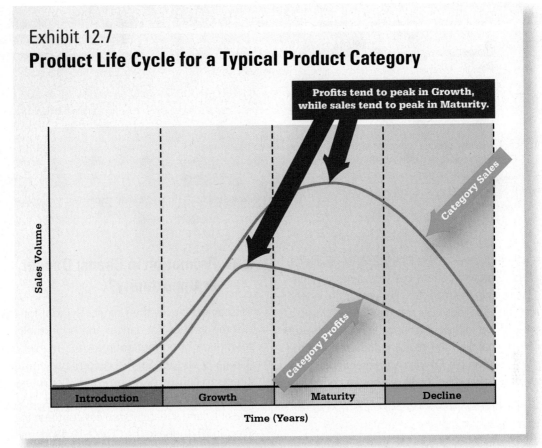

**product life cycle**: a pattern of sales and profits that typically changes over time. The life cycle can be dramatically different across individual products and product categories, and predicting the exact shape and length of the life cycle is virtually impossible. But most product categories do move through the four distinct stages shown in Exhibit 12.7.

- **Introduction:** This is a time of low sales and nonexistent profits as companies invest in raising awareness about the product and the product category. Some categories, such as the microwave, languish in this phase for years, while other categories, such as computer memory sticks, zoom through this phase. And some categories never get beyond introduction. (Think clear beers.)

- **Growth:** During the growth period, sales continue to rise, although profits usually peak. Typically, competitors begin to notice emerging categories in the growth phase. They enter the market—often with new variations of existing products—which further fuels the growth. Electric cars, streaming video services, personal drones, and driverless cars are currently in the growth phase, and a number of competitors have recently entered the market.

- **Maturity:** During maturity, sales usually peak. Profits continue to decline as competition intensifies. Once a market is mature, the only way to gain more users is to steal them from competitors rather than to bring new users into the category. Weaker players begin to drop out of the category. Gasoline-powered cars, sugared soda, and network TV are in maturity in the United States.

- **Decline:** During this period, sales and profits begin to decline, sometimes quite rapidly. The reasons usually relate to either technological change or change in consumer needs. For instance, the introduction of word processing pushed typewriters into decline, and a change in consumer taste and habits pushed hot cereal into decline. Competitors continue to drop out of the category.

Familiarity with the product life cycle helps marketers plan effective strategies for existing products and identify profitable categories for new products. Exhibit 12.8 summarizes typical marketing strategies and offers examples for each phase.

> **product life cycle** A pattern of sales and profits that typically changes over time.

## Exhibit 12.8  The Product Life Cycle and Marketing Strategies

| Phase | Examples | Sales/Profits | Key Marketing Strategies |
|---|---|---|---|
| Introduction | Virtual reality games, fuel cell technology, driverless vehicles | Low sales, low profits | Build awareness, trial, and distribution |
| Growth | Electric cars, mini tablets, fitness trackers, vegan food, wellness apps | Rapidly increasing sales and profits | Reinforce brand positioning, often through heavy advertising |
| Maturity | Airlines, personal computers, online stock trading, flavored sparkling water, coffee shops | Flat sales and declining profits | Target competitors, while defending franchise with new product features, competitive advertising, promotion, and price cuts |
| Decline | Landline phones, MP3 players, DVDs | Declining sales and profits | Reduce spending and consider terminating the product |

Individual products also have life cycles that usually follow the category growth pattern but sometimes vary dramatically. Clearly, it's in the marketer's best interest to extend the profitable run of an individual brand as long as possible. There are several ways to make this happen: finding new uses for the product, changing the product, and changing the marketing mix. For example, *Dancing with the Stars* has maintained interest in its franchise for 30 seasons by continually introducing new celebrity dancers and judges each season.

 ## 12-4  Promotion: Influencing Consumer Decisions

**Promotion** is the power to influence consumers—to remind them, to inform them, to persuade them. The best promotion goes one step further, building powerful consumer bonds that draw your customers back to your product again and again. But don't forget that great promotion only works with a great product. Bill Bernbach, an ad industry legend, captures this concept by noting, "A great ad campaign will make a bad product fail faster. It will get more people to know it's bad."

Marketers can directly control most promotional tools. From TV advertising to telephone sales, the marketer creates the message and communicates it directly to the target audience. But ironically, marketers *cannot* directly control the most powerful promotional tools: publicity, such as a comment on *The View* or a review in *Consumer Reports*, and word-of-mouth, such as a recommendation from a close friend or even a casual acquaintance. Marketers can only influence these areas through creative promotional strategies.

**promotion** Marketing communication designed to influence consumer purchase decisions through information, persuasion, and reminders.

### 12-4a Promotion in Chaos: Danger or Opportunity?

Not coincidentally, the Chinese symbol for crisis resembles the symbols for danger and opportunity—a perfect description of promotion in today's market. The pace of change is staggering. Technology has empowered consumers to choose how and when they interact with media, and they are grabbing control with dizzying speed. Digital TV and streaming movies continue to grow explosively. In 2020, due to the COVID-19 pandemic lockdowns, streaming services grew an unprecedented +37%, fueled largely by the well-funded introduction of Disney+. As media splinter across an array of entertainment options, usage patterns have changed as well: tech-savvy viewers are more prone to consume media in on-the-fly snacks rather than sit-down meals. Also, services such as Netflix streaming and Hulu Plus have led to an increase in binge viewing of entire seasons of TV shows. Rising consumer power and the breakneck pace of technology have created a growing need—and a stunning opportunity—for marketers to zero in on the right customers, at the right time, with the right message.[9]

### 12-4b Integrated Marketing Communication: Consistency and Focus

How many marketing messages have you gotten in the past 24 hours? Did you flip on the TV or radio? Surf the web? Notice a billboard? Glance at the logo on a T-shirt or cap? Chat with a friend about some product they like? Marketing exposure quickly snowballs: the typical consumer receives about 3,000 promotional messages each day. Some of those messages are hard to avoid as marketers find new, increasingly creative ways to promote their products to a captive audience. The venues include elevators, taxicabs, golf carts, and other surprising settings.[10]

Given the confounding level of clutter, smart companies use **integrated marketing communication** to coordinate their messages through every promotional vehicle—including their advertising, website, and salespeople—creating a coherent impression in the minds of their customers. Why bother coordinating all of these elements? The answer is clear. Consumers don't think about the specific source of the communication; instead, they combine—or integrate—the messages from *all* the sources to form a unified impression about your product. If the messages are out of sync or confusing, busy consumers won't bother to crack the code. They'll simply move on to the next best option.

Can you really control every message that every consumer sees or hears about your product? It's not likely. But if you accurately identify the key points of contact between your product and your target market, you can focus on those areas with remarkable effectiveness. For instance, the most common points of contact for McDonald's are probably advertising and the in-store experience. From upbeat commercials to smiling employees, to bright, cheerful uniforms, McDonald's spends millions of dollars to support its core message of fast, tasty, high value food in a clean, friendly environment—heavily concentrated in the areas that are key to its brand.

Other companies are likely to encounter the bulk of their customers through different channels. You'd probably learn about Dell computers, for example, through either its website or word of mouth. Dell has invested heavily in both areas. The company maintains an innovative, user-friendly website that allows even novice users to create customized systems. And Dell delivers award-winning customer service and technical support, which gets its customers to recommend its products to family and friends.

With so much clutter in the marketplace, coordinating messages can be a real challenge.

### 12-4c Coordinating the Communication

Even after you've identified the key points of contact, coordinating the messages remains a challenge. In many companies, completely different teams develop the different promotional areas. Salespeople and brand managers often have separate agendas, even when the same executive manages both departments. Frequently, disconnected outside agencies handle advertising, web development, and sales promotion programs. Coordinating the messages will happen only with solid teamwork, which must begin at the top of the organization.

Information also plays a crucial role. To coordinate marketing messages, everyone who creates and manages them must have free access to knowledge about the customer, the product, the competition, the market, and the strategy of the organization. Some of this information, such as strategic goals, will come from the top down, but a fair amount, such as information about the customer, should come from the bottom up. Information must also flow laterally across departments and agencies. The marketing research department, for instance, might have critical information about product performance, which might help the web management agency create a feature page that might respond to competitive threats identified by the sales force. When all parties have access to the same data, they are much more likely to remain on the same page.

## 12-5 A Meaningful Message: Finding the Big Idea

Your promotional message begins with understanding how your product is different from and better than the competition. But your **positioning statement**—a brief statement that articulates how you want your target market to envision your product relative to the competition—seldom translates directly into the promotional message. Instead, it marks the beginning of the creative development process, often spearheaded by ad agency creative professionals. When it works, the creative development process yields a *big idea*—a meaningful, believable, and distinctive

> **integrated marketing communication** The coordination of marketing messages through every promotional vehicle to communicate a unified impression about a product.
>
> **positioning statement** A brief statement that articulates how the marketer would like the target market to envision a product relative to the competition.

concept that cuts through the clutter. Big ideas are typically based on either a rational or an emotional premise. Here are a few examples from the past decade:

| Rational: | Price: | Walmart: "Save Money. Live Better." |
|---|---|---|
| | Engineering: | Bose: "Better Sound Through Research" |
| | Ingredients: | Snapple: "Made from the Best Stuff on Earth." Subway: "Eat Fresh" |
| Emotional: | Imagination: | GE: "Imagination at Work" |
| | Humor: | M&M's: "Melts in your mouth, not in your hands" |
| | Fear: | Cancer Patients Aid Association: "Cancer Cures Smoking" |
| | Energy: | Nike: "Just Do It" |
| | Self-Esteem: | L'Oréal: "Because You're Worth It." |
| | Patriotism: | The Marine Corps: "The Few. The Proud. The Marines." |

Not surprisingly, funny ads are a consumer favorite, although humor can be risky. For a number of years, Budweiser and Frito-Lay—known for using humor effectively—dominated the top ten in *USA Today*'s annual Ad Meter consumer ranking of Super Bowl ads. But Amazon's Alexa made its first appearance in the top ten with a funny ad in 2018, followed by another winning funny ad in 2021. Also in 2021, two different comical ads from Rocket Mortgage took both the number one *and* the number two slot in the Ad Meter rankings.[11]

The best big ideas have entrenched themselves in popular culture. A small sampling:

- The Energizer Bunny
- "Got Milk?"
- Budweiser: "Whassssuuup?!?!"
- GE: "We bring good things to life."
- Motel 6: "We'll leave the light on for you."

### 12-5a An International Perspective

Some big ideas translate well across cultures. The Marlboro Man now promotes rugged individualism across the globe. But other big ideas don't travel as smoothly. DeBeers tried running ads in Japan using their proven strategy in the West: fabulously dressed women smiling and kissing their husbands who have just given them glittering diamonds. The

Source: Rocket Mortgage, LLC

**When "pretty sure" isn't sure enough, Rocket Can™**

When it comes to home buying or refinancing, "pretty sure" isn't sure enough. Tracy Morgan shows you why it's better to be certain in our Super Bowl LV ads.

This hilarious Super Bowl ad cut through the clutter to create a strong impression for Rocket Mortgage among its target consumers.

ads failed in Japan because a Japanese woman would be more likely to shed a few tears and feign anger that her husband would spend so much money. The revised DeBeers campaign featured a hardworking husband and wife in their tiny apartment. Receiving a diamond, the wife chides her extravagant husband: "Oh, you stupid!" The campaign was a wild success. Taking a big idea to a foreign market can mean big money and a powerful brand, but careful research should still be your first step.[12]

### 12-6 The Promotional Mix: Communicating the Big Idea

Once you've nailed your message, you need to communicate the big idea to your target market. The traditional communication tools—or **promotional channels**—include advertising, sales promotion, direct marketing, and personal selling. But more recently, a number of new tools have emerged. The combination of communication tools that you choose to promote your product is called your "promotional mix."

### 12-6a Emerging Promotional Tools: The Leading Edge

In the past decade, the promotional landscape has changed dramatically. Consumer expectations and empowerment have skyrocketed. Consumer tolerance for impersonal corporate communication has fallen. And digital technology has surged forward at breakneck speed. As a result, new promotional tools have emerged, and previously minor tools have burst into the mainstream. This section covers several leading-edge promotional tactics, but keep in mind that other tools—such as mobile phone

**promotional channels**
Specific marketing communication vehicles, including traditional tools, such as advertising, sales promotion, direct marketing, and personal selling, and newer tools such as product placement, advergaming, and internet minimovies.

promotion, social media marketing, and widget-based marketing—are growing explosively, too.

**Internet Advertising** Internet advertising has been highly visible for more than a decade. But the industry has moved far beyond simple banner ads and annoying pop-up ads. The highest growth areas include paid search advertising, search engine optimization, and online video advertising.

Paid search advertising includes both sponsored links on Google that relate to the topic you've searched, and targeted Google text ads on a number of different websites—both of which are at the heart of Google's outsized financial success. Industry expert *eMarketer* estimates that paid search advertising, including both Google and other similar services, will top $60 billion by 2023, with much of that spending targeting mobile.[13] Paid search seems to be an especially attractive tactic during tough economic times, since it offers high accountability—marketers can tell exactly how well their limited advertising dollars are working. Analysts also predict that markets will begin to shift their paid search budgets to voice and voice-activated search via digital assistants such as Alexa.[14]

Search engine optimization (SEO) also demonstrated strong growth as the economy weakened. SEO involves taking specific steps to ensure that your website appears high on the list when customers look for your product or service via an internet search engine such as Google or Yahoo!. Typically, the higher a firm appears, the more traffic that site will receive from potential customers. Analysis from *eMarketer* suggest that most marketers worldwide do desktop SEO as a matter of course, and will turn their efforts to mobile SEO over the next few years, since that is where consumers make most of their search queries.[15]

Online video advertising represents another high-growth area. This includes the increasingly popular "pre-roll" ads, the 15- to 30-second spots that viewers often sit through before watching an online video on YouTube, Hulu, or many other sites. Experts predict that video advertising will grow at a spectacular rate, hitting $12.7 billion by 2024, and most of that growth will driven by mobile. And the big spend will be worthwhile, since research suggests that 95% of viewers retain messages they receive through video.[16]

**Social Media** Clearly, social media—including Facebook, Twitter, Blogger, Tumblr, Foursquare, and many others—are not a fad, but rather a paradigm shift in how successful businesses market themselves. According to advertising heavyweight Alex Bogusky, "You

can't buy attention anymore. Having a huge budget doesn't mean anything in social media. . . . The old media paradigm was PAY to play. Now you get back what you authentically put in." And the evidence is building that social media offer a truly impressive return on investment, especially compared to traditional media. A few examples underscore the potential return on investment:

- BlendTec increased its sales five times by running the often humorous "Will It Blend" videos on YouTube, blending everything from an iPhone to a sneaker.

- Dell sold $3,000,000 worth of computers on Twitter.

- When Gillette released a short film titled "The Best a Man Can Be" on social media in 2019 in response to the #MeToo movement, the brand sparked heavy debate about the role of marketing in social issues and garnered more than a million mentions on social media within the first 24 hours of its release.[17]

- Aiming to become the "iPhone of chicken sandwiches," Popeyes introduced its fried chicken sandwich by declaring an all-out #ChickenWar on Twitter with competitor Chick-fil-A. And it worked—Popeyes new chicken sandwich sold out in all 3,000 locations across 49 states, with customers queuing for hours to get their Popeyes fried chicken sandwich—an instant cultural phenomenon.[18]

- Debt relief firm CareOne found that customers gained through social media completed their first payment through the company, at a higher rate of 732%.

- Retailing behemoth Walmart executed a Black Friday campaign on TikTok that encouraged users to upload videos of themselves dancing in the aisles of Walmart for the chance to win a $100 gift card. The campaign received two billion hits within the first week, and campaign content garnered over 700 million impressions.[19]

Looking ahead, smart marketers of both large and small businesses are investing their limited resources in social marketing and reaping an unprecedented return, forging the future of marketing promotion.[20]

**Native Advertising** Across all media, but especially internet advertising and social media, native advertising is a burgeoning category of advertising specifically designed to mimic the user experience into which it is placed in terms of form and function (picture the "suggested posts" in your Facebook newsfeed that you as a user are much

Social media offer marketers myriad opportunities to reach consumers.

more likely to read and click on than a typical banner ad, or similarly, any of the first few options that come up on a typical Google search). Native ads are often fully integrated into a specific delivery platform and are not always identified as advertising. They *do* look like the surrounding editorial content and they typically *are* relevant to it. Analysts predict that the native advertising sector will swell nearly 400% between 2020 and 2025, hitting an absolute value of more than $400 billion. They attribute this rapid growth to demand for more engaging, less intrusive ads. Interestingly, nearly 90% of native advertising is purchased on mobile platforms. Overall, native advertising is still a relatively small part of marketers' spending plans due to concerns about ethics and budget. The FTC demands that native ads include a "clear and prominent" disclosure of their commercial nature, but the interpretation of that requirement is left to the marketer.[21]

### Product Placement

**Product placement**—the paid integration of branded products into movies and TV—exploded into big-screen prominence in 1982, when Reese's Pieces played a highly visible role in Steven Spielberg's blockbuster film *E.T.* Reese's Pieces sales shot up 65% (a major embarrassment for the marketers of M&Ms, who had passed on the opportunity). Over the years, product placement in movies has moved rapidly into the limelight. A few notable examples are:

**product placement** The paid integration of branded products into movies, television, and other media.

- *Avengers*: The blockbuster 2019 film *Avengers: Endgame* blatantly peddled Audi when Tony Stark sped up the comeback scene in his stylish new e-tronGT concept model with his costar watching in awe.

- *James Bond*: This long-standing movie icon hawked so many products in recent movies (e.g., Omega watches, Heineken beer, British Airways, and Macallan whiskey) that it triggered a backlash from annoyed moviegoers and critics.[22]

For many years, Apple has garnered top honors in the movie product placement contest, according to product placement tracking firm Concave. In 2020 alone, Apple products appeared in 30 of the 50 movies tracked by Concave, featured in over an hour of total screen time. Although many Apple products appeared in movies, the iPhone accounted for more than three-quarters of Apple's total product placement value in 2020 and received 67% share of all mobile phone product placement value. Interestingly, film director Rian Johnson recently revealed that Apple product placement contracts will not allow any sort of movie villains to be seen using their product. So, if you're watching a thriller, you know who the bad guys are if they're using PCs or Androids.[23]

In an interesting combination of promotional tactics, product placement and online video have begun to merge. In 2013, Avril Lavigne released her new single, "Rock N Roll," starting with a shot of her saying, "Oh, my new Sony phone is ringing." When she pulled the phone out of a glass of water to answer it, she effectively—and dramatically—demonstrated its new waterproof feature. According to marketing research firm Nielsen, not only do people notice brands in music videos, but also these videos can contribute to a lift of 8 percentage points, on average, in purchase intent and improved perception. The effect on a brand actually reflects how creatively it's placed, rather than the number of on-screen seconds it gets. Nielsen found that it's possible for products that have 5 seconds of exposure to create 35% (or even higher) brand lift, the same as those that are on screen for 35–60 seconds.[24]

Social media influencers are probably the biggest growth area for product placement today. These influencers, often YouTube or Instagram stars, promote products or services during their broadcasts in exchange for a fee. Since influencers tend to have an authentic relationship with their followers, they are more likely to disclose (and even joke about) the promotional relationship in order to maintain that authenticity. Product placement on TV has catapulted into the mainstream in response to the growing prominence of digital video recorders (DVRs) such as TiVo. Research suggests that 54% of U.S. households had at least one DVR in 2019, up from fewer than 10% in 2005. DVRs allow consumers not only

# Going Local!

Not surprisingly, perceptions of "classic American style" can differ dramatically around the world. World travelers have discovered—often to their amusement—that familiar products sometimes show up in very different iterations in other countries. A few examples:

- In France, the mouth-puckering candy Sour Patch Kids is called "Very Bad Kids."

- In Holland, Cool Ranch Doritos are "Cool American" flavor.

- In New Zealand, Rice Krispies are called Rice Bubbles, and in the United Kingdom, Cocoa Krispies are called Coco Pops.

- In Thailand, Lay's carries Salted Egg flavor chips.

- In China, Lay's carries "American Classic" flavor chips (plain).

- In Australia, Axe Body Spray is called Lynx.

- In the Netherlands, Red Solo cups are called "American Cups."

Kudos to each of these international marketers for researching and responding to local preferences to build their businesses in an increasingly complex world.[25]

---

to watch on their own schedule but also to zap ads. However, despite fears that DVRs would destroy television's longtime ad-supported business model—research shows that many consumers actually watch commercials when they playback programming from their DVRs; in fact, among DVR homes, commercial ratings rise 44% after three days.[26]

Product placement works best for marketers—in both movie and television—if the product seamlessly integrates into the show as a player rather than simply a prop. For instance, it was hard to miss Coke in *American Idol*. The judges were seldom without their Coca-Cola–emblazoned cups, and during the early years of the show a "Coke Couch" was used onstage. The price tag for this exposure—including commercial time and online content—was about $35 million. Media buyers often negotiate product placement deals as part of a package that includes regular ads, which reinforce the product that appeared in the program (unless, of course, the ads are zapped).[27]

Whether in TV or movies, product placement offers marketers huge sales potential in a credible environment, which may account for its huge growth rate. But product placement is risky—if your show is a dud, your placement is worthless. And the cost is high and growing, which only increases the financial risk. The benefits of product placement are tough to measure as well, especially for existing brands. But in the end, the only measure that really counts is consumer acceptance, which may disappear if

product placement intrudes too much on the entertainment value of the show.

Paramount network's hit cable drama, *Yellowstone*, offers an example of television product placement outrageously overdone from a viewer perspective. Rugged outdoor clothing brand, Carhartt, shows up on most of the characters, and the camera lingers lovingly on its details. Coors beer can be found everywhere in *Yellowstone's* Montana, even though the state's favorite beer is Rainier. Ram trucks seem to be the vehicle of choice for virtually every character—and despite the dirt and dust of rural ranch life, the Dodge Rams all stay mysteriously shiny and clean—virtually showroom ready! The internet noticed, and it was not impressed.[28]

**Buzz Marketing** A recent study defined "buzz" as the transfer of information from someone who is in the know to someone who isn't. Buzz is essentially word of mouth, which now influences two-thirds of all consumer product purchases. And it makes sense. In a world that's increasingly complex, people turn to people they know and trust to help sort the garbage from the good stuff. Other popular terms for **buzz marketing** are "guerrilla marketing" and "viral marketing."

Not surprisingly, marketers have actively pursued buzz for

> 90% of people trust online recommendations from people they know. Only 14% trust traditional TV advertisements.
>
> —Socialnomics

**buzz marketing** The active stimulation of word of mouth via unconventional, and often relatively low-cost, tactics. Other terms for buzz marketing are "guerrilla marketing" and "viral marketing."

## Scandals Might Cut Hard, but They Don't Seem to Cut Deeply

You may remember a horrifying video from 2017 where a Vietnam-born doctor was roughly dragged off a United Airlines plane—blood running down his face—so that his seat could be used by a United employee. Given the consumer outrage directed at United, one would expect, and perhaps even hope, that the incident would have a financial impact on the company. But according to financial analysts, "Incidents like this rarely pose lasting or significant financial headwinds for major transportation companies." United stock fell a bit the day the video came out, but analysts attributed that to mixed operational data released that same morning.

You may also remember that Starbucks faced a call for a boycott in 2017 after CEO Howard Schultz announced that the coffee firm would hire 10,000 refugees globally. A few months later, Schultz addressed the issue directly at the company's annual stockholder meeting: "I can unequivocally tell you that there is zero, absolutely no evidence whatsoever that there is any dilution in integrity of the Starbucks brand, reputation, or our core business as a result of being compassionate."[29]

---

their brands, especially with the rising cost and diminishing effectiveness of more traditional media channels. Innovative buzz campaigns are typically custom designed to meet their objectives, and they often cost significantly less than more traditional approaches. Here are some notable examples:

> "The best marketing of all is happy clients"
>
> —Susan Stripling, Photographer

- **Flower Drop**: In an effort to spread cheer through the city and gain good publicity, upscale retail district Liverpool ONE left hundreds of bunches of brightly colored flowers for morning commuters, packaged into pairs, encouraging people to keep a bouquet for themselves and pass the other on to a friend, colleague, or even a stranger to share the joy. The timing? Blue Monday—the third Monday in January (widely thought to be the saddest day of the year). The result? A publicity boon! Not only that, the flower drop gave both locals and those further afield a great impression, not only of Liverpool ONE but of the city as a whole.

- **Fitness First:** This Dutch health club ambushed unsuspecting commuters by displaying their weight in neon lights when they took a seat at a bus bench in Rotterdam. Yikes. Chances are good that they both gained some new customers and scarred some other potential customers for life![30]

**sponsorship** A deep association between a marketer and a partner (usually a cultural or sporting event), which involves promotion of the sponsor in exchange for either payment or the provision of goods.

- **ShareYourEars:** Unlike the previous example, some buzz campaigns are intended to spread *positive* energy. The Walt Disney Company, in partnership with the Make-A-Wish foundation, executed a campaign to raise awareness and funds for terminally-ill children. This campaign encouraged fans to share images and selfies featuring Disney's classic mouse ears on Twitter and Instagram using the #ShareYourEars hashtag. Disney pledged a $5 donation to the Make-A-Wish foundation for each participant, with a total cap of $1 million. The campaign was eventually so successful that Disney doubled its original pledge to $2 million.[31]

**Sponsorships** Sponsorships provide a deep association between a marketer and a partner (usually a cultural or sporting event). Even though sponsors can't usually provide more than simply their logo or slogan, consumers tend to view them in a positive light, since they are clearly connected to events that matter to the target audience. The best sponsorship investments, of course, occur when the target audience for the marketer completely overlaps the target audience for the event. The high level of integration between the sponsors and events can provide millions of dollars in valuable media coverage, justifying the hefty price. After the COVID-19 pandemic began, many marketers dramatically cut their sponsorship budgets as sporting and cultural event managers determined how and when to safely ramp up attendance to prepandemic levels.

# TikTok's Time Has Come

TikTok, the most recently arrived member of the social media family, has been catapulting brands to viral fame with the help of short quirky videos and a host of young users.

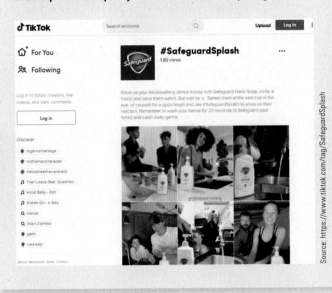

Source: https://www.tiktok.com/tag/SafeguardSplash

Although core TikTok users are from Generation Z, people of many ages have embraced the platform. All types of TikTok challenges are wildly popular, and simplicity is effective (with a 15-second video, simplicity is *crucial*!). Chipotle, the NBA, and Elf Cosmetics all leverage TikTok effectively. A couple of success stories:

■ Leading edge cosmetic company, Too Faced, became aware of the power of TikTok when it traced a surge in the sales of its lip-plumper product to a user-generated before-after video challenge on TikTok. Too Faced then decided to partner with TikTok influencer Kristen Hancher to successfully launch its Damn Girl mascara.

■ Soap may sound boring, but it was all the rage during the COVID-19 pandemic. Safeguard soap used TikTok to bolster its brand. Safeguard encouraged users to show off their handwashing moves in its genius #SafeguardSplash challenge. This lighthearted, health-focused approach became a marketing sensation and garnered 1.8 billion views.[32]

Some savvy marketers found fresh ways to activate sponsorships, such as partnering with esports leagues.[33]

## 12-6b Traditional Promotional Tools: A Marketing Mainstay

Although new tools are gaining prominence, traditional promotional tools—advertising, sales promotion, public relations, and personal selling—remain powerful. In fact, many marketers use the new tools in conjunction with the traditional to create a balanced, far-reaching promotional mix.

**Advertising** The formal definition of **advertising** is paid, nonpersonal communication, designed to influence a target audience with regard to a product, service, organization, or idea. Most major brands use advertising not only to drive sales but also to build their reputation, especially with a broad target market. Television (network broadcasts and cable combined) remains the number-one advertising medium, with magazines and newspapers following. As mass media prices increase and audiences fragment, fringe media are roaring toward the mainstream. But measurement is tough, since alternative media tactics are buried in other categories, including magazines, outdoor, and internet. The overall media spending patterns for 2019 are shown in Exhibit 12.9.

| Exhibit 12.9 | 2019 Measured Global Media Spending by Medium (Billions) | |
| --- | --- | --- |
| **Measured Media** | **2019 Spending** | **Percentage of Total** |
| **TV** | $198.7 | 31.9% |
| **Internet** | $263.5 | 42.3% |
| **Newspapers** | $50.4 | 8.1% |
| **Radio** | $36.8 | 5.9% |
| **Magazines** | $27.4 | 4.4% |
| **Outdoors and Cinema** | $44.8 | 7.2% |
| **Total** | $623 | 100% |

Source: Advertising Expenditure Forecasts, Zenith Media, https://www.zenithmedia.com/wp-content/uploads/2019/03/Adspend-forecasts-March-2019-executive-summary.pdf, accessed May 1, 2021

Note: TV includes broadcast, cable, spot, syndicated, and Spanish-language networks.

Each type of media offers advantages and drawbacks, as summarized in Exhibit 12.10. Your goal as a marketer should be to determine which media

**advertising** Paid, nonpersonal communication, designed to influence a target audience with regard to a product, service, organization, or idea.

## Exhibit 12.10 Major Media Categories

| Major Media | Advantages | Disadvantages |
|---|---|---|
| **Broadcast TV** | *Mass audience:* Top-rated shows garnered roughly 11 million viewers in 2020.<br><br>*High impact:* TV lends itself to vivid, complex messages that use sight, sound, and motion. | *Disappearing viewers:* The 100 million viewers for the top-rated show in 2012 was dwarfed by the 1983 record of 105 million viewers for the finale of M*A*S*H.<br><br>*Jaded viewers:* Consumers who aren't zapping ads with their DVR are prone to simply tuning them out.<br><br>*High cost:* A 30-second ad during Super Bowl 2021 cost a record $5.6 million, and a typical primetime ad cost nearly $500,000, depending on the show. |
| **Cable TV** | *Targeted programming:* Cable helps advertisers target highly specialized markets (Zhong Tian Channel, anyone?).<br><br>*Efficient:* The cost per contact is relatively low, especially for local buys.<br><br>*High impact:* Cable offers the same sight, sound, and motion benefits as broadcast. | *DVRs:* As with broadcast TV, many viewers simply aren't watching ads.<br><br>*Uneven quality:* Many cable ads are worse than mediocre, providing a seedy setting for quality products. |
| **Newspapers** | *Localized:* Advertisers can tailor their messages to meet local needs.<br><br>*Flexible:* Turnaround time for placing and pulling ads is very short.<br><br>*Consumer acceptance:* Readers expect, and even seek, newspaper ads. | *Short life span:* Readers quickly discard their papers.<br><br>*Clutter:* It takes two or three hours to read the average metro paper from cover to cover. Almost no one does it.<br><br>*Quality:* Even top-notch color newsprint leaves a lot to be desired. |
| **Direct Mail** | *Highly targeted:* Direct mail can reach very specific markets.<br><br>*International opportunity:* Less jaded foreign customers respond well to direct mail.<br><br>*Email option:* Opt-in email can lower direct mail costs. | *Wasted resources:* Direct mail uses a staggering amount of paper. And most recipients don't even read it before they toss it.<br><br>*High cost:* Cost per contact can be high, although advertisers can limit the size of the campaign.<br><br>*Spam:* Unsolicited email ads have undermined consumer tolerance for all email ads. |
| **Radio** | *Highly targeted:* In L.A., for example, the dial ranges from Vietnamese talk radio to urban dance music, each station with dramatically different listeners.<br><br>*Low cost:* Advertisers can control the cost by limiting the size of the buy.<br><br>*Very flexible:* Changing the message is quick and easy. | *Low impact:* Radio relies only on listening.<br><br>*Jaded listeners:* Many of us flip stations when the ads begin. |
| **Magazines** | *Highly targeted:* From Cosmopolitan to Computerworld, magazines reach very specialized markets.<br><br>*Quality:* Glossy print sends a high-quality message.<br><br>*Long life:* Magazines tend to stick around homes and offices. | *High cost:* A full-page, four-color ad in People can cost nearly $400,000.<br><br>*Inflexible:* Advertisers must submit artwork months before publication. |
| **Outdoor** | *High visibility:* Billboards and building sides are hard to miss.<br><br>*Repeat exposure:* Popular locations garner daily viewers.<br><br>*Breakthrough ideas:* Innovative approaches include cars and buses "wrapped" in ads, video billboards, and blimps. | *Simplistic messages:* Anything more than an image and a few words will get lost.<br><br>*Visual pollution:* Many consumers object to outdoor ads.<br><br>*Limited targeting:* It's hard to ensure that the right people see your ad. |
| **Internet** | *24/7 global coverage:* Offers a remarkable level of exposure.<br><br>*Highly targeted:* Search engines are especially strong at delivering the right ad to the right person at the right time.<br><br>*Interactive:* Internet ads can empower consumers. | *Intrusive:* The annoyance factor from tough-to-close pop-ups alienates consumers, infuriating many.<br><br>*Limited readership:* Web surfers simply ignore the vast majority of ads. |

options reach your target market efficiently and effectively, within the limits of your budget.

**Sales Promotion Sales promotion** stimulates immediate sales activity through specific short-term programs aimed at either consumers or distributors. Traditionally, sales promotion has been subordinate to other promotional tools, but spending has accelerated in the past decade. Sales promotion falls into two categories: consumer and trade.

**Consumer promotion** is designed to generate immediate sales. Consumer promotion tools include premiums, promotional products, samples, coupons, rebates, and displays.

- **Premiums** are items that consumers receive free of charge—or for a lower than normal cost—in return for making a purchase. Upscale cosmetics companies use the gift-with-purchase approach on a regular basis. Successful premiums create a sense of urgency—"Buy me now!"—while building the value of the brand.

- **Promotional products** are also essentially gifts to consumers of merchandise that advertises a brand name. Or pizza delivery places give away refrigerator magnets with their logo and phone number. Promotional products work best when the merchandise relates to the brand and it's so useful or fun that consumers will opt to keep it around. In 2019, for instance, Twix invented a very-limited edition of a reusable device called the Twix Meltdown that helped fans easily melt a Twix into their coffee to create a delicious new flavor. The company distributed the meltdown via a contest on Instagram.

- **Samples** reduce the risk of purchasing something new by allowing consumers to try a product before committing their cash. From 2009 to 2011, Muscle Milk hired hundreds of personal trainers to conduct promotions and distribute samples. Sampling also drives immediate purchases. At one time or another, most of us have probably bought food we didn't need after tasting a delicious morsel in the supermarket aisle. Costco and Trader Joe's do especially well with this angle on sampling.

- **Coupons** offer immediate price reductions to consumers. Instant coupons require even less effort, since they are attached to the package right there in the store. The goal is to entice consumers to try new products. But the downside is huge. Marketers who depend on coupons encourage consumers to focus on price rather than value, which makes it harder to differentiate brands and build loyalty. In categories with frequent coupons (such as soap and cereal), too many consumers wait for the coupon in order to buy. They end up getting great deals, but marketers pay the price in reduced profits.

- **Rebates**, common in the car industry and the electronics business, entice consumers with cash-back offers. This is a powerful tactic for higher-priced items, since rebates offer an appealing purchase motivator. And rebates provide an incentive for marketers as well: breakage. Most people who buy a product because of the rebate don't actually follow through and do the paperwork to get the money (some estimates suggest that breakage rates are as high as 90% to 95%). This means that marketers can offer hefty discounts without actually coughing up the cash, so it isn't surprising that rebates are a popular promotional tool!

- **Displays** generate purchases in-store. Most experts agree that consumers make a hefty chunk of their purchase decisions as they shop, which means that displays can play a crucial role in sales success. Marketers of consumer products often give prefabricated display materials to grocery stores and mass merchandisers to encourage promotion.

**Trade promotion** is designed to stimulate wholesalers and retailers to push specific products more aggressively. Special deals and allowances are the most common form of trade promotion, especially for consumer products. The idea is that if you give your distributors a temporary price cut, they will pass the savings on to consumers via a short-term "special."

Trade shows are another popular form of trade promotion. Usually organized by industry trade associations, trade shows give exhibitors a chance to display and promote their products to their distributors. They typically attract hundreds of exhibitors and thousands of attendees. Trade shows are especially common in rapidly changing industries such as toys and consumer

**sales promotion** Marketing activities designed to stimulate immediate sales activity through specific short-term programs aimed at either consumers or distributors.

**consumer promotion** Marketing activities designed to generate immediate consumer sales, using tools such as premiums, promotional products, samples, coupons, rebates, and displays.

**trade promotion** Marketing activities designed to stimulate wholesalers and retailers to push specific products more aggressively over the short term.

Companies and stores work together to create a positive message through store displays.

**public relations (PR)** The ongoing effort to create positive relationships with all of a firm's different "publics," including customers, employees, suppliers, the community, the general public, and the government.

**publicity** Unpaid stories in the media that influence perceptions about a company or its products.

response to COVID-19 concerns, with plans to return to Vegas in 2022.

Other forms of trade promotion include contests, sweepstakes, and special events for distributors. A soda company might sponsor a contest to see which grocery store can build the most creative summer display for its soda brands. Or a cable TV programmer might take a group of system managers to Key West to "learn more about their programming" (really an excuse for a great party that makes the system managers more open to the programmer's pitch).

**Public Relations** In the broadest sense, **public relations (or PR)** involves the ongoing effort to create positive relationships with all of a firm's different "publics," including customers, employees, suppliers, the community, the general public, and the government. But in a more focused sense, PR aims to generate positive **publicity**, or unpaid stories in the media that create a favorable impression about a company or its products. The endgame, of course, is to boost demand.

For the most part, the media cover companies or products that they perceive as newsworthy. To get coverage, smart firms continually scan their own companies for potential news—a hot product or a major corporate achievement—and present that news to the media. But finding news on a regular basis can be tough. To fill the gaps, innovative PR people sometimes simply create "news."

electronics. Every year the Consumer Electronics Association hosts "the world's largest annual trade show for consumer electronics!" in Las Vegas. In 2021, the Consumer Electronics Show was presented as an "all-digital experience" in

## Cheaters Never Prosper

In a massive, brand-breaking, environmentally damaging scandal, Volkswagen (VW) admitted in 2015 that the company fit millions of cars with devices to mask the amount of pollutants that they spewed into the environment. In other words, VW knowingly cheated on standardized emissions tests so its cars would appear road-ready when they were anything but. Not surprisingly, this sizable scandal carried a sizable price for VW. Within a month of the cheating coming to light, Volkswagen sales plummeted 225%. What's more, the EPA levied fines against VW of up to $37,500 per car—more than the cost of each car affected—amounting to a total penalty of up to $18 billion. Five years after the scandal broke, in 2020, yet another of the former Volkswagen executives went on trial for his role in the scandal. In 2020, VW stock was still 35% below its prescandal price. And VW dropped from the world's 18th most valuable brand to the 25th. The scandal also damaged its German brand, which had a global reputation for unsurpassed global engineering prowess. It's hard to imagine how the Volkswagen brand will recover, but it may take even longer for overall trust in automobile environmental claims to recover.[34]

PR guru Bill Stoller offers some interesting ideas for how to invent stories that will grab media attention:

- **Launch a Hall of Fame:** Induct some luminaries from your industry, create a simple website, and send your press release to the media. Repeat each year, building your reputation along the way.

- **Make a List:** The best, the worst, the top ten, the bottom ten—the media loves lists, and the possible topics are endless! Just make sure that your list is relevant to your business.

- **Create a Petition:** The Web makes this tactic easy. Harness a growing trend or identify a need in your industry and launch your petition. The more signatures you get, the better your chances for publicity.[35]

The biggest advantage of publicity is that it is usually credible. Think about it: Are you more likely to buy a product featured on the news or a product featured in a 30-second ad? Are you more likely to read a book reviewed by the *New York Times* or featured on a billboard? Publicity is credible because most people believe that information presented by the media is based on legitimate opinions and facts rather than on the drive to make money. And it also helps that publicity is close to free (excluding any fees for a PR firm).

But publicity has a major downside: the marketer has no control over how the media present the company or its products. For example, in an effort to protect customers from a growing tide of solicitors in front of its stores, Target banned Salvation Army bell ringers in front of all its stores in 2004. The press cried foul, focusing not on the service to consumers, but rather on the disrespect to a venerable charity. Target's archrival Walmart, spotting an opportunity for itself at Target's expense, announced that it would match customer donations to the Salvation Army at all of its locations.

**Personal Selling** **Personal selling**—the world's oldest form of promotion—is person-to-person presentation of products to potential buyers. But successful selling typically begins long before the actual presentation and ends long afterward. In today's competitive environment, selling means building relationships on a long-term basis.

Creating and maintaining a quality sales force is expensive. Experts estimate that each business-to-business

> ## "More than 85 percent of customers have a negative view of all salespeople."
>
> —Bill Brooks,
> The Brooks Group

sales call costs nearly $400. So why are so many people employed in sales?[36] Because nothing works better than personal selling for high-ticket items, complex products, and high-volume customers. In some companies, the sales team works directly with customers; in other firms, the sales force works with distributors who buy large volumes of products for resale.

Salespeople fall along a spectrum that ranges from order takers who simply process sales to order seekers who use creative selling to persuade customers. Most department stores hire order takers who stand behind the counter and ring up sales. But Nordstrom hires creative order seekers who actively garner sales by offering extra services such as tasteful accessory recommendations for a clothing shopper.

A separate category of salespeople focuses on *missionary selling*, which means promoting goodwill for a company by providing information and assistance to customers. The pharmaceutical industry hires a small army of missionary salespeople who call on doctors to explain and promote its products, even though the actual sales move through pharmacies.

The sales process typically follows six key stages. Keep in mind that well before the process begins, effective salespeople seek a complete understanding of their products, their industry, and their competition. A high level of knowledge permeates the entire selling process.

1. **Prospect and Qualify:** Prospecting means identifying potential customers. Qualifying means choosing those who are most likely to buy your product. Choosing the right prospects makes salespeople more efficient, since it helps them focus their limited time in areas that will yield results. Companies find prospects in a number of different ways, from trade shows to direct mail, to cold calling. In a retail environment, everyone who walks in the door is a prospect, so salespeople either ask questions or look for visual cues to qualify customers.

2. **Prepare:** Before making a sales call, research is critical, especially in a business-to-business environment. What are your prospect's wants and needs? What are their current product lines? Who are the key competitors? What are the biggest internal and external challenges? How much time is your prospect willing to give you? The answers to these

> **personal selling** The person-to-person presentation of products to potential buyers.

questions will help you customize your presentation for maximum effectiveness.

3. **Present:** You've probably heard that you don't get a second chance to make a good first impression, and that's especially true in sales. With so many options and so little time, buyers often look for reasons to eliminate choices; a weak first impression provides an easy reason to eliminate you. Your presentation itself should match the features of your product to the benefits that your customer seeks (a chance to use all that preparation). Testimonials, letters of praise from satisfied current customers, can push forward the sale by reducing risk for your prospect. A demonstration can be the clincher. When test-driving cars, a demonstration is a no-brainer. But in other categories, technology can help demonstrate products that are too big to move.

4. **Handle Objections:** The key to success here is to view objections as opportunities rather than criticism. Objections give you a chance to learn more about the needs of your prospects and to elaborate on the benefits of your product. You should definitely anticipate as many objections as possible and prepare responses. One response may be connecting prospects with others in your company who can better handle their concerns. This approach offers the additional benefit of deepening ties between your prospect and your company.

5. **Close Sale:** Closing the sale—or asking the prospect to buy—is at the heart of the selling process. The close should flow naturally from the prior steps, but often it doesn't—sealing the deal can be surprisingly tough. One approach may be a trial close: "Would you like the 15-inch screen or the 17-inch screen?" If your prospect is still reluctant to buy, you may want to offer another alternative or a special financial incentive. Even if the prospect doesn't actually make the purchase, remember that they may be willing in the future, so keep the door open.

6. **Follow-up:** The sales process doesn't end when the customer pays. The quality of service and support plays a crucial role in future sales from the same customer, and getting those sales is much easier than finding brand-new prospects. Great relationships with current customers also lead to testimonials and referrals that build momentum for long-term sales success.

Two personal selling trends are gathering momentum in a number of organizations: consultative selling and team selling. *Consultative selling* involves shifting the focus from the products to the customers. On a day-to-day basis, the practice involves a deep understanding of customer needs. Through lots and lots of active listening, consultative salespeople offer practical solutions to customer problems—solutions that use their products. While consultative selling generates powerful customer loyalty, it involves a significant—and expensive—time investment from the sales force.

*Team selling* tends to be especially effective for large, complex accounts. The approach includes a group of specialists from key functional areas of the company—not just sales but also engineering, finance, customer service, and others. The goal is to uncover opportunities and respond to needs that would be beyond the capacity of a single salesperson. In these situations, a key part of the salesperson's role is to connect and coordinate the right network of contacts.

## 12-6c Choosing the Right Promotional Mix: Not Just a Science

There are no fail-safe rules for choosing the right combination of promotional tools. The mix varies dramatically among various industries but also within specific industry segments. The best approach may simply be to consider the following questions in developing the mix that works best for your products.

- **Product Characteristics:** How can you best communicate the features of your product? Is it simple or complex? Is it high priced or inexpensive? A specialized, high-priced item, for example, might require an investment in personal selling, whereas a simple, low-cost product might lend itself to billboard advertising.

- **Product Life Cycle:** Where does your product stand in its life cycle? Are you developing awareness? Are you generating desire? What about driving purchases? And building loyalty? The answers will clearly affect your promotional focus. For instance, if you're developing awareness, you might focus more on advertising, but if you're aiming to drive immediate sales, you'll probably emphasize sales promotion.

- **Target Audience:** How big is your target audience? Where do they live and work? A small target audience—especially if it's geographically dispersed—would lend itself to personal selling or direct mail. A sizable target audience might suggest advertising as an effective way to reach large numbers. Audience expectations should also play a role in your promotional mix decisions.

- **Push versus Pull:** Does your industry emphasize push or pull strategies? A **push strategy** involves motivating distributors to "push" your product to the final consumers, usually through heavy trade promotion and personal selling. A **pull strategy** involves creating demand from your final consumers so that they "pull" your products through the distribution channels. Many successful brands use a combination of push and pull strategies to achieve their goals. P&G, for example, ran a consumer marketing campaign for Crest toothpaste featuring an "Irresistibility IQ" quiz for club-goers, but it also promotes heavily to dentists, hoping that those dentists will recommend Crest to their patients.

- **Competitive Environment:** How are your key competitors handling their promotional strategies? Would it make more sense for you to follow their lead or to forge your own promotional path? If all your competitors offer coupons, for instance, your customers may expect you to offer them as

well. Or if the environment is cluttered, you might want to focus on emerging promotional approaches such as TikTok.

- **Budget:** What are your promotional goals? How much money will it take to achieve them? (Answering this question is tough, but it's clearly important.) How much are your competitors spending in each area of the mix? And how much money do you have for promotion? Even though available budget shouldn't drive the promotional mix, it plays a crucial role, especially for smaller businesses.

> **push strategy** A marketing approach that involves motivating distributors to heavily promote—or "push"—a product to the final consumers, usually through heavy trade promotion and personal selling.
>
> **pull strategy** A marketing approach that involves creating demand from the ultimate consumers so that they "pull" your products through the distribution channels by actively seeking them.

## The Big Picture

The possibilities in both product development and promotional strategy have rapidly multiplied in the past few years alone. But companies can't deliver on the potential without well-oiled teamwork throughout the organization. For instance, the operations group must focus on quality, the accounting group must focus on cost, and the finance group must focus on funding—but from a big-picture standpoint, all groups must work toward the same overarching goal: maximizing customer value. Promotion also requires coordination within the organization and among the outside suppliers who provide promotional services. Finally, the best ideas for both product and promotion can come from any department. Marketers who stay ahead of the curve will only sharpen their competitive edge in the decade to come.

## Careers in Product and Promotion

### Pharmaceutical Sales Representative

Build effective long-term business relationships with healthcare providers. Develop and deliver sales presentations to healthcare professionals. Distribute product information and samples in order to encourage more prescriptions and recommendations. Answer questions from healthcare professionals in a timely manner. Keep current about clinical data, competitive offerings, and healthcare organizations, issues, and events, particularly in area of specialty. Organize group events for healthcare professionals. Create and maintain detailed records of all contacts and meetings.

# 13 | Distribution and Pricing:
## Right Product, Right Person, Right Place, Right Price

## Learning Objectives

After studying this chapter, you will be able to:

**13-1** Differentiate between channels of distribution and physical distribution

**13-2** Describe the various types of wholesale distributors

**13-3** Discuss strategies and trends in store and nonstore retailing

**13-4** Explain the key factors in physical distribution

**13-5** Outline core pricing objectives and strategies

**13-6** Discuss pricing in practice, including the role of consumer perceptions

## 13-1 Distribution: Getting Your Product to Your Customer

Next time you go to the grocery store, look around—the average U.S. supermarket carries more than 40,000 products.[1] Is your favorite brand of soda part of the mix? Why? How did it get from the factory to your neighborhood store? Where else could you find that soda? How far would you be willing to go to get it? These are marketing distribution questions that contribute directly to the **distribution strategy**: getting the right product to the right person at the right place at the right time.

**distribution strategy**
A plan for delivering the right product to the right person at the right place at the right time.

**channel of distribution**
The network of organizations and processes that links producers to consumers.

**physical distribution**
The actual, physical movement of products along the distribution pathway.

**direct channel** A distribution process that links the producer and the customer with no intermediaries.

The distribution strategy has two elements: channels of distribution and physical distribution. A **channel of distribution** is the path that a product takes from the producer to the consumer, while **physical distribution** is the actual movement of products along that path. Some producers choose to sell their products directly to their customers through a **direct channel**. No one stands between the producer and the customer. Examples range from Dell computers to local farmers markets, to factory outlet stores. But most producers use

**channel intermediaries** to help their products move more efficiently and effectively from their factories to their consumers. Hershey's, for example, sells chocolate bars to Sam's Club—a channel intermediary—which may, in turn, sell them to you.

### 13-1a  The Role of Distributors: Adding Value

You might be asking yourself why we need distributors. Wouldn't it be a lot less expensive to buy directly from the producers? The answer, surprisingly, is no. Distributors add value—additional benefits—to products. They charge for adding that value, but typically they charge less than it would cost for consumers or producers to add that value on their own. When distributors add to the cost of a product without providing comparable benefits, the intermediaries don't stay in business. Fifteen years ago, for instance, most people bought plane tickets from travel agents. But when the internet reduced the cost and inconvenience of buying tickets directly from airlines, thousands of travel agencies lost their customers.

One core role of distributors is to reduce the number of transactions—and the associated costs—for goods to flow

> ## "We now live in an age of surreal abundance."
>
> —Jonah Lehrer, Author

from producers to consumers. As you'll see in Exhibit 13.1, even one marketing intermediary in the distribution channel can funnel goods from producers to consumers, with far fewer costly transactions.

Distributors add value, or utility, in a number of different ways: form, time, place, ownership, information, and service. Sometimes the distributors deliver the value (rather than adding it themselves), but often they add new utility that wouldn't otherwise be present. As you read through the various types of utility, keep in mind that they are often interrelated, building on each other to maximize value.

*Form utility* provides customer satisfaction by converting inputs into finished products. Clearly, form utility is primarily a part of manufacturing.

> **channel intermediaries**
> Distribution organizations that facilitate the movement of products from the producer to the consumer.

# The Case of the Missing Toilet Paper

In the first couple of months of the COVID-19 pandemic, toilet paper disappeared from store shelves—suddenly, massively, and decisively. What in the world was going on? Were people using more toilet paper? Seemed unlikely since the virus was respiratory, not digestive. And the data suggested otherwise: the average American usage remained around 141 rolls per year (compared with 134 rolls in Germany and just 49 rolls in China). But more and more of those rolls were being used at home as the economy shut down. So why couldn't suppliers just reroute commercial toilet paper for home usage? One reason was that commercial toilet paper is typically thinner and rougher than plush home toilet paper. Also, institutional rolls tend to be larger, so cleaning staff don't have to refill them as often and people don't steal them. Well, couldn't companies have just made more toilet paper for the home market? Not really. The three biggest U.S. toilet paper companies were already running their toilet paper plants 24 hours a day before the pandemic hit. That's the only way they can make a profit on such a low-margin product. An additional culprit in the shortage was hoarding, which is a common reaction in times of crisis, when consumers feel a

need for control and security. By the end of 2020, the toilet paper market was back in balance, at least until the next time things go sideways![2]

Kevin McGovern/Shutterstock.com

## Exhibit 13.1
## Reducing Transactions through Marketing Intermediaries

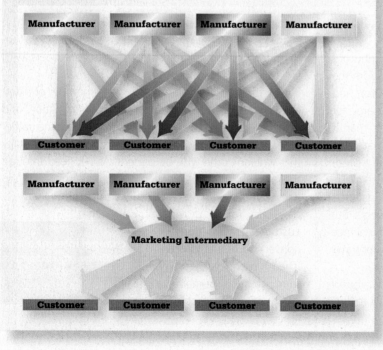

PepsiCo, for instance, provides form utility by transforming water, chemicals, and aluminum into cans of soda. But retailers can add form utility as well. McDonald's, for instance, converts syrup, bubbly water, and paper into cups of soda.

*Time utility* adds value by making products available at a convenient time for consumers. In our 24/7 society, consumers feel entitled to instant gratification, a benefit that distributors can provide more easily than most producers. Consider one-hour dry cleaning, or vending machines at your school. These distributors provide options for filling your needs at a time that works for you.

*Place utility* satisfies customer needs by providing the right products in the right place. Gas stations and fast food, for instance, often cluster conveniently at the bottom of freeway ramps. ATMs—essentially electronic distributors—are readily available in locations that range from grocery stores to college cafeterias.

*Ownership utility* adds value by making it easier for customers to actually possess the

Although Nintendo typically uses cargo ships to move products from Japan to the United States, the video game manufacturer changed its distribution method to airplane—to the tune of $45 per unit—to meet unexpectedly high demand for its new Switch console.

goods and services that they purchase. Providing credit, cashing checks, delivering goods, and installing products are all examples of how distributors make it easier for customers to own their products.

*Information utility* boosts customer satisfaction by providing helpful information. Zappos.com, for instance, hires customer service experts to guide its customers through its website to the perfect pair of shoes. Similarly, most skateboard stores hire skater salespeople who gladly help customers find the best board for them.

*Service utility* adds value by providing fast, friendly, personalized service. Examples include placing a special order for that part you need to customize your computer, or choosing just the right gift in your local clothing boutique. Distributors that provide service utility typically create a loyal base of customers.

**The Members of the Channel: Retailers versus Wholesalers** Many producers sell their goods through multiple channels of distribution. Some channels have many members, while others have only a few. The main distinction among channel members is whether they are retailers or wholesalers. **Retailers** are the distributors that most of us know and use on a daily basis. They sell products directly to final consumers. Examples include 7-Eleven markets, Starbucks, and Urban Outfitters. **Wholesalers**, on the other hand, buy products from the producer and sell them to businesses (or other nonfinal users, such as hospitals, nonprofits, and the government). The businesses that buy from wholesalers can be retailers, other wholesalers, or business users. To complicate this fairly simple concept, some distributors act as both wholesalers and retailers. Costco, for example, sells directly to businesses *and* to consumers. Nike offers another example, selling its sneakers to a wide range of shoe stores, but also selling directly to final users (or resellers) via its website or its NikeTown stores.

## 13-2 Wholesalers: Sorting Out the Options

Some wholesalers are owned by producers, while others are owned by retailers, but the vast majority—accounting for about two-thirds of all the wholesale trade—are **independent wholesaling businesses**. These companies represent a number of different producers, distributing their goods to a range of customers. Independent wholesalers fall into two categories: (1) **merchant wholesalers**, who take legal possession, or title, of the goods they distribute, and (2) **agents/brokers**, who don't take title of the goods.

### 13-2a Merchant Wholesalers

Merchant wholesalers comprise about 80% of all wholesalers. By taking legal title to the goods they distribute, merchant wholesalers reduce the risk of producers' products

**retailers** Distributors that sell products directly to the ultimate users, typically in small quantities, that are stored and merchandized on the premises.

**wholesalers** Distributors that buy products from producers and sell them to other businesses or nonfinal users such as hospitals, nonprofits, and the government.

**independent wholesaling businesses** Independent distributors that buy products from a range of different businesses and sell those products to a range of different customers.

**merchant wholesalers** Independent distributors who take legal possession, or title, of the goods they distribute.

**agents/brokers** Independent distributors who do not take title of the goods they distribute (even though they may take physical possession on a temporary basis before distribution).

being damaged or stolen—or even that they just won't sell. Taking title also allows merchant wholesalers to develop their own marketing strategies, including pricing.

- Full-service merchant wholesalers provide a complete array of services to the retailers or business users who typically purchase their goods. This includes warehousing, shipping, promotional assistance, product repairs, and credit.

- Limited-service merchant wholesalers provide fewer services to their customers. For example, some might warehouse products, but not deliver them. Others might warehouse and deliver, but not provide credit or marketing assistance. The specific categories of limited-service merchant wholesalers include the following:

  - *Drop Shippers:* Drop shippers take legal title of the merchandise, but they never physically process it. They simply organize and facilitate product shipments directly from the producer to their customers. Drop shippers are common in industries with bulky products, such as coal or timber. Amazon, however, successfully pioneered the use of drop shipping in e-commerce, where it has become a standard shipping method for a number of major websites.

  - *Cash and Carry Wholesalers:* These distributors service customers who are too small to merit in-person sales calls from wholesaler reps. Customers must make the trip to the wholesaler themselves and cart their own products back to their stores. Costco and Staples are both examples.

  - *Truck Jobbers:* Typically working with perishable goods such as bread, truck jobbers drive their products to their customers, who are usually smaller grocery stores. Their responsibilities often include checking the stock, suggesting reorder quantities, and removing out-of-date goods.

## 13-2b Agents and Brokers

Agents and brokers connect buyers and sellers and facilitate transactions in exchange for commissions. But they do not take legal ownership of the goods they distribute. Many insurance companies, for instance, distribute via agents, while brokers often handle real estate and seasonal products such as fruits and vegetables.

**multichannel retailing**
Providing multiple distribution channels for consumers to buy a product.

Shopping malls allow customers to visit several store retailers under one roof—but their days may be numbered in the wake of a dramatic retail restructuring.

## 13-3 Retailers: The Consumer Connection

Retailers represent the last stop on the distribution path, since they sell goods and services directly to final consumers. Given their tight consumer connection, retailers must keep in especially close touch with rapidly changing consumer needs and wants.

Smart retailers gain a competitive edge by providing more utility, or added value, than their counterparts. Low prices are only part of the equation. Other elements clearly include customer service, product selection, advertising, and location. The look and feel of the retailer—whether online or on-ground—is another critical element.

Retailing falls into two main categories: store and nonstore. But as we discuss each type, keep in mind that the lines between them are not always clear. In fact, **multichannel retailing**—or encouraging consumers to buy through different venues—is an increasingly common phenomenon. Some marketers have sold their products through multiple channels for many years. For example, on any given day, you could purchase a Coke from a grocery store, a restaurant, or a vending machine. But the emergence of the internet has provided a host of new opportunities for firms that hadn't previously considered a multichannel approach. In fact, an active relationship between on-ground and online outlets may well be *essential* for successful retailers, since Walmart CEO shared that customers who shop at Walmart both in-store and online spend roughly twice as much money.[3]

## Exhibit 13.2 Retail Store Categories

| Store Type | Store Description | Examples |
|---|---|---|
| **Category Killer** | Dominates its category by offering a huge variety of one type of product. | OfficeMax, Best Buy, Staples, PetSmart, Dick's Sporting Goods |
| **Convenience Store** | Sells a small range of everyday and impulse products at easy-to-access locations with long hours and quick checkout. | 7-Eleven, AM/PM markets, Circle K, and a wide range of local stores |
| **Department Store** | Offers a wide variety of merchandise (e.g., clothes, furniture, cosmetics), plus (usually) a high level of service. | Nordstrom, Macy's |
| **Discount Store** | Offers a wide array of merchandise at significantly lower prices and with less service than most department stores. | Target, Walmart, 99 Cents Only Stores |
| **Outlet Store** | Producer-owned store sells directly to the public at a huge discount. May include discontinued, flawed, or overrun items. | Nordstrom Rack, J. Crew Factory, T. J. Maxx |
| **Specialty Store** | Sells a wide selection of merchandise within a narrow category, such as auto parts. | Barnes & Noble, Victoria's Secret, Claire's, AutoZone, LensCrafters, Bath & Body Works |
| **Supermarket** | Offers a wide range of food products, plus limited nonfood items (e.g., toilet paper). | Kroger, Safeway, Albertsons, Whole Foods, Trader Joe's |
| **Supercenter** | Sells a complete selection of food and general merchandise at a steep discount in a single enormous location. | Walmart Supercenters, Super Target |
| **Warehouse Club** | Sells discounted food and general merchandise to club members in a large warehouse format. | Costco, Sam's Club |

## 13-3a Store Retailers

While other retail channels are growing, traditional stores remain the 800-pound gorilla of the retail industry, accounting for roughly 79% of total retail in 2020. Stores range in size from tiny mom-and-pop groceries to multi-acre superstores dwarfed only by their parking lots.[4] Exhibit 13.2 highlights examples of different store types.

In the decade leading up to the global pandemic, the retail industry faced a period of dramatic restructuring that some analysts called a retail apocalypse. Brick-and-mortar stores began closing at a record pace while online shopping continued to grow explosively. But online shopping wasn't the only force at work. Traditional retailers faced an influx of new fast fashion and bargain priced chains, leading to a brutally competitive retail landscape. The social environment changed and mall traffic fell, since consumers no longer viewed most malls as entertainment destinations. By 2019, retail stores that were household names such as Blockbuster, Payless, Borders, Sports Authority, Toys "R" Us, and Gymboree were gone…and then the COVID-19 pandemic hit. The year 2020 saw the shuttering of Pier-1 Imports, Party City, and many Victoria's Secret and Bath & Body Works stores.[5]

> When supermarkets double the size of the shopping carts, consumers buy 40% more.
>
> —CNBC

Both retailers and the producers who distribute through them must carefully consider their distribution strategy. The three key strategic options are intensive, selective, and exclusive.

**Intensive Distribution** Intensive distribution involves placing your products in as many stores as possible (or placing your stores themselves in as many locations as possible). This strategy makes the most sense for low-cost convenience goods that consumers won't travel too far to find. Marketers have chosen this strategy for Snickers candy bars, Dial soap, and *Sports Illustrated* magazine, among thousands of other items.

**Selective Distribution** Selective distribution means placing your products only with preferred retailers (or establishing your stores only in limited locations). This approach tends to work best for medium- and higher-priced products or stores that consumers don't expect to find on every street corner. Marketers have chosen this strategy for Trader Joe's, Jones Soda, and most brands of paintball equipment, for instance.

**Exclusive Distribution** Exclusive distribution means establishing only one retail outlet in a given area. Typically, that one retailer has exclusive distribution rights and provides exceptional service and selection. This strategy tends to work for luxury-goods providers with a customer base that actively seeks their products. Examples include top-end cars such as Tesla and fashion trendsetters such as Raf Simons.

The **wheel of retailing** offers another key strategic consideration. The wheel is a classic theory that suggests retail firms—sometimes even entire retail categories—become more upscale as they go through their life cycles. For instance, it's easiest to enter a business on a shoestring, gaining customers by offering low prices. But eventually businesses trade up their selection, service, and facilities to maintain and build their customer base. Higher prices then follow, creating vulnerability to new, lower-priced competitors. And thus the wheel keeps rolling.

Although the wheel of retailing theory does describe many basic retail patterns, it doesn't account for stores that launch at the high end of the market (e.g., Whole Foods) and those that retain their niche as deep discounters (e.g., Dollar General or Taco Bell). But the wheel theory does underscore the core principle that retailers must meet changing consumer needs in a relentlessly competitive environment.

## 13-3b Nonstore Retailers

While most retail dollars flow through brick-and-mortar stores, a growing number of sales go through other channels, or nonstore retailers. The key players represent e-commerce, m-commerce, direct-response retailing, direct selling, and vending.

**E-Commerce:** Fueled by the COVID-19 pandemic, e-commerce surged an unprecedented +44% in 2020, hitting $861 billion and accounting for roughly 21% of total retail sales, up from 5% a decade earlier. Analysts anticipate that the growth will continue but at a more moderate pace going forward.[6]

> "Leaders win through logistics. Vision, sure. Strategy, yes. But when you go to war, you need to have both toilet paper and bullets at the right place at the right time. In other words, you must win through superior logistics."
>
> —Tom Peters, Business Writer

**M-Commerce:** Mobile commerce—which refers to shopping via a mobile device such as a phone or a tablet—has been rising alongside overall e-commerce. *Business Insider* predicts that m-commerce will represent 44% of overall e-commerce by 2024. Although they have historically suffered poor click-to-purchase conversion rates due to customer frustration at checking out on a small screen, smartphones have become the driving force behind m-commerce growth. One reason is that many retailers have introduced one-click checkout to their sites. This method requires shoppers to enter their payment information once, and then they can use the one-click option to make purchases without having to re-enter it at a later time. Also, tech savvy millennials and Gen Z consumers—who are gaining spending power—are likely to do a wider share of shopping on their smartphones.[7]

Online retailers, like their on-ground counterparts, have learned that great customer service can be a powerful differentiator. Simply "getting eyeballs" isn't enough, since—depending on the industry—fewer than 5% of the people visiting a typical website convert into paying customers. Optimizing one's conversion rate through excellent online customer service can dramatically increase both sales and profitability. One way of improving online service is by using a live chat greeting. You have likely encountered a box that pops up a few minutes after you've been browsing a retail website with a prompt asking if an agent can help you find what you need. Research suggests that visitors invited to chat are 6.3 times more likely to convert into customers than ones who aren't. What's more, 61% of those customers convert within the first chat! For higher-value products and services that entail greater levels of commitment, the conversation might start via chat and then move to a click-to-call channel when the visitor's interest in the product is confirmed. However, in the online environment—as in any business environment—a customer service agent's knowledge, training, and skills make all the difference between a satisfied customer

**wheel of retailing** A classic distribution theory that suggests that retail firms and retail categories become more upscale as they go through their life cycles.

oatawa/Shutterstock.com

and a dissatisfied one. Online retailers who invest in top-tier customer service in chat and beyond position themselves to achieve breakthrough success. For marketers who cannot afford fully trained and highly available customer service agents, chatbots can be a reliable, effective, and affordable alternative. [8]

Despite the advantages, online retailers face two major hurdles. The first is that products must be delivered, and even the fastest delivery services typically take at least a couple of days. But the truly daunting hurdle is the lack of security on the web. As online retailers and software developers create increasingly secure systems, hackers develop more sophisticated tools to crack their new codes.

**Direct Response Retailing** This category includes catalogs, telemarketing, and advertising (such as infomercials) meant to elicit direct consumer sales. According to Direct Marketing Association, consumers who received catalogs spent an average of $850 per year on catalog purchases, and 31% of shoppers have a catalog with them when they make an online purchase.[9]

Telemarketing, both inbound and outbound, also remains a potent distribution channel, despite the popular National Do Not Call list established in 2003.

**Direct Selling** This channel includes all methods of selling directly to customers in their homes or workplaces. Door-to-door sales has enjoyed a resurgence in the wake of the National Do Not Call list, but the real strength of direct selling lies in **multilevel marketing**, or **MLM**. Multilevel marketing involves hiring independent contractors to sell products to their personal network of friends and colleagues and to recruit new salespeople in return for a percentage of their commissions. Mary Kay Cosmetics and The Pampered Chef have both enjoyed enormous success in this arena, along with pioneering companies such as Tupperware.

**Vending** Until about a decade ago, vending machines in the United States sold mostly soft drinks and snacks. But more recently, the selection has expanded (and the machines have gone more upscale) as marketers recognize the value of providing their products as conveniently as possible to their target consumers. The Maine Lobster Game, for example, allows customers to catch their own fresh lobster dinner with a metal claw in restaurants and bars. But other countries are far ahead of the United States in the vending arena. In Japan, for instance, people buy everything from blue jeans to beef from vending machines. In China, a vending machine at a main subway station in Nanjing sells an average of 200 live hairy crabs every day. And vending machines in Puerto Rico dispense free tubes of Colgate along with candy bars, plus an LED message that says "Don't forget

to brush."[10] As technology continues to roll forward, U.S. consumers are likely to see a growing number of vending machines for products as diverse as "fresh-baked" pizza, digital cameras, and specialty coffee drinks.

## 13-4 Physical Distribution: Planes, Trains, and Much, Much More

Determining the best distribution channels for your product is only the first half of your distribution strategy. The second half is the physical distribution strategy: determining how your product will flow through the channel from the producer to the consumer.

The **supply chain** for a product includes not only its distribution channels but also the string of suppliers who deliver products to the producers. (Refer to Exhibit 13.3.) Planning and coordinating the movement of products along the supply chain—from the raw materials to the final consumers—is called **supply chain management** or **SCM**. **Logistics** is a subset of SCM that focuses more on tactics (the actual movement of products) than on strategy.

At one time, relationships among the members of the supply chain were contentious. But these days, companies that foster collaboration, rather than competition, have typically experienced more success. Vendor-managed inventory is an emerging strategy—pioneered by Walmart—that allows suppliers to determine buyer needs and automatically ship product. This strategy saves time and money but also requires an extraordinary level of trust and information-sharing among members of the supply chain.

In our turbocharged 24/7 society, supply chain management has become increasingly complex. Gap, for instance, contracts with more than 3,000 factories in more than 50 different countries, and distributes its products to about 3,000 stores in eight different countries. The coordination

**multilevel marketing (MLM)** Involves hiring independent contractors to sell products to their personal network of friends and colleagues and to recruit new salespeople in return for a percentage of their commissions.

**supply chain** All organizations, processes, and activities involved in the flow of goods from the raw materials to the final consumer.

**supply chain management (SCM)** Planning and coordinating the movement of products along the supply chain, from the raw materials to the final consumers.

**logistics** A subset of supply chain management that focuses largely on the tactics involved in moving products along the supply chain.

## Exhibit 13.3
## Elements of the Supply Chain

**The supply chain highlights the links among the various organizations in the production and distribution process.**

Raw Materials

Logistics (transportation, coordination, etc.)

Warehouse/Storage

Production

Warehouse/Storage

Logistics (transportation, coordination, etc.)

Distributors—Marketing and Sales

- **Order Processing:** How should we manage incoming and outgoing orders? What would be most efficient for our customers and suppliers?

- **Customer Service:** How can we serve our customers most effectively? How can we reduce waiting times and facilitate interactions?

- **Transportation:** How can we move products most efficiently through the supply chain? What are the key tradeoffs?

- **Security:** How can we keep products safe from vandals, theft, and accidents every step of the way?

And fragile or perishable products require even more considerations.

### 13-4a Transportation Decisions

Moving products through the supply chain is so important that it deserves its own section. The various options—trains, planes, and railroads, for instance—are called **modes of transportation**. To make smart decisions, marketers must consider what each mode offers in terms of cost, speed, dependability, flexibility, availability, and frequency of shipments. The right choice depends on the needs of the business and on the product itself. Refer to Exhibit 13.4 for a description of the transportation options.

Depending on factors such as warehousing, docking facilities, and accessibility, many distributors use several different modes of transportation. If you owned a clothing boutique in Las Vegas, for example, chances are that much of your merchandise would travel by boat from China to Long Beach, California, and then by truck from Long Beach to Las Vegas.

requirements are mind-boggling. Key management decisions include the following considerations:

- **Warehousing:** How many warehouses do we need? Where should we locate our warehouses?

- **Materials Handling:** How should we move products within our facilities? How can we best balance efficiency with effectiveness?

- **Inventory Control:** How much inventory should we keep on hand? How should we store and distribute it? What about costs such as taxes and insurance?

### Exhibit 13.4 Modes of Transportation

| Mode | Percentage of U.S. Volume Based on 2007 Ton-Miles | Cost | Speed | On-Time Dependability | Flexibility in Handling | Frequency of Shipments | Availability |
|---|---|---|---|---|---|---|---|
| Rail | 39.5% | Medium | Slow | Medium | Medium | Low | Extensive |
| Truck | 28.6% | High | Fast | High | Medium | High | Most extensive |
| Ship | 12.0% | Lowest | Slowest | Lowest | Highest | Lowest | Limited |
| Plane | 0.3% | Highest | Fastest | Medium | Low | Medium | Medium |
| Pipeline | 19.6% | Low | Slow | Highest | Lowest | Highest | Most limited |

Source: Table 1-46b: U.S. Ton-Miles of Freight (BTS Special Tabulation), 2007 data, Bureau of Transportation website, https://www.bts.gov/publications/national_transportation_statistics/html/table_01_46b.html, accessed September 5, 2017.

### 13-4b Proactive Supply Chain Management

A growing number of marketers have turned to supply chain management to build a competitive edge through greater efficiency. But given the complexity of the field, many firms choose to outsource this challenge to experts rather than handling it internally. Companies that specialize in helping other companies manage the supply chain—such as UPS—have done particularly well in today's market.

## 13-5 Pricing Objectives and Strategies: A High-Stakes Game

Pricing strategy clearly has a significant impact on the success of any organization. Price plays a key role in determining demand for your products, which directly influences a company's profitability. Most people, after all, have a limited amount of money and a practically infinite number of ways they could spend it. Price affects their spending choices at a more fundamental level than most other variables.

But ironically, price is perhaps the toughest variable for marketers to control. Both legal constraints and marketing intermediaries (distributors) play roles in determining the final price of most products. Marketers must also consider costs, competitors, investors, taxes, and product strategies.

In today's frenetic environment, stable pricing is no longer the norm. Smart marketers continually evaluate and refine their pricing strategies to ensure that they meet their goals. Even the goals themselves may shift in response to the changing market. Common objectives and strategies include building profitability, boosting volume, matching the competition, and creating prestige.

Many firms express long-term profitability goals in terms of either return on investment or return on sales.

### 13-5a Building Profitability

Since long-term profitability is a fundamental goal of most businesses, profitability targets are often the starting point for pricing strategies. Many firms express these goals in terms of either return on investment (ROI) or return on sales (ROS). Keep in mind that profitability is the positive difference between revenue (or total sales) and costs. Firms can boost profits by increasing prices or decreasing costs, since either strategy will lead to a greater spread between the two. Doing both is tricky, but companies that succeed—such as Apple—typically dominate their markets.

### 13-5b Boosting Volume

Companies usually express volume goals in terms of market share—the percentage of a market controlled by a company or a product. Amazon.com, for example, launched with volume objectives. Its goal was to capture as many "eyeballs" as possible, in hopes of later achieving profitability through programs that depend on volume, such as advertising on its site. A volume objective usually leads to one of the following strategies.

**Penetration Pricing** Penetration pricing, a strategy for pricing new products, aims to capture as much of the market as possible through rock-bottom prices. Each individual sale typically yields a tiny profit; the real money comes from the sheer volume of sales. One key benefit of this strategy is that it tends to discourage competitors, who may be scared off by the slim margins. But penetration pricing makes sense only in categories that don't have a significant group of consumers who would be willing to pay a premium (otherwise, the marketer would be leaving money on the table). For obvious reasons, companies that use penetration pricing are usually focused on controlling costs. JetBlue is a key example. Its prices are often unbeatable, but it strictly controls costs by using a single kind of jet, optimizing turnaround times at the gate, and using many non-major airports.

**Everyday-Low Pricing** Also known as "sustained discount pricing," **everyday-low pricing (EDLP)** aims to achieve long-term profitability through volume.

---

**modes of transportation** The various transportation options—such as planes, trains, and railroads—for moving products through the supply chain.

**penetration pricing** A new product pricing strategy that aims to capture as much of the market as possible through rock-bottom prices.

**everyday-low pricing (EDLP)** Long-term discount pricing, designed to achieve profitability through high sales volume.

# So What's the Trick to Getting College Students to Eat Healthier?

The answer may be in the pricing. A recent study at Belgium University found that increasing the price of meals sold with fries significantly reduced the sale of fries, while offering discounts for choosing fruit for dessert increased fruit sales.

Before the experiment, more than half of students (53%) chose meals with fries. During the experiment, the price of meals with fries was raised 10% one week and 20% the next if students chose fries instead of rice or mashed potatoes with lunch meals. About 42% of students chose fries when the cost was 10% higher, and 31% chose them when the cost was 20% higher. A second experiment offered meals with fruit instead of pastries for dessert. Before the experiment, 37% of students chose meals with fruit. During the experiment, the price of meals with fruit was discounted 10% one week and 20% the next. About 62% of students chose fruit when it was discounted 10%, and about 79% chose fruit when the discount grew to 20%.

Interestingly, reducing the price of a healthy food had a greater impact on students' behavior than increasing the price of an unhealthy food. No gender differences were found. On campuses where students do more of their eating from vending machines, the lessons from this study could be applied quickly and effectively.[11]

Walmart became the king of EDLP with their classic slogan, "Always low prices. *Always!*" But Costco uses the same strategy to attract a more-upscale audience. Costco customers are typically seeking everyday discounts because they want to, not because they need to. The product mix—eclectic and upscale—reflects the customer base. (Costco sells discounted fine wine, low-priced rotisserie chickens, fresh king crab legs, and high-end electronics.)

**High/Low Pricing** The **high/low pricing** strategy tries to increase traffic in retail stores by special sales on a limited number of products, and higher everyday prices on others. Often used—and overused—in grocery stores, drug stores, and department stores, this strategy can alienate customers who feel cheated when a product they bought for full price goes on sale soon afterward. High/low pricing can also train consumers to buy only when products are on sale.

**Loss-Leader Pricing** Closely related to high/low

> "If automobiles had followed the same development cycle as the computer, a Rolls-Royce would today cost $100, get a million miles per gallon, and explode once a year, killing everyone inside."
>
> —Robert Cringely, Technology Journalist

pricing, **loss-leader pricing** means pricing a handful of items—or loss leaders—temporarily below cost to drive traffic. The retailer loses money on the loss leaders but aims to make up the difference (and then some) on other purchases. To encourage other purchases, retailers typically place loss leaders at the back of the store, forcing customers to navigate past a tempting array of more profitable items. The loss-leader strategy has been used effectively by producers, as well. Gillette, for instance, gives away some shavers practically for free but reaps handsome

**high/low pricing** A pricing strategy designed to drive traffic to retail stores by special sales on a limited number of products, and higher everyday prices on others.

**loss-leader pricing** Closely related to high/low pricing, loss-leader pricing means pricing a handful of items—or loss leaders—temporarily below cost to drive traffic.

# Is Price Gouging Illegal? Is Price Gouging Immoral? Can Price Gouging Be a Good Thing?

Nobody loves the business that doubles the price of bottled water right after a hurricane or the individual who overcharges for generators in the wake of an earthquake. To discourage both businesses and individuals from raising prices after an emergency, many states have passed anti-price gouging laws. These laws are quite popular among consumers, but according to economists, they may exacerbate the supply problems that cause inconvenience—and even suffering—after natural disasters. For example, anti–price gouging laws tend to encourage hoarding. People at the front of the line may buy more cases of water than they actually need, leaving nothing for those at the back of the line. Anti–price gouging laws also remove the incentive for both businesses and individuals to replenish supply. Why go to the extra effort or incur the extra risks of bringing in extra inventory if you can't charge more to get extra profits? Nevertheless, most states *do* have anti–price gouging laws due to their overwhelming popularity with voters. If the price-gouging retailer finds himself at the wrong end of a natural disaster, he might end up being thankful for such laws as well.[12]

profits as consumers buy replacement blades. Similarly, Microsoft has sold its Xbox systems at a loss to increase potential profits from high-margin video games. But the loss-leader strategy can't be used everywhere, since a number of states have made loss leaders illegal for anti-competitive reasons.[13]

### 13-5c Matching the Competition

The key goal is to set prices based on what everyone else is doing. Usually, the idea is to wipe out price as a point of comparison, forcing customers to choose their product based on other factors. Examples include Coke and Pepsi, Honda and Toyota, Chevron and Mobil, and Delta and United. But sometimes one or two competitors emerge that drive pricing for entire industries. Marlboro, for instance, leads the pack in terms of cigarette pricing, with other brands falling into place behind.

### 13-5d Creating Prestige

The core goal is to use price to send consumers a message about the high quality and exclusivity of a product—the higher the price, the better the product. Of course, this strategy works only if the product actually delivers top quality; otherwise, nobody would buy more than once (and those who do so would clearly spread the word). Rolex watches, Mont Blanc pens, and Bentley cars all use prestige pricing to reinforce their image.

**Skimming Pricing** This new product pricing strategy is a subset of prestige pricing. **Skimming pricing** involves offering new products at a premium price. The idea is to entice price-insensitive consumers—music fanatics, for example—to buy high when a product first enters the market. Once these customers have made their purchases, marketers will often introduce lower-priced versions of the same product to capture the bottom of the market. Apple used this strategy with its iPod, introducing its premium version for a hefty price tag. Once it had secured the big spenders, Apple introduced the lower-priced iPod Nanos and Shuffles with a powerful market response. But keep in mind that skimming works only when a product is tough to copy in terms of design, brand image, technology, or some other attribute. Otherwise, the fat margins will attract a host of competitors.

## 13-6 Pricing in Practice: A Real-World Approach

At this point, you may be wondering about economic theory. How do concepts such as supply and demand and price elasticity affect pricing decisions?

Even though most marketers are familiar with economics, they often don't have the information they need to apply the theories to their specific pricing strategies. Collecting data for supply and demand curves is expensive and time consuming, which may be unrealistic for rapidly changing markets. From a real-world standpoint, most marketers consider market-based factors—especially customer expectations and competitive prices—but they rely on cost-based pricing. The key question is: What price levels will allow me to cover my costs and achieve my objectives?

> **skimming pricing** A new product pricing strategy that aims to maximize profitability by offering new products at a premium price.

# Does Your Privacy Matter to You as Much as Cheap Prices?

Years ago, anyone willing to scour coupons, search for deals, and shop often could make use of the lowest prices at the grocery store. But those days are disappearing as quickly as your internet privacy. A number of large grocers are now implementing personalized pricing programs that create unique offers and prices tailored to shoppers' individual behaviors and needs, ultimately bumping up the grocers' profit margins. Soon, such personalized pricing programs might well displace standardized price tags. For example, a shopper who has a history of purchasing alcohol and barbecue sauces may receive a coupon designed to encourage them to purchase a brand-new high margin Kentucky bourbon sauce. Some customized coupons are offered on-the-spot via mobile apps that are loaded with customer data, while others are sent in the mail. According to shopper Ainy Kazmi, "It's a little bit creepy, but I figure they're checking anything anyway—I might as well get a good deal out of it."[14]

Prostock-studio/Shutterstock.com

## 13-6a Breakeven Analysis

**Breakeven analysis** is a relatively simple process that determines the number of units a firm must sell to cover all costs. Sales above the breakeven point will generate a profit; sales below the breakeven point will lead to a loss. The actual equation looks like this:

$$\text{Breakeven Point (BP)} = \frac{\text{Total fixed costs (FC)}}{\text{Price/unit (p)} - \text{Variable costs/unit (VC)}}$$

If you were selling customized nachos, for example, your fixed costs might be $400,000 per year. Fixed costs stay the same regardless of how many servings of nachos you sell. Specific fixed costs might include the mortgage, equipment payments, advertising, insurance, and taxes. Suppose your variable cost per serving—the cost of the ingredients and the cost of wages for the cook—were $5 per serving. If your customers would pay $12 per serving, you could use the breakeven equation to determine how many servings of nachos you'd need to sell in a year so that your total sales were equal to your total expenses. Remember: a company that is breaking even is not making a profit.

> **breakeven analysis**
> The process of determining the number of units a firm must sell to cover all costs.

Here's how the breakeven analysis would work for our nacho business:

$$BP = \frac{FC}{P - VC} = \frac{\$400{,}000}{\$12 - \$5} = \frac{\$400{,}000}{\$7} = 57{,}143 \text{ Servings Nachos}$$

Over a one-year horizon, 57,143 servings of customized nachos would translate to about 157 servings per day. Is that reasonable? Could you do better? If so, start thinking of some names for your nachos! If not, you have several choices, each with its own set of considerations:

- **Raise Prices:** How much do other snack-like meals in your neighborhood cost? Are your nachos better in some way? Would potential customers be willing to pay more?

- **Decrease Variable Costs:** Could you use less expensive ingredients? Is it possible to hire less expensive help? How would these changes affect quality and sales?

- **Decrease Fixed Costs:** Should you choose a different location? Can you lease cheaper equipment? Would it make sense to advertise less often? How would these changes affect your business?

Clearly, there isn't one best strategy, but a breakeven analysis helps marketers get a sense of where they stand and the hurdles they need to clear before actually introducing a product.

# Pricing Sleight of Hand

As a consumer, does it ever seem to you as though marketers use magic to separate you from your money? As a marketer, it may be helpful to know some pricing tricks that marketers use to maximize revenue. Here are some examples, used especially well by Apple:

■ **Establish a high reference point:** Research suggests that most consumers need a reference point to determine whether a given price is reasonable. For instance, the iPhone cost $599 when it first launched, which helps make an iPhone today at $199 seem like a bargain.

■ **Obscure the reference point:** Apple products look so unique that it's impossible to compare them accurately to anything else on the market. Similarly, candy and other treats in movie theaters are tough to accurately price-compare to goodies at other outlets, because they tend to come in unusual, large boxes that are shaped nothing like what you see at other stores.

■ **Hide price components in bundles:** Not just Apple, but most electronic devices, count on downstream data fees over the course of a contract to supplement the cost of the device itself. For instance, computer printers are relatively cheap, but manufacturers rely on anticipated sales from proprietary ink cartridges. Ink revenue adds up quickly—especially over the full life of a printer.

Each of these strategies is legally sound, but they may be a bit ethically shaky. Being aware is a crucial part of being a smart consumer. And making pricing information transparent is part of being an ethical marketer.[15]

Ljupco Smokovski/Shutterstock.com

## 13-6b Fixed Margin Pricing

Many firms determine upfront how much money they need to make for each item they sell. The **profit margin**—which is the gap between the cost and the price on a per-product basis—can be expressed as a dollar amount but more often is expressed as a percent. There are two key ways to determine margins.

1. **Cost-Based Pricing:** The most popular method of establishing a fixed margin starts with determining the actual cost of each product. The process is more complex than it may initially seem, since fixed costs must be allocated on a per-product basis, and some variable costs fluctuate dramatically on a daily or weekly basis. But once the per-product cost is set, the next step is to layer the margin on the cost to determine the price. Costco, for instance, has a strict policy that no branded item can be marked up by more than 14%, and no private-label item by more than 15%. Supermarkets, on the other hand, often markup merchandise by 25%, and department stores by 50% or more. Margins in other industries can be much thinner.[16]

2. **Demand-Based Pricing:** This approach begins by determining what price consumers would be willing to pay. With that as a starting point, marketers subtract their desired margin,

which yields their target costs. This method is more market-focused than cost-based pricing, but it's also more risky, since profits depend on achieving those target costs. A number of Japanese companies, such as Sony, have been very successful with this approach, achieving extraordinarily efficient production.

## 13-6c Consumer Pricing Perceptions: The Strategic Wild Card

You just don't know if you've found the right price until you figure out how consumers perceive it. And those perceptions can sometimes defy the straightforward logic of dollars and cents. Two key considerations are price–quality relationships and odd pricing.

The link between price and perceived quality can be powerful. Picture yourself walking into a local sporting goods store, looking for a new snowboard. They have several models of your favorite brand, most priced at around $450. But then you notice another option—same brand, same

> There are two kinds of fools in any market. One doesn't charge enough. The other charges too much.
>
> —Russian Proverb

**profit margin** The gap between the cost and the price of an item on a per-product basis.

style—marked down to $79. Would you buy it? If you were like most consumers, you'd probably assume that something was wrong with a board that cheap. Would you be right? It's hard to know. Sometimes the relationship between price and quality is clear and direct, but that is not always the case. Regardless, consumers will use price as an indicator of quality unless they have additional information to guide their decision. Savvy marketers factor this tendency into their pricing strategies.

Marketers also must weigh the pros and cons of **odd pricing**, or ending prices in numbers below even dollars and cents. A micro stereo system at Target, for instance, might cost $99.99 instead of an even $100. Gasoline uses odd pricing to 99/100ths of a cent. But wouldn't round numbers be easier? Does that extra penny really make a difference? While the research is inconclusive, many marketers believe that jumping up to the "next" round number sends a message that prices have hit a whole new level. In other words, they believe that the *perceived* gap between $99.99 and $100.00 is much greater than the *actual* gap of 0.0001%. And it certainly makes sense from an intuitive standpoint.

Odd prices have also come to signal a bargain, which is often—but not always—a benefit for the marketer. For instance, a big-screen TV for $999.99 might seem like a great deal, while knee surgery for $4,999.99 sounds kind of scary—you'd probably rather that your doctor

Olivier Le Moal/Shutterstock.com

Many marketers use odd pricing because the perceived gap between $1.00 and $0.99 is much greater than the actual gap between these two prices.

> **odd pricing** The practice of ending prices in numbers below even dollars and cents in order to create a perception of greater value.

charge $5,000. Likewise, a fast-food joint might charge $3.99 for its value meal, while fine restaurants almost always end their prices in zeros. Marketers can determine whether odd pricing would work for them by evaluating the strategy in light of the messages it sends to the target market.

## The Big Picture

Distribution and pricing are two fundamental elements of the marketing mix. In today's frenzied global economy, marketers are seeking a competitive edge through distribution management. Creating a profitable presence in multiple retail venues requires constant focus throughout the organization. And managing the supply chain—how products move along the path from raw materials to the final consumer—plays a crucial role in controlling costs and providing great customer service. Integrating effective technology during the entire process can separate the winners from the losers.

Pricing objectives and strategies are also pivotal since they directly impact both profitability and product image. As the market changes, successful companies continually reevaluate and modify their approach, working hand in hand with their accountants.

Looking ahead, a growing number of companies will probably move toward collaboration, rather than competition, as they manage their supply chains. And pricing will likely become even more dynamic in response to the changing market.

## Warehouse Manager

Oversee the safe receipt, storage, retrieval, and timely transmission of goods. Oversee computerized inventory management system. Comply with federal, state, and local laws regarding warehousing, material handling, and shipping. Plan the arrangement of goods within the warehouse, and handle requirements for specialized stock (e.g., chilled goods or fragile products). Keep current with all relevant legislation and industry trends. Ensure security in all aspects of warehouse operation. Maintain physical condition of warehouse. Create and track warehousing budget to meet financial objectives. Hire, manage, and motivate warehouse staff.

# 14 Management, Motivation, and Leadership:
## Bringing Business to Life

### Learning Objectives

After studying this chapter, you will be able to:

**14-1** Discuss the importance of management to organizational success

**14-2** Explain key theories and current practices of motivation

**14-3** Explain business planning, especially strategic planning

**14-4** Discuss the organizing function of management

**14-5** Explain the role of managerial leadership and the key leadership styles

**14-6** Describe the management control process

## 14-1 Bringing Resources to Life

To grow and thrive, every business needs resources—money, technology, materials—and an economic system that helps enterprise flourish. But those resources, or factors of production, are nothing without **management** to bring them to life. Managers provide vision and direction for their organizations, they decide how to use resources to achieve goals, and they inspire others—both inside and outside their companies—to follow their lead. By formal definition, managers achieve the goals of an organization through planning, organizing, leading, and controlling organizational resources, including people, money, time, and technology.

**management** Achieving the goals of an organization through planning, organizing, leading, and controlling organizational resources including people, money, and time.

**planning** Determining organizational goals and action plans for how to achieve those goals.

**organizing** Determining a structure for both individual jobs and the overall organization.

**leading** Directing and motivating people to achieve organizational goals.

**controlling** Monitoring performance and making adjustments as needed.

In simple terms, **planning** means figuring out where to go and how to get there. **Organizing** means determining a structure for both individual jobs and the overall organization. **Leading** means directing and motivating people to achieve organizational goals. And **controlling** means monitoring performance and

making adjustments as needed. In today's chaotic, hyper-competitive business environment, managers face daunting challenges. But for the right people, management positions can provide an exhilarating—though sometimes exhausting—career.

As the business pace accelerates and the environment continues to morph—especially in the wake of economic turmoil—the role of management is also radically transforming. The successful manager has changed from boss to coach, from disciplinarian to motivator, from dictator to team builder. But the bottom-line goal remains the same: to create value for the organization.

In late 2017, management became more complex, with the reemergence of the #MeToo movement, which shined bright light on sexual harassment and assault in the workplace. Hundreds of women in prominent positions came forward publicly with their stories of harassment. Public opinion, the press, their employers, and in many cases, even the law, rallied behind them with strong support—punishing the perpetrators, and establishing new safeguards to prevent future abuse. In 2020, equity, diversity, and inclusion gained increased prominence in American culture. And many companies made far-reaching efforts to weave these values into their business culture and practices. Managers in today's workplace

> "Just because you are CEO, don't think you have landed. You must continually increase your learning, the way you think, and the way you approach the organization."
>
> —Indra Nooyi, Former Chair and CEO, Pepsico

must be hyperaware of how they treat all employees—always keeping absolute fairness and transparency at the forefront of their actions and perspective. Please refer to Chapter 15 for more detail on this issue.

### 14-1a Management Hierarchy: Levels of Responsibility

Most medium-sized and large companies have three basic levels of management: **top management**, **middle management**,

> **top management**
> Managers who set the overall direction of the firm, articulating a vision, establishing priorities, and allocating time, money, and other resources.
>
> **middle management**
> Managers who supervise lower-level managers and report to a higher-level manager.

# Starting Early and Staying Strong

Some people seem compelled to succeed no matter what ... and those are the folks who tend to drive the economy. A quick survey of some well-known super-achievers suggests that a high level of motivation was part of their personalities from the very beginning:

- *Mark Zuckerberg, Facebook founder*: Before he went to college, Mark was recruited to work for Microsoft and AOL. As a toddler, he found a screwdriver and dismantled his crib when he thought he was too old for a "baby bed."

- *Palmer Luckey, 23-year-old founder of Oculus Rift*: Luckey experimented with building coil guns in his parents' garage when he was a teenager. "Looking back," he says, "it's honestly a miracle I am not dead."

- *Oprah Winfrey, media mogul*: Winfrey began working at the corner grocery store next to her father's barber shop, and she "hated every minute of it." Winfrey wasn't allowed to talk to the customers, which she understandably found "very, very, very hard."

- *Jeff Bezos, Amazon founder*: As a teenager, Jeff built amateur robots and an assortment of other electronic inventions.

- *Warren Buffett, founder of Berkshire Hathaway*: One of the richest people in the world, Warren began delivering papers on his bicycle at the age of 13. By the time he finished high school in 1947, Buffett had earned $5,000, which is the equivalent of $54,000 today.

- *Richard Branson, Virgin Group CEO*: Branson attributes at least some of his motivation to his mom: When he was six, she would shove him out of the car and tell him to find his own way home.

- *Chris Rock, comedian*: Chris' first job was at Red Lobster. "The thing about Red Lobster is that if you work there, you can't afford to eat there," he once told Jay Leno. "You're making minimum wage. A shrimp costs minimum wage."

But keep in mind that some high achievers don't gear up until well after childhood. True motivation requires clear goals, which people can develop at any point in their lives. When meaningful goals merge with energy and determination, anything becomes possible.[1]

son Photo/Shutterstock.com

---

and **first-line (or supervisory) management**. The levels typically fall into a pyramid of sorts, with a small number of top managers and a larger number of supervisory managers. Responsibilities shift as managers move up the hierarchy, and the skills that they use must shift accordingly. Here are the differences between three key levels:

- **Top management** sets the overall direction of the firm. Top managers must articulate a vision, establish priorities, and allocate time, money, and other resources. Typical titles include chief executive officer (CEO), president, and vice president.

- **Middle management** manages the managers. (Say that three times!) Middle managers must communicate up and down the pyramid, and their primary contribution often involves coordinating teams and special projects with their peers from other departments. Typical titles include director, division head, and branch manager.

> **first-line (supervisory) management** Managers who directly supervise nonmanagement employees.

- **First-line (supervisory) management** manages the people who do the work. First-line managers must train, motivate, and evaluate nonmanagement employees, so they are heavily involved in day-to-day production issues. Typical titles include supervisor, foreman, and section leader.

- **Smaller companies** usually don't have a hierarchy of management. Often the owner must act as the top-, middle-, and first-line manager, all rolled into one. This clearly requires enormous flexibility and well-developed management skills.

## 14-1b Management Skills: Having What It Takes to Get the Job Done

Given the turbulence of today's business world, managers must draw on a staggering range of skills to do their jobs efficiently and effectively. Most of these abilities cluster into three broad categories: technical skills, human skills, and conceptual skills.

### Bad Decisions, Big Impacts

Every day, managers around the globe make high-stakes decisions, from expanding overseas, to introducing new products, to closing factories. The great decisions have become the stuff of legends, shaping the business world as we know it today. Bad choices also abound. Consider these business decisions that made history for their silliness:

- Faced with the opportunity to buy rights to the telephone in 1876, Western Union, the telegraph behemoth, rejected the newfangled device: "This 'telephone' has too many shortcomings to be seriously considered as a means of communication. The device is inherently of no value to us."

- In 1899, two young attorneys approached Asa Candler—owner of the briskly selling new fountain drink Coca-Cola—with an innovative proposal to bottle the beverage. Chandler sold them exclusive rights to bottle Coke across most of the United States for the grand sum of $1. Oops.

- In the 1970s, Milwaukee-based Schlitz beer was number two in the market, giving Budweiser a run for their money. Then the owner decided to compete with cheaper ingredients that gave the beer an unfortunate resemblance to snot. By the time Schlitz finally recalled the product, it had plummeted out of the top three in the beer market and was forced to close its flagship Milwaukee plant. AaaChooo!

- In 1977, the executives at 20th Century Fox exhibited overconfidence in their deal-making abilities, and far too little confidence in director George Lucas's filmmaking and business savvy. In exchange for a paltry $20,000 payment, they signed over to Lucas all product merchandising rights for the current and all future Star Wars films. The combined revenue from merchandising is estimated to have exceeded $3 billion, and continues to grow annually, making it the most lucrative deal ever struck between an individual and a corporate studio in entertainment history. Seemed like a good idea at the time....

- In 1999, fledgling search engine Excite rejected an offer to buy Google because it considered the $1 million asking price to be too high. Google is now worth nearly $300 billion, and Excite is defunct.

- In 2016, Mylan pharmaceuticals raised the price of the EpiPen, a life-saving drug delivery system, from $57 to more than $500. After the news broke, Mylan's stock price dropped from almost $58 a share to around $38 per share—a loss of more than 34%—suggesting that sometimes increased profits just aren't worth as much as they may seem.

- Also in 2016, Samsung *twice* had to halt production and undergo a massive and expensive recall of its Galaxy Note 7 phone, which had the inconvenient and potentially deadly problem of heating up and catching fire. The cost of the recall may ultimately exceed $17 billion, which is potentially more than the phone would've attracted in the first place. Clearly, taking a product to market without thoroughly testing it first is not always worth the potential costs.

- Mike Smith, one of the executives in charge of evaluating new talent for the London office of Decca Records, rejected the Beatles in 1962 with the now infamous line: "Groups are out; four-piece groups with guitars particularly are finished." Not so much....

In hindsight, momentous decisions may seem almost inevitable. But these bloopers clearly show that in the fog of the moment, the right choice can be anything but clear.[2]

---

1. **Technical Skills:** **Technical skills** refer to expertise in a specific functional area or department. Keep in mind that technical skills don't necessarily relate to technology. People can have technical skills—or specific expertise—in virtually any field, from sales, to copywriting, to accounting, to airplane repair, to computer coding.

2. **Human Skills:** **Human skills** refer to the ability to work with and through other people in a range of different relationships. Human skills include communication, leadership, coaching, empathy, and team building. A manager with strong human skills can typically mobilize support for initiatives and find win–win solutions for conflicts.

3. **Conceptual Skills:** **Conceptual skills** refer to the ability to grasp a big-picture view of the overall organization and the relationship between its various parts. Conceptual skills also help managers understand how their company fits into the broader competitive environment. Managers with strong conceptual skills typically excel at strategic planning.

All three categories of skill are essential for management success. But their importance varies according to the level of the manager. Front-line managers must have a

**technical skills** Expertise in a specific functional area or department.

**human skills** The ability to work effectively with and through other people in a range of different relationships.

**conceptual skills** The ability to grasp a big-picture view of the overall organization, the relationships among its various parts, and its fit in the broader competitive environment.

high degree of technical skills, which help them hire, train, and evaluate employees; avoid mistakes; and ensure high-quality production. Middle-level managers need an especially high level of human skills. They typically act as the bridge between departments, coordinating people and projects that sometimes have mismatched priorities. Top-level managers must demonstrate excellent conceptual skills in order to formulate a vision, interpret marketplace trends, and plan for the future. To move up in an organization, managers must constantly learn and grow, nurturing skills that reflect their new tasks.

Across all three skill sets, critical thinking and decision-making abilities have become increasingly important. Critical thinking helps managers find value even in an overload of information. Part of how information overload plays out is in email management; according to *Fortune* magazine, the average knowledge worker now spends an astounding 28% of their work time managing email. Simply deleting unwanted emails could take more than 16 hours per year! Strong decision-making skills help managers respond wisely and rapidly to all this information, with an unwavering focus on customer satisfaction.

Managers who expect to grow in the company hierarchy must expect to foster new skills. Too often, workers get promotions because of great technical skills—for example, the top salesperson lands the sales manager slot—but they struggle to move further because they don't fully develop their human and conceptual skills.

**Maslow's hierarchy of needs theory** A motivation theory that suggests that human needs fall into a hierarchy and that as each need is met, people become motivated to meet the next-highest need in the pyramid.

## 14-2  Motivation: Lighting the Fire

Standout managers motivate others to reach for their best selves—to accomplish more than they ever thought possible. Motivated workers tend to feel great about their jobs, and workers who feel great tend to produce more. But the thinking about *how* to motivate workers has changed dramatically over time. In the early 1900s, key management thinkers focused on efficiency and productivity, dictating precisely how workers should do each element of their jobs. But more recent research suggests that people's thoughts and feelings play a vital role in motivation, which leads to a range of new theories.

### 14-2a  Theories of Motivation

**Maslow's Hierarchy of Needs Theory** Noted psychologist Abraham Maslow theorized that people are motivated to satisfy only unmet needs. He proposed a hierarchy of human needs—from basic to abstract—suggesting that as each need is met, people become motivated to meet the next-highest need in the pyramid. Maslow's five specific needs are shown in Exhibit 14.1. While his theory was not based on the workplace, Maslow's ideas can illuminate the needs behind motivation at work.

From a workplace perspective, the idea that people are motivated only by unmet needs clearly holds true for the first two levels of the hierarchy. Finding a job that pays the bills, for instance, is the primary motivator for most people who don't have any job at all. People who have a job but no healthcare would find health insurance much more motivating than, say, a company picnic geared toward meeting social needs.

But after physiological and safety needs are met, the other needs are motivating to different degrees in different

| Exhibit 14.1 | Maslow's Hierarchy of Needs and the Workplace | |
|---|---|---|
| **Maslow's Need** | **Description** | **Workplace Examples** |
| **Self-Actualization** | Need for fulfillment—the need to realize one's fullest potential | Challenging, creative jobs; meaningful work that ties to a greater good; volunteer opportunities |
| **Esteem** | Need for self-respect and respect from others—recognition and status | Acknowledgment, feedback, promotions, perks, raises |
| **Social (Belonging)** | Need to feel connected to others— accepted by family and friends | Teamwork, positive corporate culture, company lunchroom, uniforms, department outings |
| **Safety** | Need to feel secure—free of harm and free of fear | Safety equipment, healthcare plans, life insurance, retirement plans, job security, gym membership |
| **Physiological** | Need for basic survival—food, water, clothing, and shelter | A job with enough pay to buy the basics |

## Exhibit 14.2 Theory X and Theory Y

| Theory X Assumptions about Workers | Theory Y Assumptions about Workers |
|---|---|
| ■ Workers dislike work and will do everything they can to avoid it. | ■ Work is as natural as play or rest—workers do not inherently dislike it. |
| ■ Fear is motivating—coercion and threats are vital to get people to work toward company goals. | ■ Different rewards can be motivating—people can exercise self-direction and self-control to meet company goals. |
| ■ People prefer to be directed, avoiding responsibility and seeking security. | ■ People can accept and even seek responsibility. |
| | ■ The capacity for imagination, creativity, and ingenuity is widely distributed in the population. |
| | ■ The intellectual capacity of the average worker is underutilized in the workplace. |

people. An employee with strong social connections outside work might be more motivated by a promotion that meets esteem needs than by a company outing that meets social needs. A number of firms actually use self-actualization needs as a starting point for motivating employees, by creating a mission statement that communicates the importance of the work. The House of Blues inspires employees through its lofty purpose: to promote racial and spiritual harmony through love, peace, truth, righteousness, and nonviolence.

### 14-2b Theory X and Theory Y

Psychologist Douglas McGregor, one of Maslow's students, studied workplace motivation from a different angle. He proposed that management attitudes toward workers would directly affect worker motivation. His research suggested that management attitudes fall into two opposing categories, which he called **Theory X and Theory Y**, described in Exhibit 14.2.

McGregor proposed that managers should employ Theory Y assumptions to capitalize on the imagination and intelligence of every worker. In American business today, some organizations use a Theory X approach, but a growing number have begun to at least experiment with Theory Y, tapping into a rich pool of employee input.

**Job Enrichment** A number of researchers have focused on creating jobs with more meaningful content, under the assumption that challenging, creative work will motivate employees to give their best effort. **Job enrichment** typically includes the following factors:

1. **Skill Variety:** Workers can use a range of different skills.

2. **Task Identity:** Workers complete tasks with clear beginnings and endings.

3. **Task Significance:** Workers understand the impact of the task on others.

4. **Autonomy:** Workers have freedom and authority regarding their jobs.

5. **Feedback:** Workers receive clear, frequent information about their performance.

Richard Branson, maverick founder of the Virgin Group, relies on job enrichment, especially autonomy and feedback, to keep people motivated at his 350-company empire (which includes a startling range of firms, such as Virgin Atlantic Airlines, Virgin Music, Virgin Wines, and Virgin Galactic space travel). Branson gives his managers a stake in their companies and then tells them "to run it as if it's their own." He says, "I have to be good at helping people run the individual businesses, and I have to be willing to step back. The company must be set up so it can continue without me." According to Virgin's website, "we pretty much practice a collaborative and supportive style of custodianship." Due in large part to Branson's motivational approach, the Virgin workforce is fully engaged with the company, contributing to its remarkable long-term success.[3]

### Expectancy Theory

Usually attributed to researcher Victor Vroom, **expectancy theory** deals with the relationship among individual effort, individual performance, and individual reward. The key concept is that a worker will be motivated if they believe that effort will lead to performance, and performance will lead to a meaningful reward.

Effort → Performance → Reward

**Theory X and Theory Y** A motivation theory that suggests that management attitudes toward workers fall into two opposing categories based on management assumptions about worker capabilities and values.

**job enrichment** The creation of jobs with more meaningful content, under the assumption that challenging, creative work will motivate employees.

**expectancy theory** A motivation theory that concerns the relationship among individual effort, individual performance, and individual reward.

The theory suggests that if any link in the chain is broken, the employee will not be motivated.

Imagine if your professor announced on the first day of class that they had never given any student an A, as a matter of principle. Would you be motivated to perform in class? Not likely—the link between performance and reward would be broken. Retailer Hot Topic has done a particularly strong job implementing the link between effort and performance. A Hot Topic employee describes the connection, saying, "I've worked for HT for five years, and the best thing I've learned is that if you work hard enough and dedicate enough of yourself to something, you can achieve your goals!" Hot Topic has also established strong links between performance and rewards. Perhaps it's no coincidence that Hot Topic is one of the few retail chains that continues to perform well, even as many other chains shutter their locations. According to Hot Topic CEO, Steve Vranes, "To our customers, Hot Topic is more than a retailer," said Vranes. "We represent community and self-expression."[4]

**Equity Theory** Pioneered by J. Stacy Adams, **equity theory** proposes that perceptions of fairness directly affect worker motivation. The key idea is that people won't be motivated if they believe that the relationship between what they contribute and what they earn is different from the relationship between what others contribute and what others earn. For example, if you worked

> **equity theory** A motivation theory that proposes that perceptions of fairness directly affect worker motivation.

> "If we are not making mistakes, we're not trying hard enough."
>
> —James Quincey, CEO, Coca-Cola

ten-hour days, and earned less than your friend in the next cube who works seven-hour days doing the same job, you'd probably think it was pretty unfair. To restore a sense of balance, you might:

- Demand a raise
- Start coming in late, leaving early, and taking extra-long lunch hours
- Convince yourself that your friend is about to be fired (or try to get them fired)
- Look for another job

The response to perceived inequity almost always involves trying to change the system, changing your own work habits, distorting your perceptions, or leaving the company.

But keep in mind that equity theory is based on perceptions, which are not always on the mark. People are all too prone to overestimate their own contributions, which throws perceived equity out of balance. The best way to combat equity issues is through clear, open communication from management.[5]

### 14-2c Motivation Today

Companies today use a range of approaches to motivation, although several key themes have emerged. Most firms no longer seek to make their employees happy; instead, they want their workers to be productive and engaged. Yet, for employees, work is about more than just productivity. University of Michigan business school professor David Ulrich

## Change That Can't Be Spared

President John F. Kennedy once said "Change is the law of life, and those who look only to the past and present are certain to miss the future." Kennedy's words are especially meaningful in today's postpandemic business world. One of the critical roles of management is to envision and lock in positive organizational change in the face of a tumultuous business environment. But organizational change can be tough. One reason is that a critical mass of workers can be deeply resistant to any attempt to pull them out of their comfort zone. Interestingly, recent research suggests that the more change workers face, the less change they are able to effectively absorb. The result is "change fatigue," which manifests in reactions such as burnout, frustration, or apathy. So what

can managers to do move forward? Experts recommend some combination of the following:

- Engage employees in planning the change.
- Gain staff commitment to the change and its eventual benefits.
- Introduce change in small increments.
- Encourage open, authentic communication about the process.
- Celebrate achievement of milestones along the way.

Successful change management will lead to a productive organization that can thrive in the face of whatever the future holds.[6]

points out that even in today's hyper-competitive environment, "people still want to find meaning in their work and in the institutions that employ them."[7]

A growing emphasis on corporate culture has captured the best of both worlds for companies that do it right. A look at *Fortune* magazine's 100 Best Companies to Work for in 2021 demonstrates that a distinctive, positive culture tends to create productive employees who are deeply attached to their work and their companies. The winners tend to emphasize the health and well-being of their employees and to offer strong commitments to make the world a better place. Cisco, number one on the list in 2021, made an especially strong showing during the COVID-19 pandemic, ramping up communications, expanding benefits and access to mental health services, and providing multiple "Days for Me" for employees to step back and recharge. Long known for its community engagement, Cisco also created a website to help remote students and donated unused videoconferencing gear to bolster telemedicine offerings at local medical facilities.

Unsurprisingly, compensation plays an important role at the 100 best firms to work for. Employees at

Alexander Tolstykh/Shutterstock.com

Google, which spent many years on the list—often in the number one slot—offers employees a famous set of perks at their Silicon Valley headquarters, including on-site haircutting, massage services, game facilities, and 25 cafés companywide, all free. But by 2018, Google had lost its coveted status as one of the *Fortune* 100 best places to work. In the wake of both high growth (doubling in size) and several high-profile scandals, the culture at Google transformed from an aura of exceptionalism to a sense of poorly concealed dissatisfaction and resentment.[8]

Edward Jones mention regular bonuses and overnight family retreats as examples of "meaningful recognition." Hyatt Hotel employees appreciate generous bonuses and the opportunity for housekeeping staff to clean more to earn more. Playful and thoughtful perks make a difference as well in creating a culture that works for employees. Workday, an enterprise software provider, offers unlimited time off, on-site car washes, bike repair, and manicures, and it has a slide in its San Francisco office. Quicken Loans encourages all employees to submit innovative ideas about how to improve the business to its Cheese Factory in the interest of continually "building a better mousetrap," and it actually implements hundreds of those ideas.[9]

In 2020, *Fortune* also published a list of the 75 best large workplaces for millennials—those (born between 1981 and 1997) who are known for appreciating firms with strong values and for changing jobs frequently. Many of the companies on the list in 2021 featured a diverse workforce and focused on respecting the individual employee. A happy employee at Progressive Insurance (number 7 on the list) explains, "People are encouraged to bring their whole selves to work. I value a company devoted to diversity and inclusion and it gives me great pride that we are encouraged to give back to our community." Another key theme among the companies is a strong focus on employee work/life balance. Allianz Life Insurance (number 40 on the list) offers a strong example. An employee elaborates, "The company has the best work/life balance I have ever seen. They encourage to put your family and your health as a priority above the business." Last but not least many firms on the list have created fun work cultures that their employees enjoy. A worker at AppFolio explains, "People work hard without being workaholics. It's FUN to work here."[10]

## 14-3 Planning: Figuring Out Where to Go and How to Get There

The planning function—figuring out where to go and how to get there—is the core of effective management. A survey in the *Wall Street Journal* found that 80% of executives identify planning as their most valuable management tool. But even though planning is critical, it's also highly risky in light of cutthroat competition, rapid change, and economic uncertainty. The best plans keep the organization on track without sacrificing flexibility and responsiveness; they incorporate ways to respond to change both inside and outside the organization.[11]

Exhibit 14.3    Managerial Planning

| Type of Planning | Management Level | Scope of Planning | Examples of Planning Questions and Concerns |
|---|---|---|---|
| **Strategic Planning** | Senior management | Typically five-year time frame | Should we acquire a new company? <br> Should we begin manufacturing in China? <br> Should we expand to overseas markets? <br> Should we take our company public? |
| **Tactical Planning** | Middle management | Typically one-year time frame | Should we spend more time servicing each customer? <br> Should we hire a public relations agency to handle PR? <br> Should we spend fewer ad dollars on TV and more on the Web? |
| **Operational Planning** | First-line management | Daily, weekly, and monthly time frame | How should we schedule employees this week? <br> When should we schedule delivery for each batch of product? <br> How should customer service people answer the phones? |

Although all managers engage in planning, the scope of the process changes according to the manager's position, as shown in Exhibit 14.3. Top-level managers focus on **strategic planning**. They establish a vision for the company, define long-term objectives and priorities, determine broad action steps, and allocate resources. Middle managers focus on **tactical planning**, or applying the strategic plan to their specific areas of responsibility. And first-line managers focus on **operational planning**, or applying the tactical plans to daily, weekly, and monthly operations. Successful firms often encourage a flow of feedback up and down the organization to ensure that all key plans are sound and that all key players "buy in." Some typical planning decisions and time frames are shown in Exhibit 14.3.

A fourth category of planning has gained new prominence in the past decade: **contingency planning**, or planning for unexpected events. Senior management usually spearheads contingency planning but with input from the other levels of management. Contingency plans consider what might go wrong—both inside the business and with the outside environment—and develop responses. Potential issues include:

- How should we respond if our competitors knock off our best-selling product?

- What should we do if the government regulates our industry?

- How should we respond if our data management/computer system fails?

- How can we restart our business if a natural disaster destroys our plant or supply channels?

- How will we evacuate employees if terrorists strike our headquarters?

- And of course, how do we manage in the face of a global pandemic?

Clearly, anticipating every potential problem is impossible (and impractical). Instead, effective contingency plans tend to focus only on the issues that are most probable, most potentially harmful, or both (refer to Exhibit 14.4). For example, a Southern California amusement park (e.g.,

**strategic planning** High-level, long-term planning that establishes a vision for the company, defines long-term objectives and priorities, determines broad action steps, and allocates resources.

**tactical planning** More specific, shorter-term planning that applies strategic plans to specific functional areas.

**operational planning** Very specific, short-term planning that applies tactical plans to daily, weekly, and monthly operations.

**contingency planning** Planning for unexpected events, usually involving a range of scenarios and assumptions that differ from the assumptions behind the core plans.

Effective planning can be complex and time-consuming.

fizkes/Shutterstock.com

## Exhibit 14.4
## Contingency Planning Paradigm

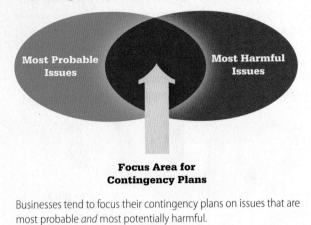

Most Probable Issues

Most Harmful Issues

**Focus Area for Contingency Plans**

Businesses tend to focus their contingency plans on issues that are most probable *and* most potentially harmful.

| Exhibit 14.5 | Examples of Mission Statements |
|---|---|
| **Company** | **Mission Statement** |
| **Levi Strauss & Co.** | We will market the most appealing and widely worn casual clothing in the world. We will clothe the world. |
| **IKEA** | To create a better everyday life for the many people. Our business idea supports this vision by offering a wide range of well-designed, functional home furnishing products at prices so low that as many people as possible will be able to afford them. |
| **Foot Locker** | To fuel a shared passion for self-expression. |
| **Warby Parker** | To offer designer eyewear at a revolutionary price, while leading the way for socially conscious businesses. |

Disneyland Park) might concentrate its contingency plans on earthquake response, while an online retailing firm might focus its plans on responding to a computer hacker attack.

### 14-3a Strategic Planning: Setting the Agenda

Strategic planning is the most fundamental part of the planning process, since all other plans—and most major management decisions—stem from the strategic plan. The strategic planning process typically includes these steps:

1. Define the mission of the organization.
2. Evaluate the organization's competitive position.
3. Set goals for the organization.
4. Create strategies for competitive differentiation.
5. Implement strategies.
6. Evaluate results, and incorporate lessons learned.

**Defining Your Mission** The mission of an organization articulates its essential reason for being. The **mission** defines the organization's purpose, values, and core goals, providing the framework for all other plans (refer to Exhibit 14.5). Most large companies present their mission as a simple, vivid, compelling statement that everyone involved with the company—from the janitor to the CEO, from customers to investors—can easily understand. Mission statements tend to vary in their length, their language, and even their names, but they share a common goal: to provide a clear, long-term focus for the organization.

**Evaluating Your Competitive Position** Strategy means nothing in a vacuum—every firm must plan

| Exhibit 14.6 | SWOT Analysis | |
|---|---|---|
| **Potential Internal Strengths** | | **Potential External Opportunities** |
| Premium brand name | | Higher consumer demand |
| Proven management team | | Complacent competitors |
| Lower costs/higher margins | | Growth in foreign markets |
| Diverse workforce | | New social trends |
| **Potential Internal Weaknesses** | | **Potential External Threats** |
| Low employee satisfaction | | A powerful new competitor |
| Inadequate financial resources | | A deep recession |
| Poor location | | New government regulations |
| Bad safety record | | Significant new taxes |

in the context of the marketplace. Many companies use a **SWOT analysis** (strengths, weaknesses, opportunities, and threats) to evaluate where they stand relative to the competition. Strengths and weaknesses are internal to the organization, and they include factors that would either build up or drag down the firm's performance. Opportunities and threats are external, and they include factors that would affect the company's performance but are typically out of the company's control. Exhibit 14.6 offers some examples.

> **mission** The definition of an organization's purpose, values, and core goals, which provides the framework for all other plans.
>
> **SWOT analysis** A strategic planning tool that helps management evaluate an organization in terms of internal strengths and weaknesses, and external opportunities and threats.

## Say What???

Generation Z, born in the year 2000 and later, is the largest generation in human history. Over the next 10 years, 1.3 billion of its members will enter the global workforce. Business communication between these new hires and their older-generation managers may be fraught with difficulty. Traditional "business speak" relies on email, and can appear overly prim and formal to Gen Z workers who are accustomed to incorporating and interpreting emojis in quickly dashed-off, informal texts. Supporting self-expression of Gen Z workers is a critical part of supporting diversity, which is a fundamental value for this uniquely diverse generation. Business psychologist Nicky Thompson explains, "Creating a more diverse and inclusive workspace is about language, tone, who I am as a person, and being able to actually express that in the workplace."

So how can older generation managers help? The first step may be to simply acknowledge and appreciate that Gen Z workers are digital natives, and they innately know more about navigating the contemporary world than any generation before

them. As such, they offer enormous potential value. Another possibility is to align older and younger generations in two-way mentorship programs. Management could also develop and distribute a style guide for business communication. Perhaps, most importantly, older-generation managers can model that the overall goal of business communication is connection, which matters more than style, regardless of generation.[12]

Vitalii Vodolazskyi/Shutterstock.com

---

Initial information about internal strengths and weaknesses usually comes from careful analysis of internal reports on topics such as budget and profitability. But to better understand strengths and weaknesses, executives should actively seek firsthand information—on a personal basis—from key people throughout the company, from front-line workers to the board of directors.

Gathering information about external opportunities and threats can be more complex, since these areas include both current and potential issues (which can be tough to predict). Information about external factors can come from many different sources, including the news, government reports, customers, and competitors.

**Setting Your Goals Strategic goals** represent concrete benchmarks that managers can use to measure performance in each key area of the organization. They must fit the firm's mission and tie directly to its competitive position. The most effective goals have three characteristics:

1. **Specific and Measurable:** Whenever possible, managers should define goals in clear numerical terms that everyone understands.

2. **Tied to a Time Frame:** To create meaning and urgency, goals should be linked to a specific deadline.

3. **Realistic but Challenging:** Goals that make people stretch can motivate exceptional performance.

Exhibit 14.7 offers examples of how weak goals can transform into powerful goals.

**Creating Your Strategies Strategies** are action plans that help the organization achieve its goals by forging the best fit between the firm and the environment. The underlying aim, of course, is to create a significant advantage versus the competition. Sources of competitive advantage vary, ranging from better product quality to better technology, to more motivated employees. The most successful

> **strategic goals** Concrete benchmarks that managers can use to measure performance in each key area of the organization.
>
> **strategies** Action plans that help the organization achieve its goals by forging the best fit between the firm and the environment.

| Exhibit 14.7 | Goal Setting: Getting It Right |
|---|---|
| **Weak Goal** | **Powerful Goal** |
| **Become More Innovative.** | Introduce one new product each quarter for the next three years. |
| **Reduce Delinquent Accounts.** | Reduce delinquent accounts to no more than 1% of the total by the next quarter. |
| **Increase Market Share.** | Become the #1 or #2 brand in each market where we compete by the end of 2030. |

companies build their advantage across several fronts. Southwest Airlines, for example, has a more motivated workforce and a lower cost structure. H&M has lower prices and more fashionable clothing choices. And Procter & Gamble has more innovative new products and strong core brands.

The specifics of strategy differ by industry and by company, but all strategies represent a roadmap. The SWOT analysis determines the starting point, and the objectives signify the immediate destination. Since speed matters, you must begin mapping the next leg of the journey even before you arrive. For added complexity, you never know—given the turbulent business environment—when you might hit roadblocks. This means that strategies must be dynamic and flexible. Top managers have responded to this challenge by encouraging front-line managers to participate in the process more than ever before.

**Implementing Your Strategies** Implementation should happen largely through tactical planning. Middle managers in each key area of the company must develop plans to carry out core strategies in their area. If the strategic plan, for example, calls for more new products, marketing would need to generate ideas, finance would need to find funding, and sales would need to prepare key accounts. And all of these steps would require tactical planning.

**Evaluating Your Results and Incorporating Lessons Learned** Evaluation of results should be a continual process, handled by managers at every level as part of their controlling function, covered further in this chapter. But for evaluation to be meaningful, the lessons learned must be analyzed objectively and factored back into the next planning cycle.

## 14-4 Organizing: Fitting Together the Puzzle Pieces

The organizing function of management means creating a logical structure for people, their jobs, and their patterns of interaction. And clearly, the pieces can fit together in a number of different ways. In choosing the right structure for a specific company, management typically considers many factors, including the goals and strategies of the firm, its products, its use of technology, its size, and the structure of its competitors. Given the potential for rapid change in each of these factors, smart companies continually reexamine their structure and make changes whenever necessary. Microsoft, for instance, restructures its organization every couple of years as new challenges emerge.

But to be effective, reorganizations—and their purpose—must be clear to employees throughout the company. Former Xerox CEO Anne Mulcahy learned the hard way. Her comments: "During the 1990s, we had lots of consultants on organizational effectiveness. We sliced and diced the business into industries, product lines, and geographies . . . you name it. It looked good on paper, but fell apart in implementation. I found myself in a job where I couldn't look anybody in the eye and feel clear accountability for anything . . . I'll trade off organizational design for clarity and accountability any day of the week!"[13]

To help employees understand how they and their jobs fit within the broader organization, most firms issue an **organization chart**, or a visual representation of the company's formal structure, as shown in Exhibit 14.8.

Looking at the company represented by Exhibit 14.8, you would probably assume that the vice president of production has more power than a regular employee in the marketing department. And in terms of formal power, you'd be absolutely right. But if the marketing employee babysits on the weekend for the president's granddaughter, the balance of power may actually be a bit different than it seems.

**organization chart** A visual representation of the company's formal structure.

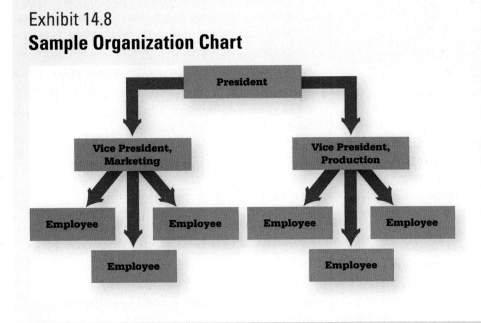

## Exhibit 14.8
## Sample Organization Chart

President

Vice President, Marketing

Vice President, Production

Employee

Employee

Employee

Employee

Employee

Employee

Make no mistake: The formal structure matters. But knowing how power flows on an informal basis could dramatically increase your effectiveness as well, by helping you target your ideas to the right managers and marshal the support of the most influential employees.

## 14-4a Key Organizing Considerations

In developing the organizational structure, management must make decisions about the degree of centralization, the span of management control, and the type of departmentalization that makes the most sense at any given time.

**Centralization** The **degree of centralization** relates directly to the source of power and control. In centralized companies, a small number of people at the top of the organization have the power to make decisions. This approach is simple and efficient, and the result tends to be a strong corporate image and a uniform customer approach across the front lines. But the downside is that centralized companies typically respond more slowly to customer needs and have lower employee morale. The tradeoff may be worthwhile in steady, stable markets, but those are rare.

Faced with today's turbulent environment—especially in the wake of the COVID-19 pandemic—many firms are seeking to redesign themselves in an effort to speed up operations. The key elements of redesign include flatter structures, greater decentralization, better teamwork, and pushing power to the lower levels of the organization. Employees with the power to make decisions can respond to customer needs more quickly and effectively. They can also capitalize on opportunities that would likely vaporize in the time it would take to get permission to act. But for decentralization to work, every employee must fully understand the firm's mission, goals, and strategy; otherwise, the company could develop a fragmented image, which would undermine its long-term strength. Also, active communication across departments is essential so that all employees can benefit from innovations in other parts of the organization.[14]

**Span of Control** The **span of control**, or span of management, refers to the number of people a manager supervises. There is no ideal number for every manager. The "right" span of control varies, based on the abilities of both the manager and the subordinates, the nature of the work being done, the location of the employees, and the need for planning and coordination. Across industries, the general trend has moved toward wider spans of control as a growing number of companies have pruned layers of middle management to the bare minimum.

**Departmentalization** Departmentalization means breaking workers into logical groups. A number of different options make sense, depending on the organization.

- **Functional:** Dividing employees into groups based on area of expertise, such as marketing, finance, and engineering, tends to be efficient and easy to coordinate. For those reasons, it works especially well for small- to medium-sized firms.

- **Product:** Dividing employees into groups based on the products that a company offers helps workers develop expertise about products that often results in especially strong customer relations.

- **Customer:** Dividing employees into groups based on the customers that a company serves helps companies focus on the needs of specific customer groups. Many companies have separate departments for meeting the needs of business and consumer users. This approach is related to product departmentalization.

- **Geographical:** Dividing employees into groups based on where customers are located can help different departments better serve specific regions within one country. Similarly, many international firms create a separate department for each different country they serve.

- **Process:** Dividing into groups based on what type of work employees do is common in manufacturing, where management may divide departments by processes such as cutting, dyeing, and sewing.

As companies get larger, they usually adopt several different types of departmentalization at different levels of the organization. This approach, shown in Exhibit 14.9, is called "hybrid departmentalization."

## 14-4b Organization Models

Company structures tend to follow one of three different patterns: line organizations, line-and-staff organizations, and matrix organizations. But these organizational models are not mutually exclusive. In fact, many management teams build their structure using elements of each model at different levels of the organization.

**Line Organizations** A **line organization** typically has a clear, simple chain of command from top to bottom.

**degree of centralization** The extent to which decision-making power is held by a small number of people at the top of the organization.

**span of control** Span of management; refers to the number of people a manager supervises.

**departmentalization** The division of workers into logical groups.

**line organizations** Organizations with a clear, simple chain of command from top to bottom.

## Exhibit 14.9
## An Example of Hybrid Departmentalization

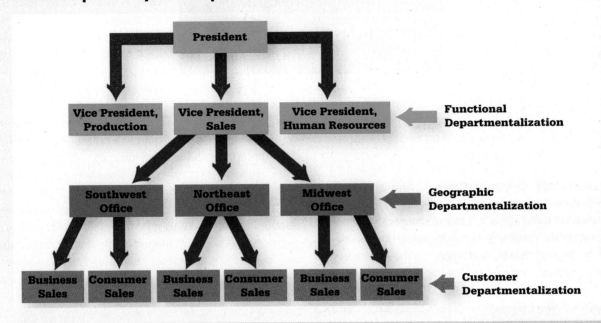

# Wanna Be More Productive? Relax!!

Ironically, a growing body of research suggests rather strongly that the best way to get more done may be to spend more time doing less, which may include daytime workouts, short afternoon naps, longer sleep hours at night, and longer, more frequent vacations. Despite misguided efforts to make it otherwise, time is definitely finite; energy, on the other hand, can be renewed. A recent study on the economic costs of insufficient sleep (less than six hours per night) found that a lack of sleep among the U.S. workforce is costing businesses about $411 billion in lost productivity each year. The study, which spanned the United States, the United Kingdom, Canada, Germany, and Japan, found that the United States sustained the highest economic losses due to sleep deprivation by far.

Studies of vacation show that taking more vacation days has a dramatic positive impact on worker performance. Unfortunately, whether it's obsession, dedication, or fear of unreasonable bosses, a recent study showed that the average American leaves four full days of paid vacation on the table each year. That's still better than South Korea, where workers throw an average 11 of their 15 available days of paid vacation away. Europeans, on the other hand, tend to use all of their 30 days of paid vacation—leading to a much healthier work-life balance. Like sleep deprivation, not taking vacation days can be bad for the economy. Project: Time Off estimates that servicing the needs of those unused American vacation days could have created 1.6 million jobs, resulting in $65 billion in additional income. If Americans used just one more day of vacation per year, the economy would see a $34 billion jump in total spending.

CEO Tony Schwartz attempts to run his business on the principle that the energy people bring to their jobs is more important than the number of hours they work. He and his management team have policies in place that reflect the idea that, "When we're renewing, we're truly renewing, so when we're working, we can really work." Partly because of this ethos, in the decade that his firm has been in business, no one has chosen to leave the company. If more CEOs communicated this message, chances are that more vacation time would actually be used. Eighty percent of employees surveyed by Project: Time Off said that if they felt fully supported and encouraged by their boss, they would be more likely to take more time off. A growing number of high-profile companies, such as Virgin Group and Netflix, are offering employees unlimited or unmonitored vacation days to encourage time off and rejuvenation.[15]

New Africa/Shutterstock.com

Each person is directly accountable to the person immediately above, which means quick decision making and no fuzziness about who is responsible for what. The downside is a lack of specialists to provide advice or support for line managers. This approach tends to work well for small businesses, but for medium-sized and large companies, the result can be inflexibility, too much paperwork, and even incompetence, since experts aren't available to give their input on key decisions.

**Line-and-Staff Organizations** A **line-and-staff organization** incorporates the benefits of a line organization without all the drawbacks. **Line managers** supervise the functions that contribute directly to profitability: production and marketing. **Staff managers**, on the other hand, supervise the functions that provide advice and assistance to the line departments. Examples include legal, accounting, and human resources. In a line-and-staff organization, the line managers form the primary chain of authority in the company. Staff departments work alongside line departments, but there is no direct reporting relationship (except at the top of the company). Since staff people don't report to line people, their authority comes from their know-how. This approach, which overlays fast decision-making with additional expertise, tends to work well for medium-sized and large companies. But in some firms, the staff departments gain so much power that they become dictatorial, imposing unreasonable limitations on the rest of the company.

**Matrix Organizations** **Matrix organizations** build on the line-and-staff approach by adding a lot more flexibility. A matrix structure brings together specialists from different areas of the company to work on individual projects on a temporary basis. A new-product-development team, for instance, might include representatives from sales, engineering, finance, purchasing, and advertising. For the course of the project, each specialist reports to the project manager and to the head of their own department (e.g., the vice president of marketing). The matrix approach has been particularly popular in the high-tech and aerospace industries.

The matrix structure offers several key advantages. It encourages teamwork and communication across the organization. It offers flexibility in deploying key people. It lends itself to innovative solutions. And not surprisingly—when managed well—the matrix structure creates a higher level of motivation and satisfaction for employees. But these advantages have a clear flip side. The need for constant communication can bog down a company in too many meetings. The steady state of flux can be overwhelming for both managers and employees. And having two bosses can cause conflict and stress for everyone.

> "Management is doing things right; leadership is doing the right things."
> —Peter Drucker, Management Researcher, Writer, and Speaker

## 14-5 Leadership: Directing and Inspiring

While most people easily recognize a great leader, defining the qualities of leaders can be more complex since successful leaders have a staggering range of personalities, characteristics, and backgrounds. Most researchers agree that true leaders are trustworthy, visionary, and inspiring. After all, we don't follow people who don't know where they're going, and we definitely don't follow people we don't trust. Other key leadership traits include empathy, courage, creativity, intelligence, and fairness.

### 14-5a Leadership Style

How a leader uses power defines their leadership style. While the range of specific styles is huge, most seem to cluster into three broad categories: autocratic, democratic, and free-rein. The categories fall along a continuum of power, with the manager at one end and the employees at the other, as shown in Exhibit 14.10.

**Autocratic leaders** hoard decision-making power for themselves, and they typically issue orders without consulting their followers. **Democratic leaders** share

---

**line-and-staff organization** An organization with line managers forming the primary chain of authority in the company, and staff departments working alongside line departments.

**line managers** Managers who supervise the functions that contribute directly to profitability: production and marketing.

**staff managers** Managers who supervise the functions that provide advice and assistance to the line departments.

**matrix organizations** Organizations with a flexible structure that brings together specialists from different areas of the company to work on individual projects on a temporary basis.

**autocratic leaders** Leaders who hoard decision-making power for themselves and typically issue orders without consulting their followers.

**democratic leaders** Leaders who share power with their followers. While they still make final decisions, they typically solicit and incorporate input from their followers.

## Exhibit 14.10
## The Continuum of Leadership and Power

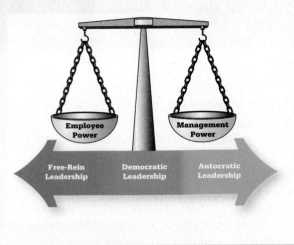

Employee Power — Management Power

Free-Rein Leadership | Democratic Leadership | Autocratic Leadership

power with their followers. Even though they still make final decisions, they typically solicit and incorporate input from their followers. **Free-rein leaders** set objectives for their followers but give them freedom to choose how they accomplish those goals.

Interestingly, the most effective leaders don't use just one approach. They tend to shift their leadership style, depending on the followers and the situation. When a quick decision is paramount, autocratic leadership may make the most sense. An army officer, for example, probably shouldn't take a vote on whether to storm a hill in the middle of a firefight. But when creativity is the

The most effective leaders are typically comfortable using a range of different leadership styles.

Fizkes/Shutterstock.com

top priority—during new-product brainstorming, for instance—free-rein management would probably work best. Likewise, a brand-new worker might benefit from autocratic (but friendly) management, while a talented, experienced employee would probably work best under free-rein leadership.

Another vital consideration is the customer. When the customer seeks consistency in the delivery of the product—in fast food, for instance—the autocratic leadership style may be appropriate. But when the customer needs flexibility and problem-solving assistance—a consulting client, for example—the free-rein leadership style may be most effective. The democratic leadership style typically provides customers with a balance of consistency and flexibility, which works across a wide range of industries.

## 14-6 Controlling: Making Sure It All Works

Controlling may be the least glamorous of the management functions, but don't be fooled: It's critically important. Controlling means monitoring performance of the firm—or individuals within the firm—and making improvements when necessary. As the environment changes, plans change. And as plans change, the control process must change as well, to ensure that the company achieves its goals. The control process includes three key steps:

1. Establish clear performance standards.

2. Measure actual performance against standards.

3. Take corrective action if necessary.

Establishing clear standards—or performance goals—begins with planning. At every level of planning, objectives should emerge that are consistent with the company's mission and strategic plan. The objectives must be (1) specific and measurable, (2) realistic but challenging, and (3) tied to a time frame. Individual managers may need to break these goals into smaller parts for specific employees, but the subgoals should retain the same three qualities as the original objective.

Measuring performance against standards should happen well before the end of the time frame attached to the goal. A strong information-tracking system is probably management's best tool in this phase of the control process.

If the company or individual is not on track to meet the goals, management's

**free-rein leaders** Leaders who set objectives for their followers but give them freedom to choose how they will accomplish those goals.

> The control process includes three key steps:
>
> 1. Establish clear performance standards
>
> 2. Measure actual performance against standards
>
> 3. Take corrective action if necessary

Nerthuz/Shutterstock.com

first response should be communication. Employees with full information are far more likely to improve their performance than employees who never learn that they're falling behind. But sometimes workers need more than information—they may need additional resources or coaching to meet their goals. Apple's Steve Jobs was often accused of being a tyrannical boss—especially in the employee-evaluation process—but he defended himself by saying, "My job is not to be easy on people. My job is to make them better." If they still don't succeed, perhaps the goals themselves need reexamination as part of a dynamic planning process. Given the expense in both human and financial terms, disciplining employees for poor performance should come only after exploring the reasons for not meeting goals and making changes if necessary.

## The Big Picture

In the past decade, management has become more complex and demanding than ever before. Managers in every area of the business must carry out their roles—planning, organizing, leading, and controlling—in a relentlessly fast-paced world, seething with constant change. While management isn't for everyone, it's often a fit for people with vision, courage, integrity, energy, and a passionate commitment to their companies.

Looking forward, the role of management will continue to evolve in response to the environment. Regardless of how the changes unfold, several key factors will be absolutely vital for successful managers in the twenty-first century: a constant focus on the customer, a commitment to globalization, excellent judgment, and the right mix of talented, motivated employees.

## Careers in Management

### Manager

Define strategic and tactical objectives for the organization or business unit. Develop plans to meet those objectives. Coach, counsel, motivate, and develop employees. Maintain and allocate resources as necessary to attain goals. Monitor achievement of objectives and make changes as necessary. Create and oversee a business unit budget. Ensure product and service quality by setting and enforcing standards. Foster a business culture that aligns with the broader organizational culture. Communicate and collaborate as appropriate throughout the organization. Maintain current professional and technical knowledge.

# 15 | Human Resource Management:
## Building a Top-Quality Workforce

### Learning Objectives
After studying this chapter, you will be able to:

**15-1** Explain the importance of human resources to business success

**15-2** Discuss key human resource issues in today's economy

**15-3** Outline challenges and opportunities that the human resources function faces

**15-4** Discuss human resource planning and core human resources responsibilities

**15-5** Explain the key federal legislation that affects human resources

**15-6** Explain the role of diversity in contemporary business

Mavo/Shutterstock.com

## 15-1 Human Resource Management: Bringing Business to Life

As competition accelerates across the globe, leading firms in every business category have recognized that a quality workforce can vault them over the competition. Southwest Airlines was early to recognize the untapped potential of its people. Southwest founder Herb Kelleher declared, "We value our employees first. They're the most important, and if you treat them right, then they treat the customers right, and if you treat the customers right, then they keep coming back and shareholders are happy." His attitude has more than paid off. Southwest Airlines posted profits for 47 consecutive years, even as other airlines spiraled into decline. The Southwest Airlines profitability streak didn't snap until the entire travel industry collapsed with the COVID-19 pandemic in 2020. Even through the most tumultuous times, managing human resources remains a top priority for Southwest CEO Gary Kelly. He maintains, "Our people-first approach, which has guided our company since it was founded,

means when our company does well, our people do really, really well. Our people work incredibly hard and deserve to share in Southwest's success." Perhaps due to this attitude and a history of commensurate actions, nearly 28% of Southwest's workforce agreed to take either voluntary exit or extended unpaid time off packages, allowing the airline to avoid furloughs, layoffs, pay rate cuts, or benefits cuts through 2020, giving it a shot at recovering from the COVID-19 pandemic.[1]

> "If something goes wrong, it's my problem; if something goes *right*, it's their success."
>
> —Pamela Fields, former CEO, Stetson

Companies that get the most from their people often consider their human resources their biggest investment. They view the core goal of **human resource (HR) management** in a similar light: to nurture their human investment so that it yields the highest possible return. HR can achieve that goal by recruiting world-class talent, promoting career development, and boosting organizational effectiveness. But clearly, this can happen only in partnership with key managers throughout the company, especially senior executives. (In smaller companies, the owners usually handle HR management in addition to their other responsibilities.)

> **human resource (HR) management** The management function focused on maximizing the effectiveness of the workforce by recruiting world-class talent, promoting career development, and determining workforce strategies to boost organizational effectiveness.

## 15-2 Human Resource Management Challenges: Major Hurdles

Building a top-quality workforce can be tougher than it may initially seem. Human resource managers—and their counterparts throughout the company—face huge challenges. The best strategies still aren't clear, but forward-thinking firms tend to experiment with new approaches.

### 15-2a Outsourcing

As high-tech, high-end jobs follow low-tech, low-end jobs out of the country—or even just to local contractors and consultants, as part of a growing phenomenon called domestic outsourcing—human resources find themselves in turmoil. How can businesses boost the morale and the motivation level of the employees who are left behind? Does less job security translate to less worker loyalty? How can human resources continue to add value as the ground shifts beneath them—and as they wonder how long their own jobs will last? Despite robust employment rates, the number of outsourced American jobs continues to grow due to the benefits it offers businesses in terms of much lower costs and access to a global talent pool. Functions that are most often affected include manufacturing, technology, and ironically, human resources.[2]

### 15-2b Wage Gap

Comparing CEO pay to worker pay demonstrates a startling wage gap, bigger in the United States than in any other developed country. In 2019, the average CEO at America's top 350 firms earned 320 times what the average employee earned. This means that top CEOs make much more in two days than an average employee does in one year.[3] And the pay gap continued to grow in 2020, despite massive pay cuts, furloughs, and layoffs in the face of the COVID-19 economic shutdowns. Of the 200 companies with the largest CEO pay packages included in a *New York Times* survey, 68% had larger gaps between CEO pay and worker pay in 2020 than they did before the pandemic—CEO pay rose 14.1% in 2020 from 2019, while median worker pay rose just 1.9% during the same period. Eight executives surveyed by the *New York Times* earned more than $100 million in

2020, compared to just one in 2019. Most observers don't object to the CEO-worker pay gap when top CEO pay is tied to top performance. But the *Harvard Business Review* suggests that performance-based pay can actually have dangerous outcomes for companies that implement it. In jobs that require learning and creativity—such as top management positions—tying pay to performance can actually harm the company. How so? Suppose a CEO's performance rating is tied to the company's stock price, so they cut back on research and development spending in order to meet short-term stock price goals. This move is in the CEO's best interest personally, but it could devastate the company in the long run. Performance-based pay also increases the likelihood that a top-level manager is willing to "cook the books" to achieve their performance goals. Untangling these sorts of issues is a real strategic challenge for HR management.[4]

### 15-2c Older Workers

As the "forever young" baby boomer generation has begun to hit the traditional retirement age, their employers—which include virtually every major American company—face a potential crisis: the loss of key talent and experience through massive retirements. Beginning January 1, 2011, every day more than 10,000 baby boomers reached the age of 65, and that will continue to happen every day until 2030. Enlightened companies have responded with programs to retain their best employees through flexible schedules, training opportunities, and creative pay schedules. But to the surprise of many analysts, the actual wave of retirements was much lower than they projected. According to Pew Research, boomers have been exiting the workforce at an actual rate of roughly 5,900 per day. Pew also reports that 45% of boomers surveyed in 2016 expected to retire *after* age 65. But the issue of a "knowledge gap" remains—how can companies help pass the high levels of institutional knowledge and experience (since many of those boomers work in management) to the next generations? Some practical steps human resources professionals can take include the following:

- Organize semistructured intergenerational mentoring relationships.
- Work with functional managers to ensure the younger generation has

> If forced to choose, 40% of Gen Z workers would choose lower pay for more free time, versus 53% of millennial workers.
>
> —Commericial Café

a development plan so the path to their next career step is clear. Proactively identify team members capable of advancing to leadership positions.

■ Communicate respectfully and consistently with boomer (and all) team members to understand their plans and not be caught off guard by a seemingly sudden decision to retire.[5]

### 15-2d Younger Workers

As younger workers enter the workforce, they often bring optimism, open minds, technological know-how, a team orientation, a proven ability to multitask, and a multicultural perspective. But a number of them also bring an unprecedented sense of entitlement. This can translate into startlingly high expectations for their pay, their responsibilities, and their job flexibility, but little willingness to "pay dues." Many have no expectation that their employers will be loyal to them, and they don't feel that they owe their companies strong loyalty. Managing this group can sometimes be a challenge, but companies that do it well stand to deliver results for years to come.[6]

### 15-2e Women Workers

Over the past few decades, women have made enormous strides in terms of workplace equality. But several large-scale studies confirm that women continue to face daunting discrimination in terms of both pay and promotions. While unfair treatment has been an issue for many years, recent legal changes have made it easier for women to sue, costing companies millions of dollars in the past decade alone. And the flood of lawsuits shows no signs of slowing. Many women have responded to the unfriendly business environment by leaving the workforce; droves of highly qualified, professional women step out of the workforce early— usually to raise children, start their own companies, or pursue other interests. As a result, we are experiencing a harmful, ongoing brain drain. Human resource managers can help mitigate this issue by implementing specific retention plans for valued women workers and by taking proactive steps to reintegrate returning women back into the workforce.[7]

In late 2017, the #MeToo movement made clear that women face issues of sexual harassment and assault in the workplace to a greater degree than most people realized. As awareness grew, human resources professionals took

> **Frivolous lawsuits cost American businesses over $865 billion per year.**
> —Pacific Research Institute

responsibility for training the workforce and establishing new safeguards to prevent future abuse. For the most part, absolute fairness and transparency have been at the forefront of their actions and perspective. Transparency can be a particularly tricky issue for human resources professionals with regard to sexual harassment. Employees who bring forward complaints would of course like to know what actions are being taken, but in fairness to the accused, HR must sometimes keep them in the dark, which can at times make HR appear insensitive.

### 15-2f Work–Life Balance

Over the past couple of decades, workers across all ages and genders have actively pursued more flexibility and work–life balance in their jobs. But in times of economic turmoil, companies tend to cut back on these initiatives, describing them as "nice to have" programs in a time when "need to have" goals—such as meeting payroll each month—are tough to attain. Middle-level managers are also apt to demonstrate bias against worker flexibility, even when top management actively supports work–life balance programs. A recent study showed that younger workers, although they tend to work fewer hours and less overtime, also tend to be more stressed and fairly unsatisfied with their work–life balance. One reason for their bleak outlook may be that many of these tech savvy workers always stay connected to the office, letting work intrude on their personal lives and turning work–life balance into what some call a work–life blend. The pivot to remote work—spurred by the COVID-19 pandemic—certainly didn't help. In spite of these issues, insightful HR managers try hard to offer enough flexibility to keep their best workers without jeopardizing their company's business goals.[8]

### 15-2g Lawsuits

The United States has become a wildly litigious society, with employees, customers, and shareholders levying lawsuit after lawsuit against firms of all sizes. Even though many of the lawsuits are legitimate—some profoundly important—a good number are just plain silly. But even if a lawsuit is frivolous, and even if it's thrown out of court, it can still cost a company millions of dollars. Even more importantly, a frivolous lawsuit can cost a business its reputation. Avoiding employee lawsuits by knowing the law and encouraging legal practices is a growing human resources challenge.

# Do as I Say, Not as I Do...

Huge high-tech companies are among the first to denounce racism and sexism and to hail diversity. Every year since 2014, the major tech companies have filed reports on their number of women and employees of color to the Equal Employment Opportunity Commission in a public display that some have called "diversity theater." Although the display is impressive—the actual results are disheartening.

Apple, for example, showed zero growth in its percentage of Black technical workers, which remained at 6% for all of the years that it reported, and only 3% for leadership roles. Facebook showed the smallest increase in Black employees, going from 3% to 3.8% in five years. The number of Latinx workers rose only 2% during that same time period. At the most recent count, Google listed only five Black female executives among its top 357 officers—a mere 1.4%.

So why is there such a disconnect between the PR message from Big Tech and their real-world actions? It seems as though tech leadership may have missed the memo that diversity is good for business. A study published in 2018 demonstrated that more racially and ethnically diverse companies earn profits that are 43% higher than their more homogenous counterparts. Diversity also offers a chance to get first dibs on top job candidates in a tight labor market, since 67% of people on the job market state that racial and gender diversity is an important factor in their job search.

When Big Tech closes the gap between their words and their actions with regard to diversity, they can expect to garner a rich array of benefits from greater profitability to a more engaged workforce.[9]

ImageFlow/Shutterstock.com

## 15-3   Human Resources Managers: Corporate Black Sheep?

Human resources management suffers from a reputation problem in many organizations. Workers and even managers in other parts of the company tend to regard them as a nuisance at best (all that paperwork, and those *rules*!) and a money pit at worst. But the good news is that human resources has the potential and the tools to play a vitally important role in virtually every organization.

### 15-3a The Problem

The human resource management function is clearly critical, but human resources departments—and the people who work in them—face major challenges. Leading-edge firms expect every department to offer "big picture," strategic contributions that boost company value. But a report in *Fast Company* suggests that most HR professionals lack sufficient strategic skills. Among other data, the report quotes a respected executive at a top U.S. company:

"Business acumen is the single biggest factor that HR professionals in the U.S. lack today."[10]

But even highly qualified, strategically focused HR managers face daunting perception problems. A management professor at a leading school comments, "The best and the brightest just don't go into HR." Once in the workforce, many employees see the human resources department as irrelevant, a nuisance—or even worse, as the enemy. This perception clearly undermines their effectiveness. Business history indicates that companies seem to value HR most when workers are scarce (unemployment is low). But there are still steps proactive HR managers can take in the meantime to bolster their perception within the rest of the organization.[11]

### 15-3b The Solution

To gain respect from both senior management and their peers, human resources executives must earn a seat at the table. The first step is to know the company. What are the strategic goals? Who is the core customer? Who is the competition? One potential source of value is the company's employee database, which HR can leverage by developing analytics to predict good hires, build strong teams, manage healthcare costs, and identify top performers. Respected HR departments typically figure out ways to quantify their impact on the company in dollars and cents. They determine how to raise the value of the firm's human capital, which in turn increases the value of the firm itself. Effective HR people also remain open to exceptions even as they enforce broad company policies.

But clearly, these solutions will work only if senior management recognizes the potential value of effective human resource management. One simple test of senior management commitment is the reporting relationship. If the HR department reports to the CFO, it may be on the fast track to outsourcing. But if the HR department reports to the CEO, the strategic possibilities are unlimited.

## 15-4 Human Resource Planning: Drawing the Map

Great human resource management begins with great planning: Where should you go? And how should you get there? Your objectives should flow from the company's master plan, and your strategies must reflect company priorities.

One of the first steps in the HR planning process should be to figure out where the company stands in terms of human resources. What skills does the workforce already have? What skills does it need? A company-wide **job analysis** often goes hand in hand with evaluating the current workforce. Job analysis examines what exactly needs to be done in each position to maximize the effectiveness of the organization—independent of who might be holding each job at any specific time. Smaller companies often handle job analysis on an informal basis, but larger companies typically specify a formal **job description** and **job specifications** (or "**specs**").

A job description defines the jobholder's responsibilities, and job specs define the qualifications for doing the job. Consider the job of band manager. The job description might include finding engagements for the band and settling disputes among band members. The job specs might include the type of education and experience required. Taken together, the two might look something like Exhibit 15.1.

The next step is to forecast future human resource requirements. The forecasting function requires a deep understanding of the company's goals and strategies. HR managers must also assess the future supply of workers. Assessing supply can be a real challenge, since the size and quality of the workforce shift continually. But key considerations should include retirement rates, graduation rates in relevant fields, and the pros and cons of the international labor market.

A complete HR plan—which falls under the company's strategic planning umbrella—must cover each core area of human resource management (refer to Exhibit 15.2):

- Recruitment
- Selection
- Training
- Evaluation
- Compensation
- Benefits
- Separation

### 15-4a Recruitment: Finding the Right People

Finding people to hire is often easy—especially when the unemployment rate is high—but finding *qualified* employees is almost always a daunting challenge. The U.S. Census Bureau points out that a college degree typically doubles earning power, and the U.S. Bureau of Labor Statistics attests that most of the

**job analysis** The examination of specific tasks that are assigned to each position, independent of who might be holding the job at any specific time.

**job description** An explanation of the responsibilities for a specific position.

**job specifications (specs)** The specific qualifications necessary to hold a particular position.

| Exhibit 15.1 | Job Description and Job Specifications: Band Manager |
| --- | --- |

| Job Description | Job Specifications |
| --- | --- |
| Work with the music group to help make major decisions regarding the creative and business direction of the band | A bachelor's degree in music management |
| Negotiate recording contracts and engagement fees | A minimum of three years' experience managing a high-profile band |
| Help band members understand their rights and responsibilities | Excellent communication and networking skills |

## Exhibit 15.2
## Human Resource Management

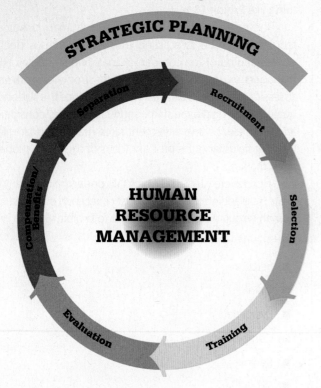

STRATEGIC PLANNING

Separation

Recruitment

Compensation/Benefits

**HUMAN RESOURCE MANAGEMENT**

Selection

Evaluation

Training

right person within their organization. The firm may be too small, or perhaps no one has the right set of skills to fill the immediate needs. Or maybe the firm needs the fresh thinking and energy that can come only from outside. When this is the case, companies turn to **external recruitment**.

External recruitment, or looking for employees outside the firm, usually means tapping into a range of different resources. The possibilities include employment websites, newspaper ads, job fairs, trade associations, college and university employment centers, and employment agencies. But the most promising source of new hires may be referrals from current employees. A growing number of organizations offer their current employees a cash bonus—typically $1,000 to $2,000—for each person they refer to the company who makes it past a probationary period. As an added benefit, employees who come through referrals have an excellent chance at success, since the person who recommended them has a stake in their progress. Employee-referral programs also represent a real bargain for employers, compared to the average cost per new hire of more than $4,000. Not surprisingly, a higher level of employee referrals correlates to a higher level of shareholder returns, although lack of diversity may become a long-term problem with relying on employee referrals.[13]

### 15-4b Selection: Making the Right Choice

Once you have a pool of qualified candidates, your next step is to choose the best person for the job. This, too, is more easily said than done, yet making the right selection is crucial. The costs of a bad hire—both the direct

Job fairs are a popular external recruitment tool for companies looking to hire large numbers of entry-level employees.

fastest-growing fields in the next five years will require college graduates. But only one-third of adults in America ages 25–29 have a college degree. And as highly trained, highly educated baby boomers hit retirement, HR recruiters may face a hiring crunch. In addition to finding qualified hires, recruiters also must find new employees who fit with the company culture in terms of both personality and style.[12]

New employees come from two basic sources: internal and external. **Internal recruitment** involves transferring or promoting employees from other positions within the company. This approach offers several advantages:

■ Boosts employee morale by reinforcing the value of experience within the firm

■ Reduces risk for the firm, since current employees have a proven track record

■ Lowers costs of both recruitment and training

But companies often find that they don't have the

**internal recruitment** The process of seeking employees who are currently within the firm to fill open positions.

**external recruitment** The process of seeking new employees from outside the firm.

costs such as placing ads, and the intangibles such as lost productivity and morale—can drain company resources. A typical selection process includes accepting applications, interviewing, testing, checking references and background, and making the job offer. Keep in mind that small businesses often follow a more streamlined process.

**Applications** Many companies use written applications simply as an initial screening mechanism. Questions about education and experience will determine whether a candidate gets any further consideration. In other words, the application is primarily a tool to reject unqualified candidates, rather than to actually choose qualified candidates.

**Interviews** Virtually every company uses interviews as a central part of the selection process. In larger companies, the HR department does initial interviews and then sends qualified candidates to the hiring manager for the actual selection. The hiring manager usually recruits coworkers to participate in the process.

Although employers frequently give interviews heavy weight in hiring decisions, interviews often say surprisingly little about whether a candidate will perform on the job. Too many managers use the interview as a get-to-know-you session rather than focusing on the needs of the position. To help ensure that interviews better predict performance, experts recommend a **structured interview** process: developing a list of questions beforehand and asking the same questions to each candidate. The most effective questions are typically behavioral: they ask the candidate to describe a situation that they faced at a previous job—or a hypothetical situation at the new job—and to explain the resolution. Interviewers should gear the specific questions toward behaviors and experiences that are key for the new position. Consider the following examples of how these questions could be worded:

- Describe a time when you had to think "outside the box" to find a solution to a pressing problem.

- Describe a situation that required you to do a number of things at the same time. How did you handle it? What was the outcome?

- If you realized that a coworker was cheating on their expense report, how would you handle the situation?

- What would you do if your boss asked you to complete a key project within an unreasonable time frame?

Cultural differences also affect interview performance. As the U.S. labor pool becomes

> **"More than 70% of HR managers say that employee referral job candidates get high priority in job searches."**
>
> *—Los Angeles Times*

more diverse, even domestic companies must be aware of cultural differences. And it isn't simply a matter of legality or ethics. Firms that hire the best people regardless of cultural background will gain a critical edge in our increasingly competitive world.

Most colleges and universities offer comprehensive career services. Especially in today's competitive labor market, you would be wise to visit your career center early in your college career and use those services to prepare yourself for a smooth transition into the workforce.

**Testing** Either before or after the interview process (and sometimes at both points), a growing number of companies have instituted employment testing of various sorts. The main categories include skills testing, personality testing, drug testing, and physical exams. Skills testing and personality testing carry a fair amount of legal risk, since these tests must measure skills and aptitudes that relate directly to the job itself. Virtually 100% of Fortune 500 companies conduct pre-employment drug testing, as do most other companies. Physical exams are also standard but are highly regulated by state and federal law to ensure that firms don't use them just to screen out certain individuals.

**References and Background Checks** Even if you feel absolutely certain that a candidate is right for the job, don't skip the reference check before you make an offer. Research from the Society for Human Resource Managers suggests that more than 50% of job candidates lie on their résumé in some way. Although it may be tough to verify contributions and accomplishments at former jobs, it's pretty easy to uncover lies about education, job titles, and compensation. And it's quite worthwhile, given that the costs of bringing an unethical employee on board can be staggering. Furthermore, if you happen to hire a

> **"External hires get paid 18–20% more than staff promoted from within."**
>
> *—Matthew Bidwell,*
> *Wharton Business School*

**structured interviews**
An interviewing approach that involves developing a list of questions beforehand and asking the same questions in the same order to each candidate.

truly dangerous employee, you can open the door to negligent-hiring lawsuits for not taking "reasonable care." But surprisingly—despite the high risk—employment expert James Challenger estimates that only about 25% of candidates are thoroughly vetted by the companies that consider them.[15]

**Job Offers** After you find the right person, the next hurdle is to design the right job offer and get your candidate to accept it. To hook an especially hot contender, you may need to get creative. A phone call from top management, the royal treatment, and special perks go a long way, but most superb candidates also want to know in very specific terms how their contributions would affect the business. And no matter how excited you are about your candidate, be certain to establish a **probationary period** up front. This means a specific time frame (typically three to six months) during which a new hire can prove their worth on the job. If everything works out, the employee will move from conditional to permanent status; if not, the company can fire the employee fairly easily.

**Contingent Workers** Companies that experience a fluctuating need for workers sometimes opt to hire **contingent workers**—or employees who don't expect regular, full-time jobs—rather than permanent, full-time workers. Specifically, contingent employees include temporary full-time workers, independent contractors, on-call workers, and temporary agency or contract agency workers. As a group, contingent workers account for more than a third of U.S. employment.[16]

Employers appreciate contingent workers because they offer flexibility, which can lead to much lower costs. But the hidden downside can be workers who are less committed and less experienced. Too much reliance on contingent workers could unwittingly sabotage company productivity and the customer experience. Also, contingency workers tend to suffer from significantly higher poverty rates, mostly because they are typically paid less than standard full-time workers, but also because they are more than three times as likely to be laid off when times are tough.[17]

### 15-4c Training and Development: Honing the Competitive Edge

For successful companies in virtually every field, training and development have become an ongoing process

**probationary period** A specific time frame (typically three to six months) during which a new hire can prove their worth on the job before they become permanent.

**contingent workers** Employees who do not expect regular, full-time jobs, including temporary full-time workers, independent contractors, and temporary agency or contract agency workers.

rather than a one-time activity. Retraining and "upskilling" the workforce has gained particular urgency in light of the inexorable advances of artificial intelligence. Analysts suggest that by 2030, as many as 325 million, or roughly 14% of the global workforce, may need to switch occupations. This change is as profound as the large-scale shift from agricultural to manufacturing work that occurred in North America and Europe in the early nineteenth century.[18]

Even in a recession, training and development must gather speed for companies and individuals to maintain their competitive edge. Experts offer five key reasons that relate directly to a healthy bottom line:

1. Increased innovation in strategies and products

2. Increased ability to adopt new technologies

3. Increased efficiency and productivity

4. Increased employee motivation and lower employee turnover

5. Decreased liability (e.g., sexual harassment lawsuits)

Training programs take a number of different forms, from orientation to skills training, to management development, depending on the specific employee and the needs of the organization.

**Orientation** Once you hire new employees, **orientation** should be the first step in the training and development process. Effective orientation programs typically focus on introducing employees to the company culture (but without sacrificing need-to-know administrative information). Research consistently shows that strong orientation programs significantly reduce employee turnover, which lowers costs.

The Boeing aerospace company has mastered the art of employee orientation. Boeing Military Aircraft and Missile Systems revamped its orientation process to include mentoring, meetings with senior executives, and an after-work social program. One highlight of the orientation—meant to crystallize the "wow" factor of working at Boeing—is the chance to take the controls of an F/A-18 fighter plane flight simulator. Management rightfully sees the program as a chance to develop "future leaders . . . the ones who will make sure that Boeing continues to be a great place to work."[19]

**On-the-Job Training** On-the-job training is popular because it's very low-cost. Employees simply begin their jobs—sometimes under the guidance of more experienced employees—and learn as they go. For simple jobs, this can make sense, but simple jobs are disappearing from the U.S. market due to the combined impact of offshoring and technology. On-the-job training can also compromise the customer experience. Have you ever waited much too long in a short line at the grocery store because the clerk

On-the-job training often works best for relatively simple jobs.

couldn't figure out how to use the cash register? Multiplied across hundreds of customers, this kind of experience undermines the value of a company's brand.

Formal apprenticeship programs tend to be a more effective way of handling on-the-job training. **Apprenticeship** programs mandate that each beginner serve as an assistant to a fully trained worker for a specified period of time before gaining full credentials to work in the field. In the United States, apprenticeships are fairly common in trades such as plumbing and bricklaying. But in Europe, apprenticeships are much more common across a wide range of professionals, from bankers to opticians.

**Off-the-Job Training** Classroom training happens away from the job setting but typically during work hours. Employers use classroom training—either on-site or off-site—to teach a wide variety of topics from new computer programming languages, to negotiation skills, to stress management, and more. Going one step further than classroom training, some employers train workers off-site on "real" equipment (e.g., robots) similar to what they would actually use on the job. This approach is called "vestibule training." Police academies often use vestibule training for firearms. Job simulation

**orientation** The first step in the training and development process, designed to introduce employees to the company culture and provide key administrative information.

**on-the-job training** A training approach that requires employees to simply begin their jobs—sometimes guided by more experienced employees—and to learn as they go.

**apprenticeships** Structured training programs that mandate that each beginner serve as an assistant to a fully trained worker before gaining full credentials to work in the field.

goes even further than vestibule training, by attempting to duplicate the exact conditions that the trainee will face on the job. This approach makes sense for complex, high-risk positions such as astronaut or airline pilot.

**Computer-Based Training** Computer-based training—mostly delivered via the Web—now plays a crucial role in off-the-job training. Broadband technology has turbocharged audio and visual capabilities, which support engaging and interactive online training programs. Online training also standardizes the presentation of the material, since it doesn't depend on the quality of the individual instructor. And the Web helps employers train employees wherever they may be in the world, at their own pace and convenience. But there is a key drawback: it takes a lot of discipline to complete an online program, and some people simply learn better through direct human interaction.

**Management Development** As the bulk of top-level U.S. executives move toward retirement (or lose their jobs in the recession), developing new leaders has become a priority in many organizations. **Management development** programs help current and potential executives develop the skills they need to move into leadership positions. These programs typically cover specific issues that the business faces but also less-tangible—yet equally important—topics, such as communication, planning, business-analysis, change-management, coaching, and team-building skills.

### 15-4d Evaluation: Assessing Employee Performance

Straightforward, frequent feedback is a powerful tool to improve employee performance. The best managers provide informal feedback on a constant basis so that employees always know where they stand. But most companies also require that managers give formal feedback through periodic **performance appraisals**, usually every six months or once a year. Typically, managers conduct the appraisals by sitting down with each employee on a one-to-one basis and comparing actual results to expected results. The performance appraisal affects decisions regarding compensation, promotions, training, transfers, and terminations.

> **management development**
> Programs to help current and potential executives develop the skills they need to move into leadership positions.

> **performance appraisal** A formal feedback process that requires managers to give their subordinates feedback on a one-to-one basis, typically by comparing actual results to expected results.

The HR role in performance appraisals begins with the strategic process of creating evaluation tools that tie directly into the company's big-picture objectives. Then, on a day-to-day basis, HR coordinates the actual appraisal process, which typically involves volumes of paperwork. HR must also ensure that managers are trained in providing relevant, honest, objective feedback, and that workers at every level know how to respond if they believe their appraisal is not fair.

Both giving and receiving evaluations tend to be awkward for everyone involved, and unfortunately, uncomfortable people tend to make mistakes. As you read the following list, you'll probably find that you've been on the receiving end of at least a couple of the most common appraisal goofs.

1. **Gotcha!** Too many managers use the performance appraisal as a chance to catch employees doing something wrong rather than doing something right.

2. **The Once-a-Year Wonder** Many companies mandate annual reviews, but some managers use that as an excuse to give feedback only once a year.

3. **Straight from the Gut** Although "gut feel" can have real value, it's no substitute for honest, relevant documentation of both expectations and accomplishments.

4. **What Have You Done for Me Lately?** Many managers give far too much weight to recent accomplishments, discounting the early part of the review period.

5. **The "Me Filter"** While appraisals are a bit subjective by their very nature, some managers filter every comment through their personal biases. Here are some examples:

   ■ **Positive Leniency:** "I'm nice, so I give everyone great scores."

- **Negative Leniency:** "I have high expectations, so I give everyone low scores."

- **Halo Effect:** "I like this employee, so I'll give them top scores across the board."

For a performance appraisal to be effective, the manager must focus on fairness, relevance, objectivity, and balance. Equally important, the manager should give feedback on a continual basis to eliminate surprises and maximize performance.

### 15-4e Compensation: Show Me the Money

The term **compensation** covers both pay and benefits, but when most people think about compensation, they think about cash. Yet your paycheck is only part of the picture. Many companies also offer noncash benefits such as healthcare, which can be worth up to 30% of each employee's pay. Researching, designing, and managing effective compensation systems are core HR functions.

From a company perspective, compensation—both cash and noncash—represents a big chunk of product costs, especially in labor-intensive businesses such as banks, restaurants, and airlines. Although many firms opt to cut labor costs as far as possible, others boost compensation above the norm to find and keep the best workers. In fact, research suggests that companies offering higher-than-average compensation generally outperform their competitors in terms of total return to shareholders—both stock price and dividend payouts.[20]

Regarding specific individuals and positions, companies typically base compensation on a balance of the following factors:

- **Competition:** How much do competing firms offer for similar positions?

- **Contribution:** How much does a specific person contribute to the bottom line?

- **Ability to Pay:** How much can the company afford?

- **Cost of Living:** What would be reasonable in light of the broader local economy?

- **Legislation:** What does the government mandate?

The most common compensation systems in the United States are wages and salaries. **Wages** refer to pay in exchange for the number of hours or days that an employee works. Variations can be huge, starting at the federal minimum wage of $7.25 per hour (as of June 2021) and ranging up to more than $50 per hour. Jobs that require less education—such as flipping burgers—typically pay hourly wages. Federal law requires companies to pay nonexempt wage earners overtime, 50% more than their standard wage, for every hour worked over 40 hours per week.

| Exhibit 15.3 | Performance Pay Options |
| --- | --- |
| **Variable Pay System** | **Description** |
| *Commission* | Commission involves payment as a percentage of sales. Usually, larger commissions go with smaller base pay. |
| *Bonuses* | Bonuses are lump-sum payments, typically to reward strong performance from individual employees. |
| *Profit Sharing* | Profit-sharing plans reward employees with a share of company profits above and beyond predetermined goals. |
| *Stock Options* | Stock options are the right to buy shares of company stock at some future date for the price of the shares on the day that the company awarded the options. |
| *Pay for Knowledge* | This approach involves awarding bonuses and pay increases in exchange for increases in knowledge such as earning an MBA. |

**Salaries**, on the other hand, cover a fixed period, most often weekly or monthly. Most professional, administrative, and managerial jobs pay salaries. While salaries are usually higher than wages, salaried workers do not qualify for overtime, which means that sometimes a low-level manager's overall pay may be less than the pay of wage-based employees who work for that manager.

**Pay for Performance** In addition to wages and salaries, many organizations link some amount of worker pay directly to performance. The idea is to motivate employees to excel. Exhibit 15.3 lists some common approaches.

As you look over the range of variable pay options, which would you find most motivating? Why? What type of business might use each form of variable pay? Why?

### 15-4f Benefits: From Birthday Cakes to Death Benefits

**Benefits** represent a significant chunk of money for employers, but for many years, workers took benefits for granted. No longer. As the unemployment rate skyrocketed in 2009, employees began to appreciate their benefits more

**compensation** The combination of pay and benefits that employees receive in exchange for their work.

**wages** The pay that employees receive in exchange for the number of hours or days that they work.

**salaries** The pay that employees receive over a fixed period, most often weekly or monthly.

**benefits** Noncash compensation, including programs such as health insurance, vacation, and childcare.

# Won't Work for Coffee...

As the economy roared back to life in the wake of the COVID-19 pandemic, beleaguered restaurant and retail employees began quitting their jobs in record numbers. The quit rate hit 5.6% in April, 2021, a record high for the food service and accommodations sector. According to *Business Insider*, the final straw for one Starbucks employee was realizing that the prices of the fancy coffees she sold were getting uncomfortably close to her hourly wage. It took her a "literal day" to find a better job. A significant chunk of retail and food service workers took the opportunity of the booming labor market to move into completely different fields such as non-customer-facing warehouse jobs. Between low pay and difficult customers, it's hard to blame them. A Service Employees International Union survey of 4,187 McDonald's workers in the summer of 2020 found that nearly half of respondents said that they had been physically or verbally assaulted. Some businesses responded to the labor crunch by offering perks, benefits, and bonuses to potential employees to get them in the door for interviews.

Others, such as Chipotle, raised wages to attract and retain workers. Flipping burgers and pouring coffee may finally get the respect they deserve.[21]

Rawpixel.com/Shutterstock.com

than ever, recognizing that healthcare, dental care, paid sick days, retirement plans, and other perks add enormous value to their paychecks—and can be yanked at the discretion of their employer.[22]

In fact, a number of budget-minded employers already stick to the legally mandated basics: Social Security and Medicare contributions, payments to state unemployment and workers' compensation programs, and job protection per the Federal Family and Medical Leave Act. However, socially responsible employers—and companies that seek a competitive advantage through a top-notch workforce—tend to offer far more. Optional benefits usually include some or all of the following:

- Paid vacation days and holidays
- Paid sick days
- Health insurance
- Retirement programs
- Product discounts

A smaller number of companies also offer less traditional benefits such as backup childcare options, free massage, pet health insurance, tuition reimbursement, and paid time off for volunteering. During tight economic times, companies that offer "extras" focus extra attention on perks that boost morale without an outrageous price tag.[23]

In the past decade, a growing number of companies have begun to offer **cafeteria-style benefits**. This approach involves giving their employees a set dollar amount per person that they must spend on company benefits. The key to these plans is choice, which allows employees to tailor their benefits to their individual needs.

Over the past couple of decades, employees across the U.S. economy have demanded more flexibility from their employers, and companies have responded. Flexible scheduling options include flextime, remote work, and job-sharing plans, discussed in detail below.

**Flextime** A **flextime** plan gives workers some degree of freedom in terms of when they start and finish their workday, as long as they complete the required number of hours. Typically, companies with flextime scheduling oblige their employees to start work between mandated hours in the morning—say, anytime between 7 A.M. and 10 A.M.—to take lunch between certain hours in the middle of the day, and to complete work at the end of eight hours. This approach ensures that everyone is present during core hours for communication and coordination, but it provides choice outside those parameters. Flextime tends to increase employee

**cafeteria-style benefits**
An approach to employee benefits that gives all employees a set dollar amount that they must spend on company benefits, allocated however they wish within broad limitations.

**flextime** A scheduling option that allows workers to choose when they start and finish their workdays, as long as they complete the required number of hours.

morale and retention, but it makes less sense in jobs that entail extensive teamwork and customer interaction. It also requires careful management to avoid abuse.

The **compressed workweek**, another version of flextime scheduling, allows employees to work a full-time number of hours in less than the standard workweek. The most popular option is to work four ten-hour days rather than five eight-hour days. Major companies, such as Intel, have developed successful compressed workweek programs at a number of their facilities.

**Remote Work**  Booming technological advances make it possible for many employees to "commute" to the office via phones, videoconferencing, and broadband networks. The global business community underwent a massive experiment with **remote work** when economies around the world shut down in response to the COVID-19 pandemic in 2020, and all but essential workers began working remotely. Remote work offers both benefits and drawbacks to employees and employers alike, as you'll see in Exhibit 15.4 below. As the pandemic subsided, research from Stanford University suggested that more than 70% of organizations were looking for the best of both worlds by planning for some type of hybrid work plan, giving employees the autonomy to choose the environment that's best for them. But this may not be the straightforward answer it initially sounds like. Those requesting to work from home—who tend to be women with children—have a 50% lower chance of promotion than their office-based colleagues.[24]

In addition to the benefits listed in the exhibit, remote work offers benefits to society. Research suggests that if every American worker who *could* work remotely did so just half the time, the nation would save almost 90,000 people from traffic-related injury or death. Accident-related costs would be reduced by more than $10 billion a year. And greenhouse gases would decrease by 54 million tons—the equivalent of taking almost 10 million cars (the entire New York State workforce) off the road for a year.[25]

**Job Sharing**  Job sharing allows two or more employees to share a single full-time job. Typically, job-share participants split the salary equally, but they often need to allocate full benefits to just one of the partners. On a nationwide basis, at least 22% of employers (e.g., American Express, PricewaterhouseCoopers, and some departments of the U.S. federal government) offer job-sharing programs and reap the benefits such as higher morale and better retention.[26]

## 15-4g Separation: Breaking Up Is Hard to Do

Employees leave jobs for a number of different reasons. Experiencing success, they may be promoted or lured to another firm. Experiencing failure, they may be fired. Or in response to changing business needs, their employer might transfer them or lay them off. And employees also leave jobs for completely personal reasons such as family needs, retirement, or a change in career aspirations.

When companies terminate employees, they must proceed very carefully to avoid wrongful-termination lawsuits. The best protection is honesty and documentation. Employers should always document sound business reasons for termination and share those reasons with the employee.

But employees can still lose their jobs for reasons that have little or nothing

---

**compressed workweek** A version of flextime scheduling that allows employees to work a full-time number of hours in less than the standard workweek.

**remote work** Working outside a traditional office setting via telephone, videoconferencing, and broadband networks.

---

| Exhibit 15.4 | An Analysis of Remote Work | |
|---|---|---|
| | **Benefits** | **Drawbacks** |
| **Organization** | ■ Lower costs for office space, equipment, and upkeep<br>■ Higher employee productivity due to better morale, fewer sick days, and more focused performance<br>■ Access to a broader talent pool (not everyone needs to be local) | ■ Greater challenges maintaining a cohesive company culture<br>■ Greater challenges fostering teamwork<br>■ Greater challenges monitoring and managing far-flung employees |
| **Employee** | ■ Much more flexibility<br>■ Zero commute time (less gas money)<br>■ Better work–family balance<br>■ Every day is casual Friday (or even pajama day!)<br>■ Fewer office politics and other distractions | ■ Less fast-track career potential<br>■ Less influence within the organization<br>■ Weaker connection to the company culture<br>■ Isolation from the social structure at work |

Source: Flexible Hours and Telecommuting—Not the Ticket to the Top of Corporate America, Five Questions for Susan DePhillips, Workforce Management, September 2005, https://www.workforce.com/section/02 /article/24/14/66.html.

# What Your Boss REALLY Thinks of Your Tattoo

It doesn't really matter what your boss thinks of your tattoo—as long as your boss *can't see* your tattoo. But as climate change brings warmer temperatures, keeping your tattoo covered up may not always be an option, even if you are so inclined. Even in an age of relaxed attitudes about tattoos, this may pose a problem in the mainstream workplace. About 30% of college graduates (and 47% of millennials) sport at least one tattoo. However, 37% of HR managers cite tattoos as the third most likely physical attribute to limit career potential (behind bad breath and non-traditional piercings). There are currently no laws protecting people with tattoos from discrimination in the hiring process, but it's not all bad news if you're forced (or you choose) to show your ink. A number of top companies are known for being tattoo friendly, including Whole Foods, Google,

Trader Joe's, Target, Home Depot, and Barnes & Noble. Ninety-four percent of people with tattoos would hire someone with tattoos, so as ink becomes more common in the workplace, tattoo-based discrimination may soon be a thing of the past.[27]

FXQuadro/Shutterstock.com

---

to do with their individual performance. In response to the COVID-19 pandemic, unemployment hit a sudden, unexpected high of 14.8% in April 2020, remaining at a relatively high 6.1% a year later. About half of those who remained unemployed were pessimistic about finding a job and about two-thirds had seriously considered changing their occupation or field of work. As companies have become leaner, the remaining workers have experienced enormous stress. Managers can mitigate the trauma most effectively by showing empathy and concern for their employees, and by treating any laid-off employees with visible compassion.[28]

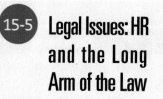 **15-5** Legal Issues: HR and the Long Arm of the Law

Even when the company is right—even when the company wins—employment lawsuits can cost millions of dollars and deeply damage the reputation of an organization, as we briefly discussed earlier in this chapter. To avoid employment lawsuits, most firms rely on HR

to digest the complex, evolving web of employment legislation and court decisions, and to ensure that management understands the key issues.

The bottom-line goal of most employment legislation is to protect employees from unfair treatment by employers. Some would argue that the legislation goes so far that it hinders the ability of companies to grow. But regardless of your personal perspective, the obligation of an ethical employer is to understand and abide by the law as it stands—even if you're working within the system to change it.

The most influential piece of employment law may be the **Civil Rights Act of 1964**. **Title VII** of this act—which applies only to employers with 15 or more workers—outlaws discrimination in hiring, firing, compensation, apprenticeships, training, terms, conditions, or privileges of employment based on race, color, religion, sex, or national origin. Over time, Congress has supplemented Title VII with legislation that prohibits discrimination based on pregnancy, age (40+), and disability.

Title VII also created the **Equal Employment Opportunity Commission (EEOC)** to enforce its provisions. And in 1972, Congress beefed up the EEOC with additional powers to regulate and to enforce its mandates, making the EEOC a powerful force in the human resources realm.

Here are some additional key pieces of employment legislation:

- **Fair Labor Standards Act of 1938:** Established a minimum wage and overtime pay for employees working more than 40 hours a week.

---

**Civil Rights Act of 1964** Federal legislation that prohibits discrimination in hiring, firing, compensation, apprenticeships, training, terms, conditions, or privileges of employment based on race, color, religion, sex, or national origin.

**Title VII** A portion of the Civil Rights Act of 1964 that prohibits discrimination in hiring, firing, compensation, apprenticeships, training, terms, conditions, or privileges of employment based on race, color, religion, sex, or national origin for employers with 15 or more workers.

**Equal Employment Opportunity Commission (EEOC)** A federal agency designed to regulate and enforce the provisions of Title VII.

- **Equal Pay Act of 1963:** Mandated that men and women doing equal jobs receive equal pay.

- **Occupational Safety and Health Act of 1970:** Required safety equipment for employees and established maximum exposure limits for hazardous substances.

- **Immigration Reform and Control Act of 1986:** Required employers to verify employment eligibility for all new hires.

- **Americans with Disabilities Act of 1990:** Prohibited discrimination in hiring, promotion, and compensation against people with disabilities and required employers to make "reasonable" accommodations for them.

- **Family and Medical Leave Act of 1993:** Required firms with 50 or more employees to provide up to 12 weeks of job-secure, unpaid leave on the birth or adoption of a child or the serious illness of a spouse, child, or parent.

### 15-5a Affirmative Action: The Active Pursuit of Equal Opportunity

The term **affirmative action** refers to policies meant to increase employment and educational opportunities for historically marginalized groups—especially groups defined by race, ethnicity, or gender. Emerging during the American civil rights movement in the 1960s, affirmative action seeks to make up for the systematic discrimination of the past by creating more opportunities in the present.

Over the past couple of decades, affirmative action has become increasingly controversial. Opponents have raised concerns that giving preferential treatment to some groups amounts to "reverse discrimination" against groups who do not get the same benefits. They claim that affirmative action violates the principle that all individuals are equal under the law. But supporters counter that everyone who benefits from affirmative action must—by law—have relevant and valid qualifications. They argue that proactive measures are the only workable way to right past wrongs and to ensure truly equal opportunity.

> ## About 12 workers are killed on the job in the United States every day.
>
> —Occupational Safety and Health Administration

Recent U.S. Supreme Court decisions have supported affirmative action, pointing out that government has a "compelling interest" in ensuring racial diversity. But the Court has rejected "mechanistic" affirmative action programs that amount to quota systems based on race, ethnicity, or gender.

The long-term fate of affirmative action remains unclear, but achieving the underlying goal—a diverse workplace with equal opportunity for all—stands to benefit both business and society as a whole.

### 15-5b Sexual Harassment: Eliminating Hostility

**Sexual harassment**—which violates Title VII of the Civil Rights Act of 1964—involves discrimination against a person based on their gender. According to the EEOC, sexual harassment can range from requests for sexual favors to the presence of a hostile work environment. The EEOC also points out that a sexual harasser may be of any gender, and the harasser doesn't need to be the victim's supervisor. The victim could be anyone affected—either directly or indirectly—by the offensive conduct. And clearly, to qualify as sexual harassment, the conduct must be unwelcome. The total number of sexual harassment charges filed with the EEOC in the past decade has stayed relatively steady. Interestingly, the percentage of charges filed by men has also stayed relatively steady at just over 16%.[29]

Not just the perpetrator is liable for sexual harassment; employers may share accountability if they did not take "reasonable care" to prevent and correct sexually harassing behavior, or if they did not provide a workable system for employee complaints. Simply adopting a written policy against sexual harassment is not enough. Taking "reasonable care" also means taking proactive steps—such as comprehensive training—to ensure that everyone in the organization understands (1) that the firm does not tolerate sexual harassment and (2) that the firm has a system in place for complaints and will not tolerate retaliation against those who complain.[30]

The #MeToo movement in late 2017 highlighted the unfortunate prevalence of sexual harassment and assault in the workplace, and human resources is the first line of defense. Handling sexual harassment complaints can be especially thorny for human resources, particularly on behalf of younger workers—since the conventional understanding of sexual harassment does not typically match the legal definition of sexual harassment.

**affirmative action** Policies meant to increase employment and educational opportunities for historically marginalized groups—especially groups defined by race, ethnicity, or gender.

**sexual harassment** Workplace discrimination against a person based on their gender.

## 15-6 Diversity in Contemporary Business

In the spring and summer of 2020, a series of high-profile unjust shootings of Black people fueled a heightened national awareness of systemic racism; a number of U.S. businesses responded by examining their policies and products in an effort to root out racism. The efforts were especially clear in human resources. A couple of prominent examples:

■ **Starbucks:** In 2020, Starbucks hired their first chief inclusion and diversity officer, Nzinga "Zing" Shaw, and committed $1 million in Neighborhood Grants to promote racial equity and create more inclusive and just communities.[31]

■ **Pfizer:** In 2021, Pfizer created a new position of Global Chief Diversity, Equity, and Inclusion (DEI) Officer, and hired Ramcess Jean-Louis, Esq. to make sure that Pfizer "continues to enhance the type of culture where every person is seen, heard, and cared for."[32]

According to Yolanda Conyers, Chief Diversity Officer at Lenovo, the question for Human Resources now needs to be: "How do you create a sense of belonging, an environment of respect, so that you can really tap into those skills and experiences that diversity brings to a company?" Businesses that answer that question effectively will ultimately leverage deeper talent pools and gain access to a broader range of markets.[33]

## The Big Picture

Effective human resource management can create an unbeatable competitive edge—a fair, productive, empowering workplace pays off in bottom-line results. In good times, one core HRM goal is to find, hire, and develop the best talent. While that function remains crucial in tough economic times, the focus changes to managing HR costs while maintaining morale. Looking forward, a growing number of firms will most likely outsource traditional HR tasks such as payroll and benefits administration to companies that specialize in these areas. HR departments could then focus on their core mission: working with senior management to achieve business goals by cultivating the firm's investment in human resources.

## Careers in Human Resources

### Human Resources Manager

Plan, organize, lead, and coordinate the personnel, or labor relations activities of an organization. Identify staff vacancies and recruit, interview, and select applicants, ensuring a strong match between personnel and positions. Establish, maintain, and implement a competitive pay and benefit structure, and ensure that policies remain in compliance with federal, state, and local laws. Establish and conduct employee orientation and training programs. Provide current and prospective employees with information about company policies, pay, benefits, and promotional opportunities. Counsel and coach management as necessary on human resources issues. Maintain accurate human resources records. Keep current regarding professional and technical knowledge.

# 16 | Managing Information and Technology:
## Finding New Ways to Learn and Link

**Learning Objectives**

After studying this chapter, you will be able to:

**16-1** Describe the basic elements of computer technology—including hardware, software, and networks—and key trends in each area

**16-2** Discuss the reasons for the increasing popularity of cloud computing

**16-3** Describe how data become information and how decision support systems can provide high-quality information that helps managers make better decisions

**16-4** Explain how internet-based technologies have changed business-to-consumer and business-to-business commerce

**16-5** Describe the problems posed by the rapid changes in internet-based technologies and the ways to address these problems

FrameStockFootages/Shutterstock.com

## 16-1 Information Technology: Explosive Change

Over the last 75 years, computer and communications hardware and software have changed dramatically. Hardware capabilities have increased by orders of magnitude. In the late 1950s, for example, you would have needed fifty 24-inch disks—costing tens of thousands of dollars—to store just 5 megabytes of data. Today you can buy a flash memory device, about the same size as a postage stamp, which stores 256 gigabytes of data for under $40—over 51,000 times more than that entire 1950s disk array. And in terms of processing power and performance, consider Apple's new M1 chip (adapted from the Bionic chips used in iPads), which delivers 11 trillion mathematical operations per second. Apple's $1,300 M1 MacBook Pro (MBP) laptops are three times faster and use 75% less power than MBPs using PC-based chips made by Intel. The battery life of M1-based MBPs has doubled to 16 hours and their chip speed and graphics performance match those

found on $10,000 Mac pros using high-end graphics cards and Intel's fastest desktop chips.[1] This much computing power has never been available to the average computer user at so little cost. And while more difficult to quantify with specific statistics, it's also clear that software has become more powerful, more flexible, and easier to use.

Perhaps an even more important development than more powerful hardware and software is the degree to which today's technology is linked by high-speed networks. These networks allow businesses to coordinate internal functions, reach customers, and collaborate with suppliers and partners in ways that could not have been envisioned a

quarter of a century ago. Networks have not only improved the efficiency and effectiveness of existing businesses, but they've also opened up entirely new business opportunities. Do-it-yourselfers, independent auto repair shops, and restorers of older cars have long turned to local junk yards to find cheaper auto parts or parts for older cars that are no longer made. Exponential increases in broadband internet speeds, however, allowed New Jersey–based Copart to become a global, billion-dollar "junk yard." As described by *Forbes'* Giacomo Tognini, "This is no ordinary junkyard. Everything is coordinated electronically: The forklift drivers follow a meticulous schedule laid out on a tablet. Each [junked] car, be it a lightly battered BMW or a totaled Toyota, has a numerical code on the windshield so it can be digitally identified, inventoried, and then moved to its corresponding spot in the sales area. In the squat, one-story building out front, customers who bought a vehicle online wait to pick up their newly purchased wreck after scanning a QR code on their phones."[2] As CEO Jay Adair says, "We took a relatively unsophisticated business where they were selling cars over an [in-person] oral auction, and turned that into a business that receives a hundred billion dollars a year in bids and is doing 100% of it online."[3] Company founder Willis Johnson said, "Nobody has to be at our yard. When we're having an auction online, it doesn't matter if Florida is having a tornado; we're selling cars."[4] Auto industry analyst Craig Kennison explains that "Once Copart moved onto the internet, they were able to discover a massive number of buyers… And now it's at a global scale where they have buyers literally all over the world."[5]

Of course, global high-speed networks pose challenges and threats as well as benefits and opportunities. Fifty years ago, computer users, whose machines were *not* connected to any networks, didn't have to contend with computer viruses, spyware, phishing, ransomware, or spam (except for the Hormel meat product variety). Over the course of this chapter, we'll take a look at both sides of this rapidly changing story.

### 16-1a  Hardware and Software

**Hardware** refers to the physical components used to collect, input, store, and process data, and to display and distribute information. This hardware includes the various components of a computer system as well as communications and network equipment. Examples include barcode scanners, hard drives, printers, routers, and smartphones.

**Software** refers to the programs that provide instructions to a computer so that it can perform a desired task. There are two broad categories of software: system software and application software. Both types of software have used the tremendous increase in hardware capabilities to become more powerful and easier to use.

**System software** performs the critical functions necessary to operate a computer at the most basic level. The fundamental form of system software is the operating system which controls the overall operation of the computer, such as Windows, Mac OS, and Linux for computers, or iOS or Android for smartphones and tablets. Operating system software implements vital tasks, such

as managing the file system, reading programs and data into main memory, and allocating system memory among various tasks to avoid conflicts. And unlike in the past where users paid for significant annual or generational upgrades to systems software, today those upgrades are usually free for individuals (Microsoft charges businesses for system software upgrades). But that wasn't always the case. Apple, for example, charged $129 for operating system upgrades, and then dropped the price to $29 and $19 before making annual upgrades free in 2013.[6]

Operating system software also provides the interface that enables users to interact with their computers. Early operating systems required users to type complex commands with very precise syntax to carry out tasks such as running programs or opening, saving, or deleting files. For example, to copy a file to another directory (what we call "folders"), you might type:

c:\>  copy  c:\documents\research\cats1.doc  c:\websites\writing\cats1.doc

This copies the cats1.doc from the "research" subfolder in your "documents folder" to the "writing" subfolder in the "websites" folder. If you made a typing error, which was common, your computer would just sit there until you typed the command, the folder structures, and file names correctly. Today's operating systems use *graphical user interface* (or GUI—pronounced "gooey") where clicking or tapping application icons, dragging file icons from one folder to another, or clicking application menus is much simpler, faster, and more intuitive.

Utility programs supplement operating system software in ways that increase the security or abilities of the computer system. Examples include firewalls, antivirus software, and antispyware programs. Over the years, operating systems have incorporated many features that were originally provided by utility programs, such as the Windows Defender for malware and viruses or MacOS Filevault for securely encrypting the contents of your hard drive.

**Applications software** is software that helps users perform a desired task. Horizontal applications software, such as word processing, spreadsheet, and personal information management software, is used by many different businesses and occupations. Vertical application software is designed for specific industries or professions. For example, Dealertrack is vertical application software for automobile dealers. Dealertrack handles digital processing of new car and traded-in titles, in- and out-of-state auto registrations, digital marketing and retailing, and business issues such as managing costs, reducing employee turnover, and maximizing profits. It also helps dealers by automating and tracking the procedures used to secure

**hardware** The physical tools and equipment used to collect, input, store, organize, and process data and to distribute information.

**software** Programs that provide instructions to a computer so that it can perform a desired task.

**system software** Software that performs the critical functions necessary to operate the computer at the most basic level.

**applications software** Software that helps a user perform a desired task.

approval for customers' auto loans. Dealertrack's "live funding checklist" ensures all forms are completed properly, starting with credit checks and ending with digital signing of loan documents.[7]

## 16-1b Networks

Today, most firms (and households) use networks that allow users to communicate with each other and share both files and hardware resources. A network links computer resources, using either a wired or wireless connection. Firms usually want to prevent outsiders from obtaining access to their networks for privacy and security reasons, but they sometimes allow customers or suppliers partial access to their private networks to strengthen their relationships with these important stakeholders.

**The Internet and the World Wide Web** The development and growth of the **internet** is one of the great networking stories of the past three decades. The internet is often referred to as the world's largest computer network. It's actually a network of networks, consisting of hundreds of thousands of smaller networks operating under a common set of protocols (rules) so that they can communicate with each other.

One common way to experience the internet is through the World Wide Web. But while the internet supports the web and provides access to it, only about 6.6% of the global traffic on the internet involves the web. Still, the web is an incredibly rich environment of 5.45+ billion indexed pages of documents written and linked together using Hypertext Markup Language (HTML).[8] Video streaming (57.6%) like Netflix, Amazon Prime, Disney+, Hulu, YouTube, and TikTok, social networking (10.7%) like Facebook, marketplaces (5%) like eBay, messaging (4.9%) like WhatsApp, file sharing (4.6%) like Dropbox, video games (4.2%) like Xbox, PlayStation, and mobile gaming account for 95% of global internet traffic. The apps/services using the most data on the internet are YouTube, which accounts for 15% of all global network traffic, followed by Netflix at 11%.[9]

The increased availability of broadband and wireless internet connections have fueled the popularity of internet applications. A **broadband internet connection** has the capacity to transmit large amounts of data very quickly, allowing users to quickly download large files such as music, games, and movies. A survey by the Pew Research Center, summarized in Exhibit 16.1, found that access to broadband internet connections grew rapidly over the last two decades. As Exhibit 16.1 shows, only 1% of American adults had access to high-speed internet at home in 2000, but by 2019 that figure had climbed to 73%.[10] Exhibit 16.1 also shows that while 96% of Americans have cell phones, 84% now have smartphones with fast cellular internet service, up from 33% in 2011.[11] Smartphones are likely why growth in home broadband has leveled off. Thirty-seven percent of U.S. adults primarily use their smartphones when accessing the internet, up from 19% in 2013. Forty-five percent of those without home broadband say they don't need it because they can do everything they need to do online with their smartphones. Finally, 80% of those without home broadband aren't interested in getting it. Growing access to 5G service for smartphones may make home broadband even less attractive to those who don't have it, given that in daily use 5G is 5x to 10x faster than 4G and as fast (and perhaps faster) than WiFi powered by basic broadband.[12]

From a business perspective, the growth in high-speed internet access via broadband, smartphones, and now 5G allows companies to offer richer, more interactive experiences to customers who visit their websites or use their apps, no matter where they're located.

But even today's broadband connections are too slow and inefficient for some data-intensive business and scientific applications. Beginning in 1996, several leading research universities, corporations, and other organizations formed a coalition to create a new generation of internet technology in the United States based on fiber-optic cable. The

**internet** The world's largest computer network; essentially a network of computer networks all operating under a common set of rules that allow them to communicate with each other.

**broadband internet connection** An internet connection that is capable of transmitting large amounts of information very quickly.

## Exhibit 16.1
## Growth in Broadband and Smartphone Internet Access

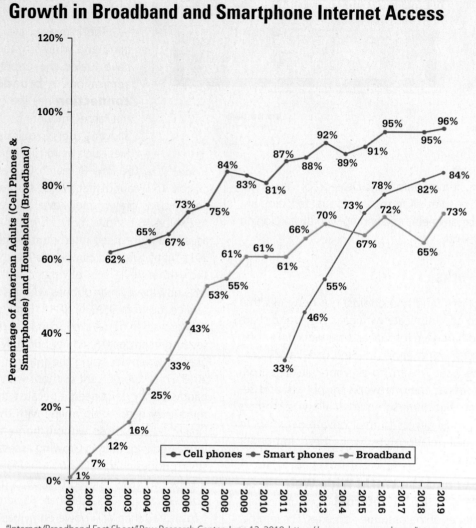

"Internet/Broadband Fact Sheet," Pew Research Center, June 12, 2019, https://www.pewresearch.org/internet/fact-sheet/internet-broadband/, accessed February 20, 2021; M. Anderson, "Mobile Technology and Home Broadband 2019," Pew Research Center, June 13, 2019, https://www.pewresearch.org/internet/2019/06/13/mobile-technology-and-home-broadband-2019/, accessed February 20, 2021.

resulting network became known as **internet2** (or "**I2**"). Today, I2 can reliably deliver internet speeds between 10 and 100 gigabits per second, which is at least 100 to 1,000 times faster than standard broadband.[13]

Today the I2 consortium consists of over 320 major universities as well 56 leading high-tech corporations, 60 government agencies, 44 regional and state networks, and research and educational networks in 100+ countries.[14] But under an initiative begun in 2001, members of the I2 consortium can sponsor access to the network for other research and educational organizations that otherwise would be unable to qualify for membership. This initiative has given 1,000+ community institutions such as elementary schools, high schools, community colleges, libraries, and museums access to I2 resources.[15]

Internet2 isn't simply a faster way to surf the web or send email. In fact, such routine uses of the current internet

**internet2 (I2)** A new high-tech internet with access limited to a consortium of member organizations (and other organizations these members sponsor). I2 utilizes technologies that give it a speed and capacity far exceeding the current internet.

# Bots and Scalpers: Why You Couldn't Find a NextGen Videogame Console

The Sony PlayStation 5 and Microsoft Xbox Series X and S next-generation videogame consoles launched in fall 2020. Before they went on sale (only online), eager video gamers double checked or opened accounts at Sony, Microsoft, Amazon, Walmart, Target, BestBuy, and GameStop, making sure their accounts were active, their addresses were correct, and their credit card information was up-to-date.

On launch day, they logged onto those accounts in separate browser windows and preloaded the PlayStation or Xbox web pages (all showing zero inventory), doing the same on their tablets and smartphones. At the precise second sales opened, they hit reload on all of their devices… and waited. Eventually, after numerous page reloads, if they were lucky, a page opened showing an in-stock console, which they added to their cart, crossing their fingers as they clicked "buy."

Were they able to get one at launch? Probably not. Even after adding game consoles to their carts, many came away empty handed. Why? Digital robots, or bots, armed with multiple credit cards, checked hundreds of retail websites around the globe, finding and buying momentarily in-stock consoles in the blink of an eye. Cybersecurity firm Netacea found that a bot using 300 computers made 1 million tries in six hours to buy PlayStation 5s.

Could retailers have prevented this? Not really. Despite Walmart's servers blocking 20 million bot attempts in just 30 minutes, and Japanese retailer Nojima manually reviewing each order, bots bought enough consoles for the scalpers who used them to make $35 million in profit on PlayStation 5s and $24 million in profit on new Xboxes in just one month.

Can the scalper bots be beaten, or at least matched? Yes, grab the OctoShop Chrome browser extension to run your own bot. OctoShop notifies you when consoles (or other items) are in stock, automatically reloads pages, and puts the power of bots to use for regular consumers.[16]

Source: Google, Inc.

---

aren't even allowed. Instead, it is a noncommercial network that uses high-speed connectivity to improve education, research, and collaboration. Member organizations see internet2 as a way to bring together their researchers, scientists, and engineers at various locations in a way that allows real-time collaboration on complex and important topics. It also allows corporations to collaborate with other companies, universities, and organizations located thousands of miles apart. One of the missions of the internet2 consortium is to "facilitate the development, deployment, and use of revolutionary internet technologies."[17] So, the benefits of internet2 will eventually become commonplace on the internet that the rest of us use.

**Intranets and Extranets** An **intranet** is a private network that has the same look and feel as the web and uses the same web browser software to display documents, but limits access to the employees of a single firm (or members of a single organization). When properly implemented, intranets enhance communication and collaboration among employees and provide an effective way to distribute information and applications throughout the organization. Employees can usually log onto their company's intranet from remote locations using password-protected internet access, allowing them to use company resources when working on the road or from home. Exhibit 16.2 illustrates an example from Igloo Software, a leading provider of intranet software. On this screen, employees on a marketing team can find team members, communicate with them via Slack (a team communication tool), share organized notes with others using

> **intranet** A private network that has the look and feel of the internet and is navigated using a web browser, but which limits access to a single firm's employees (or a single organization's members).

## Exhibit 16.2
## Igloo Software Intranet

OneNote, see new postings or news via Recent Activity, access and share files via Dropbox, see what's coming up on the team calendar, and "publish" content to multiple digital locations (Slack, Dropbox, Microsoft 365, and Workday) with one click using "Add to digital workplace."

Firms sometimes also create **extranets** by giving key stakeholders, such as suppliers or customers, limited access to certain areas of their intranet. Extranets enable firms to provide additional services and information to their external stakeholders. For example, the firm might allow customers to check on the status of their order, or suppliers to check on the state of the firm's inventory to plan shipments of parts and materials.

### 16-1c The Role of the IT Department

Many business organizations have an information technology (IT) department to manage their information resources. But the role of this department varies significantly from one company to another. In some firms, the IT department plays a strategic role, making and implementing key decisions about the technologies the firm will use. In other organizations, the role of IT is largely operational; managers in functional departments make the key decisions about the computer and information resources their areas need, and the IT department maintains these resources and provides technical support to employees.

**extranet** An intranet that allows limited access to a selected group of stakeholders, such as suppliers or customers.

**cloud computing** The use of internet-based storage capacity, processing power, and computer applications to supplement or replace internally owned information technology resources.

### 16-2 Cloud Computing: The Sky's the Limit!

In most companies, employees have used applications and accessed data stored on their own computers or their companies' servers. But "cloud computing" is changing that approach. **Cloud computing** means using internet-based storage capacity, applications, and processing power to supplement or replace internally owned computer resources.

You're already familiar with consumer-focused cloud computing services if you backup, organize, and share your photos on Google Photos; stream music from Spotify; or use a service like Dropbox or Google Docs or Apple's iCloud to access and share documents and files. These services clearly offer significant benefits, such as the ability to store large files without taking up valuable space on your computer's hard drive and the convenience of being able to access your documents, music, and photos from anywhere via any computer or mobile device with an internet connection.

Until recently, most businesses were reluctant to embrace cloud computing, citing concerns about security and reliability. But that is quickly changing. A 2020 survey of 551 IT managers found that spending on cloud services accounted for one-third of their total IT budgets. But over the next 18 months they plan to move even more IT services to the cloud. The percentage of companies managing all of their own IT equipment and services in-house will decline from 8% to 5%. The share of firms that are mostly in-house with some cloud services will decline from 54% to 36%. Companies that are mostly cloud with some in-house equipment and services will grow from 29% to 43%. Finally, the percentage of companies that are currently all cloud will rise from 9% to 16% over the next year and a half.[18] For example, global communications company Nokia Oyj is moving all of its IT data and services to Google Cloud. Ravi Parmasad, Nokia Oyj's vice president of global IT infrastructure, said, "Every few years you have to go and invest in all of this hardware, so we get to break that cycle [by moving to Google Cloud]."[19]

And for many organizations, moving to the cloud may actually increase data security.[20]

- First, data are encrypted in the cloud *and,* then when uploaded and downloaded from the cloud.

- Second, cloud service providers automatically apply security patches and operating system updates to cloud servers, while simultaneously pushing updates to users' computers, tablets, and smartphones. Unpatched vulnerabilities, which are easily identified and compromised by hackers, are one of the biggest threats to data security.

- Third, major cloud services are much less likely to make configuration errors when setting up data storage systems. Eric Knorr, editor in chief at *InfoWorld*, says, "In defending against threats, the major clouds are much more secure than the average enterprise data center. The real issues center on proper configuration of cloud security controls, to ensure the policies and access controls codified by an organization extend to its public cloud platform."[21]

- Fourth, major cloud service providers attract and retain top cybersecurity talent. With 74% of cybersecurity professionals reporting that the long-term shortage of well-trained, experienced cybersecurity workers has prevented them from utilizing security technologies to their fullest potential, it makes more sense to rely on cloud service providers who are able to pay, train, and retain top cybersecurity talent.[22]

If you share photos on Facebook, store your music on Apple's iCloud storage services, or use Dropbox to access and share documents and files, you're already using cloud computing.

Besides greater security, the cloud offers to its users the ability to:

- Access a vast array of computing resources without the need to invest heavily in expensive new hardware, software, and IT personnel. Thomas Publishing Co., which got its start more than a century ago publishing its "big green books," provides a comprehensive registry of U.S. manufacturers. Thomas moved its data online in 2006, running its own data centers and services. But now, Thomas uses Amazon Web Services' cloud. Chief Technical Officer Hans Wald explained, "We want to be out of the business of running data centers."[23]

- Allow lower costs and excess capacity by only paying for the computer resources they need or use. When *Conde Nast*, the travel publisher, moved all of its data online, data costs dropped by 40%.[24]

- Use a wide variety of sophisticated cloud-based apps and tools that cloud services offer to clients. For example, Exhibit 16.3 shows the 26 categories of apps and tools offered on Amazon Web Services, the largest cloud provider in the world. Client companies can choose from analytics to business applications to machine learning (artificial intelligence) to robotics to VR & AR (virtual reality and augmented reality). For example, clicking on the "Front-End Web & Mobile" icon reveals more apps and tools, such as the "AWS Device Farm," to "test Android, iOS, and web apps on real devices in the AWS cloud," a

"There are only two industries that refer to their customers as 'users.'"

—Edward Tufte, Statistician

## Exhibit 16.3
## Amazon Web Services Cloud Apps and Tools

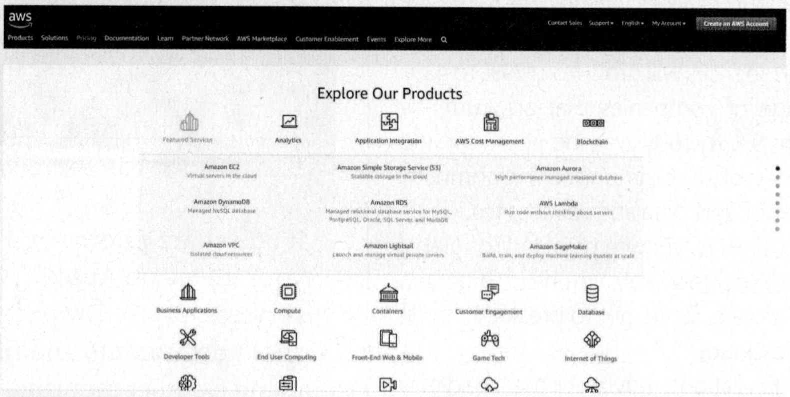

Source: Amazon Inc.

capability that most companies would want but that few could develop for themselves.[25]

■ Take advantage of incredible gains in processing speed via *massively parallel computing* that simultaneously combines the processing power of hundreds (or even thousands) of computers. By combining computing power, data processing projects can be completed in 70% to 80% less time. Online crafts e-commerce site Etsy uses Google Cloud's data analysis and machine learning to conduct "experiments" in which it compares different ways to sort product reviews or various methods of alerting customers to new products that might interest them. Chief technology officer Mike Fisher explained that because of Etsy's move to Google Cloud, "Now, our engineers can run the data, get it processed and be ready to train their models in a day or two. The speed of innovation is so much faster now."[26]

## 16-3 Information Technology and Decision Making: A Crucial Aid

One of the vital functions of information technology—at least in relationship to business—is to transform data into useful information for decision makers. In order to make decisions, managers must have information about the current state of their business, their competitive environment, and

**data** Raw, unprocessed facts and figures.

**information** Data that have been processed in a way that make them meaningful to their user.

the trends and market conditions that offer new opportunities. Where does this information come from? How can it be made more useful? How can managers process the information to make better decisions?

### 16-3a Data and Information

Let's start by distinguishing between data and information. **Data** are the facts and figures a firm collects. Data in their raw form have limited usefulness because they lack the context needed to give them meaning. For example, over the course of a lifetime you're probably treated by dozens of different medical providers, from the pediatrician who takes care of you when you're young, to specialists like cardiologists and oncologists who treat heart disease and cancer, to the gerontologist who takes care of you in your old age. The promise of electronic health records (EHRs) is that they can capture all of the data from every doctor's appointment, every medical and lab test, and every hospital stay in just one database available to all medical practitioners and organizations.

The problem with centralized EHRs, however, is they have *too much* data. Clinicians reviewing EHRs often struggle to find the relevant data they need to form a medical diagnosis and choose a proper treatment. In other words, while EHRs are bursting with data, they often lack information. Data become **information** when they are processed, organized, and presented in a way that makes them useful to a decision maker. Which is why the Mayo Clinic's Intensive Care Unit (ICU) conducted 1,500 interviews with ICU clinicians to identify the 60 pieces of information, such as blood pressure, medications, cough strength, or difficulties with previous endotracheal intubations (used in emergency situations to open airways when people can't breathe on their own), that are critical to making high pressure, split-second, life-saving decisions in ICUs. Then to make that information even more useful, they developed 1,000+ algorithmic rules that filter those 60 pieces of information down to a smaller set of the most critical, relevant information for each patient that it calls "single patient view." For example, if an ICU patient is at risk of acute bleeding, Mayo's system shows continuously monitored visual displays for changes in blood hemoglobin, platelets, and coagulation.[27] ICUs using Mayo's Ambient Warning and Response Evaluation (AWARE) system cut death rates in half and reduced the length of ICU stays by 50%, hospital stays by 37% and total hospital costs by 30%.[28] Dr. John Litell, a critical care physician at Abbott Northwestern Hospital in Minneapolis, said, "Unlike any other system I've used, AWARE shows me what I need to see, at the point of care, organized in the way that I think."[29]

Sometimes firms can obtain useful information from external sources, but sometimes they must create information by processing their own data. Given today's competitive environment, the speed with which managers obtain good-quality information can be a crucial competitive advantage.

Internally, every department of an organization generates facts and figures that the firm must store and track. Every time a financial transaction is completed, for example, the firm's accounting system must record the specific accounts affected. Similarly, a firm's human resources department must enter new data every time an employee is hired, fired, promoted, changes jobs, or retires. Firms must also keep track of the names, addresses, and credit information of each customer. This is hardly a complete list, but you get the picture; firms must store mountains of data and convert them into useful information.

Typically, today's businesses store their data in **databases**, which are files of related data organized according to a logical system and stored on hard drives or some other computer-accessible storage media. It isn't unusual for a company to have many different databases, each maintained by a different department or functional area to meet its specific needs. For example, the human resources department might have a database of employee pay rates, and the marketing department may have another database of customer history.

Once all these data are stored, the firm must convert them into information. One common method is to query a database. A query is a request for the database management software to search the database for data that match criteria specified by the user. Suppose, for instance, that a

marketing manager plans to introduce a product upgrade. She can enter a query asking for the email addresses of every customer who purchased the product in the last year and then send a targeted email message promoting the upgrade to them, because they are most likely to buy it.

### 16-3b Characteristics of Good Information

We've seen that businesses have many sources of information. But not all information is of good quality. High-quality information is:

- Accurate: It should be free of errors and biases.

- Relevant: It should focus on issues that are important to decision makers.

- Timely: It should be available in time to make a difference.

- Understandable: It must help the user grasp its meaning.

- Secure: Confidential information must be secure from hackers and competitors.

It has been standard practice for those with Type 1 diabetes to prick their fingers numerous times a day to test blood glucose levels—before meals and snacks, sometimes after meals, before exercise (and after any prolonged activity), when going to bed, and when experiencing shakiness or irregular heartbeats due to low blood sugar.[30] With extreme cases, such as 14 year-old Raynham McArthur who woke up at midnight and 3 a.m. to test the effectiveness of her insulin pump, the frequent finger pricks resulted in bloody and bruised fingers. But thanks to 14-day disposable sensors, basically coin-sized skin patches with tiny needles that continuously test and report insulin levels to smartphone apps, Raynham and her parents sleep throughout the night.[31] With accurate, relevant, timely, understandable, and secure information (the newest models have cybersecurity protections), people with Type 1 diabetes increased their time within recommended glucose ranges by 40% while reducing the time outside of recommended glucose ranges (hyperglycemia) by 44%.[32]

**database** A file consisting of related data organized according to a logical system and stored on a hard drive or some other computer-accessible media.

## 16-3c Using Information Technology to Improve Decision Making

A company's information technology (IT) department frequently works closely with managers throughout the organization to support decision making. In fact, many companies develop **decision support systems (DSS)** that give managers access to large amounts of data and the processing power to convert the data into high-quality information quickly and efficiently.

Over the past two decades, a new class of decision support system has evolved to take advantage of the dramatic increase in data storage and processing capabilities. Called **business intelligence systems**, these systems help businesses discover subtle and complex relationships hidden in their data. Such systems can be a source of competitive advantage for the businesses that develop them. Freight rail companies, which ship 40% of goods nationwide, use business intelligence systems to predict problems before they become safety issues. For example, a freight train can derail when one or more of the eight steel wheels on one of its freight cars breaks, possibly causing a massive loss of life and property. Every year, an average of 400 train wheels break, creating the possibility for 400 disasters. But with 12 million freight train wheels on 1.5 million freight rail cars in the United States, there is less than a 0.0033% chance of predicting when and where a wheel could break. Thanks to business intelligence systems, freight rail companies are frequently able to predict when a steel wheel needs fixing or replacing. As a result, the accident rate for freight trains has dropped 80% since 1980 and 45% since 2000.[33]

One of the most common approaches to implementing a business intelligence system is to create a data warehouse and use data mining to discover unknown relationships. A **data warehouse** is a very large, organization-wide database that provides a centralized location for storing data from both the organization's own databases and external

An expert system helps managers make better decisions by asking a series of questions until enough information is gathered to reach a decision.

sources. Why do companies need data warehouses? Because smart phones alone generate 18 exabytes of data each month. How big is that? An exabyte is 1,000 petabytes, which is 1,000 terabytes, which is 1,000 gigabytes. Most of us can conceptualize a gigabyte because of the gigabytes of storage on our smartphones, tablets, laptops, and gaming platforms.[34] Scott Dietzen is the former CEO and now board chair of Pure Storage, which makes data storage systems capable of holding five times more information than conventional technology. Dietzen says that the amount of data recorded today is so overwhelming that "[n]o one can look at all their data anymore; they need algorithms just to decide what to look at."[35]

**Data mining** uses powerful statistical and mathematical techniques to analyze vast amounts of data to identify useful information that had been hidden. In recent years, data mining has had considerable success in areas as diverse as fraud and crime detection and quality control and scientific research. New York City's Human Resources Administration used data mining to identify $46.5 million in fraudulent welfare claims, up 60% from before. Commissioner Steven Banks says data mining "allows us to zero in on likely fraud so we don't divert resources to finding what otherwise might be a needle in a haystack."[36]

## 16-3d Expert Systems

Managers who use decision support systems usually already know quite a bit about the problem and how they

**decision support system (DSS)** A system that gives managers access to large amounts of data and the processing power to convert these data into high-quality information, thus improving the decision-making process.

**business intelligence system** A sophisticated form of decision support system that helps decision makers discover information that was previously hidden.

**data warehouse** A large, organization-wide database that stores data in a centralized location.

**data mining** The use of sophisticated statistical and mathematical techniques to analyze vast amounts of data to discover hidden patterns and relationships, thus creating valuable information.

want to solve it. They just need access to the right data and a system to "crunch the numbers" in a way that provides relevant, accurate, and timely information to help them make their decisions. But what happens when the problem is beyond the expertise of the manager? One way to deal with this problem is to set up an **expert system (ES)** to guide the manager through the decision-making process.

To develop expert systems, programmers ask experts in the relevant area to explain how they solve problems. They then devise a program to mimic the expert's approach, incorporating various rules or guidelines that the human expert uses. The finished program will ask a user a series of questions, basing each question on the response to the previous question. The program continues to ask questions until it has enough information to reach a decision and make a recommendation. Doctors at a large New York hospital system use an expert system to help determine if a coughing patient has pneumonia. The expert system asks the doctor whether the patient "has a fever and rapid heart rate," and if the doctor hears, "a 'crackle' in the lungs."[37] High scores indicate immediate treatment, while low scores suggest pneumonia isn't the issue.

Expert systems routinely solve problems in areas as diverse as medical diagnoses, fraud detection, and consumer credit evaluation. The troubleshooting systems that many companies have on the customer-support pages of their websites are another type of expert system. If your product doesn't work, the troubleshooter will ask a series of questions designed to diagnose the problem and suggest solutions. Based on your responses to each question, the system selects the next question as it starts narrowing down the possible reasons for the problem until it identifies the cause and offers a solution. Often you can solve your problem without waiting on hold to talk to a human expert over the phone.[38]

Despite impressive results in many fields, expert systems have their limitations. Programming thousands of decision rules into the system can be time-consuming, complicated, and expensive. In fact, it's sometimes impossible because the experts themselves can't clearly explain how they make their decisions—they just "know" the answer based on their years of experience. If the experts can't clearly explain how they reach their conclusions, then programmers can't include the appropriate decision rules in the system. Finally, an expert system has little flexibility and no common sense. It probably won't be able to find a solution to a problem that deviates in any significant way from the specific type of problem it was programmed to solve.[39]

## 16-4 Information Technology and the World of E-Commerce

Advances in information technology have had dramatic and widespread effects on how companies conduct their business. But in this section of the chapter, we'll focus on one key area: the growth and development of e-commerce.

**E-commerce** refers to marketing, buying, selling, and servicing of products over a network (usually the internet). You're probably most familiar with **business-to-consumer (B2C) e-commerce**. You participate in this form of e-commerce when you order something from Amazon, use Expedia to make travel arrangements, or buy stocks through an online broker such as Charles Schwab. However, **business-to-business (B2B) e-commerce**, which consists of markets where businesses sell supplies, components, machinery, equipment, or services to other businesses, actually accounts for a much larger volume of e-commerce.

While both B2C and B2B involve exchanging goods over the internet, they differ in some important ways, as shown in Exhibit 16.4. Given these structural differences, it isn't surprising that the two markets operate so differently.

While B2B and B2C are the most obvious forms of e-commerce, they aren't the *only* forms. For example, inC2C (consumer-to-consumer) e-commerce, consumers buy from and sell to other consumers—think eBay and Craigslist. And in B2G (business-to-government), e-commerce businesses sell information, goods, and services to government agencies.

### 16-4a Using Information Technology in the B2C Market

Firms in the B2C market use information technology in a variety of ways. In this section, we'll describe how firms use technology in general (and the internet in particular) to attract new customers and strengthen the loyalty of existing customers.

**expert system (ES)** A decision support system that helps managers make better decisions in an area where they lack expertise.

**e-commerce** The marketing, buying, selling, and servicing of products over a network (usually the internet).

**business-to-consumer (B2C) e-commerce** E-commerce in which businesses and final consumers interact.

**business-to-business (B2B) e-commerce** E-commerce in markets where businesses buy from and sell to other businesses.

**Exhibit 16.4  Key Differences between B2C and B2B E-Commerce**

| | B2C | B2B |
|---|---|---|
| **Type of Customers** | Individual final consumers | Other businesses |
| **Number of Customers in Target Market** | Very large | Often limited to a few major business customers |
| **Size of Typical Individual Transaction** | Relatively small (usually a few dollars to a few hundred dollars) | Potentially very large (often several thousand dollars, sometimes several million dollars) |
| **Customer Behavior** | May do some research, but many purchases may be based on impulse. | Usually does careful multiple research and compares vendors. May take bids. |
| **Complexity of Negotiations** | Purchase typically involves little or no negotiation. Customer usually buys a standard product and pays the listed price. | Often involves extensive negotiation over specifications, delivery, installation, support, and other issues. |
| **Nature of Relationship with Customers** | Firm wants to develop customer loyalty and repeat business but seldom develops a close working relationship with individual customers. | Buyers and sellers often eventually develop close and long-lasting relationships that allow them to coordinate their activities. |

**Web 2.0** One major goal for most firms today is to develop stronger relationships with their customers. The internet has proven to be an excellent tool for fostering such relationships—though it took a while for businesses to discover the best way to do so. In the early days of e-commerce, most companies tried to maintain tight control over the content presented on their websites. These websites presented information about products and allowed customers to place orders for goods and services, but offered little opportunity for user participation or involvement. However, by the early years of the twenty-first century, innovative businesses were developing ways to make e-commerce more interactive and collaborative. In doing so, they not only forged stronger relationships with the customers who posted this content, they also created a richer, more interesting, and more useful experience for *others* who visited the site. This approach became known as **Web 2.0**.

Many Web 2.0 sites rely on users (or members) to provide most of their content. For instance, the online encyclopedia Wikipedia uses wiki software to allow users to comment on and contribute to its articles. And social networking sites such as Facebook and Twitter wouldn't exist without content posted and created by users. The more users who participate on these sites, the more useful (and entertaining) they become—and the easier it is to attract even more visitors and contributors.

Interestingly, many companies have found that techniques used to encourage collaboration among their customers can be used to accomplish the same result with their employees. Nearly all major corporations use Web 2.0 techniques to help their employees work together more effectively. The use of Web 2.0 technologies within organizations is called Enterprise 2.0.[40] We see this today in the surging popularity of discussion channels and chat rooms such as Slack, Microsoft Teams, or Google Chat. **Discussion channels and chat rooms** use web- or app-based communication tools to hold department, team, or private discussions based on topics, projects, or clients. Team room channels are often restricted to team members working together, while private discussions are typically invitation-only for teams or for one-to-one work sessions. Discussion channels and chat rooms, all of which are standard features in Slack, Microsoft Teams, or Google Chat, allow the sharing of expertise, avoid duplicating solutions already discovered by others, and provide a historical database for people dealing with particular problems. They promote collaborative discussion via participant comments and through document sharing and editing.[41]

**Digital Advertising** Many B2C companies have large target markets, so digital advertising is an important part of their marketing strategy. Digital advertising is omnichannel, which means that today's B2C companies advertise on websites, podcasts, social media, and even within digital apps. Our limited discussion of digital

**Web 2.0** Websites that incorporate interactive and collaborative features to create a richer, more interesting, and more useful experience for their users.

**discussion channels and chat rooms** The use of web- or app-based communication tools to hold department-based, topic/project/client-based, team, or private discussions.

advertising will review the basics involved with search engine optimization, opt-in email, social media, social media influencers, and affiliate marketing.

- There are two kinds of internet searches: paid and organic. Companies pay Google and other search engines to put their links at the top of search results. When I searched for "best laptops" on Google, paid ads were shown at the top of the search results page for Microsoft, HP, Samsung, and Acer. Below those, however, were organic unpaid links that best matched the search; for example, "Best Laptops 2021" at Laptopmag.com. Google defines **search engine optimization (SEO)** as "the practice of continuously optimizing a website for higher rankings in the organic search results...."[42] SEO is complex, and ranges from basics like keyword selection in web content, page titles, and URLs to meta descriptions and structured data. (Lost you on those last two, right?) See "Search Engine Optimization (SEO) Starter Guide" at https://developers.google.com/search/docs/beginner/seo-starter-guide if you want to learn more.

- Firms in B2C markets also use opt-in email that consumers explicitly choose to receive. Opt-in landing pages ask for permission to send product or service information in exchange for consumers' names and email addresses. Conversion rates, the rate at which potential customers become paying customers, are quite high with opt-in emails, most likely because only very interested consumers opt in.[43] Newsletters, first-purchase discounts, sales, new products, or new blog entries are commonly communicated via opt-in emails. Sophisticated email marketing software, such as MailChimp, HubSpot, or Campaigner, makes opt-in email a powerful and effective advertising method.[44]

- Social media, in which users share, comment on, or create content, includes Facebook, Twitter, LinkedIn, Instagram, Snapchat, Reddit, YouTube, and TikTok. Spending on social media advertising grew from 13% of total marketing budgets in 2019 to 23% in 2020.[45] While some argue that Facebook usage has peaked, 67% of advertisers agree that Facebook is the most effective social media platform on which to advertise.[46] With 2+ billion active users, even the smallest business can reach an enormously large audience on Facebook. Furthermore, Facebook advertising, which can be targeted and measured with sophisticated tools, is often less expensive than other social media

alternatives. The steps to set up an Ad on Facebook are choose your objective (brand awareness vs. sales conversions), select your audience, decide where to run the ad (Facebook, Instagram, Messenger, Facebook's Mobile App, or all four), set a budget, pick a format (photos, videos, stories, etc.), place the order, and then measure and manage the ad's effectiveness.[47] Similar tools exist on other social media platforms.

- Social media influencers, such as Jack Morris (@doyoutravel) for travel, Chiara Ferragni (@chiaraferragnibrand) for fashion, and Joanna Gaines (@joannagaines) of TV show *Fixer Upper* for home design and furnishings, typically have large groups of dedicated followers who trust their recommendations and opinions. Whether its technology, fashion, video games, or even niche markets such as @tractortimewithtim, a tractor and tractor attachment YouTuber, influencers have remarkable effects on consumer buying. For example, Twitter found that 40% of Twitter users have made purchases because of influencer Tweets.[48] Companies can work with influencers by paying travel costs so influencers can attend new product launches, giving them early access to new products, advertising on influencers' social media channels, or formally partnering with influencers to promote their brands (many influencers, however, do not accept sponsor payment, believing it compromises their objectivity and independence). A survey of chief marketing officers shows that spending on social media influencers is expected to double from 6.5% to 12.7% of total marketing budgets over the next few years.[49]

- Affiliate marketing is when businesses pay affiliates, such as influencers, websites, Instagrammers, or YouTubers, to put ads for their products or services on the influencers' digital media. Affiliates get paid when followers click those ads or when consumers click those ads and subsequently purchase those products or services. For example, Amazon's large affiliate program pays affiliates sales commissions up to 10% of the product sales price.[50] Affiliate programs give businesses much broader reach with their digital advertising. eBay's Partner Network affiliate program has 1.4 billion listings to advertise that reach 183 million buyers in 190 markets.[51] Think of it this way. Instead

**search engine optimization** Optimizing a website for higher rankings in organic search results.

# We're Still Having Problems with Passwords!!!

**Most Popular (Failed) Passwords.** In a database of 275 million breached passwords—passwords that did NOT keep hackers out—the top five most popular passwords were: 123456 (used 2.5 million times!), 123456789, Picture1, password, and 12345678 (for those who found 123456789 too complex!).

**Lost Bitcoin Passwords.** Passwords aren't just a problem for "ordinary" users. Some Bitcoin investors are locked out of their bitcoin accounts because of lost passwords. (Bitcoin, without getting too detailed, is sort of like digital gold. With a fixed number of Bitcoins, the price largely depends on demand.) Stefan Thomas owned 7,002 bitcoins worth $304 million dollars the day this was written. But Thomas cannot find the password to the IronKey hard drive containing the password to his Bitcoin wallet. And he's already entered eight incorrect passwords trying to access the IronKey drive. Which means he has just two more attempts before the drive permanently encrypts its contents. Thomas said, "I would just lay in bed and think about it. Then I would go to the computer with some new strategy, and it wouldn't work, and I would be desperate again." Unfortunately, Thomas has lots of company, as the owners of 18.5 million Bitcoins, roughly 20% of the overall supply, are locked out of their Bitcoin wallets. Because of Bitcoin's decentralized encryption technology, there's no central database to help Bitcoin buyers retrieve lost passwords.

**Even Data Breaches Can't Get People to Change Their Passwords.** When Yahoo! accounts were famously breached several years ago, the news coverage was hard to miss. Most Yahoo! users knew their accounts had been compromised. But researchers found that only one-quarter of Yahoo! users went back to their Yahoo! logins to change their passwords. And of those who changed their passwords, only a third made their new passwords stronger by making them longer or adding numbers or special characters.

**Is There Any Good News?** Because of security concerns, many systems require users to reset passwords every three to six months. Ironically, that leads to simpler, easier-to-remember passwords! But cybersecurity researchers have found that promising people they could keep stronger passwords for longer periods is a strong incentive. Here's how it worked: "As they typed, text displayed just below the password entry field told them how long it would be before the password expired. For example, the password "123456" would only be valid for two weeks, whereas a good password like "I ate 8 marshmallows at the BBQ" would expire after six months. As the password got stronger, the time to expiration became greater."[52]

Rawpixel.com/Shutterstock.com

of putting an ad for your business on one billboard in one city, affiliate programs give you the chance to put billboards on dozens of streets in each major city in the world!

> The average American spends 50 minutes on Facebook every day.
>
> —Facebook CEO, Mark Zuckerberg

**Handling Payments Electronically** B2C e-commerce normally requires customers to pay at the time the purchase is made. Clearly, the use of cash and paper checks isn't practical. Most payments in the B2C market are made by credit cards. To ensure that such transactions are secure, most sites transmit payment information using a secure socket layer (SSL) protocol. You can tell if a site on which you're doing business is using SSL in two fairly subtle ways. First, the URL will begin with https:// instead of simply http://. (Note the "s" after http in the address.) Second, a small, closed lock icon will appear near the bottom of your web browser (the exact location depends on the specific browser you are using).

Another increasingly common method of payment is via **digital wallets** that are used for secure electronic transfer of funds for e-commerce transactions. By far the best-known digital wallets are PayPal, which also operates Braintree (to handle companies' web and mobile payments), and Apple Pay, Google Pay, and Samsung Pay. The primary advantage of digital wallets is they make transactions more secure. While there are a number of ways this is done, the primary method is to not use the customer's credit card number on the e-commerce site where the purchase is being made. So, how does this work? PayPal does this by transferring consumers to their website or app during online purchases, authenticating the payment from your credit card or bank using their more secure PayPal systems, and then depositing payment into the e-commerce seller's PayPal account.[53] By contrast, after using face ID or fingerprint scans or device PIN numbers on smartphones to authenticate that you're really you, Apple Pay, Google Pay, and Samsung send a token or transaction-specific dynamic security code in place of your credit card number.[54] Transaction-specific means that it's only used once. Dynamic means that it's different each time. So, the code used to buy your latte in the morning will be different than the code used when you buy your sandwich at lunch.

How important are digital wallets to e-commerce? According to figures on its website, in 2020 PayPal had 377 million active accounts that handled $936 billion in annual payments in 200 countries and 25 currencies, up by 31% from 2019.[55] Globally the number of people using digital wallets to make e-commerce purchases is predicted to grow from 2.3 billion per year to almost 4 billion in 2024, or nearly half the people on earth.[56]

### 16-4b Using Information Technology in the B2B Market

B2B e-commerce generally requires a very different approach than B2C e-commerce. Not only do B2B transactions often involve much larger sums of money and require much more negotiation than B2C transactions, they also often result in long-term supply chain relationships that require close collaboration between buyer and seller. A *supply chain* is the network of organizations and activities needed to obtain materials and other resources, produce final products, and get those products to their final users. Forging tight and efficient supply chain relationships can be a key competitive advantage for firms.

An effective supply chain requires close coordination between a company and its suppliers. Information technology can provide the tools needed to foster this coordination. The extranets we mentioned earlier can allow suppliers to keep tabs on their customers' inventories, thus anticipating when to make shipments of parts or materials. Moderna, one of the primary companies behind the COVID-19 vaccines that were designed, tested, and delivered in just 11 months, relied on a special kind of extranet called supply chain software. *Supply chain software* provides a standard platform to handle communication, track orders, and predict how much is needed at each step of the supply chain to deliver then 30 to 45 million vaccinations needed each month. This allowed Moderna to work efficiently with the suppliers who handled different sections of the supply chain, from using bioreactors to produce the main vaccine ingredient, to formulating that ingredient into a liquid, to packaging the liquid vaccine into glass vials, to storing the vaccine in freezers, to finally delivering vials to the hospitals, clinics, and pharmacies where people go to get vaccinated.[57] Neel Jones Shah, executive vice president and global head of airfreight at Flexport, a freight-forwarding company, explained that, "No one company can own the end-to-end vaccine supply chain. Collaboration will be critical." Supply chain software made that collaboration possible.[58]

Many firms involved in B2B business also make use of specialized internet sites, called **e-marketplaces**, which provide a platform for businesses in specific B2B markets to interact. These platforms generally allow buyers in the market to solicit bids by posting requests for proposals (RFPs) on the site. Suppliers can then respond by bidding on RFPs that interest them. Alibaba.com, the world's largest B2B e-marketplace for "global wholesale trade," sells millions of products from 40 categories in 190 countries.[59] ThomasNet.com is the largest B2B e-marketplace for industrial manufacturers, bringing together 1.2 businesspeople and 500,000 suppliers who make 6 million industrial products.[60]

> **digital wallet** A method used for secure electronic transfer of funds for e-commerce transactions.
>
> **e-marketplace** A specialized internet site where buyers and sellers engaged in business-to-business e-commerce can communicate and conduct business.

E-marketplaces provide a number of advantages to their participants:

- Compared to older methods, they reduce the time, effort, and cost of doing business for both buyers and sellers.

- Because they are internet-based, they don't require expensive dedicated connections between firms, so even smaller firms can afford to participate.

- They enable sellers and buyers to contact and negotiate with a large number of market participants on the other side of the market, thus maximizing the chances of finding good matches.

- They often provide additional services—beyond simple trade—that allow firms to exchange information and collaborate, thus forging tighter supply chain relationships.

In recent years, many firms have begun using another information technology known as **radio frequency identification (RFID)** to improve the efficiency of their supply chains. This technology stores information on a microchip and transmits it to a reader when it's within range—up to several thousand feet. The chips can be extremely small—some are difficult to see with the naked eye—and can be embedded in most types of tangible products. The chips are usually powered by the energy in the radio signal sent by the reader, so they don't need batteries.

**radio frequency identification (RFID)**
A technology that stores information on small microchips that can transmit the information when they are within range of a special reader.

RFID chips can store and transmit all sorts of information, but most commonly they transmit a serial number that uniquely identifies a product, vehicle, or piece of equipment. This type of information can be used to help track goods and other resources as they move through a supply chain. Deliveries can be recorded automatically and electronically without the need to make manual records. The chips also can make taking inventory much quicker and simpler, since the items in stock identify themselves to readers. And the chips can be used to reduce the chances of theft. The results of these advantages are lower costs and a more efficient supply chain.

Disney World uses RFID chips in MagicBands, bracelets that serve as park visitors' admission tickets, hotel keys, and credit cards at shops and restaurants.[61] Because they contain RFID chips, Disney can track where the park is busy and then add more staff at those rides and restaurants. And with the ability to shift staff precisely where they are most needed, Disney World can now easily admit 3,000 more people to the park each day. One example of how Disney guests benefit from MagicBands is faster food service. For instance, after park guests Jason and Melissa McInerney entered their lunch orders into a touch screen kiosk, the screen directed them to sit wherever they liked. Just after they sat down at their table, their food server brought them their sandwiches and drinks. Thanks to the MagicBands, the kitchen and their server knew what they ordered and where they were sitting.[62]

## 16-5 Challenges and Concerns Arising from New Technologies

So far, we've concentrated on the benefits of advances in information technology—and it's clear that these benefits are enormous. But rapid technological advances also pose challenges and create opportunities for abuse. These problems affect businesses, their customers, and their employees, as well as the general public. In this section, we'll look at annoyances, security concerns, and legal and ethical issues.

### 16-5a Malware

The internet—for all its advantages—creates the possibility that unwanted files and programs may land on your computer. In many cases, this happens without

# When Can Artificial Intelligence Help Your Business?

*Artificial intelligence*, or *AI*, is the capability of computerized systems to learn and adapt through experience.[63] AI learns by feeding information into the AI system, analyzing that information for patterns, making decisions (do this or that) or categorical distinctions (this is a picture of a wolf, not a dog), and then telling the AI system when it was right or wrong. AI beats people in complex games like chess, sophisticated simulations such as F-16 jet dogfights, or advanced language skills such as reading comprehension. While impressive, that doesn't help the average businessperson figure out if AI can help their business.

Here's where AI can help:

**Associations.** AI excels at detecting patterns (i.e., when we do X, what typically happens?). For example, $11 billion of farm-raised salmon are exported from Norway each year. Not surprisingly, fish food accounts for 40% of the cost. But figuring out the right amount of food is tricky. Feed the fish too little and the fish will be undersized. Overcorrect by feeding them too much and you not only waste food but harm the fish's environment. AI-linked video cameras are monitoring fish behavior to see how changing the frequency of fish feeding affects their health and growth. Imagine watching thousands of hours of video of millions of fish and trying to determine if feeding frequency changed what you saw. People can't do that, but AI can.

**Step 1: AI. Step 2: Humans. Step 3: Customer Satisfaction.** AI is also good at determining when things are different, which can help businesses adjust products and services to different customer needs. Investment firm Vanguard is using AI for its Personal Advisor Services (PAS). AI is used for initial steps, such as analyzing questionnaire responses regarding financial goals, routine steps, such as rebalancing a portfolio by buying or selling stocks, or generating visual displays for what-if scenarios for customers thinking about changing investment strategies. PAS advisors, by contrast, handle the more personal and complex issues associated with further customizing AI-developed plans, working through the complexities of retirement income and spending plans, and coaching clients through changing market conditions.

AI was once too complex and costly for most businesses. Today, good AI tools are widely available and dropping in cost. Your challenge is determining where AI can best help your business.[64]

sdecoret/Shutterstock.com

---

your knowledge, much less your permission. Some of these files and programs are relatively benign (even useful), but others can create major problems. Software that is created and distributed with malicious intent is called **malware** (short for "malicious software"). Spyware, computer viruses, and worms are all examples of malware.

**Spyware** is software that installs itself on your computer without permission and then tracks your computer behavior in some way. It might track which internet sites you visit to learn more about your interests and habits in order to send you targeted ads. Or, more alarmingly, it might log every keystroke (thus capturing passwords, account numbers, and usernames to accounts as you enter them), allowing someone to steal your identity. Some spyware even goes beyond passive watching and takes control of your computer, perhaps sending you to websites you didn't want to visit.

**Computer viruses** are programs that install themselves on computers without the users' knowledge or permission and spread—sometimes very rapidly—by attaching themselves to other files that are transferred from computer to computer. Viruses are often attached to emails, instant messages, or files downloaded from the internet. Some viruses are little more than pranks, but others can cause great harm. They can erase or modify data on your hard drive, prevent your computer from booting up, or

**malware** A general term for malicious software, such as spyware, computer viruses, and worms.

**spyware** Software that is installed on a computer without the user's knowledge or permission to track the user's behavior.

**computer virus** Computer software that can be spread from one computer to another without the knowledge or permission of the computer users by attaching itself to emails or other files.

find and send personal information you've stored on your computer to people who want to use it for identity theft. **Worms** are similar to viruses, except that they are independent programs that often use well-known vulnerabilities (unsecured points) to enter computers networks and spread across computer networks.

How can you protect yourself from spyware, viruses, and worms? Take these commonsense steps:

- Perform regular backups. This can come in handy should a virus tamper with (or erase) the data on your hard drive. Store the backed-up data in a separate place.

- Install high-quality antivirus and antispyware software, and keep it updated. (Today's internet security software usually has the ability to download and install updates automatically, but may need to be configured to do so.)

- Update your operating system regularly so that any security holes it contains are patched as soon as possible.

- Don't open email messages or attachments if you don't know and trust the sender.

- Don't download files from websites unless you are sure they are legitimate. And be sure to read the licensing agreement of any programs you install—especially those of freeware you download from the internet. The wording of these agreements will often indicate if other programs (such as spyware) will be installed along with your free program.

## 16-5b Spam, Phishing, and Pharming

**Spam** refers to unsolicited commercial emails, usually sent to huge numbers of people with little regard for whether they are interested in the product or not. It's estimated that 50% or more of all email traffic is spam. Some spam messages contain malicious email attachments that download ransomware to unknowing users' computers.[65] Spam filters are highly effective at screening the 306 billion emails sent every day.[66] Google's Gmail, for instance, claims that that only 0.1% of spam gets past its spam filters to Gmail users. If all spam filters were that effective (they aren't), 306 million spam messages would still be delivered to email inboxes every day. And unfortunately, that would mean more false positives, whereby a spam filter wrongly screens out legitimate email messages (Gmail's false positive rate is 0.05%).[67]

The U.S. Congress enacted the Controlling the Assault of Non-Solicited Pornography and Marketing Act (usually called the CAN-SPAM Act) in 2003. This act requires senders of unsolicited commercial email to label their messages as ads and to tell the recipient how to unsubscribe from further messages. It also prohibits the use of false or deceptive subject lines in email messages. But the rapid increase in the amount of spam in recent years suggests this law hasn't been an effective deterrent.

**Phishing** is another common use of spam. Phishers send email messages that appear to come from a legitimate business, such as a bank, credit card company, or retailer. The email attempts to get recipients to disclose personal information, such as their social security or credit card numbers, by claiming that there is a problem with their account—or that the account information needs to be verified or updated. The messages appear authentic; in addition to official-sounding language, they often include official-looking corporate logos. The email also usually provides a link to a website where the recipient is supposed to log in and enter the desired information. When the victims of the scam click on this link, they go to a website that can look amazingly like the site for the real company—but it's not. It's a clever spoof of the site where the phishers collect personal information and use it to steal identities. Exhibit 16.5 shows a highly sophisticated phishing attack using Google's Gmail service. A number of Gmail users received a convincing email that looked like it was sent from someone they knew. When the users clicked on an attachment included with the email (in the form of a Google-looking graphic), a new tab opened in their web browsers (Gmail is largely web-based). As Exhibit 16.5 shows, the Gmail users were then prompted to sign into their accounts again "to continue to Gmail." While careful email users would have noticed that the URL begins "data:text/html,https://accounts.google.com" instead of "https:accounts.google.com," many Gmail users were fooled. When they mistakenly signed into their accounts again, what they were actually doing was giving hackers their Google account passwords. The result was that their Gmail and Google accounts were soon, if not immediately, compromised.[68]

One of the best ways to avoid such scams is to be skeptical of email requests for personal information; reputable businesses almost *never* ask you to divulge such information via email. Also, never click on a link in an email message to go to a website where you have financial

**worm** Malicious computer software that, unlike viruses, can spread on its own by using well-known vulnerabilities (unsecured points) to enter computer networks without being attached to other files.

**spam** Unsolicited email advertisements usually sent to very large numbers of recipients, many of whom may have no interest in the message.

**phishing** A scam in which official-looking emails are sent to individuals in an attempt to get them to divulge private information such as passwords, usernames, and account numbers.

## Exhibit 16.5
## Gmail Phishing Example

**Google**

# One account. All of Google.

Sign in to continue to Gmail

Enter your email

**Next**

Need help?

Source: M. Maunder, "Wide Impact: Highly Effective Gmail Phishing Technique Being Exploited," Wordfence, January 12, 2017, https://www.wordfence.com/blog/2017/01/gmail-phishing-data-uri/#officialupdate, accessed February 13, 2017.

accounts—if the message is from a phisher, that link is used to direct you to the fake site (as in the Gmail phishing attack shown in Exhibit 16.5) where the phishers hope that you'll mistakenly enter your username and password. Instead, use a link to the site that you've bookmarked, or type in the link to the real site yourself.

Not content with phishing expeditions, some scam artists have now taken to **pharming**. Like phishing, pharming uses fake websites to trick people into divulging personal information. But pharming is more sophisticated and difficult to detect than phishing because it doesn't require the intended victim to click on a bogus email link. Instead, it uses techniques to redirect internet traffic to the fake sites. Thus, even if you type in the *correct* URL for a website you want to visit, you still might find yourself on a very realistic-looking pharming site. One way to check the validity of the site is to look for the indications that the site is secure, such as the https:// in the URL and the small, closed lock icon mentioned earlier.[69]

Computers aren't the only devices plagued by these threats and annoyances. Cell phone users are facing increasing problems with spam delivered via text messaging. Even more alarming, some scammers have found ways to take their phishing expeditions to cell phones—a practice known as "SMiShing," or SMS phishing. One typical SMiShing ploy is to use text messaging to entice cell phone users to visit the scammer's fake website asking you to provide personal or financial information.[70]

### 16-5c Hackers: Break-Ins in Cyberspace

**Hackers** are skilled computer users who have the expertise to gain unauthorized access to other people's computers. Not all hackers intend to do harm, but some—called "black hat hackers" (or "crackers")—definitely have malicious intent. They may attempt to break into a computer system to steal identities or to disrupt a business.

Protecting against hackers requires individuals and businesses to be security conscious. Some of the precautions used against hackers, such as making frequent backups, are similar to those used to protect against viruses. Another key to protecting against hackers is to make sure that all data transmitted over a network are encrypted or sent in encoded form that can only be read by those who have access to a key. Security experts also suggest that organizations restrict access to computer resources by requiring users to have strong passwords. According to Microsoft, strong passwords are at least 14 characters in length; include a mix of letters, numbers, and special characters; and don't contain any common words or personal information.[71] MIT researchers have found, however, that making passwords longer by "adding a word or two" is more effective than adding numbers or upper-case letter. Their finding is that longer passwords are safer because they're much more difficult to crack.[72]

Unfortunately, users struggle to remember strong passwords, so they reuse one or two passwords. "Having the same password for everything is like having the same key for your house, your car, your gym locker, your

> **pharming** A scam that seeks to steal identities by routing internet traffic to fake websites.
>
> **hacker** A skilled computer user who uses their expertise to gain unauthorized access to the computer (or computer system) of others, sometimes with malicious intent.

# Pixels: The Sneaky, but Clever Way Your Email Is Tracked

Your email is definitely being tracked by spammers, advertisers, people you know, or the companies who send you monthly bills. How? Pixels. Every time you open an email with pictures, pixels are downloaded from a server (similar to web pages). When that happens, they know you've opened their email—and where—and on what device.

The sneaky way to do "open mail tracking" is by inserting a miniature 1 × 1 pixel so small that it goes unnoticed in URL links or words with larger fonts (such as headings). Eighty-five percent of the 14,000 most popular websites use pixel tracking in their emails. Furthermore, says Florian Seroussi, founder of global marketing company Omnicom, "One out of six people that emails you is sending a tracker, and it's real life. It could be your friend, your wife, your boss, this number is really mind boggling—you give up a lot of privacy just opening emails."

Other than knowing what you looked at in your email inbox, Seroussi explains that open email tracking could be used by "stalkers, harassers, even thieves who might be sending you spam emails just to see if you're home."

What's the fix? Image blocking. Every email app has the option to prevent images from automatically loading. If there's an image you want to see, click to download it. But otherwise, with image blocking activated, your email can't be tracked—and neither can you.[73]

Turn off Open Mail Tracking by changing the settings in your Mail app. Here, as shown in Apple Mail on a Mac, you would uncheck "Load remote content in messages." Similar settings are available in other Mail apps, and for Windows computers, too.

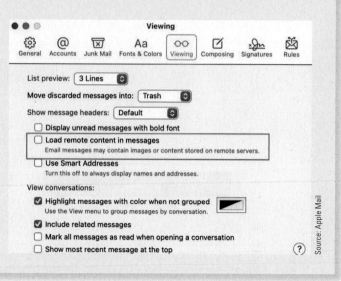

Source: Apple Mail

office," says PayPal's Michael Barrett. With password management software, such as 1Password, users memorize just one master password. 1Password works with any browser on any computer, tablet, or smartphone. It generates unique, strong passwords, synchronizes encrypted data across devices, and autofill forms so you don't have to manually enter personal information or passwords.[74] It also issues warnings when the same password has been used for different accounts, or when new passwords are needed because a website has been compromised.[75]

**Firewalls** are another important tool to guard against hackers and other security threats. A firewall uses hardware or software (or sometimes both) to create a barrier that prevents unwanted messages or instructions from entering a computer system. As threats from spyware, hackers, and other sources have developed, the use of firewalls has become commonplace.

**firewall** Software and/or hardware designed to prevent unwanted access to a computer or computer system.

## 16-5d Ethical and Legal Issues

Information technology raises a number of legal and ethical challenges, such as the need to deal with privacy issues and to protect intellectual property rights. These issues are controversial and don't have simple solutions.

**Personal Privacy** Firms now have the ability to track customer behavior in ways that were never before possible. This has advantages for you because it allows firms to offer better, more personalized service. But all this extra information comes at the expense of your privacy. Does the fact that firms know so much about your preferences and behavior make you a bit nervous?

Does it bother you that your email messages lack confidentiality? When you send an email, it is stored on several computers: your personal computer, the server of your email provider, the server of your recipient's provider, and your recipient's own computer. If you send the email from your company's system, it's also likely to be stored when the company backs up its information. If you thought that deleting an email message from your own computer erased it permanently and completely, you need to think again.

The list of other ways in which information technology can erode your personal privacy is long and getting longer. For example, anyone who carries a smartphone, and 84% of us do, leaves a data trail that is legal to collect, use, and sell to others. From location data that shows where you've been, to what-you-thought was-personal information such as the websites you look at, the apps you use and how you use them, a terrifying amount of detailed information about your behavior and habits is available to others. In 2019, the *New York Times* Privacy Project obtained such data from 12 million smartphones to see how much could be discovered from supposedly anonymous data. Their conclusion: "If you could see the full trove [of information about you], you might never use your phone the same way again."[76] While people believe that such data are anonymous and secure, the *Times* found that "it's child's play to connect real names to the dots that appear on the maps."[77] "With the help of publicly available information, like home addresses, we easily identified and then tracked scores of notables. We followed military officials with security clearances as they drove home at night. We tracked law enforcement officers as they took their kids to school. We watched high-powered lawyers (and their guests) as they traveled from private jets to vacation properties." Unless you turn off your smartphone or carry a burner phone that you bought with cash, assume that most of what you do and where you go can be figured out by accessing the digital breadcrumbs from your smartphone.

The bottom line is that there's no simple way to solve privacy concerns. Privacy is an elusive concept, and there is no strong consensus about how much privacy is enough.

## Protecting Intellectual Property Rights

**Intellectual property** refers to products that result from creative and intellectual efforts. There are many types of intellectual property, but we'll focus on forms of intellectual property that are protected by copyright law, such as books, musical works, computer programs, video games, and movies. Copyright law gives the creators of this property the exclusive right to produce, record, perform, and sell their work for a specified time period.

*Piracy* of intellectual property occurs when someone reproduces and distributes copyrighted work without obtaining permission from—or providing compensation to—the owner of the copyrighted material. When piracy becomes widespread, creators of intellectual property receive much less income for their efforts. This can substantially reduce their incentive to continue developing creative material.

A growing trend in intellectual property crime is the illegal use of internet protocol television (IPTV) to stream pay-per-view events, movies, and live television channels. Some black market retailers have even begun selling set-top boxes preconfigured to play illegal streams.

The Business Software Alliance estimates that, globally, 37% of all business software installed on personal computers in 2018 was pirated, resulting in the loss of over $46 billion in revenue to software companies. In several smaller countries, including Libya and Venezuela, the rate of piracy was over 89%. Among larger nations, the piracy rate in China exceeded 66%, while in India it was 56%. The good news is that the piracy rate was much lower in the United States at 15%. But given the huge size of the U.S. software market, even this relatively low rate of piracy still resulted in losses of over $9.5 billion in revenue for software companies. Faced with such a widespread problem, many software publishers have become very aggressive at prosecuting firms and individuals engaged in software piracy.[78]

Music studios, TV and motion picture producers, and videogame developers also face significant problems with piracy. In the United States alone, piracy costs the music industry $2.7 billion a year and 71,000 jobs.[79] Globally, the TV and motion picture industries are predicted to lose $51.6 billion to piracy in 2022.[80] Current estimates regarding videogame piracy are difficult to find, but one older study estimated that there were 2.4 billion illegal downloads of videogames

**intellectual property**
Property that is the result of creative or intellectual effort, such as books, musical works, inventions, and computer software.

in 2014.[81] While it's unclear how much piracy affects the videogame industry today, pirate servers in 2020 allowed 20,000 gamers per day to illegally play World of Warcraft without paying monthly subscription fees.[82] Furthermore, hackers use crowdsourced funding and advertising on pirate game sites to fund their efforts to crack Denuvo, the videogame industry's digital rights management technology.[83] But even the makers of Denuvo admit that delaying videogame piracy is their goal. Denuvo's Elmar Fischer said, "Our goal, and it's still the goal, is to protect initial sales. Of course, we would like to have it [where games are] uncracked forever, but that just doesn't happen in the games industry."[84]

Given how lucrative piracy can be, it's unlikely that this problem will go away anytime soon. You can expect the companies hurt by these practices to continue aggressively prosecuting pirates and to work on new technologies that make pirating digital media more difficult.

---

## The Big Picture

Information technology plays a vital role in virtually every aspect of business operations. For instance, marketing managers use information technology to learn more about customers, reach them in novel ways, and forge stronger relationships with them—as we showed in our discussion of Web 2.0. Operations managers use RFID technologies to coordinate the movement of goods within supply chains and to keep more accurate inventory records. And financial managers use IT to track financial conditions and identify investment opportunities. Managers in all areas of a business can use decision support systems to improve their decision making. They also can apply techniques such as data mining to obtain interesting new insights hidden in the vast streams of data that flow into their companies.

Cloud computing represents the newest and one of the most exciting new approaches to how companies acquire and utilize IT resources. The use of cloud-based resources has the potential to not only lower costs and increase flexibility but also significantly magnify computation power. If cloud computing can overcome concerns about security and stability, it is likely to continue growing in popularity, which could result in significant changes to the role IT departments play within their organizations.

The rapid changes in IT in recent years—especially those related to the rise of the Internet as a business venue—have opened up exciting new commercial opportunities. But these changes have also created a host of legal and ethical challenges and security questions. One thing is certain: business organizations that find ways to leverage the advantages of new IT developments while minimizing the accompanying risks are most likely to enjoy competitive success.

---

## Careers in Information Technology

### Information Technology Support Specialist

Responsible for installing and configuring software, responding to employee and customer issues within the ticket management system, interacting with sales, engineering, and product managers to address complex customer issues, escalating relevant problems to appropriate functional and management teams, contributing potential technical workarounds, and acting as a technical expert for IT solutions within a global IT team. The ideal candidate has a bachelor's degree in computer science or information technology, at least one year of experience with Windows and Unix/Linux administrative services, web services, configuration and release management, possesses strong analytical, problem solving, and customer communication skills, and is self-motivated and works effectively with little instruction.

# 17 | Operations Management:
## Putting It All Together

Rawpixel.com/Shutterstock.com

### Learning Objectives

After studying this chapter, you will be able to:

**17-1** Define operations management and how the role of operations management has changed over the last five decades

**17-2** Discuss the key responsibilities of operations managers

**17-3** Describe how operations managers face the special challenges posed by the provision of services

**17-4** Explain how changes in technology have revolutionized operations management

**17-5** Describe the strategies operations managers have used to improve the quality of goods and services

**17-6** Explain how lean and green practices can help both the organization and the environment

## 17-1 Operations Management: Producing Value in a Changing Environment

**Operations management** creates value by managing the activities that produce goods and services and then distributes them to customers. When operations managers do their job well, their firms produce the *right* goods and services in the *right* quantities and distribute them to the *right* customers at the *right* time—all the while keeping quality high and costs low. While few would say the $1,900+ cost for a Peloton home exercise bike is low, Peloton's 1.3 million bike owners rave about its quality and high value, the no-cost financing, which helps with the sticker price shock, and Peloton's inspirational online classes and instructors. But the thousands of consumers who are *still* waiting for their Peloton bikes to be delivered are angry. A Facebook group of 8,400 people exists only to discuss Peloton's delivery problems, which typically take the form of buying a Peloton bike, making numerous monthly finance payments while awaiting delivery, typically 8 to 10 weeks out, and then getting

**operations management**
Creating value by managing the activities that produce goods and services and then distributing them to customers.

a message on the delivery date that delivery needs to be pushed back a month or longer.[1] Attorney Amanda Carmody ordered her Peloton on October 17 for a December 9 delivery that was delayed to December 31, then January 9 and finally February 22, after which she cancelled her order. Carmody said that, "the fact they can't give you a delivery date and stick to it, and that their customer service department is not empowered at all to find solutions to problems is the most frustrating part of this."[2]

> "Success is simple. Do what's right, the right way, at the right time."
>
> —Arnold H. Glasow,
> American Psychologist

But without the help of Peloton's operations managers who are struggling to increase production of Peloton bikes to meet surging consumer demand, there's nothing Peloton's customer service department can do. Peloton is reducing delays by incurring the high cost of flying bikes from overseas factories. Furthermore, Peloton paid $420 million to buy U.S.-based fitness machine manufacturer Precor. Peloton President William Lynch said. "Keeping up with… growth, which has been a moving target, has been a big company priority. As we've been investing in scaling our manufacturing, this is an area where Precor is very strong." Peloton is learning that operations management has a major impact on company performance.

### 17-1a Responding to a Changing Environment

The practice of operations management has changed dramatically over the past half century. New technologies, shifts in the structure of the economy, challenges posed by global competition, and concerns about the impact of production on the environment have fueled this revolution. Let's begin by identifying the key changes that have characterized the practice of operations management over the last five decades.

**From a Focus on Efficiency to a Focus on Effectiveness** To operations managers, **efficiency** means producing a product at the *lowest cost*. Global giant UPS studies every step in package delivery in pursuit of improved efficiency. Drivers walk briskly with packages, instead of running which could tire them out, and avoid left turns which are safer and take less time. But its biggest improvements come from ORION (On-Road Integrated Optimization and Navigation), a 1,000-page algorithm that finds the most efficient routes for drivers who make 135+ daily deliveries.[3] Every time a change is needed because of bad traffic or new package pickups ordered by customers, ORION considers up to 200,000 options before efficiently reorganizing the driver's route. Thanks to ORION's algorithm and its turn-by-turn navigation, UPS trucks drive 100 million fewer miles each year, thus saving 10 million gallons of fuel.[4]

**Effectiveness** means producing products that *create value* by providing customers with goods and services that offer a better relationship between price and perceived benefits. In other words, effectiveness means finding ways to give customers more for their money—while still making a profit. Technological advances create value by allowing the development of faster, cheaper products with more features and functionality every year. For example, a 1998 desktop computer with 4MB (yes, megabytes, not gigabytes) of memory, a 720MB hard drive, a 14-inch VGA screen (640x480 resolution), and a bubble jet printer (4 pages per minute) would cost $3,430 in 2021 dollars.[5] But today, a Dell desktop computer with 8GB of memory, a 1TB hard drive, a 24-inch HD touchscreen monitor (1920x1080 resolution), and a wireless inkjet printer/scanner (14 black ink pages per minute/7.5 color pages per minute) costs just $730 at Dell.com.[6] In other words, for just 21.3% of the cost of the 1998 computer package, today's consumer gets a 1,456 times larger hard drive, 2,048 times more memory, a 2.9 times larger monitor that's much easier on the eyes, and a much cheaper, higher definition printer that is 3.5 times faster.[7] That's giving customers more for their money![8]

In the 1960s, the focus of operations management was mainly on efficiency. The goal was to keep costs low so the firm could make a profit

> "Nothing is less productive than to make more efficient what should not be done at all."
>
> —Peter F. Drucker

while keeping prices competitive. In today's highly competitive global markets, efficiency remains important. But operations managers now realize that keeping costs (and prices) low are only part of the equation. Customers usually buy goods that offer the best value—and these aren't always the same as the goods that sell for the lowest price. A product that offers better features, more attractive styling, and higher quality, such as Peloton, may provide more value—and attract more customers—than a product with a lower price. Thus, today's operations managers have broadened their focus to look at benefits as well as costs.

**From Goods to Services** **Goods** are tangible products that you can see and touch. *Durable goods* are expected to last three years or longer; examples include furniture, cars, and appliances. *Nondurable goods*, such as toothpaste, apples, and paper towels, are used up more quickly and are often perishable. **Services** are activities that yield benefits but don't directly result in a physical product. Examples include legal advice, entertainment, and medical care. Goods are consumed, while services are experienced.

In the 1960s, the U.S. economy was a manufacturing powerhouse, with more than a third of its labor force employed in the goods-producing sector. But over the last five decades, the American economy has experienced a fundamental shift away from the production of goods and toward the provision of services. By the end of 2020, 14% of the nonfarm labor force worked in the goods-producing sector. By contrast, employment in the service sector had risen to 86% of the labor force.[9]

**From Mass Production to Mass Customization** Fifty years ago, one common production strategy was to keep costs low by producing large quantities of standardized products. The goal of this *mass production* strategy was to achieve reductions in average cost by taking advantage of specialization and the efficient use of capital. But today's technologies allow many firms to pursue *mass customization*—the production of small quantities of customized goods and services that more precisely meet the needs of specific customers—with very little increase in costs. Starbucks, for example, claims that there are 87,000 different drink combinations that a customer can order. Health reporter Julie Beck writes, "You've got your non-fat milk, full-fat milk, soy milk, and coconut milk; espresso shots; all the different flavored syrups, some of which are sugar-free; whipped cream; iced, hot, or "extra hot" if you've got a Kevlar tongue; different sizes; different roasts of coffee; and on and on and on."[10] Sophie Egan, former program director at the Culinary Institute of America, says, "Mass customization [is] a desire within our hyper industrialized food system to have something that feels like it meets my personal taste profile. We have access to customized and personalized food experiences at the restaurant level, at the fast casual level, and at the packaged food level and it has only increased."[11]

**From Local Competition to Global Competition** For the first 25 years after World War II, American firms dominated key markets. This strength was based partly on the fact that the United States possessed a rich base of natural resources, a growing and increasingly well-educated labor force, an excellent infrastructure, and the strong incentive system inherent in a market economy. But it also reflected the fact that the production facilities and infrastructure in many European and Asian nations had been severely damaged during the war.

By the early 1970s, the economies of Japan, Germany, and other war-ravaged nations had been rebuilt, with many of their major companies boasting efficient new production facilities with state-of-the-art technology based on world-class operations management techniques, all of which greatly improved the quality of their products and helped them regain market share from American firms. For example, in 1950, five years after the end of World War II, gross domestic product per capita, which represents national economic output per person, was 6.1 times higher in the United States than in Japan.

# Why You Can't Find Dumbbell Weights

The COVID-19 pandemic transformed regular gym goers into stay-at-home exercisers overnight. When they went online in search of dumbbells and weight equipment, they found little inventory and prices 6 to 7 times pre-pandemic levels (which later settled at 2.5 to 3 times regular prices).

## What happened?

**Exploding demand.** Phil Patti, global development director of American Barbell, a designer and manufacturer of premium fitness equipment, says the pandemic was a crisis for the company for about a week. Then one of his partners told him, "We have $4 million in internet orders." Patti explained that, "In 2019 we did about $1 million to $1.5 million in total [online]. Now we had $4 million all at once."

**China was closed.** Ninety-five percent of dumbbells are made in China, the first country to close because of the virus. With Chinese citizens and factories in lockdown from January to April, no new dumbbells were made for four months.

**Manufacturing and shipping lead times.** It takes a month to make large orders of dumbbells and transport them from inland China to seaside ports. From China, it takes three weeks on a container ship to Los Angeles or 35 days to New York. Then add 7-14 days stateside for handling and trucking. In short, no new dumbbells came out of China to the U.S. for six months or longer.

**Adding manufacturing capacity takes time.** John Fread, director of global marketing at Nautilus, a manufacturer of fitness equipment which saw sales double, said, "We had to triple our capacity for the second half of this year and have spent the last few months seeking out new factories to work with. For reference, it can take up to months—if not longer—to ramp up a new factory. Globally, product demand continues at a high level, so we're constantly making changes to our operations to deliver products as fast as possible."

So why couldn't you find dumbbells? Demand suddenly spiked. Chinese factories were closed. Manufacturing and shipping take two months. And adding new manufacturing capacity to meet higher demand takes even longer. The best inventory and operations management practices make huge differences in firm performance, but even they could not have prevented this dumbbell shortage.[12]

By 1980, with Japan's post war economic recovery largely complete, U.S. GDP per capita was only 1.5 times higher than Japan's.[13] In more recent decades, firms in Korea, India, and China have also become formidable global competitors. As a result, the U.S. share of global GDP declined from 40% in 1960 to 24% in 2019.[14]

**From Simple Supply Chains to Complex Value Chains** Over the last five decades, the increasingly competitive and global nature of markets has brought about major changes in how firms produce and distribute their goods and services. Many supply chains today span multiple organizations located in many different countries. For example, Nutella, the chocolate and hazelnut spread, is based in Italy, has factories in Europe, Russia, North America, and Australia, and gets hazelnuts from Turkey, palm oil from Malaysia, cocoa from Nigeria, sugar from Brazil and vanillin from France.[15] The shift from a cost perspective to a value perspective has led operations managers to extend their view beyond the traditional supply chain to encompass a broader range of processes and organizations known as a *value chain*.

**From Exploiting the Environment to Protecting the Environment** In the 1960s, many operations managers viewed the natural environment as something to exploit. The emphasis on keeping costs low made it tempting to dispose of waste as cheaply as possible—often by dumping it into rivers, lakes, or the atmosphere. But the serious consequences of environmental pollution became increasingly apparent. Operations managers at socially responsible companies responded by adopting a variety of green practices to produce goods and services in more environmentally responsible ways. From roads and bridges to home foundations to factory floors and walls, concrete is the most used construction material on earth. But concrete manufacturers are the second largest producers of global $CO_2$ emissions, with every ton of concrete releasing a ton of $CO_2$ into the atmosphere.[16] Solidia, based in Piscataway, NJ, has developed a concrete manufacturing process that reduces $CO_2$ emissions by 70%.[17] Solidia's process actually uses $CO_2$ to cure concrete products in 24 hours (compared to the standard 28 days) and dramatically reduces the amount of water needed to make concrete. Solidia's approach, which can be adapted to existing concrete plants, would, if broadly adopted by concrete manufacturers, reduce the industry's $CO_2$ emissions by 70%, save 3 trillion gallons of water a year, slash annual energy consumption by 260 million barrels of oil, and prevent 100 million tons of concrete from ending up in landfills.[18]

Exhibit 17.1 summarizes the discussion of the key ways in which operations management has changed over the last five decades. We'll look at these changes in greater detail as we move through this chapter. But first let's take a look at the some of the key tasks operations managers perform.

## Exhibit 17.1
## Operations Management: Five Decades of Change

| Characteristics of Operations Management in 1962 | Factors Promoting Change | Characteristics of Operations Management |
|---|---|---|
| • Focus on Minimizing Costs<br>• Production of Goods<br>• Mass Production<br>• Simple Supply Chains<br>• Exploit the Environment | • Improvements in Production and Information Technologies<br>• Rise of Global Competition and Global Opportunities<br>• Recognition of Quality as a Source of Competitive Advantage<br>• Adoption of Marketing Perspective and Customer Focus<br>• Recognition of Serious Environmental Problems | • Focus on Creating Value<br>• Provision of Services<br>• Mass Customization<br>• Complex Value Chains<br>• Sustain the Environment |

## 17-2 What Do Operations Managers Do?

Understanding the marketing definition of *product* plays a pivotal role in understanding what operations managers do. A product consists of all of the tangible and intangible features (sometimes called the *customer benefit package*) that create value for consumers by satisfying their needs and wants. For example, when you purchase a car made by General Motors, you not only get the physical automobile, you also get (among other things) a warranty and (for many models) up to two years of OnStar services.[19] Likewise, when an airline purchases an Airbus passenger jet, it can include training in the purchase. Airbus trains pilots, mechanics, and flight crews on six continents. Airbus pilot training, for example, has 30 full-flight simulators for basic pilot training to achieve initial flight qualification on Airbus jets and extended pilot training to recertify already qualified pilots.[20]

Marketing research typically determines which features a product should include to appeal to its target customers. Although operations managers don't normally have the primary responsibility for designing these goods and services, they provide essential information and advice during the product-design process, especially regarding the challenges and constraints involved in creating actual products on time and within budget.

Once the actual goods and services are designed, operations managers must determine the processes needed to produce them and get them to the customer. A **process** is a set of related activities that transform inputs into outputs, thus adding value. Once these processes are designed, operations managers also play a key role in determining where they will be performed, what organizations will perform them, and how the processes will be organized and coordinated.

The most obvious processes are those directly involved in the production of goods and services. But there are many other processes that play necessary "supporting roles." For example, purchasing and inventory management

> ### "The other part of outsourcing is this: It simply says where the work can be done outside better than it can be done inside, we should do it."
>
> —Alphonso Roy Jackson, Former U.S. Secretary of Housing and Urban Development

Operations managers oversee the processes needed to produce products and get them to customers, including inventory control, project scheduling, and managing value chains.

processes ensure that the firm has an adequate supply of high-quality materials, parts, and components needed to produce the goods without delays or disruptions.

Let's take a closer look at some of the functions that operations managers perform to move goods and services from the drawing board to the final user.

### 17-2a Process Selection and Facility Layout

Once a product is designed, operations managers must determine the best way to produce it. This involves determining the most efficient processes, deciding the best sequence in which to arrange those processes, and designing the appropriate layout of production and distribution facilities. Well-designed processes and facility layouts enable a firm to produce high-quality products effectively and efficiently, giving it a competitive advantage. Poorly designed processes can result in production delays, quality problems, and high costs.

There are several ways to organize processes. The best approach depends on considerations such as the volume of production and the degree of standardization of the product.

- Firms often use a *product layout* when they produce goods that are relatively standardized and produced in large volumes. This type of layout organizes machinery, equipment, and other resources according

> **process** A set of related activities that transform inputs into outputs, thus adding value.

to the specific sequence of operations that must be performed. The machinery used in this type of layout is often highly specialized, designed to perform one specific task *very* efficiently. One classic example of a product layout is an assembly line, where the product being produced moves from one station to another in a fixed sequence, with the machinery and workers at each station performing specialized tasks. Services that provide a high volume of relatively standardized products also use flow-shop processes. For example, fast-food restaurants often use a simple product layout to prepare sandwiches, pizzas, or tacos in a standard sequence of steps.

- A *process layout* is used by many firms that need to produce small batches of goods that require a degree of customization. This approach arranges equipment according to the type of task performed. For example, in a machine shop, all of the drills may be located in one area, all of the lathes in another area, and all of the grinders in yet another. Unlike assembly lines and other product layouts, a process layout doesn't require work to be performed in a specific sequence; instead, the product can be moved from one type of machinery to another in whatever sequence is necessary. Thus, process layouts can be used to produce a variety of products without the need for expensive retooling. But this flexibility sometimes comes at the cost of longer processing times and more complex planning and control systems. Also, because the machinery and equipment used in a process layout is usually more general-purpose in nature and may be used to produce a greater variety of goods, the process layout requires workers to be more versatile than those employed in a product layout.

- A *cellular layout* falls between the product layout and the process layout. It groups different types of machinery and equipment into self-contained cells. A production facility might have several cells, each designed to efficiently produce a family of parts (or entire products) that have similar processing requirements. Like an assembly line, the product moves from one station in the cell to the next in a specific sequence. However, unlike most assembly lines, cells are relatively small and are designed to be operated by a few workers who perform a wider array of tasks than assembly-line workers.

- A *fixed position layout* is used for goods that must be produced at a specific site (such as a building or a bridge) or that are so large and bulky that it isn't fea-

sible to move them from station to station (such as a ship or commercial airplane). Even some services, such as concerts or sporting events that are performed at a specific location, use this approach. In a fixed position layout, the good or service stays in one place, and the employees, machinery, and equipment are brought to the fixed site when needed during various stages of the production process. For example, for its largest planes, Airbus uses separate fixed position layouts to construct the rear and front fuselage sections of passenger jets in Hamburg, Germany, the massive wings in Broughton, United Kingdom, and the final assembly process in Toulouse, France, where the wings and fuselage sections are added to each jet.[21]

## 17-2b Facility Location

There is an old saying in real estate that the three most important factors determining the value of a property are "location, location, and location." Location also matters to operations managers because the location of facilities strongly affects the efficiency and effectiveness of an organization's processes.

For some types of facilities, the location decision is dominated by one key consideration. A lithium mine to extract lithium for electrical car batteries or batteries storing solar- and wind-generated energy, for instance, must be located where there's lithium, such as Sonora, Mexico or Humboldt County, Nevada.[22] But for many other types of facilities, the decision is more complex. Exhibit 17.2 identifies some key factors that operations managers evaluate when they decide where to locate a facility, but the importance of each factor varies depending on the specific industry. For instance, many service firms place primary interest on locating close to their customers while manufacturing firms are often more concerned about the cost and availability of land and labor and access to highways, railways, and port facilities. When locating its massive warehouses, Amazon needs to balance access to highways, railways, and airports with being close to customers. Which is why after establishing three warehouses in New York City (NYC), and then building 14 warehouses with 7 million square feet in adjacent New Jersey and Long Island, it bought nine new warehouses in NYC in 2020 to better serve NYC's 8.3 million people. Because they're closer to customers, having nine additional warehouses in NYC cuts Amazon's delivery costs by 20%. And with 2.4 million packages delivered each day, those savings are substantial.[23]

## Exhibit 17.2 Factors That Affect Location Decisions

| General Location Factors | Examples of Specific Considerations |
|---|---|
| **Adequacy of Utilities** | Is the supply of electricity reliable? |
| | Is clean water available? |
| **Land** | Is adequate land available for a facility? |
| | How much does the land cost? |
| **Labor Market Conditions** | Are workers with the right skills available? |
| | How expensive is labor? |
| **Transportation Factors** | Is the location near customers and suppliers? |
| | Is appropriate transportation nearby? |
| **Quality-of-Life Factors** | What is the climate like? |
| | Are adequate healthcare facilities available? |
| **Legal and Political Environment** | Does the local government support new businesses? |
| | What are the local taxes, fees, and regulations? |

### 17-2c Inventory Control: Knowing When to Hold 'Em

**Inventories** are stocks of goods or other items held by an organization. Manufacturing firms usually hold inventories of raw materials, components and parts, work in process, and finished goods. Retail firms don't normally hold work in process or raw materials, but they do hold inventories of the finished goods they sell as well as basic supplies that they need.

Deciding how much inventory to hold can be a real challenge for operations managers because increasing (or decreasing) the amount of inventory involves both benefits and costs. For example, the benefits of holding larger inventories include:

- **Smoother Production Schedules:** A candy maker might produce more candy than it needs in August and September and hold the excess in inventory so that it can meet the surge in demand for Halloween treats without investing in more production capacity.

- **Protection against Stock-Outs and Lost Sales:** Holding larger inventories reduces the chance of stock-outs and lost sales due to supply disruptions or unexpected surges in demand (as we saw with Peloton at the beginning of the chapter).

- **Reduced Ordering Costs:** Every time a company orders supplies, it incurs paperwork and handling costs. Holding a larger average inventory reduces the number of orders the firm must make and thus reduces ordering costs.

But holding larger inventories involves costs as well as benefits:

- **Tied-Up Funds:** Items in inventory don't generate revenue until they're sold, so holding large inventories can tie up funds that could be better used elsewhere within the organization.

- **Additional Holding Costs:** Bigger inventories require more storage space, which can mean extra costs for heating, cooling, taxes, insurance, and more.

- **Increased Risk:** Holding large inventories exposes the firm to the risk of losses due to spoilage, depreciation, and obsolescence.

Operations managers determine the optimal amount of inventory by comparing the costs and benefits associated with different levels of inventory. For example, at the beginning of the COVID-19 pandemic, millions of consumers suddenly stopped eating at restaurants where they typically spent half of their food budget.[24] To make up for not eating at restaurants—and to minimize shopping trips to reduce possible exposure to the virus—they began binge buying at grocery stores. The result, according to Rollin Ford, a former Walmart executive, is that food suppliers sold three months of food products in just 10 days![25] As a result, grocery stores only had 87% of their typical inventory in stock at the beginning of the pandemic.[26] Five months later, food suppliers had increased production enough so that grocery stores had 90% of inventory on store shelves. While a 10% stockout seems small,

**inventory** Stocks of goods or other items held by organizations.

## Exhibit 17.3    Activities Involved in Presenting a Play

| Activity | Description | Immediate Predecessor(s) | Estimated Completion Time (Weeks) |
|---|---|---|---|
| A | Select Play | None | 2 |
| B | Select Cast | A (must know play to know what roles are available) | 4 |
| C | Design Sets | A (must know play before sets can be designed) | 4 |
| D | Design Costumes | A (must know play to determine what costumes are needed) | 5 |
| E | Buy Materials for Sets | C (set must be designed to determine types and quantities of materials needed to build it) | 2 |
| F | Buy Materials for Costumes | D (costumes must be designed before materials for costumes are determined) | 2 |
| G | Build Sets | E (must have materials in order to build the sets) | 4 |
| H | Make Costumes | B, F (must have materials in order to make the costumes, and must know actors' sizes to ensure that costumes fit) | 6 |
| I | Initial Rehearsals | B (actors must be selected for each role before they can rehearse their parts) | 2 |
| J | Final (Dress) Rehearsal | G, H, I (costumes and sets must be completed, and initial rehearsals performed, before the final rehearsal can occur) | 1 |
| K | Perform Play (end of project) | J | N/A |

grocery stores would lose $20 billion a year in sales at 90% inventory levels.[27] Managing inventory well is critical to customer satisfaction and company profitability.

### 17-2d   Project Scheduling

Projects such as constructing a new production facility, developing a new commercial airliner, or filming a movie are complex and expensive endeavors. It's vital to monitor them carefully to avoid major delays or cost overruns. The **critical path method (CPM)** is one of the most important tools that operations managers use to manage such projects. We can illustrate the basic idea behind this tool by looking at a simple example in which a theater company wants to stage a play. Exhibit 17.3 presents the steps involved in this project.

Notice that Exhibit 17.3 identifies **immediate predecessors** for all of the activities except activity A. *Immediate predecessors*

are activities that must be completed before another activity can begin. For example, it is clear that the cast for the play cannot be determined until the play has been selected, so activity A (selecting the play) is an immediate predecessor to activity B (selecting the cast). Similarly, since sets can't be built without lumber, paint, and other materials, activity E (buying materials for the sets) is an immediate predecessor for activity G (building the sets).

**Using the Critical Path Method to Focus Efforts**   Now refer to Exhibit 17.4, which is a CPM network for the theater project. This network shows how all of the activities in the theater project are related to each other. The direction of the arrows shows the immediate predecessors for each activity. Notice that arrows go from activities B (selecting the cast) *and* F (purchasing material for the costumes) to activity H (making the costumes). This indicates that *both* of these activities are immediate predecessors for activity H—the costumes can't be made without material, and they must be made in the correct sizes to fit the actors. But also notice that no arrow links activities B and C. This shows that these are independent activities; in other words, the theater company doesn't have to select the cast before it designs the sets (or vice versa).

**critical path method (CPM)** A project-management tool that illustrates the relationships among all the activities involved in completing a project and identifies the sequence of activities likely to take the longest to complete.

**immediate predecessors** Activities in a project that must be completed before some other specified activity can begin.

## Exhibit 17.4
## A CPM Network for Staging a Play

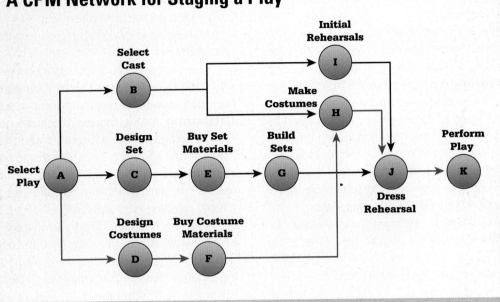

We can use Exhibit 17.4 to illustrate some basic concepts used in CPM analysis. A *path* is a sequence of activities that *must be completed in the order specified by the arrows* for the overall project to be completed. You can trace several paths in our example by following a series of arrows from start to finish. For example, one path is A → B → I → J → K, and another path is A → C → E → G → J → K.

The **critical path** consists of the sequence of activities that takes the longest to complete. A *delay in any activity on a critical path is likely to delay the completion of the entire project*. Thus, operations managers watch activities on the critical path very carefully and take actions to help ensure that they remain on schedule. We've shown the critical path for the theater project (A → D → F → H → J → K) with red arrows on our diagram.

Distinguishing between the critical path and other paths can help operations managers allocate resources more efficiently. Activities that aren't on the critical path can be delayed without causing a delay in the overall completion of the project—as long as the delay isn't too great. In CPM terminology, these activities have *slack*. When operations managers see delays in critical path activities, they may be able to keep the project on track by diverting manpower and other resources from activities with slack to activities on the critical path. For more on critical paths, refer to the "Computer Chips Disrupt Global Manufacturers' Critical Paths" boxed feature.

### 17-2e Designing and Managing Value Chains

Perhaps the most important function of operations management is the design and management of value chains. A **value chain** is the network of relationships that channels the flow of inputs, information, and financial resources through all of the processes directly or indirectly involved in producing goods and services and distributing them to customers.

An organization's value chain clearly includes its supply chain, which consists of the organizations, activities, and processes involved in the physical flow of goods, from the raw materials stage to the final consumer. In fact, some organizations use the terms *value chain* and *supply chain* interchangeably. But a value chain is a broader concept; in addition to the supply chain, it includes activities and processes involved in *acquiring customers*—such as contract negotiations and customer financing—as well as activities and processes involved in *keeping customers* by providing services after the sale, such

**critical path** The sequence of activities in a project that is expected to take the longest to complete.

**value chain** The network of relationships that channels the flow of inputs, information, and financial resources through all of the processes directly or indirectly involved in producing goods and services and distributing them to customers.

as performing warranty repairs, offering call center assistance, and helping customers recycle used goods. In a value chain, the main focus is on the customer; in contrast, the supply chain is more oriented toward traditional production relationships.[28]

One of the most important issues that operations managers examine when they design value chains is the trade-off between vertical integration and outsourcing. **Vertical integration** occurs when a firm attempts to gain more control over its value chain by either developing the ability to perform processes previously performed by other organizations in the chain or by acquiring those organizations. IKEA uses 671 million cubic feet of wood each year—roughly 1% of the world's annual supply of lumber.[29] To reduce costs and ensure access to sustainable wood, IKEA has vertically integrated its lumber supplies by buying forests in Romania, Bulgaria, Estonia, Lithuania, Latvia, and the United States (in Alabama, Georgia, Oklahoma, South Carolina, and Texas).[30] Altogether it now owns 613,000 acres of forests in the U.S. and Europe.[31] According to Professor Franck Delpal, at Paris' Institut Françaisde la Mode, "If you control the greater part of your supply chain [through vertical integration], you get [better] margins at every step, and at the end of the day, it creates big business."[32]

**Outsourcing** is essentially the opposite of vertical integration; it involves arranging for other organizations to perform value chain functions that were previously performed internally. In recent years, the trend in value chain design has been to rely more on outsourcing and less on vertical integration. Outsourcing allows a firm to shed functions it doesn't perform well in order to focus on its areas of strength. It also frees people, money, and other resources that had been tied up in the outsourced activities, allowing these resources to be employed in more profitable ways. Whether due to a focus on research and development or the increasing complexity of production, global pharmaceutical firms often outsource production of some of their drug manufacturing. Eric Langer, president of research and marketing firm BioPlan Associates says, "Essentially what's happening is everyone is scrambling for space" with contract drug manufacturers to whom they outsource production. Langer said that, "A lot of the [contract drug] companies, even pre-pandemic, were just fully booked."[33] That demand helped South Korean-based Samsung Biologics, founded in 2010, become the largest global manufacturer of biopharmaceuticals in just over a decade.[34] Samsung Biologics manufactures drugs for Bristol-Myers Squibb and Roche Holdings. With its manufacturing orders having tripled in 2020, and a new $370 million contract with GlaxoSmithKline, Samsung Biologics is building a new $2 billion production facility to meet demand.[35]

Even when a firm decides to perform processes itself, it still faces a choice: Should it perform these functions domestically, or should it offshore these activities? **Offshoring** means moving processes previously performed domestically to a foreign location. It is important to realize that offshoring is *not* the same thing as outsourcing processes to other organizations. Offshoring doesn't require outsourcing; a firm often offshores processes by directly investing in its *own* foreign facilities. Similarly, outsourcing doesn't require a firm to go offshore; activities can be outsourced to other *domestic* firms. Despite this distinction, many firms have combined these approaches by hiring organizations in other countries to perform some of the processes that they previously performed at their own domestic facilities.

It is also worth noting that offshoring can go in both directions. Just as American firms offshore processes to other countries, some foreign companies offshore some of their processes to the United States. For example, several Japanese, European, and Korean automakers have extensive design and production facilities in the United States. German-based BMW has a manufacturing plant in South Carolina which employs 11,000 people, produces 1,500 BMWs every day, is responsible for 70% of the BMWs exported to 125 countries, and has produced 5 million BMWs in its 25 years of existence.[36]

One common reason for offshoring by U.S. firms is to take advantage of less expensive labor. But other factors can also play a role. Land and other resources also may be less expensive in developing nations than in the United States. And some foreign governments, eager to attract American investments, may offer financial incentives or other inducements. In addition, many foreign markets are growing much more rapidly than the relatively mature U.S. market. Firms often find it advantageous to locate production facilities close to these rapidly growing markets.

While foreign outsourcing can often reduce costs, it also can complicate value chains and create coordination problems. And it can expose the firm to certain types of risks. When a firm outsources important functions, it may have to entrust others in its value chain with confidential information and intellectual property, such

**vertical integration**
Performance of processes internally that were previously performed by other organizations in a supply chain.

**outsourcing** Arranging for other organizations to perform supply chain functions that were previously performed internally.

**offshoring** Moving production or support processes to foreign countries.

Offshoring involves moving activities previously performed domestically to a foreign location.

as copyrighted material or patented designs. These strategic assets have less legal protection in some countries than in the United States, so providing access to foreign firms may increase the risk that the firm's intellectual property will be pirated or counterfeited. This issue has been of greatest concern when firms have outsourced some of their supply chain functions to organizations in China.[37]

Given the trend toward offshoring and outsourcing, value chains (and the supply chains at their core) have become increasingly complex, often involving many different organizations and processes located in many different countries. Modern operations managers rely on sophisticated *supply chain management software* known as **enterprise resource planning (ERP)** to streamline the communications among supply chain participants and to help them plan and coordinate their efforts. The newest versions of enterprise resource planning software take supply chain management to its highest level. ERP initially focused on integrating the flow of information among *all* aspects of a single organization's operations—accounting, finance, sales and marketing, production, and human resources. But the newest versions go beyond a single organization to help manage activities along an entire supply chain or value chain. The common information system makes it easier for organizations throughout the chain to communicate and coordinate their activities. For example, Pittsburgh-based PPG, a global supplier of paints, coatings, and specialty materials, has 47,000 employees and 156 manufacturing facilities across five continents. PPG has large industrial customers in the aerospace, automotive, building and construction, and marine industries.[38] Imagine the complexity of trying to coordinate a company

of this size with so many products in so many markets. ERP software makes this possible. Because of its size and global footprint, PPG uses a number of different incompatible ERP programs. PPG's new CIO, Bhaskar Ramachandran, is overseeing their consolidation into one ERP program for the entire company.[39]

ERP systems do have some drawbacks. They are complex, expensive, and difficult to implement, and they require users to learn new ways to enter and access data. Productivity can actually fall until users become accustomed to these new methods. But despite these challenges, ERP systems have become very popular. And they continue to evolve and take advantage of new technologies. One of the newest developments is the arrival of Web-based ERP systems that can be "rented" from online providers—a strategy that reduces the need to invest in new hardware and software. The use of Web-based ERP services is an example of cloud computing discussed in Chapter 16.[40]

## 17-3 Implications of a Service-Based Economy: Responding to Different Challenges

Exhibit 17.5 illustrates how services differ from tangible goods. These differences present a number of challenges to service providers. One key challenge arises because customers often participate in the provision of services, which means that service providers have less control over how the process is carried out, how long it takes to complete, and whether the result is satisfactory. For instance, the accuracy of a doctor's diagnosis depends on how honestly and completely the patient answers the doctor's questions. And the amount of time the doctor spends with each patient will depend on the seriousness of the problem and the complexity of the diagnosis and treatment.

### 17-3a Designing the Servicescape

Because of the interaction between customers and service providers, the design of service facilities often must take the experiences of the participants into account. A **servicescape** is the environment in which

**enterprise resource planning (ERP)** Software-based approach to integrate an organization's (and in the sophisticated versions, a value chain's) information flows.

**servicescape** The environment in which a customer and service provider interact.

## Exhibit 17.5 Differences Between Goods and Services

| Goods | Services |
|-------|----------|
| Are tangible: They have a physical form and can be seen, touched, handled, etc. | Are intangible: They can be "experienced," but they don't have a physical form. |
| Can be stored in an inventory. | Must be consumed when they are produced. |
| Can be shipped. | Must be consumed where they are provided. |
| Are produced independently of the consumer. | Often require the customer to be actively involved in their production. |
| Can have at least some aspects of their quality determined objectively by measuring defects or deviations from desired values. | Intangible nature means quality is based mainly on customer perceptions. |

the customer and service provider interact. A well-designed servicescape can have a positive influence on the attitudes and perceptions of both the customer and those who provide the service. A poor servicescape can have the opposite effect.[41]

The design of servicescapes centers on three types of factors: ambience; functionality; and signs, symbols, and artifacts.

- *Ambience* refers to factors such as decor, background music, lighting, noise levels, and even scents. For example, the ambience is quite different at fast food restaurants like McDonald's (food wrapped in paper, no servers, plasticware, bright lights, bright colors, louder music), versus casual dining restaurants like California Pizza Kitchen (servers, silverware and plates, softer lights, warmer colors, softer music, bar), or fine dining restaurants like Ruth's Chris Steak House (formally dressed servers and customers, tablecloths dressed with formal silverware and glass settings, dimmed lighting, plush seating, even softer music, bar with extensive wine cellar and premium alcohol).

- *Functionality* involves how easy it is for the customers to move through the facility and find what they are looking for.

- *Signs, symbols,* and *artifacts* convey information to customers and create impressions, Obviously, signs like "Place Your Order Here" and "Pick Up Your Order Here" provide useful information that helps consumers maneuver through the service encounter. But other signs and symbols can be used to create favorable impressions.

Taco Bell has significantly redesigned its service-scape to create its Taco Bell Cantina restaurants. These new locations are designed to compete with more upscale Chipotle Mexican restaurants. There are no drive-throughs at the Cantinas, which makes them easier to locate in city and urban locations. Menus, ordering, and payment are all digitized. Local architecture influences the interior and exterior design, thus differentiating each Cantina's look. Green design is emphasized with reclaimed materials and LED lighting. Open design kitchens permit customers to see their food prepared as it is ordered. In addition to the standard Taco Bell menu, Cantinas will serve tapas-style shareable appetizers and alcohol (beer, wine, sangria, and frozen drinks).[42] R. J. Hottovy, a financial analyst at investment data and consultancy firm Morningstar, says, "Consumers have shown a willingness to pay up for fast-casual brands such as Chipotle, Five Guys, and Panera. I think this is Taco Bell attempting to play in that space."[43]

## 17-3b How Big Is Big Enough?

Because services are intangible and often must be experienced at the time they are created, service providers can't produce the service in advance and store it to meet temporary surges in demand. This can create challenges for operations managers because the demand for many types of services varies significantly, depending on the season, the day of the week, or the time of day. During peak lunch and dinner hours, popular restaurants tend to be very busy—often with crowds waiting to get a table. The same restaurants may be nearly empty during the mid-afternoon or late at night. Given such fluctuations in demand, the selection of *capacity*—the number of customers the service facility can accommodate per time period—becomes a crucial consideration.

If the capacity of a service facility is too small, customers facing long waits during periods of peak demand may well take their business elsewhere. But a facility large enough to handle peak capacity is more expensive to build; costs more to heat, cool, and insure; and may have substantial excess capacity during off-peak periods. Operations managers must weigh these drawbacks against the ability to handle a larger number of customers during peak hours.

Many service firms try to minimize this trade-off by finding ways to spread out demand so that big surges don't occur. One way to do this is to give customers an incentive to use the service at off-peak times. Many bars and restaurants have "happy hours" or "early-bird specials." Similarly, movie theaters have lower prices for matinée showings, and resort hotels offer reduced rates during their off seasons.

# 17-4 The Technology of Operations

Now let's take a close look at how technology has revolutionized operations management. Some of the new technologies involve the increasing sophistication of machinery and equipment. Others involve advances in software and information technology. The impact of these technological advances is greatest when the automated machinery is directly linked to the new software running on powerful new computers.

Solcan Design/Shutterstock.com

## 17-4a Automation: The Rise of the Machine

For the past half century, one of the biggest trends in operations management has been increased **automation** of many processes. Automation means replacing human operation and control of machinery and equipment with some form of programmed control. The use of automated systems has become increasingly common—and increasingly sophisticated.

Automation began in the early 1950s with primitive programmed machines. But in recent decades, **robots** have taken automation to a whole new level. Robots are reprogrammable machines that can manipulate materials, tools, parts, and specialized devices in order to perform a variety of tasks. Some robots have special sensors that allow them to "see," "hear," or "feel" their environment. Many robots are mobile and can even be guided over rugged terrain.

Robots offer many advantages to firms:

- They often perform jobs that most human workers find tedious, dirty, dangerous, or physically demanding.

- They don't get tired, so they can work very long hours while maintaining a consistently high level of performance.

- They are flexible; unlike old dogs, robots *can* be taught new tricks because they are reprogrammable.

Robots are most commonly used for factory tasks such as welding, spray painting, and assembling products, but they can do many other things ranging from packaging frozen pizza to disposing of hazardous waste. However, robots are beginning to make a difference in retail settings like grocery stores and in restaurant kitchens. Robotic micro-fulfillment centers, typically 10,000 to 20,000 square feet in size and located in the back of grocery stores, use specialized multi-tier shelving with rails that enable robots to move horizontally and vertically so that grocery stores can handle the dramatic increase in online orders for parking lot pick-ups. José Vicente Aguerrevere, co-founder and chief executive of Takeoff Technologies Inc., says the advantage is that "Basically, instead of you going to a shelf to pick grocery items, the robots bring the shelf to you."[44] Fast food chain White Castle is using Miso Robotics' *Flippy* robot, which can handle 360 baskets of fried foods each day.[45] Flippy, which can also grill burgers, costs between $20,000 and $30,000 to own, but can be leased for as little as $2,000 a month.[46] Finally, Chowbotics, which is now owned by DoorDash, makes Sally, a $35,000 salad-making robot about the size of a refrigerator, that sells and makes salads, grain bowls, breakfast bowls and snacks from 22 fresh ingredients in just 90 seconds.[47] Customers can order using a touch screen or pre-order via the Chowbotics app.

## 17-4b Software Technologies

Several types of software have become common in operations management, and as the processing power of computers has improved, the capabilities of these applications have become increasingly sophisticated. Some of the most common examples include:

- **Computer-aided design (CAD)** software provides powerful drawing and drafting tools that enable users to create and edit blueprints and design drawings quickly and easily. Current CAD programs allow users to create 3-D drawings.

- **Computer-aided engineering (CAE)** software enables users to test, analyze, and optimize their designs through computer simulations. CAE software can help engineers find and correct design flaws *before* production.

- **Computer-aided manufacturing (CAM)** software takes the electronic design for a product and

**automation** Replacing human operation and control of machinery and equipment with some form of programmed control.

**robot** A reprogrammable machine that is capable of manipulating materials, tools, parts, and specialized devices in order to perform a variety of tasks.

**computer-aided design (CAD)** Drawing and drafting software that enables users to create and edit blueprints and design drawings quickly and easily.

**computer-aided engineering (CAE)** Software that enables users to test, analyze, and optimize their designs.

creates the programmed instructions that robots and other automated equipment must follow to produce that product as efficiently as possible.

Today, **computer-aided design** and **computer-aided manufacturing** software are often combined into a single system, called **CAD/CAM**. This enables CAD designs to flow directly to CAM programs, which then send instructions directly to the automated equipment on the factory floor to guide the production process.

When a CAD/CAM software system is integrated with robots and other high-tech equipment, the result is **computer-integrated manufacturing (CIM)**, in which the whole design and production process is highly automated. The speed of computers, the ability to reprogram computers rapidly, and the integration of all these functions make it possible to switch from the design and production of one good to another quickly and efficiently. CIM allows firms to produce custom-designed products for individual customers quickly and at costs almost as low as those associated with mass-production techniques, thus allowing firms to pursue the strategy of mass customization mentioned at the beginning of this chapter.

> "Customers don't expect you to be perfect. They do expect you to fix things when they go wrong."
>
> —Donald Porter, Vice President, British Airways

ways to increase quality can also lead to greater efficiency because the cost of poor quality can be very high. When a firm detects defective products, it must scrap, rework, or repair them. And the costs of poor quality can be even higher when a firm *doesn't* catch defects before shipping products to consumers. These costs include handling customer complaints, warranty repair work, loss of goodwill, and the possibility of bad publicity or lawsuits. In the long run, firms often find that improving quality reduces these costs by more than enough to make up for their investment.

These ideas aren't especially new. W. Edwards Deming, viewed by many as the father of the quality movement, first proposed the relationship between quality and business success in the early 1950s. His ideas, which came to be known as the *Deming Chain Reaction*, are summarized in Exhibit 17.6.

**computer-aided manufacturing (CAM)**
Software that takes the electronic design for a product and creates the programmed instructions that robots must follow to produce that product as efficiently as possible.

**computer-aided design/computer-aided manufacturing (CAD/CAM)** A combination of software that can be used to design output and send instructions to automated equipment to perform the steps needed to produce this output.

**computer-integrated manufacturing (CIM)** A combination of CAD/CAM software with flexible manufacturing systems to automate almost all steps involved in designing, testing, and producing a product.

**17-5 Focus on Quality**

Almost everyone agrees that quality is important. But the concept of quality is tough to define—even expert opinions differ. For our purposes, we'll adopt the view that quality is defined in terms of how well a good or service satisfies customer preferences.

Why is quality so important? First, better quality clearly improves effectiveness (creates value) since consumers perceive high-quality goods as having greater value than low-quality goods. But finding

**Exhibit 17.6**
## The Deming Chain Reaction: Improved Quality Helps the Business's Bottom Line

Improve quality

↓

Costs decrease because of less rework, fewer mistakes, fewer delays and snags, and better use of time and materials

↓

Productivity improves

↓

Capture the market with better quality and lower price

↓

Stay in business

↓

Provide jobs and more jobs

# Computer Chips Disrupt Global Manufacturers' Critical Paths

With production and project scheduling, a path is a sequence of activities that must be completed in a specified order. A *critical path* is the sequence of activities that takes longest to complete. Any delay along the critical path delays production schedules. As a result, operations managers closely monitor critical path activities and act quickly, so they remain on schedule.

Unfortunately, computer chip shortages are slowing critical paths across a number of global industries.

**Smartphones.** Apple's production of high-end 5G smartphones was slowed by "across the board" shortages of Qualcomm mobile chips.

**Computers.** Personal computer makers began feeling shortages in spring 2020, when due to the COVID-19 pandemic, millions of work-from-home employees and "zoom school" students suddenly needed separate computers for daily use.

**Gaming consoles.** Jim Ryan, president and chief executive of Sony Interactive Entertainment, which makes the PlayStation 5, warned that while chip shortages would "ease incrementally," "there are very few magic wands that can be waved."

**Automobiles.** With today's cars using 100+ computer chips, GM, Ford, Toyota, Fiat Chrysler, and Volkswagen slowed production, cut shifts, or temporarily closed plants due to chip shortages. With half a year between orders and deliveries, chip shortages may cut auto company revenues by $60 billion.

**Taiwan Semiconductor Manufacturing Co. (TSMC) is the critical path.** TMSC, the world's largest computer chip maker, increased capital spending by 47% to build additional production capacity, but chip fabrication plants are complex and take 18 to 24 months to build.

With existing factory orders completely booked one year out, industry analysts estimate that it will take two years to address critical path shortages of computer chips.[48]

franz12/Shutterstock.com

## 17-5a Waking Up to the Need for Quality

In the years immediately after World War II, most Japanese goods had a reputation for being cheap and shoddy. But during the 1950s, many Japanese firms sought advice from Deming and other U.S. quality gurus. They learned to view quality improvement as a *continuous* process that was the responsibility of all employees in the organization. During the 1950s and 1960s, the quality of Japanese goods slowly but steadily improved.

By the early 1970s, many Japanese firms had achieved a remarkable turnaround, with quality levels that exceeded those of companies in most other countries (including the United States) by a wide margin. This improved quality was a major reason why Japanese firms rapidly gained global market share, often at the expense of American firms that had faced little competition in years immediately following World War II.

## 17-5b How Global Firms Responded to the Quality Challenge

When operations managers realized how far they trailed the Japanese in quality, they made a real effort to change their ways. Like the Japanese a few decades earlier, business leaders began to view improving the quality of their goods and services as a key to regaining international competitiveness.

**Total Quality Management** The first result of this newfound emphasis on quality was the development of an approach called **total quality management (TQM)**, better known as TQM. There are several variations, but all versions of TQM share the following characteristics:

> **total quality management (TQM)** An approach to quality improvement that calls for everyone within an organization to take responsibility for improving quality and emphasizes the need for a long-term commitment to continuous improvement.

- **Customer Focus:** TQM recognizes that quality should be defined by the preferences and perceptions of customers. Most consumers have strong pizza preferences, thin or thick crust, tomato versus nontomato sauces, and pepperoni versus sausage versus vegetarian. Thirty percent of us eat pizza once a week, and when we do, 36% order pepperoni pizza.[49] For decades, lay-flat pepperoni with the sausage casing removed has been the standard at most pizzerias. But in recent years, curled pepperoni (which curls when cooked because of the *attached* sausage casing) is making a comeback. Consumer Justin Kadis says, "It's just more aesthetically pleasing. The way those little pools of grease glisten, it just enhances the appeal."[50] Anthony Panichelli, pizza toppings brand manager for Hormel Foodservice, says, "In every city where there's a pizza culture, we see people using it. It will never overtake lay-flat, because it's more costly and time-consuming to produce. But it's a great marketing tool." So, with customer preferences changing, local pizzerias like Ken's Pizza Corner in Rochester, New York and national pizza chains like Marco's now offer both.[51]

- **Emphasis on Building Quality throughout the Organization:** TQM views quality as the concern of every department and every employee.

- **Empowerment of Employees:** Most TQM programs give teams of workers the responsibility and authority to make and implement decisions to improve quality.

- **Focus on Prevention Rather than Correction:** The TQM philosophy agrees with the old adage that an "ounce of prevention is worth a pound of cure." Thus, TQM pursues a strategy of preventing mistakes that create defects. While IKEA is known for its low-cost self-assembly furniture, it is also strongly focused on quality. Karen Hopkinson Pflug, who served as IKEA's global head of quality, said she was hired "to look at quality from the supply chain right through the customer satisfaction point of view. We're focusing on quality as an enabler of lower cost."[52] Under her leadership, IKEA ran two product testing labs, one in Sweden and the other in China. Together, those labs conduct more than 100,000 quality tests each year. The focus of the product testing, Pflug said, was to "get things right at the very beginning."[53]

- **Long-Run Commitment to Continuous Improvement:** TQM requires firms to adopt a focus on making improvements in quality a way of life.

In many cases, firms using TQM attempt to reduce defects by using **poka-yokes**—the Japanese term for "mistake proofing." Poka-yokes are simple procedures built into the production process that either prevent workers from making mistakes or help workers quickly catch and correct mistakes if they do occur. One simple example of a poka-yoke would be providing assembly workers with "kits" that contain exactly enough parts to complete one unit of work at a time. If the worker completes an assembly and sees a part left over, it's clear that a mistake has been made, and he or she can correct it on the spot.[54]

**The Move to Six Sigma** During the 1990s, another approach to quality improvement, known as **Six Sigma**, became increasingly popular. Six Sigma shares some characteristics with TQM, such as an organization-wide focus on quality, emphasis on finding and eliminating causes of errors or defects (prevention rather than correction), and a long-term focus on continuous quality improvement. Also like TQM, it relies on teams of workers to carry out specific projects to improve quality. At any given time, a firm may have several Six Sigma projects under way, and the goal of each is to achieve the Six Sigma level of quality.

But Six Sigma differs from TQM in other respects. Unlike TQM, it has a single unifying measure: to reduce defects of any operation or process to a level of no more than 3.4 per million opportunities. Attaining this level of quality represents a rigorous and challenging goal. Six Sigma also differs from TQM in its reliance on extensive (and expensive) employee training and reliance on expert guidance. The techniques used in the Six Sigma approach are quite advanced, and their application requires a high level of expertise.

### 17-5c Quality Standards and Initiatives

Another way firms try to improve quality is to launch programs designed to achieve certification or recognition from outside authorities. Two common approaches are participation in the Baldrige National Quality Program and seeking certification under the International Organization for Standardization's ISO 9000 standards.

**The Baldrige National Quality Program** Congress passed the Malcolm Baldrige National Quality Improvement Act of 1987 in an effort to encourage American firms to become more competitive in the global economy

**poka-yokes** Simple methods incorporated into a production process designed to eliminate or greatly reduce errors.

**Six Sigma** An approach to quality improvement characterized by very ambitious quality goals, extensive training of employees, and a long-term commitment to working on quality-related issues.

# Where Robots Don't Work...

Using robots to automate tasks is one of the biggest trends in operations management. Robots often perform jobs that people find tedious, dirty, dangerous, or physically demanding. And with increasingly better sensors that allow them to "see,""hear," or "feel," the number of tasks robots can perform will keep growing.

But robots don't always improve operations, especially when working with people.

The Henn na Hotel—"henn na" is Japanese for strange—which opened near the Tokyo Disney Resort five years ago was staffed with 243 robots and seven people. Animatronic "humans" and robot T-Rexes checked guests into the hotel. Robot porters carried luggage to rooms. Other robots vacuumed rooms and cleaned windows. Facial recognition replaced room keys. Motion sensors controlled room lighting. "Churi," an egg-shaped voice-activated robot in each room, served as a concierge, answering guest questions and turning room appliances on and off.

Well, that was the plan. Four years later, Henn na has gotten rid of half of its 243 robots.

- Front desk robots couldn't answer guests' basic questions. One guest said, "They functioned more like life-sized dolls, rather than problem-solving miracles from the future. One thing they did exceedingly well however: give us a serious case of the heebie-jeebies."

- Room concierge Churi frequently mistook snoring for questions, waking guests up by saying, "Sorry, I couldn't catch that. Could you repeat your question?" Also, Churi couldn't answer simple queries such as what time the nearby Disney resort opened and closed.

- Robot porters could only transport luggage to 25% of the hotel's 100 rooms. Hotel guest Taishi Mito said, "They were really slow and noisy, and would get stuck trying to go past each other."

- Pet-sized "dancing" robots that were supposed to welcome guests to the lobby were frequently broken or uncharged.

How are things after the robot downsizing?

A hotel employee said, "It's easier now that we're not being frequently called by guests to help with problems with the robots." Company founder and chair Hideo Sawada agreed, "When you actually use robots you realize there are places where they aren't needed—or just annoy people."[55]

by vigorously pursuing improvements in quality and productivity. Winners of the Baldrige Award must demonstrate excellence in seven areas: leadership; strategy; customers; measurement, analysis and knowledge management; workforce; operations; and results.[56]

Firms that participate in the **Baldrige National Quality Program** receive benefits even if they don't win the award. Every participating firm receives a detailed report prepared by expert evaluators identifying areas of strength and areas where improvement is needed. Considering the normal fees that high-powered consulting firms charge for similar reports, the information and advice a firm gets for the fee charged to participate in the Baldrige

> "Quality is more important than quantity. One home run is much better than two doubles."
> —Steve Jobs, Co-Founder of Apple

program are a tremendous bargain! The cost of applying for the Baldrige Award includes a $400 eligibility fee for all organizations. Manufacturing, service, and large healthcare or nonprofit organizations also pay an application fee of $20,000 and a site visitation fee of $58,000 to $69,000. Small businesses and small healthcare, nonprofit, and education organizations also pay an application fee of $10,800 and a site visitation fee of $35,000 to $40,500. K–12 education organizations also pay an application fee of $4,800 and a site visitation fee of $17,000.[57]

**Baldrige National Quality Program** A national program to encourage American firms to focus on quality improvement.

**ISO 9000 Certification** Founded in 1947, ISO is a network of national standards institutes from more than 165 nations that have worked together to develop over 23,600 international standards for a wide array of industries, such as building and construction, chemicals, food and agriculture, mechanical engineering, ores and metals, and transport.[58] ISO standards ensure that goods produced in one country will meet the requirements of buyers in another country, that safety issues are consistently addressed, and that best practice ideas and solutions are broadly shared.[59] This benefits buyers by giving them the ability to purchase from foreign sellers with confidence, thus giving them a wider array of choices. It also benefits sellers by allowing them to compete more successfully in global markets.[60]

Most of the standards established by the ISO are industry-specific, such as medical devices, railways, or petroleum, petrochemical, and natural gas.[61] But in 1987, the ISO developed and published the **ISO 9000** family of standards. The goal of this effort was to articulate an international consensus on good quality-management practices that could be applied to virtually any company. Similar to the other quality initiatives we've discussed, ISO 9000 standards define quality in terms of the ability to satisfy customer preferences and require the firm to implement procedures for continuous quality improvement. ISO 9000 standards don't describe how to make a better-quality car, computer, or widget. Instead, they describe how companies can extensively document (and thus standardize) the steps they take to create and improve the quality of their products.[62] There are several standards in the ISO 9000 family, but the most basic is ISO 9001, which specifies the requirements for a quality-management system and "helps businesses and organizations be more efficient and improve customer satisfaction."[63]

> **ISO 9000** A family of generic standards for quality management systems established by the International Organization for Standardization.

# Can "Robots" Stop COVID-19 from Killing Saville Row's Bespoke Suit Business?

London's Saville Row has been home to the best bespoke tailors in the world for three centuries. At Huntsman, established in 1849, bespoke suits requiring 50 individual measurements, multiple fittings and adjustments, and 80 hours of handcrafting by master tailors to ensure perfect fit, *start* at $5,000. Roughly half of Huntsman's business comes from the large number of international businesspeople flowing through London, one of the world's premiere financial centers. The other half comes from trunk shows in which Huntsman tailors and client managers travel to clients in New York, Los Angeles, Shanghai, Tokyo, Dubai, and other locations.

But will Saville Row survive COVID-19? Simon Cundey, managing director of Henry Poole & Co., established in 1806, said, "Our company lived through the Boer War, World War I, the Depression, World War II, recessions.... But through all of these crises, we could visit our customers and they could visit us. This is a tragedy on a different scale."

In March 2020, Pierre Lagrange, a Belgian hedge fund manager who bought Huntsman in 2013, figured if surgeons can do online surgery, then why couldn't Huntsman find a way to do remote fitting of bespoke suits?

Huntsman's six "telepresence robots" are basically tablets and webcams mounted on mobile stands controlled by the client's "cutter" in London. With the help of an onsite Huntsman assistant who marks, measures, and adjusts the remote client's clothes at the cutter's direction, the cutter is free to communicate with the client and record measurements, photos, and video as needed.

While it's too early to determine how well this will work, Huntsman has learned it can measure and fit a suit with "telepresence robots" in 5 months, compared to the 12 months it normally takes with trunk shows or with international businesspeople in London who typically go months between fittings on Saville Road.

Lagrange is optimistic because it gives Huntsman a third, faster on-demand way to serve global clients. He said, "I don't know how fast we would have gotten here without COVID. Sometimes you need a crisis."[64]

FXQuadro/Shutterstock.com

# 17-6 The Move to Be Lean and Green: Cutting Cost and Cutting Waste

**Lean production** refers to a set of strategies and practices to eliminate waste, which is defined as any function or activity that uses resources but doesn't create value. Eliminating waste can lead to dramatic improvements in efficiency. For example, Louis Vuitton produces some of the most expensive handmade bags and purses in the world. To increase productivity, it switched to teams of 6 to 12 workers who learned to complete multiple production steps. So instead of having three workers separately gluing, stitching, and finishing the edges of a flap over and over, one worker would do all three steps. Because of that, former CEO Yves Carcelle said, "We were able to hire 300 new people without adding a factory."[65]

## 17-6a Reducing Investment in Inventory: Just-In-Time to the Rescue

One of the hallmarks of lean systems is a tight control on inventories. In part, this reflects recognition of the costs of holding large inventories that we discussed earlier. But the lean approach also offers another reason for minimizing inventories. Large inventories serve as a buffer that enables a firm to continue operations when problems arise due to poor quality, faulty equipment, or unreliable suppliers—making it easier for firms to live with these problems rather than correct them. Advocates of lean production argue that, in the long run, it is more efficient to improve quality, keep equipment in good working order, and develop reliable supply relationships than to continue compensating for these problems by holding large inventories.

Lean manufacturing avoids overproduction and holding large inventories of finished goods by using **just-in-time (JIT) production** methods. JIT produces only enough goods to satisfy current demand. This approach is called a *pull system* because actual orders "pull" the goods through the production process. The workers at the end of the production process produce just enough of the final product to satisfy actual orders and use just enough parts and materials from preceding stages of production to satisfy their needs. Workers at each earlier stage are expected to produce just enough output at their workstations to replace the amount used by the processes further along in the process—and in so doing they withdraw just the needed amount of parts and other supplies from even earlier processes.

JIT techniques obviously result in very small inventories of finished goods and work in process. But lean firms also hold only small inventories of materials and parts, counting on suppliers to provide them with these items as they need them to meet current demand. In a lean system, *all* organizations in the supply chain use the JIT approach, so that inventories are minimized at each stage. Clearly, this type of system requires incredible coordination among all parts of the supply chain; in fact, the movement toward JIT is a key reason why supply chain management has become so crucial. Spain-based Zara is a global clothing and accessories retailer. Zara's competitive advantage is fast fashion, meaning frequent introductions of new fashions that are made in small batches, delivered quickly to stores, and stocked as just-in-time inventory. It took just 25 days, for example, for a black, high collar women's wrap coat with a metal ring to end up in Zara's flagship store in New York City. The inspiration for the coat started with a Zara designer in Arteixo, Spain talking to store managers. The designer took five days to create a design prototype, which was handed over to a manufacturing pattern maker. Seamstresses at Zara's suppliers worked for 13 days to produce 8,000 coats. Six days were needed for ironing, labeling, quality checks, and transportation from Zara's distribution center in Zaragoza, Spain to the Barcelona airport to New York's JFK airport, and finally to the Zara's Fifth Avenue store. Industry analyst Anne Critchlow says, "Think of Zara not as a brand, but as speedy chameleon that adapts instantly to fashion trends."[66]

JIT does have some potential drawbacks. The most serious problem is that it can leave producers vulnerable to supply disruptions. If a key supplier is unable to make deliveries due to a natural disaster, labor strike, or other problem, the firms further along the supply chain may quickly run out of parts or materials and have to shut down production. If there's a business lesson to learn from the COVID-19 pandemic, it's that JIT-based supply chains are much more vulnerable to supply disruptions than anyone imagined. A year into the pandemic, cars, Harley-Davidson motorcycles, toilet paper and paper towels, refrigerators, clothes washers and dryers, and thousands more products were still in short supply around the world.[67] *Wall Street Journal* reporters Sharon Terlep and Annie Gasparro summarized this major weakness in JIT systems:

"The scarcity is rooted in a decades long quest by businesses at all levels, handling many different products, to eke out more profit by operating with almost no slack. Make only what you can sell quickly. Order only enough materials to keep production lines going. Have only enough railcars for a day's worth of output. Stock only enough items on a shelf to last till the next batch arrives."[68]

**lean production** An approach to production that emphasizes the elimination of waste in all aspects of production processes.

**just-in-time (JIT) production** A production system that emphasizes the production of goods to meet actual current demand, thus minimizing the need to hold inventories of finished goods and work in process at each stage of the supply chain.

JIT makes businesses more efficient and profitable. But, like falling dominoes, JIT shortages cascade from company to company across global supply chains.

## 17-6b Lean Thinking in the Service Sector

Employing lean principles in the service sector can be quite a challenge because customers often participate in providing the service. This means a service firm usually has less control over how processes are conducted. But many service firms have benefited from creatively applying lean techniques.

Kroger supermarkets used lean thinking to reduce checkout waiting times. Kroger uses Vision, a network of infrared sensors, to count the customers in a store and then determine how many checkout aisles should be opened now and in the next 30 minutes. Mike Slevin, global sales and marketing director of U.K.-based Irisys, which makes Kroger's Vision system, said, "They display our dashboard in their stores, so you'll see it on big monitors that they have above the checkout area. They show what we call the 'golden balls,' which are three circles with numbers in them showing how many lanes they should have open, how many lanes they do have, and how many lanes they should have open in 15 minutes."[69] The system dramatically slashed average checkout times from four minutes a few years ago to just 26 seconds today. As a result, customer satisfaction with checkout speed rose by 42%, while sales increased nearly 10%. Kroger former senior vice president Marnette Perry said, "There are 7 million shoppers at Kroger stores today—we'll save them 25 million minutes today."[70] Vision also proved worthwhile during the COVID-19 pandemic by automatically counting the number of customers entering and exiting each store. When capacity limits were reached, Vision alerted store managers so that customers' lines could be formed outside stores.[71]

## 17-6c Green Practices: Helping the Firm by Helping the Environment

Many of today's leading firms have also tried to become "greener" by finding environmentally friendly ways to carry out the processes needed to produce and distribute their goods and services. Green practices include designing facilities to be more energy efficient; using renewable energy sources such as wind, solar, or geothermal power when possible; making

**ISO 14000** A family of generic standards for environmental management established by the International Organization for Standardization.

Elxeneize/Shutterstock.com

Green practices aim to achieve sustainability by finding ways to meet the organization's current objectives while protecting and preserving the environment.

use of recyclable materials; switching to paints, lubricants, cleaning fluids, and solvents that are less harmful to the environment; and even providing labeling to help consumers find out which products are the most environmentally friendly. As part of a commitment to slash greenhouse gas emissions to zero by 2040, UK grocer Sainsbury will spend $1.4 billion to put LED lights in all stores, switch to electric vehicles and alternative fuels, cut food waste and water usage, and plant 1.5 million trees. The biggest savings in terms of costs and the environment, however, may come from improving refrigeration at Sainsbury's stores and warehouse facilities.[72]

The long-term goal of many green practices is to achieve *sustainability*, which means finding ways to meet the organization's current objectives while protecting and preserving the environment for future generations. One impediment to even greater acceptance of sustainability initiatives is that some sustainability efforts—such as switching to renewable sources of energy—increase costs. But many firms have found that other sustainability efforts can actually benefit the bottom line. A recent study by Aberdeen Group, a well-known technology research firm, found that firms employing best-in-class sustainability practices not only saw an 8% drop in sustainability-related costs but also experienced a 16% increase in customer retention.[73]

In the late 1990s, the International Organization for Standardization developed a set of standards called **ISO 14000**, which focus on environmental management. As with ISO 9000, the term "ISO 14000" actually refers to a family of standards. The broadest of these is ISO 14001. To receive ISO 14001 certification, a firm must:

- demonstrate the ability to identify and control the environmental impact of their activities;

- make a commitment to continually improve their environmental performance; and

- implement a systematic approach to setting environmental targets and to achieving those targets.

It is important to note that ISO 14000 standards do not establish specific goals for environmental performance; doing so would be very difficult, since ISO is intended to be a generic set of standards that apply to all industries, and each specific industry faces different environmental challenges.[74]

## The Big Picture

Operations managers are responsible for "putting it all together" by developing and implementing the processes needed to produce goods and services and distribute them to the target market. Their decisions affect both revenues and costs, going a long way toward determining whether a firm makes a profit or suffers a loss.

The responsibilities of operations managers require them to work closely with other managers throughout their organizations. For example, they must work with marketers and designers to ensure that the desired goods and services move from the drawing board to the final customer on time and within budget. They must work closely with financial managers to ensure that the company invests in the capital goods needed to produce goods and services in the most efficient manner.

And they must work effectively with human resource managers to attract and develop workers who possess the knowledge and skills needed to become world-class competitors. Operations managers must even go beyond their own organization and work effectively with the suppliers and distributors who comprise the firm's value chain.

Operations managers must continuously adapt to changes in technology and in competitive conditions. Key challenges in recent years have centered on the need to continuously improve product quality while finding ways to reduce costs and protect the environment. You can expect the goals of becoming ever leaner—and ever greener—to remain a major focus of operations managers in years to come.

## Careers in Operations Management

### Plant Supervisor

Responsible for supervising production and warehouse crews, monitoring and maintaining a safe working environment, timely completion of paperwork and records, keeping lines of communication open between the plant, management, scheduling, and sales, coordinating overtime and reviewing production schedules to make sure each piece of equipment has the appropriate number of workers, and cross-training employees for multiple tasks and jobs. The ideal candidate has a bachelor's degree, two to four years of manufacturing experience, strong interpersonal, communication, and team-building skills, good analytical and problem-solving skills, ability to analyze cost performance data to improve operations and reduce costs, and be willing to work evenings, night shifts, weekends, and holidays.

# Personal Finance Appendix

Kenchiro168/Shutterstock.com

## Learning Objectives

After studying this appendix, you will be able to:

**A-1** Apply the principles of budgeting to your personal finances

**A-2** Identify strategies to help build a sufficient savings

**A-3** Explain the importance of using credit wisely

**A-4** Discuss key wealth-building principles and the financial instruments that may be part of a wealth-building strategy

Unfortunately, two-thirds of us fail a basic financial literacy test (see how well you do on the National Financial Capability Study (NFCS) at https://www.usfinancialcapability .org/quiz.php). Many of us struggle to calculate simple interest on loans. Only 45% of our parents or guardians taught us how to manage our finances.[1] Just 28% of us have ever been offered the chance to take a class in personal finance. Yet, despite financial literacy declining by 8% over the last decade, 71% of those taking the NFCS financial literacy test rated themselves "high" on financial knowledge.[2] Unfortunately, when it comes to personal finance, many people don't know what they don't know. Financial ignorance is not bliss. With financial illiteracy so widespread—and growing—it's not surprising that Americans report that money (61%), work (58%), and the economy (50%) are significant sources of stress.[3] More specifically, 53% indicate that "thinking about my personal finances can make me feel anxious," while 44% agreed that "discussing my finances can make my heart race or make me feel stressed."[4]

If you lack confidence about your personal finances or just need a quick refresh, this appendix provides an introduction to key topics, such as budgets, building savings and managing credit cards, starting a basic financial

portfolio and investing for the long term—your retirement. Another educational resource is the Mint Grad, which financial advising firm Northwestern Mutual developed specifically for college students and recent college grads. Mint Grad uses a four-step process to help young adults master personal finance:

- Learn (budgeting, spending, practical investing, and lifestyle planning)

- Try it (quizzes, financial calculators, and budget worksheets)

- Plan (setting goals for saving, building positive credit, and paying down student debt)

- Online socializing (reading and discussing blog topics)

Other popular apps and/or websites for learning about personal finance include Nerdwallet.com, WiseBread.com, and TheBalance.com.

Let's take a look at how budgeting, building your savings, managing your credit, and investing wisely can help you meet your financial goals, and hopefully reduce the money-related stress in your life.

## A-1 Your Budget

One of the first steps to controlling your finances is developing a **budget**, which is a detailed forecast of your expected cash inflows (income) and cash outflows (expenditures). You can use your budget to develop a personal financial plan and to monitor progress toward achieving your financial goals.

### A-1a How Do I Get Started?

You can get a good handle on what should be included in your budget by carefully tracking and analyzing all of your financial transactions for several months. This takes discipline and careful record keeping, but once you know where your money comes from and where it goes, you'll have what you need to prepare your budget.

**Assessing Revenues: Where Does My Money Come From?** A budget starts with a forecast of your revenue—the money you bring in. This can come from many different sources. For most people, the paycheck from their job is their primary source of income. But the major source of revenue for entrepreneurs might be the

profits earned from their businesses. Some people also derive a substantial amount of revenue from financial investments, such as stocks and bonds, while others earn rental income. Retirees often depend on retirement accounts, Social Security, and private investments for much of their income. For most beginning investors, assessing revenues is (unfortunately) a relatively quick and easy first step.

**Assessing Expenses: Where Does It All Go?**
Once you have identified the amount of revenue you expect to receive from various sources, turn your focus to the spending side of your budget. To successfully

**budget (personal)**
A detailed forecast of financial inflows (income) and outflows (expenses) to determine your net inflow or outflow for a given period of time.

set up your budget, you'll need to be very specific about where your money goes. There are two basic approaches to assessing expenses, automatic tracking and tracking expenses by hand.

Some of the most widely used budgeting apps and websites automatically track and categorize spending and saving.[5] To do that, they require users to provide secure access to credit cards, bank statements, and retirement accounts.

- Intuit's Mint.com, the online and app-based service tracks spending, helps manage and pay bills, easily creates customized budgets, and keeps track of your credit score and investments. Mint is supported by its financial partners and advertising, so it costs you nothing. It is regularly recommended as one of the best all-in-one financial tools.

- The Digit app and website (digit.co) automates saving, investing, paying off debts, and avoiding overdrafts. Every day, after assessing your income, how much you have in the bank, upcoming bills, and expected purchases, Digit calculates how much it is "safe to save today." It then puts those daily savings toward rainy day funds, or credit card payments, or financial goals. One user said, "I've saved over $2,600 for our Vacation Fund, in the 1 year I've been using @hellodigit."[6] Another said, "My Digit savings helped me pay off a semester of tuition so I don't have to take out a loan." Digit provides the financial discipline that many people need but lack. After a free first month, users pay a small monthly fee. Acorns (acorns.com) is a similar automated savings app and website.

If you are comfortable tracking expenses by hand, then spreadsheet

apps like Microsoft Excel or app/online website YNAB are two good options. Microsoft's Templates and Themes for Office website (https://templates.office.com) has Excel budget templates for expenses, family budget planning, personal money tracking, college budgeting, and academic club budgeting to help you get started. These templates are generic, so you will want to adjust them to suit your circumstances. Some people find all of the information, charts, and graphs generated by automated expense tracking apps overwhelming and just prefer the simplicity of a spreadsheet template.

YNAB, which is short for You Need a Budget (youneedabudget.com) is a powerful "hands-on" expense tracking tool with charts, graphs, and reports as good as automate expense trackers like Mint or Digit.[7] While YNAB has sophisticated, powerful budgeting tools, it takes a proactive approach to budgeting that focuses on financial goals, planning ahead, and, yes, when needed, manually entering budget data such as spending expenses.

**Understanding Your Spending Habits** Whether expenses are tracked automatically or by hand, you'll probably be surprised by some of the spending habits you uncover. You might find that you're spending a lot more than you thought on video games, eating out, clothes, a beloved hobby or rarely used annual subscriptions or memberships. But once you discover your spending patterns, you'll be in a better position to determine the categories of spending to include in your budget and to track the amount you spend in each category.

Spending can be classified into discretionary and nondiscretionary categories. The payments you have the most control over are called your **discretionary payments**. Perhaps you like dining out, nightclubbing, or shopping. Perhaps you just have expensive taste in coffee. David Bach, author of *The Automatic Millionaire,* challenges us to look at our "latté factors," meaning the little vices we each find hard to resist. You'll find that something as seemingly minor as a $5 cup of coffee each workday costs you $1,300 a year

PathDoc/Shutterstock.com

**discretionary payments**
Expenditures for which the spender has significant control in terms of the amount and timing.

($5 × 5 days per week × 52 weeks). If instead you invested that $1,300 each year, earning a conservative 6% annual return, those investments would grow to $113,000 in 30 years! Likewise, if you spend $2 a day for bottled water 5 days a week at an annual cost of $520, you're giving up the chance to grow that pocket change into a $50,000 investment after 30 years.[8] Of course, no one is saying don't drink coffee or bottled water, just don't overpay for them. David Bach says, "I do not start my day without coffee, but I make it at home every morning for 20 cents instead of spending $5 at a cafe."[9] Likewise, pay $30 for a Takeya Actives stainless steel water bottle, keep tap water in your refrigerator, and then fill your water bottle every morning.[10] It's better for the environment, too. Once you realize the true cost of these "latté factors," you'll have a greater incentive to bring them under control.[11] Your budget can help you find the discipline you need to accomplish this goal.

**Nondiscretionary payments** are those you have little control over, such as your monthly rent or car payment, which are set by contract. Your lifestyle may also lock you into other costs that are at least partly nondiscretionary. Given your need to get to school and work, you may have to spend a significant amount of money on car payments, fuel, and car maintenance every month. But with a little flexibility and creativity, you may find that such costs aren't *completely* nondiscretionary. For instance, you might be able to significantly reduce your expenses for gas and car maintenance by carpooling or using public transportation.

You may also want to consider your attitude toward spending. Are you most likely to spend too much money when you are depressed or stressed out? Look at this aspect carefully, and try to be as honest as possible with yourself. Who are you with when you spend money? You may find that you tend to spend much more money while hanging out with certain friends. Finally, are you an impulse spender, indulging yourself with expensive goods, artisanal meals, or last-minute trips? Understanding your spending habits and your attitude toward spending are enormously important first steps to taking control of your money.

**Putting It All Together in Your Budget** Once you've gotten a handle on your revenue sources and spending habits, it's time to figure out your financial goals and put this all together in a budget. As with expense tracking, there are broadly two kinds of tools for personal budgets: automated tools and tools that require you to be

> ## "Rather go to bed without dinner than to rise in debt."
> —Benjamin Franklin

much more "hands-on" with your budget data and decisions.

Mint.com automatically tracks your spending and suggests budget levels based on that spending (which might not work well if your spending is out of control). YNAB (You Need a Budget) is very "hands-on," making you assign a spending or savings category for *every* dollar that goes in and out of your hands—and your various accounts. The next step is assigning budget goals for each category, and then tracking your spending against each budget goal. Though more complicated, YNAB forces you to decide about your spending in order "to be intentional about what you want your money to do before you spend it."[12] *New York Times* personal finance reporter Tara Siegel Bernard said, "For people who want a more proactive approach to spending and whittling down debt, there's You Need a Budget. I've come across many people in my reporting who have attested that it's life-changing."[13] While Mint is free thanks to advertising, YNAB is free to try for one month, and then $84 a year or $11.99 a month.

But if you're looking for something in between Mint and YNAB, consider Simplifi by Quicken. Like Mint, Simplifi accesses your checking, savings, and investment accounts to automatically track spending. Like Mint and YNAB, Simplifi generates sophisticated charts, tables, and reports of your financial transactions. Simplifi, for example, shows recurring bills, automatically categorized expenses, and watchlists indicating where you are or could overspend.[14] What makes Simplifi different is that rather than comparing spending to budgets in dozens of categories like YNAB, it focuses your attention on how much more money you can spend *this month* considering your income, bills, *and* what you need to put aside to meet financial goals.[15]

Whether you do a budget by hand with a spreadsheet like Microsoft Excel, or with powerful apps like Mint, YNAB, or Simplifi, you'll need to adjust your budget periodically to reflect significant changes in your lifestyle, employment status, and financial goals. So, as your life changes because of marriage or children, moving for career advancement, or deciding to go back to school for a graduate degree, adjust your budget to serve your new personal financial plans and goals. Doing so can help you spend money the "right way" when your life changes. That's important because spending money the "right way" increases personal happiness. A study of 76,000 bank records matched to personality dimensions shows that people are happiest when spending their money on things that fit

> **nondiscretionary payments** Expenditures that the spender has little or no control over.

their personalities.[16] The study's lead author, Sandra Matz, explained, "Money enables us to lead a life we want."[17] But without keeping close track of how you spend your money, you may end up spending it in ways—and amounts—that don't fit who you are or your financial goals. Indeed, the study also found that spending money in ways contrary to personality resulted in less happiness.

## A-2 Your Savings: Building a Safety Net

A **savings account** is an interest-earning account that is intended to satisfy obligations that your checking account cannot handle. Think of your savings account as a "safety net" for unexpected financial challenges, such as a major plumbing repair, the need to replace your car's transmission, or even the loss of your job. Many financial experts suggest that you have enough money in your savings to cover six months of your expenses. Marguerita Cheng, CEO of Blue Ocean Global Wealth, tells her clients to be prepared for the unexpected. She explained, "My father taught me the importance of planning for unexpected emergencies or opportunities. When I was 10 years old, my aunt passed away. She left behind four children and didn't have life insurance. My dad paid for her funeral because he knew my uncle and his family were experiencing emotional and financial trauma. He later explained to me that just because you don't plan for unfortunate events it doesn't mean they won't happen. As an adult, that lesson led me to focus on the value of building up an emergency fund and getting life insurance to give me financial peace of mind, which is priceless. I sleep better at night knowing that we have planned for the unexpected."[18]

One technique for establishing a sizable savings balance is to "pay yourself first." This concept, popularized by David Bach, suggests that you have a predetermined amount from each paycheck automatically deposited into your savings account. Once you've accumulated enough in your savings account to provide an adequate safety net, you can use the "pay yourself first" approach to achieve other financial goals.[19] For example, you can use your savings account to accumulate funds for vacations, holiday gifts, or a large down payment on a car or home. However, it's even better to pay yourself first *twice* by automatically depositing money into savings *and* retirement accounts. Why twice? Retirement savings, discussed in section A-4e of this appendix, are often matched dollar for dollar by employers. If you put in $500 a month, your employer doubles it to $1,000—and that's before it grows through investing. The other advantage of retirement accounts is that the IRS usually adds a 10% penalty for early withdrawals, which is enough to discourage most people from trying to spend those funds.[20] By contrast, savings accounts are easily "raided" for impulsive, unplanned spending.

Interest rates on savings accounts vary from bank to bank, so you should shop around to find the best rate. In recent years, online savings banks have often provided higher interest rates than traditional banks. If you can, try to find savings accounts that keep up with the rate of inflation. Doing so protects the purchasing power of those savings. Just be sure to look for reputable banks that are insured by the **Federal Deposit Insurance Corporation (FDIC)**. The FDIC is an independent agency created by Congress to maintain stability and public confidence in the nation's financial system, primarily by insuring bank deposits. The FDIC insures individual deposits up to $250,000 per account in FDIC-insured banks.[21]

## A-3 Your Credit: Handle with Care!

**Credit** refers to your ability to obtain goods or resources without having to make immediate payment. One of the most important determinants of the amount of credit you can obtain is your **credit score**, which is a numerical indicator of your creditworthiness. Currently, the most commonly used credit scoring system is the Fair, Isaac and Company (FICO) scale. The FICO scale runs from 300 to 850.[22]

Your individual FICO score is based on several factors, including your payment history (35%), the amount you owe (30%), the length of time you've held various credit accounts (15%), credit mix (10%) meaning the kind of credit you're using, and how many new credit accounts (10%) you've opened.[23] Exhibit A.1 shows how to interpret FICO scores. Very poor scores fall below 580; fair scores are 580–669; good scores are 670–739 (the average score is 711); very good scores are 740–799, and exceptional scores are 800–850.[24] A high score makes it easier to get credit on favorable terms.[25] On a $216,000, 30-year fixed mortgage,

## Exhibit A.1 What FICO Credit Scores Mean

| Score | Creditworthiness | Percentage of Consumers |
|-------|------------------|-------------------------|
| Below 580 | Very poor | 5.7% |
| 580–669 | Fair | 18.5% |
| 670–739 | Good | 22.3% |
| 740–799 | Very good | 35% |
| 800–850 | Exceptional | 18.6% |

Source: "What Is a Credit Score?" myFICO, https://www.myfico.com/credit-education/credit-scores, accessed March 17, 2021.

a borrower with a fair credit score of 620 will pay $69,120 more interest because of higher interest rates than a borrower with a very good credit score of 760.[26]

### A-3a Credit Cards: Boon or Bane?

Now let's look at a specific source of credit that is near and dear to many college students' hearts: the **credit card**. A credit card allows its holder to make a purchase now and pay the credit card issuer later.

There are several benefits to having and using credit cards. The most obvious is that credit cards are more convenient and safer than carrying a lot of cash. Credit cards also make it easy to track your expenditures, since you have access to a monthly summary of charges. And many cards offer perks, such as discounts on certain products, extended warranties on purchases, or frequent-flier miles. Another benefit of the *responsible* use of credit cards is that it can improve your credit score by allowing you to establish a history of prompt payments. This can make it easier for you to borrow money when you really need it—such as when you want to buy a car or your first home.

One downside of having a credit card is that the "buy now, pay later" aspect of credit card use makes it hard for some people to maintain financial discipline. Another problem is that interest rates on unpaid card balances tend to be very high. Many card issuers also impose a variety of fees that can make a noticeable dent in your wallet. And making late payments or failing to pay what you owe can damage your credit history, hurting your chances of getting additional credit when you need it.

### A-3b The Devil in the Details— Understanding Your Credit Card Agreement!

Before you accept a credit card, make sure you read the credit card agreement and understand the main conditions for using that card. Some things to look for include:

- **Grace period:** The period of time that you have to pay your balance before interest or fees are assessed. Most credit card companies expect to receive their payment within 21–25 days of the credit card statement date.[27] So, to avoid interest charges and other fees, be sure to pay your credit card bills on or before their due dates.

- **APR (annual percentage rate):** The percentage financing cost charged on unpaid balances. The higher the APR, the greater your interest expense on unpaid balances. Your credit card company may charge different APRs for different types of transactions.

- **Late fees:** May also be assessed if a payment is not received within the grace period. Federal law now caps late fees at $29 for a first offense and $40 for additional late payments. However, the late fee can't exceed what you owe the credit card company. So, if you were late on a $15 balance, then the fee would be limited to $15.[28]

- **Other fees:** Include *annual fees* (a charge just for the privilege of having a card, whether you use it or not), *over-the-credit-limit fees* if your charges exceed your credit limit, and *balance-transfer fees* if you transfer a balance from one card to another. This isn't a complete list, but it does reflect many of the most common types of fees you might incur. Not all cards are subject to all of these charges; the specific types and amounts of fees can

**credit card** A card issued by a bank or finance company that allows the cardholder to make a purchase now and pay the credit card issuer later.

**grace period** The period of time that the credit card holder has to pay outstanding balances before interest or fees are assessed.

**annual percentage rate (APR)** The interest expense charged on a credit card, expressed as an annual percentage.

vary considerably from one issuer to another—which is why reading the fine print is important!

### A-3c Protection for Consumers: New Laws and Regulations

The most important protection for consumers comes from the 1974 Equal Credit Opportunity Act which basically says that credit worthiness is the only factor that may be used when making decisions about individuals' credit applications. In other words, it is illegal to take race, color, religion, national origin, sex, sexual identity, marital status, or age into consideration when making lending decisions.[29] Two more recent laws, however, have also had a significant impact on credit card practices.

The Credit Card Accountability, Responsibility and Disclosure Act of 2009 (often called the CARD Act) requires issuers to give a 45-day notice before making significant changes to credit agreements. It further prohibits credit card companies from raising interest rates on existing balances unless the borrower is more than 60 days late in making required payments, the card was issued with a variable interest rate, or a lower promotional interest rate has ended.[30] It also requires anyone under the age of 21 who applies for a credit card to either verify proof of income or have an adult cosign the application. And it places caps on certain types of fees that credit card issuers can charge.[31]

New laws and regulations have changed the way many financial markets operate in recent years. The Dodd-Frank Wall Street Reform and Consumer Protection Act of 2010, passed in the wake of the financial crisis of 2008 and 2009, includes several provisions intended to protect the financial rights of consumers. One key provision of this Act is the establishment of the Consumer Financial Protection Bureau (CFPB) to eliminate confusing and potentially deceptive banking practices related to mortgages, credit cards, and other loan agreements.[32] The CFPB also makes it easier for consumers to compare the features and costs of various credit cards so that they can select the ones that best meet their needs. And if your credit application is rejected, the CFPB explains that the lender is required to:[33]

- Tell you why your credit application was rejected.

- Provide a free copy of your credit score, including the credit reporting company whose credit score was used in reviewing your credit application.

- Explain how to address possible mistakes on your credit report, or the steps you can take to make your credit report more complete.

- Allow you to dispute inaccuracies and mistakes on your credit report, should they exist.

> If you owe $5,000 on a credit card but only make minimum payments, you'll be repaying for 273 months, and pay $6,923 in interest!
>
> —Bankrate.com

And even if your credit applications are not rejected, the CFPB requires the credit score companies, Equifax, Experian, and Transunion, to each provide one free credit report a year. Go to AnnualCreditReport.com to request yours.[34]

### A-3d Using Credit Cards Wisely: The Need for Discipline

Although many young adults manage their credit cards without major problems, others are stunned when the credit card bill arrives. Many never read their credit card agreements, so they are taken by surprise by higher than expected interest charges and fees. Others simply lack discipline. They succumb to the temptations of a "buy now, pay later" mentality and run up big bills that they can't afford to pay.

The first rule when you have credit card difficulties is to "PUT THE CARD DOWN!" When you find yourself in trouble, stop using the card so you don't compound your difficulties. Make sure you don't use the card again until you've gotten your spending habits under control. If you're struggling to put the credit card down, use a task app or a reminder app to bolster your new spending habits. Researchers have found that when simple messages like "Don't swipe the small stuff. Use cash when it's under $20" are sent via email twice a month, displayed as a banner

Teerasak Ladnongkhun/Shutterstock.com

| Exhibit A.2 | Growing Your Investment: Starting Early Makes a Difference | | | |
|---|---|---|---|---|
| | **Starting Age** | | | |
| **Monthly Savings** | **20** | **30** | **40** | **50** |
| **$30** | $158,236 | $68,816 | $28,531 | $10,381 |
| **$60** | $316,472 | $137,633 | $57,062 | $20,762 |
| **$90** | $474,709 | $206,449 | $85,592 | $31,143 |
| **$120** | $632,945 | $275,266 | $114,123 | $41,525 |
| **$150** | $791,181 | $344,082 | $142,654 | $51,906 |

Note: Figures in the table show the amount accumulated at age 65. Results are based on an assumed annual rate of return of 8% compounded monthly.

ad on one's banking website, and written on a refrigerator magnet, consumers spend 2% less over six months' time.[35] Activating alerts for daily spending summaries or purchases over a certain amount can also do wonders. The idea is to use reminders and alerts to strengthen your commitment to putting the card down. Joe Pinsker, a reporter at *The Atlantic*, finds that logging his credit card use helps. He said, "After I buy something, I log the transaction on my phone, recording the price and what I bought. The idea is to increase the pain of paying, especially with a credit card, by forcing myself to take note of what I'm spending."[36] Doing so helped cut his credit card spending by 10% to 15%.

Once you've eliminated the temptation to dig a deeper hole, the next step is to make sure you consistently pay a substantial amount each month toward retiring the debt on that card. Given how high APRs are on the unpaid balances for most credit cards, it is usually a good idea to place a *very* high priority on eliminating these balances as quickly as possible. In no particular order, here are three ways to dig out.[37] To reduce what you owe, move balances from high-interest credit cards to low-interest credit cards, some of which come with introductory periods with zero interest. Or use "snowballing" to build momentum by paying off the credit card with the smallest balance, and then the next and the next. Zeroing out the debt on a credit card is a powerful reward and that happens faster with smaller balances. Or reduce your interest costs by paying off your highest interest rate credit cards or your credit cards with the highest amount of monthly interest first.

If you just can't seem to shake the habit of overspending, consider using cash or a **debit card** instead of a credit card. Although a debit card looks like a credit card, there is a big difference. When you use a debit card, money is immediately withdrawn from your bank account, so you "feel the pain" just as if you'd paid in cash. Many people spend less when they use cash or debit cards than when they use credit cards.

### A-4 Your Investments: Building for the Future

**Investing** involves reducing consumption today in order to acquire assets that build future wealth. In a very real way, investing is like the concept of sowing and reaping. A farmer plants a seed (makes an investment) in anticipation of a harvest (return) that will be much larger than the seed that was planted. When it comes to investing, early is better than late—but late is better than never.

> "The best time to plant a tree was 20 years ago. The next best time is now."
> —Chinese Proverb

### A-4a Building Wealth: The Key Is Consistency—And an Early Start!

Don't talk yourself out of investing just because you don't have much to invest. Even if you start with a small amount, your wealth will eventually grow to a significant amount as long as you stick with it. And the earlier you start, the better off you'll be. To see this, refer to Exhibit A.2, which compares how big your retirement nest egg will be at age 65 for different monthly

**debit card** A card issued by the bank that allows the customer to make purchases as if the transaction involved cash. In a debit card purchase, the customer's bank account is immediately reduced when the purchase is made.

**investing** Reducing consumption in the current time period in order to build future wealth.

investment amounts beginning at different ages (and assuming you earn an annual return of 8%). A 30-year-old who invests $60 per month will end up with $137,633 at age 65. Compare this to someone who begins investing $60 per month at age 20, and the results are startling. The investor who starts at age 20 only directly invests $7,200 more ($60 per month for 120 more months) than the investor who starts at age 30. But the earlier investor ends up with a nest egg of $316,472—almost $179,000 more than that of the investor who started at age 30.

The reason for this result is that, over time, you earn interest not only on the money you directly invest but also on the *interest* you've earned in *previous* years—a process known as *compounding*. The earlier you begin investing, the more powerful the compounding effect becomes. By the time an investor reaches age 65, any dollars invested at age 20 have been compounded for a *very long* time, resulting in a big increase in the nest egg. The message of Exhibit A.2 is clear: an early start to investing can lead to dramatically more money when it comes time to retire. Which is why, after seeing a YouTube video about investing by one of his favorite video gamers, Cornell University graduate Dray Farley began thinking about retirement accounts in his teens. He explained, "It was how to get rich in 22 years, and the general math and concept of compound interest, the snowball effect, and how eventually your gains are making gains."[38] So even though he had little to invest, he opened an investment account at 19, buying two shares of an index fund. He continued investing while in college with the earnings from two internships and working as a residential advisor. "I have been fixated on putting in as much as I can, as soon as I can, into securities."[39]

### Financial Securities: What Are My Investment Options?

Now that we've demonstrated the importance of investing, let's look at some specific types of financial instruments you might want to include in your investment portfolio. Our brief discussion can't hope to cover all of the possibilities, so we'll focus only on some of the most common choices. Keep in mind that, in addition to the financial instruments we describe in this section, many people also hold much of their wealth in other assets. The largest single asset for many households is the equity they have in their home.

Let's begin by looking at *common stock*, which represents ownership in a corporation. Common stock offers the possibility of two types of financial returns. The first, called a *dividend*, is a distribution of profits paid out to the stockholders. Dividends are paid only if the corporation's board of directors declares them—and there is no legal requirement for them to do so. If a corporation is in poor financial shape, its board of directors may decide that it is unable to pay a dividend. But even if a company is highly profitable, its board may decide to reinvest (retain) its profits rather than pay dividends to stockholders.

Investors can earn a second type of return, called a capital gain, if the market price of their stock rises relative to the price they paid for it. But stock prices can go down as well as up—as many investors painfully discover! Thus, it is possible for investors to experience *capital losses* as well as capital gains. For example, while the average compound return from S&P 500 stocks was 11.57% a year from 1928 to 2020, the S&P 500 suffered a compound loss of −6.63% from March 2004 to March 2009.[40] Clearly, investing in common stock entails a significant degree of risk. But historically the average rate of return on stocks has been better than the return on many other types of investments.

In addition to common stock, some corporations also offer another type of stock, called *preferred stock*. The two types of stock have some important differences. From the perspective of many investors, the most important distinction is that owners of preferred stock are more likely to receive a dividend than owners of common stock. Preferred stock is normally issued with a stated dividend, and common stockholders can't be paid *any* dividend until the preferred dividend is paid in full. Still, even preferred stockholders have no guaranteed legal right to receive a dividend. Whether your dividends come from common or preferred stock, you almost always have the option to use dividends to buy more shares of the same company. If your dividends are too small to buy a full share of stock, chances are you can be issued a fractional share, such as a tenth of a share.[41] Search for "dividend reinvestment" on your stockbroker's website. Then check the box to automatically grow your portfolio whenever you're paid dividends.

A *corporate bond* is another type of corporate security, but it is quite different from stock. A bond is a formal IOU issued by a corporation. While stockholders are the owners of a corporation, bondholders are its creditors. Most bonds are long-term debts that mature (come due) 10 to 30 years after they are issued, though bonds with shorter and longer maturities are sometimes issued.

As creditors, bondholders are legally entitled to receive interest payments from the issuing corporation every year until the bond matures, and to receive an amount known as the *principal* (or "face value") when the bond matures. But bondholders don't have to hold their bonds until they mature. Like stocks, bonds can be bought and sold on securities markets, and their price can rise and fall. So, like stockholders, bondholders can experience capital gains or losses.

Because the issuing corporation is legally required to pay interest and principal on a fixed schedule, the returns on bonds are more predictable than returns on stocks. However, even bonds pose some risk. During the COVID-19 pandemic, many firms defaulted on (failed to make) their legally required bond payments. Bondholders recovered just 55 cents to 60 cents on the dollar on those bond defaults.[42]

*Government securities* are IOUs issued by government entities when they borrow money. As with corporate bonds, government securities normally pay their holders a stated rate of interest until they mature. State and local governments often issue bonds. In fact, many investors like to invest in municipal bonds because interest income earned on these bonds is usually exempt from federal income taxes. But the biggest single issuer of government securities is the federal government. The U.S. Treasury markets a variety of securities, from long-term bonds that mature in 30 years to short-term treasury bills (popularly called "T-bills") that can mature in as little as four weeks. Historically, securities issued by the federal government have been viewed as very safe investments. But in recent years, the rapid growth in federal debt has led some securities rating services to question this view.[43]

Branislav Nenin/Shutterstock.com

For many users today, a mobile app may be the most intuitive way to start investing. According to financial advice website NerdWallet, TD Ameritrade, Charles Schwab, and Fidelity Investments offer the best all-around mobile stock trading apps.[44] NerdWallet's top brokers for new investors are again TD Ameritrade, Charles Schwab, and Fidelity Investments, as well as InteractiveBrokers.[45]

*Certificates of deposit* (CDs) are offered by banks and other depository institutions like credit unions. They are similar to savings accounts but are issued for a fixed term—which could be as short as three months or as long as five years. The rate of interest paid on CDs is often slightly higher than the rate on a regular savings account but usually lower than the interest rate on corporate bonds and most government securities. CDs with longer maturities typically earn a higher interest rate than CDs that have shorter terms. You can cash in a CD before it matures, but you'll incur a substantial penalty if you do.

One advantage of CDs is that they are insured by the FDIC. Because of this insurance and their predictable rate of return, CDs are considered to be among the safest investment options. The trade-off is that they offer lower returns than most other types of investments.

*Mutual funds* sell shares to investors and pool the resulting funds to invest in financial instruments such as corporate stocks, corporate bonds, government securities, or other assets. Some mutual funds invest mainly in bonds, others invest mainly in stocks, and others in government securities. Some invest in specific sectors of the economy, such as technology, energy, or healthcare, while others invest in broader portfolios.

Many mutual funds are professionally managed, with the fund's manager selecting the specific securities that the fund will hold. This professional management appeals to many investors who don't have the time or expertise to evaluate investment alternatives. But it is also expensive—mutual funds charge fees to cover the cost of managing the fund and to meet other expenses. Investors must pay these fees even if the funds perform poorly.

*Exchange Traded Funds* (ETFs) are similar to mutual funds in that they represent ownership in a broad portfolio of securities. However, unlike most mutual funds, they are bought and sold just like shares of corporate stock. ETFs are a relatively new investment vehicle (first marketed in 1993), but they have become quite popular in recent years.

## A-4b Acquiring Financial Assets: The Role of a Broker

Investors normally acquire many of their financial assets, including shares of common and preferred stocks, corporate bonds, and certain other financial assets (such as ETFs),

Full-service brokers provide financial planning, tax advice, and research to identify good investment opportunities.

by purchasing them in securities markets. However, individual investors can't directly participate in these markets. Instead, they normally rely on the services of a brokerage firm to buy and sell securities.

When choosing a broker, it's important to consider both the costs and the level of service. *Discount brokers* provide the basic services needed to buy and sell stocks, mutual funds, exchange-traded funds, and bonds and bond funds. For most investors, that's all they'll need, especially with the easy access and extensive information provided by discount brokers' websites and apps. Vanguard is the quintessential discount broker.[46]

By contrast *full-service brokers* provide a wide range of services—such as market research, personalized investment advice, and tax planning. In addition to executing standard trades, full-service brokers allow investors to buy and sell foreign securities, stock options, foreign exchange (currencies) and buy on margin (putting say, 10% down to buy securities and then borrowing the remaining 90% from the broker). E*TRADE and TD Ameritrade (now owned by Charles Schwab) and Merrill Lynch are full-service brokers.

Discount brokers used to charge significantly lower prices than full-service brokers, but in the last decade fees and commissions have dropped dramatically at all brokers. Today, many charge nothing for online trades that customers make themselves (using broker websites and apps) or for buying and selling the broker's own investment funds (which are often very good investments). But if you need

broker assistance to buy or sell an investment, expect to pay something like $25 per trade. Likewise, less expensive flat fees, such as E*TRADE's $6.95 fee for OTC trades, have replaced more expensive commission fees based on a percentage of the value of the securities bought or sold.[47]

The result is that today's investors have excellent options when choosing brokers. Full-service firms have lowered fees or eliminated commissions to stop clients from defecting to discount brokers. Discount brokers have cut their prices even more and have broadened the range of basic services they offer. Many brokerage firms, such as Charles Schwab or Fidelity, go even further, offering investors their choice of either discount or full-service accounts. So investing is much less expensive than it used to be. But brokerage firms aren't free. All brokers, discount or full-service, charge a variety of fees, such as annual fees, maintenance fees for Individual Retirement Accounts (IRAs), minimum balance fees, and, sometimes, "inactivity fees" if you don't place enough orders!

Robo advisors are a third option for acquiring and managing financial assets. These automated advisors help people set, track, stick to (that's the hard part), and eventually achieve their financial goals. Wealthfront and Betterment, two of the largest robo advisor services, use computer algorithms to automatically invest clients' wealth in a way that maximizes returns and minimizes taxes. Based on criteria set by the user, these services automatically deposit bank funds into retirement accounts each month; retrieve and then invest extra cash that would otherwise not earn a return; and rebalance stock portfolios by selling fast-moving stocks (capturing the gains) and investing in underweighted (and perhaps cheaper) stocks. Not only do robo advisors do all this automatically and based on individualized financial goals, they do so with lower annual fees than traditional advisors. Robo advisors typically charge 0.25% to 0.50% of assets, compared to 1% to 2% among human advisors.[48]

Before entrusting a brokerage firm and your broker with your financial transactions, you should check out their background. The Financial Industry Regulatory Authority's (FINRA's) BrokerCheck website (https://brokercheck.finra .org/) is a good place to start. This site offers very detailed background information on more than 1.3 million current and former FINRA-registered brokers and more than 17,400 FINRA-registered brokerage firms.

### A-4c Building a Portfolio: A Few Words about Diversification, Risk, and Return

The financial securities we've described are not mutually exclusive. It is possible—and usually desirable—to invest in a diversified financial portfolio consisting of a variety of stocks, bonds, CDs, government securities, and other assets. Brian Walsh, Jr. a senior financial advisor at Walsh & Nicholson Financial Group in Wayne, Pennsylvania recommends a popular approach called the "three-bucket strategy". He says, "A short-term bucket should have one to two years of expenses in short-term instruments such as cash or short duration bonds. An intermediate-term bucket should be for monies not needed for two to five years, such as core bond funds. A long-term bucket should consist of money not needed for at least five years and can be invested in equities."[49]

The main advantage offered by diversification is that it reduces your risk. If you put a large part of your wealth into one specific investment, you could be wiped out if that investment goes sour. If you invest in several different assets, then losses in some are likely to be offset by gains in others. But diversification also has a downside—it not only reduces risk but also reduces the possibility of earning exceptionally high returns.

One widely accepted financial principle is that a trade-off exists between risk and return; in other words, investments with the potential for generating high returns tend to be riskier than investments that offer lower returns. For example, stock prices sometimes decline sharply, so investing in stocks is considered quite risky. But historically, the long-run average return on stocks has been significantly higher than the average return on bonds, which offer safer, more predictable returns.

In general, younger investors are less concerned about risk than older investors. When you are young, you have more time to recover from adverse results, so you may be willing to take more risks and be more aggressive in pursuit of higher returns. If you invest mostly in stocks when you are young, and the stock market crashes, you still have time to recoup your losses and take advantage of future increases in stock prices. But older investors who hold a lot of stock might find that the same crash wiped out much of the wealth just when they were counting on it to supplement their retirement income. Older investors often become more conservative, adjusting their portfolio to include a greater percentage of relatively safe assets such as government securities, bonds of corporations with strong credit ratings, and CDs.

### A-4d But What Is My Best Investment? (Hint: Look in the Mirror!)

So far, we have focused on investing in financial assets. But in many ways, the most important investment you can make is in yourself, by devoting your time, effort, and money to your education, training, health, and fitness. The Bureau of Labor Statistics reports that the median weekly earnings of high-school graduates in the fourth quarter of 2020 was $781, while for workers with bachelor's degrees, the figure was $1,421—a difference of $640 a week.[50] Over a typical worker's 40-year career, this amounts to a difference in earnings of over $1.33 million! And higher education not only increases your income, it also gives you more job security. In March 2021, the unemployment rate for workers with a high-school education was 7.2% while the unemployment rate for workers with at least a bachelor's degree was 3.8%.[51]

**Strategies to Become More Marketable** One way to increase your marketability and your starting salary is to secure an internship during your college years. Internships give students a chance to gain firsthand experience that supplements what they learn in the classroom and helps them determine whether a specific career is right for them. And the internship experience looks great on a résumé.

**Other Work Opportunities** Don't despair if you are unable to secure an internship. There are other ways to gain experience in your field of interest. Consider taking a (gulp) pay cut from your temporary *job* to get experience in your *career* field. Or perhaps consider doing volunteer work in that field—not only will you be doing a good deed, you'll also be learning the ropes in your chosen field. Taking a temporary pay cut to gain relevant work experience often pays for itself many times over when you leave college and pursue a full-time position.

Kirill makarov/Shutterstock.com

Kenary820/Shutterstock.com

taxes on the money received from a traditional IRA when you begin making withdrawals. On the other hand, the contributions you make to a Roth IRA are *not* tax deductible at the time you make them, but earnings on these contributions are tax-free, and you pay no taxes on the distributions you receive from a Roth IRA after you retire.

One drawback to both traditional and Roth IRAs is that the amount that individuals can contribute each year is relatively small. In 2021, the maximum contribution for both types of plans was $6,000. (Individuals over the age of 50 contribute up to $7,000.)[53]

The **401(k), 403(b), and 457 plans** are employee-contribution retirement plans that are named for the sections of the IRS tax code where they are described. These plans are similar in many respects; the main differences are in who qualifies for each type of plan. The 401(k) plans are offered to employees of private-sector businesses, while 403(b) plans are for employees of certain types of nonprofit organizations such as schools, religious organizations, and charities. The 457 plans are primarily for state and local government employees and nonprofit organizations. Some employees in the nonprofit sector qualify for both 403(b) and 457 plans.

Unlike IRAs, all of these plans are implemented through a payroll-deduction process. Also, these plans have much higher contribution limits than traditional and Roth IRAs. In 2021, for example, employees could contribute up to $19,500 in a 401(k) plan, with individuals over 50 allowed to contribute up to an additional $6,500 *if* their employer's plan contained a "catch-up" provision.[54] Other potential advantages of these plans include:

- **Tax advantages:** Any income employees invest in traditional 401(k), 403(b), and 457 plans is tax deductible, and the earnings on these investments are tax deferred. This reduces current taxes and allows the funds to grow more rapidly. However, retirees must pay taxes on funds distributed from their fund when they make withdrawals. As with IRAs, there are Roth versions of these plans. Employees who choose the Roth version pay taxes on the income they contribute, but earnings on these contributions and distributions after retirement are tax exempt.

- **Company matching:** Some employers match employee contribution either dollar for dollar or with a percentage of each dollar you contribute up to a limit. This can be a big advantage of these plans over IRAs. If your company matches your 401(k) or 403(b) or 457 contributions, you should consider

## A-4e Investing for the Long Term: Planning for Your Retirement

One of the most important reasons people invest is to build up a nest egg for retirement. While your retirement might seem like it is a long way off, investing for your golden years now can really pay off, since it allows you to take advantage of the compounding effects we talked about earlier.

One of the most popular ways to build wealth for retirement is to set up an individual retirement account, or **IRA**. There are several types of IRAs; the two most popular are the *traditional IRA* and the *Roth IRA*. Both types of IRAs are individual investments—you make the decisions about how much to invest (subject to maximum allowable contributions) and what specific investments to make. You can put your IRA money into stocks, government securities, CDs, mutual funds, or other types of financial securities.

Both traditional and Roth IRAs offer tax advantages intended to provide an incentive for people to invest for their retirement. But the nature and timing of the tax advantages are different. With a traditional IRA, the contributions you make reduce your taxable income in the same tax year, and the earnings on your contributions are tax deferred, allowing them to grow more rapidly.[52] But you must pay

**IRA** An individual retirement account that provides tax benefits to individuals who are investing for their retirement.

**401(k), 403(b), and 457 plans** Employee payroll-deduction retirement plans that offer tax benefits.

**company matching** An amount contributed by the employer to an employee's retirement account, matching the employee's retirement contributions either dollar-for-dollar or based on a percentage of each dollar contributed by the employee.

# Cruddy Cars, Renting, Delivery Apps, and Automating Good Financial Habits

**Drive a Cruddy Car.** Mauldin Economics' Jared Dillian tells clients to give up large luxuries, not small ones. He says, "A car is basically a huge waste of money. Where else can you take $40,000 and set it on fire in seven years? And pay a bunch of interest to the bank in the process? What a disaster." Dillian says have $1 million in retirement funds before springing for a new car. Till then, drive a cruddy one.

**Rent it.** If something is expensive and infrequently used, rent it, don't buy it. Instead of buying expensive designer clothing, get eight items a month from Rent The Runway for $99. Choose from 700+ designers, wear and return those clothes, then pick more (dry cleaned after every customer). Yes, that's still $1,200 a year. But that infinitely cheaper than buying designer fashions and you can cancel your membership at any time. Going camping? Rent your tent, backpacks, sleeping bags, chairs, trekking poles, headlamps, and stove from REI. Just remember that renting's advantages over buying evaporate the longer you keep items, especially if they have good resale value.

**Skip the Delivery App.** When ordering food via delivery apps, expect to pay significantly more. After all, you're paying the restaurant, the driver, the food delivery app plus tips. A $42 meal from Panda Express, for example, cost $58 from GrubHub, and roughly $62 from DoorDash, Postmates and Uber Eats. Save your hard-earned money by grabbing takeout directly from the restaurant or cooking your meal at home.

**Put Good Financial Habits on Automatic.** It's like finding a $20 bill in an old pair of pants. As soon extra money hits your checking account, you'll be tempted to spend it. Prevent that from happening by automatically putting your money toward your long-term financial goals. At work, maximize your retirement contributions (and your employer's match) by having the money automatically withdrawn each month. Set up automatic recurring monthly transfers from checking to savings to fund vacations, to save for a down payment on a house, or to your broker for additional long-term investing. If it's not in your checking account, you won't miss it.[55]

A key to a comfortable retirement is to start saving early.

contributing as much as you can up to the maximum your company will match—it's like getting free money for your retirement.

There are also some important restrictions on these plans. First, not all employers offer these plans. Second, if your employer does offer a plan that offers matching contributions, you won't be entitled to all of the matching funds unless you've remained employed with the company for a stated period of time called the **vesting period**. The length of time for full vesting varies depending on the employer, but it is usually several years. Finally, keep in mind that these are *retirement* plans. There are restrictions on withdrawing the money in these plans prior to retirement, and you may pay significant penalties if you do.

**vesting period** A specified period of time for which an employee must work for an employer in order to receive the full advantage of certain retirement benefits.

## The Big Picture

Making sound personal financial decisions requires careful thought and discipline. You should start by establishing a budget; doing so will help you understand your current financial situation, plan for the future, and monitor your progress toward achieving your goals. One of your first goals should be to set aside enough savings to provide adequate protection against unforeseen financial challenges. One good strategy to build your savings is to "pay yourself first." Another key to financial success is to make careful decisions with respect to your use of credit cards and other forms of credit. Next, you should turn your attention to investing to build your wealth over time. You'll discover many different investment opportunities, each with its own pros and cons. No single investment strategy is foolproof, but two principles that have stood the test of time are (1) start investing early to take full advantage of compounding, and (2) diversify your investments to protect against risk.

# Chapter 1

1. https://stories.starbucks.com/press/2020/the-starbucks-foundation-awards-neighborhood-grants-to-advance-racial-equity/g, accessed January 5, 2021.

2. https://www.nbcnews.com/news/us-news/aunt-jemima-brand-will-change-name-remove-image-quaker-says-n1231260, accessed January 5, 2021.

3. https://www.sportingnews.com/us/nfl/news/redskins-name-change-options/17addpgbo88h51kkj1cgouwrgm, accessed January 5, 2021.

4. "Mistakes in Advertising," *English Learning Network*, https://www.learnenglish.de/mistakes/HorrorMistakes.html, accessed February 2, 2015.

5. "State of Entrepreneurship Address," Kauffman Foundation, January 19, 2010, https://www.kauffman.org/newsroom/entrepreneurs-expect-to-limit-hiring-in-2010-according-to-new-kauffman-foundation-poll.aspx, accessed January 13, 2011.

6. Soner Alemdar, https://www.perzonalization.com/blog/social-media-fails/, accessed January 5, 2021; Craig Donofrio. "15 Outrageous Business Blunders and PR Disasters." August 12, 2019, https://www.workandmoney.com/s/outrageous-business-blunders-pr-disasters-b72972d6e6ba425f, accessed January 5, 2021; "McDonald's Worst Ad Campaign," https://klintmarketing.com/corona-virus-ad-campaigns/, accessed January 5, 2021.

7. Ian Altman, "Top 10 Business Trends that Will Drive Success in 2016," *Forbes*, December 1, 2015, https://www.forbes.com/sites/ianaltman/2015/12/01/top-10-business-trends-that-will-drive-success-in-2016/#45212d2a5571, accessed January 25, 2016; "Seth Godin's Rules for Marketing in the New Economy," *SAS*, https://www.sas.com/en_us/insights/articles/marketing/seth-godins-rules-for-marketing-in-the-new-economy.html, accessed January 25, 2016.

8. "ESports is the New ESPN: Gaming Expert by Julia Limitone," FoxBusiness, May 16, 2018, https://www.foxbusiness.com/features/esports-is-the-new-espn-gaming-expert, accessed January 6, 2021; personal interview with Zandr Rose, January 6, 2021.

9. "GNI Per Capita 2007," World Bank Data, October 17, 2008, https://siteresources.worldbank.org/DATASTATISTICS/Resources/GNIPC.pdf, accessed January 19, 2009; "East and Southeast Asia: China," *The World Factbook, CIA*, updated December 18, 2008, https://www.cia.gov/library/publications/the-world-factbook/geos/ch.html, accessed January 19, 2009; "Central Asia: Russia," *The World Factbook, CIA*, updated December 18, 2008, https://www.cia.gov/library/publications/the-world-factbook/geos/rs.html, accessed January 19, 2009; "East and Southeast Asia: Hong Kong," *The World Factbook, CIA*, updated December 18, 2008, https://www.cia.gov/library/publications/the-world-factbook/geos/hk.html, accessed January 19, 2009.

10. "ChartBook: Tracking the Post-Recession Economy," Center on Budget and Policy Priorities, December 10, 2020, https://www.cbpp.org/research/economy/chart-book-tracking-the-post-great-recession-economy, accessed January 6, 2021.

11. "American Customer Satisfaction Index, 2011 Results," *ACSI*, https://www.theacsi.org/index.php?option=com_content&view=article&id=12&Itemid=110, accessed January 14, 2012.

12. DigitalCommerce360 Website, https://www.digitalcommerce360.com/2020/10/01/68-of-shoppers-buy-groceries-online-for-home-delivery-during-the-pandemic/, accessed January 6, 2021.

13. Joanna Glasner, "Why Webvan Drove Off a Cliff," *Wired News,* July 10, 2001, https://www.wired.com/techbiz/media/news/2001/07/45098.

14. Steven Levy, "Honey, I Shrunk the iPod. A Lot.," *Newsweek*, September 19, 2005; John Boddie, "Behind Apple's Strategy: Be Second to Market," *Harvard Business School Working Knowledge*, August 29, 2005, https://hbswk.hbs.edu/item.jhtml?id=4970&t=technology; John Letzing, "What's to Become of Microsoft's Answer to the iPod?," *Marketwatch*, July 29, 2009, https://www.marketwatch.com/story/microsofts-zune-continues-to-struggle-2009-07-29, accessed April 1, 2010.

15. Ibid.

16. Andrew Chamberlain, "6 Studies Showing Satisfied Employees Drive Business Results," December 6, 2017, *Glassdoor*, https://www.glassdoor.com/research/satisfied-employees-drive-business-results/#, accessed January 6, 2021.

17. Andrew Chamberlain, "Does Company Culture Pay Off? Analyzing Stock Performance of 'Best Places to Work' Companies," *GlassDoor*, March 2015, https://glassdoor.app.box.com/s/49y1ulkftvbpsbqjgeo1zh3lvijbb9uo, accessed January 29, 2016.

18. "Baby Boomers Retire," Pew Research Center, January 17, 2011, https://pewresearch.org/databank/dailynumber/?NumberID=1150, accessed January 11, 2011.

19. Michael Sheetz, "How SpaceX, Virgin Galactic, Blue Origin and Others Compete in the Growing Space Tourism Market," CNBC, September 26, 2020, https://www.cnbc.com/2020/09/26/space-tourism-how-spacex-virgin-galactic-blue-origin-axiom-compete.html, accessed January 8, 2020; Jonathan O'Callahan, "2019 Is the Year that Space Tourism Finally Becomes a Reality. No, Really," *WIRED*, January 24, 2019, https://www.wired.co.uk/article/spacex-blue-origin-space-tourism, accessed January 8, 2020.

20. Jeffrey Grau, "Retail E-Commerce Update," eMarketer, December 2008, https://www.emarketer.com/Reports/All/Emarketer_2000545.aspx, accessed January 19, 2009; David Kaplan, "eMarketer: E-Commerce Expected to Grow Double Digits through 2012," PaidContent, March 17, 2011, https://paidcontent.org/article/419-emarketer-e-commerce-expected-to-grow-double-digits-through-2012/, accessed January 15, 2012.

21. William Frey, "The U.S. Will Become Minority White in 2045, Census Projects," The Avenue, March 14, 2018, https://www.brookings.edu/blog/the-avenue/2018/03/14/the-us-will-become-minority-white-in-2045-census-projects/, accessed January 7, 2021.

22. "U.S. Census Bureau Projections Show a Slower Growing, Older, More Diverse Nation a Half Century from Now," *Census Bureau Press Release*, December 12, 2012, https://www.census.gov/newsroom/releases/archives/population/cb12-243.html, accessed January 9, 2013; "Net Migration from Mexico Falls to Zero and Perhaps Less," Pew Hispanic Center Report, 2012, https://s3.documentcloud.org/documents/346357/mexican-migration.pdf, accessed January 9, 2013; Jeffrey S. Passel & D'Vera Cohn, "U.S. Population Projections: 2005–2050," Pew Research Center, February 11, 2008, https://pewhispanic.org/files/reports/85.pdf, accessed January 17, 2011.

23. "Lynx Helped Panasonic Become a Major Player in the Hispanic Market," Lynx Hispanic Marketing Case Studies, 2013, https://www.lynxhispanicmarketing.com/case-studies/panasonic.php, accessed January 9, 2013; "Translating Hispanic Marketing Into Shareholder Value," Hispanic PR Wire/Business Wire, December 4, 2006, https://www.hispanicprwire.com/print.php?l=in&id=7660; Andrew Adam Newman, "Kraft Aims Kool-Aid Ads at a Growing Hispanic Market," *The New York Times*, May 26, 2011, https://www.nytimes.com/2011/05/27/business/media/27adco.html, accessed January 16, 2012; Elli Bishop, "6 Brands That Succeed at Understanding Hispanic Marketing," *Business to Community*, October 7, 2014, https://www.business2community.com/marketing/6-brands-succeed-understanding-hispanic-marketing-01030311, accessed January 29, 2016.

24. "In Trendy World of Fast Fashion, Styles Aren't Made to Last," *NPR*, March 11, 2013, https://www.npr.org/2013/03/11/174013774/in-trendy-world-of-fast-fashion-styles-arent-made-to-last, accessed February 3, 2015; Shannon Whitehead, "5 Truths the Fast Fashion Industry Doesn't Want You to Know," *The Huffington Post*, October 14, 2014, https://www.huffingtonpost.com/shannon-whitehead/5-truths-the-fast-fashion_b_5690575.html, accessed February 3, 2015.

25. Jessica Guynn, "Facebook Diversity Report: Efforts Still Failing Black and Hispanic Employees, Especially Women," *USA TODAY*, July 15, 2020, https://www.usatoday.com/story/tech/2020/07/15/facebook-diversity-african-american-black-hispanic-latino-employees/5430124002/, accessed January 7, 2021.

26. Shoshy Cimet, "We Got a Look at the 32-Page Internal Deck Adidas Workers Used to Pressure Leadership to Rally Against Racism. Here's What It Said and Why Employees Say the Response Fell Short," *BusinessInsider*, June 11, 2020, https://www.businessinsider.com/adidas-employees-call-out-racism-32-page-deck-sent-leadership-2020-6, accessed January 7, 2021.

27. "Diversity Awareness," Hershey Foods Corporation, https://www.hersheysjobs.com/Career/ControlPanel.aspx?ModuleCategoryID=1999999, accessed October 4, 2005.

28. "Attitudes of Young People Toward Diversity," CIRCLE fact sheet, February 2005, https://www.civicyouth.org/PopUps/FactSheets/Attitudes%202.25.pdf.

29. "U.S. Census Bureau Projections Show a Slower Growing, Older, More Diverse Nation a

Half Century from Now," *Census Bureau Press Release*, December 12, 2012, https://www.census.gov/newsroom/releases/archives/population/cb12-243.html, accessed January 9, 2013; "China Seeks Ways to Manage Ageing Population Crisis," *BBC News*, September 21, 2012, https://www.bbc.co.uk/news/world-asia-china-19662365, accessed January 9, 2013; Jeffrey S. Passel & D'Vera Cohn, "U.S. Population Projections: 2005–2050," Pew Research Center, February 11, 2008, https://pewhispanic.org/files/reports/85.pdf, accessed January 17, 2011; Toshiko Kaneda, "China's Concern Over Population Aging and Health," Population Reference Bureau, https://www.prb.org/Articles/2006/ChinasConcernOverPopulation AgingandHealth.aspx, accessed January 17, 2011.

30. Bureau of Labor Statistics News Release, September 20, 2020, https://www.bls.gov/news.release/pdf/tenure.pdf, accessed January 23, 2021.

31. Taylor Soper, "Amazon, Google Employees Ranked as 'least loyal,'" *GeekWire*, July 24, 2013, https://www.geekwire.com/2013/amazon-google-employees-ranked-least-loyal/#disqus_thread, accessed January 9, 2014; Sue Shellenbarger, "Pending Job Flexibility Act Received Mixed Reviews," *WSJ Career Journal*, https://www.careerjournal.com/columnists/workfamily/20010426-workfamily.html, accessed October 4, 2005; Les Christie, "Bad Attitudes in the Workplace," *CNNMoney*, September 6, 2005, https://money.cnn.com/2005/08/24/pf/workplace_morale/?section=money_pf; John Ellis, "Inspiring Worker Loyalty One Tough Job," *East Bay Business Times*, July 1, 2005, https://www.bizjournals.com/eastbay/stories/2005/07/04/focus1.html; Laura Petrecca, "Employee Loyalty Is at a Three-Year Low," *USA Today*, March 28, 2011, https://www.usatoday.com/money/workplace/2011-03-26-employees-less-loyal.htm, accessed January 16, 2012.

32. "Sustainability: Balancing Opportunity and Risk in the Consumer Products Industry, 2007 Report," Deloitte, https://www.deloitte.com/dtt/cda/doc/content/us_cb_sustainability-study_june2007opt.pdf, accessed January 20, 2009; Sarah Fister Gale, "While Everything Else Stops, Green Still Means Go," Green-Biz, January 19, 2009, https://www.planetthoughts.org/?pg=pt/Whole&qid=2675, accessed June 1, 2011.

33. "Manufacturing Labor Costs per Hour: China, Vietnam, Mexico, 2016-2020," *Statistica* website, https://www.statista.com/statistics/744071/manufacturing-labor-costs-per-hour-china-vietnam-mexico/, accessed January 22, 2021.

34. Marc Weirsum, "China's Manufacturing Wages Rise to $7,000 Per Year: Baidu Benefits," *Market Realist*, April 22, 2014, https://marketrealist.com/2014/04/chinas-manufacturing-wages-rise-7000-per-year-baidu-benefits/, accessed February 5, 2015; "Wages in China," *China Labour Bulletin*, June 10, 2013, https://www.clb.org.hk/en/content/wages-china, accessed January 10, 2014; Keith Bradsheir, "Even as Wages Rise, China Exports Grow," *The New York Times*, January 9, 2014, https://www.nytimes.com/2014/01/10/business/international/chinese-exports-withstand-rising-labor-costs.html?hpw&rref=business&_r=0, accessed January 10, 2014; "United States Average Hourly Wages in Manufacturing," *Trading Economics*, January 11, 2014, https://www.tradingeconomics.com/united-states/wages-in-manufacturing, accessed January 10, 2014; Louis Uchitelle, "Factory Jobs Gain But Wages Retreat," *The New York Times*, December 29, 2011, https://www.nytimes.com/2011/12/30/business/us-manufacturing-gains-jobs-as-wages-retreat.html?pagewanted=all, accessed January 9, 2013; David Luhnow & Bob Davis, "For Mexico, an Edge on China," *The Wall Street Journal*, September 16, 2012, https://online.wsj.com/article/SB10000872396390444318104577587191288101170.html, accessed January 9, 2013; Dexter Roberts, "How Rising Wages Are Changing the Game in China," *BusinessWeek*, March 27, 2006, https://www.businessweek.com/magazine/content/06_13/b3977049.htm, accessed January 20, 2009; Richard McCormack, "Good Luck Competing Against Chinese Labor Costs, Mfg. Job Growth in China Is Headed Up, Not Down; 109 Million Mfg. Workers in China Dwarfs Number in U.S.," *Manufacturing and Technology News*, May 2, 2006, https://www.manufacturingnews.com/news/06/0502/art1.html, accessed January 20, 2009; Scott Tong, "Cost of Chinese Labor Is on the Rise," *Marketplace*, July 6, 2007, https://marketplace.publicradio.org/display/web/2007/07/06/cost_of_chinese_labor_is_on_the_rise/, accessed January 20, 2009; Judith Banister, "Manufacturing in China Today: Employment and Labor Compensation," The Conference Board, September 2007, https://www.conference-board.org/economics/workingpapers.cfm, accessed January 20, 2009; Bill Powell, "The End of Cheap Labor in China," *Time* magazine, June 26, 2011, https://www.time.com/time/magazine/article/0,9171,2078121,00.html, accessed January 16, 2012.

35. Jason Beaubien, "Asian Tsunami Devastates Sri Lankan Fishing Industry," *NPR*, Morning Edition, January 10, 2005, https://www.npr.org/templates/story/story.php?storyId=4276161; Sally Pook, "Phuket Tourism Industry Crippled by Mass Cancellations," Cyber Diver News Network, January 8, 2005, https://www.cdnn.info/news/travel/t050111.html; Veronique de Rugy, "Homeland Security Scuffle," *National Review*, October 15, 2004, https://www.nationalreview.com/comment/rugy200410150840.asp; "Bush Brushes Aside Rebuilding Cost Concerns," Reuters News Service, MSNBC, September 19, 2005, https://www.msnbc.msn.com/id/9374106/.

36. Daniel Pink, "Pomp and Circumspect," *The New York Times*, June 4, 2005, https://select.nytimes.com/gst/abstract.html?res=F60C1FFD3F5C0C778CDAF0894DD404482.

Pg. 13 Fact: https://www.newsweek.com/rise-fierce-yet-fragile-superpower-94963, accessed January 19, 2021.

# Chapter 2

1. "B–1.—Gross Domestic Product, 1959–2008, Economic Report of the President: 2009 Spreadsheet Tables," Government Printing Office, updated January 14, 2009, https://www.gpoaccess.gov/eop/tables09.html, accessed January 20, 2009.

2. "How Much Is a Trillion Dollars?," *The Mansfield North Central Ohio Tea Party Association*, https://americaneedsyounow.org/howmuch.htm, accessed July, 2013.

3. "U.S. Foreclosure Activity Decreases 14 Percent in June to Lowest Level Since December 2006 Despite 34 Percent Jump in Judicial Scheduled Foreclosure Auctions," *RealtyTrac*, July 11, 2013, https://www.realtytrac.com/Content/foreclosure-market-report/midyear-2013-us-foreclosure-market-report-7794, accessed January 12, 2014; Amy Hoak, "More Foreclosures Expected in 2011," *The Wall Street Journal*, December 12, 2010, https://online.wsj.com/article/SB10001424052748703518604576014011451160994.html?mod=googlenews_wsj, accessed January 24, 2011; RealtyTrac Staff, "RealtyTrac's James J. Saccacio to Discuss Foreclosure Crisis Fallout at AFSA State Government Affairs Forum," *RealtyTrac*, October 1, 2008, https://www.realtytrac.com/ContentManagement/pressrelease.aspx?ChannelID=9&ItemID=5284&accnt=64847, accessed January 22, 2009; RealtyTrac Staff, "REALTYTRAC® Year-end Report Shows Record 2.8 Million U.S. Properties With Foreclosure Filings in 2009," *RealtyTrac*, January 14, 2010, https://www.realtytrac.com/contentmanagement/pressrelease.aspx?itemid=8333, accessed April 21, 2010; "RealtyTrac: 2011 National Foreclosure Rate Lowest Since 2007," Commercial Record, January 12, 2012, https://www.commercialrecord.com/news148166.html, accessed January 18, 2012; *CoreLogic National Foreclosure Report*, CoreLogic, January 2014, https://www.corelogic.com/research/foreclosure-report/national-foreclosure-report-january-2014.pdf, accessed February 6, 2015.

4. Chris Isidore, "7.9 Million Jobs Lost—Many Forever," *CNNMoney*, July 2, 2010, https://money.cnn.com/2010/07/02/news/economy/jobs_gone_forever/index.htm, accessed January 24, 2011.

5. Credit Crisis—The Essentials, *The New York Times*, updated January 20, 2009, https://www.nytimes.com/topic/subject/economic-crisis-and-market-upheavals, accessed January 20, 2009; Sharon Silke Carty & Barbara Hagenbaugh, "Automakers Say If They Go, Millions of Jobs Will Vanish," *USA Today* website, https://www.usatoday.com/money/autos/2008-11-17-automakers-bailout-impact_N.htm, accessed January 21, 2009; "Auto Industry Bailout Overview," *The New York Times*, updated January 20, 2009, https://topics.nytimes.com/topics/reference/timestopics/subjects/c/credit_crisis/index.html, accessed January 21, 2009.

6. Jackie Calmes, "TARP Bailout to Cost Less Than Once Anticipated," *The New York Times*, October 1, 2010, https://dealbook.nytimes.com/2010/10/01/tarp-bailout-to-cost-less-than-once-anticipated/.

7. Michael Grunwald, "One Trillion Dollars," January 26, 2009, *Time*, pp. 27–31, https://www.time.com/time/politics/article/0,8599,1871769,00.html, accessed February 5, 2011; Jeannine Aversa & Christopher S. Rugaber, "Economy Adds Jobs at Fastest Pace in Three Years," *Associated Press*, April 2, 2010, https://www.google.com/hostednews/ap/article/ALeqM5gNiyJ905Ho0Ur96V2TQhsBX19lGwD9 ER6P402, accessed April 20, 2010; Greg Robb, "Bernanke Declares 'recession is very likely over,'" MarketWatch, September 15, 2009, https://www.marketwatch.com/story/bernanke-declares-the-recession-over-2009-09-15, accessed April 20, 2010; Eric Morath, "Jobs Report: Solid Job Gains Belie Economic Unease," *The Wall Street Journal*, November 7, 2014, https://www.wsj.com/articles/jobs-report-economy-adds-214000-jobs-1415367269, accessed May 5, 2016.

8. Jeanne Sahadi, "Debt Ceiling FAQs: What You Need to Know," *CNN Money*, May 18, 2011, https://money.cnn.com/2011/01/03/news/economy/debt_ceiling_faqs/index.htm, accessed January 20, 2013; Michael Grunwald, "Cliff Dweller," *Time*, January 14, 2013, https://www.time.com/time/magazine/article/0,9171,2132749,00.html, accessed January 20, 2013; Andrew Taylor, "Congress Averts Shutdown; Fight Continues over Pandemic Aid," Federal News Network, December 18, 2020, https://federalnewsnetwork.com/government-shutdown/2020/12/snags-on-covid-19-relief-may-force-weekend-sessions/, accessed January 10, 2021.

9. Rebecca Blumenstein & Natalia Drozdiak, "Airbus to Join Forces with Uber for On-Demand Helicopter Service, CEO Says," *The Wall Street Journal*, January 18, 2016, https://www.wsj.com/articles/airbus-to-join-forces-with-uber-for-on-demand-helicopter-service-ceo-says-1453048668, accessed January 25, 2017; Sara Salinas, "Uber

and Lyft Are Racing to Own Every Mode of Transportation—They're Getting Close," CNBC Website, June 9, 2018, https://www.cnbc.com/2018/06/09/uber-and-lyft-are-racing-to-own-every-mode-of-transportation.html; Brendan Dorsey, "We Tried Uber's New Helicopter Service from Manhattan to JFK," The Points Guy blog, October 4, 2019, https://thepointsguy.com/news/we-tried-ubers-helicopter-service-new-york-jfk/, accessed January 11, 2021.

10. U.S. debt clock, https://www.usdebtclock.org/index.htmlhttps://www.usdebtclock.org/index.html, accessed April 19, 2018.

11. VanEck, "Will Tax Reform Add to US Debt Concerns?" January 29, 2018, https://marketrealist.com/2018/01/will-tax-reform-add-u-s-debt-woes, accessed April 18, 2018.

12. "Economic Research for the Federal Reserve Bank of St. Louis," January 7, 2021, https://fred.stlouisfed.org/series/M2, https://fred.stlouisfed.org/series/M1, accessed January 11, 2021.

13. "Historical Changes of the Target Federal Funds and Discount Rates," *Federal Reserve Bank of New York*, https://www.newyorkfed.org/markets/statistics/dlyrates/fedrate.html, accessed January 22, 2009.

14. Shira Ovide, "Why the Government Is Suing Google," *The New York Times*, October 20, 2020, www.nytimes.com/2020/10/20/technology/google-lawsuit.html, accessed January 11, 2021.

15. "21 Meaningful, Trend-Driven Innovation Opportunities," *Trendwatching*, 2021, https://info.trendwatching.com/news/21-trends-for-21-is-here, accessed January 11, 2021; Sally Ho, "Just Salad Becomes First U.S. Restaurant Chain To Carbon Label Its Entire Menu," Green Queen, August 3, 2020, https://www.greenqueen.com.hk/just-salad-becomes-first-us-restaurant-chain-carbon-label-its-entire-menu/, accessed January 11, 2021; Lucy Handley, "Allbirds Wants People to Understand Their Sneakers' Carbon Footprint like They Do Calories in Food," CNBC, September 28, 2020, https://www.cnbc.com/2020/09/28/allbirds-company-wants-people-to-understand-shoes-carbon-footprint.html, accessed January 11, 2021.

16. Steven Levitt, "Scarecrows Work on People Too," *Freakonomics,* June 28, 2006, https://freakonomics.com/2006/06/28/scarecrows-work-on-people-too/, accessed February 7, 2016.

17. "OK Federal Government, Excluding Postal Services," U.S. Department of Labor Bureau of Labor Statistics, March 12, 2008, https://stats.bls.gov/oco/cg/cgs041.htm, accessed August 16, 2008; "Postal Service Workers," U.S. Department of Labor Bureau of Labor Statistics, December 18, 2007, https://stats.bls.gov/oco/ocos141.htm, accessed August 16, 2008; "Job Opportunities in the Armed Forces," U.S. Department of Labor Bureau of Labor Statistics, December 18, 2007, https://stats.bls.gov/oco/ocos249.htm, accessed August 16, 2008.

18. Daniel J. Mitchell, "Russia's Flat Tax Miracle," The Heritage Foundation, March 24, 2003, https://www.heritage.org/Press/Commentary/ed032403.cfm; Deroy Murdock, "Russians Do Taxes Right," *National Review Online*, March 1, 2002, https://www.nationalreview.com/murdock/murdock030102.shtml; "Russia: Income Taxes and Tax Laws," Worldwide-Tax, July 2005, https://www.worldwide-tax.com/russia/russia_tax.asp; "History of the U.S. Tax System," U.S. Department of the Treasury, https://www.treasury.gov/resource-center/faqs/Taxes/Pages/historyrooseveltmessage.aspx, accessed May 21, 2017.

19. Eli Stokols, "Socialism, Capitalism Seen in New Light by Younger Americans," December 6, 2017, https://www.wsj.com/articles/socialism-capitalism-seen-in-new-light-by-younger-americans-1512561601, accessed April 19, 2018; Gary Hamel & Michele Zanini, "The Biggest Problem with Capitalism? Not Enough Capitalists," Fortune, November 21, 2020, https://fortune.com/2020/11/21/capitalism-entrepreneurship-economic-inequality-us-bureaucracy/, accessed January 12, 2021.

20. "Gross Domestic Product," Economic Research, Federal Reserve Bank of St. Louis, https://research.stlouisfed.org/fred2/series/GDP, accessed May 10, 2016.

21. Bureau of Labor Statistics, https://data.bls.gov/timeseries/LNS14000000, accessed April 19, 2018.

22. "Labor Force Statistics from the Current Population Survey," Bureau of Labor Statistics, https://data.bls.gov/timeseries/LNU04000000?years_option=all_years&periods_option=specific_periods&periods=Annual+Data, accessed January 14, 2014; Rana Foroohar, "The Flat Paycheck Recovery," *Time* Magazine, January 13, 2014, https://content.time.com/time/magazine/article/0,9171,2161670,00.html, accessed January 14, 2014; Leslie Kwoh, "News and Trends in Management," *The Wall Street Journal*, February 13, 2012, https://online.wsj.com/article/SB10001424052970204642604577215372010543642.html, accessed January 21, 2013; Jeevan Vasagar, "Graduates Warned of Record 70 Applicants for Every Job," *The Guardian*, July 6, 2010, https://www.guardian.co.uk/education/2010/jul/06/graduates-face-tougher-jobs-fight, accessed January 26, 2011.

23. "Labor Force Statistics from the Current Population Survey: Unemployment Rate Table," U.S. Department of Labor, Bureau of Labor Statistics, https://data.bls.gov/PDQ/servlet/SurveyOutputServlet?data_tool=latest_numbers&series_id=LNS14000000, accessed January 22, 2009.

24. The U.S. Inflation Calculator Website, https://www.usinflationcalculator.com/inflation/current-inflation-rates/, accessed January 12, 2021.

Pg. 27 Fact: Rana Foroohar, "Open the Door and Let 'Em In," *Time* Magazine, July 22, 2013, https://content.time.com/time/magazine/article/0,9171,2147289,00.html, accessed September 2014.

Pg. 35 "Fact: Parents Projected to Spend $245,340 to Raise a Child Born in 2013, According to USDA Report," USDA News Report, August 18, 2014, https://www.usda.gov/wps/portal/usda/usdahome?contentidonly=true&contentid=2014/08/0179.xml, accessed September 2014.

# Chapter 3

1. Jill Disis, "Trump Promised to Win the Trade War with China. He Failed," *CNN Business*, October 25, 2020, https://www.cnn.com/2020/10/24/economy/us-china-trade-war-intl-hnk/index.html, accessed January 14, 2021; https://apnews.com/article/donald-trump-virus-outbreak-global-trade-trade-policy-mexico-39aadae9a6d18de2b91889f1e552b605, accessed January 14, 2021; Paul Wiseman, "Trump Trade Policy: 4 Years of High Drama. Limited Results," *APNews*, October 27, 2020, https://apnews.com/article/donald-trump-virus-outbreak-global-trade-trade-policy-mexico-39aadae9a6d18de2b91889f1e552b605, accessed January 14, 2021; Heather Long, "Trump Has Officially Put More Tariffs on U.S. Allies than on China,"

*The Washington Post*, May 31, 2018, https://www.washingtonpost.com/news/wonk/wp/2018/05/31/trump-has-officially-put-more-tariffs-on-u-s-allies-than-on-china/?noredirect=on, accessed January 14, 2021.

2. World Bank Macro Trends, World GDP Growth Rate 1961-2021, https://www.macrotrends.net/countries/WLD/world/gdp-growth-rate, accessed January 15, 2021.

3. Sources: World Economic Outlook Update, June 2020, International Monetary Fund, https://www.imf.org/en/Publications/WEO/Issues/2020/06/24/WEOUpdateJune2020, accessed January 17, 2021; "Morgan Stanley Projects Strong Global GDP Growth of 6.4% for 2021—Led First by Emerging Markets, Followed by Reopening Economies in the U.S. and Europe—In a Macro Outlook that Diverges from the Consensus," Morgan Stanley, https://www.morganstanley.com/ideas/global-economic-outlook-2021, accessed January 17, 2021; "World Bank Africa Overview October 22, 2020," The World Bank, https://www.worldbank.org/en/region/afr/overview, accessed January 18, 2021; "Developing Asia to Contract 0.4% in 2020, Grow by 6.8% in 2021," Asian Development Bank News Release, December 10, 2021, Asian Development Bank, https://www.adb.org/news/developing-asia-contract-2020-grow-2021, accessed January 17, 2021; John Campbell, "How to Think About Africa's 'Rising Middle Class' Amid COVID-19," Council on Foreign Relations, July 7, 2020, https://www.cfr.org/blog/how-think-about-africas-rising-middle-class-amid-covid-19, accessed July 17, 2021; Bukola Adebayo, "Nigeria Overtakes India in Extreme Poverty Ranking," CNN, June 26, 2018, https://www.cnn.com/2018/06/26/africa/nigeria-overtakes-india-extreme-poverty-intl/index.html, accessed January 17, 2021.

4. Raymond Zhong, "In Halting Ant's I.P.O., China Sends a Warning to Business," *The New York Times* , November 20, 2020, https://www.nytimes.com/2020/11/06/technology/china-ant-group-ipo.html, accessed January 16, 2020; Alison Tudor-Ackroyd & Chad Bray, "What Is Jack Ma's Ant Group and How Does It Make Money?" *South China Morning Post*, https://www.scmp.com/business/banking-finance/article/3107294/what-jack-mas-ant-group-and-how-does-it-make-money, accessed January 16, 2020; Katie Canales, "China Just Suspended Ant Group's $34 Billion IPO, the Largest in History. Here's How the Company Was Spun out of Jack Ma's Alibaba and Has Transformed the Global Fintech market," *Business Insider*, November 4, 2020 https://www.businessinsider.com/what-is-ant-group-china-jack-ma-digital-payment-2020-7#:~:text=A%20holding%20company%20called%20Ant,serves%20%22the%20little%20guys.%22, accessed January 16, 2020.

5. Natasha Lomas, "ABI: Africa's Mobile Market to Pass 80% Subscriber Penetration in Q1 Next Year; 13.9% of Global Cellular Market by 2017," TechCrunch, November 28, 2012, https://techcrunch.com/2012/11/28/abi-africas-mobile-market-to-pass-80-subscriber-penetration-in-q1-next-year-13-9-of-global-cellular-market-by-2017/, accessed January 24, 2013; Pia Heikkila, "1B Cell Phone Users and no Apple iPhone in India's Breakneck Mobile-Apps Market," *International Business Times*, September 15, 2012, https://www.ibtimes.com/1b-cellphone-users-and-no-apple-iphone-indias-breakneck-mobile-apps-market-789460, accessed January 24, 2013; Sumnina Udas, "Bringing Toilets and Dignity to India's Poor," *CNN*, September 17, 2012, https://www.cnn.com/2012/09/17/world/asia/india-open

-toilets-udas/index.html, accessed January 24, 2013; BankMyCell January 2021 Mobile User Statistics, https://www.bankmycell.com/blog/how -many-phones-are-in-the-world, accessed January 24, 2021; Measuring Digital Development Facts and Figures 2020, ITU, https://www.itu.int/en /ITU-D/Statistics/Pages/facts/default.aspx, accessed January 24, 2021.

6. "Insperiences," Trendwatching, https://www .trendwatching.com/trends/insperience.htm, accessed January 12, 2006; "Ten Key Trends for Chocolate Products," Food and Drink Europe, January 23, 2012, https://www.foodanddrinkeurope .com/Consumer-Trends/10-key-trends-for -chocolate-products?utm_source=copyright&utm _medium=OnSite&utm_campaign=copyright, accessed February 3, 2012.

7. "Trade Shows Signs of Rebound from COVID-19, Recovery Still Uncertain," WTO Press Release, October, 6, 2020, https://www .wto.org/english/news_e/pres20_e/pr862_e.htm, accessed January 19, 2021.

8. "WTO Sees Gradual Recovery in Coming Months Despite Cut in Trade Forecasts," WTO Press Release, September 19, 2013, https://www .wto.org/english/news_e/pres13_e/pr694_e.htm, accessed January 16, 2014; "Trade to Expand by 9.5% in 2010 after a Dismal 2009," WTO Press Release, March 26, 2010, https://www.wto.org /english/news_e/pres10_e/pr598_e.htm, accessed February 9, 2010; "The World Economy: Overview," The World Factbook, CIA, updated February 2010, https://www.cia.gov/library /publications/the-world-factbook/geos/xx.html, accessed February 9, 2010; "Economy," The World Factbook, CIA, January 26, 2012, https://www .cia.gov/library/publications/the-world-factbook /geos/xx.html, accessed February 3, 2012; "Falling Import Demand, Lower Commodity Prices Push Down Trade Growth Prospects," WTO Press Release, September 30, 2015, https://www.wto.org /english/news_e/pres15_e/pr752_e.htm, accessed March 2, 2016.

9. Emily Chasan, "Currency Cost U.S. Companies at Least $4 Billion in Second Quarter," The Wall Street Journal, September 19, 2013, https://blogs.wsj.com/cfo/2013/09/19/currency -cost-u-s-companies-at-least-4-billion-in-second -quarter/, accessed January 16, 2014; Paul Ausick, "P&G Only One of Many Hit by Foreign Exchange Rates (PG, PEP, KMB, CL, KO, PM, MCD, F, CCL)," 24/7, The Wall Street Journal, June 20, 2012, https://247wallst.com/2012/06/20 /pg-only-one-of-many-hit-by-foreign-exchange -rates-pg-pep-kmb-cl-ko-pm-mcd-f-ccl/, accessed January 25, 2013.

10. Neha Gupta, "What Is Countertrade?," Barter News Weekly, March 11, 2010, https:// www.barternewsweekly.com/2010/03/11/what -is-counter-trade-1851/, accessed February 10, 2010; Dan West, "Countertrade—An Innovative Approach to Marketing," Chairman American Countertrade Association, BarterNews 36 (1996), https://barternews.com/approach_marketing. htm; Global Offset and Countertrade Association, https://www.globaloffset.org/index.htm, accessed January 27, 2006.

11. "Phthalates Found in Children at Harmful Levels in 13 out of 15 EU Countries," EEB, November 28, 2019, https://eeb.org/flood-of-toxic -chinese-toys-threatens-childrens-health/, accessed January 20, 2021.

12. "Outsourcing Costs | Call Center Pricing," Worldwide Call Centers, https://www .worldwidecallcenters.com/call-center-pricing/, accessed January 19, 2021.

13. E. Yellin, Your Call Is (Not That) Important to Us (New York: Simon Schuster, 2009); Carolyn Beeler, "Outsourced Call Centers Return, to U.S. homes," NPR, August 25, 2010, https://www.npr .org/templates/story/story.php?storyId=129406588, accessed February 10, 2010.

14. "Trading Stories: The Impact of Exports on Small Businesses Across the Nation," Office of the U.S. Trade Representative, https://ustr.gov/about-us /policy-offices/press-office/blog/2015/may/trading -stories-impact-exports-small-businesses, accessed January 21, 2021.

15. Source: Global Employment Trends for Youth 2020, International Labor Organization, ENG _ILO_Report_GlobalYouthEmployment_Layout_ InsidePages_Final.indd, accessed January 19, 2021.

16. Stacy Meichtry & John Stoll, "Fiat Nears Stake in Chrysler That Could Lead to Takeover," The Wall Street Journal, January 20, 2009, https:// online.wsj.com/article/SB123238519459294991 .html, accessed February 10, 2010; "eBay to acquire Skype," Skype Press Release, September 12, 2005, https://www.skype.com/company/news/2005/skype _ebay.html, accessed February 10, 2010.

17. David Barboza, "Intel to Build Advanced Chip-Making Plant in China," The New York Times, March 27, 2007, https://www.nytimes .com/2007/03/27/technology/27chip.html, accessed January 30, 2009.

18. Cynthia Churchwell, "Rethink the Value of Joint Ventures," Harvard Business School Working Knowledge, May 10, 2004, https://hbswk.hbs.edu /item.jhtml?id=4113&t=globalization.

19. Kinbesa, "Hyundai & Kia SUVs Combined to Post Nearly 49% Market Share in 2020," January 12, 2021, https://kinabesa.com/hyundai-kia-suvs -combined-to-post-nearly-49-market-share-in -2020/, accessed January 23, 2021.

20. Michael Schuman, "Hyundai Grows Up," Time Global Business, July 2005, https://www.time.com /time/globalbusiness/article/0,9171,1074141,00 .html; Cathie Gandel, "At 5 Feet 10 Inches, I Was Too Tall for Tokyo," My Turn, Newsweek, December 12, 2005; Moon Ihlwan, "Hyundai Bets Big on India and China," BusinessWeek, January 30, 2008, https://www.businessweek.com/globalbiz /content/jan2008/gb20080130_061205.htm, accessed January 30, 2009; "Maruti, Hyundai, Tata Motors Lose Market Share to Smaller Firms in 2010," India Times, April 10, 2011, https:// economictimes.indiatimes.com/automobiles /maruti-hyundai-tata-motors-lose-market-share-to -smaller-firms-in-2010-11/articleshow/7932281.cms, accessed February 6, 2012.

21. "Rural Market India Brand Equity Foundation," IBEF, December 10, 2010, https:// www.ibef.org/artdispview.aspx?art_id=27581&cat _id=938&in=78, accessed February 10, 2010; "Selling to Rural India," Springwise Newsletter, June 2003, https://www.springwise.com /newbusinessideas/2003/06/shakti.html; "Red Herring: Selling to the Poor," The Next Practice, April 11, 2004, https://www.thenextpractice.com /news/red_herring_selling_to_the_poor.php; Tim Weber, "Are You Ready for Globalization 2.0?," BBC News, January 28, 2005, https://news.bbc .co.uk/1/hi/business/4214687.stm.

22. International Telecommunications Union, Measuring Digital Development, Facts and Figures, 2020, https://www.itu.int/en/ITU-D /Statistics/Documents/facts/FactsFigures2020.pdf, accessed January 23, 2021.

23. Ted Burnham, "What Pizza Hut's Crown Crust Pizza Says about Global Fast Food Marketing," NPR, May 2, 2012, https://www.npr.org/sections /thesalt/2012/05/01/151781785/what-pizza-huts -crown-crust-pizza-says-about-global-fast-food -marketing, accessed January 25, 2013; Nina Africano, "McDonald's International: Top Ten Most Unusual Around the World," AOL Travel, September 3, 2010, https://news.travel.aol .com/2010/09/03/mcdonald-s-international-top -ten-most-unusual-around-the-world/, accessed January 25, 2013; "McDonald's Country/Market Sites," https://www.mcdonalds.com./countries .html, accessed February 10, 2011; Domino's Pizza LLC [US], https://www.dominos.com/Public -EN/Site+Content/Secondary/Inside+Dominos /Pizza+Particulars/International+Speciality+Topp ings/; Robyn Lee, "10 Crazy Asian Pizzas," https:// slice.seriouseats.com/archives/2008/02/crazy-weird -asian-pizza-crusts-japanese-korean-hong-kong .html, accessed May 21, 2017; Editors of Publications International, "Favorite Pizza Toppings in 10 Countries," How Stuff Works Lifestyle, https:// recipes.howstuffworks.com/fresh-ideas/dinner -food-facts/favorite-pizza-toppings-in-10-countries .htm, accessed May 21, 2017; William Mellor, "McDonald's No Match for KFC in China as Colonel Rules Fast Food," Bloomberg, January 26, 2011, https://www.bloomberg.com/news/2011-01 -26/mcdonald-s-no-match-for-kfc-in-china-where -colonel-sanders-rules-fast-food.html, accessed February 6, 2012; Erik German, "Morocco Loving the McArabia," Global Post, May 30, 2010, https:// www.globalpost.com/dispatch/morocco/090825 /morocco-loving-the-mcarabia, accessed February 6, 2012.

24. "Internet World Stats," https://www.internetworld stats.com/stats.htm, accessed January 28, 2016.

25. World Bank, Doing Business 2017: Equal Opportunity for All (Washington, DC: World Bank). DOI: 10.1596/978-1-4648-0948-4. License: Creative Commons Attribution CC BY 3.0 IGO, accessed January 28, 2017.

26. "Shadow Market: 2011 Global Software Piracy Study," Business Software Alliance, May 2012, https://portal.bsa.org/globalpiracy2011/downloads /study_pdf/2011_BSA_Piracy_Study-Standard.pdf, accessed January 26, 2013.

27. Will Sarni, "Water Works," Interbrand, 2012, https://www.interbrand.com/en/best-global-brands /Best-Global-Green-Brands/2012-Report/water -works.aspx, accessed January 26, 2013; 2030: Brian Dumaine, "China's Coming Water Crisis," Fortune magazine, December 14, 2012, https://tech.fortune .cnn.com/2012/12/14/2030-chinas-coming-water -crisis/, accessed January 26, 2013; "WaterFacts," Water.Org, 2012, https://water.org/water-crisis /water-facts/water/, accessed January 26, 2013.

28. Richard Mills, "USTR Releases 2002 Inventory of Trade Barriers," Press Release, Office of the United States Trade Representative, April 2, 2002, https://ustr.gov/archive/Document_Library /Press_Releases/2002/April/USTR_Releases_2002 _Inventory_of_Trade_Barriers.html; "U.S. Targets Non-tariff Barriers to Global Trade," Press Release, Washington File, April 2, 2002, https://wfile.ait.org .tw/wf-archive/2002/020402/epf212.htm.

29. "Questions and Answers: The IMF's Response to COVID-19." IMF, www.imf.org/en/About/FAQ/imf -response-to-covid-19#Q1, accessed January 27, 2021.

30. Daniel Workman, "Top 10 Exporting Countries Causing the US Trade Deficit," Suite101, April 27, 2010, https://www.suite101.com/content/top -10-exporting-countries-causing-the-us-trade -deficit-a226747, accessed February 11, 2011.

31. "European Union," The World Factbook, The Economy Overview: CIA, February 2011, https:// www.cia.gov/library/publications/the-world -factbook/geos/ee.html, accessed February 11, 2011.

32. Tiffany May & Mike Ives, "Hong Kong Arrests Nine Over Protesters' Escape by Speedboat," *The New York Times*, October 10, 2020, https://www.nytimes.com/2020/10/10/world/asia/hong-kong-arrests-protests.html, accessed January 24, 2021; Alexandra Stevenson, "Business Embraces Hong Kong's Security Law. The Money Helps," The New York Times, June 30, 2020, https://www.nytimes.com/2020/06/30/business/china-hong-kong-security-law-business.html, accessed January 24, 2021.

33. Steven Erlanger, "'Brexit': Explaining Britain's Vote on European Union Membership," *The New York Times*, June 16, 2016, https://www.nytimes.com/interactive/2016/world/europe/britain-european-union-brexit.html?_r=1, accessed July 31, 2016; Everrett Rosenfeld, "Brexit 101: What Just Happened, and Why It's Important for Americans," June 24, 2016, https://www.cnbc.com/2016/06/24/brexit-101-what-just-happened-and-why-its-important-for-americans.html, accessed July 31, 2016.

34. Rebecca Flood, "REVEALED: Which Countries Could Be Next to Leave the EU?," *Express*, October 2, 2016, https://www.express.co.uk/news/world/716421/EU-referendum-Brexit-leave-vote-country-Merkel-superstate-Italy, accessed January 31, 2017; Alex Hunt & Brian Wheeler, "Brexit: All You Need to Know About the UK Leaving the EU," *BBC News*, June 21, 2018, https://www.bbc.com/news/uk-politics-32810887, accessed July 2, 2018.

Pg. 44 Fact: Stephen Gandel, "This Time for Africa?," *Time* magazine, November 1, 2010, https://content.time.com/time/magazine/article/0,9171,2026897,00.html, accessed October 19, 2016.

Pg. 53 Fact: Human Development Reports, http://hdr.undp.org/en/2020-MPI, accessed January 23, 2021.

# Chapter 4

1. "Uber and Lyft to Continue Treating Drivers as Independent Contractors," NPR, November 20, 2020, https://www.npr.org/2020/11/04/931435959/uber-and-lyft-to-continue-treating-drivers-as-independent-contractors, accessed January 27, 2021; Megan Cerullo, "Uber Drivers Are Independent Contractors, Not Employees, Says National Labor Relations Board," CBS News, May 14, 2019, https://www.cbsnews.com/news/uber-drivers-are-independent-contractors-not-employees-says-national-labor-relations-board/, accessed January 27, 2021.

2. Ryan Prior, "This Breast Cancer Advocate Says She Discovered a Facebook Flaw That Put the Health Data of Millions at risk," *CNN*, March 6, 2020, https://www.cnn.com/2020/02/29/health/andrea-downing-facebook-data-breach-wellness-trnd/index.html, accessed January 27, 2021.

3. Craig Downden, "Forget Ethics Training: Focus on Empathy," *Financial Post*, June 21, 2013, https://business.financialpost.com/2013/06/21/forget-ethics-training-focus-on-empathy/, accessed January 24, 2014.

4. Josh Levs, "Big Three Auto CEOs Flew Private Jets to Ask for Taxpayer Money," *CNN*, November 19, 2008, https://www.cnn.com/2008/US/11/19/autos.ceo.jets/, accessed February 2, 2009.

5. Samantha Schmidt, "Lululemon CEO Resigns. Unspecified Conduct 'Fell Short' of Standards," *The Washington Post*, February 6, 2018, https://www.washingtonpost.com/news/morning-mix/wp/2018/02/06/lululemon-ceo-resigns-unspecified-conduct-fell-short-of-standards/, accessed January 27, 2021; "Barnes & Noble Says Former C.E.O. Demos Parneros Was Fired for Sexual Harassment by Tiffany Hsu & Alexandra Alter," *The New York Times*, August 28, 2018, https://www.nytimes.com/2018/08/28/business/barnes-noble-ceo-sexual-harassment-lawsuit.html, accessed January 27, 2021.

6. Barney Gimbel, "Why We'll Miss the Disney Trial," *Fortune*, CNNMoney, December 27, 2004, https://money.cnn.com/magazines/fortune/fortune_archive/2004/12/27/8217949/index.htm; Peter Bart, "Disney's Basket Cases," *Variety*, March 7, 2004, https://www.variety.com/article/VR1117901299.html?categoryid=1&cs=1.

7. "Pierre Omidyar: Tufts President Lawrence S. Bacow Awarded Pierre Omidyar an Honorary Degree During the University's 155th Commencement Ceremonies on Sunday," *TuftsNow*, May 22, 2011, https://now.tufts.edu/commencement-2011/pierre-omidyar, accessed February 24, 2013; Skye Malmberg, "The Rise and Fall of Elizabeth Holmes, Founder of Theranos," *The Western Journal*, June 16 2020,, https://www.westernjournal.com/rise-fall-elizabeth-holmes-founder-theranos/, accessed February 1, 2021, Annie Palmer, "Read the Memo Jeff Bezos Sent to Amazon Employees About Coronavirus Safety at Warehouses," *CNBC*, March 21, 2020, https://www.cnbc.com/2020/03/21/jeff-bezos-memo-about-coronavirus-safety-at-amazon-warehouses.html, accessed February 7, 2021; "Bezos' Amazon Launches US$2 Billion Housing Equity Fund," January 7, 2021, *CEO Magazine*, https://www.theceomagazine.com/business/news/amazon-housing-equity/, accessed February 1, 2021; "Coronavirus Update: Defiant Musk Confirms Tesla Fremont Plant Reopening; Gov. Newsom Unaware," *CBS San Francisco*, May 11, 2020, https://sanfrancisco.cbslocal.com/2020/05/11/coronavirus-update-workers-return-to-tesla-fremont-assembly-plant-elon-musk-files-lawsuit-against-alameda-county/, accessed February 1, 2021: Our Response to COVID-19, https://www.honest.com/blog/lifestyle/family/our-response-to-covid-19/03182020.html, accessed February 1, 2021.

8. "Global Business Ethics Survey, 2020, Report Number One," Ethics & Compliance Initiative™ https://www.ethics.org/wp-content/uploads/Global-Business-Ethics-Survey-2020-Report-1-Final.pdf, accessed January 28, 2021.

9. Report to the Nations, 2020 Global Study on Occupational Fraud and Abuse, Association of Certified Fraud Examiners, https://acfepublic.s3-us-west-2.amazonaws.com/2020-Report-to-the-Nations.pdf, accessed January 28, 2021.

10. Bob Lane, "The Role of Tone from the Top," Ethisphere, December 28, 2009, https://ethisphere.com/the-role-of-tone-from-the-top/, accessed February 21, 2011.

11. "Supplemental Research Brief, Ethics and Employee Engagement, 2009 National Business Ethics Survey," Ethics Resource Center, https://www.ethics.org/files/u5/NBESResearchBrief2.pdf, accessed February 6, 2013.

12. Nicole Schuman, "Kraft Navigates Social Backlash from 'Send Noods' Campaign," October 15, 2020, https://www.prnewsonline.com/kraft-send-noods-social-backlash/, accessed January 29, 2021; Evan Comen & Thomas Frohlich, "The Biggest Corporate Scandals of the Decade," 24/7 Wall Street, December 20, 2019, https://247wallst.com/special-report/2019/12/20/the-biggest-corporate-scandals-of-the-decade/5/, accessed January 2021; "What We're Doing About Our Plastic Problem," Patagonia, https://www.patagonia.com/stories/what-were-doing-about-our-plastic-problem/story-72799.html, accessed January 29, 2021; Eve Batey, "NorCal Lawsuit Claims Subway's Tuna 'Is Not Fish'," Eater San Francisco, January 28, 2021, https://sf.eater.com/2021/1/28/22254853/subway-fish-concoction, accessed January 29, 2021.

13. Felicity Barringer, "Clorox Courts Sierra Club, and a Product Is Endorsed," *The New York Times*, March 26, 2008, https://www.nytimes.com/2008/03/26/business/businessspecial2/26cleanser.html, accessed February 24, 2013; Tyson Foods Homepage, https://www.tyson.com/About-Tyson.aspx, accessed February 24, 2013; Andrea Tse, "Will Supreme Court Hear Farmer's Case Against Tyson Foods?," *The Street*, January 24, 2011, https://www.thestreet.com/story/10982877/1/will-supreme-court-hear-farmers-case-against-tyson-foods.html, accessed February 24, 2011; Sarah Ellison, "Kraft Limits on Kids' Ads May Cheese Off Rivals," *The Wall Street Journal*, January 13, 2005, https://www.aef.com/industry/news/data/2005/3076, accessed February 24, 2013; Megan Chuchmach, "Bailed Out Bank of America Sponsors Super Bowl Fun Fest," *ABC News*, February 2, 2009, https://abcnews.go.com/Blotter/story?id=6782719&page=1, accessed February 24, 2013; Jane Akre, "Crash That Led to Toyota Recall 'Inconclusive,'" Legal Examiner, December 8, 2009, https://news.legalexaminer.com/crash-that-led-to-toyota-recall-inconclusive.aspx?googleid=275542, accessed February 24, 2013. Felicity Barringer, "Clorox Courts Sierra Club, and a Product Is Endorsed," *The New York Times*, March 26, 2008, https://www.nytimes.com/2008/03/26/business/businessspecial2/26cleanser.html, accessed February 24, 2013; Tyson Foods Homepage, https://www.tyson.com/About-Tyson.aspx, accessed February 24, 2013; Andrea Tse, "Will Supreme Court Hear Farmer's Case Against Tyson Foods?," *The Street*, January 24, 2011, https://www.thestreet.com/story/10982877/1/will-supreme-court-hear-farmers-case-against-tyson-foods.html, accessed February 24, 2011; Sarah Ellison, "Kraft Limits on Kids' Ads May Cheese Off Rivals," *The Wall Street Journal*, January 13, 2005, https://www.aef.com/industry/news/data/2005/3076, accessed February 24, 2013; Megan Chuchmach, "Bailed Out Bank of America Sponsors Super Bowl Fun Fest," *ABC News*, February 2, 2009, https://abcnews.go.com/Blotter/story?id=6782719&page=1, accessed February 24, 2013; Jane Akre, "Crash That Led to Toyota Recall 'Inconclusive,'" Legal Examiner, December 8, 2009, https://news.legalexaminer.com/crash-that-led-to-toyota-recall-inconclusive.aspx?googleid=275542, accessed February 24, 2013.

14. Gillian White, "Can Wells Fargo Ever Make Amends?" *The Atlantic*, April 11, 2017, https://www.theatlantic.com/business/archive/2017/04/wells-fargo-apology-tour/522558/, accessed February 8, 2021.

15. Equifax Data Breach Settlement, January 2020, FTC, https://www.ftc.gov/enforcement/cases-proceedings/refunds/equifax-data-breach-settlement, accessed February 9, 2021; How the Equifax hack happened, and what still needs to be done By Alfred Ng, September 7, 2018, CNet website, https://www.cnet.com/news/equifaxs-hack-one-year-later-a-look-back-at-how-it-happened-and-whats-changed/, accessed February 9, 2021.

16. Mylan CEO on EpiPen drug price controversy, "I get the outrage"," *CBS*, January 27, 2017, https://www.cbsnews.com/news/epipen-price-hike-controversy-mylan-ceo-heather-bresch-speaks-out/, accessed February 9, 2021.

17. Maria Leighton, "B Corps Are Businesses Committed to Using Their Profit for Good—These

14 Make Products We Love," December 8, 2020, https://www.businessinsider.com/b-corp-retail-companies, accessed January 29, 2021.

18. *Giving USA 2020:* Charitable Giving Showed Solid Growth, Climbing to $449.64 Billion in 2019, One of the Highest Years for Giving on Record," Giving USA, June 16, 2020, https://givingusa.org/giving-usa-2020-charitable-giving-showed-solid-growth-climbing-to-449-64-billion-in-2019-one-of-the-highest-years-for-giving-on-record/, accessed January 29, 2021.

19. Todd Henneman, "Patagonia Fills Payroll with People Who Are Passionate," Workforce, November 5, 2011, https://www.workforce.com/articles/patagonia-fills-payroll-with-people-who-are-passionate, accessed January 25, 2013.

20. "Starbucks Focuses Hiring Strategy on Veterans and Military Spouses," Starbucks, November 6, 2013, https://news.starbucks.com/news/starbucks-focuses-hiring-strategy-on-veterans-and-military-spouses, accessed January 25, 2014.

21. "BP CEO Apologizes for "Thoughtless" Oil Spill Comment," Reuters, June, 2, 2010, https://www.reuters.com/article/us-oil-spill-bp-apology/bp-ceo-apologizes-for-thoughtless-oil-spill-comment-idUSTRE6515NQ20100602, accessed January 31, 2021.

22. Derek Hawkins, "'Re-accommodate'? United Ridiculed for Corporate Speak Response to Passenger Dragging," *The Washington Post*, April 11, 2017, https://www.washingtonpost.com/news/morning-mix/wp/2017/04/11/re-accommodate-united-gets-lampooned-for-its-awkward-response-to-passenger-dragging/, accessed January 13, 2021.

23. "Our Planet," McDonald's, https://corporate.mcdonalds.com/corpmcd/our-purpose-and-impact/our-planet.html.

24. Jan Hoffman, "Cheating's Surprising Thrill," *The New York Times*, October 7, 2013, https://well.blogs.nytimes.com/2013/10/07/in-bad-news-cheating-feels-good/, accessed January 28, 2014; Romeo Vitelli, "Is There a 'Cheater's High'?," Psychology Today, October 14, 2013, https://www.psychologytoday.com/blog/media-spotlight/201310/is-there-cheaters-high, accessed January 28, 2014; Nicole E. Reudy, Celia Moore, Francesca Gino & Maurice E. Schweitzer, "The Cheater's High: The Unexpected Affective Benefits of Unethical Behavior," *Journal of Personality and Social Psychology* (September 2, 2013), https://www.apa.org/pubs/journals/releases/psp-a0034231.pdf, accessed March 16, 2015; Yoni Blumberg, "Companies with More Female Executives Make More Money—Here's Why," CNC, March 2, 2018, https://www.cnbc.com/2018/03/02/why-companies-with-female-managers-make-more-money.html, accessed January 31, 2021; Stephanie Creary, Mary-Hunter McDonnell, Saakshi Ghai & Jared Scruggs, "When and Why Diversity Improves Your Board's Performance," *Harvard Business Review*, March 27, 2019, https://hbr.org/2019/03/when-and-why-diversity-improves-your-boards-performance, accessed February 8, 2021; Jill Goldsmith, "Debra Lee, Former BET Networks CEO, Launches New Search Firm to Boost Diversity on Corporate Boards," Deadline, January 19,2021, https://deadline.com/2021/01/debra-lee-former-bet-ceo-launches-search-firm-to-boost-diversity-on-corporate-boards-1234675917/, accessed February 8, 2021.

25. Michelle Chapman, "General Motors Sets Goal of Going Largely Electric by 2035,"January 30, 2021, https://www.seattletimes.com/business/gm-sets-goal-of-going-carbon-neutral-by-2040/, accessed January 30, 2021.

26. "'Carbon Footprint' Gaining Business Attention," Press Release, Conference Board, October 18, 2006, https://www.conference-board.org/UTILITIES/pressDetail.cfm?press_ID=2985, accessed February 4, 2009; Jeffery Ball, "Green Goal of 'Carbon Neutrality' Hits Limit," *The Wall Street Journal*, December 30, 2008, https://online.wsj.com/article/SB123059880241541259.html, accessed February 4, 2009; Andrew Martin, "How Green Is My Orange?" *The New York Times*, January 22, 2009, https://www.nytimes.com/2009/01/22/business/22pepsi.html?_r=1&scp=1&sq=How%20green%20is%20my%20orange&st=cse, accessed February 4, 2009.

27. Jena McGregor, "The Oddest, Worst and Most Memorable CEO Apologies of the Year," *The Washington Post*, December 23, 2014, https://www.washingtonpost.com/blogs/on-leadership/wp/2014/12/23/the-oddest-worst-and-most-memorable-ceo-apologies-of-the-year/, accessed March 15, 2015; Eun Kyung Kim, "Lululemon Co-founder Steps Down in Wake of 'Women's Bodies' Remark," Today Money, December 10, 2013, https://www.today.com/money/lululemon-co-founder-steps-down-wake-womens-bodies-remark-2D11721314, accessed March 15, 2015; Mark Thompson & Chris Liakos, "Volkswagen CEO Quits Over 'Grave Crisis,'" CNN, September 23, 2015, https://money.cnn.com/2015/09/23/news/companies/volkswagen-emissions-crisis/, accessed March 17, 2016.

28. Quad Sustainability Symposium Day 2: Don't Sacrifice Progress for Perfection, October 23, 2020, https://www.quad.com/resources/quad-sustainability-symposium-day-2-dont-sacrifice-progress-for-perfection/, accessed January 31, 2021.

29. Marcus Noland & Tyler Moran, "Firms with More Women in the C-Suite Are More Profitable," *Harvard Business Review*, February 8, 2016, https://hbr.org/2016/02/study-firms-with-more-women-in-the-c-suite-are-more-profitable, accessed March 27, 2017.

30. Price Benowitz, https://whitecollarattorney.net/fcpa/famous-cases/, accessed January 31, 2021.

31. Kay Johnson, "Marketing. Selling to the Poor," Time Bonus Section, May 2005; C. K. Prahalad & Allen Hammond, "Serving the World's Poor, Profitably—The Payoff for Investing in Poor Countries," Harvard Business School Working Knowledge, https://hbswk.hbs.edu/item.jhtml?id=3180&t=nonprofit&noseek=one.

32. Nathaniel Parish Flannery, "Has Ralph Lauren Learned That Bribery Is a Bad Business Strategy in Latin America?," *Forbes*, April 24, 2013, https://www.forbes.com/sites/nathanielparishflannery/2013/04/24/bribery-a-bad-business-strategy-in-latin-america/, accessed January 26, 2014; Juan Gonzalez & Amy Goodman, "Walmart Is Now Under Investigation in Mexican 'Bribery Aisle' Scandal," Truthout, December 21, 2012, https://truth-out.org/news/item/13469-the-bribery-aisle-how-walmart-used-payoffs-to-bribe-its-way-through-expansion-in-mexico, accessed February 6, 2013; Joe Palazzolo, Emily Galzer & Joann Lublin, "Prosecutors Ask to Meet Jung in Avon Bribe Probe," *The Wall Street Journal*, July 29, 2012, https://online.wsj.com/article/SB10000872396390444840104577553683406542666.html, accessed February 6, 2013; "Bribe Payers Index 2011," Transparency International, https://bpi.transparency.org/results/, accessed March 24, 2012; Stephen Gandel, "Not Just Wal-Mart: Dozens of U.S. companies face bribery suspicions," Fortune, April 26, 2012, https://fortune.com/2012/04/26/not-just-wal-mart-dozens-of-u-s-companies-face-bribery-suspicions/, accessed March 16, 2015.

33. Patagonia Supplier Code of Conduct, https://www.patagonia.com/on/demandware.static/-/Library-Sites-PatagoniaShared/default/dwa5177359/PDF-US/Patagonia_COC_English_02_13.pdf, accessed May 2, 2021)

34. Gap, Inc. Social Reporting Award, *Business Ethics,* December 20, 2004, https://www.business-ethics.com/annual.htm#Gap%20Inc.

# Chapter 5

1. Erin Meyer, "The Culture Map: Breaking through the Invisible Boundaries of Global Business," Public Affairs, 2014.

2. "Experts Say… Is Communication Really Only 7% Verbal? Truth vs. Marketing," Neurodata Lab, November 16, 2018, https://medium.com/@neurodatalab/experts-say-is-communication-really-only-7-verbal-truth-vs-marketing-9a8e7428fd0f, accessed February 4, 2021.

3. Claire Atkinson, "Fake News Can Cause 'Irreversible Damage' to Companies—And Sink Their Stock Price," *NBCNews*, April 25, 2019, https://www.nbcnews.com/business/business-news/fake-news-can-cause-irreversible-damage-companies-sink-their-stock-n995436, accessed February 4, 2021.

4. Eugene Raudsepp, "Body Language Tactics That Sway Interviewers," *The Wall Street Journal Career Journal*, December 5, 2002, https://www.careerjournal.com/jobhunting/interviewing/20021205-raudsepp.html.

5. Michael McCarthy, "Lance Armstrong Blew His Last Chance Experts Say," *Advertising Age*, January 19, 2013, https://adage.com/article/media/lance-armstrong-blew-chance-experts/239295/, accessed February 20, 2013; Brigid Schulte, "Dominance and Empathy," *The Washington Post*, February 13, 2013, https://www.washingtonpost.com/local/body-language-experts-say-obama-exuded-dominance-and-empathy/2013/02/13/7755207e-7590-11e2-95e4-6148e45d7adb_story.html, accessed March 21, 2015.

6. Michael Purdy, "The Listener Wins," Monster, https://featuredreports.monster.com/career-advice/article/the-listener-wins, accessed August 22, 2006; Stephen D. Boyd, "The Human Side of Business," *Agency Sales*, February 2004, p. 35, accessed via Infotrac College Edition.

7. Harvey Mackay, We Learn More by Listening Than Talking,", *The Daily Herald*, January 16, 2005, page E6[SB14], https://old.heraldextra.com/modules.php?op=modload&name=News&file=article&sid=45313; "Listening Factoids," International Listening Association, https://www.listen.org/pages/factoids.html, accessed August 22, 2006.

8. Stephen D. Boyd, "The Human Side of Business," *Agency Sales*, February 2004, page 35, accessed via Infotrac College Edition; Marjorie Brody, "Learn to Listen: Closing the Mouth and Opening the Ears Facilitates Effective Communication," Incentive, May 2004, page 57, accessed via Business and Company Resource Center.

9. Zoom Meetings: Etiquette and Best Practices, University of Pittsburg information Technology, https://www.technology.pitt.edu/blog/zoom-tips, accessed February 13, 2021; "Meeting and Webinar Best Practices and Resources," Zoom, https://support.zoom.us/hc/en-us/articles/209743263-Meeting-and-Webinar-Best-Practices-and-Resources, accessed February 13, 2021; Andrii Parkhomenko, "Op-Ed: How Remote Working in the Post-COVID-19 Era Could Transform L.A. and Other Cities," December 20, 2020, Los Angeles Times, https://www.latimes.com/opinion/story/2020-12-20/covid-los-angeles-cities-remote-work, accessed February 13, 2021.

10. Katie Sehl, "Top Twitter Demographics That Matter to Social Media Marketer," May 28, 2020, Hootsuite blog, https://blog.hootsuite.com/twitter -demographics/, accessed February 15, 2021.

11. Employers Continue Rejecting Jobseekers Because of Social Media Content, CBBIA, August 16, 2018, https://www.cbia.com/news/hr-safety /employers-continue-rejecting-jobseekers -social-media/, accessed February, 15, 2021 "Employers Reveal the Social Media Gaffes That Tank Your Chances of Getting the Job," July 24, 2014, Workopolis, https://careers.workopolis.com /advice/employers-reveal-the-social-media-gaffes -that-tank-your-chances-of-getting-the-job-724201/, accessed February 15, 2021; Lauren Theisen, "Employee Says He Was Fired After Anger Over $6 BBQ Sauce Gift," New York Daily News, January 5, 2020, https://www.nydailynews.com/news/national/ny -employee-says-he-was-fired-after-anger-over-bbq -sauce-gift-20200106-3ztdia6xlvejxmrntowbug7hw4 -story.html, accessed February 20, 2021.

12. Brendan Greenley, "Forget 'Best' or 'Sincerely,' This Email Closing Gets the Most Replies," January 31, 2017, Boomerang Website, https://blog .boomerangapp.com/2017/01/how-to-end-an-email -email-sign-offs/#footnotes, accessed April 6, 2017.

13. Edward P. Bailey, Writing and Speaking at Work (Prentice Hall, 2005), pp. 82–89.

14. Kevin Sintumuang, "Tech Etiquette: 21 Do's and Don'ts for 2015," The Wall Street Journal, January 2, 2015, https://www.wsj.com/articles/tech-etiquette -21-dos-and-donts-for-2015-1420222724, accessed March 22, 2015; Sarah Griffiths, "Never End a Relationship by Text or Social Media," Daily Mail, February 25, 2016, https://www.dailymail.co.uk/ sciencetech/article-3463952/Thou-shalt-not-end -relationship-text-Psychologist-reveals-10-golden -rules-digital-etiquette.html, accessed April 7, 2016.

15. "Presenting Effective Presentations with Visual Aids," U.S. Department of Labor, Occupational Safety and Health Administration, https://www .osha.gov/doc/outreachtraining/htmlfiles/traintec .html, accessed August 22, 2006.

16. Philip Tucker, "Bringing the Cloud with You," Google Docs Blog, March 31, 2008, https:// googledocs.blogspot.com/2008/03/bringing-cloud -with-you.html, accessed February 13, 2009; Brian Braiker, "Living in the Clouds," Newsweek, June 10, 2008, https://www.newsweek.com/id/140864, accessed February 13, 2009; Michael Miller, "Comparing Google Docs with Competing Cloud Computing Applications," InformIT, February 9, 2009, https://www.informit.com/articles/article. aspx?p=1323244&seqNum=3, accessed February 13, 2009.

# Chapter 6

1. "Frequently Asked Questions About Small Business," U.S. Small Business Administration, Office of Advocacy, October 2019, https://cdn .advocacy.sba.gov/wp-content/uploads/2020 /11/05122043/Small-Business-FAQ-2020.pdf, accessed January 9, 2021; P. George, "The Scary Truth about Corporate Survival," Harvard Business Review, 94 (December 2016): 24–25.

2. "COVID-19 Restaurant Impact Survey V: Key Findings," National Restaurant Association, December 2, 2020, https://restaurant.org/downloads /pdfs/advocacy/covid-19-restaurant-impact-survey-v -state-results, accessed January 10, 2021.

3. Ibid.

4. J. Musto, "Facebook Survey Shows 15% of Small Businesses Collapsed in Pandemic," Fox Business,

December 9, 2020, https://www.foxbusiness.com /economy/facebook-survey-small-business-shuttered -pandemic, accessed January 10, 2021.

5. S. Kalemili-Ozcan, P. Gourinchas, V. Penciakova & N. Sander, "Covid-19 and SME Failures, Working Paper 27877," International Monetary Fund Working Paper, September 25, 2020, https://www .imf.org/en/Publications/WP/Issues/2020/09/25 /COVID-19-and-SME-Failures-49753, accessed January 10, 2021.

6. P. Aldrick, "Covid: 'At least 250,000 Small Firms Will Fold' as Restrictions Devastate Trade," The Times, January 11, 2020, https://www.thetimes.co .uk/article/covid-at-least-250-000-small-firms -will-fold-as-restrictions-devastate-trade-338xjfvqn ?utm_source=newsletter&utm_campaign =newsletter_103&utm_medium=email&utm _content=103_11789380&CMP=TNLEmail _120899_11789380_103, accessed January 11, 2021.

7. V. Romei, "Pandemic Triggers Surge in Business Start-Ups Across Major Economies," Financial Times, December 30, 2020, https://www.ft.com/content /3cbb0bcd-d7dc-47bb-97d8-e31fe80398fb ?segmentId=114a04fe-353d-37db-f705 -204c9a0a157b, accessed January 11, 2021.

8. K. Mackrael, "In the Covid Economy, Laid-Off Employees Become New Entrepreneurs," Wall Street Journal, November 18, 2020, https://www.wsj.com /articles/in-the-covid-economy-laid-off-employees -become-new-entrepreneurs-11605716565?mod =djem10point, accessed January 11, 2021.

9. "LLC Filing as a Corporation or Partnership," Internal Revenue Service, January 6, 2021, https:// www.irs.gov/businesses/small-businesses-self -employed/llc-filing-as-a-corporation-or-partnership, accessed January 9, 2021.

10. Ibid.

11. "Why States Should Adopt RULLCA," Uniform Law Commission: The National Conference of Commissioners on Uniform State Laws, https://www.uniformlaws.org/Narrative. aspx?title=Why%20States%20Should%20 Adopt%20RULLCA, accessed January 16, 2017.

12. "Table 12: Number of Business Tax Returns, by Size of Business for Income Years, 1990–2014 [1] Expanded," Internal Revenue Service, https://www .irs.gov/uac/soi-tax-stats-historical-table-12, accessed January 16, 2017.

13. J. Sparshott, "Big Growth in Tiny Businesses," The Wall Street Journal, December 28, 2016, https://www.wsj.com/articles/big-growth-in-tiny -businesses-1482953786, accessed January 16, 2017.

14. "Fortune 500 List of Companies 2020," Fortune, httpshttps://fortune.com/fortune500/2020 /search/?profitable=true, accessed January 11, 2021.

15. "Table 12: Number of Business Tax Returns, by Size of Business for Income Years, 1990–2014 [1] Expanded," Internal Revenue Service, https://www .irs.gov/uac/soi-tax-stats-historical-table-12, accessed January 16, 2017.

16. Ibid.

17. "Single Member Limited Liability Companies," Internal Revenue Service, September 20, 2020, https://www.irs.gov/businesses/small-businesses -self-employed/single-member-limited-liability -companies, accessed January 11, 2021.

18. R. Simon, "Pass-Through Businesses Are Rethinking Their Status in Wake of Tax Law," The Wall Street Journal, February 22, 2018, accessed January 9, 2021, https://www.wsj.com/articles/tax -law-leaves-business-owners-with-big-decision-to-c -or-not-to-c-151929540.

19. J. Sparshott, "Big Growth in Tiny Businesses," The Wall Street Journal, December 28, 2016,

https://www.wsj.com/articles/big-growth-in-tiny -businesses-1482953786, accessed January 16, 2017.

20. C. Winokur Munk , "Entrepreneurs Are Better Off Going It Alone, Study Says," The Wall Street Journal, April 28, 2019, https://www.wsj.com/articles /entrepreneurs-are-better-off-going-it-alone-study -says-1155650332, accessed January 12, 2021.

21. A. Bartik, M. Bertrand, Z. Cullen, E. Glaeser, M. Luca & C. Stanton, "A Way Forward for Small Businesses," Harvard Business Review, April 13, 2020, https://hbr.org/2020/04/a-way-forward-for -small-businesses, accessed January 12, 2021; A. Bartik, M. Bertrand, Z. Cullen, E. Glaeser, M. Luca & C. Stanton, "The Impact of COVID-19 on Small Business Outcomes and Expectations," Proceedings of the National Academy of Science of the United States of America, July 28, 2020, https://www.pnas.org /content/117/30/17656, accessed January 12, 2021.

22. E. Palattella, "Unpaid Wages Pile Up at Erie County Farms," GoErie, December 4, 2016, https:// www.goerie.com/news/20161204/unpaid-wages-pile -up-at-erie-county-farms, accessed January 16, 2017.

23. P. Mahler & F. Fritz, "Death of Limited Partner Disarms Derivative Action," JDSupra, February 10, 2020, https://www.jdsupra.com /legalnews/death-of-limited-partner-disarms-32017/, accessed January 13, 2021.

24. "IRS Provides Tax Inflation Adjustments for Tax Year 2021," Internal Revenue Service, October 6, 2020, https://www.irs.gov/newsroom/irs-provides-tax -inflation-adjustments-for-tax-year-2021, accessed January 17, 2021; "Tax Cuts and Jobs Act, Provision 11011 Section 199A - Qualified Business Income Deduction FAQs," Internal Revenue Service, November 24, 2020, https://www.irs.gov/newsroom /tax-cuts-and-jobs-act-provision-11011-section-199a -qualified-business-income-deduction-faqs, accessed January 17, 2021; A. Fontinelle, "Is Now the Time to Restructure Your Business?," Investopedia, January 21, 2020, https://www.investopedia.com/taxes/now-time -restructure-your-business/, accessed January 17, 2021; R. Simon, "Pass-Through Businesses Are Rethinking Their Status in Wake of Tax Law," The Wall Street Journal, February 28, 2018, https://www .wsj.com/articles/tax-law-leaves-business-owners -with-big-decision-to-c-or-not-to-c-1519295401, accessed January 17, 2021; B. Weltman, "A Guide to the Qualified Business Income Deduction (QBI Deduction)," The Blueprint (A Motley Fool Service), August 13, 2020, https://www.fool.com/the-blueprint /qualified-business-income-deduction/, accessed January 17, 2021.

25. R. Evans, S. Klevens & S. Badawi, "Three Steps to Shield Innocent Partners From Malpractice Liability," The Recorder, February 24, 2015, https://www.law.com/therecorder /almID/1202718859639/Three-Steps-to-Shield -Innocent-Partners-From-Malpractice-Liability/?/, accessed January 13, 2021.

26. "Pros and Cons of LLC vs Corporation," Upcounsel, https://www.upcounsel.com/pros-and -cons-of-llc-vs-corporation, accessed January 13, 2021; "Registered Agent: Everything You Need to Know," Upcounsel, https://www.upcounsel.com /registered-agent, accessed January 13, 2021.

27. "About the Division of Corporations," Division of Corporations - State of Delaware, https://www .corp.delaware.gov/aboutagency.shtml, accessed January 13, 2021.

28. "The Carlyle Group Announces Conversion to Full C-Corporation Reports Second Quarter 2019 Financial Results," The Carlyle Group, July 31, 2019, https://ir.carlyle.com/static-files/95e346e9 -9741-42f3-a830-476646bcc830, accessed January 13, 2021.

29. "About the Division of Corporations," Division of Corporations - State of Delaware, https://www.corp.delaware.gov/aboutagency.shtml, accessed January 13, 2021.

30. J. Cardwell, "If You Invested $100 in Visa's IPO, This Is How Much Money You'd Have Now," *The Motley Fool*, February 13, 2020, https://www.fool.com/investing/2020/02/13/if-you-invested-100-in-visa-ipo-this-is-how-much-m.aspx, accessed January 14, 2021.

31. T. Gryta & T. Francis, "GE's Top Executives Miss Out on Cash Bonuses for the First Time," *The Wall Street Journal*, March 12, 2018, https://www.wsj.com/articles/ge-didnt-pay-bonuses-to-ceo-top-executives-in-2017-1520892109, accessed January 14, 2021; "General Electric Company, Schedule 14A Information," U.S. Securities and Exchange Information, April 25, 2018, https://www.sec.gov/Archives/edgar/data/40545/000120677418000752/ge3334621-def14a.htm, accessed January 14, 2021.

32. E. Savitz, "Zoom Raised $1.75B. Morgan Stanley Says the Street Is Too Bearish," *Barron's*, January 13, 2021, https://www.barrons.com/articles/zoom-raised-1-75b-morgan-stanley-says-the-street-is-too-bearish-51610568346, accessed January 14, 2021.

33. D. Larcker & B. Tayan, "How Netflix Redesigned Board Meetings," *Harvard Business Review*, May 8, 2018, https://hbr.org/2018/05/how-netflix-redesigned-board-meetings, accessed January 17, 2021; J. Lublin, "Boards Try Buddy System to Get Newcomers Up to Speed," *The Wall Street Journal*, September 18, 2017, https://www.wsj.com/articles/boards-try-buddy-system-to-get-newcomers-up-to-speed-1505769025, accessed January 17, 2021.

34. "Form 10-K, Apple, Inc.," Securities and Exchange Commission, October 29, 2020, https://www.sec.gov/Archives/edgar/data/0000320193/000032019320000096/aapl-20200926.htm#ief781ab58e4f4fcaa872ddbd30da40e1_37, accessed January 14, 2021.

35. T. Wilde, "Analysis: Microsoft's Acquisition of Bethesda Is a Massive Disruption for the Video Game Industry," *GeekWire*, September 21, 2020, https://www.geekwire.com/2020/analysis-microsofts-acquisition-bethesda-massive-disruption-video-game-industry/, accessed January 14, 2021.

36. P. Page, "Long-Friendly Families to Unite in Truck Merger," *The Wall Street Journal*, April 10, 2017, https://www.wsj.com/articles/long-friendly-families-to-unite-in-truck-merger-1491856951, accessed January 14, 2021.

37. "About Knight Transportation – We're in It for the Long Haul," Knight Transportation, https://www.knighttrans.com/AboutKnight#; accessed January 14, 2021; "Trucking Company - Transportation and Logistics," Swift Transportation, https://www.swifttrans.com/, accessed January 14, 2021.

38. No author, "Constellation Brands (STZ) Sells Paul Masson, Concludes Divestitures," Zack's Equity Research, January 13, 2021, https://finance.yahoo.com/news/constellation-brands-stz-sells-paul-161204213.html, accessed January 14, 2021.

39. J. Walker, "Bluebird Bio to Spin Off Cancer-Drug Unit," *The Wall Street Journal*, January 11, 2021, https://www.wsj.com/articles/bluebird-bio-to-spin-off-cancer-drug-unit-11610361000, accessed January 15, 2021; Press Release, "Bluebird Bio to Separate Oncology Business into Independent Company," Bluebird Bio, Inc., January 11, 2021, https://investor.bluebirdbio.com/news-releases/news-release-details/bluebird-bio-separate-oncology-business-independent-company, accessed January 15, 2021.

40. J. Cornell, "Sharp Corporation To Carve-Out Its LCD Unit," *Forbes*, March 23, 2020, https://www.forbes.com/sites/joecornell/2020/03/23/sharp-corporation-to-carve-out-its-lcd-unit/?sh=24477ea67af5, accessed January 15, 2021.

41. J. Creswell & D. Yaffe-Bellany, "When Mac & Cheese and Ketchup Don't Mix: The Kraft Heinz Merger Falters," *The New York Times*, September 24, 2019, https://www.nytimes.com/2019/09/24/business/kraft-heinz-food-3g-capital-management.html, accessed January 18, 2021; A. Gasparro, "Kraft Heinz CEO, Pushing for Growth, Separates Winners From Losers," *The Wall Street Journal*, January 26, 2020, https://www.wsj.com/articles/kraft-heinz-ceo-pushing-for-growth-separates-winners-from-losers-11580047201, accessed January 18, 2021; A. Gasparro, "Kraft Heinz Plans $2 Billion in Cost Cuts," *The Wall Street Journal*, September 15, 2020, https://www.wsj.com/articles/kraft-heinz-plans-2-billion-in-cost-cuts-11600169462, accessed January 18, 2021; A. Lucas, "Kraft Heinz to sell part of cheese business to Lactalis in $3.2 billion deal," *CNBC*, September 15, 2020, https://www.cnbc.com/2020/09/15/kraft-heinz-to-sell-part-of-cheese-business-to-lactalis-in-3point2-billion-deal.html, accessed January 18, 2021; C. Lombardo & A. Gasparro, "Kraft Heinz to Sell Part of Cheese Business for $3.2 Billion," *The Wall Street Journal*, September 15, 2020, https://www.wsj.com/articles/kraft-heinz-nears-deal-to-sell-part-of-cheese-business-to-lactalis-11600182175, accessed January 18, 2021.

42. "Why States Should Adopt RULLCA," Uniform Law Commission: The National Conference of Commissioners on Uniform State Laws, https://www.uniformlaws.org/Narrative.aspx?title=Why%20States%20Should%20Adopt%20RULLCA, accessed January 16, 2017.

43. J. Haskins, "Reduce Self-Employment Taxes with a Corporation or LLC," LegalZoom, September 4, 2020, https://www.legalzoom.com/articles/reduce-self-employment-taxes-with-a-corporation-or-llc, accessed January 15, 2021.

44. "What's the Average Cost to Set up an LLC?" *LLC University®*, October 12, 2020, https://www.llcuniversity.com/what-is-the-average-cost-to-set-up-an-llc/, accessed January 15, 2021.

45. "LLC Annual Fees by State - All 50 States," *LLC University®*, November 10, 2020, https://www.llcuniversity.com/llc-annual-fees-by-state/, accessed January 15, 2021; "Limited Liability Company," State of California Franchise Tax Board, December 24, 2020, https://www.ftb.ca.gov/file/business/types/limited-liability-company/index.html, accessed January 15, 2021.

46. "Limited Liability Company Act, Revised," Uniform Law Commission, https://www.uniformlaws.org/committees/community-home?communitykey=bbea059c-6853-4f45-b69b-7ca2e49cf740&tab=groupdetails, accessed January 15, 2021.

47. "Why States Should Adopt RULLCA," Uniform Law Commission: The National Conference of Commissioners on Uniform State Laws, https://www.uniformlaws.org/Narrative.aspx?title=Why%20States%20Should%20Adopt%20RULLCA, accessed January 16, 2017.

48. No Author, "How Much Do Franchise Owners Make a Year?" *Franchise Business Review*, https://franchisebusinessreview.com/post/how-much-franchise-owners-make/, accessed January 18, 2021; B. Borzykowski, "This Is How Much to Pay Yourself as a Business Owner," *CNBC*, February 29, 2020, https://www.cnbc.com/2020/02/28/this-is-how-much-to-pay-yourself-as-a-business-owner.html, accessed January 18, 2021; E. Garone, "Women Flock to Franchising," *The Wall Street Journal*, December 1, 2019, https://www.wsj.com/articles/women-flock-to-franchising-11575255662, accessed January 18, 2021; P. Sullivan, "How to Get Rich by Buying a Franchise (Really)," *The New York Times*, October 25, 2019, https://www.nytimes.com/2019/10/25/your-money/franchise.html, accessed January 18, 2021.

49. "Research: Quick Facts," International Franchise Association, https://www.franchisefoundation.org/research, accessed January 15, 2021.

50. Hait, "Franchising in America: Not Just Fast-Food Restaurants," United States Census Bureau, March 28, 2018, https://www.census.gov/library/stories/2018/03/franchises.html, accessed January 15, 2021.

51. "Advanced Beverages & Bar Supplies Franchise Overview," Franchising.com, https://www.franchising.com/advancedbeveragesbarsupplies/, accessed January 15, 2021; "Advanced Beverages and Bar Supplies Franchise Costs and Franchise Info for 2020," FranchiseClique.com, https://www.franchiseclique.com/franchise/Advanced-Beverages-and-Bar-Supplies, accessed January 15, 2021.

52. "Rankings of the Top 100 Franchises of 2020," Franchise Direct, https://www.franchisedirect.com/top100globalfranchises/rankings, accessed January 15, 2021.

53. "McDonald's Franchise Information," *Entrepreneur*, October 23, 2020, https://www.entrepreneur.com/franchises/mcdonalds/282570, accessed January 15, 2021; "Subway Franchise Information," *Entrepreneur*, October 23, 2020, https://www.entrepreneur.com/franchises/subway/282839, accessed January 15, 2021; "7-Eleven Inc. Franchise Information," *Entrepreneur*, October 23, 2020, https://www.entrepreneur.com/franchises/7eleveninc/282052, accessed January 15, 2021.

54. "The Top 50 Franchises for Women," *Franchise Business Review*, https://franchisebusinessreview.com/page/top-franchises-for-women/, accessed January 16, 2021.

55. E. Garone, "Women Flock to Franchising," *The Wall Street Journal*, December 1, 2019, https://www.wsj.com/articles/women-flock-to-franchising-11575255662, accessed January 16, 2021.

56. "Minority-Owned Franchises—Where Are We Now, and What Are We Doing?" *Franchise Direct*, October 14, 2020, https://www.franchisedirect.com/blog/minority-owned-franchiseswhere-are-we-now-and-what-are-we-doing, accessed January 16, 2021.

57. J. Bourdow & M. Brewer, "Inclusion Is a Growth Strategy," *Franchising World*, (June 2013): 15–17.

58. "Sponsors and Donors | IFA Foundation," International Franchise Association Foundation, https://www.franchisefoundation.org/sponsors-and-donors, accessed January 16, 2021.

59. "Women Flock to Franchising," *The Wall Street Journal*.

60. "General FAQs," Subway, https://www.subway.com/en-US/ContactUs/SubwayFAQs#franchiseownership, accessed January 16, 2021; J. Robinson, "Subway Combines Online, In-Store and Classroom Training to Provide Effective Training for Franchisees," *Latitude Learning*, March 8, 2016, https://www.latitudelearning.com/blog/subway-combines-online-in-store-and-classroom-training-to-provide-effective-training-for-franchisees, accessed January 16, 2021.

61. "Subway," *Entrepreneur*, https://www.entrepreneur.com/franchises/subway/282839-2.html, accessed March 20, 2016.

62. No author, "Domino's Pizza Shares Fall 7% Amid Franchise Row," *BBC News*, December 10,

2018, https://www.bbc.com/news/business -46509475, accessed January 19, 2021; M. Colias, "About 150 U.S. Cadillac Dealers to Exit Brand, Rather Than Sell Electric Cars," *The Wall Street Journal*, December 4, 2020, https://www.wsj .com/articles/about-150-u-s-cadillac-dealers -to-exit-brand-rather-than-sell-electric-cars -11607111494?mod=djemlogistics_h, accessed January 19, 2021; B. Dooley & H. Ueno, "A 7-Eleven in Japan Might Close for a Day. Yes, That's a Big Deal," *The New York Times*, December 30, 2019, https://www.nytimes.com/2019/12/30 /business/7-eleven-japan-work.html, accessed January 19, 2021; H. Muramatsu, "Ex-7-Eleven Franchisee in Japan Who Cut Store Hours Sues Firm Over Contract Cancellation" *The Mainichi*, February 12, 2020, https://mainichi.jp/english /articles/20200212/p2a/00m/0na/008000c, accessed January 19, 2021; H. Ueno, "How 7-Eleven Struck Back Against an Owner Who Took a Day Off," *The New York Times*, January 6, 2020, https:// www.nytimes.com/2020/01/06/business/7-eleven -japan.html, accessed January 19, 2021; D. Walsh, "Franchise Disputes Hold Back Domino's Expansion," *The Times*, March 13, 2019, https:// www.thetimes.co.uk/article/franchise-disputes -hold-back-domino-s-expansion-tb0z9jdtq, accessed January 19, 2021.

63. Franchise Rule Compliance Guide, Federal Trade Commission, https://www.ftc.gov/bcp/edu /pubs/business/franchise/bus70.pdf, pages 20, 102–103, and 121.

Pg. 105 Fact: John McCormack, "GE Filed 57,000-Page Tax Return, Paid No Taxes on $14 Billion in Profits," *The Weekly Standard*, November 17, 2011, https://www.weeklystandard .com/blogs/ge-filed-57000-page-tax-return-paid -no-taxes-14-billionprofits_609137.html.

# Chapter 7

1. Lauren Bauer, Kristen Broady, Wendy Edelberg & Jimmy O'Donnell, "Ten Facts About COVID-19 and the U.S. Economy," September 17, 2020, https://www.brookings.edu/research/ten-facts -about-covid-19-and-the-u-s-economy/, accessed March 26, 2021; Miles Brandon, "Pandemic Sparks New Businesses," September 24, 2020, https://www .npr.org/sections/coronavirus-live-updates/2020/09 /24/916205107/pandemic-sparks-new-businesses, accessed March 26, 2021, GEM Staff, "Prior to the Pandemic, Entrepreneurship Was Surging in the United States," https://www.gemconsortium .org/news/new-gem-%2F-babson-report%3A-prior -to-pandemic%2C-entrepreneurship-was-surging- in-the-united-states, accessed March 26, 2021; Business Formation Statistic, US Census, https:// www.census.gov/econ/bfs/index.html, accessed March 26, 2021.

2. Chidike Samuelson, "How Generation Z Is Altering the Face of Entrepreneurship for Good," November 24, 2020, https://www.entrepreneur. com/article/358930, accessed March 26, 2021; Kim Parker & Ruth Igielnik, "What We Know About Gen Z so Far," May 14, 2020, https://www .pewresearch.org/social-trends/2020/05/14/on-the -cusp-of-adulthood-and-facing-an-uncertain-future -what-we-know-about-gen-z-so-far-2/, accessed March 26, 2021.

3. Matthew Miller & Duncan Greenberg (eds.), "The Forbes 400," *Forbes*, September 17, 2008, https://www.forbes.com/2008/09/16/forbes-400 -billionaires-lists-400list08_cx_mn_0917richamericans _land.html, accessed February 15, 2009.

4. "The Big Fat Story, The Geek Kings," *Newsweek*, June 5, 2011, https://www.newsweek.com/big-fat -story-geek-kings-67969, accessed February 5, 2013; "Forbes 400 Richest Americans," *Forbes*, September 2013, https://www.forbes.com/profile /dustin-moskovitz/, accessed February 19, 2014; Jason Nazar, "Surprising Past Jobs of Successful Entrepreneurs," *Business Insider*, October 31, 2013, https://www.businessinsider.com/surprising-past -jobs-of-successful-entrepreneurs-2013-10, accessed April 5, 2015.

5. "Discover Polls Reveal True Character of the American Entrepreneur," Press Release, Discover Financial Services, October 22, 2007, https:// investorrelations.discoverfinancial.com/phoenix .zhtml?c=204177&p=irol-newsArticle&ID =1065373&highlight=, accessed February 15, 2009.

6. "More than Half of Small Business Owners Work at Least Six-Day Weeks, Still Find Time for Personal Life," Wells Fargo News Release, August 9, 2005, https://www.wellsfargo.com/press/20050809 _GallupPersonalLife; "Discover Polls Reveal True Character of the American Entrepreneur," Press Release, Discover Financial Services, October 22, 2007, https://investorrelations.discoverfinancial.com /phoenix.zhtml?c=204177&p=irol-newsArticle&ID =1065373&highlight=, accessed February 15, 2009; "Small Business Owners Working Longer Hours," May 26, 2009, Rent to Own, https://rtoonline.com /Content/Article/may09/smal-business-owners-work -hours-survey-052609.asp, accessed June 12, 2012.

7. Brian Wu & Anne Marie Knott, "Entrepreneurial Risk and Market Entry," SBA Office of Advocacy, January 2005, https://www.sba .gov/advo/research/wkpbw249.pdf.

8. Ibid

9. Alice E. Vincent, "Rejection Letters: The Publishers Who Got It Embarrassingly Wrong . . . ," *The Huffington Post*, November 7, 2012, https:// www.huffingtonpost.co.uk/2012/05/16/publishers -who-got-it-wrong_n_1520190.html#slide =more226527, accessed March 15, 2013; "Failure: Use It as a Springboard to Success," U.S. SBA Online Library, https://www.sba.gov/library /successXIII/19-Failure-Use-it.doc, accessed December 28, 2005.

10. Keith McFarland, "What Makes Them Tick," Inc 500, 2005, Inc, https://www.inc.com/resources /inc500/2005/articles/20051001/tick.html; Kwame Kuadey, "Bootstrapping Your Startup? Make Money Before You Spend It," Young Entrepreneurs Council, June 12, 2012, https://theyec.org/bootstrapping-your-startup -make-money-before-you-spend-it/, accessed June 12, 2012.

11. "The Biggest Lies People Told Me About Entrepreneurship," Inc., April 4, 2017, https:// www.inc.com/cox-business/the-biggest-lie-people -told-me-about-entrepreneurship.html, accessed April 13, 2017.

12. Benjamin Ryan, "Starved of Financing, New Businesses Are in Decline," *Gallup Business Journal*, September 4, 2014, https://www.gallup.com /businessjournal/175499/starved-financing-new -businesses-decline.aspx, accessed April 5, 2015.

13. "How to Finance a New Business," *Consumer Reports*, April 2008, https://www.consumerreports .org/cro/money/credit-loan/how-to-finance-a-new -business/overview/how-to-finance-a-new-business -ov.htm, accessed March 18, 2011.

14. Frequently Asked Questions, SBA Office of Advocacy, October 2020, https://cdn.advocacy.sba .gov/wp-content/uploads/2020/11/05122043/Small -Business-FAQ-2020.pdf, accessed March 27, 2021.

15. John Tozzi, "Credit Cards Replace Small Business Loans," *BusinessWeek*, August 20, 2008, https://www.businessweek.com/smallbiz/content /aug2008/sb20080820_288348.htm?chan=smallbiz _smallbiz+index+page_top+small+business+stories, accessed February 15, 2009; Kimberly Palmer, "Can I Start a Business with Credit Cards? Meet Some Entrepreneurs Who Did," November 1, 2017, https://www.nerdwallet.com/article/credit -cards/use-credit-card-to-start-business, accessed March 27, 2021.

16. Patrick Clark, "What Do Small Businesses Need Banks for, Anyway?," *BusinessWeek*, September 10, 2013, https://www.businessweek.com /articles/2013-09-10/what-do-small-businesses -need-banks-for-anyway, accessed February 6, 2014; Frequently Asked Questions, SBA Office of Advocacy, October 2020, https://cdn.advocacy .gov/wp-content/uploads/2020/11/05122043/Small -Business-FAQ-2020.pdf, accessed March 27, 2021.

17. "Start-Up Information," Delaware Small Business Development Center, updated April 28, 2008, https://www.delawaresbdc.org/Document Master.aspx?doc=1003#6, accessed February 15, 2009.

18. Mike Freeman, "San Diego's Investing Angels," *San Diego Union Tribune*, January 32, 2013, https:// www.utsandiego.com/news/2013/jan/31/Tech-Coast -Angels-fund-local-start-ups/?page=1#article-copy, accessed March 24, 2013; "Financial Assistance," Small Business Administration, https://www.sba.gov /services/financialassistance/index.html, accessed February 15, 2009.

19. Darrah Brustein, "Growth-Hacking 101," *Entrepreneur*, August 5, 2016, https://www .entrepreneur.com/article/280130, accessed April 13, 2017; Global Crowdfunding Market Size and Growth, February 2020, https://www .marketdataforecast.com/market-reports /crowdfunding-market, accessed March 27, 2021.

20. Jane Mulkerrins, "Meet Whitney Wolfe, the Queen Bee of Digital Dating," March 4, 2017, https://www.dailymail.co.uk/home/you /article-4271840/Meet-Whitney-Wolfe-queen-bee -digital-dating.html?ITO=1490, accessed March 30, 2021; "At 31, Bumble Founder and SMU Grad Whitney Wolfe Herd Just Became Tech's Newest Self-Made billionaire," *Bloomberg Wire*, February 11, 2021, https://www.dallasnews.com/business /technology/2021/02/11/at-31-bumble-founder -whitney-wolfe-herd-just-became-techs-newest -self-made-billionaire/, accessed March 30, 2021.

21. Ryan Robinson, "5 Crowdfunded Side Projects That Became Million-Dollar Companies," September 18, 2017, https://www.forbes.com /sites/ryanrobinson/2017/09/18/crowdfunded -side-projects-that-became-million-dollar-companies /?sh=217b22a43f1d, accessed March 27, 2021.

22. Jeffrey Sohl, Wan-Chien Lien & Jianhong Chen, "The Angel Market and COVID-19, Building Bridges or Piers," May 2020, accessed March 27, 2021.

23. Jeffrey Sohl, "Angel Investor Market in Q1Q2 2011: A Return to the Seed Stage," Center for Venture Research, University of New Hampshire, October 11, 2011, https://paulcollege.unh.edu/sites /paulcollege.unh.edu/files/q1q2_2011_analysis _report_0.pdf, accessed June 12, 2012; Abby Tracy, "Angel Investments Up 40%," Inc., March 13, 2012, https://wire.inc.com/2012/03/13/angel-investments -up-40/, accessed June 12, 2012.

24. Neal Taparia, "Why Startups Need To Value Diversity More," March 26, 2021, https://www .forbes.com/sites/nealtaparia/2021/03/26/why -startups-need-to-value-diversity-more/?sh =6451fc5e7930, accessed April 1, 2021.

25. "The Steady, Strategic Assent of JetBlue Airways," Strategic Management Knowledge at Wharton, December 14, 2005–January 10, 2006, https://knowledge.wharton.upenn.edu/article/1342.cfm; Bobbie Gossage, "Charging Ahead," Inc. Magazine, January 2004, https://www.inc.com/magazine/20040101/gettingstarted.html.

26. Amplestuff, https://www.amplestuff.com/; "Kazoo v. Walmart," Reveries, November 29, 2005, https://www.reveries.com/?p=232.

27. "E-Commerce Award—June 2002," Anything Left-Handed, https://www.anythingleft-handed.co.uk/pressreleases.html, accessed May 24, 2017.

28. Rhonda Abrams, "Focus on Success, Not Failure," USA Today, May 7, 2004, https://www.usatoday.com/money/smallbusiness/columnist/abrams/2004-05-06-success_x.htm.

29. "Is Entrepreneurship for You?," U.S. Small Business Administration, https://www.sba.gov/starting_business/startup/areyouready.html, accessed December 15, 2005.

30. "Committee Examines Ways to Ease Growing Regulatory Burden on Small Businesses," U.S. House of Representatives Press Release, House of Representatives, July 30, 2008, https://www.house.gov/smbiz/PressReleases/2008/pr-7-30-08-regulatory.html, accessed February 15, 2009.

31. David Nather, "How Obamacare Affects Businesses—Large and Small," Politico, September 30, 2013, https://www.politico.com/story/2013/09/how-obamacare-affects-businesses-large-and-small-97460.html, accessed February 6, 2014; "Entrepreneurship in the 21st Century," Conference Proceedings, March 26, 2004, SBA Office of Advocacy and the Kauffman Foundation, https://www.sba.gov/advo/stats/proceedings_a.pdf; Sharon McLoone, "Health Care Costs Surface in Economic Stimulus Debate," The Washington Post, February 10, 2009, https://voices.washingtonpost.com/small-business/2009/02/health_care_costs_surface_in_e.html, accessed February 15, 2009.

32. "Inventor of the Week, Lemulson-MIT," https://web.mit.edu/invent/iow/epperson.html, accessed March 15, 2013; "10 Accidental Inventions You Won't Believe," Science Channel, https://science.discovery.com/brink/top-ten/accidental-inventions/inventions-01.html, accessed March 22, 2011.

33. "Business Plan Basics," U.S. SBA, https://www.sba.gov/starting_business/planning/basic.html, accessed February 15, 2009.

34. Frequently Asked Questions, SBA Office of Advocacy, October 2020, https://cdn.advocacy.sba.gov/wp-content/uploads/2020/11/05122043/Small-Business-FAQ-2020.pdf, accessed March 27, 2021.

35. "Frequently Asked Questions," SBA Office of Advocacy, updated September 2008, SBA, https://www.sba.gov/advo/stats/sbfaq.pdf, accessed February 17, 2009.

36. Ibid.

37. "Small Business Drives Inner City Growth and Jobs," news release, U.S. SBA Office of Advocacy, October 11, 2005, https://www.sba.gov/advo/press/05-32.html.

38. Global Entrepreneurship Monitor, 2019/2020 Global Report, Accessed March 29, 2021.

39. Niels Bosma, Zoltan J. Acs, Erkko Autio, Alicia Coduras, & Jonathan Levie, "Global Entrepreneurship Monitor, 2008 Executive Report," Global Entreprenurship Research Association, London School of Economics, January 15, 2009, https://www.gemconsortium.org/article.aspx?id=76, accessed February 17, 2009.

Pg. 129 Fact: John Greathouse, "Business Tips from College Dropouts: Zuckerberg, Jobs, Gates, Dell, Ellison, Branson and Disney," Forbes, June 5, 2012, https://www.forbes.com/sites/johngreathouse/2012/06/05/business-tips-from-college-dropouts-zuckerberg-jobs-gates-dell-ellison-branson-and-disney/, accessed November 2012; and https://www.gemconsortium.org/docs/download/260, accessed November 2012.

# Chapter 8

1. T. Kinder, "Patisserie Valerie Goes Bust as Rescue Talks Fail," The Times, January 23, 2019, https://www.thetimes.co.uk/article/patisserie-valerie-goes-bust-as-rescue-talks-fail-tv3q8v62q?region=global, accessed January 21, 2021.

2. R. Hotten, "Patisserie Valerie Collapses Into Administration as Rescue Talks Fail," BBC News, January 22, 2019, https://www.bbc.com/news/business-46965761, accessed January 21, 2021.

3. A. Ralph, "Grant Thornton Sued for £200m Over Patisserie Valerie Audit 'Negligence,'" The Times, January 8, 2021, https://www.thetimes.co.uk/article/grant-thornton-sued-for-200m-over-patisserie-valerie-audit-negligence-d5kbws9v6?region=global, accessed January 21, 2021.

4. T. Gerken, "Patisserie Valerie: Redundant staff 'Not Receiving Final Pay,'" BBC News, February 3, 2019, https://www.bbc.com/news/business-47107659, accessed January 21, 2021.

5. "Administration of Patisserie Valerie: Update - KPMG United Kingdom," January 23, 2019, https://home.kpmg/uk/en/home/media/press-releases/2019/01/administration-of-patisserie-valerie-update.html, accessed January 21, 2021; A. Graham, "Patisserie Valerie Liquidators File £200m Lawsuit Against Auditor Grant Thornton," Independent, January 8, 2021, https://www.independent.ie/world-news/patisserie-valerie-liquidators-file-200m-lawsuit-against-auditor-grant-thornton-39946999.html, accessed January 21, 2021.

6. S. Butler, "Patisserie Valerie Saved in Buyout Backed by Irish Private Equity Firm," The Guardian, February 14, 2019, https://www.theguardian.com/business/2019/feb/14/patisserie-valerie-saved-in-buyout-backed-by-irish-private-equity-firm-causeway-capital, accessed January 21, 2021; O. Gill, "Patisserie Valerie Saved by Irish Private Equity Firm," Telegraph, February 14, 2019, https://www.telegraph.co.uk/business/2019/02/14/patisserie-valerie-saved-irish-private-equity-firm/, accessed January 21, 2021.

7. "Patisserie Holdings PLC," Serious Fraud Office, November 9, 2020, https://www.sfo.gov.uk/cases/patisserie-holdings-plc/, accessed January 21, 2021.

8. A. Ralph, "Grant Thornton sued for £200m over Patisserie Valerie audit 'negligence,'" The Times, January 8, 2021, https://www.thetimes.co.uk/article/grant-thornton-sued-for-200m-over-patisserie-valerie-audit-negligence-d5kbws9v6?region=global, accessed January 21, 2021.

9. Ibid.

10. "150 Hour Requirement for Obtaining a CPA License," Association of International Certified Professional Accountants, https://www.aicpa.org/becomeacpa/licensure/:~:text=150%20Hour%20Requirement%20for%20Obtaining%20a%20CPA%20License.,hours%20of%20education%20for%20obtaining%20the%20CPA%20license.#states, accessed January 22, 2021.

11. "CMA Certification," Institute of Management Accountants, https://www.imanet.org/cma-certification?ssopc=1, accessed January 22, 2021; "The CFE Credential," Association of Certified Fraud Examiners, https://www.acfe.com/cfe-credential.aspx, accessed January 22, 2021.

12. "Final Q4 2020 Letter to Shareholders," Netflix, January 19, 2021, https://s22.q4cdn.com/959853165/files/doc_financials/2020/q4/FINAL-Q420-Shareholder-Letter.pdf, accessed January 22, 2021.

13. AFP News, "A Real Roasting: Coffee Startup Luckin Set to Overtake Starbucks in China," Yahoo!News, January 3, 2019, https://sg.news.yahoo.com/real-roasting-coffee-startup-luckin-set-overtake-starbucks-111401100.html, accessed January 26, 2021; Editorial Board, "Cleaning Up a Chinese Coffee Spill," The Wall Street Journal, May 19, 2020, https://www.wsj.com/articles/cleaning-up-a-chinese-co!ee-spill-11589930591, accessed January 26, 2021; M. Robinson, "Luckin to Pay $180 Million to Settle SEC Accounting Probe," Bloomberg, December 17, 2020, https://www.bloombergquint.com/markets/luckin-to-pay-180-million-to-settle-sec-accounting-probe, accessed January 26, 2021; S. Wang & M. Campbell, "Luckin Scandal Is Bad Timing for U.S.-Listed Chinese Companies," Bloomberg, July 31, 2020, https://www.bloombergquint.com/businessweek/luckin-coffee-fraud-behind-starbucks-competitor-s-scandal, accessed January 26, 2021; Q. Webb & J. Chiu, "Ernst & Young Says It First Found Accounting Issues at Luckin," The Wall Street Journal, April 3, 2020, https://www.wsj.com/articles/ernst-young-says-it-first-found-accounting-issues-at-luckin-11585927403, accessed January 26, 2021; J. Yang, "Behind the Fall of China's Luckin Coffee: a Network of Fake Buyers and a Fictitious Employee," The Wall Street Journal, May 28, 2020, https://www.wsj.com/articles/behind-the-fall-of-chinas-luckin-coffee-a-network-of-fake-buyers-and-a-fictitious-employee-11590682336, accessed January 26, 2021; J. Yang & H. Gillers, "Luckin Coffee's Accounting Scandal Thwarts Backer's $2.5 Billion Fund," The Wall Street Journal, April 17, 2020, https://www.wsj.com/articles/luckin-coffees-accounting-scandal-thwarts-backers-2-5-billion-fund-11587109890, accessed January 26, 2021; J. Yang & J. Steinberg, "Luckin Coffee Terminates CEO Jenny Qian Amid Investigation Into Fabricated Sales," The Wall Street Journal, May 12, 2020, https://www.wsj.com/articles/luckin-coffee-terminates-ceo-jenny-zhiya-qian-amid-investigation-into-fabricated-sales-11589297382, accessed January 26, 2021; Z. Yushuo, "China's Luckin Coffee Puts Scandal Behind It, Recruits Franchisees as Rivalry Boils Over," Yicai Global, January 19, 2021, https://www.yicaiglobal.com/news/china-luckin-coffee-puts-scandal-behind-it-recruits-franchisees-as-rivalry-boils-over, accessed January 26, 2021.

14. "About the FASB," Financial Accounting Standards Board," https://www.fasb.org/facts/, accessed January 23, 2021.

15. "Board Members," Financial Accounting Standards Board," https://www.fasb.org/cs/Satellite?c=Page&cid=1218220131802&pagename=FASB%2FPage%2FSectionPage, accessed January 23, 2021.

16. M. Maurer, "Companies' Non-GAAP Adjustments to Net Income Have Soared," The Wall Street Journal, October 18, 2019, https://www.wsj.com/articles/companies-non-gaap-adjustments-to-net-income-have-soared-11571429258?mod=djemRiskCompliance, accessed January 23, 2021.

17. Ibid.

18. S. Asper, C. McCoy & G. Taylor, "The Expanding Use of Non-GAAP Financial Measures," The CPA Journal, July 2019, https://www.cpajournal.com/2019/07/24/the-expanding-use-of-non-gaap-financial-measures/, accessed January 23, 2021

19. Ibid.

20. "Top Accounting Scandals: A Recap of the Top Scandals in the Past," Corporate Finance Institute, https://corporatefinanceinstitute.com/resources /knowledge/other/top-accounting-scandals/, accessed January 23, 2021; A. Ross Sorkin, "Graphic: A Long Line of Accounting Scandals," Dealbook, *The New York Times*, November 20, 2012, https://dealbook. nytimes.com/2012/11/20/graphic-a-long-line-of -accounting-scandals/, accessed March 5, 2013.

21. No author, "Facebook EBITDA Margin 2009-2020," *MacroTrends*, https://www .macrotrends.net/stocks/charts/FB/facebook /ebitda-margin, accessed January 27, 2021; No author, "Facebook Inc. (NASDAQ:FB) | Goodwill and Intangible Assets," *Stock Analysis on Net*, https://www.stock-analysis-on.net/NASDAQ /Company/Facebook-Inc/Analysis/Goodwill-and -Intangible-Assets#Disclosure, accessed January 27, 2021; B. Carlson, "How Tech Stocks 'Ate' the Stock Market," *Fortune*, January 21, 2021, https:// fortune.com/2021/01/21/stock-market-tech -stocks-companies-gdp-employees-us-workers -data-charts/, accessed January 27, 2021; V. Govindarajan, S. Rajgopal & A. Srivastava," Why Financial Statements Don't Work for Digital Companies," *Harvard Business Review*, February 26, 2018, https://hbr.org/2018/02/why-financial -statements-dont-work-for-digital-companies, accessed January 27, 2021; J. Khalili, "Workplace From Facebook Has a Cunning Plan to Conquer the Collaboration Market," *TechRadar*, January 12, 2021, https://www.techradar.com/news/workplace -from-facebook-has-a-cunning-plan-to-conquer -the-collaboration-market; accessed January 27, 2021; J. Lukomnik, "Will Accountants Become the Weavers of the 21st Century?" *Accounting Today*, November 19, 2018, https://www.accountingtoday. com/opinion/will-accountants-become-the -weavers-of-the-21st-century, accessed January 27, 2021; I. Lunden, "Facebook's Workplace, Now With 5M Paying Users, Adds Drop-In Video Rooms and More," *TechCrunch*, May 21, 2020, https://techcrunch.com/2020/05/21/facebooks -workplace-now-with-5m-paying-users-adds-drop -in-video-rooms-and-more/, accessed January 27, 2021; L. Trevisan, "EBITDA Multiples by Industry," *Equidam*, January 13, 2020, https:// www.equidam.com/ebitda-multiples-trbc -industries/, accessed January 27, 2021; T. Warren, "Microsoft Teams Usage Jumps 50 Percent to 115 Million Daily Active Users," *The Verge*, October 27, 2020, https://www.theverge.com/2020/10 /27/21537286/microsoft-teams-115-million-daily -active-users-stats, accessed January 27, 2021.

22. J. Kahn, "Wirecard Shows That Auditing Is Broken. Here's Why—and How to Fix It," *Fortune*, June 25, 2020, https://fortune.com/2020/06/25 /wirecard-auditing-is-broken-fintech-ey-ernst-and -young/, accessed January 28, 2021; P. Kowsmann & J. Eaglesham, "After Wirecard, Ernst & Young Says Auditors Should Focus More on Fraud Prevention," *The Wall Street Journal*, September 15, 2020, https:// www.wsj.com/articles/after-wirecard-ernst-young -says-auditors-should-focus-more-on-fraud-prevention -11600167893, accessed January 28, 2021; P. Kowsmann, P. Davies & J. Chung, "Wirecard Scandal Puts Spotlight on Auditor Ernst & Young," *The Wall Street Journal*, June 27, 2020, https://www.wsj .com/articles/wirecard-scandal-puts-spotlight-on -auditor-ernst-young-11593286933?tesla=y, accessed January 28, 2021; O. Storbeck, "Whistleblower Warned EY of Wirecard Fraud Four Years Before Collapse," *Financial Times*, September 30, 2020, https://www.ft.com/content/3b9afceb-eaeb-4dc6 -8a5e-b9bc0b16959d, accessed January 28, 2021; O. Storbeck, T. Kinder & S. Palma, "EY Failed to Check Wirecard Bank Statements for 3 Years," *Financial Times*, June 26, 2020, https://www.ft.com

/content/a9deb987-df70-4a72-bd41-47ed8942e83b, accessed January 28, 2021; N. Trentmann, "Best Points and Miles Strategy for Airlines, Hotels, Travel Credit Cards," *The Wall Street Journal*, July 6, 2020, https://www.wsj.com/articles/u-k-regulator -orders-big-four-to-separate-audit-practices -by-2024-11594070565, accessed January 28, 2021.

23. A. Ralph, "BT Auditor Highlights New Failure," *The Times*, June 8, 2020, https://www.thetimes .co.uk/article/bt-auditor-highlights-new-failure -zsrzltnkd, accessed January 24, 2021.

24. "Mission, Vision, and Values | PCAOB," Public Company Accounting Oversight Board, https:// pcaobus.org/about/mission-vision-values, accessed January 24, 2021.

25. "Accounting Class Action Filings and Settlements: 2019 Review and Analysis," Cornerstone Research, April 8, 2019, https://www .cornerstone.com/Publications/Reports/2019 -Accounting-Class-Action-Filings-and-Settlements, accessed January 24, 2021.

26. "International Code of Ethics for Professional Accountants," International Ethics Standards Boards for Accountants, https://www.ethicsboard .org/international-code-ethics-professional -accountants, accessed January 25, 2021.

27. R. Teitelbaum, "Accountants, Auditors to Get a New Ethics Rule Book," *The Wall Street Journal*, July 11, 2016, https://www.wsj.com/articles /accountants-auditors-to-get-a-new-ethics-rule-book -1468283179, accessed January 24, 2021.

28. A. Elstein, M&T Bank Reported a 'Significant Increase' in bad commercial real estate loans," *Crain's New York Business*, January 21, 2021, https://www.crainsnewyork.com/commercial -real-estate/mt-bank-reports-significant-increase -bad-real-estate-loans, accessed January 29, 2021; J. Emont, "Retailers Canceling Apparel Orders Amid Coronavirus Torments Clothes Makers," *The Wall Street Journal*, May 5, 2020, https://www.wsj.com /articles/retailers-canceling-apparel-orders-amid -coronavirus-torments-clothes-makers -11588683151?mod=djemlogistics_h, accessed January 29, 2021; J. Hagel, "Bean Counters No More, Internal Audit Embraces Broader Risk Advisory Role," *The Wall Street Journal*, November 27, 2020, https://www.wsj.com/articles/bean- counters-no-more-internal-audit-embraces-broader -risk-advisory-role-11606496400?mod=searchresults _pos3&page=1, accessed January 28, 2021; M. Maurer, "Auditors Struggle to Access Data, Count Inventory During Remote Work," *The Wall Street Journal*, September 1, 2020, https://www.wsj.com /articles/auditors-struggle-to-access-data-count -inventory-during-remote-work-11598952600, accessed January 28, 2021; M. Maurer, "Company Write-Downs Surge as Business Slows During Covid-19," *The Wall Street Journal*, August 19, 2020, https://www.wsj.com/articles/company -write-downs-surge-as-business-slows-during -covid-19-11597873913, accessed January 29, 2021.

29. "Microsoft 2020 Annual Report," Microsoft, October 13, 2020, https://www.microsoft.com /investor/reports/ar20/index.html, accessed January 24, 2021.

30. Ibid.

31. *The Essentials of Finance and Budgeting* (Boston, MA: Harvard Business School Press, 2005), pp. 177–181.

32. No author, "ABC Shells Out to Keep 'Wheel of Fortune' and 'Jeopardy' After Big Offer From Fox," *Variety*, November 5, 2018, https://variety .com/2018/tv/news/wheel-of-fortune-jeopardy-abc -fox-cbs-1203019794/, accessed January 25, 2021.

33. S. Abramovitch, "James Holzhauer Returns to 'Jeopardy!' as Insiders Reveal Financial Details of a Record Streak," *Hollywood Reporter*, May 20, 2019, https://www.hollywoodreporter.com/news /james-holzauer-returns-jeopardy-financial-details -revealed-1212143, accessed January 25, 2021.

34. A. Epstein, "Alex Trebek Helped Turn Jeopardy Into a Gargantuan TV Empire," *Quartz*, November 9, 2020, https://qz.com/1930329/alex -trebek-helped-turn-jeopardy-into-a-gargantuan -tv-empire/, accessed January 25, 2021.

35. "James Holzhauer - Jeopardy, Total Winnings & Family," *Biography*, January 15, 2020, https:// www.biography.com/personality/james-holzhauer., accessed January 25, 2021.

36. J. Pinsker, "Jeopardy's Prize Budget vs. James Holzhauer," *The Atlantic*, April 20, 2019, https:// www.theatlantic.com/entertainment/archive /2019/04/james-holzhauer-vs-jeopardys-prize -budget-game-show/587668/, accessed January 25, 2021.

37. Abramovitch, "James Holzhauer Returns to 'Jeopardy!' as Insiders Reveal Financial Details of a Record Streak."

38. J. Bursztynsky, "Coronavirus: At Least 150 Companies Have Warned of Earnings Hit," *CNBC*, March 11, 2020, https://www.cnbc.com/2020/03/11 /coronavirus-at-least-150-companies-have-warned -investors.html, accessed January 25, 2021.

39. Ibid.

40. W. Steve Albrecht, James D. Stice, Earl K. Stice & Monte R. Swain, *Accounting Concepts and Applications*, 9th ed. (Boston, MA: Cengage Learning), p. 758; "Securities and Exchange Commission: A Beginner's Guide to Financial Statements," SEC, https://www.sec.gov/investor /pubs/begfinstmtguide.htm, accessed March 29, 2009. ("Read The Footnotes" finished seventh in the 2004 Kentucky Derby.)

41. J. Creswell & P. Eavis, "Manhattan's Office Buildings Are Empty. But for How Long?" *The New York Times* , September 8, 2020, https://www.nytimes .com/2020/09/08/business/economy/new-york-office -space-coronavirus.html, accessed January 25, 2021.

42. Ibid.

43. S. Kapner & P. Ziobro, "Amazon, Walmart Tell Consumers to Skip Returns of Unwanted Items," *The Wall Street Journal*, January 10, 2021, https://www.wsj.com/articles/amazon-walmart -tell-consumers-to-skip-returns-of-unwanted -items-11610274600?mod=hp_lead_pos3, accessed January 25, 2021; C. Riley, "Online Shopping Has Been Supercharged by the Pandemic. There's No Going Back," *CNN*, October 13, 2020, https:// www.cnn.com/2020/10/11/investing/stocks-week -ahead/index.html, accessed January 25, 2021.

44. S. Kapner & P. Ziobro, "Amazon, Walmart Tell Consumers to Skip Returns of Unwanted Items."

# Chapter 9

1. K. Krader, "Restaurant Dining Bond Program Tries to Stave Devastation," *Bloomberg*, March 16, 2020, https://www.bloomberg.com/news/articles /2020-03-16/restaurant-dining-bond-program-tries -to-stave-devastation, accessed February 1, 2021.

2. K. Rogers, "Covid's Devastating Toll on Restaurants: 2.5 Million Jobs Lost," *CNBC*, January 26, 2021, https://www.cnbc.com/2021/01/26 /restaurant-industry.html, accessed February 1, 2021.

3. M. Maurer, "Domino's CFO Adopts a New Playbook For Pandemic," *The Wall Street Journal*,

April 24, 2020, https://www.wsj.com/articles
/dominos-cfo-adopts-a-new-playbook-for-pandemic
-11587771188, accessed February 1, 2021.

4. Ibid.

5. T. Huddleston, Jr., "How Tesla and SpaceX CEO
Elon Musk Spends His Billions," *CNBC*, January
12, 2021, https://www.cnbc.com/2020/08/18/how
-tesla-and-spacex-ceo-elon-musk-spends-his
-billions.html, accessed February 1, 2021;
T. Locke, "Elon Musk: There Was a Great
Chance SpaceX, Tesla Would Be Worth $0,"
*CNBC*, January 7, 2021, https://www.cnbc
.com/2020/10/02/elon-musk-there-was-a-great
-chance-spacex-tesla-would-be-worth-0.html,
accessed February 1, 2021; S. McBride & D.
Hull, "Elon Musk's Boring Co. Raises $120
Million in First Outside Investment," *Bloomberg*,
July 25, 2019, https://www.bloomberg.com
/news/articles/2019-07-25/elon-musk-s-boring
-co-raises-120-million-in-first-outside-investment
?sref=xXo7CWym, accessed February 1, 2021; J.
Wattles, "SpaceX Is Now a $46 Billion 'Unicorn,'"
*CNN*, August 19, 2020, https://www.cnn.com
/2020/08/19/tech/spacex-valuation-46-billion-scn
/index.html; accessed February 1, 2021.

6. S. Pulliam, M. Ramsey & B. Mullins, "Elon
Musk Supports His Business Empire with Unusual
Financial Moves," *The Wall Street Journal*, April
27, 2016, https://www.wsj.com/articles/elon-musk
-supports-his-business-empire-with-unusual
-financial-moves-1461781962?mod=djem10point,
accessed February 1, 2017.

7. S. Bainbridge, "A Duty to Shareholder Value,"
*The New York Times*, April 16, 2015, https://www
.nytimes.com/roomfordebate/2015/04/16/what-are
-corporations-obligations-to-shareholders/a-duty-to
-shareholder-value, accessed February 1, 2017.

8. L. Strine, "The Dangers of Denial: The Need
for a Clear-Eyed Understanding of the Power
and Accountability Structure Established by the
Delaware General Corporation Law," *Wake Forest
Law Review* 50 (2015): 761.

9. See, for example, J. R. McGuigan, R. P. Rao &
C. Moyer, *Fundamentals of Contemporary Financial
Management*, 2nd ed. (Stamford, CT: South-Western,
Cengage Learning), p. 3; Eugene F. Brigham,
*Fundamentals of Financial Management*, 11th ed.
(Stamford, CT: Cengage Learning, 2005), p. 2.

10. P. Dvorak, "Can Solar Power Compete With
Coal? In India, It's Gaining Ground," *The Wall Street
Journal*, February 17, 2020, https://www.wsj.com
/articles/solar-power-is-beginning-to-eclipse-fossil
-fuels-11581964338, accessed February 2, 2021.

11. R. Naam, "Solar's Future Is Insanely Cheap
(2020)," Ramez Naam, May 14, 2020, https://
rameznaam.com/2020/05/14/solars-future-is
-insanely-cheap-2020/, accessed February 2, 2021.

12. M. Copley, "Human Rights Allegations in
Xinjiang Could Jeopardize Solar Supply Chain,"
*S&P Global Market Intelligence*, October 21, 2020,
https://www.spglobal.com/marketintelligence/en
/news-insights/latest-news-headlines/human-rights
-allegations-in-xinjiang-could-jeopardize-solar
-supply-chain-60829945, accessed February 2, 2021.

13. A. Damodaran, "Annual Returns on Stock,
T. Bonds & T. Bills: 1928-2020," Stern School of
Business, New York University, January 1, 2021,
https://www.stern.nyu.edu/~adamodar/pc/datasets
/histretSP.xls, accessed February 2, 2021; "Risk and
Return: An Introduction," Bogleheads, August 1,
2016, https://www.bogleheads.org/wiki/Risk_and
_return:_an_introduction#cite_note-7, accessed
February 2, 2017.

14. "Industry Browser—Services—Restaurants
Industry—Company List," Yahoo! Finance, https://

finance.yahoo.com/q/ks?s=MCD+Key+Statistics,
accessed April 9, 2015; "McDonald's Corporation
Financials," *The Wall Street Journal*, https://
quotes.wsj.com/MCD/financials/Ratios, accessed
April 9, 2015; "McDonald's Financial Ratios
MCD," *The Motley Fool*, https://www.fool.com
/quote/nyse/mcdonalds/mcd/financial-ratios,
accessed April 9, 2015; "McDonald's Visual
Financials," ADVFN, https://www.advfn.com
/stock-market/NYSE/MCD/financials, accessed
April 9, 2015; "Overview Industry Profile:
Fast-Food & Quick-Service Restaurants," First
Research, https://mergent.firstresearch-learn.
com/industry_detail.aspx?pid=433&chapter=7,
accessed April 9, 2015.

15. J. Ballard, "Activision Blizzard Is Set for
Outperformance," *The Motley Fool*, December 28,
2016, https://www.fool.com/investing/2016/12/28
/activision-blizzard-is-set-for-outperformance
.aspx, accessed February 2, 2017; D. Gallagher,
"Tracking Videogame Sales Is Tougher Than You
Think," *The Wall Street Journal*, July 26, 2016, C8.

16. M. Dealessandri, "2020 Sees Record US
Games Spending at $56.9bn: US Annual Report,"
*GamesIndustry.biz*, January 15, 2021, https://www
.gamesindustry.biz/articles/2021-01-15-2020
-sees-record-us-games-spending-at-usd56-9bn
-us-annual-report, accessed February 2, 2021;
E. Makuch, "Top-Selling Games And Consoles Of
2020 Revealed for the US," *GameSpot*, January 15,
2021, https://www.gamespot.com/articles
/top-selling-games-and-consoles-of-2020-revealed
-for-the-us/1100-6486361/, accessed February 2,
2021; W. Witkowski, "Videogames Are a Bigger
Industry Than Movies and North American Sports
Combined, Thanks to the Pandemic," *MarketWatch*,
January 2, 2021, https://www.marketwatch.com/story
/videogames-are-a-bigger-industry-than-sports
-and-movies-combined-thanks-to-the-pandemic
-11608654990, accessed February 2, 2021.

17. T. Mochizuki, "Sony Hikes Profit Outlook 34%
in Bet on Game, iPhone Demand," *Bloomberg*,
February 3, 2021, https://www.bloomberg.com
/news/articles/2021-02-03/sony-boosts-forecasts-as
-profits-smash-estimates?sref=xXo7CWym,
accessed February 3, 2021.

18. E. Fung, "Mall Landlord Simon Property Suing
Retailer Gap Over Missed Rent," *The Wall Street
Journal*, June 4, 2020, https://www.wsj.com/articles
/mall-landlord-simon-property-suing-retailer-gap
-over-missed-rent-11591295748?mod=article
_inline, accessed February 3, 2021.

19. K. Roof, "Greylock Partners Raises $1 Billion
for Venture Capital Fund," *Bloomberg*, September
15, 2020, https://www.bloomberg.com/news
/articles/2020-09-15/greylock-partners-raises-1
-billion-for-venture-capital-fund?sref=xXo7CWym,
accessed February 3, 2021.

20. T. Mohamed, "A Legendary Venture-Capital
Firm Bought Airbnb Shares for $0.01 Each in 2009,"
*Markets Insider*, December 11, 2020, https://markets
.businessinsider.com/news/stocks/airbnb-investor
-sequoia-capital-bought-shares-1-cent-now-140-2020
-12-1029885671, accessed February 3, 2021.

21. C. Driebusch, "Coronavirus Cash Needs
Prompt Companies to Rethink Investments," *The
Wall Street Journal*, June 22, 2020, https://www
.wsj.com/articles/coronavirus-cash-needs-prompt
-companies-to-rethink-investments-11592818201,
accessed February 5, 2021; E. Fung, "Landlords,
Companies Clash Over Rent Payments Amid
Coronavirus," *The Wall Street Journal*, April 14,
2020, https://www.wsj.com/articles/landlords-
companies-clash-over-rent-payments-during-
coronavirus-11586865600, accessed February 5,
2021; I. Pacheco & S. Stamm, "How Coronavirus

Spread Through Corporate America," *The Wall
Street Journal*, April 13, 2020, https://www.wsj.com
/graphics/how-coronavirus-spread-through
-corporate-america/, accessed February 5, 2021.

22. The approximate "finance charge" of not taking
the discount on credit can be computed using the
following formula:

$$= \frac{\% \text{ discount}}{(100 - \% \text{ discount})} \times \frac{365}{(\text{Credit\_Period} - \text{Discount\_Period})}$$

where % discount is the discount the buyer receives
for paying on or before the last day the discount
is available and the Credit Discount Period is the
number of days before payment of full invoice
amount is due.

23. R. Cole, "Bank Credit, Trade Credit or No
Credit: Evidence from the Surveys of Small Business
Finances," Office of Advocacy, Small Business
Administration, June 2010, https://www.sba.gov/sites
/default/files/rs365tot.pdf, accessed February 2, 2017.

24. E. Dou & G. Wong, "Hon Hai Banks on
Finance—The iPhone Assembler Now Provides
Loans to Electronics Industry," *The Wall Street
Journal*, November 18, 2015, p. B6.

25. "Annual Asset-Based Lending and Factoring
Survey Highlights, 2018," Secured Finance
Network, https://www.sfnet.com/docs/default
-source/data-files-and-research-documents/sfnet
-abl-and-factoring-survey-highlights-2018.pdf?Stat
us=Temp&sfvrsn=5efa6553_2, accessed February
3, 2021µ.

26. J. Franklin & D. Henry, "U.S. Companies Draw
on Credit Lines, Fearing They May Lose Them,"
*Reuters*, March 13, 2020, https://www.reuters.com
/article/us-health-coronavirus-creditlines-idUSKB
N2100YQ, accessed February 3, 2021.

27. N. Trentmann, "Companies Issue New Bonds
to Pay Down Short-Term Debt Amid Pandemic,"
*The Wall Street Journal*, September 2, 2020, https://
www.wsj.com/articles/companies-issue-new-bonds
-to-pay-down-short-term-debt-amid-pandemic
-11599039003?mod=hp_minor_pos8, accessed
February 3, 2021.

28. M. Pilon, "What Is Commercial Paper and Why
Does It Matter?" *The Wall Street Journal*, October
7, 2008, https://blogs.wsj.com/wallet/2008/10/07
/what-is-commercial-paper-and-why-does-it-matter
/tab/print/, accessed March 24, 2013.

29. "Commercial Paper Rates and Outstanding
Summary: Derived from Data Supplied by the
Depository Trust & Clearing Corporation," Board
of Governors of the Federal Reserve System,
February 3, 2021, https://www.federalreserve.gov
/releases/cp/rates.htm, accessed February 3, 2021.

30. J. White, "Cash Managers Favored Commercial
Paper in January," *The Wall Street Journal*,
February 6, 2013, https://blogs.wsj.com/cfo/2013
/02/06/cash-managers-favored-commercial
-paper-in-january/, accessed March 24, 2013;
J. Willhite, "Finance Execs Dumped Commercial
Paper in December—The CFO Report, " January 22,
2015, https://blogs.wsj.com/cfo/2015/01/22/
finance-execs-dumped-commercial-paper-in
-december/?KEYW-ORDS=%22commercial
+paper%22, accessed April 9, 2015; T. Shumsky,
"Companies Pare Government Bond Holdings,
Favor Commercial Paper in August—CFO
Journal," *The Wall Street Journal*, August 8, 2016,
https://blogs.wsj.com/cfo/2016/08/08/companies
-pare-government-bond-holdings-favor-commercial
-paper-in-august/, accessed February 2, 2017.

31. B. Novick, T. Callahan, J. Pucci, T. Kinnally, K. Fulton, S. DeZur, J. Steel & T. Meyer, "Lessons from COVID-19: U.S. Short-Term Money Markets," BlackRock, July 2020, https://www.blackrock.com/corporate/literature/whitepaper/viewpoint-lessons-from-covid-19-us-short-term-money-markets-july-2020.pdf, accessed February 3, 2021.

32. D. Hull, "Tesla Raising Up to $5 Billion in Third Share Sale This Year," *Bloomberg*, December 8, 2020, https://www.bloomberg.com/news/articles/2020-12-08/tesla-raising-up-to-5-billion-in-third-capital-raise-this-year?sref=xXo7CWym, accessed February 4, 2021.

33. T. Lee, "Tesla Reports Its First Annual Profit," *Ars Technica*, January 27, 2021, https://arstechnica.com/cars/2021/01/tesla-reports-its-first-annual-profit/, accessed February 4, 2021.

35. "Berkshire Hathaway Inc., Historical Prices, February 3, 2004 to February 2, 2017," Google Finance, https://www.google.com/finance/historical?cid=4376&startdate=Feb%203%2C%202004&enddate=Feb%203%2C%202017&num=30&ei=CZiUWKCbK4e62Aam_4XoCQ&start=0, accessed February 3, 2017.

36. "Why Do companies Issue Debt and Bonds? Can't They Just Borrow from the Bank?, Investopedia, https://www.investopedia.com/ask/answers/05/reasonforcorporatebonds.asp, accessed on February 3, 2017.

37. M. Smith, "T-Mobile Sells $19 Billion of Bonds to Finance Sprint Takeover," *Bloomberg*, April 2, 2020, https://www.bloomberg.com/news/articles/2020-04-02/t-mobile-kicks-off-five-part-jumbo-bond-sale-for-sprint-takeover?sref=xXo7CWym, accessed February 4, 2021.

38. No author, "Netflix Q4 2020 Letter to Shareholders," Netflix, January 19, 2021, https://s22.q4cdn.com/959853165/files/doc_financials/2020/q4/FINAL-Q420-Shareholder-Letter.pdf, accessed February 6, 2021; No author, "Netflix Raises Price of Standard Monthly Plan in U.S. to $14 per Month," *Variety*, October 29, 2020, https://variety.com/2020/digital/news/netflix-increases-prices-us-monthly-plans-1234819132/, accessed February 6, 2021; B. Barrett, "Netflix Raises Prices to Stockpile for the Streaming Wars," *Wired*, January 15, 2019, https://www.wired.com/story/netflix-price-hike/, accessed February 6, 2021; E. Lee, "Netflix Will No Longer Borrow, Ending Its Run of Debt," *The New York Times*, January 19, 2021, https://www.nytimes.com/2021/01/19/business/netflix-earnings-debt.html, accessed February 6, 2021; D. Ng, "Netflix Is on the Hook for $20 Billion. Can It Keep Spending Its Way to Success?" *Los Angeles Times*, July 29, 2017, https://www.latimes.com/business/hollywood/la-fi-ct-netflix-debt-spending-20170729-story.html, accessed February 6, 2021; E. Savitz, "Netflix Has Turned the Corner. Why It's Time for the Skeptics to Concede," *Barron's*, January 22, 2021, https://www.barrons.com/articles/netflix-has-vanquished-the-critics-whats-next-for-the-stock-51611354742, accessed February 6, 2021; M. Smith, "Netflix (NFLX) to Sell $2 Billion Bonds to Help Fund More Content," *Bloomberg*, April 23, 2019, https://www.bloomberg.com/news/articles/2019-04-23/netflix-to-sell-2-billion-of-bonds-to-help-fund-more-content?sref=xXo7CWym, accessed February 6, 2021.

39. R. Smith, J. Rennison & N. Asgari, "Debt Investors Lay Claim to Islands, Cruise Ships and Theme Parks," *Financial Times*, May 21, 2020, https://www.ft.com/content/79cd7d89-3d61-4383-8abf-a2396a846f42, accessed February 4, 2021.

40. A. Gladstone & S. Kapner, "J.C. Penney Skips Bond Payment, Starting Bankruptcy Clock," *The Wall Street Journal*, April 15, 2020, https://www.wsj.com/articles/j-c-penney-skips-bond-payment-starting-bankruptcy-clock-11586979911, accessed February 4, 2021; S. Kapner & A. Scurria, "J.C. Penney, Pinched by Coronavirus, Files for Bankruptcy," *The Wall Street Journal*, May 15, 2020, https://www.wsj.com/articles/j-c-penney-pinched-by-coronavirus-files-for-bankruptcy-11589582224, accessed February 4, 2021.

41. A. Gladstone, "J.C. Penney Settles With Holdout Lenders, Easing Chapter 11 Sale," *The Wall Street Journal*, November 2, 2020, https://www.wsj.com/articles/j-c-penney-settles-with-holdout-lenders-easing-chapter-11-sale-11604333972?mod=searchresults_pos11&page=2, accessed February 4, 2021.

42. L. Fichenscher, "JCPenney Exits Bankruptcy With Sale to Biggest Landlords," *New York Post*, December 7, 2020, https://nypost.com/2020/12/07/jcpenney-exits-bankruptcy-with-sale-to-biggest-landlords/, accessed February 4, 2021.

43. P. Clark, M. Smith & J. Surane, "Hilton Selling $1 Billion Loyalty Points to American Express," Bloomberg, April 16, 2020, https://www.bloomberg.com/news/articles/2020-04-16/hilton-selling-1-billion-in-loyalty-points-to-american-express?sref=xXo7CWym, accessed February 6, 2021; C. Driebusch, "Coronavirus Cash Needs Prompt Companies to Rethink Investments," *The Wall Street Journal*, June 22, 2020, https://www.wsj.com/articles/coronavirus-cash-needs-prompt-companies-to-rethink-investments-11592818201, accessed February 6, 2021; T. Gryta & T. Francis, "Cash Remains King as Companies Close a Dismal Second Quarter," *The Wall Street Journal*, June 21, 2020, https://www.wsj.com/articles/cash-remains-king-as-companies-close-a-dismal-second-quarter-11592737200, accessed February 6, 2021.

44. Chris Arnold, "Financial Sectors' New Buzzword Is Deleverage," *NPR*, https://www.npr.org/templates/story/story.php?storyId=94795760, accessed August 9, 2009; James Saft, "Deleveraging, Now Only in Early Stages, Will Transform the Banking Industry," *The New York Times*, https://www.nytimes.com/2008/06/26/business/worldbusiness/26iht-col27.1.14006619.html?_r=1, accessed August 9, 2009; "Deleveraging: A Fate Worse than Debt," *Economist*, https://www.economist.com/businessfinance/displaystory.cfm?story_id=12306060, accessed August 9, 2009.

45. "Brief Summary of the Dodd-Frank Wall Street Reform and Consumer Protection Act," United States Senate Committee on Banking, Housing and Urban Affairs, https://banking.senate.gov/public/_files/070110_Dodd_Frank_Wall_Street_Reform_comprehensive_summary_Final.pdf; Michael Rapoport & Rachael King, "For Heavily Indebted Firms Like Dell, Tax Bill Delivers a Downside," *The Wall Street Journal*, December 21, 2017, https://www.wsj.com/articles/downside-of-tax-bill-hits-dell-other-heavily-indebted-companies-1513852200, accessed February 12, 2018; W. Richter, "What Will the Tax Law Do to Over-Indebted Corporate America?" *Wolf Street*, December 22, 2017, https://wolfstreet.com/2017/12/22/what-will-the-tax-law-do-to-over-indebted-corporate-america/, accessed February 12, 2018; J. Lahart, "The One Tax Change That Really Bites Businesses," *The Wall Street Journal*, December 19, 2017, https://www.wsj.com/articles/the-one-tax-change-that-really-bites-businesses-1513708835, accessed February 12, 2018.

46. K. Hankins & M. Petersen, "Why Are Companies Sitting on So Much Cash?" *Harvard Business Review*, January 17, 2020, https://hbr.org/2020/01/why-are-companies-sitting-on-so-much-cash, accessed February 5, 2021.

47. "Vanguard Cash Reserves Federal Money Market Fund (VMMXX)," Vanguard, January 1, 2021, https://investor.vanguard.com/mutual-funds/profile/performance/vmmxx, accessed February 5, 2021.

48. Ibid.

49. "Janus Henderson Global Dividend Index, Edition 28," Janus Henderson, November 2020, https://cdn.janushenderson.com/webdocs/Report+28_US.pdf, accessed February 7, 2021; C. Hughes, "Coronavirus: Three Cheers for the Pandemic Dividend Cutters," *Bloomberg*, April 16, 2020, https://www.bloomberg.com/opinion/articles/2020-04-16/coronavirus-three-cheers-for-the-pandemic-dividend-cutters?sref=xXo7CWym, accessed February 7, 2021; E. Smith, "Paying Dividends Is a 'Moral Imperative' to Support People's Retirement, CEO Says," *CNBC*, April 16, 2020, https://www.cnbc.com/2020/04/16/skeoch-paying-dividends-a-moral-imperative-to-support-peoples-retirement.html, accessed February 7, 2021; R. Wigglesworth, K. Martin & M. Darbyshire, "How Covid-19 Sparked a Dividend Drought for Investors," *Financial Times*, September 10, 2020, https://www.ft.com/content/2719966c-b228-4300-bdc0-dcbe2f7050fd?segmentId=bf7fa2fd-67ee-cdfa-8261-b2a3edbdf916, accessed February 7, 2021.

50. N. Trentmann, "Levi's CFO Picks Up the Phone to Remind Retailers to Pay Their Bills," *The Wall Street Journal*, May 7, 2020, https://www.wsj.com/articles/levis-cfo-picks-up-the-phone-to-remind-retailers-to-pay-their-bills-11588883356?mod=djemCFO, accessed February 5, 2021.

51. J. Ewing & D. Clark, "Lack of Tiny Parts Disrupts Auto Factories Worldwide," *The New York Times*, January 13, 2021, https://www.nytimes.com/2021/01/13/business/auto-factories-semiconductor-chips.html#:~:text=Lack%20of%20Tiny%20Parts%20Disrupts%20Auto%20Factories%20Worldwide,factories%20in%20China%2C%20Europe%20and%20the%20United%20States, accessed February 5, 2021.

52. Ibid.

53. Ibid.

54. No author, "Office Tour: Behind the Scenes at Spotify's Creative, Collaborative NYC HQ," Spotify, April 2, 2018, https://newsroom.spotify.com/2018-04-02/office-tour-behind-the-scenes-at-spotifys-creative-collaborative-nyc-hq/, accessed February 5, 2021; Press Release, "Spotify Spotify Technology S.A. Announces Financial Results for Fourth Quarter 2020," Spotify, February 3, 2021, https://investors.spotify.com/financials/press-release-details/2021/Spotify-Technology-S.A.-Announces-Financial-Results-for-Fourth-Quarter-2020/default.aspx, accessed February 5, 2021;

# Chapter 10

1. "Zoom Video Communications, Inc., 'Zoom Announces Closing of $2.0 Billion Public Offering,'" GlobeNewsWire, January 15, 2021, https://www.globenewswire.com/news-release/2021/01/15/2159603/0/en/Zoom-Announces-Closing-of-2-0-Billion-Public-Offering.html, accessed February 15, 2021; C. Driebush, "Companies Raised Record Amounts by Selling Stock During Covid-19 Crisis," *The Wall Street Journal*, July 9, 2020, https://www.wsj.com/articles/companies-raised-record-amounts-by-selling-stock-during-covid-19-crisis-11594292401?mod=djemCFO, accessed February 9, 2021; D. Sebastian,

"Zoom Aims to Raise $1.5 Billion Through Stock Offering," *The Wall Street Journal*, January 12, 2021, https://www.wsj.com/articles/zoom-aims-to-raise-1-5-billion-through-stock-offering-11610461335?mod=searchresults_pos4&page=1, accessed February 9, 2021.

2. Press Release, "ZoomInfo Announces Pricing of $350 Million of 3.875% Senior Notes Due 2029," *Business Wire*, January 28, 2021, https://www.businesswire.com/news/home/20210128006154/en/, accessed February 9, 2021.

3. A. Root, "How to Make $41 Million From $3,000: Investing Lessons From a Century," *Barron's*, January 10, 2021, https://www.barrons.com/articles/how-to-make-41-million-from-3-000-investing-lessons-from-a-century-51610283600?mod=hp_LATEST, accessed February 9, 2021.

4. "Investment Calculator," Calculator.net, https://www.calculator.net/investment-calculator.html, accessed February 9, 2021.

5. "Form S-1 Registration Statement," U.S. Securities and Exchange Commission, April 8, 2019, https://investors.zoom.us/static-files/37c6efa3-7516-42c7-a9b6-7a3e69b899f3, accessed February 15, 2021; A. Levy, "Zoom Plans $1.5 Billion Share Sale at 10 Times Its IPO Price," *CNBC*, January 12, 2021, https://www.cnbc.com/2021/01/12/zoom-plans-1point5-billion-share-sale-at-10-times-its-ipo-price.html, accessed February 15, 2021; J. Novet, "Zoom Rocketed 72% on First Day of Trading," CNBC, April 18, 2019, https://www.cnbc.com/2019/04/18/zoom-ipo-stock-begins-trading-on-nasdaq.html, accessed February 15, 2021.

6. Financial Accounts of the United States: Flow of Funds, Balance Sheets, and Integrated Macroeconomic Accounts, L.110 Private Depository Institutions (1), Federal Reserve Statistical Release, September 21, 2020, https://www.federalreserve.gov/releases/z1/20200921/z1.pdf, accessed February 9, 2021.

7. "How Is a Credit Union Different Than a Bank?," MyCreditUnion.gov, https://www.mycreditunion.gov/about-credit-unions/Pages/How-is-a-Credit-Union-Different-than-a-Bank.aspx, accessed February 8, 2017.

8. Financial Accounts of the United States: Flow of Funds, Balance Sheets, and Integrated Macroeconomic Accounts, Table L.114 Credit Unions, Federal Reserve Statistical Release, September 21, 2020, https://www.federalreserve.gov/releases/z1/20200921/z1.pdf, accessed February 9, 2021.

9. "Mortgage Debt Outstanding," Board of Governors of the Federal Reserve System, December 2016, https://www.federalreserve.gov/econresdata/releases/mortoutstand/current.htm, accessed February 8, 2017.

10. T. Curry & L. Shibut, "The Cost of the Savings & Loan Crisis: Truth and Consequences," *FDIC Banking Review*, December 2000, https://www.fdic.gov/bank/analytical/banking/2000dec/brv13n2_2.pdf, accessed March 28, 2016.

11. M. Fitzgerald, "Charles Schwab Q4 2020 Earnings," *CNBC*, January 19, 2021, https://www.cnbc.com/2021/01/19/charles-schwab-q4-2020-earnings-.html, accessed February 9, 2021; J. McCrank, "Factbox: The U.S. Retail Trading Frenzy in Numbers," *US News & World Report*, January 29, 2021, https://www.usnews.com/news/top-news/articles/2021-01-29/factbox-the-us-retail-trading-frenzy-in-numbers, accessed February 9, 2021.

12. "The Goldman Sachs Group, Inc., Form 8-K," U.S. Securities and Exchange Commission, January 19, 2021, https://www.goldmansachs.com/investor-relations/financials/current/8k/8k-01-19-21.pdf, accessed February 9, 2021.

13. Press Release, "JPMorgan Chase Reports Fourth-Quarter 2020 Net Income/Full-Year 2020 Net Income," January 15, 2021, https://www.jpmorganchase.com/content/dam/jpmc/jpmorgan-chase-and-co/investor-relations/documents/quarterly-earnings/2020/4th-quarter/276305ed-730d-4acc-887c-1671d6c39e53.pdf, accessed February 9, 2021.

14. M. Egan, "Fed Dusts Off 2008 Playbook to Avoid Another Financial Crisis," *CNN*, March 19, 2020, https://www.cnn.com/2020/03/19/business/fed-2008-playbook-coronavirus/index.html, accessed February 10, 2021.

15. "The Cost of the Savings and Loan Crisis: Truth and Consequences," *FDIC Banking Review*.

16. "Deposit Insurance FAQs," Federal Deposit Insurance Corporation, May 13, 2020, https://www.fdic.gov/deposit/deposits/faq.html, accessed February 10, 2021.

17. News Release, "GameStop Reports Fourth Quarter and Fiscal 2019 Results Ahead of Earnings Expectations," GameStop Corp., March 26, 2020, accessed June 17, 2020, https://news.gamestop.com/news-releases/news-release-details/gamestop-reports-fourth-quarter-and-fiscal-2019-results-ahead; M. Darbyshire, R. Wigglesworth, A. Kantor & A. Kasumov, "'Moment of Weakness': Amateur Investors Left Counting GameStop Losses," *Financial Times*, February 5, 2021, https://www.ft.com/content/04e6c524-389b-47fc-afaa-eb52c1e76048, accessed February 16, 2021; R. Ensign, "GameStop Investors Who Bet Big—And Lost Big," *The Wall Street Journal*, February 15, 2021, https://www.wsj.com/articles/gamestop-investors-who-bet-bigand-lost-big-11613385002, accessed February 16, 2021; C. Morgan, "Will GameStop Survive in a Digital Future?" *Business Insider*, May 20, 2019, https://www.businessinsider.com/gamestop-video-games-gaming-survive-digital-future-2019-5, accessed March 16, 2020; C. Ostroff & P. Santilli, "The Rise and Fall of the GameStop Frenzy," *The Wall Street Journal*, February 11, 2021, https://www.wsj.com/articles/the-rise-and-fall-of-the-gamestop-frenzy-11613083164, accessed February 16, 2021; M. Quiroz-Gutierrez, "Is GameStop a Bubble? History's Spectacular Crashes, From Tulips to Beanie Babies," *The Wall Street Journal*, February 6, 2021, https://www.wsj.com/articles/is-gamestop-a-bubble-historys-spectacular-crashes-from-tulips-to-beanie-babies-11612607400, accessed February 16, 2021; P. Thomas, "GameStop Shares Fall as Company Turns to Store Closures," *The Wall Street Journal*, September 11, 2019, https://www.wsj.com/articles/gamestop-shares-fall-as-company-turns-to-store-closures-11568230146?mod=djemRiskCompliance, accessed March 16, 2020; J. Valinsky, "GameStop Is Closing Hundreds More Stores," CNN, September 10, 2020, https://www.cnn.com/2020/09/10/investing/gamestop-store-closures/index.html, accessed February 16, 2021.

18. J. Browning, "Walid Choucair: Convicted London Trader Forfeits $5.4 Million in Profits," *Bloomberg*, January 21, 2021, https://www.bloomberg.com/news/articles/2021-01-21/convicted-london-trader-forfeits-5-4-million-in-profits?sref=xXo7CWym, accessed February 10, 2021.

19. "About the PCAOB," Public Company Accounting Oversight Board, https://pcaobus.org/About, accessed February 8, 2017.

20. "Brief Summary of the Dodd-Frank Wall Street Reform and Consumer Protection Act," U.S. Senate Committee on Banking, Housing and Urban Affairs, https://banking.senate.gov/public/_files/070110_Dodd_Frank_Wall_Street_Reform_comprehensive_summary_Final.pdf, accessed April 13, 2015; "About FSOC," Financial Stability Oversight Council, https://www.treasury.gov/initiatives/fsoc/about/Pages/default.aspx, accessed February 8, 2017.

21. Press Release, "Shareholders Approve the Proposed Merger Between FCA and Groupe PSA, Which Plan to Finalize Their Merger on January 16, 2021," *Média Stellantis*, January 4, 2021, https://archives-media.stellantis.com/fr/node/90080300, accessed February 10, 2021.

22. L. Strauss, "Comcast, Kimberly-Clark, and 7 Other Companies That Raised Dividends This Week," *Barron's*, January 30, 2021, https://www.barrons.com/articles/comcast-kimberly-clark-stock-dividends-51611955464, accessed February 10, 2021.

23. N. Fildes, "Vodafone Slashes Dividend 40% to Bolster Balance Sheet," *Financial Times*, May 14, 2019, https://www.ft.com/content/dd5b9854-760f-11e9-be7d-6d846537acab, accessed February 10, 2021.

24. "Peloton Interactive, Inc." *Yahoo! Finance*, https://finance.yahoo.com/quote/PTON/history?p=PTON, accessed February 10, 2021.

25. A. Barry, "Banks Are Taking Advantage of Low Rates to Issue Preferred Shares," *Barron's*, February 8, 2021, https://www.barrons.com/articles/banks-are-taking-advantage-of-low-rates-to-issue-preferred-shares-51612804961, accessed February 10, 2021.

26. Press Release, "Chesapeake Energy Corporation Reinstates Payment of Quarterly Preferred Stock Dividends," Chesapeake Energy, January 20, 2017, https://www.chk.com/media/news/press-releases/Chesapeake+Energy+Corporation+Reinstates+Payment+Of+Quarterly+Preferred+Stock+Dividends+1+20+2017+, accessed February 8, 2017; L. Cook, "Oil Patch Is Bracing For Further Cuts in Jobs," *The Wall Street Journal*, July 27, 2015, p. B1; B. Levisohn, "Chesapeake Energy: Sending Signals—Stocks to Watch," *Barron's*, January 23, 2017, https://blogs.barrons.com/stockstowatchtoday/2017/01/23/chesapeake-energy-sending-signals/, accessed February 8, 2017.

27. Some preferred stock contains a "participating" feature on its dividend. This means that if the dividend paid to common stockholders exceeds some specified amount, the board must also raise the dividend to preferred stockholders. See Participating Preferred Stock, Investopedia, https://www.investopedia.com/terms/p/participating preferredstock.asp, accessed April 13, 2015.

28. Zacks Equity Research, "Iron Mountain Upsizes Notes Offering to $2.4M, To Repay Debt," *Yahoo!Finance*, June 18, 2020, https://finance.yahoo.com/news/iron-mountain-upsizes-notes-offering-121012554.html, accessed February 11, 2021.

29. Ibid.

30. "Boeing Inc.DL-Notes 2020(20/2407) Bond," *Markets Insider*, February 11, 2021, https://markets.businessinsider.com/bonds/boeing_codl-notes_202020-40-bond-2040-us097023cv59, accessed February 11, 2021.

31. A. Gladstone & S. Kapner, "J.C. Penney Skips Bond Payment, Starting Bankruptcy Clock," *The Wall Street Journal*, April 15, 2020, https://www.wsj.com/articles/j-c-penney-skips-bond-payment-starting-bankruptcy-clock-11586979911, accessed February 4, 2021; S. Kapner & A. Scurria, "J.C. Penney, Pinched by Coronavirus, Files for Bankruptcy," *The Wall Street Journal*, May 15, 2020, https://www.wsj.com/articles/j-c-penney-pinched

-by-coronavirus-files-for-bankruptcy-11589582224, accessed February 4, 2021.

32. R. Lehmann, "The Coming Bond Default Wave," *Forbes*, September 8, 2008, https://www.forbes.com/free_forbes/2008/1013/130.html, accessed February 8, 2017.

33. J. Hill & M. Reyes, "Bond Defaults Deliver 99% Losses in New Era of U.S. Bankruptcies," *Bloomberg*, October 26, 2020, https://www.bloomberg.com/news/articles/2020-10-26/bond-defaults-deliver-99-losses-in-new-era-of-u-s-bankruptcies?sref=xXo7CWym, accessed February 10, 2021.

34. "Berkshire Hathaway's Class A Stock," Microsoft Bing, https://www.bing.com/search?q=Berkshire+Hathaway%E2%80%99s+Class+A+stock&form=APMCS1&PC=APMC, accessed February 10, 2021; "Berkshire's Class B Stock," Microsoft Bing, https://www.bing.com/search?q=Berkshire%E2%80%80%99s+Class+B+stock&form=APMCS1&PC=APMC, accessed February 10, 2021; N. Friedman, "Berkshire's B Shares Are Second Class No More—MoneyBeat," *The Wall Street Journal*, December 14, 2016, https://blogs.wsj.com/moneybeat/2016/12/14/berkshires-b-shares-are-second-class-no-more/, accessed February 9, 2017.

35. J. Franklin, "Silver Lake Cashes Out on AMC for $713 Million After Reddit-Fueled Rally," *Yahoo!Finance*, January 29, 2021, https://finance.yahoo.com/news/silver-lake-cashes-amc-713-001059970.html, accessed February 11, 2021; A. Gladstone, "Silver Lake Nets $113 Million Profit After Liquidating Entire AMC Stake," *The Wall Street Journal*, January 29, 2021, https://www.wsj.com/articles/silver-lake-nets-113-million-profit-after-liquidating-entire-amc-stake-11611966061, accessed February 11, 2021.

36. A. Gladstone & S. Biswas, "Silver Lake Converts AMC Debt to Equity After Dazzling Stock Rally," *The Wall Street Journal*, January 28, 2021, https://www.wsj.com/articles/silver-lake-converts-amc-debt-to-equity-as-cinema-chains-stock-price-soars-11611842367?mod=djem10point, accessed February 11, 2021.

37. J. Carpenter, "When the Robinhood Crowd Buys for the Long Haul," *The Wall Street Journal*, December 12, 2020, https://www.wsj.com/articles/when-the-robinhood-crowd-buys-for-the-long-haul-11607769001, accessed February 16, 2021; T. Demos, "Free Trading's Costs Come Into Focus," *The Wall Street Journal*, February 3, 2021, https://www.wsj.com/articles/free-tradings-costs-come-into-focus-11612375679?mod=djemMoneyBeat_us, accessed February 16, 2021; M. Egkolfopoulou & S. Ponczek, "Robinhood Crisis Reveals Hidden Costs in Zero-Fee Trading Model," *Bloomberg*, February 3, 2021, https://www.bloomberg.com/news/articles/2021-02-03/robinhood-crisis-reveals-hidden-costs-in-zero-fee-trading-model?sref=xXo7CWym, accessed February 16, 2021; J. Zweig, "I Started Trading Hot Stocks on Robinhood. Then I Couldn't Stop," *The Wall Street Journal*, December 4, 2020, https://www.wsj.com/articles/robinhood-day-trade-i-started-trading-hot-stocks-then-i-couldnt-stop-11607095765, accessed February 16, 2021.

38. No author, "How to Invest in a Closed-End Fund," *The Wall Street Journal*, https://guides.wsj.com/personal-finance/investing/how-to-invest-in-a-closed-end-fund/, accessed February 11, 2021.

39. "Build a Diversified Portfolio with Just a Few Vanguard Funds," The Vanguard Group, https://personal.vanguard.com/pdf/s050.pdf?2210105586, accessed February 9,

2017; "Vanguard Total Stock Market Index Fund," Vanguard, December 31, 2020, https://institutional.vanguard.com/iippdf/pdfs/FS585.pdf, accessed February 11, 2021.

40. D. Carlson, "8 Facts to Know About Mutual Fund Fees: Mutual Fund Fees are Falling," U.S. News & World Report, October 24, 2019, https://money.usnews.com/investing/funds/slideshows/facts-to-know-about-mutual-fund-fees?slide=6, accessed February 11, 2021.

41. "First Trust NASDAQ CEA Cybersecurity ETF," ETF Database, https://etfdb.com/etf/CIBR/#etf-ticker-profile, accessed February 11, 2021; "First Trust NASDAQ Clean Edge Smart Grid Infrastructure Index Fund," ETF Database, First Trust NASDAQ Clean Edge Smart Grid Infrastructure Index Fund, accessed February 11, 2021.

42. E. Griffeth, "Snowflake Stock More Than Doubles in IPO Debut," *The New York Times*, September 17, 2020, https://www.nytimes.com/2020/09/16/technology/snowflake-tech-ipo.html, accessed February 12, 2021.

43. "ICE Exchanges & Clearing," Intercontinental Exchange, February 2021, https://www.theice.com/about/exchanges-clearing, accessed February 12, 2021; "New York Stock Exchange (NYSE)," TradingHours, https://www.tradinghours.com/markets/nyse, accessed February 12, 2021.

44. "NASDAQ Stock Exchange (NASDAQ)," TradingHours, https://www.tradinghours.com/markets/nasdaq, accessed February 12, 2021; "Home - Statistics Portal," World Federation of Exchanges, https://statistics.world-exchanges.org/, accessed February 12, 2021.

45. "Market Data," OTC Markets, https://www.otcmarkets.com/market-data/overview, accessed February 12, 2021.

46. M. Frankel, "Vanguard 2021 update Review: Pros, Cons, and More," *The Ascent by Motley Fool*, January 14, 2021, https://www.fool.com/the-ascent/buying-stocks/vanguard-brokerage-review/, accessed February 12, 2021.

47. "E°TRADE Fees and Rates | Pricing for Investing & Trading," E°TRADE, https://us.etrade.com/what-we-offer/pricing-and-rates, accessed February 12, 2021.

48. L. Kramer and S. Smith, "Can Robo Advisers Replace Human Financial Advisers?," *The Wall Street Journal*, February 28, 2016, https://www.wsj.com/articles/can-robo-advisers-replace-human-financial-advisers-1456715553, accessed April 6, 2016; P. Sullivan, "The Computer as a Financial Planner," *The New York Times*, June 20, 2015, B5; R. Powell, "Behavioral Economist Richard Thaler on the Key to Retirement Savings," *The Wall Street Journal*, November 29, 2015, accessed March 22, 2016, https://www.wsj.com/articles/behavioral-economist-richard-thaler-on-the-key-to-retirement-savings-1448852602; "SmartDeposit: Auto-Deposit, But Smarter," Betterment, https://www.betterment.com/resources/inside-betterment/product-news/smartdeposit-auto-deposit-but-smarter/, accessed April 5, 2016.

49. N. Jasinki, "This New Way of Taking a Company Public Has Little Pop, and That's a Good Thing for Investors," *Barron's*, December 31, 2020, https://www.barrons.com/articles/this-new-way-of-taking-a-company-public-has-little-pop-and-thats-a-good-thing-for-investors-51609443905, accessed February 16, 2021; N. Jasinki, "Bypassing the Traditional IPO Route May Become More Popular in 2020," *Barron's*, January 3, 2020, https://www.barrons.com/articles/bypassing-the-traditional-ipo-

route-may-become-more-popular-in-2020-51578054600, accessed February 16, 2021; C. Tse, "Roblox Switches to Direct Listing From IPO With Investment," *Bloomberg Quint*, January 7, 2021, https://www.bloombergquint.com/business/roblox-plans-to-go-public-via-direct-listing-instead-of-ipo, accessed February 16, 2021.

50. K. Amadeo, "Black Monday in 1929, 1987, 2015, and 2020," The Balance, March 13, 2020, https://www.thebalance.com/what-is-black-monday-in-1987-1929-and-2015-3305818, accessed February 14, 2021.

51. C. Mullen, "Buying the Dip Works Nicely, a 30-Year History of Routs Shows," *Bloomberg*, February 6, 2018, https://www.bloomberg.com/news/articles/2018-02-07/buying-the-dip-works-nicely-a-30-year-history-of-routs-shows?sref=xXo7CWym, accessed February 14, 2021.

52. N. Maggiulli, "Even God Couldn't Beat Dollar-Cost Averaging," *Of Dollars And Data*, February 5, 2019, https://ofdollarsanddata.com/even-god-couldnt-beat-dollar-cost-averaging/, accessed February 14, 2021.

53. "Dogs of the Dow Explained: Dog Steps," *Dogs of the Dow*, https://www.dogsofthedow.com/dogsteps.htm, accessed February 14, 2021.

54. No author, "Dogs of the Dow Stock List: How the Dogs of the Dow Strategy Works," *MarketBeat*, February 14, 2021, https://www.marketbeat.com/market-data/dogs-of-the-dow-stocks/, accessed February 14, 2021.

55. D. Butler, "Startups Success Rates And Repositioning for the New Normal," *Forbes*, May 27, 2020, https://www.forbes.com/sites/donbutler/2020/05/27/startups-success-rates-and-repositioning-for-the-new-normal/?sh=11638a957a61, accessed February 14, 2021.

56. J. Zweig, "The Panic of 2020? Oh, I Made a Ton of Money—and So Did You," *The Wall Street Journal*, March 20, 2020, https://www.wsj.com/articles/the-panic-of-2020-oh-i-made-a-ton-of-moneyand-so-did-you-11584716442, accessed February 14, 2021.

# Chapter 11

1. Derek Thompson, "War and Peace in 30 Seconds: How Much Does the Military Spend on Ads?" *The Atlantic*, January 30, 2012, https://www.theatlantic.com/business/archive/2012/01/war-and-peace-in-30-seconds-how-much-does-the-military-spend-on-ads/252222/, accessed February 9, 2014; Stuart Elliott, "Army to Use Webcasts From Iraq for Recruiting," *The New York Times*, November 10, 2008, https://www.nytimes.com/2008/11/11/business/media/11adco.html, accessed February 22, 2009; "Army Strong! Army Smash!" Armchair Generalist, October 11, 2006, https://armchairgeneralist.typepad.com/my_weblog/2006/10/army_strong_arm.html, accessed April 19, 2011; "U.S. Army Searches New Agency, Defines Hispanic Market as Key Target," Portada, August 12, 2010, https://www.portada-online.com/article.aspx?aid=6604, accessed April 19, 2010; Andrew McMains, "U.S. Army Puts Marketing in Play," *AdWeek*, August 11, 2010, https://www.adweek.com/news/advertising-branding/us-army-puts-marketing-play-103040, accessed June 16, 2012.

2. Jordan Valinsky, "Kim Kardashian West Is Officially a Billionaire, Says Forbes," *CNNBusiness*, April 7, 2021, https://www.cnn.com/2021/04/06

/business/kim-kardashian-west-billionaire-forbes /index.html, accessed April 12, 2021; Thomas Frank, "Former Wells Fargo CEO John Stumpf Barred from Industry, to pay $17.5 Million for Sales Scandal," January 23, 2020, https://www.cnbc .com/2020/01/23/former-wells-fargo-ceo-stumpf -barred-from-industry-to-pay-17point5-million -over-sales-scandal.html, accessed April 12, 2021; Debbie White, "RECORD BREAKER How Old Is Alexandria Ocasio-Cortez and What's Her Net Worth?" February 22, 2021, https://www.the-sun .com/news/2255480/how-old-alexandria-ocasio -cortez-what-net-worth/, accessed April 12, 2021; Political Marketing – 5 Incredible Campaign Examples You Should Learn From, April 26, 2020, https://callhub.io/political-marketing/, accessed April 12, 2021; Erandi Palitlakara, "Why the Kardashian Marketing Strategy Is One for the Books," February 4, 2016, https://www.huffpost .com/entry/why-the-kardashian-market_b_9136006, accessed April 12, 2021.

3. Al Ries, "What Marketers Can Learn from Obama's Campaign," *Advertising Age*, November 5, 2008, https://adage.com/moy2008/article?article _id=131810, accessed February 22, 2009.

4. Thomas Moore, "Tourism Officials Report Record 42.9M Las Vegas Visitors in 2016," *Las Vegas Sun*, January 10, 2017, https://lasvegassun .com/news/2017/jan/10/tourism-officials-report -record-429m-las-vegas-vis/, accessed April 21, 2017.

5. Matt Villano, "Las Vegas Is Set to Come Out of Pandemic Better than Ever," April 14, 2021, https:// www.cnn.com/travel/article/las-vegas-new-casinos -attractions-covid/index.html, accessed April 14, 2021.

6. American Customer Satisfaction Index, 2020, https://www.theacsi.org/acsi-benchmarks /benchmarks-by-industry, accessed April 13, 2021.

7. Rama Ramaswami, "Eight Reasons to Keep Your Customers Loyal," Mulitchannel Merchant, January 12, 2005, https://multichannelmerchant .com/opsandfulfillment/advisor/Brandi-custloyal, accessed February 24, 2009.

8. Kim Bhesin & Olga Kharif, "Nike Gains After China and E-Commerce Fuel Return to Growth," December 18, 2020, https://www.bloomberg.com /news/articles/2020-12-18/nike-gains-as-china -and-online-sales-help-results-top-estimates, accessed April 13, 2021; Andria Cheng, "Three Takeaways from Nike's Earnings Beyond US-China Tariffs," January 27, 2019, https://www.forbes .com/sites/andriacheng/2019/06/27/tariffs -and-other-takeaways-from-nikes-earnings/?sh =44db2c7d4ce9, accessed April 13, 2021.

9. June Campbell, "The Psychology of Color in Marketing," 4hb, https://www.4hb.com/0107psysoc olormarket.html, accessed May 22, 2017; Al Martinovic, "Color psychology in marketing," ImHosted, June 21, 2004, https://developers.evrsoft .com/article/web-design/graphics-multimedia -design/color-psychology-in-marketing.shtml; Suzanne Roman, "Colors that Sell," ImHosted, November 29, 2004, https://developers.evrsoft.com /article/web-design/graphics-multimedia-design /colors-that-sell.shtml; Pam Belluck, "Reinvent Wheel? Blue Room. Defusing a Bomb? Red Room," *The New York Times*, February 6, 2009, https://www.nytimes.com/2009/02/06/science /06color.html, accessed February 26, 2009.

10. Uniquely Generation Z, 2016, https://www .ibm.com/downloads/cas/9PPL5YOX, accessed April 14, 2021; Kim Parker & Ruth Igielnik, "On the Cusp of Adulthood and Facing an Uncertain Future," May 14, 2020, https://www.pewresearch .org/social-trends/2020/05/14/on-the-cusp-of -adulthood-and-facing-an-uncertain-future-what -we-know-about-gen-z-so-far-2/, accessed April 14,

2021; Thomas Law, "Ten Vital Strategies to Use When Marketing to Generation Z," November 3, 2020.

11. "Facebook: Friend, Foe, or Frenemy?" *Newsweek*, May 27, 2010, https://www .newsweek.com/blogs/techtonic-shifts /2010/05/26/facebook-friend-foe-or-frenemy -.html, accessed April 11, 2010.

12. Dan Patterson, "Facebook Data Privacy Scandal: A Cheat Sheet," July 30, 2020, https://www.techrepublic.com/article/facebook -data-privacy-scandal-a-cheat-sheet/, accessed April 14, 2021.

13. Kristien Matelski, "2018 Social Media Wins & Fails," October 19, 2018, https://www.vizion .com/blog/2018-social-media-wins-fails/, accessed April 14, 2021; Huge Companies, "29 Huge Social Media Gaffes," October 18, 2017, https:// www.cracked.com/pictofacts-811-29-huge-social -media-gaffes-by-huge-companies/, accessed April 14, 2021; Jennifer Calfas, "Education Department Misspells W.E.B. Du Bois's Name in Tweet," February 2, 2017, https://thehill. com/blogs/blog-briefing-room/news/319132 -education-department-misspells-web-du-bois -name-in-tweet, accessed April 14, 2021.

14. "The Problem with Sustainability Marketing? Not Enough Me, Me, Me," March 9, 2015, https://www.theguardian.com/sustainable -business/behavioural-insights/2015/mar/09 /problem-sustainability-marketing-not-enough -me, accessed April 22, 2017.

15. Yuri Kagiyama, "Toyota Profits up Amid Solid Recovery From Pandemic Fallout," February 9, 2021, https://abcnews.go.com/ International /wireStory/toyota-profits-amid-solid-recovery -pandemic-fallout-75794831, accessed April 14, 2021.

16. "Environment a Fair-weather Priority for Consumers," Press Release, Penn, Schoen & Bergland, June 3, 2008, https://www .psbresearch.com/press_release_Jun3-2008 .htm, accessed February 24, 2009; Gloria Sin, "Green Fashion: Is It More Than Marketing Hype?," *Fast Company*, May 28, 2008, https:// www.fastcompany.com/articles/2008/05/green -fashion-hype.html, accessed February 24, 2009; "'Green Fashion,' Formerly Hippie, Now Hip!," *CBS News*, February 21, 2008, https://www.cbsnews.com/stories/2008/02/21 /earlyshow/living/beauty/main3855868.shtml, accessed February 24, 2009.

Pg. 216 Fact: Marketing Charts staff, "Facebook Posts Get Half Their Reach Within 30 Minutes of Being Published, "November 2, 2012, MarketingCharts, https://www.marketing charts.com/online/facebook-posts-get-half -their-reach-within-30-minutes-of-being -published-24453/, accessed September 2014.

# Chapter 12

1. Melissa Sowry, "The Ultimate Energy Drink: Cocaine?," *ABCNews*, September 18, 2006, https://abcnews.go.com/Health/story?id =2459718&page=1#.UU45fjcwok9, accessed March 20, 2013; "Top 25 Biggest Product Flops of All Time," *DailyFinance*, https:// www.dailyfinance.com/photos/top-25-biggest -product-flops-of-all-time/#slide=3662621, accessed March 20, 2013.

2. "Characteristics of a Great Name," The Brand Name Awards, Brighter Naming, https://www. brandnameawards.com/top10factors .html, accessed April 10, 2005.

3. Mura Dominko, "Eat This, Not That! 20 Beloved Snacks Vanishing From Grocery Shelves This Year," October 16, 2020, https:// www.eatthis.com/snacks-vanishing-from -grocery-stores-this-year/, accessed April 29, 2021.

4. Adam Bass, "Brand Extensions: Marketing in Inner Space," Brand Channel, https://www .brandchannel.com/papers_review.asp?sp _id=296, accessed March 25, 2007; Reena Jana, "Brand Extensions We Could Do Without," *BusinessWeek*, August 7, 2006, https://www .businessweek.com/magazine/content/06 _32/b3996420.htm; "The 20 Worst Product Failures," Sales HQ, https://saleshq.monster .com/news/articles/2655-the-20-worst-product -failures, accessed June 20, 2012.

5. Alex Palmer, "Private Label Growing Rapidly," AdWeek, September 22, 2009, https://www .adweek.com/brand-marketing/private-label -growing-rapidly-105007/, accessed June 14, 2010; Christopher Durham, "Ten Private Brand Trends that Shook North America," My[Private] Brand, December 9, 2010, https://mypbrand .com/2010/12/09/10-private-brand-trends-that -shook-north-america/, accessed May 2, 2011; "IRI: Fewer Shoppers Buying Private Label Versus Last Year," Store Brands Decisions, https:// www.storebrandsdecisions.com/news/2011/04/05 /iri-fewer-shoppers-buying-private-label-versus -last-year, posted April 5, 2011, accessed May 2, 2011; Christopher Durham, "Private Brand Sales Outpace National Brands—PLMA's 2013 Private Label Yearbook," My Private Brand, June 28, 2013, https://mypbrand.com/2013/06/28/private -brands-sales-outpace-national-brands-plmas -2013-private-label-yearbook/, accessed February 12, 2014.

6. "The USA Apparel Market Research Report," Informat Fashion, June 2010, https://www.infomat .com/fido/getpublication.fcn?&type=research&Sear chString=apparel&id=737870ST0000927&start=1& tr=17Infomat, accessed June 14, 2010.

7. "Not on the List? The Truth About Impulse Purchases," Knowledge@Wharton, January 7, 2009, https://knowledge.wharton.upenn.edu /article.cfm?articleid=2132, accessed February 28, 2009.

8. "3M: Commitment to Sustainability," GreenBiz Leaders website, 1999.

9. Dawn C. Chmielewski, "Binge-Viewing Is Transforming the Television Experience," *The Los Angeles Times*, February 1, 2013, https://articles .latimes.com/2013/feb/01/entertainment/la-et-ct -binge-viewing-20130201, accessed March 20, 2013; David Hinkley, "Americans Spend 34 Hours a Week Watching TV, According to Nielsen Numbers," *Daily News*, September 19, 2012, https://www.nydailynews.com/entertainment /tv-movies/americans-spend-34-hours-week -watching-tv-nielsen-numbers-article-1.1162285, accessed March 20, 2013; Stine Thorhauge, "How People Spend Their Time Online," Mind-Jumpers, May 24, 2012, https://www.mindjumpers.com /blog/2012/05/time-spend-online/, accessed March 20, 2013; "U.S. Consumer Online Behavior Survey Results 2007 Part One: Wireline Usage," International Data Corporation, February 19, 2008, https://www.idc.com/getdoc.jsp?containerId =prUS21096308, accessed March 3, 2009; Dan Frommer, "Why Video On Demand Is Still Cable's Game to Lose," *The Business Insider*, September 5, 2008, https://www.businessinsider

.com/2008/9/why-video-on-demand-is-still-cable
-s-game-to-lose, accessed March 3, 2009; Glenn
Abel, "Streaming Vids Boost Netflix Profits,"
Download Movies 101, January 29, 2009, https://
downloadmovies101.com/wordpress-1/2009/01/29
/streaming-vids-boost-netflix-profits/, accessed
March 3, 2009; "Casting the Big Movie Download
Roles," eMarketer, September 7, 2007, https://www
.emarketer.com/Article.aspx?id=1005346, accessed
March 3, 2009; Clark Fredricksen, "Time Watching
TV Still Tops Internet," December 15, 2010,
eMarketer Blog, https://www.emarketer.com/blog
/index.php/time-spent-watching-tv-tops-internet/,
accessed May 4, 2011; "Average Time Spent Online
Per U.S. Visitor in 2010," ComScore Data Mine,
January 11, 2011, https://www.comscoredatamine
.com/2011/01/average-time-spent-online-per-u
-s-visitor-in-2010/, accessed May 4, 2011; Erick
Schonfeld, "How People Watch TV Online and
Off," TechCrunch, January 8, 2012, https://
techcrunch.com/2012/01/08/how-people-watch-tv
-online/, accessed June 20, 2012.

10. William C. Taylor, "Permission Marketing,"
Fast Company, December 18, 2007, https://www
.fastcompany.com/magazine/14/permission.html,
accessed March 3, 2009.

11. Rick Suter, "The Top 10 Super Bowl LV Ads,
According to USA TODAY Ad Meter," February 8,
2021, https://admeter.usatoday.com/2021/02/08/the
-top-10-super-bowl-2021-commercials/, accessed
April 29, 2021.

12. Professor Paul Herbig, Tristate University,
International Marketing Lecture Series, Session 6,
International Advertising, https://www.tristate.edu
/faculty/herbig/pahimadvstg.htm, accessed June 1,
2005; Karl Moore & Mark Smith, "Taking Global
Brands to Japan," The Conference Board, https://
www.conference-board.org/worldwide/worldwide
_article.cfm?id=243&pg=1, accessed June 1, 2005.

13. "US Digital Display Ad Spending to Surpass
Search Ad Spending in 2016," eMarketer, January 11,
2016, https://www.emarketer.com/Article/US
-Digital-Display-Ad-Spending-Surpass-Search-Ad
-Spending-2016/1013442, accessed April 29, 2017.

14. "Mobile Gets One Out of Five Paid Search
Clicks," eMarketer, May 6, 2013, https://www
.emarketer.com/Article/Mobile-Gets-One-of-Five
-Paid-Search-Clicks/1009865, accessed February
13, 2014; "Steady Gains for Mobile Paid Search,"
eMarketer, February 22, 2013, https://www
.emarketer.com/Article/Steady-Gains-Mobile-Paid
-Search/1009686, accessed June 20, 2013; "Search
Marketing Trends: Back to Basics," eMarketer,
February 2009, https://www.emarketer.com/Report
.aspx?code=emarketer_2000559, accessed June
18, 2010; Leah McBride Mensching, "eMarketer:
Display ad Growth Catching Up with Search,"
December 16, 2010, sfnblog, https://www.sfnblog
.com/advertising/2010/12/emarketer_display_ad
_growth_catching_up.php, accessed May 11, 2011;
"US Online Ad Spend Poised to Grow 20% in 2011,"
eMarketer, June 8, 2011, https://www.emarketer
.com/Article.aspx?R=1008431, accessed June 20,
2012; Forrester: Digital marketing spend to reach
$146B by 2023, but search landscape is changing
by Erica Sweeny, February 27, 2019, https://www
.marketingdive.com/news/forrester-digital
-marketing-spend-to-reach-146b-by-2023-but
-search-lands/549285/, accessed May 2, 2021.

15. "Mobile Requires Revamped SEO, SEM
Strategy," eMarketer, April 18, 2013, https://www.
emarketer.com/Article/Search-Gets-Mobile
-Makeover/1009822, accessed February 13, 2014;
Pamela Parker, "eMarketer: Among Online Ads,
Search to Gain Most New Dollars in 2011,"
SearchEngine Land, June 11, 2008, https://
searchengineland.com/emarketer-among-online

-ads-search-to-gain-most-new-dollars-in-2011
-80707, accessed March 20, 2013; Adweek staff,
"eMarketer: Search Is Vital in a Recession,"
Brandweek, February 25, 2009, https://www
.brandweek.com/bw/content_display/news
-and-features/digital/e3i195c363ab252f976a2
dabde4d8ef2549, accessed March 3, 2009.

16. "Online Video Advertising Moves Front and
Center," eMarketer, May 14, 2013, https://www
.emarketer.com/Article/Online-Video-Advertising
-Moves-Front-Center/1009886, accessed February
13, 2017; "U.S. Online Advertising Video Spending
2007–2013," eMarketer, August 2008, https://www
.marketingcharts.com/television/emarketer-revises
-online-video-ad-spend-projections-downward-5679
/emarketer-online-video-ad-spend-us-2007-2013jpg/,
accessed June 18, 2010; David Hallerman,
"Promises, Promises: Will Online Video Ads
Deliver this Year?," December 9, 2010, The
eMarketer Blog, https://www.emarketer.com
/blog/index.php/promises-promises-online-video
-ads-deliver-year/, accessed May 11, 2011; "US
Online Ad Spend Poised to Grow 20% in 2011,"
eMarketer, June 8, 2011, https://www.emarketer
.com/Article.aspx?R=1008431, accessed June 20,
2012; Video Advertising Trends Going Into 2021
By Linden Skeens, October 12, 2020, https://www
.forbes.com/sites/forbesbusinesscouncil/2020/10/12
/video-advertising-trends-going-into-2021/?sh
=5403dcf47761, accessed June 13, 2021.

17. Successful Social Media Campaigns to Learn
from in 2021, https://www.plannthat.com/social
-media-campaigns-2020/, accessed April 29, 2021.

18. Ibid.

19. "Master TikTok Influencer Marketing with
These success stories,"IZEA, August 24, 2020,
https://izea.com/2020/08/24/master-tiktok-influencer
-marketing-with-these-success-stories/, accessed
April 29, 2021.

20. Meghan Keane, "Social Media Claims More of
Our Attention. But Email's Not Dead Yet," August
2, 2010, eConsultancy, https://econsultancy.com/us
/blog/6366-social-media-might-claim-a-lot-of-our
-attention-but-email-s-not-dead-yet, accessed
May 11, 2011; Erik Qualman, "Social Media ROI
Examples & Video," Socialnomics, Social Media
Blog, November 12, 2009, https://socialnomics.
net/2009/11/12/social-media-roi-examples-video/,
accessed June 28, 2010; Lauren Fisher, "The
ROI of Social Media: 10 Case Studies," The Next
Web, July 16, 2011, https://thenextweb.com/
socialmedia/2011/07/16/the-roi-of-social-media
-10-case-studies/, accessed June 21, 2012.

21. "Infographic: Native Advertising Grows Despite
Budget and Transparency Concerns," Adweek,
February 16, 2015, https://www.adweek.com/news
/technology/infographic-native-advertising-grows
-despite-budget-and-transparency-concerns-162963,
accessed April 25, 2015; Native Advertising: A
Guide for Business, https://www.ftc.gov/tips-advice
/business-center/guidance/native-advertising-guide
-businesses, accessed April 30, 2021; John Glenday,
"Native Advertising Sector Predicted to Be Worth
$400 Billion by 2025," March 6, 2019, https://www
.thedrum.com/news/2019/03/06/native-advertising
-sector-predicted-be-worth-400bn-2025, accessed
April 30, 2021.

22. Margot Peppers, "Crocs Get a Stylish Make-
over as Brand Hopes to DOUBLE Sales in Five
Years—But Can the Foam Shoe Move on from
Its Ugly Past?," Daily Mail, July 19, 2013, https://
www.dailymail.co.uk/femail/article-2370360/Crocs
-stylish-make-brand-hopes-DOUBLE-sales-years
--foam-shoe-ugly-past.html, accessed February 15,
2013; "Pizza and a Movie, Time Pop Chart," Time
Magazine, June 3, 2013, https://content.time.com

/time/magazine/article/0,9171,2144105,00.html,
accessed February 15, 2014.

23. "Top 10 Product Placement Brands in 2020
Movies," Concave Brand Tracking, https://
concavebt.com/top-10-product-placement-brands-
in-2020-movies/, accessed April 30, 2021; "Apple
Does Not 'Let Bad Guys Use iPhones on Screen,'"
The Guardian, February 26, 2020, https://www
.theguardian.com/technology/2020/feb/26/apple
-does-not-let-bad-guys-use-iphones-on-screen,
accessed April 30, 2021.

24. David Bakula, "Behind the Music (Video): How
Important Are Videos to Both Artists and Brands?"
April 22, 2014, https://www.nielsen.com/us/en
/insights/article/2014/behind-the-music-video-how
-important-are-videos-to-both-artists-and-brands/,
accessed April 30, 2021.

25. "31 American Things That Look a Whole
Lot Different in Other Countries," https://www
.boredpanda.com/american-food-products
-abroad/?utm_source=duckduckgo&utm
_medium=referral&utm_campaign=organic,
accessed April 30, 2021.

26. Colin Dixon, "US TV Homes, Devices, and
Services," September 2, 2019, https://nscreenmedia
.com/us-tv-homes-devices-services/, accessed April 30,
2021; "DVR Use in the US," December 2010,
https://www.nielsen.com/wp-content/uploads/sites
/3/2019/04/DVR-State-of-the-Media-Report.pdf,
accessed April 30, 2021.

27. Abe Sauer, "Product Placement Sees Global
Rise as Fans Face Saturated Entertainment,"
BrandChannel, April 24, 2013, https://www
.brandchannel.com/home/post/2013/04/24/Product
-Placement-On-The-Rise-042413.aspx, accessed
February 13, 2014; Abe Sauer, "Announcing
the 2013 BrandCameo Product Placement
Award Winners," BrandChannel, February 25,
2013, https://www.brandchannel.com/home
/post/2013/02/25/Brandchannel-9th-Brandcameo
-Product-Placement-Awards-022513.aspx, accessed
March 20, 2013; "PQ Media Market Analysis Finds
Global Product Placement Spending Grew 37% in
2006; Forecast to Grow 30% in 2007, Driven by
Relaxed European Rules, Emerging Asian Markets;
Double-Digit Growth in U.S. Decelerates," PQ
Media, March 14, 2007, https://www.pqmedia.com
/about-press-20070314-gppf.html, accessed
September 4, 2008; Jose Fermoso, "DVR
Households Swelling Ranks," Portfolio, December 16,
2008, https://www.portfolio.com/views/blogs/the
-tech-observer/2008/12/16/dvr-households
-swelling-ranks, accessed March 4, 2009; "FCC
Opens Inquiry Into Stealthy TV Product Placement,"
USA Today, June 26, 2008, https://www.usatoday
.com/life/television/2008-06-26-fcc-advertising_N
.htm, accessed March 4, 2009; Bill Gorman, "DVRs
Now in 30.6% of U.S. Households," TV by the
Numbers, April 30, 2009, https://tvbythenumbers
.com/2009/04/30/dvrs-now-in-306-of-us-households
/17779, accessed June 16, 2010; Andrew Hampp,
"Product Placement Dipped Last Year for the First
Time," AdAge, June 29, 2010, https://adage.com
/article/madisonvine-news/product-placement
-dipped-year-time/144720/, accessed May 11,
2011; Robert Seidman, "DVR Penetration Grows
to 39.7% of Households, 42.2% of Viewers,"
TV by the Numbers, March 23, 2011, https://
tvbythenumbers.zap2it.com/2011/03/23/dvr
-penetration-grows-to-39-7-of-households-42
-2-of-viewers/86819/, accessed May 11, 2011;
Joseph Plambeck, "Product Placement Grows in
Music Videos," The New York Times, July 5, 2010,
https://www.nytimes.com/2010/07/06/business
/media/06adco.html?_r=1, accessed June 21, 2012;
Bill Carter & Brian Stelter, "DVRs and Streaming
Prompt a Shift in the Top-Rated TV Shows," The

*New York Times*, March 4, 2012, https://www
.nytimes.com/2012/03/05/business/media/dvrs-and
-streaming-prompt-a-shift-in-the-top-rated-tv
-shows.html?pagewanted=all, accessed June 21,
2012.

28. Robert Balkovitch, "The Ridiculous Product
Placements You Never Noticed in Yellowstone,"
October 22, 2020, https://www.looper.com/265843
/the-ridiculous-product-placements-you-never
-noticed-in-yellowstone/, accessed April 30, 2021.

29. Susan Gunelius, "Ford, Coke & AT&T Pay
More to Sponsor American Idol," *Bizzia*, January 18,
2008, https://www.bizzia.com/brandcurve
/ford-coke-att-pay-more-to-sponsor-american
-idol/, accessed March 4, 2009; Amy Johannes,
"Global Paid Product Placement to Reach $7.6
Billion by 2010: Report," PromoMagazine, August
17, 2006, https://promomagazine.com/research
/paidplacementreport/, accessed June 16, 2010.

30. Lisa Evans, "Fitness First—Wait Watching,"
*The Cool Hunter*, March 17, 2009, https://www
.thecoolhunter.co.uk/article/detail/1504/fitness
-first-wait-watching, accessed March 30, 2013;
"UNICEF Finland: Mom," I Believe in Advertising,
March 31, 2009, https://www.ibelieveinadv
.com/2009/03/unicef-finland-mom/, accessed
March 30, 2013; Melanie Wells, "Kid Nabbing,"
*Forbes*, February 2, 2004, https://www.forbes
.com/free_forbes/2004/0202/084.html; Tremor,
https://tremor.com/index.html, accessed March 5,
2009; Elaine Wong, "General Mills, Kraft Launch
Word of Mouth Networks," *BrandWeek*, October 5,
2008, https://www.brandweek.com/bw/content
_display/news-and-features/packaged-goods/e3i2db03
fb29d573ec52722456845f5c274, accessed March 5,
2009; "The World's Weird America: How Some of Our
Most Popular Products Are Seen Overseas," *Pacific
Standard*, February 26, 2014, https://psmag.com
/the-world-s-weird-america-how-some-of-our-most
-popular-products-are-seen-overseas-1d4a6b1732c0#
.38jodwtwf, accessed May 7, 2016.

31. Aaron Agius, "The 10 Best Social Media
Marketing Campaigns of 2016 So Far," *Social
Media Today*, July 28, 2016, https://www
.socialmediatoday.com/marketing/10-best-social
-media-marketing-campaigns-2016-so-far, accessed
April 30, 2017.

32. Chantal India, "The Best Brands on TikTok: 10
Accounts to Inspire Your Strategy," March 12, 2021,
https://www.cyberclick.net/numericalblogen
/the-best-brands-on-tiktok-10-accounts-to-inspire
-your-strategy, accessed May 1, 2021; "Master
TikTok Influencer Marketing with These Success
Stories," IZEA, August 24, 2020, https://izea
.com/2020/08/24/master-tiktok-influencer
-marketing-with-these-success-stories/, accessed
May 1, 2021.

33. Alex Brownsell, "How Sponsorship Marketing
Can Rediscover Its Stride in 2021," November 26,
2020, https://www.warc.com/newsandopinion
/opinion/how-sponsorship-marketing-can
-rediscover-its-stride-in-2021/3958, May 1, 2021.

34. Shawn Paul Wood, "Emissions Scandal Took
the Air Out of Volkswagen Sales in November,"
AdWeek, December 2, 2015, https://www.adweek
.com/prnewser/emissions-scandal-took-the-air-out
-of-volkswagen-sales-in-november/119765, accessed
May 15, 2016; Geoff Colvin, "5 Years in, Damages
from the VW Emissions Cheating Scandal Are Still
Rolling in," October 6, 2020, https://fortune
.com/2020/10/06/volkswagen-vw-emissions
-scandal-damages/, accessed May 1, 2020.

35. Bill Stoller, "Publicity from Thin Air (Don't
Just Wait for News to Happen)," ArticlesClick.com,
https://articlesclick.com/articles/public-relations
/publicity-from-thin-air.php, accessed June 15, 2005.

36. "The Employment Situation—April 2011,"
Bureau of Labor Statistics News Release, Bureau
of Labor Statistics, May 6, 2011, https://www.bls
.gov/news.release/pdf/empsit.pdf, accessed
May 16, 2011.

Pg. 235 Fact: Erik Qualman, "Social Media
Video 2013," *Socialnomics*, January 1, 2013,
https://www.socialnomics.net/2013/01/01/social
-media-video-2013/, accessed September 2014.

# Chapter 13

1. "Supermarket Facts, Industry Overview
2008," Food Marketing Institute, https://www.
fmi.org/facts_figs/?fuseaction=superfact,
accessed June 30, 2010; Brandon Gaille,
"Fascinating Grocery Industry Statistics,"
https://brandongaille.com/11-grocery-industry
-statistics/, accessed May 16, 2021.

2. AP, "How a Global Pandemic Led to a Toilet
Paper Shortage—And When It Gets Better," April 9,
2020, https://nypost.com/2020/04/09/how-a-global
-pandemic-lead-to-a-toilet-paper-shortage/,
accessed June 11, 2021.

3. Greg Petro, "Do Consumers Really Want to Shop
Online?" December 4, 2020, https://www.forbes
.com/sites/gregpetro/2020/12/04/do-consumers
-really-want-to-shop-online/?sh=7065f7436cf4,
accessed May 16, 2021.

4. Fareeha Ali, "A Decade in Review: Ecommerce
Sales vs. Retail Sales, 2007 – 2020," January 29,
2021, https://www.digitalcommerce360.com/article
/e-commerce-sales-retail-sales-ten-year-review/,
accessed May 16, 2021.

5. Nathan Bomey & Kelly Tyko, "More Store
Closings in 2021?", December 20, 2020, https://www
.usatoday.com/story/money/2020/12/30/store-closures
-2021-macys-jcpenney-among-vulnerable-retailers
/3974684001/, accessed May 15, 2021; Kelly
Tyko, "Retailers Lost in the Last Decade: Toys R
Us, Sports Authority, Blockbuster, Borders and
Payless," December 29, 2019, https://www.usatoday
.com/story/money/2019/12/29/decade-store-closings
-biggest-retailers-lost-decade/2750954001/,
accessed May 15, 2021.

6. Fareeha Ali, "A Decade in Review: Ecommerce
Sales by 2007–2020," January 29, 2021, https://www
.digitalcommerce360.com/article/e-commerce-sales
-retail-sales-ten-year-review/, accessed May 17, 2021.

7. Andrew Meola, "Rise of M-Commerce: Mobile
Ecommerce Shopping Stats & Trends in 2021,"
December 30, 2020, https://www.businessinsider
.com/mobile-commerce-shopping-trends-stats?op=1,
accessed May 17, 2021.

8. Miranda Hobbs, "How Does Real-time Online
Support Boost Conversion Rates and Ensure a
Purchase Sticks?," iAdvize blog, April 16, 2015,
https://www.iadvize.com/blog/en/en-conversion-rate
-optimisation-live-chat/, accessed May 5, 2017;
Justyna Kraszewska, "Why Should I Set Up Chat
Greetings," Live Chat, https://www.livechatinc.com
/kb/why-should-i-set-up-chat-greetings/, 7.

9. Megan Conley, "Direct Marketing, Brand
Association and Revenue: Why a Catalog Might Be
Your Next Best Marketing Bet," https://www
.bigcommerce.com/blog/catalog-marketing/,
accessed June 10, 2021.

10. Christian Storm, "30 Bizarre Vending Machines
from Around the World," *Business Insider*,
November 10, 2014, https://www.businessinsider
.com/most-unique-vending-machines-2014-11,
accessed April 27, 2015.

11. "Sales Soften at Costco," Retail Analysis,
IGD, March 4, 2009, https://www.igd.com/analysis
/channel/news_hub.asp?channelid=1&channelitemi
d=9&nidp=&nid=5616, accessed March 13, 2009.

12. Loss Leader Strategy, Investopedia website (a
Forbes Digital Company), https://www.investopedia
.com/terms/l/lossleader.asp, accessed March 14, 2009;
Al Norman, "Walmart Not Crying Over Spilt Milk,"
*The Huffington Post*, August 22, 2008, https://
www.huffingtonpost.com/al-norman/wal-mart
-not-crying-over_b_120684.html, accessed March 14,
2009.

13. Rafi Mohammed, "The Problem with Price
Gouging Laws," *Harvard Business Review*, July 23,
2013, https://hbr.org/2013/07/the-problem
-with-price-gouging-laws, accessed May 6, 2017;
Jeffrey Dorfman, "Price Gouging Laws Are Good
Politics But Bad Economics," *Forbes*, September 23,
2016, https://www.forbes.com/sites/jeffreydor
fman/2016/09/23/price-gouging-laws-are-good
-politics-but-bad-economics/#2a5aebc264d3,
accessed May 6, 2017.

14. Stephanie Clifford, "Shopper Alert: Price
May Drop for You Alone by Stephanie Clifford,"
*The New York Times*, August 9, 2012 https://www
.nytimes.com/2012/08/10/business/supermarkets
-try-customizing-prices-for-shoppers.html, accessed
May 6, 2017.

15. Ben Kunz, "How Apple Plays the Pricing
Game," *Bloomberg Businessweek*, October, 6, 2010,
https://www.nbcnews.com/id/38980367/ns/business
-us_business/t/how-apple-plays-pricing-game/#.
UWInbjcwok9, accessed April 7, 2013.

16. Steven Greenhouse, "How Costco Became
the Anti Walmart," *The New York Times*, July 17,
2005, https://www.nytimes.com/2005/07/17
/business/yourmoney/17costco.html?adxnnl=1&
pagewanted=1&adxnnlx=1122004143-8VFn2DFl
1MJfern M1navLA; Matthew Boyle, "Why Costco
Is So Addictive," *CNNMoney*, October 25, 2006,
https://money.cnn.com/magazines/fortune/fortune
_archive/2006/10/30/8391725/index.htm, accessed
March 14, 2009.

Pg. 249 Fact: Tyler Mathisen, "Supermarkets Wage
War for Your Dollars," January 27, 2011, https://www
.today.com/id/wbna41259243#.VPD9KGSbbmA?utm_
source=aol-df&utm_medium=guest&utm_campaign
=10-tricks-stores-use-to-get-you-to-spend-more-
money, accessed May 16, 2021.

Pg. 257 Fact: Russian proverb.

# Chapter 14

1. Stephanie Vozza, "The Surprising First Jobs of
10 Famous CEOS," Fast Company, https://www
.fastcompany.com/3027074/dialed/the-surprising
-first-jobs-of-10-famous-ceos#1, accessed May 1,
2015; "First Jobs of the Rich and Famous," *Parade*,
https://www.parade.com/celebrity/slideshows
/flashback/stars-first-jobs.html#?slideindex=0,
accessed April 7, 2013; "The Importance of Being
Richard Branson, Leadership and Change,"
Knowledge@Wharton, January 12, 2005, https://
knowledge.wharton.upenn.edu/article/1109.cfm;
Jeffrey Kluger, "Ambition: Why Some People
Are Most Likely to Succeed," *Time* Magazine,
November 14, 2005, pp. 48–59, https://www.time
.com/time/archive/preview/0,10987,1126746,00
.html; "Jeff Bezos," Reference for Business, https://
www.referenceforbusiness.com/businesses/A-F
/Bezos-Jeff.html, accessed June 24, 2012; Matt
Melvin2011, "The Roller Coaster Ride of Mark
Zuckerberg," Teen Ink, https://www.teenink
.com/nonfiction/academic/article/292857/The,
accessed June 24, 2012; "Reagan Trail Days," The
Ronald Reagan Trail, https://www.ronaldreagantrail
.net/Pages/ReaganTrail.php?city=2&page=Dixon,

accessed June 24, 2012; "Celebrities' First Jobs," Oprah.com, https://www.oprah.com/entertainment /Oprahs-Live-Newscast-and-Celebrities-First -Jobs, accessed September 4, 2016; David Kushner, "Will Virtual Reality Change Your Life?," *Rolling Stone*, May 23, 2016, https://www.rollingstone .com/culture/features/will-virtual-reality-change -your-life-20160523, accessed September 4, 2016.

2. Erika Anderson, "It Seemed Like a Good Idea at the Time: 7 of the Worst Business Decisions Ever Made," *Forbes*, October 4, 2013, https:// www.forbes.com/sites/erikaandersen/2013/10/04 /it-seemed-like-a-good-idea-at-the-time-7-of-the -worst-business-decisions-ever-made/, accessed March 1, 2014; "The Worst Business Decisions of All Time," 24/7 *The Wall Street Journal*, October 4, 2013, https://247wallst.com/2012/10/17/the -worst-business-decisions-of-all-time/3/, accessed April 7, 2013; "Top Ten Bad Business Decisions," Business Excellence, October 10, 2010, https://www .bus-ex.com/article/top-ten-bad-business-decisions, accessed June 24, 2012; Peter Roesler, "8 of the Biggest Business Mistakes in History," Inc., April 20, 2015, https://www.inc.com/peter-roesler/8-of -the-biggest-business-mistakes-in-history.html, accessed June 1, 2016; "The Stupidest Business Decisions in History," April 15, 2008, https://www .neatorama.com/2008/04/15/the-stupidest-business -decisions-in-history/, accessed June 11, 2021.

3. "The Importance of Being Richard Branson," Leadership and Change, Knowledge@Wharton, January 12, 2005, https://knowledge.wharton.upenn .edu/article/1109.cfm.

4. "Hot Topic, Inc. Reports Fourth Quarter EPS Increases 19% to $0.32 Per Diluted Share; Provides Guidance for the 1st Quarter of 2009," News Blaze, March 11, 2009, https://newsblaze.com/story /2009031112554500001.pz/topstory.html, accessed March 25, 2009.

5. Steve Lohr, "A New Game at the Office: Many Young Workers Accept Fewer Guarantees," *The New York Times*, December 5, 2005, https://select .nytimes.com/gst/abstract.html?res=F00F12FE385 50C768CDDAB0994DD404482.

6. Susan Heathfield, "Use These Tips From HR Pros to Plan and Implement Changes at Work," February 1, 2021, https://www.thebalancecareers .com/change-management-tips-1917809, accessed June 13, 2021; Change management trends to watch in 2021 by Mary Beth Gibson, December 15, 2020, https://www.logic2020.com/insight/change -management-trends-2021, accessed June 13, 2021.

7. Jeremy Morgan, "Uber Was Right to Hustle, but Here's Where Its Leadership Blew It," *Fortune*, March 22, 2017, https://fortune.com/2017/03/22 /uber-president-resigns-travis-kalanick/, accessed May 14, 2017; Dinah Eng, "For Which Wich, Success Is in the Bag," April 22, 2017, https:// fortune.com/2017/04/22/which-wich-sandwiches -jeff-sinelli/, accessed May 14, 2017.

8. Caterina Bulargella, "From Exceptionalism to Unrest: Why Google's Culture Is Changing," February 19, 2020, https://www.forbes.com/sites /caterinabulgarella/2020/02/19/from-exceptionalism -to-unrest-why-googles-culture-is-changing/?sh =cd0bb003560c, accessed June 11, 2021.

9. "Fortune 100 Best Companies to Work for," https://fortune.com/best-companies/2021/, accessed June 11, 2021.

10. "75 Best Large Workplaces for Millennials," https://fortune.com/best-workplaces-millennials /2020/search/, accessed June 11, 2021.

11. Darrell Rigby, "Don't Get Hammered by Management Fads," *The Wall Street Journal*, May 21, 2001.

12. Kate Morgan, "How Young Workers Are Changing the Rules of 'Business Speak,'" December 9, 2020, https://www.bbc.com/worklife/article /20201204-how-young-workers-are-changing-the -rules-of-business-speak, accessed June 12, 2021.

13. "The Cow in the Ditch: How Anne Mulcahy rescued Xerox," Special Section: Knowledge at Wharton, November 16–29, 2005, https://knowledge .wharton.upenn.edu/index.cfm?fa=viewArticle&id =1318&specialId=41.

14. "Ready, Set, Go: Reinventing the Organization for Speed in the Post-COVID-19 Era," June 26, 2020, https://www.mckinsey.com/business-functions /organization/our-insights/ready-set-go-reinventing -the-organization-for-speed-in-the-post-covid-19 -era, accessed June 12, 2021.

15. Amy Langfield, "Unused Vacation Days at 40-year High," *CNBC*, October 23, 2014, https://www .cnbc.com/id/102110867, accessed May 4, 2015; Tony Schwartz, "Relax! You'll Be More Productive," *The New York Times*, February 9, 2013, https://www .nytimes.com/2013/02/10/opinion/sunday/relax -youll-be-more-productive.html?pagewanted=all& _r=0, accessed April 8, 2013; Chris Morris, "The Average American Throws Away 4 Vacation Days a Year," *Fortune*, November 17, 2015, https://fortune .com/2015/11/17/vacation-paid-time-americans -survey/, accessed June 5, 2016; Suyin Hayes, "Lack of Sleep Costs U.S. About $411 Billion in Lost Productivity, Study Finds," *Fortune*, November 30, 2016, https://fortune.com/2016/ 11/30/sleep-productivity-rand-corp-411-billion/, accessed May 14, 2017; "The State of American Vacation: How Vacation Became a Casualty of Our Work Culture," Project: Time Off, https://www .projecttimeoff.com/research/state-american -vacation-2016, accessed May 14, 2017.

# Chapter 15

1. No furloughs for Southwest in 2020, thanks to nearly 17K voluntary departures by Edward Russell, July 26, 2020, https://www.msn.com/en-us/travel /news/no-furloughs-for-southwest-in-2020-thanks -to-nearly-17k-voluntary-departures/ar-BB16YJh6, accessed June 17, 2021; David Shepardson, "Southwest Airlines CEO Calls Idea of Profit This Year 'Unrealistic'," August 12, 2020, https://www .nasdaq.com/articles/southwest-airlines-ceo-calls-idea -of-profit-this-year-unrealistic-2020-08-12, accessed June 17, 2021.

2. Anna Brown & Eileen Patten, "The Narrowing, But Persistent, Gender Gap in Pay," Fact Tank, Pew Research Center, April 3, 2017, https://www .pewresearch.org/fact-tank/2017/04/03/gender-pay -gap-facts/, accessed May 21, 2017; 26 Must-Know Outsourcing Statistics and Trends in 2021by Darko Jacimovic, March 30, 2021, https://whattobecome. com/blog/outsourcing-statistics/, accessed June 17, 2021; Domestic Outsourcing in the United States, January 31, 2018, https://www.dol.gov/sites/dolgov /files/OASP/legacy/files/Domestic-Outsourcing -in-the-United-States.pdf, accessed June 17, 2021; IT Outsourcing Trends in 2021 by Kateryna Kachkovska, December 17, 2020, https://www .daxx.com/blog/development-trends/it-outsourcing -trends, accessed June 17, 2021.

3. Grace Donnelly, "Top CEOs Make More in Two Days Than An Average Employee Does in One Year," July 20, 2017, https://fortune.com/2017/07/20 /ceo-pay-ratio-2016/, accessed May 28, 2018.

4. Kathryn Dill, "Report: CEOs Earn 331 Times as Much as Average Workers, 774 Times as Much as Minimum Wage Earners," *Forbes*, April 15, 2014, https://www.forbes.com/sites/kathryndill/2014/04/15 /report-ceos-earn-331-times-as-much-as-average -workers-774-times-as-much-as-minimum-wage -earners/, accessed Mary 10, 2015; Talib Visram, "CEOs Now Earn 320 Times More Than Average Workers," August 19, 2020, https://www.fastcompany .com/90541658/ceos-now-earn-320-times-more -than-average-workers, accessed June 18, 2021; Sarah Hansen, "Gap Between CEO Pay and Worker Pay Continued to Widen During The Pandemic, New Survey Finds," June 11, 2021, https:// www.forbes.com/sites/sarahhansen/2021/06/11 /gap-between-ceo-pay-and-worker-pay-continued -to-widen-during-the-pandemic-new-survey -finds/?sh=210c766810fa, accessed June 18, 2021.

5. Adam Burroughs, "How Baby Boomer Retirements Are Threatening Organizational Knowledge," July 1, 2017, https://www.sbnonline. com/article/baby-boomer-retirements-threatening -organizational-knowledge/, accessed June 19, 2021; Richard Fry, "Baby Boomers Are Staying in the Labor Force at Rates Not Seen in Generations for People Their Age," July 24, 2019, https://www .pewresearch.org/fact-tank/2019/07/24/baby-boomers -us-labor-force/z, accessed July 19, 2021.

6. Steve Greenhouse, "The Age Premium: Retaining Older Workers," *The New York Times*, May 14, 2014, https://www.nytimes.com/2014 /05/15/business/retirementspecial/the-age-premium -retaining-older-workers.html, accessed May 15, 2017.

7. Betsy Morris, "How Corporate America Is Betraying Women," *Fortune*, January 10, 2005; "Jane Drain—Women Leaving Your Workforce," Smart Manager, https://www.smartmanager.com.au /web/au/smartmanager/en/pages/89_jane_drain —women_leaving_workforce.html, accessed July 5, 2011; Tiziana Barghini, "Educated Women Quit Work as Spouses Earn More," Reuters, March 8, 2012, https://www.reuters.com/article/2012/03/08 /us-economy-womenidUSBRE8270AC20120308, accessed June 25, 2012; "Highly Achieved Women Leaving the Traditional Workforce, Final Report March 2008," U.S. Department of Labor, https:// www.choose2lead.org/Publications/Are%20We%20 Losing%20the%20Best%20and%20the%20 Brightest.pdf, accessed June 25, 2012.

8. "Featured Employee Rap Sheet," Hot Topic, https://www.hottopic.com/community/rapsheets /emp_jodi.asp?LS=0&, accessed April 11, 2006; Steve Lohr, "A New Game at the Office: Many Young Workers Accept Fewer Guarantees," *The New York Times*, December 5, 2005, https://select.nytimes.com/gst/abstract.html?res =F00F12FE38550C768CDDAB0994DD404482; Andrea Shim, "Work-life Benefits Fall Victim to Sloweconomy," *Los Angeles Times*, April 4, 2009, https://www.latimes.com/business/la-fi-flexible 42009apr04,0,4344887.story, accessed April 4, 2009; Sue Shellenbarger, "Pending Job Flexibility Act Received Mixed Reviews," *WSJ Career Journal*, https://www.careerjournal.com/columnists/workfamily /20010426-workfamily.html, accessed August 9, 2005; "Work-Life Balance Survey: Gen Z, Millennials Are the Unhappiest Generations," March 26, 2019, https://www.commercialcafe.com/blog/work-life -balance-survey-2019/, accessed June 19, 2021.

9. Sidney Fussell, "Black Tech Employees Rebel Against 'Diversity Theater,'" March 8, 2021, https:// www.wired.com/story/black-tech-employees -rebel-against-diversity-theater/, accessed June 23, 2021; Ashley Stahl, "What's to Come in 2021 for Diversity, Equity and Inclusion in the Workplace," April 14, 2021, https://www.forbes.com/sites /ashleystahl/2021/04/14/whats-to-come-in-2021-for -diversity-equity-and-inclusion-in-the-workplace /?sh=51e4a8417f26, accessed June 23, 2021; Kate Rooney & Yasmin Khorram, "Tech Companies

Say They Value Diversity, but Reports Show Little Change in Last Six Years," June 12, 2020, https://www.cnbc.com/2020/06/12/six-years-into-diversity-reports-big-tech-has-made-little-progress.html, accessed June 23, 2021.

10. Keith W. Hammonds, "Why We Hate HR," Fast Company, December 19, 2007, https://www.fastcompany.com/magazine/97/open_hr.html?page=0%2C1, accessed April 4, 2009.

11. Peter Capelli, "Why We Love to Hate HR… and What HR Can Do About It," August 2015, https://hbr.org/2015/07/why-we-love-to-hate-hr-and-what-hr-can-do-about-it, accessed June 19, 2021.

12. Mary Beth Marklein, "One-Third of Young People Have a Bachelor's," USA Today, November 5, 2012, https://www.usatoday.com/story/news/nation/2012/11/05/college-graduates-pew/1683899/, accessed April 9, 2013; "Table 1. The 30 Fastest Growing Occupations Covered in the 2008–2009 Occupational Outlook Handbook," Economic News Release, Bureau of Labor Statistics, December 18, 2007, https://www.bls.gov/news.release/ooh.t01.htm, accessed April 7, 2009; "Census Bureau Data Underscore Value of College Degree," U.S. Census Bureau News, October 26, 2006, https://www.census.gov/Press-Release/www/rel-eases/archives/education/007660.html, accessed April 7, 2009; Derek Quizon, "Increasing Share of Adults Have College Degrees, Census Bureau Finds," The Chronicle of Higher Education, April 26, 2011, https://chronicle.com/article/Increasing-Share-ofAdults/127264/, accessed July 5, 2011.

13. "SHRM Human Capital Benchmarking Study," 2008 Executive Summary, page 14, SHRM, https://www.shrm.org/Research/Documents/2008%20Executive%20Summary_FINAL.pdf, accessed April 7, 2009; "Effective Recruiting Tied to Stronger Financial Performance," News Release, Watson Wyatt Worldwide, August 16, 2005, https://www.watsonwyatt.com/news/press.asp?ID=14959, accessed April 7, 2009.

14. "CareerBuilder Releases Annual List of Strangest Interview and Body Language Mistakes," CareerBuilder January 12, 2017, https://www.careerbuilder.com/share/aboutus/pressreleasesdetail.aspx?ed=12%2F31%2F2017&id=pr984&sd=1%2F12%2F2017, accessed May 20, 2017; "Top 10 Unbelievable Interview Blunders," CareerBuilder, https://employer.careerbuilder.com/jobposter/small-business/article.aspx?articleid=ATL_0174INTERVIEWBLUNDERS, accessed May 20, 2017.

15. Jeanne Sahadi, "Top Five Resume Lies," CNN Money, December 9, 2004, https://money.cnn.com/2004/11/22/pf/resume_lies/.

16. Elaine Pofeldt, "Source: Shocker: 40% of Workers Now Have 'Contingent' Jobs, Says U.S. Government," May 25, 2015, https://www.forbes.com/sites/elainepofeldt/2015/05/25/shocker-40-of-workers-now-have-contingent-jobs-says-u-s-government/, accessed May 20, 2017.

17. Contingent Workforce: Size, Characteristics, Earnings, and Benefits April 20, 2015, https://www.gao.gov/products/gao-15-168r, accessed June 20, 2021.

18. "Retraining and Reskilling Workers in the Age of Automation," January 22, 2018, https://www.mckinsey.com/featured-insights/future-of-work/retraining-and-reskilling-workers-in-the-age-of-automation, accessed June 21, 2021.

19. Matt DeLuca, "Orientation: Not Just a Once-over-Lightly Anymore," HRO Today, April/May 2005, https://www.hrotoday.com/Magazine.asp?artID=928; Leslie Gross Klaff, "New Emphasis on First Impressions," Workforce Management,

March 2008, https://www.workforce.com/archive/feature/25/41/58/index.php?ht=, accessed April 7, 2009; Leon Rubis, "Show and Tell—Disney Institute's Four-Day Seminar on HR Management," HR Magazine, April 1998; Daryl Stephenson, "New Employee Experience Aims for Excitement Beyond the First Day," Boeing Frontiers Online, May 2002, https://www.boeing.com/news/frontiers/archive/2002/may/i_mams.html.

20. Sean McFadden, "Labor-Intensive," Boston Business Journal, November 19, 2004, https://www.bizjournals.com/boston/stories/2004/11/22/smallb1.html; Stanley Holmes & Wendy Zelner, "The Costco Way; Higher Wages Mean Higher Profits. But Try Telling Wall Street," Business-Week, April 12, 2004; Todd Raphael, "Study: Moderation in Hiring Practices Boosts Business Performance," Workforce Management, August 19, 2005, https://www.workforce.com/section/00/article/24/14/03.html.

21. Mary Meisendahl, "Restaurant Workers Are Quitting at Record-High Rates, and It Could Force Their Employers to Raise Wages, Experts Say," June 13, 2021, https://www.businessinsider.com/restaurant-workers-are-quitting-at-record-rates-2021-6?nr_email_referer=1&utm_source=Sailthru&utm_medium=email&utm_content=Business_Insider_select&pt=385758&ct=Sailthru_BI_Newsletters&mt=8&utm_campaign=Insider%20Select%202021-06-14&utm_term=INSIDER%20SELECT%20-%20ENGAGED%2C%20ACTIVE%2C%20PASSIVE%2C%20DISENGAGED%2C%20NEW, accessed June 23, 2021.

22. Carroll Lachnit, "Appreciating Benefits as Times Gets Tough," Blog: The Business of Management, Workforce Management, March 24, 2009, https://www.workforce.com/article/20090324/BLOGS02/303249999/appreciatingbenefits-as-times-gets-tough, accessed April 9, 2009.

23. Sue Shellenbarger, "Perking Up: Some Companies Offer Surprising New Benefits," The Wall Street Journal, March 18, 2009, https://online.wsj.com/article/SB123733195850463165.html, accessed April 9, 2009.

24. Adi Gaskell, "A Hybrid Workforce May Not Be the Panacea After All," June 2021, https://www.forbes.com/sites/adigaskell/2021/06/17/a-hybrid-workforce-may-not-be-the-panacea-after-all/?sh=1611e243411b, accessed June 21, 2021.

25. Kenneth Rapoza, "One in Five Americans Work from Home, Numbers Seen Rising Over 60%," Forbes, February 18, 2013, https://www.forbes.com/sites/kenrapoza/2013/02/18/onein-five-americans-work-from-home-numbersseen-rising-over-60/, accessed March 30, 2014; Rick Hampson, "The Work-from-Home Tug of War," USA Today, March 11, 2013, https://www.usatoday.com/story/news/nation/2013/03/11/the-work-from-home-tug-ofwar/1979457/, accessed March 30, 2014; "Global Workplace Analytics and the Telework Research Network," Telework Research Network, https://www.teleworkresearchnetwork.com/pros-cons, accessed April 10, 2013; Mary C. Noonan & Jennifer L. Glass, "The Hard Truth About Telecommuting," Monthly Labor Review, June 2012, https://www.bls.gov/opub/mlr/2012/06/art3full.pdf, accessed April 10, 2013; Ted Samson, "Give Telecommuting the Green Light," InfoWorld, June 7, 2007, https://www.infoworld.com/d/green-it/givetelecommuting-green-light-628, accessed April 10, 2009; Brendan I. Koerner, "Home Sweet Office: Telecommute Good for Business, Employees, and Planet," Wired, September 22, 2008, https://www.wired.com/culture/culturereviews/magazine/16-10/st_essay, accessed April 10, 2009; Ginger Christ, "Skype: More Companies Allow Telecommuting," Dayton Business Journal, April 5, 2011, https://

www.bizjournals.com/dayton/news/2011/04/05/more-companies-allowtelecommuting.html, accessed July 5, 2011; "Costs and Benefits, Advantages of Telecommuting for Companies," Telework Research Network, https://www.teleworkresearchnetwork.com/costsbenefits, accessed July 5, 2011.

26. Michelle V. Rafter, "The New Job Sharers," Workforce Management, May 2008, https://www.workforce.com/archive/feature/25/53/28/index.php, accessed April 10, 2009; Stephen Miller, "Study Attempts to Dispel Five Myths of Job Sharing," Society for Human Resource Management, May 9, 2007, https://moss07.shrm.org/Publications/HRNews/Pages/XMS_021497.aspx, accessed April 10, 2009; Job Sharing: Twice the Benefits or Double the Problems?https://edwardlowe.org/job-sharing-twice-the-benefits-or-double-the-problems-2/, accessed June 21, 2021.

27. Jacquelyn Smith, "Here's What Hiring Managers REALLY Think of Your Tattoos," Business Insider, January 5, 2016, https://www.businessinsider.com/what-hiring-managers-really-think-of-yourtattoos-2016-1, accessed June 12, 2016; Authur Zuckerman, "38 Tattoo Statistics; 2020\2021, Industry Trends and Demographics," May 13, 2020, https://comparecamp.com/tattoo-statistics/, accessed June 21, 2021.

28. Rex Nutting, "5.1 Million Jobs Lost in This Recession so Far," MarketWatch, April 3, 2009, https://www.marketwatch.com/news/story/51-million-jobs-lost-recession/story.aspx?guid={CF54164C-6F7B-4501-B6FB-D7D1C8D710B9}&dist=msr_8, accessed April 10, 2009; "Boost Employee Morale After Layoffs," Workforce Management, https://www.workforce.com/archive/article/22/14/10.php, accessed April 10, 2009; Kim Parker, "Unemployed Americans Are Feeling the Emotional Strain of Job Loss; Most Have Considered Changing Occupations," February 10, 2021, https://www.pewresearch.org/fact-tank/2021/02/10/unemployed-americans-are-feeling-the-emotional-strain-of-job-loss-most-have-considered-changing-occupations/, accessed June 21, 2021.

29. "Charges Alleging Sexual Harassment FY 2010–FY 2015," EEOC, https://www.eeoc.gov/eeoc/statistics/enforcement/sexual_harassment_new.cfm, accessed June 12, 2016.

30. "Sexual Harassment," US Equal Employment Opportunity Commission, updated March 11, 2009, https://www.eeoc.gov/types/sexual_harassment.html, accessed April 10, 2009.

31. Starbucks, https://stories.starbucks.com/press/2020/the-starbucks-foundation-awards-neighborhood-grants-to-advance-racial-equity/g, accessed January 5, 2021.

32. Cedric Thornton "Pfizer Announces Ramcess Jean-Louis as Global Chief Diversity, Equity and Inclusion Officer," June 18, 2021, https://www.blackenterprise.com/pfizer-announces-ramcess-jean-louis-as-global-chief-diversity-equity-and-inclusion-officer/, accessed June 21, 2021.

33. The Lenovo Way: Yolanda Conyers on Transforming Corporate Culture by Sarah Thurmond, April 16, 2020, https://www.cognitivetimes.com/2020/04/yolanda-conyers-on-transforming-corporate-culture/, accessed June 21, 2021.

Pg. 280 Fact: "Work-Life Balance Survey: Gen Z, Millennials Are the Unhappiest Generations," March 26, 2019, https://www.commercialcafe.com/blog/work-life-balance-survey-2019/, accessed June 17, 2021.

Pg. 281 Fact: "Frivolous Lawsuits," America's Best, April 2008, https://www.americasbestcompanies

.com/magazine/articles/frivolous-lawsuits.aspx, accessed November 27, 2012.

Pg. 285 Fact: Walter Hamilton, "Few Firms Recruiting Liberal Arts Majors," *Los Angeles Times*, May 21, 2014, https://www.latimes.com/business /la-fi-companies-hiring-liberal-arts-majors-jobs 20140521-story.html, accessed May 10, 2015.

Pg. 293 Fact: "Occupational Safety and Health Administration Statistics," Occupational Safety and Health Administration, https://www.osha.gov /oshstats/commonstats.html, accessed September 2014.

# Chapter 16

1. "Buy 13-inch MacBook Pro," Apple, https:// www.apple.com/shop/buy-mac/macbook-pro/13 -inch, accessed February 19, 2021; "Apple M1 Chip," Apple, https://www.apple.com/mac /m1/, accessed February 19, 2021; H. Casey, "MacBook Air and MacBook Pro M1 Battery Life Tested— This Is Amazing," *Tom's Guide*, November 18, 2020, https://www.tomsguide.com /news/macbook-air-and-macbook-pro-m1-battery -life-tested-this-is-amazing, accessed February 19, 2021; C. Gartenberg, "Apple's First-Gen M1 Chips Have Already Upended Our Concept of Laptop Performance," The Verge, November 19, 2020, https://www.theverge.com/2020/11/19/21574057 /apple-m1-chips-laptop-performance-intel-qualcomm -competition, accessed February 19, 2021.

2. G. Tognini, "How Copart Is Making A Billion Dollars From a Junkyard," *Forbes*, November 16, 2020, https://www.forbes.com/sites/giacomotognini /2020/11/16/how-to-make-a-billion-dollars-junkyard -cars-copart-salvage/?sh=7b4a969a7498; accessed February 19, 2021.

3. Ibid.

4. Ibid.

5. Ibid.

6. R. Tate, "Apple Just Ended the Era of Paid Operating Systems," *Wired*, October 22, 2013, https://www.wired.com/2013/10/apple-ends-paid -oses/, accessed February 19, 2021.

7. "Dealertrack: Application Processing," Dealer Track, https://us.dealertrack.com/content/dealer track/en/originations-solutions.html, accessed February 20, 2021.

8. "The Size of the World Wide Web (The Internet)," WorldWideWebSize, February 20, 2021, https://www .worldwidewebsize.com/, accessed February 20, 2021.

9. "The Global Internet Phenomena Report: COVID-19 Spotlight," Sandvine Intelligent Broadband Networks, May 2020, https://www .sandvine.com/covid-internet-spotlight-report, accessed February 19, 2021.

10. No author, "Internet/Broadband Fact Sheet," Pew Research Center, June 12, 2019, https:// www.pewresearch.org/internet/fact-sheet /internet-broadband/, accessed February 20, 2021; M. Anderson, "Mobile Technology and Home Broadband 2019," Pew Research Center, June 13, 2019, https://www.pewresearch.org /internet/2019/06/13/mobile-technology-and-home -broadband-2019/, accessed February 20, 2021.

11. Ibid.

12. C. McGarry, "5G Speed: 5G vs 4G Performance Compared," Tom's Guide, January 20, 2021, https://www.tomsguide.com/features/5g-vs -4g, accessed February 20, 2021.

13. "Advanced Layer 1 Service: Control Your Own Network—Without Building It," Internet2, https:// internet2.edu/wp-content/uploads/2020/10/IS -advanced-layer-1-service-20160429.pdf, accessed February 20, 2021.

14. "About Us - Internet2," Internet2, https:// internet2.edu/community/about-us/, accessed February 20, 2021.

15. Ibid.

16. W. Bedingfield, "The Race Is On to Stop Scalping Bots From Buying All the PS5s," *Wired UK*, February 2, 2021, https://www.wired.com /story/scalping-bots-buying-all-the-ps5s/, accessed February 27, 2021; M. Jeffery, "How to Beat PlayStation 5 Scalpers and Find Your Next-Gen Console," *GamingIntel*, November 14, 2020, https://gamingintel.com/how-to-beat-playstation -5-scalpers-and-find-your-next-gen-console/, accessed February 27, 2021; T. Mochizuki (Bloomberg News), "'This Is a Launch Disaster.' Here's Why You Can't Find a PlayStation 5," *Chicago Tribune*, December 17, 2020, https:// www.chicagotribune.com/business/ct-biz-playstation -5-ps5-xbox-shortage-20201217-enxdgcnydvhbhm4 p3uxdk6xetu-story.html, accessed February 27, 2021.

17. E. Boyd, "Internet2 Technology Update," Internet 2, January 21, 2008, https://www.internet2 .edu/presentations/jt2008jan/20080121-boyd.ppt, accessed February 11, 2017.

18. E. Knorr, "The 2020 IDG Cloud Computing Survey," *InfoWorld*, June 8, 2020, https://www .infoworld.com/article/3561269/the-2020-idg-cloud -computing-survey.html, accessed February 21, 2021.

19. T. Seal, "Nokia Ditches Data Centers for Google Cloud in Five-Year Deal," *Bloomberg*, October 14, 2020, https://www.bloomberg.com /news/articles/2020-10-14/nokia-ditches-data -centers-for-google-cloud-in-five-year-deal?sref=xX o7CWym, accessed February 21, 2021.

20. J. Konstantas, "7 Reasons Why The Cloud Is More Secure," *Oracle Cloud Security Blog*, September 16, 2019, https://blogs.oracle.com /cloudsecurity/7-reasons-why-the-cloud-is-more -secure, accessed February 22, 2021.

21. "The 2020 IDG Cloud Computing Survey," *InfoWorld*.

22. J. Oltsik, "Is the cybersecurity skills shortage getting worse?" *CSO Online*, May 10, 2019, https://www.csoonline.com/article/3394876/is-the -cybersecurity-skills-shortage-getting-worse.html, accessed February 22, 2021.

23. J. Greene, "Amazon to Offer Cloud-Migration Service," *The Wall Street Journal*, March 15, 2016, p. B4.

24. S. Ovide & C. Boulton, "Flood of Rivals Could Burst Amazon's Cloud," *The Wall Street Journal*, July 26, 2014, p. B4.

25. "Cloud Computing Services," Amazon Web Services (AWS), https://aws.amazon.com/, accessed February 21, 2021.

26. S. Castellanos, "Etsy Accelerates AI Experimentation Thanks to Cloud," *The Wall Street Journal*, February 19, 2020, https://www.wsj.com /articles/etsy-accelerates-ai-experimentation-thanks -to-cloud-11582144740?mod=djemCIO, accessed February 21, 2021.

27. V. Herasevich, B. Pickering & O. Gajic, "How Mayo Clinic Is Combating Information Overload in Critical Care Units," *Harvard Business Review*, March 22, 2018, https://hbr.org/2018/03/how -mayo-clinic-is-combating-information-overload-in -critical-care-units, accessed February 21, 2021.

28. Ibid.

29. "Predictive Analytics in Healthcare: AWARE Testimonials," Ambient Clinical Analytics, https:// ambientclinical.com/solution/aware-critical-care/, accessed February 21, 2021.

30. A. Hess, "Blood Glucose Monitoring: Expert Tips for People With Diabetes - How Often, Where to Test and How to Reduce Pain From Finger Pricks," OnTrack Diabetes, August 15, 2019, https://www.ontrackdiabetes.com/blood-glucose /blood-glucose-monitoring-tips-people-diabetes, accessed February 22, 2021.

31. P. Loftus, "For Many Diabetes Patients, Skin Patches and Phones Are Replacing Finger Pricks," *The Wall Street Journal*, July 29, 2019, https://www. wsj.com/articles/devices-for-diabetes-patients-spur -growth-at-medical-firms-11564392603?mod =djemwhatsnews, accessed February 22, 2021.

32. T. Dunn, Y. Xu, G. Hayter & R. Ajjan, "Real-World Flash Glucose Monitoring Patterns and Associations Between Self-Monitoring Frequency and Glycemic Measures: A European Analysis of Over 60 Million Glucose Tests," *Diabetes Research and Clinical Practice* 137 (2018): 37-46.

33. T. Sultana, "Big Data Is Driving Safety on Freight Railroads," RealClearTechnology, January 27, 2016, https://www.realcleartechnology.com/articles /2016/01/27/big_data_is_driving_safety_on_freight _railroads_1271.html, accessed February 12, 2017.

34. Q. Hardy, "As a Data Deluge Grows, Companies Rethink Storage," *The New York Times*, March 14, 2016, https://www.nytimes.com/2016/03/15/technology /as-a-data-deluge-grows-companies-rethink-storage .html?_r=0, accessed February 12, 2017.

35. Ibid.

36. N. Singer, "Bring Big Data to the Fight Against Benefits Fraud," *The New York Times*, February 20, 2015, https://www.nytimes.com/2015/02/22 /technology/bringing-big-data-to-the-fight-against -benefits-fraud.html, accessed April 15, 2015.

37. L. Lagnado, "Doctors Test Tools to Predict Your Odds of a Disease," *The Wall Street Journal*, May 30, 2016, https://www.wsj.com/articles /doctors-test-tools-to-predict-your-odds-of-a -disease-1464633980, accessed February 12, 2017.

38. Effy Oz, *Management Information Systems*, 5th ed., Course Technology (Stamford, CT: Cengage Learning, 2006), pp. 332–338; Jack Copeland, "What Is Artificial Intelligence," AlanTuring.Net, May 2000, https://www.cs.usfca.edu/www.AlanTuring.net /turing_archive/pages/Reference%20Articles /what_is_AI/What%20is%20AI07.html.

39. David M. Kroenke, *Experiencing MIS* (Upper Saddle River, NJ: Pearson Prentice Hall, 2008): pp. 340–341; "What Are Expert Systems?," Thinkquest.org, https://library.thinkquest .org/11534/expert.htm, accessed May 24, 2009.

40. D. Nations, "What Is Enterprise 2.0? Enterprise 2.0 Explained," About Tech, https:// webtrends.about.com/od/office20/a/enterprise -20.htm, accessed April 16, 2015; D. Nation, "What Is Web 2.0—How Web 2.0 Is Defining Society," About Tech, https://webtrends.about .com/od/web20/a/what-is-web20.htm, accessed April 16, 2015.

41. C. Williams, "Chapter 15 Communication," *MGMT 12e* (Boston, MA: Cengage Publishing, 2021).

42. "Google SEO 2021: Complete SEO Beginner's Guide," Google, https://backlinko.com/google-seo -guide, accessed February 24, 2021.

43. A. Raza, "Effective Internet Marketing Tactics You Need in 2020," *Influencive*, November 7, 2020, https://www.influencive.com/effective-internet -marketing-tactics-you-need-in-2020/, accessed February 24, 2021.

44. M. McLaughlin & G. Sevilla, "The Best Email Marketing Software for 2021," *PC Mag*, September 2, 2020, https://www.pcmag.com/picks/the-best -email-marketing-software, accessed February 24, 2021.

45. C. Moorman & T. McCarthy, "CMOs: Adapt Your Social Media Strategy for a Post-Pandemic World," *Harvard Business Review*, January 19, 2021, https://hbr.org/2021/01/cmos-adapt-your-social-media-strategy-for-a-post-pandemic-world, accessed February 24, 2021.

46. "Effective Internet Marketing Tactics You Need in 2020," *Influencive*.

47. "Facebook Ads: Online Advertising on Facebook," Facebook for Business, https://www.facebook.com/business/ads, accessed February 24, 2021.

48. K. Aka, New Research: The Value of Influencers on Twitter," Twitter, May 10, 2016, https://blog.twitter.com/en_us/a/2016/new-research-the-value-of-influencers-on-twitter.html, accessed February 24, 2021.

49. C. Moorman, "Covid-19 and the State of Marketing: Highlights & Insights Report," The CMO Survey, June 2020, https://cmosurvey.org/wp-content/uploads/2020/06/The_CMO_Survey-Highlights-and_Insights_Report-June-2020.pdf, accessed February 25, 2021.

50. "Recommend Products. Earn Commissions – Amazon's Affiliate Marketing Program," Amazon Associates, https://affiliate-program.amazon.com/, accessed February 24, 2021.

51. "Welcome to the eBay Partner Network," eBay Partner Network, https://partnernetwork.ebay.com/, accessed February 25, 2021.

52. C. Cimpanu, "After a Breach, Users Rarely Change Their Passwords, Study Finds," *ZDNet*, June 1, 2020, https://www.zdnet.com/article/after-a-breach-users-rarely-change-their-passwords-study-finds/, accessed February 28, 2021; S. Ferdowsi, "The 200 Most Common Online Passwords of 2020 Are Awful," *Vice*, November 18, 2020; N. Popper, "Lost Passwords Lock Millionaires Out of Their Bitcoin Fortunes," *The New York Times*, January 12, 2021, https://www.nytimes.com/2021/01/12/technology/bitcoin-passwords-wallets-fortunes.html, accessed February 28, 2021.

53. PayPal Editorial Staff, "How Credit Card Processing With PayPal Works for Your Business," PayPal, May 17, 2019, https://www.paypal.com/us/brc/article/how-paypal-works-for-sellers, accessed February 25, 2021.

54. L. Savvides & V. Hand Orellana, "Apple Pay vs. Samsung Pay vs. Google Pay: Which Mobile Payment System Is Best?" *CNET*, June 17, 2019, https://www.cnet.com/news/apple-pay-google-pay-samsung-pay-best-mobile-payment-system-compared-nfc/, accessed February 25, 2021.

55. "Fourth Quarter and Full Year 2020 Results," PayPal, February 3, 2021, https://s1.q4cdn.com/633035571/files/doc_financials/2020/q4/Q4-FY-20-PayPal-Earnings-Release.pdf, accessed February 25, 2021; "PayPal Global - All Countries and Markets," PayPal, https://www.paypal.com/us/webapps/mpp/country-worldwide, accessed February 25, 2021.

56. D. Bourguetts, "B2B Digital Payments Stats for Merchants to Know in 2020," Paystand, July 30, 2020, https://www.paystand.com/blog/b2b-digital-payment-statistics-2020, accessed February 25, 2021.

57. E. Chen, "Drugmakers Race to Build Covid-19 Vaccine Supply Chains," *The Wall Street Journal*, July 30, 2020, https://www.wsj.com/articles/drugmakers-race-to-build-covid-19-vaccine-supply-chains-11596101586, accessed February 25, 2021.

58. Ibid.

59. "About Alibaba.com," Alibaba, https://activities.alibaba.com/alibaba/following-about-alibaba.php?tracelog=footer_alibaba, accessed February 26, 2021.

60. "About Us: Thomas," Thomasnet.com®, https://business.thomasnet.com/about, accessed February 26, 2021.

61. "MagicBands & Admission Cards," Walt Disney World Resort, https://disneyworld.disney.go.com/plan/my-disney-experience/bands-cards/, accessed February 26, 2021.

62. "Disney Bets Big on Visitor-Tracking Technology," *Bloomberg Businessweek/MSN Money*, March 10, 2014, https://money.msn.com/technology-investment/post--disney-bets-big-on-visitor-tracking-technology, accessed March 31, 2014.

63. "AI Definition from PC Magazine Encyclopedia," PC Magazine, accessed May 7, 2017, https://www.pcmag.com/encyclopedia/term/37613/ai.

64. A. Cuthbertson, "AI Pilot Thoroughly Beats Human in F-16 Dogfight, Marking Major Breakthrough for Artificial Intelligence," *The Independent*, August 21, 2020, https://www.independent.co.uk/life-style/gadgets-and-tech/news/ai-pilot-dogfight-artificial-intelligence-darpa-a9681346.html, accessed February 28, 2021; T. Davenport & R. Ronanki, "3 Things AI Can Already Do for Your Company," *Harvard Business Review*, January-February 2018, https://hbr.org/2018/01/artificial-intelligence-for-the-real-world, accessed February 28, 2021; T. Ghose, "Artificial Intelligence Beats 'Most Complex Game Devised by Humans,'" *Live Science*, January 27, 2016, https://www.livescience.com/53497-ai-defeats-human-go-player.html, accessed February 28, 2021; B. Lynn, "Artificial Intelligence Beats Humans in Major Reading Test," *Learning English*, January 23, 2018, https://learningenglish.voanews.com/a/ai-beats-human-scores-in-major-reading-test/4215369.html, accessed February 28, 2021; B. Suh, "When Should You Use AI to Solve Problems?" *Harvard Business Review*, February 17, 2021, https://hbr.org/2021/02/when-should-you-use-ai-to-solve-problems, accessed February 28, 2021; C. Stupp, "AI Could Help Find Cheaper and Smarter Ways to Raise Fish," *The Wall Street Journal*, September 30, 2020, https://www.wsj.com/articles/ai-could-help-find-cheaper-and-smarter-ways-to-raise-fish-11601458200?mod=djemCIO, accessed February 28, 2021.

65. T. Kulikov, T. Shcherbakova & T. Sidorina, "Spam and Phishing in 2020," *Securelist*, February 15, 2021, https://securelist.com/spam-and-phishing-in-2020/100512/, accessed February 26, 2021.

66. H. Tankovska, "E-mail Usage in the United States - Statistics & Facts," *Statista*, February 17, 2021, https://www-statista-com.ezproxy.butler.edu/topics/4295/e-mail-usage-in-the-united-states/, accessed February 26, 2021.

67. Metz, "Google Says Its AI Catches 99.9 Percent of Gmail Spam," *Wired*, July 9, 2015, https://www.wired.com/2015/07/google-says-ai-catches-99-9-percent-gmail-spam/, accessed February 13, 2017.

68. M. Maunder, "Wide Impact: Highly Effective Gmail Phishing Technique Being Exploited," Wordfence, January 12, 2017, https://www.wordfence.com/blog/2017/01/gmail-phishing-data-uri/#officialupdate, accessed February 13, 2017.

69. "Pharming: Is Your Trusted Website a Clever Fake?" Microsoft, January 3, 2007, https://www.microsoft.com/protect/yourself/phishing/pharming.mspx; "Online Fraud: Pharming," Symantec, https://www.symantec.com/norton/cybercrime/pharming.jsp, accessed May 24, 2009; "Advisory: Watch Out for Drive-by-Pharming Attacks," Pharming.org, https://www.pharming.org/index.jsp, accessed May 24, 2009.

70. M. Huffman, "'Smishing' Emerges as New Threat to Cell Phone Users," *Consumer Affairs*, https://www.consumeraffairs.com/news04/2006/11/smishing.html, accessed May 22, 2009; E. Millis, "'SMiShing' Fishes for Personal Data Over Cell Phone," *CNet*, February 24, 2009, https://news.cnet.com/8301-1009_3-10171241-83.html, accessed April 2, 2013; L. Musthaler, "How to Avoid Becoming a Victim of SMiShing (SMS Phishing)," NetworkWorld, March 7, 2013, https://www.networkworld.com/newsletters/techexec/2013/030813bestpractices.html, accessed April 2, 2013.

71. "Create and Strong Passwords," Microsoft Support, https://support.microsoft.com/en-us/windows/create-and-use-strong-passwords-c5cebb49-8c53-4f5e-2bc4-fe357ca048eb, accessed February 26, 2021.

72. T. Simonite, "You've Been Misled About What Makes a Good Password," *MIT Technology Review*, October 19, 2015, https://www.technologyreview.com/s/542576/youve-been-misled-about-what-makes-a-good-password/, accessed February 13, 2017.

73. K. Bell, "Yes, Your Emails Are Being Tracked. Here's How to Stop It," *Mashable*, July 7, 2019, https://mashable.com/article/how-to-block-email-pixel-tracking/, accessed February 28, 2021; Verge Staff, "What Is a Tracking Pixel and Can Strangers Really Spy on Me Through Email?" *The Verge*, July 3, 2019, https://www.theverge.com/2019/7/3/20681508/tracking-pixel-email-spying-superhuman-web-beacon-open-tracking-read-receipts-location, accessed February 28, 2021; Wired Staff, "You Give Up a Lot of Privacy Just Opening Emails. Here's How to Stop It," *Wired*, December 11, 2017, https://www.wired.com/story/how-email-open-tracking-quietly-took-over-the-web/, accessed February 28, 2021.

74. R. Myers, "The Best Password Manager (and Why You Need One): 1Password," September 12, 2016, https://thesweetsetup.com/apps/best-password-manager-and-why-you-need-one/, accessed February 13, 2017.

75. "1Password Watchtower," 1Password, https://watchtower.1password.com/, accessed February 26, 2021.

76. Times Opinion, "Twelve Million Phones, One Dataset, Zero Privacy," *The New York Times*, December 19, 2019, https://www.nytimes.com/interactive/2019/12/19/opinion/location-tracking-cell-phone.html, accessed February 26, 2021.

77. Ibid.

78. "Software Management: Security Imperative, Business Opportunity: BSA Global Software Survey," BSA: The Software Alliance, June 2018, https://gss.bsa.org/wp-content/uploads/2018/05/2018_BSA_GSS_Report_en.pdf, accessed February 26, 2021.

79. S. Siwek, "The True Cost of Sound Recording Piracy to the U.S. Economy," Recording Industry Association of America, https://www.riaa.com/reports/the-true-cost-of-sound-recording-piracy-to-the-u-s-economy/, accessed February 26, 2021.

80. Statista, "Media Piracy in the U.S. and Worldwide," *Statista*, 2018, https://www.statista.com/study/42923/media-piracy-worldwide/, accessed February 26, 2021.

81. I. Birnbaum, "The state of PC piracy in 2016," *PC Gamer*, August 10, 2016, https://www.pcgamer.com/the-state-of-pc-piracy-in-2016/, accessed February 27, 2021.

82. E. Van der Sar, "Gaming Giants Highlight the Latest Piracy Threats," *TorrentFreak*, October 4, 2019, https://torrentfreak.com/gaming-giants-highlight-the-latest-piracy-threats-191004/, accessed February 27, 2021.

83. C. Hoffman, "What Is Denuvo, and Why Do Gamers Hate It?" *How-To Geek*, December 30, 2018, https://www.howtogeek.com/400126/what-is-denuvo-and-why-do-gamers-hate-it/, accessed February 27, 2021.

84. H. Taylor, "Denuvo: " There Is No Uncrackable Game. What We Do Is Protect the Initial Sales," GamesIndustry.biz, August 29, 2018, https://www.gamesindustry.biz/articles/2018-08-29-denuvo-and-irdeto-on-protecting-early-sales-from-piracy, accessed February 27, 2021.

# Chapter 17

1. S. Maheshwari & E. Griffith, "Peloton's Rapid Rise Is Threatened by Its Slow Delivery," *New York Times*, January 17, 2021, https://www.nytimes.com/2021/01/17/business/peloton-slow-delivery.html, accessed March 3, 2021.

2. Ibid.

3. P. Sawers, "UPS Will Now Use Dynamic Routing to Get Parcels to You on Time," *VentureBeat*, January 29, 2020, https://venturebeat.com/2020/01/29/ups-will-now-use-dynamic-routing-to-get-parcels-to-you-on-time/, accessed March 4, 2021.

4. Press Release, "UPS: UPS to Enhance Orion with Continuous Delivery Route Optimization," *Bloomberg*, January 29, 2020, https://www.bloomberg.com/press-releases/2020-01-29/ups-ups-to-enhance-orion-with-continuous-delivery-route-optimization?sref=xXo7CWym, accessed March 4, 2021.

5. "Find US Dollar's Value from 1913-2021," US Inflation Calculator, https://www.usinflationcalculator.com/, accessed March 4, 2021.

6. "Epson WorkForce WF-2860 Wireless All-In-One Inkjet Printer," Dell USA, https://www.dell.com/en-us/shop/epson-workforce-wf-2860-wireless-all-in-one-inkjet-printer-black/apd/aa198966/printers-ink-toner, accessed March 4, 2021; "Inspiron 24 5000 All-in-One," Dell USA, https://www.dell.com/en-us/shop/serviceselection/na5400ekphh?cartitemid=a5aea343-1fbc-4f9b-87cf-3f3d06f3f131, accessed March 4, 2021.

7. "Byte Converter: Bytes to KB to MB to GB to TB [Calculator]," *Whatsabyte*, https://whatsabyte.com/P1/byteconverter.htm, accessed March 4, 2021; "Screen Size Comparison," *Screen Innovations*, https://www.screeninnovations.com/tools/screen-size-comparison/, accessed March 4, 2021.

8. M. Perry, "Technology Has Advanced So Rapidly That a Laptop Computer Today Is 96% Cheaper than a 1994 Model and 1,000x Better," American Enterprise Institute, May 25, 2016, https://www.aei.org/publication/technology-has-advanced-so-rapidly-that-a-laptop-computer-today-is-96-cheaper-than-a-1994-model-and-1000x-better/, accessed March 4, 2021.

9. "Establishment Data Employment-Table B-1a. Employees on Nonfarm Payrolls by Industry Sector and Selected Industry Detail, Seasonally Adjusted," Current Employment Statistics—CES (National): Bureau of Labor Statistics, February 5, 2021, https://www.bls.gov/web/empsit/ceseeb1a.htm, accessed March 4, 2021.

10. "Starbucks' Secret Menu—The Drinks You Didn't Know You Can Ask For," *The Telegraph*, February 15, 2017, https://www.telegraph.co.uk/finance/picture-galleries/11375182/Revealed-The-drinks-you-didnt-know-you-could-order-at-Starbucks.html, accessed February 15, 2017.

11. J. Beck, "Starbucks Orders and the Mass Customization of American Food," *The Atlantic*, May 13, 2016, https://www.theatlantic.com/health/archive/2016/05/food-customization-america/482073/, accessed February 15, 2017.

12. "Distances & Time," SeaRates, https://www.searates.com/services/distances-time/, accessed March 10, 2021; A. Abad-Santos, "The Extremely Profitable (And Ethically Murky) Business of Reselling Dumbbells," *Vox*, September 23, 2020, https://www.vox.com/the-goods/21443765/buying-dumbbells-online-expensive-resellers, accessed March 10, 2021; A. Abad-Santos, "Why It's So Hard to Find Dumbbells in the US," *Vox*, August 24, 2020, https://www.vox.com/the-goods/21396116/dumbbell-set-shortage-nordictrack-bowflex, accessed March 10, 2021; M. Garcia, "Prices on Free Weights are Skyrocketing Because of Coronavirus," *Fox 25 KOKH*, April 8, 2020, https://okcfox.com/news/consumer-watch/prices-on-free-weights-are-skyrocketing-because-of-coronavirus; T. Garrity, "Making Sense of the Dumbbell Shortage in America," *InsideHook*, August 25, 2020, https://www.insidehook.com/daily_brief/health-and-fitness/dumbbell-shortage-america, accessed March 10, 2021.

13. "GDB Per Capita, 1823 to 2016," Our World In Data, https://ourworldindata.org/economic-growth, accessed March 6, 2021.

14. "Visualizing the U.S. Share of the Global Economy Over Time," *Visual Capitalist*, January 14, 2021, https://www.visualcapitalist.com/u-s-share-of-global-economy-over-time/, accessed March 6, 2021.

15. "Our Quality and Ingredients," Nutella® USA, https://www.nutella.com/us/en/inside-nutella/quality-and-ingredients, accessed March 6, 2021.

16. "Impact Statement," Solidia, https://assets.ctfassets.net/jv4d7wct8mc0/4LwjKXYDVgu9KVuDbrMcEq/6119b7ef7efdb4aba7b1dab5b1b1fa5b/Solidia_Technologies_Impact_Statement_9.6.19.pdf, accessed March 7, 2021.

17. S. Reed, "Betting On a New Way to Make Concrete That Doesn't Pollute," *The New York Times*, December 2, 2018, https://www.nytimes.com/2018/12/02/climate/betting-on-a-new-way-to-make-concrete-that-doesnt-pollute.html, accessed March 7, 2021.

18. "Solidia® – A Giant Step That Leaves a Small Footprint," Solidia, https://www.solidiatech.com/impact.html, accessed March 7, 2021.

19. "OnStar: Vehicle Technology | Cadillac Ownership," Cadillac, https://www.cadillac.com/ownership/vehicle-technology/onstar, accessed March 7, 2021.

20. "Flight Crew Pilot Training," Airbus Services, https://services.airbus.com/en/flight-operations/pilot-and-flight-operations-training/flight-crew-training-courses/pilot-flight-crew-training.html, accessed March 7, 2021.

21. "Production - How Is an Aircraft Built," Airbus, https://www.airbus.com/aircraft/how-is-an-aircraft-built/production.html, accessed March 7, 2021.

22. No author, "Top Ten Biggest Lithium Mines in the World Based on Reserves," *Mining Technology*, December 4, 2020, https://www.mining-technology.com/features/top-ten-biggest-lithium-mines/, accessed March 7, 2021.

23. M. Haag & W. Hu, "Amazon Went on a New York Buying Spree as Online Shopping Surged," *The New York Times*, March 4, 2021, https://www.nytimes.com/2021/03/04/nyregion/amazon-in-new-york.html., accessed March 7, 2021.

24. V. Chamlee, "Americans Now Spend More at Restaurants Than Grocery Stores," *Eater*, June 16, 2016, https://www.eater.com/2016/6/16/11954062/restaurant-spending-outpaces-grocery-stores, accessed March 7, 2021.

25. A. Gasparro, J. Smith & J. Kang, "Grocers Stopped Stockpiling Food. Then Came Coronavirus," *The Wall Street Journal*, March 23, 2020, https://www.wsj.com/articles/grocers-stopped-stockpiling-food-then-came-coronavirus-11584982605, accessed March 7, 2021.

26. A. Gasparro & S. Stamm, "Why Are Some Groceries Still So Hard to Find During Covid?" *The Wall Street Journal*, August 10, 2020, https://www.wsj.com/articles/why-are-some-groceries-still-so-hard-to-find-during-covid-11597069761, accessed March 7, 2021.

27. Ibid.

28. D. Collier & J. Evans, *OM*, 2nd ed. (Mason, OH: South-Western, Cengage Learning, 2010): 27–28.

29. A. Kirkman, "IKEA's Ambitious Plan To Make Its Cheap Furniture Last Forever," *HuffPost*, February 10, 2021, https://www.huffpost.com/entry/ikea-plan-cheap-furniture-last-climate-footprint_n_6021a3a3c5b6173dd2f8b30b, accessed March 8, 2021.

30. Press Release, "Ingka Investments Acquires Forestland in US from the Conservation Fund," *IKEA*, https://www.ikea.com/us/en/this-is-ikea/newsroom/ingka-investments-acquires-forestland-in-united-states-from-the-conservation-fund-pub70656d40, accessed March 8, 2021; D. DiFurio, "Why is IKEA Buying Up Thousands of Acres of Forestland in East Texas?" *Dallas Morning News*, November 22, 2019, https://www.dallasnews.com/business/retail/2019/11/22/why-is-ikea-buying-up-thousands-of-acres-of-forestland-in-east-texas/, accessed March 8, 2021; A. Peters, "Why IKEA Just Bought an 11,000-Acre Forest in Georgia," *Fast Company*, January 14, 2021, https://www.fastcompany.com/90594218/why-ikea-just-bought-an-11000-acre-forest-in-georgia, accessed March 8, 2021.

31. "IKEA's Ambitious Plan To Make Its Cheap Furniture Last Forever," *HuffPost*.

32. M. Elwood, "Luxury Brands Buy Supply Chains to Ensure Meeting Demand," *The New York Times*, November 15, 2018, https://www.nytimes.com/2018/11/15/business/luxury-brands-buy-supply-chains-to-ensure-meeting-demand.html, accessed March 8, 2021.

33. E. Koh, "Samsung's Drugmaking Future Includes a $2 Billion 'Super Plant' Bigger Than the Louvre," *The Wall Street Journal*, September 3, 2020, https://www.wsj.com/articles/samsungs-drugmaking-future-includes-a-2-billion-super-plant-bigger-than-the-louvre-11599125658, accessed March 8, 2021.

34. Ibid.

35. Ibid.

36. "Plant Spartanburg," BMW Group, https://www.bmwgroup-werke.com/spartanburg/en.html/, accessed March 8, 2021.

37. "Outsourcing: Ripoff Nation," BW Smallbiz Front Line, Winter 2006, *BusinessWeek*, https://www.businessweek.com/magazine/content/06_52/b4015435.htm?chan=rss_topStories_ssi_5; Steve Dickinson, "Outsourcing in China: Five Basic Rules for Reducing Risk," Ezine Articles, https://ezinearticles.com/?Outsourcing-in-China:-Five-Basics-for-Reducing-Risk&id=17214, accessed March 3, 2021.

38. "Facts About PPG," PPG, https://news.ppg.com/facts-about-ppg/default.aspx, accessed March 8, 2021.

39. J. McCormick, "PPG Names Tech Veteran to Head Its IT Efforts," *The Wall Street Journal*, February 9, 2021, https://www.wsj.com/articles/ppg-names-tech-veteran-to-head-its-it-efforts-11612910384?mod=searchresults_pos2&page=1, accessed March 8, 2021.

40. David Stodder, "ERP and Cloud Computing: Delivering a Virtual Feast," Information Week, May 20, 2010, https://www.informationweek.com/news/software/bi/224701329, accessed December 6, 2011.

41. M. Bitner, "Servicescapes: The Impact of Physical Surroundings on Customers and Employees," *Journal of Marketing*, April 1992: 57–71.

42. Press Release, "Taco Bell New Urban Restaurant Concept Redefines Fast Food Experience," Taco Bell, September 15, 2015, https://www.tacobell.com/news/taco-bell-new-urban-restaurant-concept-redefines-fast-food-experience, accessed February 17, 2017; J. Jargon, "Taco Bell to Open Upscale 'Cantina' Restaurants," *The Wall Street Journal*, September 15, 2015, https://www.wsj.com/articles/taco-bell-to-open-upscale-cantina-restaurants-1442330973, accessed February 17, 2017.

43. Khouri, "Chalupas and Beer? Taco Bell to Serve Alcohol at New Cantina Restaurants," *The Los Angeles Times*, September 15, 2015, https://www.latimes.com/business/la-fi-taco-bell-cantinas-20150915-story.html, accessed February 16, 2017.

44. A. Loten, "Calling All Robots: Businesses Automate the Battle Against Coronavirus," *The Wall Street Journal*, April 6, 2020, https://www.wsj.com/articles/calling-all-robots-businesses-automate-the-battle-against-coronavirus-11586170801, accessed March 8, 2021.

45. E. Demaitre, "White Castle to Expand Deployment of Miso's Flippy ROAR to 10 Sites," *The Robot Report*, October 27, 2020, https://www.therobotreport.com/white-castle-expand-deployment-miso-robotics-flippy-roar-10-sites/, accessed March 9, 2021.

46. Ibid.

47. "Sally the Robot: The First Fresh Food Robot," Chowbotics, https://www.chowbotics.com/our-solutions/, accessed March 9, 2021; D.-A. Durbin & T. Chea (Associated Press), "Demand for Robot Cooks Rises as Kitchens Combat COVID-19," *CTV News*, July 15, 2020, https://www.ctvnews.ca/sci-tech/demand-for-robot-cooks-rises-as-kitchens-combat-covid-19-1.5023490, accessed March 9, 2021; R. Wilmer, "Chowbotics Is Now Part of the DoorDash Team," Chowbotics, February 8, 2021, https://www.chowbotics.com/chowbotics-is-now-part-of-the-doordash-team/, accessed March 9, 2021.

48. T. Bradshaw, "Chip Shortage Threatens PlayStation 5 Supply as Demand Races Ahead," *Financial Times*, February 23, 2021, https://www.ft.com/content/f7c089dc-515e-4387-82fd-ea0a49998650, accessed March 11, 2021; M. Colias, "Ford Expected to Slash Vehicle Production over Chip Shortage," *The Wall Street Journal*, February 4, 2021, https://www.wsj.com/articles/fords-2021-to-do-list-is-topped-by-fixing-quality-problems-11612450536, accessed March 11, 2021; J. Ewing & D. Clark, "Lack of Tiny Parts Disrupts Auto Factories Worldwide," *The New York Times*, January 13, 2021, https://www.nytimes.com/2021/01/13/business/auto-factories-semiconductor-chips.html, accessed March 11, 2021; A. Fitch & E. Koh, "Chips Are in Hot Demand—And That's a Problem," *The Wall Street Journal*, January 14, 2021, https://www.wsj.com/articles/chips-are-in-hot-demandand-thats-a-problem-11610630859, accessed March 11, 2021; C. Rogers, "Chip Shortage Hits General Motors, Leads to Production Cuts," *The Wall Street Journal*, February 3, 2021, https://www.wsj.com/articles/chip-shortage-hits-general-motors-leads-to-production-cuts-11612382359, accessed March 11, 2021; M. Wayland, "How Covid Led to a $60 Billion Global Chip Shortage for Automakers," *CNBC*, February 11, 2020, https://www.cnbc.com/2021/02/11/how-covid-led-to-a-60-billion-global-chip-shortage-for-automakers.html, accessed March 11, 2021; D. Wu, V. Aavov & T. Mochizuki, "Chip Shortage Spirals Beyond Cars To Phones And Game Consoles," *Bloomberg Quint*, February 9, 2021, https://www.bloombergquint.com/global-economics/chip-shortage-spirals-beyond-cars-to-phones-and-game-consoles, accessed March 11, 2021.

49. N. Roesler, "Inside the Pizza Market's Continued Growth," *Food Business News*, April 10, 2020, https://www.foodbusinessnews.net/articles/15801-inside-the-pizza-markets-continued-growth, accessed March 9, 2021.

50. P. Lukas, "The Great Pepperoni Debate: Should It Lie Flat on Your Pizza Or Curl Up?" *The Wall Street Journal*, March 12, 2019, https://www.wsj.com/articles/the-great-pepperoni-debate-should-it-lay-flat-on-your-pizza-or-curl-up-11552410779, accessed March 9, 2021.

51. Ibid.

52. S. Chaudhuri, "At IKEA, Ensuring 'Quality as an Enabler of Lower Cost'—Corporate Intelligence," *The Wall Street Journal*, June 17, 2015, https://blogs.wsj.com/corporate-intelligence/2015/06/17/at-ikea-ensuring-quality-as-an-enabler-of-lower-cost/, accessed February 17, 2017.

53. Ibid.

54. K, Simon, "How Mistake Proof Are Your Processes?" iSixSigma, https://www.isixsigma.com/tools-templates/poka-yoke/how-mistake-proof-are-your-processes/, accessed February 17, 2017; M. Hendricks, "Make No Mistake," *Entrepreneur Magazine*, October 1996, https://www.entrepreneur.com/magazine/entrepreneur/1996/october/13430.html, accessed February 17, 2017.

55. A. Gale & T. Mochizuki, "Robot Hotel Loses Love for Robots," *The Wall Street Journal*, January 14, 2019, https://www.wsj.com/articles/robot-hotel-loses-love-for-robots-11547484628, accessed March 12, 2021; E. Hertzfeld, "Japan's Henn na Hotel Fires Half Its Robot Workforce," *Hotel Management*, January 31, 2019, https://www.hotelmanagement.net/tech/japan-s-henn-na-hotel-fires-half-its-robot-workforce, accessed March 12, 2021; D. Kikuchi, "'Strange' Hotel, Run by Robots, Opens Near Tokyo; More to Come," *Japan Times*, March 15, 2017, https://www.japantimes.co.jp/news/2017/03/15/business/strange-hotel-run-by-robots-opens-near-tokyo-more-to-come/, accessed March 11, 2021; B. Yeong, "I Stayed In Japan's Robot Hotel And Got A Glimpse Of Our Possible Future In 10 Years," *The Smart Local – Singapore*, October 8, 2019, https://thesmartlocal.com/read/robot-hotel-japan/, accessed March 12, 2021; G. Zarkadakis, R. Jesuthasan & T. Malcolm, "The 3 Ways Work Can Be Automated," *Harvard Business Review*, October 13, 2016, https://hbr.org/2016/10/the-3-ways-work-can-be-automated, accessed March 11, 2021.

56. Source: "Baldrige Criteria Commentary: Baldrige Criteria for Performance Excellence Categories and Items," Baldrige Performance Excellence Program, November 15, 2019, https://www.nist.gov/baldrige/baldrige-criteria-commentary, accessed March 9, 2021.

57. "Baldrige Award Process Fees," National Institute of Standards and Technology, November 15, 2019, https://www.nist.gov/baldrige/baldrige-award/award-process-fees, accessed March 9, 2021; C. Williams, "Managing Service and Manufacturing Operations," (Chapter 18), in *MGMT* (Boston, MA: Cengage, 2021).

58. "ISO - About Us," International Organization for Standardization, https://www.iso.org/about-us.html, accessed March 9, 2021; "ISO in Figures, 2020," International Organization for Standardization, https://www.iso.org/files/live/sites/isoorg/files/about%20ISO/iso_in_figures/docs/ISO-in-Figures_2020.pdf, accessed March 9, 2021.

59. "ISO in Brief: Great Things Happen When the World Agrees," International Organization for Standardization, https://www.iso.org/files/live/sites/isoorg/files/store/en/PUB100007.pdf, accessed March 9, 2021.

60. "ISO Standards," ISO, https://www.iso.org/iso/home/standards.htm, accessed February 17, 2017.

61. "ISO 9000 family — Quality Management," International Organization for Standardization, https://www.iso.org/iso-9001-quality-management.html, accessed March 9, 2021.

62. "Managing Service and Manufacturing Operations," (Chapter 18), in *MGMT*.

63. "ISO 9001: Debunking the Myths," International Organization for Standardization, https://www.iso.org/files/live/sites/isoorg/files/store/en/PUB100368.pdf, accessed March 9, 2021.

64. B. Browne, "How Savile Row Is Planning for Life After Covid-19," *Robb Report*, May 14, 2020, https://robbreport.com/style/fashion/how-savile-row-is-planning-for-life-after-covid-2921040/, accessed March 12, 2021; K. Dunn, "London's Savile Row Exported Bespoke British Suits to the 1%. Can It Survive in a Socially Distanced World?" *Fortune*, May 30, 2020, https://fortune.com/2020/05/30/london-savile-row-british-suits-reopen-coronavirus-covid-19-pandemic/, accessed March 12, 2021; C. Hyde, R. Bostick & K. Leinz, "Pierre Lagrange on Innovation in Tailoring," *Bloomberg*, December 18, 2020, https://www.bloomberg.com/news/videos/2020-12-18/pierre-lagrange-on-innovation-in-tailoring-video?sref=xXo7CWym, accessed March 12, 2021; D. Segal, "To Survive the Pandemic, Savile Row Cuts a Bespoke Strategy," *The New York Times*, November 15, 2020, https://www.nytimes.com/2020/11/15/business/savile-row-covid.html, accessed March 12, 2021.

65. "At Vuitton, Growth in Small Batches—Luxury-Goods Maker's New French Factory Adds to Capacity but Sticks to Strategy of Tight Rein," *The Wall Street Journal*, June 27, 2011, p. B1.

66. P. Kowsmann, "Fast Fashion: How a Zara Coat Went From Design to Fifth Avenue in 25 Days," *The Wall Street Journal*, December 6, 2016, https://www.wsj.com/articles/fast-fashion-how-a-zara-coat-went-from-design-to-fifth-avenue-in-25-days-1481080981, accessed February 17, 2017.

67. N. Naughton & A. Hufford, "Why You Might Have Trouble Getting the Refrigerator, Can of Paint or Car You Want," *The Wall Street Journal*, October 25, 2020, https://www.wsj.com/articles/factories-rush-to-keep-up-with-post-lockdown-shopping-11603627201, accessed March 9, 2021; J. Wieczner, "How The Toilet Paper Sales Surge Exposed U.S. Supply Chain Weaknesses Amid Coronavirus Pandemic," *Fortune*, May 18, 2020, https://fortune.com/2020/05/18/toilet-paper-sales-surge

-shortage-coronavirus-pandemic-supply-chain
-cpg-panic-buying/, accessed March 9, 2021.

68. S. Terlep & A. Gasparro, "Why Are There Still Not Enough Paper Towels?" *The Wall Street Journal*, August 21, 2020, https://www.wsj.com/articles/why-arent-there-enough-paper-towels-11598020793, accessed March 9, 2021.

69. A. Kleckler, "People Counting Technology Beyond COVID-19," *Progressive Grocer*, May 4, 2020, https://progressivegrocer.com/people-counting-technology-beyond-covid-19, accessed March 10, 2021.

70. A. Coolidge, "New Technology Helps Kroger Speed Up Checkout Times," *USA Today*, June 20, 2013, https://www.usatoday.com/story/money/business/2013/06/20/new-technology-helps-kroger-speed-up-checkout-times/2443975/, accessed April 1, 2014.

71. J. Wells, "Kroger Will Use Checkout Technology to Limit Customer Traffic," *Grocery Dive*, April 7, 2020, https://www.grocerydive.com/news/kroger-will-use-checkout-technology-to-limit-customer-traffic/575578/, accessed March 10, 2021.

72. A. Marsh & D. Hipwell, "Sainsbury to Spend $1.3 Billion on 2040 Net Zero Carbon Target," *Bloomberg*, January 27, 2020, https://www.bloomberg.com/news/articles/2020-01-28/sainsbury-to-spend-1-3-billion-on-2040-net-zero-carbon-target?sref=xXo7CWym, accessed March 10, 2021.

73. "Sustainability Initiatives Cut Costs 6–10%," Environmental Leader, https://www.environmentalleader.com/2009/06/09/sustainability-initiatives-cut-costs-by-6-10/, accessed April 6, 2013.

74. "ISO 14000—Environmental Management," ISO, https://www.iso.org/iso/home/standards/management-standards/iso14000.htm, accessed April 17, 2015.

# Personal Finance Appendix

1. "Infographic: Financial Capability in the United States 2016, from the National Financial Capability Study," FINRA Investor Education Foundation, www.usfinancialcapability.org/downloads/2015_Study_Infographic.pdf, accessed February 24, 2017.

2. "The State of U.S. Financial Capability: The 2018 National Financial Capability Study," FINRA Investor Education Foundation, June 2019, https://www.usfinancialcapability.org/downloads/NFCS_2018_Report_Natl_Findings.pdf, accessed March 13, 2021.

3. "Stress in America: Part 1," American Psychological Association, February 15, 2017, www.apa.org/news/press/releases/stress/2016/coping-with-change.pdf, accessed February 24, 2017.

4. "The State of U.S. Financial Capability: The 2018 National Financial Capability Study," FINRA Investor Education Foundation.

5. J. Berman, "Where Millennials Go for Financial Advice," *Wall Street Journal*, December 14, 2015, R8; A. Tugend, "A Smarter App Is Watching Your Wallet," *New York Times*, March 9, 2021, https://www.nytimes.com/2021/03/09/business/apps-personal-finance-budget.html, accessed March 14, 2021.

6. "Digit," Digit.co, https://digit.co/, accessed March 14, 2021.

7. J. Duffy, "The Best Personal Finance Services of 2017," *PC Mag*, January 10, 2017, http://www.pcmag.com/article2/0,2817,2407617,00.asp, accessed February 24, 2017.

8. C. Kornelis, "The Biggest Ways People Waste Money," *The Wall Street Journal*, June 14, 2019, https://www.wsj.com/articles/the-biggest-ways-people-waste-money-11560523181, accessed March 16, 2021.

9. Ibid.

10. E. O'Neill, "The 8 Best Water Bottles," Reviews by Wirecutter, March 27, 2020, https://www.nytimes.com/wirecutter/reviews/best-water-bottle/, accessed March 16, 2021.

11. D. Bach, *The Automatic Millionaire*, Broadway Books (New York): 2004.

12. "Gain Total Control of Your Money," YNAB, https://www.learnvest.com/wp-content/uploads/2016/12/LearnVest-Financial-Plan-Sample-Only.pdf, accessed February 24, 2017.

13. T. Siegel Bernard, "Spending Is as Easy as Pushing a Button. The Hard Part? Keeping Track," *New York Times*, March 13, 2019, https://www.nytimes.com/2019/03/13/technology/personaltech/spending-is-as-easy-as-pushing-a-button-the-hard-part-keeping-track.html, accessed March 16, 2021.

14. "Features," Simpifi, https://simplifimoney.com/features, accessed March 16, 2021.

15. T. Tepper, "The Best Budgeting Apps and Tools for 2021," Reviews by Wirecutter, July 29, 2020, https://www.nytimes.com/wirecutter/reviews/best-budgeting-apps-and-tools/#our-pick-you-need-a-budget, accessed March 16, 2021.

16. S. Matz, J. Gladstone & D. Stillwell, "Money Buys Happiness When Spending Fits Our Personality," *Psychological Science*, v. 27 no. 5 (2016): 715–725.

17. K. Newman, "How Spending Influences Happiness," *Greater Good*, June 6, 2016, http://greatergood.berkeley.edu/article/item/how_spending_influences_happiness, accessed February 24, 2017.

18. M. Cheng, "Be Prepared for the Unexpected: The Best Financial Advice I Ever Got," *The Wall Street Journal*, June 16, 2019, https://www.wsj.com/articles/the-best-financial-advice-i-ever-got-11560737220?mod=djemwhatsnews, accessed March 17, 2021.

19. "Hardships, Early Withdrawals and Loans," Internal Revenue Service, May 26, 2016, https://www.irs.gov/retirement-plans/hardships-early-withdrawals-and-loans, accessed February 24, 2017.

20. "Early Withdrawals from Retirement Plans | Internal Revenue Service," Internal Revenue Service, September 24, 2020, https://www.irs.gov/newsroom/early-withdrawals-from-retirement-plans, accessed March 18, 2021.

21. FDIC, "What's Covered," https://www.fdic.gov/deposit/covered/, accessed February 24, 2017; FDIC, "How Are My Deposit Accounts Insured by the FDIC?," https://www.fdic.gov/deposit/covered/categories.html, accessed February 24, 2017.

22. "What is a Credit Score?" *myFICO*, https://www.myfico.com/credit-education/credit-scores, accessed March 17, 2021.

23. "What's In Your FICO Scores?," *myFICO*, https://www.myfico.com/credit-education/whats-in-your-credit-score, accessed March 17, 2021; P. Curry, "How Credit Scores Work, How a Score Is Calculated," Bankrate.com, http://www.bankrate.com/brm/news/credit-scoring/20031104a1.asp, accessed February 24, 2017.

24. E. Dornhelm, "Average U.S. FICO Score at 711, But Uncertainty Abounds," *FICO*, October 19, 2020, https://www.fico.com/blogs/average-us-fico-score-711-uncertainty-abounds, accessed March 17, 2021.

25. "About Credit Scores," Money-Zine.com, http://www.money-zine.com/financial-planning/debt-consolidation/about-credit-scores/, accessed February 24, 2017.

26. "Get the Score Lenders Use to Evaluate Your Home Mortgage Loan," *myFICO*, https://www.myfico.com/loancenter/mortgage/step1/getthescores.aspx, accessed March 17, 2021.

27. L. Irby, "Credit Card Grace Period Explained," *theBalance*, March 25, 2020, https://www.thebalance.com/credit-card-grace-period-explained-960699, accessed March 17, 2021.

28. L. Irby, "Late Fees on Credit Cards," *theBalance*, February 9, 2021, https://www.thebalance.com/what-is-a-late-fee-960701, accessed March 17, 2021.

29. "The Equal Credit Opportunity Act," U.S. Department of Justice, July 22, 2020, https://www.justice.gov/crt/equal-credit-opportunity-act-3, accessed March 17, 2021; "CFPB Clarifies That Discrimination by Lenders on the Basis of Sexual Orientation and Gender Identity Is Illegal," Consumer Financial Protection Bureau, March 5, 2021, https://www.consumerfinance.gov/about-us/newsroom/cfpb-clarifies-discrimination-by-lenders-on-basis-of-sexual-orientation-and-gender-identity-is-illegal/, accessed March 17, 2021.

30. L. Irby, "Know Your Rights under the Credit Card Act," *theBalance*, February 5, 2020, https://www.thebalance.com/credit-card-accountability-responsibility-disclosure-act-2009-4061197#citation-2, accessed March 18, 2021.

31. "An Overview of the Regulation Z Rules Implementing the CARD Act - Consumer Compliance Outlook: First Quarter 2010 - Philadelphia Fed," Consumer Compliance Outlook (U.S. Federal Reserve System), First Quarter 2010, https://consumercomplianceoutlook.org/2010/first-quarter/regulation-z-rules/, accessed March 18, 2021; C. Prater, "12 Consumer Protections in the Credit CARD Act," CreditCards.com, January 28, 2016, http://www.creditcards.com/credit-card-news/help/card-act-12-consumer-protections-6000.php, accessed February 24, 2017.

32. "We're On Your Side," Consumer Financial Protection Bureau, https://www.consumerfinance.gov/, accessed February 24, 2017.

33. "My Credit Application Was Denied Because of My Credit Report. What Can I Do?," Consumer Financial Protection Bureau, June 8, 2017, https://www.consumerfinance.gov/ask-cfpb/my-credit-application-was-denied-because-of-my-credit-report-what-can-i-do-en-1253/, accessed March 18, 2021.

34. "How Do I Get a Copy of My Credit Reports?" Consumer Financial Protection Bureau, March 29, 2019, https://www.consumerfinance.gov/ask-cfpb/how-do-i-get-a-copy-of-my-credit-reports-en-5/, accessed March 18, 2021.

35. A. Carrns, "A Little Nagging Can Help Reduce Credit Card Debt," *The New York Times*, September 9, 2016, https://www.nytimes.com/2016/09/10/your-money/a-little-nagging-can-help-reduce-credit-card-debt.html, accessed February 24, 2017.

36. J. Pinsker, "To Cut My Spending, I Used Behavioral Economics on Myself," *The Atlantic*, September 7, 2018, https://www.theatlantic.com/family/archive/2018/09/spending-personal-finance-pain-of-paying/569575/, accessed March 18, 2021.

37. T. Tepper, "3 Ways to Retrain Your Mind to Get Out of Credit Card Debt," *The New York Times*, January 15, 2021, https://www.nytimes.com/2020/02/12/smarter-living/how-to-get-out-of-credit-card-debt.html, accessed March 18, 2021.

38. E. Harris, "In Their 20s and Saving for Retirement: How It Started, How It's Going," *The New York Times*, November 27, 2020, https://www.nytimes.com/2020/11/27/business/millennials-retirement-saving.html, accessed March 18, 2021.

39. Ibid.

40. A. Damodaran, "Annual Returns on Stock, Bonds and T. Bills: 1928–2020," Stern School of Business, New York University, January 1, 2021, http://www.stern.nyu.edu/~adamodar/pc/datasets/histretSP.xls, accessed March 19, 2021; P. Lach, "What's the 'Long Run' for Investing? Longer Than You Think," *The Wall Street Journal*, February 15, 2017, http://blogs.wsj.com/experts/2017/02/15/whats-the-long-run-for-investing-longer-than-you-think/, accessed February 25, 2017.

41. M. DiLallo, "Dividend Reinvestment," *The Motley Fool*, October 12, 2020, https://www.fool.com/investing/stock-market/types-of-stocks/dividend-stocks/dividend-reinvestment/, accessed March 18, 2021.

42. J. Hill & M. Reyes, "Bond Defaults Deliver 99% Losses in New Era of U.S. Bankruptcies," *Bloomberg*, October 26, 2020, https://www.bloomberg.com/news/articles/2020-10-26/bond-defaults-deliver-99-losses-in-new-era-of-u-s-bankruptcies?sref=xXo7CWym, accessed February 10, 2021.

43. A. Lee and J. Hook, "Fresh Downgrade Threat to U.S. Debt," *The Wall Street Journal,* June 9, 2011, http://online.wsj.com/article/SB10001424052702304778304576373992711772366.html, accessed April 21, 2013.

44. "11 Best Investment Apps of 2021," *NerdWallet*, March 8, 2021, https://www.nerdwallet.com/best/investing/investment-apps, accessed March 18, 2021.

45. "11 Best Online Stock Brokers for Beginners of March 2021," *NerdWallet*, March 9, 2021, https://www.nerdwallet.com/best/investing/online-brokers-for-beginners?trk=nw_gn_5.0, accessed March 18, 2021.

46. M. Frankel, "Vanguard 2021 update Review: Pros, Cons, and More," *The Ascent by Motley Fool,* January 14, 2021, https://www.fool.com/the-ascent/buying-stocks/vanguard-brokerage-review/, accessed February 12, 2021.

47. "E°TRADE Fees and Rates | Pricing for Investing & Trading," E°TRADE, https://us.etrade.com/what-we-offer/pricing-and-rates, accessed February 12, 2021.

48. J. F. Podovin, "Can Robo Advisers Replace Human Financial Advisers?," *The Wall Street Journal*, February 28, 2016, http://www.wsj.com/articles/can-robo-advisers-replace-human-financial-advisers-1456715553, accessed April 6, 2016; P. Sullivan, "The Computer as a Financial Planner," *The New York Times*, June 20, 2015, B5; Robert Powell, "Behavioral Economist Richard Thaler on the Key to Retirement Savings," *The Wall Street Journal*, November 29, 2015, http://www.wsj.com/articles/behavioral-economist-richard-thaler-on-the-key-to-retirement-savings-1448852602, accessed March 22, 2016; "SmartDeposit: Auto-Deposit, But Smarter," *Betterment*, https://www.betterment.com/resources/inside-betterment/product-news/smartdeposit-auto-deposit-but-smarter/, accessed April 5, 2016.

49. B. Walsh, Jr., "15 Personal-Finance Lessons We Can All Learn from the Year of COVID-19: You Should Have a Three-Bucket Strategy," *The Wall Street Journal*, January 24, 2021, https://www.wsj.com/articles/15-personal-finance-lessons-we-can-all-learn-from-the-year-of-covid-19-11611493201, accessed March 18, 2021.

50. "Table 5. Quartiles and Selected Deciles of Usual Weekly Earnings of Full-Time Wage and Salary Workers by Selected Characteristics, Fourth Quarter 2020 Averages, Not Seasonally Adjusted," Economic News Release, Bureau of Labor Statistics, January 21, 2021, http://www.bls.gov/news.release/wkyeng.t05.htm, accessed March 18, 2021.

51. "Table A-4. Employment Status of the Civilian Population 25 Years and Over by Educational Attainment," Economic News Release, Bureau of Labor Statistics, March 5, 2021, http://www.bls.gov/news.release/empsit.t04.htm/, accessed March 18, 2021.

52. M. Kirchner, "Venmo Doesn't Make People Jerks," *New York Magazine*, May 23, 2016, http://nymag.com/selectall/2016/05/its-not-venmos-fault-if-your-friends-are-jerks.html, accessed February 25, 2017; K. Paul, "Venmo is Turning Our Friends into Petty Jerks," *Quartz*, May 19, 2016, https://qz.com/687395/venmo-is-turning-our-friends-into-petty-jerks/, accessed February 25, 2017; S. Pizzi, "Technology Is Changing Student Spending," *Villanovan*, February 27, 2017, http://www.villanovan.com/news/view.php/1027533/Technology-is-changing-student-spending, accessed February 25, 2017.

53. "Retirement Topics - IRA Contribution Limits," Internal Revenue Service, December 15, 2020, https://www.irs.gov/retirement-plans/plan-participant-employee/retirement-topics-ira-contribution-limits, accessed March 18, 2021.

54. "Retirement Topics - 401(k) and Profit-Sharing Plan Contribution Limits," Internal Revenue Service, November 10, 2020, https://www.irs.gov/retirement-plans/plan-participant-employee/retirement-topics-401k-and-profit-sharing-plan-contribution-limits, accessed March 18, 2021.

55. B. Chen, "Up to 91% More Expensive: How Delivery Apps Eat Up Your Budget," *The New York Times*, February 26, 2020, https://www.nytimes.com/2020/02/26/technology/personaltech/ubereats-doordash-postmates-grubhub-review.html, accessed March 19, 2021; J. Dillian, "Opinion: The Road to Riches Is This Simple: Drive a Crappy Car," *MarketWatch*, June 21, 2019, https://www.marketwatch.com/story/the-road-to-riches-is-this-simple-drive-a-crappy-car-2019-06-21, accessed March 18, 2021; T. Louderback, "Ramit Sethi's Best Money Advice Isn't Mystery or Magic—It's Math," *Business Insider*, May 25, 2019, https://www.businessinsider.com/personal-finance/best-money-advice-automate-your-money-2019-5, accessed March 19, 2021; S. Maheshwari, "They See It. They Like It. They Want It. They Rent It," *The New York Times*, June 8, 2019, https://www.nytimes.com/2019/06/08/style/rent-subscription-clothing-furniture.html, accessed March 19, 2021.

# Glossary

## 401(k), 403(b), and 457 plans
Employee payroll-deduction retirement plans that offer tax benefits.

## absolute advantage
The benefit a country has in a given industry when it can produce more of a product than other nations using the same amount of resources.

## accounting
A system for recognizing, organizing, analyzing, and reporting information about the financial transactions that affect an organization.

## accounting equation
Assets = Liabilities + Owners' Equity

## accredited investor
An organization or individual investor who meets certain criteria established by the SEC and so qualifies to invest in unregistered securities.

## accrual-basis accounting
The method of accounting that recognizes revenue when it is earned and matches expenses to the revenues they helped produce.

## acquisition
A corporate restructuring in which one firm buys another.

## active listening
Attentive listening that occurs when the listener focuses their complete attention on the speaker.

## active voice
Sentence construction in which the subject performs the action expressed by the verb (e.g., The accountant did the taxes.). The active voice works better for the vast majority of business communication.

## activity-based costing (ABC)
A technique to assign product costs based on links between activities that drive costs and the production of specific products.

## administrative law
Laws that arise from regulations established by government agencies.

## advertising
Paid, nonpersonal communication, designed to influence a target audience with regard to a product, service, organization, or idea.

## affirmative action
Policies meant to increase employment and educational opportunities for historically marginalized groups—especially groups defined by race, ethnicity, or gender.

## agent
A party who agrees to represent another party, called the principal.

## agents/brokers
Independent distributors who do not take title of the goods they distribute (even though they may take physical possession on a temporary basis before distribution).

## angel investors
Individuals who invest in start-up companies with high growth potential in exchange for a share of ownership.

## annual percentage rate (APR)
The interest expense charged on a credit card, expressed as an annual percentage.

## applications software
Software that helps a user perform a desired task.

## apprenticeships
Structured training programs that mandate that each beginner serve as an assistant to a fully trained worker before gaining full credentials to work in the field.

## arbitration
A process in which a neutral third party has the authority to resolve a dispute by rendering a binding decision.

## articles of incorporation
The document filed with a state government to establish the existence of a new corporation.

## asset management ratios
Financial ratios that measure how effectively a firm is using its assets to generate revenues or cash.

## assets
Resources owned by a firm.

## autocratic leaders
Leaders who hoard decision-making power for themselves and typically issue orders without consulting their followers.

## automation
Replacing human operation and control of machinery and equipment with some form of programmed control.

## balance of payments
A measure of the total flow of money into or out of a country.

## balance of payments deficit
Shortfall that occurs when more money flows out of a nation than into that nation.

## balance of payments surplus
Overage that occurs when more money flows into a nation than out of that nation.

## balance of trade
A basic measure of the difference in value between a nation's exports and imports, including both goods and services.

## balance sheet
A financial statement that reports the financial position of a firm by identifying and reporting the value of the firm's assets, liabilities, and owners' equity.

## Baldrige National Quality Program
A national program to encourage American firms to focus on quality improvement.

## Banking Act of 1933
The law that established the Federal Deposit Insurance Corporation (FDIC) to insure bank deposits. It also prohibited commercial banks from selling insurance or acting as investment banks.

## behavioral segmentation
Dividing the market based on how people behave toward various products. This category includes both the benefits that consumers seek from products and how consumers use the products.

## benefits
Noncash compensation, including programs such as health insurance, vacation, and childcare.

## bias
A preconception about members of a particular group. Common forms of bias include gender bias; age bias; and race, ethnicity, or nationality bias.

## board of directors
The individuals who are elected by stockholders of a corporation to represent their interests.

## bond
A formal debt instrument issued by a corporation or government entity.

## boycott
A tactic in which a union and its supporters and sympathizers refuse to do business with an employer with which they have a labor dispute.

## brand
A product's identity—including product name, symbol, design, reputation, and image—that sets it apart from other players in the same category.

## brand equity
The overall value of a brand to an organization.

## brand extension
A new product, in a new category, introduced under an existing brand name.

## breach of contract
The failure of one party to a contract to perform their contractual obligations.

## breakeven analysis
The process of determining the number of units a firm must sell to cover all costs.

## broadband internet connection
An internet connection that is capable of transmitting large amounts of information very quickly.

## budget (personal)
A detailed forecast of financial inflows (income) and outflows (expenses) to determine your net inflow or outflow for a given period of time.

## budget deficit
Shortfall that occurs when expenses are higher than revenue over a given period of time.

## budget surplus
Overage that occurs when revenue is higher than expenses over a given period of time.

## budgeted balance sheet
A projected financial statement that forecasts the types and amounts of assets a firm will need to implement its future plans and how the firm will finance those assets. (Also called a pro forma balance sheet.)

## budgeted income statement
A projection showing how a firm's budgeted sales and costs will affect expected net income. (Also called a pro forma income statement.)

## budgeting
A management tool that explicitly shows how a firm will acquire and use the resources needed to achieve its goals over a specific time period.

**business**

Any organization or activity that provides goods and services in an effort to earn a profit.

**business buyer behavior**

Describes how people act when they are buying products to use either directly or indirectly to produce other products.

**business cycle**

The periodic contraction and expansion that occur over time in virtually every economy.

**business environment**

The setting in which business operates. The five key components are economic environment, competitive environment, technological environment, social environment, and global environment.

**business ethics**

The application of right and wrong, good and bad, in a business setting.

**business format franchise**

A broad franchise agreement in which the franchisee pays for the right to use the name, trademark, and business and production methods of the franchisor.

**business intelligence system**

A sophisticated form of decision support system that helps decision makers discover information that was previously hidden.

**business law**

The application of laws and legal principles to business relationships and transactions.

**business marketers (also known as business-to-business or B2B)**

Marketers who direct their efforts toward people who are buying products to use either directly or indirectly to produce other products.

**business plan**

A formal document that describes a business concept, outlines core business objectives, and details strategies and timelines for achieving those objectives.

**business products**

Products purchased to use either directly or indirectly in the production of other products.

**business technology**

Any tools—especially computers, telecommunications, and other digital products—that businesses can use to become more efficient and effective.

**business-to-business (B2B) e-commerce**

E-commerce in markets where businesses buy from and sell to other businesses.

**business-to-consumer (B2C) e-commerce**

E-commerce in which businesses and final consumers interact.

**buzz marketing**

The active stimulation of word of mouth via unconventional, and often relatively low-cost, tactics. Other terms for buzz marketing are "guerrilla marketing" and "viral marketing."

**C corporation**

The most common type of corporation, which is a legal business entity that offers limited liability to all of its owners, who are called stockholders.

**cafeteria-style benefits**

An approach to employee benefits that gives all employees a set dollar amount that they must spend on company benefits, allocated however they wish within broad limitations.

**cannibalization**

When a producer offers a new product that takes sales away from its existing products.

**capital budgeting**

The process a firm uses to evaluate long-term investment proposals.

**capital gain**

The return on an asset that results when its market price rises above the price the investor paid for it.

**capital structure**

The mix of equity and debt financing a firm uses to meet its permanent financing needs.

**capitalism**

An economic system—also known as the private enterprise or free market system—based on private ownership, economic freedom, and fair competition.

**carbon footprint**

Refers to the amount of harmful greenhouse gases that a firm emits throughout its operations, both directly and indirectly.

**case law (also called common law)**

Laws that result from rulings, called precedents, made by judges who initially hear a particular type of case.

**cash budget**

A detailed forecast of future cash flows that helps financial managers identify when their firm is likely to experience temporary shortages or surpluses of cash.

**cash equivalents**

Safe and highly liquid assets that many firms list with their cash holdings on their balance sheet.

**cause-related marketing**

Marketing partnerships between businesses and nonprofit organizations, designed to spike sales for the company and raise money for the nonprofit.

**certificate of deposit (CD)**

An interest-earning deposit that requires the funds to remain deposited for a fixed term. Withdrawal of the funds before the term expires results in a financial penalty.

**channel intermediaries**

Distribution organizations that facilitate the movement of products from the producer to the consumer.

**channel of distribution**

The network of organizations and processes that links producers to consumers.

**Chapter 11 bankruptcy**

A form of bankruptcy used by corporations and individuals that allows the debtor to reorganize operations under a court-approved plan.

**Chapter 13 bankruptcy**

A form of bankruptcy that allows individual debtors to set up a repayment plan to adjust their debts.

**Chapter 7 bankruptcy**

A form of bankruptcy that discharges a debtor's debts by liquidating assets and using the proceeds to pay off creditors.

**Civil Rights Act of 1964**

Federal legislation that prohibits discrimination in hiring, firing, compensation, apprenticeships, training, terms, conditions, or privileges of employment based on race, color, religion, sex, or national origin.

**closed shop**

An employment arrangement in which the employer agrees to hire only workers who already belong to the union.

**cloud computing**

The use of internet-based storage capacity, processing power, and computer applications to supplement or replace internally owned information technology resources.

**cobranding**

When established brands from different companies join forces to market the same product.

**code of ethics**

A formal, written document that defines the ethical standards of an organization and gives employees the information they need to make ethical decisions across a range of situations.

**cognitive dissonance**

Consumer discomfort with a purchase decision, typically for a higher-priced item.

**collective bargaining**

The process by which representatives of union members and employers attempt to negotiate a mutually acceptable labor agreement.

**commercial banks**

Privately owned financial institutions that accept demand deposits and make loans and provide other services for the public.

**commercial paper**

Short-term (and usually unsecured) promissory notes issued by large corporations.

**common market**

A group of countries that have eliminated tariffs and harmonized trading rules to facilitate the free flow of goods among the member nations.

**common stock**

The basic form of ownership in a corporation.

**communication**

The transmission of information between a sender and a recipient.

**communication barriers**

Obstacles to effective communication, typically defined in terms of physical, language, body language, cultural, perceptual, and organizational barriers.

**communication channels**

The various ways in which a message can be sent, ranging from one-on-one in-person meetings to internet message boards.

**communism**

An economic and political system that calls for public ownership of virtually all enterprises, under the direction of a strong central government.

**company matching**

An amount contributed by the employer to an employee's retirement account, matching the employee's retirement contributions either dollar-for-dollar or based on a percentage of each dollar contributed by the employee.

**comparative advantage**

The benefit a country has in a given industry if it can make products at a lower opportunity cost than other countries.

**compensation**

The combination of pay and benefits that employees receive in exchange for their work.

**compensatory damages**

Monetary payments that a party who breaches a contract is ordered to pay in order to compensate the injured party for the actual harm suffered by the breach of contract.

**compressed workweek**

A version of flextime scheduling that allows employees to work a full-time number of hours in less than the standard workweek.

**computer virus**

Computer software that can be spread from one computer to another without the knowledge or permission of the computer users by attaching itself to emails or other files.

**computer-aided design (CAD)**

Drawing and drafting software that enables users to create and edit blueprints and design drawings quickly and easily.

**computer-aided design/computer-aided manufacturing (CAD/CAM)**

A combination of software that can be used to design output and send instructions to automated equipment to perform the steps needed to produce this output.

**computer-aided engineering (CAE)**

Software that enables users to test, analyze, and optimize their designs.

**computer-aided manufacturing (CAM)**

Software that takes the electronic design for a product and creates the programmed instructions that robots must follow to produce that product as efficiently as possible.

**computer-integrated manufacturing (CIM)**

A combination of CAD/CAM software with flexible manufacturing systems to automate almost all steps involved in designing, testing, and producing a product.

**conceptual skills**

The ability to grasp a big-picture view of the overall organization, the relationships among its various parts, and its fit in the broader competitive environment.

**conglomerate merger**

A combination of two firms that are in unrelated industries.

**consideration**

Something of value that one party gives another as part of a contractual agreement.

**constitution**

A code that establishes the fundamental rules and principles that govern a particular organization or entity.

**consumer behavior**

Description of how people act when they are buying, using, and discarding goods and services for their own personal consumption. Consumer behavior also explores the reasons behind people's actions.

**consumer marketers (also known as business-to-consumer or B2C)**

Marketers who direct their efforts toward people who are buying products for personal consumption.

**consumer price index (CPI)**

A measure of inflation that evaluates the change in the weighted-average price of goods and services that the average consumer buys each month.

**consumer products**

Products purchased for personal use or consumption.

**consumer promotion**

Marketing activities designed to generate immediate consumer sales, using tools such as premiums, promotional products, samples, coupons, rebates, and displays.

**consumerism**

A social movement that focuses on four key consumer rights: (1) the right to be safe, (2) the right to be informed, (3) the right to choose, and (4) the right to be heard.

**contingency planning**

Planning for unexpected events, usually involving a range of scenarios and assumptions that differ from the assumptions behind the core plans.

**contingent workers**

Employees who do not expect regular, full-time jobs, including temporary full-time workers, independent contractors, and temporary agency or contract agency workers.

**contract**

An agreement that is legally enforceable.

**contraction**

A period of economic downturn, marked by rising unemployment and falling business production.

**controlling**

Monitoring performance and making adjustments as needed.

**convertible security**

A bond or share of preferred stock that gives its holder the right to exchange it for a stated number of shares of common stock.

**copyright**

The exclusive legal right of an author, artist, or other creative individual to use, copy, display, perform, and sell their own creations and to license others to do so.

**corporate bylaws**

The basic rules governing how a corporation is organized and how it conducts its business.

**corporate philanthropy**

All business donations to nonprofit groups, including money, products, and employee time.

**corporate responsibility**

Business contributions to the community through the actions of the business itself rather than donations of money and time.

**corporation**

A form of business ownership in which the business is considered a legal entity that is separate and distinct from its owners.

**cost**

The value of what is given up in exchange for something.

**countertrade**

International trade that involves the barter of products for products rather than for currency.

**coupon rate**

The interest paid on a bond, expressed as a percentage of the bond's par value.

**covenant**

A restriction lenders impose on borrowers as a condition of providing long-term debt financing.

**craft union**

A union comprising workers who share the same skill or work in the same profession.

**credit**

Allows a borrower to buy a good or acquire an asset without making immediate payment and to repay the balance at a later time.

**credit card**

A card issued by a bank or finance company that allows the cardholder to make a purchase now and pay the credit card issuer later.

**credit score**

A numerical measure of a consumer's creditworthiness.

**credit union**

A depository institution that is organized as a cooperative, meaning that it is owned by its depositors.

**crime**

A wrongful act against society, defined by law and prosecuted by the state.

**critical path**

The sequence of activities in a project that is expected to take the longest to complete.

**critical path method (CPM)**

A project-management tool that illustrates the relationships among all the activities involved in completing a project and identifies the sequence of activities likely to take the longest to complete.

**current yield**

The amount of interest earned on a bond, expressed as a percentage of the bond's current market price.

**customer benefit**

The advantage that a customer gains from specific product features.

**customer loyalty**

When customers buy a product from the same supplier again and again—sometimes paying even more for it than they would for a competitive product.

**customer relationship management (CRM)**

The ongoing process of acquiring, maintaining, and growing profitable customer relationships by delivering unmatched value.

**customer satisfaction**

When customers perceive that a good or service delivers value above and beyond their expectations.

**data**

Raw, unprocessed facts and figures.

**data mining**

The use of sophisticated statistical and mathematical techniques to analyze vast amounts of data to discover hidden patterns and relationships, thus creating valuable information.

**data warehouse**

A large, organization-wide database that stores data in a centralized location.

**database**

A file consisting of related data organized according to a logical system and stored on a hard drive or some other computer-accessible media.

**debit card**

A card issued by the bank that allows the customer to make purchases as if the transaction involved cash. In a debit card purchase, the customer's bank account is immediately reduced when the purchase is made.

**debt financing**

Funds provided by lenders (creditors).

**decision support system (DSS)**

A system that gives managers access to large amounts of data and the processing power to convert these data into high-quality information, thus improving the decision-making process.

**deflation**

A period of falling average prices across the economy.

**degree of centralization**

The extent to which decision-making power is held by a small number of people at the top of the organization.

**demand**

The quantity of products that consumers are willing to buy at different market prices.

**demand curve**

The graphed relationship between price and quantity from a customer demand standpoint.

**democratic leaders**

Leaders who share power with their followers. While they still make final decisions, they typically solicit and incorporate input from their followers.

**demographic segmentation**

Dividing the market into smaller groups based on measurable characteristics about people, such as age, income, ethnicity, and gender.

**demographics**

The measurable characteristics of a population. Demographic factors include population size and density, as well as specific traits such as age, gender, and race.

**departmentalization**

The division of workers into logical groups.

**depository institution**

A financial intermediary that obtains funds by accepting checking and savings deposits and then lending those funds to borrowers.

**depression**

An especially deep and long-lasting recession.

**digital wallet**

A method used for secure electronic transfer of funds for e-commerce transactions.

**direct channel**

A distribution process that links the producer and the customer with no intermediaries.

**direct cost**

Costs that are incurred directly as the result of some specific cost object.

**direct investment**

(or foreign direct investment) When firms either acquire foreign firms or develop new facilities from the ground up in foreign countries.

**discount rate**

The rate of interest that the Federal Reserve charges when it loans funds to banks.

**discretionary payments**

Expenditures for which the spender has significant control in terms of the amount and timing.

**discussion channels and chat rooms**

The use of web- or app-based communication tools to hold department-based, topic/project/client-based, team, or private discussions.

**disinflation**

A period of slowing average price increases across the economy.

**distribution strategy**

A plan for delivering the right product to the right person at the right place at the right time.

**distributive bargaining**

The traditional adversarial approach to collective bargaining.

**distributorship**

A type of franchising arrangement in which the franchisor makes a

product and licenses the franchisee to sell it.

**divestiture**

The transfer of total or partial ownership of some of a firm's operations to investors or to another company.

**Dodd–Frank Act**

A law enacted in the aftermath of the financial crisis of 2008–2009 that strengthened government oversight of financial markets and placed limitations on risky financial strategies such as heavy reliance on leverage.

**Dow Jones Industrial Average (DJIA)**

An index that tracks stock prices of 30 large, well-known U.S. corporations.

**dynamic delivery**

Vibrant, compelling presentation delivery style that grabs and holds the attention of the audience.

**e-commerce**

The marketing, buying, selling, and servicing of products over a network (usually the internet).

**e-marketplace**

A specialized internet site where buyers and sellers engaged in business-to-business e-commerce can communicate and conduct business.

**economic system**

A structure for allocating limited resources.

**economics**

The study of the choices that people, companies, and governments make in allocating society's resources.

**economy**

A financial and social system of how resources flow through society, from production to distribution, to consumption.

**effectiveness**

Using resources to create value by providing customers with goods and services that offer a better relationship between price and perceived benefits.

**efficiency**

Producing output or achieving a goal at the lowest cost.

**electronic communications network (ECN)**

An automated, computerized securities trading system that automatically matches buyers and sellers, executing trades quickly and allowing trading when securities exchanges are closed.

**embargo**

A complete ban on international trade of a certain item, or a total halt in trade with a particular nation.

**employment at will**

A legal doctrine that views employment as an entirely voluntary rela-

tionship that both the employee and employer are free to terminate at any time and for any reason.

**enterprise resource planning (ERP)**

Software-based approach to integrate an organization's (and in the sophisticated versions, a value chain's) information flows.

**entrepreneurs**

People who risk their time, money, and other resources to start and manage a business.

**environmental scanning**

The process of continually collecting information from the external marketing environment.

**Equal Employment Opportunity Commission (EEOC)**

A federal agency designed to regulate and enforce the provisions of Title VII.

**equilibrium price**

The price associated with the point at which the quantity demanded of a product equals the quantity supplied.

**equity financing**

Funds provided by the owners of a company.

**equity theory**

A motivation theory that proposes that perceptions of fairness directly affect worker motivation.

**ethical dilemma**

A decision that involves a conflict of values; every potential course of action has some significant negative consequences.

**ethics**

A set of beliefs about right and wrong, good and bad.

**European Union (EU)**

The world's largest common market, composed of 27 European nations.

**everyday-low pricing (EDLP)**

Long-term discount pricing, designed to achieve profitability through high sales volume.

**exchange rate**

A measurement of the value of one nation's currency relative to the currency of other nations.

**exchange traded fund (ETF)**

Shares traded on securities markets that represent the legal right of ownership over part of a basket of individual stock certificates or other securities.

**expansion**

A period of robust economic growth and high employment.

**expectancy theory**

A motivation theory that concerns the relationship among individual

effort, individual performance, and individual reward.

**expenses**

Resources that are used up as the result of business operations.

**expert system (ES)**

A decision support system that helps managers make better decisions in an area where they lack expertise.

**exporting**

Selling products in foreign nations that have been produced or grown domestically.

**external locus of control**

A deep-seated sense that forces other than the individual are responsible for what happens in their life.

**external recruitment**

The process of seeking new employees from outside the firm.

**extranet**

An intranet that allows limited access to a selected group of stakeholders, such as suppliers or customers.

**factor**

A company that provides short-term financing to firms by purchasing their accounts receivables at a discount.

**factors of production**

Four fundamental elements—natural resources, capital, human resources, and entrepreneurship—that businesses need to achieve their objectives.

**federal debt**

The sum of all the money that the federal government has borrowed over the years and not yet repaid.

**Federal Deposit Insurance Corporation (FDIC)**

A federal agency that insures deposits in banks and thrift institutions for up to $250,000 per customer, per bank.

**Federal Deposit Insurance Corporation (FDIC)**

An independent agency created by Congress to maintain stability and public confidence in the nation's financial system, primarily by insuring bank deposits.

**Federal Reserve Act of 1913**

The law that established the Federal Reserve System as the central bank of the United States.

**finance**

The functional area of business that is concerned with finding the best sources and uses of financial capital.

**financial accounting**

The branch of accounting that prepares financial statements for use by owners, creditors, suppliers, and other external stakeholders.

**Financial Accounting Standards Board (FASB)**

The private board that establishes the generally accepted accounting principles used in the practice of financial accounting.

**financial budgets**

Budgets that focus on the firm's financial goals and identify the resources needed to achieve these goals.

**financial capital**

The funds a firm uses to acquire its assets and finance its operations.

**financial diversification**

A strategy of investing in a wide variety of securities in order to reduce risk.

**financial leverage**

The use of debt in a firm's capital structure.

**financial markets**

Markets that transfer funds from savers to borrowers.

**financial ratio analysis**

Computing ratios that compare values of key accounts listed on a firm's financial statements.

**Financial Services Modernization Act of 1999**

An act that overturned the section of the Banking Act of 1933 that prohibited commercial banks from selling insurance or performing the functions of investment banks.

**firewall**

Software and/or hardware designed to prevent unwanted access to a computer or computer system.

**first-line (supervisory) management**

Managers who directly supervise nonmanagement employees.

**fiscal policy**

Government efforts to influence the economy through taxation and spending.

**fixed costs**

Costs that remain the same when the level of production changes within some relevant range.

**flextime**

A scheduling option that allows workers to choose when they start and finish their workdays, as long as they complete the required number of hours.

**foreign franchising**

A specialized type of foreign licensing in which a firm expands by offering businesses in other countries the right to produce and market its products according to specific operating requirements.

**foreign licensing**

Authority granted by a domestic firm to a foreign firm for the rights to produce and market its product or to use its trademark/patent rights in a defined geographical area.

**foreign outsourcing**

(also contract manufacturing) Contracting with foreign suppliers to produce products, usually at a fraction of the cost of domestic production.

**franchise**

A licensing arrangement under which a franchisor allows franchisees to use its name, trademark, products, business methods, and other property in exchange for monetary payments and other considerations.

**franchise agreement**

The contractual arrangement between a franchisor and franchisee that spells out the duties and responsibilities of both parties.

**Franchise Disclosure Document (FDD)**

A detailed description of all aspects of a franchise that the franchisor must provide to the franchisee at least 14 calendar days before the franchise agreement is signed.

**franchisee**

The party in a franchise relationship that pays for the right to use resources supplied by the franchisor.

**franchisor**

The business entity in a franchise relationship that allows others to operate its business using resources it supplies in exchange for money and other considerations.

**free trade**

The unrestricted movement of goods and services across international borders.

**free-rein leaders**

Leaders who set objectives for their followers but give them freedom to choose how they will accomplish those goals.

**General Agreement on Tariffs and Trade (GATT)**

An international trade treaty designed to encourage worldwide trade among its members.

**general partnership**

A partnership in which all partners can take an active role in managing the business and have unlimited liability for any claims against the firm.

**generally accepted accounting principles (GAAP)**

A set of accounting standards that is used in the preparation of financial statements.

**geographic segmentation**

Dividing the market into smaller groups based on where consumers live. This process can incorporate countries, cities, or population density as key factors.

**goods**

Tangible products.

**grace period**

The period of time that the credit card holder has to pay outstanding balances before interest or fees are assessed.

**green marketing**

Developing and promoting environmentally sound products and practices to gain a competitive edge.

**green marketing**

Developing and promoting environmentally sound products and practices to gain a competitive edge.

**grievance**

A complaint by a worker that the employer has violated the terms of the collective bargaining agreement.

**gross domestic product (GDP)**

The total value of all final goods and services produced within a nation's physical boundaries over a given period of time.

**hacker**

A skilled computer user who uses their expertise to gain unauthorized access to the computer (or computer system) of others, sometimes with malicious intent.

**hardware**

The physical tools and equipment used to collect, input, store, organize, and process data and to distribute information.

**high/low pricing**

A pricing strategy designed to drive traffic to retail stores by special sales on a limited number of products, and higher everyday prices on others.

**horizontal analysis**

Analysis of financial statements that compares account values reported on these statements over two or more years to identify changes and trends.

**horizontal merger**

A combination of two firms that are in the same industry.

**human resource (HR) management**

The management function focused on maximizing the effectiveness of the workforce by recruiting world-class talent, promoting career development, and determining workforce strategies to boost organizational effectiveness.

**human skills**

The ability to work effectively with and through other people in a range of different relationships.

**hyperinflation**

An average monthly inflation rate of more than 50%.

**immediate predecessors**

Activities in a project that must be completed before some other specified activity can begin.

**implicit cost**

The opportunity cost that arises when a firm uses owner-supplied resources.

**importing**

Buying products domestically that have been produced or grown in foreign nations.

**income statement**

The financial statement that reports the revenues, expenses, and net income that resulted from a firm's operations over an accounting period.

**independent wholesaling businesses**

Independent distributors that buy products from a range of different businesses and sell those products to a range of different customers.

**indirect costs**

Costs that are the result of a firm's general operations and are not directly tied to any specific cost object.

**industrial union**

A union comprising workers employed in the same industry.

**inflation**

A period of rising average prices across the economy.

**information**

Data that have been processed in a way that make them meaningful to their user.

**infrastructure**

A country's physical facilities that support economic activity.

**initial public offering (IPO)**

The first time a company issues stock that may be bought by the general public.

**institutional investor**

An organization that pools contributions from investors, clients, or depositors and uses these funds to buy stocks and other securities.

**integrated marketing communication**

The coordination of marketing messages through every promotional vehicle to communicate a unified impression about a product.

**intellectual property**

Property that is the result of creative or intellectual effort, such as books, musical works, inventions, and computer software.

**intercultural communication**

Communication among people with differing cultural backgrounds.

**interest-based bargaining**

A form of collective bargaining that emphasizes cooperation and problem solving in an attempt to find a win–win outcome.

**internal locus of control**

A deep-seated sense that the individual is personally responsible for what happens in their life.

**internal recruitment**

The process of seeking employees who are currently within the firm to fill open positions.

**International Monetary Fund (IMF)**

An international organization of 190 member nations that promotes international economic cooperation and stable growth.

**internet**

The world's largest computer network; essentially a network of computer networks all operating under a common set of rules that allow them to communicate with each other.

**internet2 (I2)**

A new high-tech internet with access limited to a consortium of member organizations (and other organizations these members sponsor). I2 utilizes technologies that give it a speed and capacity far exceeding the current internet.

**intranet**

A private network that has the look and feel of the internet and is navigated using a web browser, but which limits access to a single firm's employees (or a single organization's members).

**inventory**

Stocks of goods or other items held by organizations.

**investing**

Reducing consumption in the current time period in order to build future wealth.

**investment bank**

A financial intermediary that specializes in helping firms raise financial capital by issuing securities in primary markets.

**IRA**

An individual retirement account that provides tax benefits to individuals who are investing for their retirement.

**ISO 14000**

A family of generic standards for environmental management established by the International Organization for Standardization.

**ISO 9000**

A family of generic standards for quality management systems established by the International Organization for Standardization.

**job analysis**

The examination of specific tasks that are assigned to each position, independent of who might be holding the job at any specific time.

**job description**

An explanation of the responsibilities for a specific position.

**job enrichment**

The creation of jobs with more meaningful content, under the assumption that challenging, creative work will motivate employees.

**job specifications**

The specific qualifications necessary to hold a particular position.

**joint ventures**

When two or more companies join forces—sharing resources, risks, and profits, but not actually merging companies—to pursue specific opportunities.

**just-in-time (JIT) production**

A production system that emphasizes the production of goods to meet actual current demand, thus minimizing the need to hold inventories of finished goods and work in process at each stage of the supply chain.

**labor union**

A group of workers who have organized to work together to achieve common job-related goals, such as higher wages, better working conditions, and greater job security.

**Labor–Management Relations Act (Taft–Hartley Act)**

Law passed in 1947 that placed limits on union activities, outlawed the closed shop, and allowed states to pass right-to-work laws that made union shops illegal.

**laws**

Rules that govern the conduct and actions of people within a society that are enforced by the government.

**leading**

Directing and motivating people to achieve organizational goals.

**lean production**

An approach to production that emphasizes the elimination of waste in all aspects of production processes.

**leverage ratios**

Ratios that measure the extent to which a firm relies on debt financing in its capital structure.

**liabilities**

Claims that outsiders have against a firm's assets.

**licensing**

Purchasing the right to use another company's brand name or symbol.

**limit order**

An order to a broker to buy a specific stock only if its price is below a certain level, or to sell a specific stock only if its price is above a certain level.

**limited liability**

When owners are not personally liable for claims against their firm. Owners with limited liability may lose their investment in the company, but their other personal assets are protected.

**limited liability company (LLC)**

A form of business ownership that offers both limited liability to its owners and flexible tax treatment.

**limited liability partnership (LLP)**

A form of partnership in which all partners have the right to participate in management and have limited liability for company debts.

**limited partnership**

A partnership that includes at least one general partner who actively manages the company and accepts unlimited liability and one limited partner who gives up the right to actively manage the company in exchange for limited liability.

**line extensions**

Similar products offered under the same brand name.

**line managers**

Managers who supervise the functions that contribute directly to profitability: production and marketing.

**line of credit**

A financial arrangement between a firm and a bank in which the bank preapproves credit up to a specified limit, provided that the firm maintains an acceptable credit rating.

**line organizations**

Organizations with a clear, simple chain of command from top to bottom.

**line-and-staff organizations**

Organizations with line managers forming the primary chain of authority in the company, and staff departments working alongside line departments.

**liquid asset**

An asset that can quickly be converted into cash with little risk of loss.

**liquidity ratios**

Financial ratios that measure the ability of a firm to obtain the cash it needs to pay its short-term debt obligations as they come due.

**lockout**

An employer-initiated work stoppage.

**logistics**

A subset of supply chain management that focuses largely on the tactics involved in moving products along the supply chain.

**loss**

When a business incurs expenses that are greater than its revenue.

**loss-leader pricing**

Closely related to high/low pricing, loss-leader pricing means pricing a handful of items—or loss leaders—temporarily below cost to drive traffic.

**M1 money supply**

Includes all currency plus checking accounts and traveler's checks.

**M2 money supply**

Includes all of M1 money supply plus most savings accounts, money market accounts, and certificates of deposit.

**macroeconomics**

The study of a country's overall economic dynamics, such as the employment rate, the gross domestic product, and taxation policies.

**malware**

A general term for malicious software, such as spyware, computer viruses, and worms.

**management**

Achieving the goals of an organization through planning, organizing, leading, and controlling organizational resources including people, money, and time.

**management development**

Programs to help current and potential executives develop the skills they need to move into leadership positions.

**managerial (or management) accounting**

The branch of accounting that provides reports and analysis to managers to help them make informed business decisions.

**market makers**

Securities dealers that make a commitment to continuously offer to buy and sell the stock of a specific corporation listed on the NASDAQ exchange or traded in the OTC market.

**market niche**

A small segment of a market with fewer competitors than the market as a whole. Market niches tend to be quite attractive to small firms.

**market order**

An order telling a broker to buy or sell a specific security at the best currently available price.

**market segmentation**

Dividing potential customers into groups of similar people, or segments.

**market share**

The percentage of a market controlled by a given marketer.

**marketing**

An organizational function and a set of processes for creating, communicating, and delivering value to customers and for managing customer relationships in ways that benefit the organization and its stakeholders.

**marketing concept**

A business philosophy that makes customer satisfaction—now and in the future—the central focus of the entire organization.

**marketing mix**

The blend of marketing strategies for product, price, distribution, and promotion.

**marketing plan**

A formal document that defines marketing objectives and the specific strategies for achieving those objectives.

**marketing research**

The process of gathering, interpreting, and applying information to uncover marketing opportunities and challenges, and to make better marketing decisions.

**Maslow's hierarchy of needs theory**

A motivation theory that suggests that human needs fall into a hierarchy and that as each need is met, people become motivated to meet the next-highest need in the pyramid.

**mass customization**

The creation of products tailored for individual consumers on a mass basis.

**master budget**

A presentation of an organization's operational and financial budgets that represents the firm's overall plan of action for a specified time period.

**matrix organizations**

Organizations with a flexible structure that brings together specialists from different areas of the company to work on individual projects on a temporary basis.

**maturity date**

The date when a bond will come due.

**mediation**

A method of dealing with an impasse between labor and management by bringing in a neutral third party to help the two sides reach agreement by reducing tensions and making suggestions for possible compromises.

**merchant wholesalers**

Independent distributors who take legal possession, or title, of the goods they distribute.

**merger**

A corporate restructuring that occurs when two formerly independent business entities combine to form a new organization.

**microeconomics**

The study of smaller economic units such as individual consumers, families, and individual businesses.

**middle management**

Managers who supervise lower-level managers and report to a higher-level manager.

**mission**

The definition of an organization's purpose, values, and core goals, which provides the framework for all other plans.

**mixed economies**

Economies that embody elements of both planned and market-based economic systems.

**modes of transportation**

The various transportation options—such as planes, trains, and railroads—for moving products through the supply chain.

**monetary policy**

Federal Reserve decisions that shape the economy by influencing interest rates and the supply of money.

**money**

Anything generally accepted as a medium of exchange, a measure of value, or a means of payment.

**money market mutual funds**

A mutual fund that pools funds from many investors and uses these funds to purchase very safe, highly liquid securities.

**money supply**

The total amount of money within the overall economy.

**monopolistic competition**

A market structure with many competitors selling differentiated products. Barriers to entry are low.

**monopoly**

A market structure with one producer completely dominating the industry, leaving no room for any significant competitors. Barriers to entry tend to be virtually insurmountable.

**multichannel retailing**

Providing multiple distribution channels for consumers to buy a product.

**multilevel marketing (MLM)**

Involves hiring independent contractors to sell products to their personal network of friends and colleagues

and to recruit new salespeople in return for a percentage of their commissions.

**mutual fund**

An institutional investor that raises funds by selling shares to investors and uses the accumulated funds to buy a portfolio of many different securities.

**national brands**

Brands that the producer owns and markets.

**National Labor Relations Act (Wagner Act)**

Landmark pro-labor law enacted in 1935. This law made it illegal for firms to discriminate against union members and required employers to recognize certified unions and bargain with them in good faith.

**natural monopoly**

A market structure with one company as the supplier of a product because the nature of that product makes a single supplier more efficient than multiple, competing ones. Most natural monopolies are government sanctioned and regulated.

**negligence**

An unintentional tort that arises due to carelessness or irresponsible behavior.

**net asset value per share**

The value of a mutual fund's securities and cash holdings minus any liabilities, divided by the number of shares of the fund outstanding.

**net income**

The difference between the revenue a firm earns and the expenses it incurs in a given time period.

**net present value (NPV)**

The sum of the present values of expected future cash flows from an investment, minus the cost of that investment.

**noise**

Any interference that causes the message you send to be different from the message your audience understands.

**nondiscretionary payments**

Expenditures that the spender has little or no control over.

**nonprofit corporation**

A corporation that does not seek to earn a profit and differs in several fundamental respects from C corporations.

**nonprofits**

Business-like establishments that employ people and produce goods and services with the fundamental goal of contributing to the community rather than generating financial gain.

**nonverbal communication**

Communication that does not use words. Common forms of nonverbal communication include gestures,

posture, facial expressions, tone of voice, and eye contact.

**observation research**

Marketing research that does not require the researcher to interact with the research subject.

**odd pricing**

The practice of ending prices in numbers below even dollars and cents in order to create a perception of greater value.

**offshoring**

Moving production or support processes to foreign countries.

**oligopoly**

A market structure with only a handful of competitors selling products that can be similar or different. Barriers to entry are typically high.

**on-the-job training**

A training approach that requires employees to simply begin their jobs—sometimes guided by more experienced employees—and to learn as they go.

**open market operations**

The Federal Reserve function of buying and selling government securities, which include treasury bonds, notes, and bills.

**open shop**

An employment arrangement in which workers are not required to join a union or pay union dues.

**operating budgets**

Budgets that communicate an organization's sales and production goals and the resources needed to achieve these goals.

**operational planning**

Very specific, short-term planning that applies tactical plans to daily, weekly, and monthly operations.

**operations management**

Creating value by managing the activities that produce goods and services and then distributing them to customers.

**opportunity cost**

The opportunity of giving up the second-best choice when making a decision.

**organization chart**

A visual representation of the company's formal structure.

**organizing**

Determining a structure for both individual jobs and the overall organization.

**orientation**

The first step in the training and development process, designed to introduce employees to the company culture and provide key administrative information.

## out-of-pocket cost

A cost that involves the payment of money or other resources.

## outsourcing

Arranging for other organizations to perform supply chain functions that were previously performed internally.

## over-the-counter (OTC) market

The market where securities that are not listed on exchanges are traded.

## owners' equity

The claims a firm's owners have against their company's assets (often called "stockholders' equity" on balance sheets of corporations).

## par value (of a bond)

The value of a bond at its maturity; what the issuer promises to pay the bondholder when the bond matures.

## partnership

A voluntary agreement under which two or more people act as co-owners of a business for profit.

## passive voice

Sentence construction in which the subject does not do the action expressed by the verb; rather, the subject is acted upon (e.g., The taxes were done by our accountant.) The passive voice tends to be less effective for business communication.

## patent

A legal monopoly that gives an inventor the exclusive right over an invention for a limited time period.

## penetration pricing

A new product pricing strategy that aims to capture as much of the market as possible through rock-bottom prices.

## performance appraisal

A formal feedback process that requires managers to give their subordinates feedback on a one-to-one basis, typically by comparing actual results to expected results.

## personal selling

The person-to-person presentation of products to potential buyers.

## pharming

A scam that seeks to steal identities by routing internet traffic to fake websites.

## phishing

A scam in which official-looking emails are sent to individuals in an attempt to get them to divulge private information such as passwords, usernames, and account numbers.

## physical distribution

The actual, physical movement of products along the distribution pathway.

## picketing

A union tactic during labor disputes in which union members walk near the entrance of the employer's place of business, carrying signs to publicize their position and concerns.

## planned obsolescence

The strategy of deliberately designing products to fail in order to shorten the time between purchases.

## planning

Determining organizational goals and action plans for how to achieve those goals.

## poka-yokes

Simple methods incorporated into a production process designed to eliminate or greatly reduce errors.

## positioning statement

A brief statement that articulates how the marketer would like the target market to envision a product relative to the competition.

## preferred stock

A type of stock that gives its holder preference over common stockholders in terms of dividends and claims on assets.

## present value

The amount of money that, if invested today at a given rate of interest (called the discount rate), would grow to become some future amount in a specified number of time periods.

## primary data

New data that marketers compile for a specific research project.

## primary securities market

The market where newly issued securities are traded. The primary market is where the firms that issue securities raise additional financial capital.

## principal

A party who agrees to have someone else (called an agent) act on their behalf.

## principal–agent relationship

A relationship in which one party, called the principal, gives another party, called the agent, the authority to act in place of, and bind, the principal when dealing with third parties.

## private placement

A primary market issue that is negotiated between the issuing corporation and a small group of accredited investors.

## privatization

The process of converting government-owned businesses to private ownership.

## probationary period

A specific time frame (typically three to six months) during which a new hire can prove their worth on the job before they become permanent.

## process

A set of related activities that transform inputs into outputs, thus adding value.

## producer price index (PPI)

A measure of inflation that evaluates the change over time in the prices that business pay each other for goods and services on a weighted average.

## product

Anything that an organization offers to satisfy consumer needs and wants, including both goods and services.

## product consistency

How reliably a product delivers its promised level of quality.

## product differentiation

The attributes that make a good or service different from other products that compete to meet the same or similar customer needs.

## product features

The specific characteristics of a product.

## product life cycle

A pattern of sales and profits that typically changes over time.

## product line

A group of products that are closely related to each other, either in terms of how they work or the customers they serve.

## product mix

The total number of product lines and individual items sold by a single firm.

## product placement

The paid integration of branded products into movies, television, and other media.

## productivity

The basic relationship between the production of goods and services (output) and the resources needed to produce them (input) calculated via the following equation: output/input = productivity.

## profit

The money that a business earns in sales (or revenue), minus expenses, such as the cost of goods and the cost of salaries. Revenue − Expenses = Profit (or Loss).

## profit margin

The gap between the cost and the price of an item on a per-product basis.

## profitability ratios

Ratios that measure the rate of return a firm is earning on various measures of investment.

## promotion

Marketing communication designed to influence consumer purchase decisions through information, persuasion, and reminders.

## promotional channels

Specific marketing communication vehicles, including traditional tools, such as advertising, sales promotion, direct marketing, and personal selling, and newer tools such as product placement, advergaming, and internet minimovies.

## property

The legal right of an owner to exclude nonowners from having control over a particular resource.

## protectionism

National policies designed to restrict international trade, usually with the goal of protecting domestic businesses.

## psychographic segmentation

Dividing the market into smaller groups based on consumer attitudes, interests, values, and lifestyles.

## public offering

A primary market issue in which new securities are offered to any investors who are willing and able to purchase them.

## public relations (PR)

The ongoing effort to create positive relationships with all of a firm's different "publics," including customers, employees, suppliers, the community, the general public, and the government.

## publicity

Unpaid stories in the media that influence perceptions about a company or its products.

## pull strategy

A marketing approach that involves creating demand from the ultimate consumers so that they "pull" your products through the distribution channels by actively seeking them.

## pure competition

A market structure with many competitors selling virtually identical products. Barriers to entry are quite low.

## pure goods

Products that do not include any services.

## pure services

Products that do not include any goods.

## push strategy

A marketing approach that involves motivating distributors to heavily promote—or "push"—a product to the final consumers, usually through heavy trade promotion and personal selling.

## quality level

How well a product performs its core functions.

**quality of life**

The overall sense of well-being experienced by either an individual or a group.

**quotas**

Limitations on the amount of specific products that may be imported from certain countries during a given time period.

**radio frequency identification (RFID)**

A technology that stores information on small microchips that can transmit the information when they are within range of a special reader.

**recession**

An economic downturn marked by a decrease in the GDP for two consecutive quarters.

**recovery**

A period of rising economic growth and employment.

**registration statement**

A long, complex document that firms must file with the SEC when they sell securities through a public offering.

**remote work**

Working outside a traditional office setting via telephone, videoconferencing, and broadband networks.

**reserve requirement**

A rule set by the Fed, which specifies the minimum amount of reserves (or funds) a bank must hold, expressed as a percentage of the bank's deposits.

**retailers**

Distributors that sell products directly to the ultimate users, typically in small quantities, that are stored and merchandized on the premises.

**retained earnings**

The part of a firm's net income it reinvests.

**revenue**

Increases in a firm's assets that result from the sale of goods, provision of services, or other activities intended to earn income.

**revolving credit agreement**

A guaranteed line of credit in which a bank makes a binding commitment to provide a business with funds up to a specified credit limit at any time during the term of the agreement.

**right-to-work law**

A state law that makes union shops illegal within that state's borders.

**risk**

The degree of uncertainty regarding the outcome of a decision.

**risk-return trade-off**

The observation that financial opportunities that offer high rates of return are generally riskier than opportunities that offer lower rates of return.

**robot**

A reprogrammable machine that is capable of manipulating materials, tools, parts, and specialized devices in order to perform a variety of tasks.

**S corporation**

A form of corporation that avoids double taxation by having its income taxed as if it were a partnership.

**salaries**

The pay that employees receive over a fixed period, most often weekly or monthly.

**sale**

A transaction in which the title (legal ownership) to a good passes from one party to another in exchange for a price.

**sales promotion**

Marketing activities designed to stimulate immediate sales activity through specific short-term programs aimed at either consumers or distributors.

**Sarbanes–Oxley Act**

Federal legislation passed in 2002 that sets higher ethical standards for public corporations and accounting firms. Key provisions limit conflict-of-interest issues and require financial officers and CEOs to certify the validity of their financial statements.

**savings account**

An interest-bearing account holding funds not needed to meet regular expenditures.

**savings and loan association**

A depository institution that has traditionally obtained most of its funds by accepting savings deposits, which have been used primarily to make mortgage loans.

**scope of authority (for an agent)**

The extent to which an agent has the authority to act for and represent the principal.

**SCORE (Service Corps of Retired Executives)**

An organization—affiliated with the Small Business Administration—that provides free, comprehensive business counseling for small business owners from qualified volunteers.

**search engine optimization**

Optimizing a website for higher rankings in organic search results.

**secondary data**

Existing data that marketers gather or purchase for a research project.

**secondary securities market**

The market where previously issued securities are traded.

**Securities Act of 1933**

The first major federal law regulating the securities industry. It requires firms issuing new stock in a public offering to file a registration statement with the SEC.

**Securities and Exchange Act of 1934**

A federal law dealing with securities regulation that established the Securities and Exchange Commission to regulate and oversee the securities industry.

**Securities and Exchange Commission**

The federal agency with primary responsibility for regulating the securities industry.

**securities broker**

A financial intermediary who acts as an agent for investors who want to buy and sell financial securities. Brokers earn commissions and fees for the services they provide.

**securities dealer**

A financial intermediary who participates directly in securities markets, buying and selling stocks and other securities for its own account.

**services**

Intangible products.

**servicescape**

The environment in which a customer and service provider interact.

**sexual harassment**

Workplace discrimination against a person based on their gender.

**Six Sigma**

An approach to quality improvement characterized by very ambitious quality goals, extensive training of employees, and a long-term commitment to working on quality-related issues.

**skimming pricing**

A new product pricing strategy that aims to maximize profitability by offering new products at a premium price.

**Small Business Administration (SBA)**

An agency of the federal government designed to maintain and strengthen the nation's economy by aiding, counseling, assisting, and protecting the interests of small businesses.

**Small Business Development Centers (SBDCs)**

Local offices—affiliated with the Small Business Administration—that provide comprehensive management assistance to current and prospective small business owners.

**social audit**

A systematic evaluation of how well a firm is meeting its ethics and social responsibility goals.

**social responsibility**

The obligation of a business to contribute to society.

**socialism**

An economic system based on the principle that the government should own and operate key enterprises that directly affect public welfare.

**sociocultural differences**

Differences among cultures in language, attitudes, and values.

**software**

Programs that provide instructions to a computer so that it can perform a desired task.

**sole proprietorship**

A form of business ownership with a single owner who usually actively manages the company.

**spam**

Unsolicited email advertisements usually sent to very large numbers of recipients, many of whom may have no interest in the message.

**span of control**

Span of management; refers to the number of people a manager supervises.

**specific performance**

A remedy for breach of contract in which the court orders the party committing the breach to do exactly what the contract specifies.

**speed-to-market**

The rate at which a new product moves from conception to commercialization.

**sponsorship**

A deep association between a marketer and a partner (usually a cultural or sporting event), which involves promotion of the sponsor in exchange for either payment or the provision of goods.

**spontaneous financing**

Financing that arises during the natural course of business without the need for special arrangements.

**spyware**

Software that is installed on a computer without the user's knowledge or permission to track the user's behavior.

**staff managers**

Managers who supervise the functions that provide advice and assistance to the line departments.

**stakeholders**

Any groups that have a stake—or a personal interest—in the performance and actions of an organization.

**Standard & Poor's 500**

A stock index based on prices of 500 major U.S. corporations in a variety of industries and market sectors.

**standard of living**

The quality and quantity of goods and services available to a population.

**statement of cash flows**

The financial statement that identifies a firm's sources and uses of cash in a given accounting period.

**statute of frauds**

A requirement that certain types of contracts must be in writing in order to be enforceable.

**statute of limitations**

The time period within which a legal action must be initiated.

**statutory close (or closed) corporation**

A corporation with a limited number of owners that operates under simpler, less formal rules than a C corporation.

**statutory law**

Law that is the result of legislative action.

**stock (or securities) exchange**

An organized venue for trading stocks and other securities that meet its listing requirements.

**stock index**

A statistic that tracks how the prices of a specific set of stocks have changed.

**stockholder**

An owner of a corporation.

**store brands**

Brands that the retailer both produces and distributes (also called private-label brands).

**strategic alliance**

An agreement between two or more firms to jointly pursue a specific opportunity without actually merging their businesses. Strategic alliances typically involve less formal, less encompassing agreements than partnerships.

**strategic goals**

Concrete benchmarks that managers can use to measure performance in each key area of the organization.

**strategic planning**

High-level, long-term planning that establishes a vision for the company, defines long-term objectives and priorities, determines broad action steps, and allocates resources.

**strategies**

Action plans that help the organization achieve its goals by forging the best fit between the firm and the environment.

**strike**

A work stoppage initiated by a union.

**structured interviews**

An interviewing approach that involves developing a list of questions beforehand and asking the same questions in the same order to each candidate.

**supply**

The quantity of products that producers are willing to offer for sale at different market prices.

**supply chain**

All organizations, processes, and activities involved in the flow of goods from the raw materials to the final consumer.

**supply chain management (SCM)**

Planning and coordinating the movement of products along the supply chain, from the raw materials to the final consumers.

**supply curve**

The graphed relationship between price and quantity from a supplier standpoint.

**survey research**

Marketing research that requires the researcher to interact with the research subject.

**sustainable development**

Doing business to meet the needs of the current generation, without harming the ability of future generations to meet their needs.

**SWOT analysis**

A strategic planning tool that helps management evaluate an organization in terms of internal strengths and weakness, and external opportunities and threats.

**system software**

Software that performs the critical functions necessary to operate the computer at the most basic level.

**tactical planning**

More specific, shorter-term planning that applies strategic plans to specific functional areas.

**target market**

The group of people who are most likely to buy a particular product.

**tariffs**

Taxes levied against imports.

**technical skills**

Expertise in a specific functional area or department.

**Theory X and Theory Y**

A motivation theory that suggests that management attitudes toward workers fall into two opposing categories based on management assumptions about worker capabilities and values.

**time value of money**

The principle that a dollar received today is worth more than a dollar received in the future.

**title**

Legal ownership.

**Title VII**

A portion of the Civil Rights Act of 1964 that prohibits discrimination in hiring, firing, compensation, apprenticeships, training, terms, conditions, or privileges of employment based on race, color, religion, sex, or national origin for employers with 15 or more workers.

**top management**

Managers who set the overall direction of the firm, articulating a vision, establishing priorities, and allocating time, money, and other resources.

**tort**

A private wrong that results in physical or mental harm to an individual, or damage to that person's property.

**total quality management (TQM)**

An approach to quality improvement that calls for everyone within an organization to take responsibility for improving quality and emphasizes the need for a long-term commitment to continuous improvement.

**trade credit**

Spontaneous financing granted by sellers when they deliver goods and services to customers without requiring immediate payment.

**trade deficit**

Shortfall that occurs when the total value of a nation's imports is higher than the total value of its exports.

**trade promotion**

Marketing activities designed to stimulate wholesalers and retailers to push specific products more aggressively over the short term.

**trade surplus**

Overage that occurs when the total value of a nation's exports is higher than the total value of its imports.

**trademark**

A mark, symbol, word, phrase, or motto used to identify a company's goods.

**trading bloc**

A group of countries that have reduced or even eliminated tariffs, allowing for the free flow of goods among the member nations.

**U.S. Treasury bills (T-bills)**

Short-term marketable IOUs issued by the U.S. federal government.

**underwriting**

An arrangement under which an investment banker agrees to purchase all shares of a public offering at an agreed-upon price.

**unemployment rate**

The percentage of people in the labor force over age 16 who do not have jobs and are actively seeking employment.

**Uniform Commercial Code (UCC)**

A uniform act governing the sale of goods, leases, warranties, transfer of funds, and a variety of other business-related activities.

**union shop**

An employment arrangement in which a firm can hire nonunion workers, but these workers must join the union within a specified time period to keep their jobs.

**United States–Mexico–Canada Agreement (USMCA)**

The treaty among the United States, Mexico, and Canada that eliminated trade barriers and investment restrictions over a 15-year period starting in 1994.

**universal ethical standards**

Ethical norms that apply to all people across a broad spectrum of situations.

**unlimited liability**

When businesses formed as sole proprietorships or business partnerships cannot pay their bills, all or part of the business owner's personal financial assets, such as cash, bank accounts, investments, or homes, can be seized to pay the business debts.

**utility**

The ability of goods and services to satisfy consumer "wants."

**value**

The relationship between the price of a good or a service and the benefits that it offers its customers.

**value chain**

The network of relationships that channels the flow of inputs, information, and financial resources through all of the processes directly or indirectly involved in producing goods and services and distributing them to customers.

**variable costs**

Costs that vary directly with the level of production.

**venture capital firms**

Companies that invest in start-up businesses with high growth potential in exchange for a share of ownership.

**vertical integration**

Performance of processes internally that were previously performed by other organizations in a supply chain.

**vertical merger**

A combination of firms at different stages in the production of a good or service.

**vesting period**

A specified period of time for which an employee must work for an employer in order to receive the full advantage of certain retirement benefits.

**voluntary export restraints (VERs)**

Limitations on the amount of specific products that one nation will export to another nation.

**wages**

The pay that employees receive in exchange for the number of hours or days that they work.

**Web 2.0**

Websites that incorporate interactive and collaborative features to create a richer, more interesting, and more useful experience for their users.

**wheel of retailing**

A classic distribution theory that suggests that retail firms and retail categories become more upscale as they go through their life cycles.

**whistle-blowers**

Employees who report their employer's illegal or unethical behavior to either the authorities or the media.

**wholesalers**

Distributors that buy products from producers and sell them to other businesses or nonfinal users such as hospitals, nonprofits, and the government.

**World Bank**

An international cooperative of 189 member countries, working together to reduce poverty in the developing world.

**World Trade Organization (WTO)**

A permanent global institution to promote international trade and to settle international trade disputes.

**worm**

Malicious computer software that, unlike viruses, can spread on its own by using well-known vulnerabilities (unsecured points) to enter computer networks without being attached to other files.

# Index